MBTI Manual

MBTI Manual

A Guide to the Development and Use of the Myers-Briggs Type Indicator

Third Edition

Isabel Briggs Myers
Mary H. McCaulley
Naomi L. Quenk
Allen L. Hammer

CONSULTING PSYCHOLOGISTS PRESS, INC.
Palo Alto, California

Consulting Psychologists Press, Inc.
3803 East Bayshore Road, Palo Alto, CA 94303
800-624-1765
www.mbti.com

02 01 00 99   10 9 8 7 6 5 4 3
Printed in the United States of America

ISBN 0-89106-130-4

Myers-Briggs Type Indicator, MBTI, and *Introduction to Type* are registered trademarks of Consulting Psychologists Press, Inc.

California Psychological Inventory, CPI, *Fundamental Interpersonal Relations Orientation-Behavior,* and FIRO-B are trademarks of Consulting Psychologists Press, Inc.

Strong Interest Inventory® of the *Strong Vocational Interest Blanks*®, Form T317. Copyright © 1933, 1968, 1974, 1981, 1994 by the Board of Trustees of The Leland Stanford Junior University. All rights reserved. *Strong Interest Inventory* and *Strong Vocational Interest Blanks* are registered trademarks of Stanford University Press. Printed and scored under license from Stanford University Press, Stanford, California, 94305.

EQI is a trademark of Multi-Health Systems, Inc.

GRE is a registered trademark of Educational Testing Service (ETS).

SAT is a registered trademark of the College Entrance Examination Board.

LSAT is a trademark of the Law School Admission Council (LSAC).

Microsoft and Windows are registered trademarks of Microsoft Corporation.

Millon Index of Personality Styles and MIPS are trademarks of The Psychological Corporation.

Minnesota Multiphasic Personality Inventory and MMPI are registered trademarks of The Regents of the University of Minnesota.

The *NEO Personality Inventory* and NEO-PI are trademarks of Psychological Assessment Resources, Inc.

16 Personality Factors Questionnaire and 16PF are registered trademarks of Institute for Personality and Ability Testing, Inc.

Wechsler Adult Intelligence Scale is a registered trademark of The Psychological Corporation.

Director of Test Publishing & Information Services: T. R. Prehn
Senior Project Director: Peggy Alexander
Managing Editor: Jill L. Anderson-Wilson
Developmental Editor: Kathleen Simon
Copyeditor: Jean Schiffman
Proofreader: Pat Harris
Indexer: Shirley Manley
Cover Art: © Linda Levin, *Paese dei Sogni,* 1990
Cover Design: Big Fish
Interior Designer: Mark Ong, Side By Side Studios
Director of Design & Production: Laura Ackerman-Shaw
Production: Elysia Cooke
Manufacturing Manager: Gloria Forbes

Contents

Tables

Chapter 13

Chapter 14

Figures

Foreword

The revision of the *MBTI Manual: A Guide to the Development and Use of the Myers-Briggs Type Indicator* has been driven by a carefully formulated mission statement and philosophy. This has been true of all work in the research, development, and application of the *Myers-Briggs Type Indicator* carried out under the auspices of Consulting Psychologists Press. The philosophy embodies a combination of tradition and change.

The value of tradition and the commitment to change are based on the vision, mission, and goals of Katharine Cook Briggs and her daughter, Isabel Briggs Myers, in their collaboration to create an instrument to identify Jungian personality type.

The shared vision of Katharine Briggs and Isabel Myers was "to enable individuals to grow through an understanding and appreciation of individual differences in healthy personality and to enhance harmony and productivity among diverse groups." Briggs and Myers believed that Carl Jung's understanding of human development, his theoretical model encompassing psychological type, his concept of the process of individuation, and his structure of the psyche offered the most promising approach. Their mission was to give the *individual* access to the benefits of this understanding.

In following this tradition we have placed special emphasis on holding to the spirit of Jung, Briggs, and Myers in their never-ending quest for deeper understanding of emerging ideas, the possibilities of new and untried methods, and the insights of expanding knowledge—thus our commitment to a "tradition of change." The development of both the instrument and the theory should be viewed as an ongoing process.

This ongoing process is richly illustrated in the *MBTI Manual*. Since the death of Isabel Myers in 1980, much has been learned from a large body of new research, from the experience of thousands of practitioners, from developments in effective feedback, and from refinements in Jungian theory coupled with insights from complementary theories. In addition, new technology and psychometric methodology have made significant contributions.

For those of us who remember Isabel Myers working in relative isolation from early in the morning until late at night for nearly four decades, the phenomenon of the large group of talented, knowledgeable people who worked together on this manual and the new Form M seems awesome and wondrous. It has been an exciting project for those involved; the authors, editors, coordinators, and production team. We are proud of the fine collaborative spirit displayed throughout and the wonderful relationships that have developed. For many years, Isabel Myers was the primary researcher. This manual pulls together the work of hundreds of researchers and practitioners. We are indebted to each of them.

Katharine Downing Myers
Peter Briggs Myers
June 1998

Preface

Test manuals are revised periodically in order to give users access to new knowledge that has accumulated from research and practitioner experience. This purpose, together with the introduction of Form M of the *Myers-Briggs Type Indicator®*, was central to the development of this new edition of the *MBTI® Manual*. A second, even more powerful, objective of this revision was to reinforce the connection of the MBTI to its roots in the psychological type theory of Carl G. Jung.

One consequence of the popularity of the MBTI is that it has become increasingly detached from psychological type theory—often to the detriment of the individuals whom it is intended to benefit. Reconnecting the MBTI to type theory has critical practical implications and applications. In this regard, the overall goal of this edition is identical to that of the two editions that preceded it, and indeed to that of the Indicator itself: to make the theory of psychological types described by Jung understandable and useful in people's lives.

In this edition the registered trademark notation appears and the MBTI is described as a "personality inventory." These additions are not without significance. The trademark addresses a second consequence of popularity—the need to ensure that the origins and ownership of the MBTI are acknowledged and protected. Specifying that the MBTI is a personality inventory rather than some other kind of assessment tool discourages its misuse as a test of skills or abilities or as a simple measure of a particular construct, such as "cognitive styles." Such possible misunderstanding is just one problematic result of detaching the instrument from its theoretical roots. An associated and far more serious issue is mistaking the MBTI for a personality trait measure rather than a dynamic typology. Readers will find many references to and clarifications of this issue in the chapters making up all five parts of the manual.

As the essential reference for users of the MBTI, the manual is organized with the goal of promoting maximum understanding and ease of application. Part I, "Introduction," gives a broad overview of the distinctive features of the MBTI and its basis in Jung's type theory, details the 50-year development of the instrument, and explores the rationale and purposes behind the development of the new standard Form M. Part II, "Theory," explains Jung's dynamic theory of type and the ways in which Myers and Briggs extended and clarified it when they created their instrument. Combinations of preferences and the 16 types are described and research evidence is summarized to help make the dynamic core of psychological type accessible and meaningful to users. Part III, "Administration and Interpretation," gives practitioners the basic information necessary to use the MBTI effectively and offers practical insights into issues that influence these two critical areas. Part IV, "Research," covers the wealth of information relevant to the psychometric features of the MBTI with regard to its construction, reliability, and validity. It describes the new method of selecting items for and scoring Form M through item response theory (IRT) and contrasts it with the prediction ratio method used for previous forms of the Indicator. The focus on type dynamics and whole types that permeates Parts I through IV culminates in Part V, "The Uses of Type," which provides hands-on, practical guidance to those using the MBTI in counseling and psychotherapy, education, career counseling, organizations, multicultural settings, and, by extension, other applications yet to be discovered.

In the first (1962) manual, Isabel Myers acknowledged her mother, Katharine C. Briggs, coauthor of the MBTI, for her original theory of type that predated her discovery of Jung's theory, for "her penetrating analysis of the part played by the judgment–perception preference in her structure of Jungian types, and for her indispensable collaboration in the writing of the Type Indicator and support in its development." In the acknowledgments to the 1985 *Manual*, Mary McCaulley commented, "The influence of Isabel Myers permeates this volume. Some sections of this manual were written by her. In other sections, her ideas are summarized, using written records supplemented by notes of hundreds of hours of discussions over the decade the two authors worked together. . . . This work reflects Myers' six decades of interest in Jung's theory of psychological types and four decades of research to develop a way of putting Jung's theory to practical use."

When Isabel Myers died in 1980, Mary McCaulley took on the immense revision task that culminated in the 1985 *Manual*. Her extensive knowledge of the MBTI and her commitment to Myers' vision of a world able to make "constructive use of differences" enabled her to produce an outstanding work almost singlehandedly. It covered all the professional requirements for a psychological test manual with great clarity and precision. It was unique, however, in being accessible to both the professional psychologists for whom it was intended and laypeople who had little or no psychological training. As such, the 1985 *Manual* was the training vehicle for thousands of professionals now using the *Myers-Briggs Type Indicator.*

The goal of addressing the needs of both psychological professionals and the variety of professionals in other fields who use the Indicator was central to the writing of every chapter in this manual. To further address this need, a comprehensive glossary of terms appears at the end of the manual. The Glossary covers all relevant terms that appear in the manual, including guidelines for using terminology in a consistent and accurate manner. Also included are items that are not referred to explicitly in the manual, but that are relevant and useful to professionals interested in the MBTI, such as *Isabel Briggs Myers Memorial Library* and *CAPT-MBTI Data Bank*. To accommodate users in other countries, the glossary includes definitions of such terms as *grade point average* and *middle school*.

This 1998 revision of Isabel Briggs Myers' monumental life's work both celebrates the centennial of her birth and moves her accomplishments into the twenty-first century. It is our hope that it will bring us closer to Myers' vision of a world in which Jung's theory of type promotes, through the MBTI, the constructive use of differences.

Naomi L. Quenk
Allen L. Hammer
June 1998

Acknowledgments

In producing this revision, no single author could have hoped to duplicate Mary McCaulley's (1985) accomplishment. The depth and especially the breadth of knowledge about the MBTI and its applications that are necessary 13 years later are beyond the scope of one person. Thus the volume reflects major efforts from a number of people who either revised existing chapters or wrote new ones. All contributed within the tradition established by Myers and McCaulley, and they made every effort to retain the original language wherever possible.

Martha Wilson Alcock, R. J. Harvey, and Wayne D. Mitchell contributed significantly to the chapters in Part IV. Martha Wilson Alcock provided expertise in the area of brain functioning in relation to type, R. J. Harvey contributed his knowledge and research methods in using item response theory in the construction and analysis of Form M, and Wayne Mitchell contributed his research and interpretation of studies on type dynamics and whole type.

A number of individuals either revised chapters extensively or created new chapters for Part V. All authors accomplished the daunting task of distilling vast amounts of information into a form that would be clear, accessible, and usable by practitioners. Chapter 10 was revised by Naomi Quenk, Chapter 11 was revised by John DiTiberio, Chapter 12 was revised by Jean Kummerow, Chapter 13 was contributed by Linda Kirby, Nancy Barger, and Roger Pearman, and Chapter 14 was contributed by Linda Kirby and Nancy Barger.

Many members of the type community generously volunteered their time and expertise in critiquing selected parts of the manuscript. Their individual and combined contributions have considerably strengthened the work. Peter B. Myers, Isabel Myers' son, and Katharine D. Myers, her daughter-in-law, carefully reviewed the entire manuscript as it was being written. They provided invaluable information and insights that ensure that the legacy of Isabel Myers has been preserved.

The manual could never have been completed without the dedicated and unstinting efforts of the many individual members of the CPP manual team. Tom Prehn, Director of Test Publishing and Information Services, successfully balanced the enormous time-and-effort requirements of the revision process within the larger context of CPP's publishing commitments. Peggy Alexander, Senior Project Director, accomplished the daunting task of coordinating the many interdependent and intersecting elements of the revision process. Kathleen Simon, Developmental Editor, both provided substantive content editing at the larger organizational level and kept close watch over matters of clarity and specificity of language. Jill Anderson-Wilson, Managing Editor, used her depth of understanding and meticulous attention to detail to help hone the final edited text. Laura Ackerman-Shaw, Director of Design and Production, in addition to executing an outstanding design, exerted superhuman efforts in keeping everyone and everything on track. Superior proofreading was provided by Pat Harris, ably assisted by Karen Stough and Stacey Lynn. Jean Schiffman, copy editor, and Shirley Manley, indexer, masters of their respective crafts, went out of their way to accommodate the ever-changing schedule that was inevitable in a work of this complexity. Consulting editor Anne Scanlan-Rohrer was responsible for coordinating the many tables. Cici Arabian, Editorial Assistant, cheerfully and efficiently managed all of the many details associated with permissions, captions, references, and other elements. Elysia Cooke, graphic artist, worked feverishly to lay out the pages, input the hundreds of changes made to the manuscript and galleys, and bring the production process to completion. Gloria Forbes and Jennifer Cass, both in Manufacturing, ensured that the printed and bound book became a reality.

Judy Chartrand, Research Scientist, was responsible for analyzing the massive amounts of data collected on the national sample and other related research efforts, and for completing all analyses within very tight time constraints. She was assisted by Mark Majors, who was both flexible and thorough in the many analysis projects he undertook. Charles Junn, Research Associate, efficiently and conscientiously coordinated and managed all the data used in the analyses. These data were collected by a number of people who generously volunteered their time and effort. Among them are Barb Krantz, Kevin Nutter, Dennis Gailbreath, Jane Tibbs, Ron Seel, Gina Zanardelli, Karen Salazar, Roger Pearman, Jesse Holschbach, and the staff of Trinity Lutheran Church.

Each of the individuals who participated in the many aspects of the revision demonstrated dedication, energy, and commitment to the goal that is now realized in this new edition of the manual.

Introduction

The two chapters in Part I provide a broad yet sufficiently detailed overview of the manual so that readers will have both an accurate anticipation of the material that follows and a practical grasp of its usefulness.

Chapter 1, "Overview," covers all of the features of the *Myers-Briggs Type Indicator®* (MBTI®) that are critical for understanding its position as a theory-based instrument and how it differs from other personality instruments. The chapter succinctly encapsulates much of the material that follows in the remaining chapters, giving readers a useful preview of what is to come. As you read Chapter 1, you will become aware of the following:

- The MBTI identifies preferences rather than competencies.
- The eight characteristics that are defined in the MBTI are not traits that vary in quantity; they are dichotomous constructs that describe equally legitimate but opposite ways in which we use our minds.
- The MBTI describes a dynamic personality system such that the 16 types are greater than the sum of their parts.
- The dynamic and developmental approach of the MBTI involves the interplay of the dominant, auxiliary, tertiary, and inferior functions that were specified by Jung.
- The new standard Form M uses a different statistical method for scoring from the one used in earlier forms.
- There are five major fields in which the MBTI is currently being used.

Chapter 2, "A Tradition of Change," focuses on the essential features of the MBTI as an implementation of Jung's theory. The chapter describes the 50-year development of the Indicator, the rigorous requirements in the construction of its various forms, and the factors that led to the new standard Form M, with its revised items and new scoring method. As you read Chapter 2, you will become aware of the following:

- Item selection—that is, deleting, revising, and adding items to Form M of the Indicator—was based on both theoretical and empirical criteria.
- Separate scoring keys for males and females on the Thinking–Feeling dichotomy are no longer needed.

- The 1998 revision adhered firmly to Myers' focus on types rather than traits and on normal, adaptive behavior rather than pathology.
- A national random sample was used to revise the MBTI.

People who are new to type will find many terms in these two chapters that are either unfamiliar or defined in different and special ways. People familiar with type will also find some new words. All of these important words and terms are explained and clarified in the Glossary at the end of the manual.

Overview 1

The purpose of the *Myers-Briggs Type Indicator* (MBTI) personality inventory is to make the theory of psychological types described by C. G. Jung (1921/1971) understandable and useful in people's lives. The essence of the theory is that much seemingly random variation in behavior is actually quite orderly and consistent, being due to basic differences in the way individuals prefer to use their perception and judgment.

Perception involves all the ways of becoming aware of things, people, happenings, or ideas. Judgment involves all the ways of coming to conclusions about what has been perceived. If people differ systematically in what they perceive and in how they reach conclusions, then it is only reasonable for them to differ correspondingly in their interests, reactions, values, motivations, and skills.

In developing the *Myers-Briggs Type Indicator,* the aim of Isabel Briggs Myers and her mother, Katharine Briggs, was to make the insights of type theory accessible to individuals and groups. They addressed two related goals in the development and application of the MBTI instrument:

1. **The identification of basic preferences on each of the four dichotomies specified or implicit in Jung's theory.** The MBTI personality inventory (also referred to as "the Indicator") is based on Jung's ideas about how different ways of perceiving and judging, in combination with different attitudes, describe different types of people. Perception and judgment are conceived of as *mental functions;* the term *attitudes* refers to orientation of energy and orientation to the

external world. Personality types result from inter-actions among the four MBTI dichotomies. These dichotomies encompass four opposite domains of mental functioning: opposite ways of perceiving, opposite ways of judging, opposite attitudes in which preferred perception and preferred judgment are typically used, and opposite ways of relating to the world.

2. **The identification and description of the 16 distinctive personality types that result from interactions among the preferences.** A type is not created by simply adding the four preferred ways of functioning. Each type described by Jung and Myers is *greater than the sum of its parts* because of the different interactions among the four preferences that make up a type. By identifying the preferences, the combinations of preferences, and how the combined preferences operate as whole dynamic types, researchers can establish effects and put them to practical use.

Because the MBTI is based on a theory and because of the variety of ways in which it has been applied, this manual has four equally important goals:

■ To provide users with an adequate understanding of psychological type theory

■ To explain the psychometric properties of the instrument that are a direct consequence of the theory upon which it is based, which requires the identification of qualitatively different types rather than the more commonly measured universal traits

■ To present the research that demonstrates the reliability, validity, and psychometric soundness of the instrument

■ To serve as an essential handbook for using the MBTI in a wide variety of settings

The goal of this chapter is to provide readers with the orientation needed to make maximum use of the remaining chapters. The chapter therefore covers the intended uses of the manual, a general overview of Jung's psychological type theory, issues in identifying MBTI preferences, and the varied uses of the MBTI.

How to Use This Manual

This third edition of *The MBTI Manual: A Guide to the Development and Use of the Myers-Briggs Type Indicator* is a revision of the 1985 edition and covers information relevant to understanding and using type as obtained from the new standard Form M, which replaces Form G. Extended forms of the Indicator (Forms J and K) that give respondents individualized type results on component parts of each type dichotomy have been published. Separate manuals are available for these extended forms of the MBTI (Mitchell, in press; Saunders, 1987, 1989).

Readers of this manual who are new to the MBTI instrument will want to pay careful attention to the sections on Jung's theory and the modifications of the theory contributed by Myers and Briggs (Chapters 3 and 4). Experienced users of the Indicator will be particularly interested in the sections that describe why the MBTI was revised (Chapter 2) and how the revision relates to the construction and properties (Chapter 7) and the reliability and validity (Chapters 8 and 9) of the MBTI.

Both new and seasoned MBTI practitioners will benefit from a careful review of the theoretical and psychometric differences between the MBTI and other personality instruments. Chapters 3 and 4 provide the theoretical foundation for the Indicator, and Chapter 7 its essential psychometric features. In addition, theoretical and psychometric differences between the MBTI and other instruments have important implications for both the administration of the instrument (Chapter 5) and its interpretation to clients (Chapter 6). Familiarity with all of these differences will ensure effective use of the instrument with clients in all areas in which the MBTI is appropriately applied. In addition, researchers will profit from the detailed explanation of the distinctive psychometric features (Chapters 7, 8, and 9) of the Indicator, as this will enable them to use the most appropriate research designs and data analysis techniques. The varied ways in which the Indicator is effectively applied appear in Chapters 10 through 14. These chapters give detailed information about the way the MBTI has been used in each application setting and a summary of relevant research.

As compared with previous editions, the emphasis throughout this edition of the manual is on the dynamic character of whole, four-letter types with correspondingly less attention given to evidence concerning the preferences that make up single dichotomies. This emphasis characterizes all or most of the chapters that cover theoretical considerations, psychometric analyses, and research on applications in the many areas relevant to type.

Differences Between the MBTI and Other Instruments

The MBTI differs from most other personality instruments in that the theory upon which it is based postulates dichotomies. These dichotomies are believed to reflect innate psychological or mental dispositions. The requirement that the instrument reflect these dichotomies has been a major factor in the design of items, use of numerical information to determine type preferences, general psychometric properties, and interpretation of results of the MBTI. The following points summarize the instrument's important distinguishing features.

- The MBTI is different from typical trait approaches to personality that measure variation along a continuum; instead, the Indicator seeks to identify a respondent's status on either one or the other of *two opposite personality categories,* both of which are regarded as neutral in relation to emotional health, intellectual functioning, and psychological adaptation. Each of the categories specified in the instrument represents a multifaceted *domain of psychological functioning.* The assumption is that one of each pair of categories is inherently more appealing than the other to a particular respondent. Thus the forced-choice format of items is designed to reveal a preference between equally viable mental processes and attitudes. In contrast, trait-based instruments typically define a dimension or scale as a single trait.

- The type-trait distinction leads to quite different meanings for the scores of trait instruments and MBTI preference clarity indexes. For example, a person with a high score on the *Extraversion* scale of the *NEO Personality Inventory*™ (NEO-PI™), a trait instrument (Costa & McCrae, 1985), is seen as having *more Extraversion* than a person with a low score on that scale, and a person with a low score on the scale may be viewed as having a *deficit* of the identified personality trait of Extraversion. In contrast, MBTI preference clarity indexes indicate *how clearly* a respondent prefers one of two opposite poles of a dichotomy, not how much of that pole she or he has. Each preference in a pair is a construct with its own legitimate content that is separate and distinct from the content of the opposite preference. Opposite preferences are not adequately described by using one or the other as the definitive criterion. For example, Introversion is not described as a lack of Extraversion, nor is Extraversion seen as a deficit in Introversion.

- Because the requirement is to *sort* individuals into opposite categories rather than to *measure* an amount or degree of a trait as is done in trait-based instruments, the numerical preference clarity index on the MBTI *reflects the degree of confidence in the accuracy of placement of a respondent into a particular type category.* Chapter 6 provides guidelines for estimating degrees of confidence in category placements.

- As a self-reported indicator of complex underlying psychological processes, preference clarity indexes associated with MBTI type categories are properly viewed as trustworthy indications of the accuracy of an individual's results. However, the focus of the MBTI is on its usefulness to respondents. Therefore, verification of the accuracy of the indicated type *by the respondent* is essential. MBTI results do not "tell" a person who she or he is. Rather, individual respondents are viewed as experts who are best qualified to judge the accuracy of the type descriptions that result from their self-report. Chapter 6 covers recommended techniques and procedures for helping clients assess the accuracy of their reported MBTI type and identify the type that best fits them.

- Based on the theory, there are specific dynamic relationships among the four preferences (Extraversion or Introversion, Sensing or Intuition, Thinking or Feeling, Judging or Perceiving) that lead to the descriptions and characteristics of the 16 personality types. Further, although the four dichotomies identified by the MBTI are psychometrically independent of each other, the dynamic characteristics of each type are not reflected in a simple summation of an individual's four preferences. Rather, each of the 16 types results from a specified interaction that is consistent with the Jung and Myers theory. Understanding these dynamic interactions aids the interpretation and verification process and provides critical information for applications and research.

- The type descriptions are designed to reflect a theory that includes a model of development that continues throughout the lifespan. As a result, specific hypotheses relevant to different ages and stages of life can be made and tested empirically. For example, the theory predicts that younger persons are generally less clear and consistent in their preferences than are mature individuals. As a result, we expect lower reliability coefficients when testing samples of young people and higher reliabilities with older subjects. This hypothesis is clearly confirmed in a number of samples in the 1985 *Manual,* although sufficiently large samples of young people are not yet available on Form M to allow for a definite conclusion. In coming to conclusions about the reliability of the Indicator, therefore, it is important to recognize that samples that include a wide range of ages will demonstrate lower reliabilities than samples limited to mature, well-functioning adults. Whereas such a result helps validate the developmental aspect of the theory, failure to recognize the basis for differential reliabilities can lead to an erroneous conclusion regarding the overall reliability of the instrument.

- The MBTI dichotomies are concerned with basic attitudes and mental functions that enter into almost every aspect of behavior; therefore the scope of practical applications is broad rather than narrow and includes quite varied aspects of living. This is evident in the number of different applications covered in Part V of this manual, "The Uses of Type."

Overview of Psychological Type Theory

Type theory as used in this manual refers to Jung's theory as interpreted by Isabel Myers and Katharine Briggs in the *Myers-Briggs Type Indicator* personality inventory. The dynamic character specified by type theory involves the interaction of a person's four basic preferences. This section describes the opposites that make up each dichotomy and the 16 types that result from interactions among the four preferences.

The Four Preferences That Make Up a Type

The MBTI instrument identifies four separate dichotomies: Extraversion versus Introversion, Sensing versus Intuition, Thinking versus Feeling, and Judging versus Perceiving. An individual is assumed to have a preference for one of each pair of opposites over the other. The four preferences direct the characteristic use of perception and judgment by an individual. The particular preferences that interact in a person affect not only *what is attended to* in any given situation but also how conclusions are drawn about what has been perceived. The four dichotomies of the MBTI are described in the following sections and are outlined in Table 1.1. The MBTI classifies the first and fourth dichotomies listed as *attitudes* or *orientations* and the middle two dichotomies as *functions* or *processes*. *Attitude* and *orientation* are used interchangeably throughout this manual, as are *function* and *process*.

Table 1.1 The Four Dichotomies of the MBTI	
Extraversion–Introversion Dichotomy (attitudes or orientations of energy)	
Extraversion (E)	Introversion (I)
Directing energy mainly toward the outer world of people and objects	Directing energy mainly toward the inner world of experiences and ideas
Sensing–Intuition Dichotomy (functions or processes of perception)	
Sensing (S)	Intuition (N)
Focusing mainly on what can be perceived by the five senses	Focusing mainly on perceiving patterns and interrelationships
Thinking–Feeling Dichotomy (functions or processes of judging)	
Thinking (T)	Feeling (F)
Basing conclusions on logical analysis with a focus on objectivity and detachment	Basing conclusions on personal or social values with a focus on understanding and harmony
Judging–Perceiving Dichotomy (attitudes or orientations toward dealing with the outside world)	
Judging (J)	Perceiving (P)
Preferring the decisiveness and closure that result from dealing with the outer world using one of the Judging processes (Thinking or Feeling)	Preferring the flexibility and spontaneity that results from dealing with the outer world using one of the Perceiving processes (Sensing or Intuition)

Extraversion or Introversion (E–I) The E–I dichotomy is designed to reflect whether a person prefers Extraversion or Introversion in the sense intended by Jung (1921/1971). Extraverts are oriented primarily toward the outer world; thus they tend to focus their energy on people and objects. Introverts are oriented primarily toward the inner world; thus they tend to focus their energy on concepts, ideas, and internal experiences. Jung regarded Extraversion and Introversion as "mutually complementary" attitudes whose differences "generate the tension that both the individual and society need for the maintenance of life" (p. 160). Jung thus saw both Extraversion and Introversion as necessary for psychological adaptation.

Sensing or Intuition (S–N)[1] The S–N dichotomy is designed to reflect a person's preference between two opposite ways of perceiving. A person may rely primarily upon the process of Sensing (S), which attends to observable facts or happenings through one or more of the five senses, or a person may rely more upon the less obvious process of Intuition (N), which attends to meanings, relationships, and/or possibilities that have been worked out beyond the reach of the conscious mind.

Thinking or Feeling (T–F) The T–F dichotomy is designed to reflect a person's preference between two contrasting ways of making a judgment. A person may rely primarily on Thinking (T) to decide impersonally on the basis of logical consequences, or a person may rely primarily on Feeling (F) to decide primarily on the basis of personal or social values. In Jung's and Myers' approaches, the term *Thinking* does not imply intelligence or competence, and the term *Feeling* is not to be confused with *emotional*. Intelligence and emotional expression are independent of psychological typology.

Judging or Perceiving (J–P) The J–P dichotomy is designed to identify the process a person tends to use in dealing with the outer world, that is, with the extraverted part of life. A person who prefers using a Judging (J) process typically uses either Thinking or Feeling (the Judging processes) when dealing with the outer world. A person who prefers a Perceiving (P) process reports a preference for using either Sensing or Intuition (the perceiving processes) when dealing with the outer world. It should be noted that Myers and Briggs believed this dichotomy was implicit in Jung's theory, but it was not explicitly described in Jung's writings. Chapter 3 elucidates Briggs and Myers' extension of type theory in this regard.

It is important to note that a preference for one alternative of each dichotomy does not mean that the opposite, less-preferred alternative is never used. Both the theory and practical observations describe individuals as using each of the eight preference categories at least some of the time. Thus a person who typically uses Thinking (T) when extraverting—a person with a Judging (J) attitude—may at times extravert the preferred or even less-preferred Perceiving (P) process, even though such an approach may not be typical for the person.

The 16 Types

According to theory, each of the 16 types results from a preference for one pole of each of the four dichotomies over the opposite pole. A preference on any one dichotomy is designed to be psychometrically independent of the preferences on the other three dichotomies.[2] Therefore, preferences on the four dichotomies yield 16 possible combinations called *types,* which are denoted by the four letters identifying the poles preferred (e.g., ESTJ, INFP).

The theory postulates specific dynamic relationships among the preferences. For each type, one process is the leading, or *dominant,* process and a second process serves as an *auxiliary* process that provides balance in the personality. Each type has its own pattern of dominant and auxiliary processes and the attitudes (E or I) in which these are habitually used. Determining these dynamic relationships is enabled by the J–P dichotomy of the MBTI and is fully explained in Chapter 3. The distinctive characteristics of each type follow from the dynamic interplay of processes and attitudes.

In terms of the theory, people may reasonably be expected to develop greater comfort and facility with the processes they prefer to use and with the attitudes in which they prefer to use them. For example, if they prefer the Extraverted (E) attitude, they are likely to be more confident and effective in dealing with the outer world than with the Introverted (I) world of concepts, ideas, and inner experiences. If they prefer the perceiving process of Sensing (S), they are likely to be more confident and effective in dealing with facts and realities than in dealing with theories and possibilities, which are in the sphere of Intuition (N). If they prefer the judgment process of Thinking (T), they are likely to rely more heavily on objective Thinking judgments than on the values that underlie Feeling (F) judgments. And if they prefer to use Judging (J) rather than Perceiving (P) in interacting with the world around them, they are likely to be more comfortable when they can organize the events of their lives than when they can only experience and adapt to them. On the other hand, if a person prefers Introversion, Intuition, Feeling, and Perceiving (INFP), then the converse of the description above is likely to be true.

The preferences and the specific dynamics of their interactions are discussed further in Chapters 3 and 4 of this book, in *Gifts Differing* (Myers with Myers, 1980/1995), in *Introduction to Type Dynamics and Development* (Myers & Kirby, 1994), and in other publications.

Identifying MBTI Preferences

The main objective of the MBTI is to identify which of two opposite categories is preferred on each of the four dichotomies. The Indicator obtains a numerical score based on responses favoring one pole versus its opposite. These calculations are designed *not* as scales for measurement of traits or behaviors but rather as indications of preference for one pole of a dichotomy or its opposite. The letters E or I, S or N, T or F, and J or P are used to designate which of the opposite sides of a respondent's nature are preferred. The intent is to reflect a habitual choice between rival alternatives, analogous to right-handedness or left-handedness. One expects to use both the right and left hands, even though one reaches first with the preferred hand. Similarly, everyone is assumed to use both sides of each of the four dichotomies but to respond first, most often, and most comfortably with the preferred functions and attitudes.

Items and Preference Clarity Index

The MBTI items require forced choices between the poles of the dichotomy at issue. Choices are between seemingly inconsequential everyday events, chosen by Myers as stimuli to evoke the more comprehensive underlying type preferences. All choices reflect the two poles of the same dichotomy, that is, E or I, S or N, T or F, J or P. On the computer-scored version of Form M, responses that best predict to total preference carry greater weight. On the template- and self-scorable versions, all the items have the same weight and are simply counted to determine which preference received the most answers. Technical details of item construction and weighting as developed and tested by Myers, as well as the methodology used in the current revision of the instrument, appear in Chapters 2 and 7.

Form M computer-scored versions yield preferences based on an established midpoint. When a respondent's score is to the right of the midpoint, the preference indicated is I, N, F, or P. When the score is to the left of the midpoint, the person's preference is E, S, T, or J. Tied scores are designated as I, N, F, or P in both the Myers and Form M scoring. The preference letters indicate which of each pair of opposites the person prefers and presumably has developed or is likely to develop to a greater degree. For example, a preference letter E suggests that the person prefers extraverting to introverting and probably has spent more time extraverting than introverting. Consequently, that person is likely to seek out and be more comfortable with activities that call for Extraversion than activities that call for Introversion. For instance, such a person will presumably find greater satisfaction in a career that requires more extraverting than introverting.

As evidence that a preference has been accurately reported, MBTI results include an indication of clarity of preference termed a *preference clarity index.* Preference clarity indexes range from 1 to 30 on each of the four dichotomies.

The higher the index, the greater the clarity of preference that can be assumed. For example, a person whose preference clarity index for Thinking is T 28 could be said to be much more clear in this preference than a person with T 9—at least based on responses to the Indicator items. The characteristics associated with a preference *may* be (but are not necessarily) less apparent when a low clarity index is associated with a preference. A low preference clarity index results from almost equal votes for each opposite pair in a dichotomy. It is incorrect to assume, however, that the person with, for example, N 30 has greater facility with, confidence in, or keenness of Intuition than the person reporting N 15. *Similar cautions apply to all eight preferences identified by the preference clarity indexes of the MBTI.* Thus unlike trait scores, health, competence, or maturity cannot be inferred from the numerical preference clarity index of the MBTI. Chapter 6 discusses these issues in greater detail.

Assumptions Underlying the Types

Each pole of a dichotomy is perceived as valuable and at times indispensable in its own area of operation. The theory assumes that all types can deal effectively with life in general and in their own areas of potential talent in particular. All types are viewed as necessary in a complex world that relies on diversity and specialization to progress toward important personal and societal goals. Each type has its own special gifts and strengths, its own areas of vulnerability, and its own pathway for development.

The *type description* presents these relationships in everyday terms. Each type is described in terms of effective use of the functions and attitudes and also in terms of the specific difficulties arising when type is less developed or not used effectively. The four letters that designate a type provide a compact definition of each type (e.g., ESTJ, INFJ, ESFP). The dynamic interrelationships of the preferences are described in Chapter 3 along with the behavioral characteristics associated with each preference pattern.

Uses of the MBTI Instrument

The differences described by the MBTI are a familiar part of everyday life. Jung's theory offers an explanation for these differences that makes it easier to recognize them and to use them in constructive ways. The theory is indispensable for understanding and using the MBTI, but the majority of people who have found the MBTI interesting and valuable did not have an original interest in Jung. Rather, general interest in the MBTI is due to the fact that almost every human experience involves either perception or judgment and is played out in either the extraverted world of action or the introverted world of reflection. There is therefore a broad range of human activities where type differences are apparent. A good deal of research that examines the ways the MBTI has been applied in the years since publication of the 1985 *MBTI Manual* appears in *MBTI Applications: A Decade of Research on the Myers-Briggs Type Indicator* (Hammer, 1996b). The five applications chapters that appear in Part V of this manual cover the major ways the MBTI is currently being used.

Conclusion

This chapter has provided the context for understanding and using the MBTI. Users can effectively consult one or another chapter as appropriate to their stage of research or particular application. However, familiarity with the development and construction of the instrument (Chapters 2 and 7) and the theory underlying the instrument (Chapters 3 and 4) will maximize the explanatory and predictive potential of the MBTI. Reviewing these chapters is therefore recommended.

A Tradition of Change   2

The implementation of Jung's theory of psychological type by Isabel Briggs Myers and Katharine Briggs in the *Myers-Briggs Type Indicator* has endured for more than 50 years. Today the MBTI is the most widely used personality instrument in the world—2 million administrations are given each year. The history of the MBTI has been marked by evolving ideas of type theory interpretation, application of the instrument in new areas, and nearly constant research. Isabel Briggs Myers herself continually tinkered with the items and the scoring procedures. Yet the assumptions underlying the initial construction of the MBTI have formed the foundation for the continued development of the instrument. These assumptions, and the construction procedures that follow from them, represent the rich tradition that has grounded all changes to the instrument. Change, in the sense of constant improvement and development, has always been part of the tradition of the MBTI personality inventory.

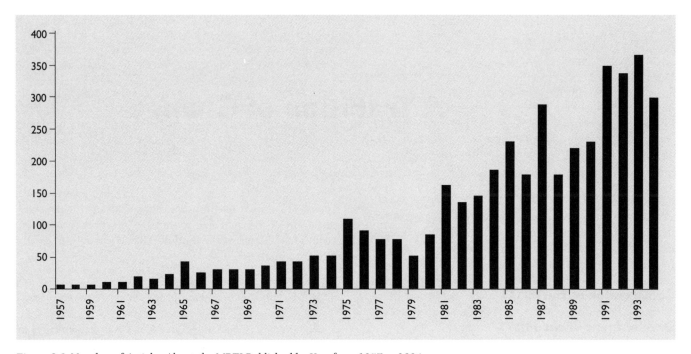

Figure 2.1 Number of Articles About the MBTI Published by Year from 1957 to 1994

Source: From *MBTI applications: A decade of research on the Myers-Briggs Type Indicator* (p. 2), A. L. Hammer (Ed.), 1996. Palo Alto, CA: Consulting Psychologists Press. Copyright 1996 by Consulting Psychologists Press. Used with permission.

Since its introduction, the Indicator has continued to mature through 11 revised forms and alternative methods for administering and scoring those forms (e.g., self-scorable, mail-in, template scoring). Between 1988 and 1997, there were four forms of the *Myers-Briggs Type Indicator* in wide use—Forms F, G, J, and K—and three levels of interpretation. These three levels are referred to as Steps I, II, and III. The MBTI Step I consists of four separate scales designed to determine a person's preferences on four dichotomies, E–I, S–N, T–F, and J–P. The result of Step I scoring of the MBTI is a four-letter type, e.g., ENFP. Two scoring variations were created in the 1980s, using Forms J and K, that extended the original research by Isabel Briggs Myers and focused on the measuring of individual differences within type. These two scoring methodologies—now called the MBTI Step II (formerly the Expanded Analysis Report, or EAR) and the MBTI Step III (formerly the *Type Differentiation Indicator*, or TDI)—add depth to the exploration of type dynamics and type development by the addition of subscales or facets associated with each of the dichotomous preferences. Finally, inspired by the observed and potential benefits derived from understanding type differences in educational settings, the *Murphy-Meisgeier Type Indicator for Children* (MMTIC) was developed in 1987 by Elizabeth Murphy and Charles Meisgeier. Its purpose is to make type concepts available to younger respondents and to aid teachers in understanding various learning styles.

As the use of the MBTI has grown, so have the applications of the instrument. The original use of the Indicator was in personal counseling, career counseling, and education. There has been considerable growth of the Indicator into new areas such as organizations, leadership, management development, and multicultural settings.

Research on the instrument has kept pace with the applications, with more than 4,000 research studies, journal articles, and dissertations written on the Indicator since the publication of the first MBTI manual in 1962. This explosion of research represents one of the most extensive empirical foundations for any psychometric personality assessment. Figure 2.1 shows the number of publications per year. Many of the studies conducted since the publication of the 1985 *MBTI Manual* are summarized in the book *MBTI Applications: A Decade of Research on the Myers-Briggs Type Indicator* (Hammer, 1996b).

The purpose of this chapter is to briefly summarize what has and has not changed with the 1998 revision of the MBTI. Longtime users of the instrument will find this material useful in quickly orienting themselves to the revised instrument. New users may not need to read this chapter, although they may find it interesting. To place this revision in its proper context, we first discuss the principles of construction, including the underlying assumptions guiding the development of the instrument. This is followed by a review of past developments in the history of the instrument. We then introduce the 1998 revision, followed by a brief summary of the revision process. All of the topics discussed in this chapter are presented in more detail in Chapter 7 of this manual, and users are urged to read that chapter carefully.

Construction of the MBTI

At all stages in its development, construction of the MBTI was governed by unusual requirements imposed by a working hypothesis. The hypothesis is that certain valuable differences in normal people result from their preferred ways of using perception and judgment. Each of these preferences, being a choice between opposites, is by nature "either-or," that is, a dichotomy. The MBTI Step I contains four separate scales designed to determine a person's preferences on four dichotomies, E–I, S–N, T–F, and J–P. Each dichotomy, according to the hypothesis, produces two categories of people. An individual will belong to one or the other category based on his or her makeup and inclination. The object of the MBTI is to ascertain, as accurately as possible, the four categories to which the respondent naturally belongs, for instance ENTP or ISFJ. This basic working hypothesis has remained as the foundation of the 1998 revision.

Underlying Assumptions

Jung's theory of psychological types provided the assumptions and set the tasks for the initial construction of the MBTI and for all of the revisions that have been made since, including the current one. These assumptions are as follows:

- "True preferences" actually exist. These preferences can be more confidently identified in persons with good type development (see Chapter 3 for an explanation of type development), than in persons with inadequate type development. However, any instrument must maximize the probability that persons unsure of their preferences will be correctly assigned to a category.
- Persons can give an indication of the preferences that combine to form type, directly or indirectly, on a self-report inventory.
- The preferences are dichotomized, and the two poles of a preference are equally valuable, each in its own sphere.

Types, Not Traits

The assumptions stated above are not typical of most psychological measures. Most current measures of personality hypothesize the existence of one or more psychological "traits." In the trait model, the person is assumed to "have" varied amounts of these characteristics. The instruments designed to assess traits are thus intended to measure how much of the particular characteristic the person possesses. In this model, one end of the trait dimension is usually considered to be good, or better than the other, and the other end to be "bad," or at least less good. Furthermore, in many trait models, having too much or too little of the characteristic (depending on which one is being measured) can be viewed as being neurotic. For example, a trait often found on trait-based personality measures is "dominance." Based on their responses to test items, people are assigned a score that is

assumed to indicate how much dominance they "have." A reasonably high score on a dominance scale might be interpreted as positive, suggesting that the person demonstrates appropriate "amounts" of assertion or leadership. Too high of a score on dominance, however, may be interpreted as indicating an aggressive or controlling approach to social or work situations. Likewise, a low score on the dominance scale may be labeled "submissive" and carry a negative connotation.

In contrast, the intent of the *Myers-Briggs Type Indicator* is specifically not to measure traits, but rather to sort people into equally valuable groups to which, in accordance with Jung's theory, they already belong. These groups are the 16 types. This intent has important implications for the construction of the instrument and the interpretation of the results, as well as for the kind of evidence sought to establish its validity.

Major Tasks Involved in Construction

The foregoing basic assumptions have guided the construction of the Indicator at each stage in its long history, including the present revision. Although each revision has been the result of a lengthy and complicated process, the following outline provides a simple description of the major tasks involved in the construction of the instrument:

1. Determine items to reflect preferences described by Jung for Extraversion or Introversion (E–I), Sensing or Intuition (S–N), and Thinking or Feeling (T–F). Also, determine items for the J–P scale, which was created by Myers to identify preferences for the Judging or Perceiving attitudes in their extraverted appearance, so that this information could be used to determine a dominant function.
2. Write, test, weight, and select items that would achieve the widest separation and least overlap between the two kinds of people preferring opposite poles of each scale.
3. Maximize precision in the center, or midpoint, of the scale, so that persons reporting indeterminate preferences would be more likely to be classified according to their "true" preference on each dichotomy.

Development of the MBTI

The MBTI has been developing since 1942, continuing to the present revision and publication of Form M in 1998. (A more complete history of the construction of the Indicator is found in Chapter 7 of this manual.) Over this period, improvements to and development of the MBTI have occurred in the following areas: language of the items, number of items, item format, item weights and scoring method, gender differences, tie-breaking method, location of the division point, expansion beyond Step I into additional scoring methods, and composition of the standardization group. Each of these is briefly reviewed in the following sections.

Language of the Items

The language of the items has been changed periodically to reflect usage current at the time, and items have sometimes been modified to eliminate ambiguity or awkward alternatives. In making changes to items, the guiding principle has been that the content of the item is less important than the need for the words and form of the sentence to serve as a "stimulus to evoke a type response." What has remained constant is that the responses for each item have been written to appeal to the appropriate types. For example, when writing an item for the J–P scale, every effort has been made to make the Perceiving response to a J–P item as attractive to Perceiving types as the Judging response is to Judging types. The success of the item in evoking a response from the person for whom it was intended has always been considered more important than content coverage of Jung's theory.

For Form M, a thorough review of all of the items contained in Form J of the MBTI was performed to identify those with outdated or awkward language. Form J was used because it contained all of the items that had ever been considered in years of testing by Myers.

Number of Items

Prior to the publication of Form M, the number of items across the various forms of the Indicator varied from as few as 94 in the self-scoring version of Form G to 290 in Form J. Not all of these items have been used in scoring for type, however; some have been included on various forms for research purposes. For example, Form G contains 126 items, 94 of which are scored for type and 32 of which are unscored research items. Also, items on some forms that are not scored for type are used to score the subscales in Step II and Step III scoring procedures.

Form M contains 93 items, all of which are scored for type.

Item Format

Originally all MBTI items were phrase questions, followed by a choice of two or more responses. Word-pair questions were added for Forms E and F. The instructions in parentheses for word pairs were added for Form G because interviews with persons taking Form F revealed that some had answered some of the word pairs on the basis of the sound or appearance of the words, not their meaning.

Form M contains both word-pair and phrase questions.

Item Weights and Scoring Method

In Forms A and B of the Indicator, the items all had the same weight, and overall preference was determined by simply adding up the number of items indicated for each preference for each scale. Beginning with Form C, a new scoring system was used, called the *prediction ratio* (PR) method. The prediction ratio shows the probability that, say, a response designed for Judging types is in fact given by Judging types and is not given by Perceiving types. This method yields separate prediction ratios for each of the two responses to the items. In this manner, it takes social desirability into account. This method was employed to arrive at the four letters of type for all forms of the Indicator from Form C through Form K.

Form M uses a method called *item response theory* (IRT) to score for type. Research conducted for the revision suggests that IRT provides a more precise indication of preference, particularly around the midpoint of the scale, than does the prediction ratio method. The new scoring method is described in detail in Chapter 7 of this manual.

Differential Weights by Gender

Throughout the development of the MBTI, all item analyses were computed separately for males and females. In the early forms, separate scoring keys for males and females were used for E–I, S–N, T–F, and J–P. Beginning with Forms E and F, the same keys were used for both genders because item analyses showed that item popularity and prediction ratios were comparable on E–I, S–N, and J–P. On the T–F scale, it was evident that females, even those who in their behavior and attitudes indicated a clear preference for Thinking, had a greater tendency to give certain Feeling responses than did males. The difference was ascribed either to the possibility that certain Feeling responses were more socially desirable for females than for males or to the effect of social training. Separate weights were assigned to T–F items for each sex, based on the prediction ratios for each item, with checks that the criterion groups were assigned the correct preference.

For Form M, all of the items in the initial item pool were analyzed using a technique derived from IRT called *differential item functioning*. All items from any scale that demonstrated significant differential responses by gender were eliminated from the item pool. This in turn eliminated the need for differential item weights on Form M.

Tie-Breaking Method

In the early stages of the MBTI development, equal points for the poles of the same scale were designated by an x; thus a type might be designated IxTJ or ENFx. With Form F, a tie-breaking formula was adopted. If the raw points derived from adding the weights for the item responses associated with each preference were equal, the tie was broken in the favor of I, N, F, or P, depending on the scale. The rationale for this method was that, given U.S. culture, social desirability may affect a person's responses in the direction of E, S, T, or J. Thus any ties may be the result of responding in a socially desirable manner.

The use of IRT to score the MBTI inventory makes it nearly impossible for a score to land exactly at the midpoint of the scale. On the extremely rare occasion when this happens, a tie-breaker continues to be used with Form M.

On Form M, all ties are broken in the same direction as with previous forms of the Indicator: I, N, F, or P.

Locating the Division Point

In Form A, where all items had equal weight, the division point was the point on a scale where half the items were answered for each pole. By definition this point was the boundary between people showing one preference and people showing the opposite preference. Later, external criteria were employed to help determine the exact location of the division point. For example, E–I continuous scores were regressed onto a rating of gregariousness. Significant changes in the level and slope of the regression line helped indicate the location on the E–I continuum that provided maximum separation between Extraverts and Introverts. This and other external criteria are reviewed in Chapter 7.

For Form M, the division point was set based on the results of a best-fit type study. For each scale, the location of the point was chosen to maximize agreement between the best-fit and the Form M scored preference.

Step II and Step III Scoring Methods

In the late 1980s, two new scoring methods were developed that have come to be known as Step II and Step III. These methods both include subscales that show facets or a more fine-grained structure within the four dichotomous scales. These scoring systems are described in their respective manuals (Saunders, 1987, 1989) and are not covered in the present manual.

Since Form M is a Step I scoring method, that is, it is scored only for the four letters of type, it does not include any of the subscales.

Standardization Groups

Katharine Briggs and Isabel Briggs Myers first tested the initial items that became the MBTI on a small criterion group of about 20 of their relatives and friends whose type preferences seemed to them to be clearly evident from a 20-year period of observing their behavior. As data on the item responses started to accumulate, larger samples were used to check or determine item weights in later forms of the Indicator. These initial criterion samples mainly included adults because adults were expected to have reached higher levels of type development and therefore to be clearer about their preferences and better able to report them. However, a sample of students—the Swarthmore class of 1943—was also included in the initial criterion groups. Later, additional student samples were included.

Between 1975 and 1977, a new standardization of items was carried out. The new analyses seemed appropriate to ensure that cultural changes had not decreased the utility of items and to make some minor modifications that two decades of experience had suggested were desirable. As a result of the analyses of the restandardization, the scoring weights for the T–F scale were modified for Form F, and a new revision of the Indicator, Form G, was published in 1977.

The standardization sample for Form M is based on a national representative sampling of adults over the age of 18 years. This is the first time that the item weights for the MBTI inventory have been based on a large national sampling. The characteristics of this sample are described in Chapter 7 of this manual.

The 1998 Revision

As is evident from the brief history of the development of the MBTI inventory outlined above, the instrument has a long tradition of change, adjustment, and refinement. All of the changes made have been in the service of improving the psychometric properties of the instrument while remaining true to Jung's theory of types. These changes have resulted in an instrument that more consistently and correctly identifies people's preferences. The 1998 revision of the MBTI Step I continues this tradition.

In this section, we present the rationale for the 1998 revision, followed by the specific goals that provided the targets for the research efforts. The revision process is then described, followed by a brief overview of the changes made.

Rationale for the Revision

People who take the MBTI inventory may make important life decisions based on the results. These results can have a significant impact on a person's self-understanding and self-esteem. Many current MBTI practitioners, in fact, became interested in the instrument after seeing the positive effect an interpretation could have on their clients. Organizations that use the instrument may base important business decisions on the outcomes. Results can affect how individuals on teams interact with one another or can help identify sources of job satisfaction. Because of the importance that is placed on the results, it is essential that they be as accurate and precise as possible. This was the overarching motivation driving all revision activities. Within this context, a number of events, observations, and research results suggested that it was time to examine the possibility of making some refinements or improvements to the Indicator.

Cultural Changes Cultural changes over the past 20 years indicated that item endorsement rates should be re-examined. The rationale was that such changes might affect how certain words or phrases are interpreted, which might affect responses to the items, which in turn might lead to changes in the item weights. Also, the prediction ratios used to derive the weights for Form G were based largely on samples of high school and college students, and it was desirable, given that more working adults are taking the Indicator, to base weights on a more representative sample. It was also desirable to have various culturally diverse groups reflected in the standardization sample.

Cultural changes in the roles of women in society indicated that the separate weights used to score responses for males and females on the T–F scale should be examined. Research supported this observation. Harris and Carskadon (1988) suggested that the old Form F weights were more valid for men than were the Form G weights. Also, application of IRT-based differential item functioning techniques (Greenberg & Harvey, 1993) led the authors to conclude that separate weights were not needed for this scale.

New Research Research had also shown that the internal consistency reliabilities of the Thinking–Feeling scale were typically among the lowest (Myers & McCaulley, 1985), suggesting that the issue of using separate weights on this scale needed to be reexamined. Researchers also realized, however, that the lower reliabilities on this scale might involve issues of type development as much as issues of measurement and scoring procedures.

Test-retest reliabilities for whole types were lower than hoped for (Myers & McCaulley, 1985), although the percent agreement varies widely across studies. The meta-analysis by Harvey (1996) shows that the agreement across all four scales was 36% for studies in which the retest period was greater than nine months and 51% for studies in which the retest period was less than nine months. (Harvey's summary was based on Table 10.6, page 173, of the 1985 *Manual*.) It is hypothesized that one reason for the low percent agreement is the possibility of misclassification around the midpoints of the separate scales. Note that since the four preferences that constitute a type are measured on four separate scales, only a small percentage of misclassifications on each scale can add up across all four scales to yield a lower than desired agreement on whole types. For example, the average test-retest agreement on each of the E–I, S–N, T–F, and J–P preference scales for periods of less than nine months is 82%, 87%, 82%, and 83%, respectively.

A number of studies have compared reported or MBTI type with "best-fit" type. Percent agreement in these studies ranges from 64% to 85%. When there has been disagreement between the type reported by the MBTI and the type verified by the individual, it almost always has occurred on those scales on which the person reported only a slight preference on the instrument.

A review conducted in 1994 of Form J, which contains all of the MBTI items developed by Myers, suggested that a small but potentially significant portion of the items used vocabulary that was colloquial or subject to possible social desirability response sets, particularly for young people.

Research by Harvey and his colleagues (Harvey & Murry, 1994; Harvey, Murry, & Markham, 1994) suggested that measurement error on the MBTI scales may have been particularly troublesome around the midpoints of the scales, which would affect test-retest and best-fit type congruencies. A study by Thomas and Harvey (1995) suggested that the addition of new items to the MBTI item pool may improve the accuracy of the type classifications by increasing the precision around the midpoint when using IRT to select and score items.

Goals of the 1998 Revision

The fact remains that the current MBTI forms in use before the revision work as intended, and they work quite well. The data in the 1985 *Manual* and the review of most of the studies conducted since its publication (reviewed in *MBTI Applications*, Hammer, 1996b) support this conclusion. However, the cultural changes and new research discussed in the preceding section suggested that certain improvements might be possible. Therefore, the purpose of the 1998 revision of the MBTI was to balance the dual goals of preserving the integrity of the instrument and making psychometric improvements.

Preserving the Integrity of the MBTI Inventory The need for preservation should be obvious. The Indicator has been used successfully for decades by millions of people. The characteristics of the instrument that have made it so useful to so many for so long should be retained if at all possible. These features include the following:

- A focus on positive, normal, healthy behavior
- A foundation in the theories of Jung and Myers
- The measurement of type as opposed to traits

Improving the Instrument On the other hand, changes in culture and language, and advances in survey and test construction methodologies, suggested that certain innovations might be possible. Therefore, the following specific objectives were targeted for research for the 1998 revision:

- To update item wording and remove outdated language
- To increase the capacity of the instrument to differentiate, particularly around the midpoint of each scale
- To base the item weights of the MBTI on the responses from a national representative sample of adults
- To decrease the number of items necessary for determining a four-letter type
- To improve item-to-scale correlations
- To lower scale intercorrelations

- To eliminate separate gender scoring
- To minimize the influence of social desirability in responses to the items for different age and gender groups
- To remove all items with more than two response options
- To explore state-of-the-art scoring methodologies consistent with the above goals
- To achieve improved validity of predicting "verified type" as an outcome of the hoped-for increased precision

Overview of Changes

The process used to move toward these goals involved many steps of item writing, item selection, research with different samples, and testing of various item sets. This process is described in detail in Chapter 7 of this manual. Here, however, we will present an overview of the 1998 revision and highlight the changes that resulted in a new form of the MBTI—Form M. This overview deals primarily with four issues: changes in the wording of the items, item selection criteria, changes in the scoring, and changes in the standardization sample.

Item Wording To examine the effect of item language, a number of items were revised and some new items were added to the tryout pool. The initial pool consisted of the 290 items from Form J, 200 revised items (Thomas, 1996a), and an additional 90 items written by two experts in the theory and use of type, making a total of 580 items.

A number of items in this pool were then modified before testing. Some of the items that had been written in true/false format were changed to fit the format of MBTI items already in existence. All items with three or more response options were changed to allow only two response options. Both of these changes were made for consistency both within the item pool and with the theory.

In revising items or writing new ones, the focus was on changes or additions that the item writers felt would better separate people with particular preferences into the appropriate categories. This emphasis follows the techniques used by Myers in her many revisions and changes to the items. The content of a question was only a stimulus to evoke a type reaction; it was not determined by requirements to provide a specified level of coverage of all of Jung's concepts related to that dichotomous preference. Nor were the content areas reflected in the questions meant to cover all domains of the preference. The intent was rather to identify any clues about preference that would empirically distinguish the two groups. The interest in questions was not in the superficial behavior reported but in the evidence the questions could provide about the underlying preferences.

While this method governed the item-writing phase, some effort was made during item selection to ensure that the final set of items did provide good coverage of the domain of that dichotomy, at least as determined by the number of and the particular subscales covered by the items. For example, the E–I questions touch on Extraverted and Introverted differences in sociability, friendship, intimacy, detachment or involvement, and outspokenness or reserve.

Item Selection Item selection was based on multiple criteria, which are detailed in Chapter 7 of this manual. Basically, there were two sets of criteria: theoretical and empirical. Theoretical criteria demanded that items be congruent with Jung's and Myers' theories of psychological opposites. Empirical criteria primarily centered on prediction ratios and item parameters derived from item response theory.

Jung's theory of type posits that people make choices between two opposite ways of perceiving and judging. For example, to function well, a person comes to prefer one of the two opposite ways of perceiving, Sensing or Intuition, because these two distinct ways of perceiving the world "compete" for the person's attention (Myers with Myers, 1980/1995). So, because type theory postulates dichotomies, the tradition of presenting questions in forced-choice format was retained. However, since every person uses all eight of the preferences at different times, if each choice were presented separately, both poles could be chosen and one could not know which pole was preferred.

To be consistent with the forced-choice format, all Form J items that had more than two response options were either eliminated or rewritten so that there were only two response choices. Those two responses that had the greatest weights associated with them were retained, as these responses did the best job of discriminating between people at the opposite poles of the dichotomy. An example of such an item is the following:

> Does the idea of making a list of what you should get done over the weekend
>
> (A) appeal to you, or
> (B) leave you cold, or
> (C) positively depress you?

As illustrated in this example, response (C) was deleted and the item was placed in the initial pool for further testing with only the (A) and (B) responses, which are keyed to the J and P preferences, respectively.

Another theoretical criterion that was used to guide item selection was the need to have the item pool for each scale reflect the richness of that preference domain. As the Step II scoring of the MBTI demonstrates, each of the four preference domains can be further subdivided into a number of subscales. Each of the four dichotomies encompasses more than is represented by its five subscales—the subscales are samples of the greatly more complex preference domain. However, the subscales do provide a criterion by which the richness of the domain can be measured. Consequently, a number of items from each of the 20 subscales of Step II were included in the initial item pool, and subscale coverage also played a role in the final item selection.

Turning to the empirical criteria, the prediction ratio method was used to first eliminate items whose ratios failed to reach the current cutoffs for item weights. These were items for which the ratios for both responses were less than .62, which would lead to item weights of 0 for those responses. An obvious example of such an item is the following:

> When you have done all you can to remedy a troublesome situation, are you
> (A) able to stop worrying about it, or
> (B) still more or less haunted by it?

Items for which one of the response weights is 0 do not function well to differentiate people of opposite preferences. Almost all of these items in fact were never intended to perform this sorting function but rather were designed to measure specific subscales that appear in the Step II and Step III scoring methodologies, as the above example demonstrates (from the Worried versus Carefree Comfort/Discomfort scale found in Step III scoring).

Item response theory parameters were also used to select items. Primary considerations were the degree of discrimination and the location of the maximum discrimination. The degree of discrimination refers to the probability that the item separates people of opposite preferences into the correct categories. Location refers to where on the scale the maximum separation takes place. One of the responses to an item could be answered, for whatever reason, in the same way by almost everyone; only a few people with very clear preferences on one side of the dichotomy would answer it in the opposite direction. An example is this item from the Thinking–Feeling scale:

> Would you rather work under someone who is
> (A) always kind, or
> (B) always fair?

Almost everyone, including those with a clear preference for Thinking, chose "always kind," which is the response keyed to the Feeling preference. Only a few people who reported a very clear preference for Thinking (i.e., those who answered almost every question on the T–F scale in the Thinking direction) responded "always fair." Apparently people who very consistently prefer Thinking are willing to put up with a certain amount of unkind behavior as long as they can be assured that they are being treated fairly. Such an item is not useful for separating people at the midpoint of the dichotomy and therefore was not selected for Form M.

IRT was also used in another way to select items. Using an IRT technique called *differential item functioning* (DIF), each item in the pool was examined to determine whether gender or age was significantly related to the response to the item. The DIF method is a powerful technique that can help determine whether the response to the item is better predicted by gender, for example, than by the person's preference on a given MBTI dichotomy. Items from any of the four scales that showed differential responding by gender were eliminated. For example, the following item showed significant gender differences:

> Do you usually
> (A) show your feelings freely, or
> (B) keep your feelings to yourself?

While people of different preferences (on the E–I and also perhaps on the T–F scale) may respond differently to this item, the different response rates by preference are not as great as is the difference between males and females. This item was therefore eliminated.

Elimination of items showing gender differences means that Form M does not require separate weights for males and females on the Thinking–Feeling scale, nor on any of the other three scales. This is the first form of the MBTI for which there is no separate weighting for males and females on any of the scales.

Although age differences were also examined, not all items showing age DIF were automatically eliminated. The items that did show age differences were generally of two kinds. One set included questions that younger respondents would have trouble answering because they have not had the experience necessary to respond. For example, one of the MBTI questions includes the response "when running a business meeting . . . ," which is unlikely to be in the behavioral repertoire of an 18-year-old respondent. Another example is this word pair from the E–I scale:

> party (A)   (B) theater

Based on the response data, young people either have little idea of what a theater actually is or see this as not a very attractive choice when compared with a party. This item was therefore eliminated, as were other such items.

A second set of items showing age DIF were items that were more developmental in nature. These primarily tended to be items from the J–P scale that asked the respondent to choose between planning versus acting spontaneously. These items were retained (if they met the other criteria described in Chapter 7) in order to not eliminate items that might be sensitive to the development of preferences. A possible outcome of this decision is that test-retest reliabilities may be lower, especially over long periods, for younger respondents.

Scoring Scoring includes a decision about how to weight items and then how to summarize the responses to the items into an overall indication of preference. Since one of the primary goals of the revision was to improve the classification of people around the midpoint of each scale, scoring and weighting schemes were examined for their capacity to increase the precision around the midpoint of each dichotomous scale. Two different approaches to scoring were tested and compared: the prediction ratio method, and an approach based on item response theory. For each of these two approaches, a number of scoring alternatives were devised and tested. To determine which was the better approach, a large-scale best-fit type study was conducted.

Isabel Briggs Myers developed the earliest items of the Indicator using a select criterion group whose type preferences were clear enough to be manifest consistently in observable behavior. Purely observational data collected by means of a small criterion group, while essential to the initial stages of a personality assessment and to later validation, gave way early in Myers' research to larger, heterogeneous samples and to a reliance on determining statistical relationships among these data. However, the fundamental objective of comparing a person's knowledge and awareness of his or her best-fit type against the reported type on the Indicator—and using a sample large enough to yield ample statistical power—has been undertaken only in recent years.

The best-fit type study undertaken to test alternative scoring methods involved administering the MBTI to more than 2,400 people nationwide. (Methods and results are described in more detail in Chapter 7 of this manual.) In addition to responding to the Indicator, each person also participated in a face-to-face interpretation, either individually with the interpreter or in a group feedback setting. The interpretations covered the theory of psychological types and a description of the preferences. Each person was asked to identify the type he or she believed provided the best fit. Each person was also asked to rate, on a scale of 1 to 5, his or her level of confidence in the estimate. The best-fit type estimates were then compared with the types that were derived by applying the different scoring procedures to the item responses.

The results indicated that one of the IRT alternative scoring methods provided the highest percentage of matches with the best-fit type estimates. The sample was divided in many different ways—by clarity of preference, age, gender, ethnic group, confidence rating, and type of interpretation—and in every analysis the IRT approach provided at least a marginally better match with best-fit type. This approach was then adopted as the scoring procedure for the 1998 revision.

Standardization Sample   The item weights used to score previous versions of the Indicator were based on prediction ratios that were calculated from the responses of high school and college students. Although these samples were large and efforts were made to select samples that might provide a substantial degree of variability, a more recent and representative sample was desired. Consequently, researchers collected a national random sample. Households across the United States were selected by random-digit dialing of telephone numbers. Specific population demographic targets for the final sample were based on the latest U.S. census. More than 8,000 people were contacted; of these, about 4,000 who matched the census targets agreed to participate and were mailed copies of the MBTI research form, along with an extensive demographic questionnaire. Responses were received from about 80% of the sample who

| Table 2.1 | A Summary of What's New and What's Not: Form M |

Tradition

1. Based on the same philosophy that all preferences are equally valuable
2. Item selection based on Jung's and Myers' theories of type
3. Focus on separating people into types, not measuring traits
4. Fifty-one items with the same wording as on current forms
5. Same forced-choice item format
6. Same two-item formats: phrase questions and word pairs
7. Multiple levels of scoring: Steps I, II, and III
8. Same four dichotomous preference scales, combined to yield 16 types
9. Professional qualifications still required to purchase administration and scoring materials

Innovation

1. Forty-two items with new and updated wording
2. New scoring system based on item response theory, yielding more precise measurement, especially around the midpoint of each scale
3. New reports and support materials
4. No items with more than two possible responses
5. One less item overall
6. No separate weights for the Thinking–Feeling (or any other) scale
7. Item weights based on responses of national sample of adults
8. Improved internal consistency and test-retest reliability of each of the four preference scales

received the forms. This sample of 3,200 adults was then used to determine the item weights. (The characteristics of this sample are described in greater detail in Chapter 7 of this manual.)

Conclusion

Because one of the goals of the 1998 revision was preservation of the MBTI tradition, users will note many similarities between Form M and previous forms of the Indicator. These similarities, as well as the changes, are outlined in Table 2.1. It can be observed in this table that the basic foundations of the MBTI, those characteristics that have made it the most widely used personality test in the world, have not changed. The changes to the instrument are primarily technical and were intended to ensure that the measurement of type keeps up with and takes advantage of the latest advances in psychometrics and test development.

Theory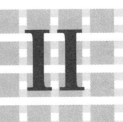

Part II of this manual comprises Chapters 3 and 4. These two chapters cover the theoretical basis of the MBTI and as such are critical to understanding the remainder of the manual and to using type in accurate and effective ways.

Chapter 3, "The Theory Behind the MBTI," puts Jung's theory and Myers and Briggs' extension of it into historical perspective, showing how Jung's initial notion of two opposite categories grew to encompass three pairs of opposites, later evolving into the four dichotomies defined by Myers and Briggs. As you read Chapter 3, you will become aware of the following:

- All of the opposite functions and attitudes are used by every individual at least some of the time.
- The Judging–Perceiving dichotomy permits two kinds of balance in our personalities.
- The theory describes the dynamic ways in which each type is likely to develop over the life span.
- The environment plays a very important role in the development and expression of type.
- A person's preference for Extraversion or Introversion and for Judging or Perceiving enables us to determine the dynamics of her or his type.
- People usually need a "good reason" for using a less-preferred function or attitude.

In reading this chapter, you may notice that you find it easier to understand and see the value of your own preferred poles of each dichotomy but that it takes more effort and objectivity to appreciate and value your less-preferred personality parts. You may also recognize as you read that one or the other pole of each dichotomy may be more generally valued within our culture or other cultures. Awareness of both personal type bias and societal type bias is central to maintaining an objective perspective as you read the second chapter in Part II.

Chapter 4, "Understanding the 16 Types," presents several approaches that will help new users begin to understand the details about the types. The chapter also provides experienced users with some new ways of understanding and explaining the dynamic aspects of the typology. Readers are shown how to read and use type tables for quick access to group type differences. This is followed by a description of and rationale for the precise terminology needed to describe different type groupings. The remainder of the chapter identifies, describes, and provides supporting research for groupings of types that consist of specific two-letter combinations. The 16 full type descriptions and supporting research summaries complete Chapter 4. As you read Chapter 4 you will become aware of the following:

■ There is a difference between, for example, dominant introverted Sensing types (ISTJ and ISFJ) and Introverts with Sensing (ISTJ, ISFJ, ISTP, and ISFP).

■ A good deal of research has been conducted with some groupings of types and very little with others.

■ The workplace accommodates the values and goals of some types more readily than it does those of other types.

■ Different types find different aspects of life more and less stressful and cope with perceived stresses in type-consistent ways.

■ Assessing the 16 types from a single-norm perspective leads to some "positive-seeming" and "negative-seeming" research results.

■ When we evaluate research, we must be careful to avoid falling into a "trait perspective" that makes some types look "better" than others.

Much material is covered in Chapter 4, and it varies in complexity. For newcomers to type, keeping type dynamics accurately in mind takes practice and repetition. They may find it difficult to fully absorb some of the information in this chapter. These readers might find it useful to revisit the chapter after they become more experienced and comfortable with the language and concepts of type.

The Theory Behind the MBTI   3

Every individual is unique. Each of us is a product of heredity and environment and, as a result, is different from everyone else. The doctrine of uniqueness, however, gives no practical help in understanding the people whom we must educate, counsel, work with, or interact with in our personal lives.

In practice we tend to assume unconsciously that other people's minds work on the same principles as our own. All too often, however, the people with whom we interact do not reason as we reason, do not value the things we value, or are not interested in what interests us. The assumption of similarity, therefore, can promote misunderstanding of the motives and behaviors of people whose minds operate quite differently from our own.

The value of the theory underlying the *Myers-Briggs Type Indicator* personality inventory is that it enables us to expect specific differences in specific people and to cope with people and their differences more constructively than we otherwise could. Briefly, the theory is that much seemingly chance variation in human behavior in fact is not due to chance; it is the logical result of a few basic, observable preferences.

In developing the Indicator, Isabel Myers' primary aim was to give individuals access to the benefits of knowing their personality type. A secondary and vital goal was to validate C. G. Jung's theory of psychological types (Jung, 1921/1971) and to put it to practical use. Jungian theory was taken into account in every question and in every step of development of the MBTI instrument. Details of the research leading up to the development of Form M are described in Chapter 7. The MBTI theory is explained in detail in *Gifts Differing* (Myers with Myers, 1980/1995), a basic reference for all who plan to use the MBTI. The dynamic and developmental nature of the theory is further explicated in *Introduction to Type® Dynamics and Development* (Myers & Kirby, 1994) and in other works that focus on specific aspects of dynamics and development (Corlett & Millner, 1993; Quenk, 1993).

A Brief History of Type Theory

When the term *type theory* is used in this manual, it refers to Jung's theory as interpreted by Isabel Myers and Katharine Briggs in the MBTI personality inventory. Jungian type theory was developed over a period of many years. Jung gradually refined the descriptive elements of the system and the dynamic interactions of the elements. Myers and Briggs further refined the approach in providing detailed, neutral descriptions of the types as well as in clarifying the rationale underlying the dynamic interactions hypothesized.

Jung's Initial Focus on Extraversion and Introversion

Jung's attempt to explain individual differences in personality initially stemmed from his observation that there were two types of people, *extraverts* and *introverts*. He described extraverts as those whose energies are primarily oriented outwardly toward people and events in their external environment and introverts as those whose energies are directed inwardly toward thoughts and experiences in their inner environment. His identification of these two types led to the detailed and broad-ranging descriptions of extraversion and introversion that he later described in *Psychological Types* (1921/1971). Jung saw extraversion and introversion as two different attitudes, with the term *attitude* defined as "a readiness of the psyche to act or react in a certain way . . . having an attitude is synonymous with an *a priori* orientation to a definite thing" (1921/1971, p. 414).[1] About 10 years after his initial studies of extraversion and introversion, Jung noted that these two types did not provide a complete picture of what he observed. He stated,

> What struck me now was the undeniable fact [that] while people may be classed as introverts or extraverts, this does not account for the tremendous differences between individuals in either class. So great, indeed, are these differences that I was forced to doubt whether I had observed correctly in the first place. It took nearly ten years of observation and comparison to clear up this doubt. (1921/1971, p. 535)

The Addition of the Four Functions

During those 10 years, Jung subdivided his initial extravert and introvert types into eight types by identifying two pairs of opposite mental functions: two opposite perceiving functions, *sensation* (called *Sensing* by Myers and Briggs) versus *intuition*; and two opposite judging functions, *thinking* versus *feeling*.[2] As stated in Chapter 1, *perceiving* refers to the gathering of information, and *judging* refers to the manner with which we come to conclusions about what we perceive. The specific meaning of each of these functions will be discussed later in this chapter. Jung defined a function as "a particular form of psychic activity that remains the same in principle under varying conditions" (Jung, 1921/1971, p. 436).

Jung further specified which of the two attitudes of extraversion and introversion was likely to be habitually used in conjunction with the *dominant* mental function in an individual. The term *dominant function* refers to the function—Sensing, Intuition, Thinking, or Feeling—that is likely to be used most enthusiastically, most often, and with the greatest confidence. The dominant function can be viewed as directing, or "dominating," the personality.

The addition of the pairs of functions to the two initial attitude types led to Jung's specification of the following eight types in *Psychological Types* (1921/1971).

- Extraverts with dominant sensing
- Introverts with dominant sensing
- Extraverts with dominant intuition
- Introverts with dominant intuition
- Extraverts with dominant thinking
- Introverts with dominant thinking
- Extraverts with dominant feeling
- Introverts with dominant feeling

Jung's system thus defined eight dominant types. They are briefly described in Table 3.1.

The Addition of the Judging–Perceiving (J–P) Dichotomy

In developing the MBTI, Myers and Briggs built on statements by Jung that related to the way Jung believed the functions interacted, that is, the dynamic character of the model. They extended Jung's model by adding the J–P dichotomy, thereby making explicit one aspect of the theory that was implicit but undeveloped in Jung's work. Specifically, they built upon Jung's description of an *auxiliary function* that supported and complemented the dominant function in every type. The addition of the J–P dichotomy in the MBTI identified the dominant and auxiliary functions for each type.[3] Thus Jung's model was refined so as to describe 16 types:

- Extraverts with dominant Sensing and auxiliary Thinking
- Extraverts with dominant Sensing and auxiliary Feeling
- Introverts with dominant Sensing and auxiliary Thinking
- Introverts with dominant Sensing and auxiliary Feeling
- Extraverts with dominant Intuition and auxiliary Thinking
- Extraverts with dominant Intuition and auxiliary Feeling
- Introverts with dominant Intuition and auxiliary Thinking
- Introverts with dominant Intuition and auxiliary Feeling

Table 3.1   The Eight Jungian Functions

Dominant Extraverted Sensing	Directing energy outwardly and acquiring information by focusing on a detailed, accurate accumulation of sensory data in the present
Dominant Introverted Sensing	Directing energy inwardly and storing the facts and details of both external reality and internal thoughts and experiences
Dominant Extraverted Intuition	Directing energy outwardly to scan for new ideas, interesting patterns, and future possibilities
Dominant Introverted Intuition	Directing energy inwardly to focus on unconscious images, connections, and patterns that create inner vision and insight
Dominant Extraverted Thinking	Seeking logical order to the external environment by applying clarity, goal-directedness, and decisive action
Dominant Introverted Thinking	Seeking accuracy and order in internal thoughts through reflecting on and developing a logical system for understanding
Dominant Extraverted Feeling	Seeking harmony through organizing and structuring the environment to meet people's needs and their own values
Dominant Introverted Feeling	Seeking intensely meaningful and complex inner harmony through sensitivity to their own and others' inner values and outer behavior

- Extraverts with dominant Thinking and auxiliary Sensing
- Extraverts with dominant Thinking and auxiliary Intuition
- Introverts with dominant Thinking and auxiliary Sensing
- Introverts with dominant Thinking and auxiliary Intuition
- Extraverts with dominant Feeling and auxiliary Sensing
- Extraverts with dominant Feeling and auxiliary Intuition
- Introverts with dominant Feeling and auxiliary Sensing
- Introverts with dominant Feeling and auxiliary Intuition

The Dynamic Character of Type Theory and the MBTI

In developing type theory, Jung, Myers, and Briggs were constantly attentive to the dynamic character of the personality types they were describing. The richness, depth, and breadth of their descriptive systems result from the dynamic interplay of the functions and attitudes inherent in each type. It is important to bear this in mind in applying type theory and interpreting the MBTI personality inventory.

When people are introduced to the MBTI, the parts of the theory—the four type dichotomies, E–I, S–N, T–F, and J–P—are generally explained first. Because these parts are interesting and useful in themselves, many people stop at this level of understanding. In doing so, they miss the broader implications and applications that are intrinsic to the dynamic character of the MBTI. Explaining the parts that contribute to the whole is, however, a necessary step in arriving at an understanding of the dynamics of type. The following discussion focuses on the four dichotomies of the MBTI.

The Four Functions

The essence of Jung's comprehensive theory of type is that everyone uses four basic mental *functions,* or *processes,* that are called Sensing (S), Intuition (N), Thinking (T), and Feeling (F). These four functions are essential for daily living. The 16 types differ in the priorities given to each function and in the attitudes of Extraversion (E) and Introversion (I) in which they typically use each function. These differences in priorities and attitudes of energy (E or I) account for the different interactions among the functions that occur in each of the 16 types. This and the next chapter describe the distinctive dynamics and development of each type.

The four functions postulated by Jung—Sensing, Intuition, Thinking, and Feeling—represent functions as they are related to consciousness. This means that any one of the four functions can be conscious in a particular individual. The function that is most conscious or dominant, that is, that has the greatest amount of conscious energy at its command, determines the degree of consciousness of the other three. For example, if Sensing is the dominant, most conscious function, the opposite, Intuition, will be the least conscious. Thinking and Feeling will be somewhere between Sensing and Intuition in available energy. The same principle applies when Intuition, Thinking, or Feeling has the largest share of psychological energy or attention.

Jung's concept of the four functions grew from his empirical observations over many years: Jung concluded, "I distinguish these functions from one another because they cannot be related or reduced to one another" (1921/1971,

p. 437). Type theory assumes, therefore, that many aspects of conscious mental activity can be subsumed under one of these four categories.

Use of the Terms *Perception* and *Judgment*

To understand Jung's theory it is important to appreciate the uses of the terms *perception* and *judgment*.

Perception means all the ways of becoming aware of things, people, events, or ideas. It includes information gathering, the seeking of sensation or of inspiration, and the selection of a stimulus to attend to.

Judgment means all the ways of coming to conclusions about what has been perceived. It includes evaluation, choice, decision making, and the selection of a response after perceiving a stimulus.

Two Kinds of Perception: Sensing (S) and Intuition (N)

Jung divided all perceiving activities into two categories—*sensation* and *intuition.* He called these *irrational functions,* by which he meant that they are attuned to the flow of events and operate most broadly when not constrained by rational direction. Freely experiencing a flood of sensations with no attempt to limit or select amongst them is an illustration of sensing as an irrational function. During such a state of free receptivity, sensations flow freely with no attempt to evaluate them. The technique of *brainstorming* illustrates intuition in the irrational sense. During brainstorming, inspirations are encouraged to flow freely, without the constraint of criticism or appraisal.

Sensing (S) *Sensing* refers to perceptions observable by way of the senses. Sensing establishes what exists. Because the senses can bring to awareness only what is occurring in the present moment, persons oriented toward Sensing tend to focus on the immediate experiences available to their five senses. They therefore often develop characteristics associated with this awareness, such as enjoyment of the present moment, realism, acute powers of observation, memory for the details of both past and present experiences, and practicality. Persons oriented to Sensing may become so intent on observing and experiencing the present moment that they do not sufficiently attend to future possibilities.

Intuition (N) *Intuition* refers to perception of possibilities, meanings, and relationships by way of insight. Jung characterized intuition as perception by way of the unconscious. Intuition may come to the surface of consciousness as a "hunch" or as a sudden discovery of a pattern in seemingly unrelated events. Intuition permits perception beyond what is visible to the senses, including possible future events. People who prefer Intuition may develop the characteristics that can follow from that emphasis and become imaginative, theoretical, abstract, future oriented, and original or creative.[4] Persons oriented toward Intuition may also become so intent on pursuing possibilities that they overlook actualities.

An Example of Sensing Versus Intuition The difference between the two perceiving functions can be illustrated by the example of an apple. When the Sensing function is used to perceive an apple, a person might describe it as "juicy," "crisp," "red," or "white with black seeds." The focus is on the sensory attributes of the apple. When the Intuitive function is used to perceive the same apple, a person may say "William Tell," "How to keep the doctor away," "Roast pig," or "My grandmother's famous pie." Here the focus is on the associations and possible meanings stimulated by the apple.

Two Kinds of Judgment: Thinking (T) and Feeling (F)

Jung used the terms *thinking* and *feeling* in specialized ways to refer to the *rational functions,* functions that can be personally directed and are in accord with the laws of reason. These rational judging functions appraise or evaluate perceptions; Thinking and Feeling judgments act as constraints or limits on the free flow of the sensations or intuitions received by the two irrational perceiving functions, which are focused entirely on the general flux of events.

Thinking Judgment (T) *Thinking* is the function that comes to a decision by linking ideas together through logical connections. Thinking relies on principles of cause and effect and tends to be objective and impersonal in the application of reason to a decision. The focus of attention of Thinking judgment is on the Sensing or Intuitive information relevant to making the particular decision at hand. Thinking judgment relies on impartiality and neutrality with respect to the personal desires and values of both the decision maker and the people who may be affected by the decision. Persons who are primarily oriented toward Thinking are likely to develop characteristics associated with this way of arriving at conclusions: analytical inclination, objectivity, concern with principles of justice and fairness, criticality, an impassive and dispassionate demeanor, and an orientation to time that is linear, that is, concerned with connections from the past through the present and toward the future.

Feeling Judgment (F) *Feeling* is the function by which one comes to decisions by weighing relative values and merits of the issues. Feeling relies on an understanding of personal values and group values; thus it is more subjective than Thinking. Nevertheless, "Feeling, like thinking, is a *rational* function, since values in general are assigned according to the laws of reason" (Jung, 1921/1971, p. 435). Because values are subjective and personal, persons making judgments with the Feeling function are more likely to be attuned to the values and feelings of others as well as to their own values and feelings. They try to understand people and to anticipate and take into account the effects of the decision at hand on the people involved and on what is important to them. They have a concern with the human as opposed to the technical aspects of problems, a desire for affiliation, warmth, and harmony, and a time orientation that includes preservation of enduring values. The focus on subjective values renders the process of making a Feeling judgment less directly observable than the linear, logical process of making a Thinking judgment. As a result, Feeling types may be at a disadvantage when asked to "justify" their judgments from the point of view of logic alone.

Although the classical distinction in psychology between "tough-minded" and "tender-minded" people is one aspect of the T–F difference, it does not follow that "thinking" people do not have "feelings" or that "feeling" people cannot follow a logical argument. Such erroneous views reflect two of the common misconceptions about people who favor one or the other of the two judging functions. Equating Feeling as a decision-making process with feeling as affect or emotion is also a common misperception. In this regard, Jung stated, "Feeling is distinguishable from affect by the fact that it produces no perceptible physical innervations, i.e., neither more nor less than an ordinary thinking process" (1921/1971, p. 434).

An Example of Thinking Versus Feeling Decision Making

An example of the difference between using Thinking judgment and using Feeling judgment is the following:

In making a decision about which of five employees should be promoted to a supervisory position, the Thinking decision process would very likely involve developing a set of explicit criteria, ranking the criteria relative to their importance to the decision, and rating each of the five employees accordingly. After deciding which candidate or candidates best met the criteria, a Thinking type might or might not use the less-preferred Feeling function to consider other factors such as personal style, acceptability to other employees, and the employee's personal circumstances. Such considerations might aid decision making when a choice must be made between equally logical alternatives. Attending to these more subjective issues might also allow the decision maker to see whether any of these factors might have a significant negative impact on the logical choice.

A Feeling decision might focus initially on the qualifications for the job, including impact on other workers and personal circumstances of the five employees, determining whether the best candidate or candidates stood out clearly as a result of this weighing of values. If two or more appropriate candidates resulted from this process, the Feeling type might use the less-preferred Thinking function to develop a set of objective criteria to aid in final decision making. If only one candidate was clearly outstanding, objective criteria would be applied to ensure that nothing important was overlooked, as well as to facilitate a smooth and harmonious transition for all employees affected by the decision.

The Roles of the Functions

The four functions direct conscious mental activity toward different goals:

- Sensing (S) seeks the fullest possible experience of what is immediate and real.
- Intuition (N) seeks the furthest reaches of the possible and imaginative.
- Thinking (T) seeks rational order in accord with the nonpersonal logic of cause and effect.
- Feeling (F) seeks rational order in accord with the creation and maintenance of harmony among important subjective values.

The key to the dynamics of the theory lies in the assumption that the four functions have different areas of specialization and therefore pull in different directions, toward different domains of mental activity. If all functions exerted equal weight, the personality would be at cross-purposes, lacking in consistent direction. To compare a personality to a ship at sea, we take it for granted that a ship needs a captain with undisputed authority to set the course and bring the ship safely to port. The ship would never reach its destination if each person at the helm in turn aimed at a different destination and altered course accordingly. In type theory, one of the four functions is the favorite, or dominant, function. This dominant function serves as the "captain" of the personality. It determines what is the necessary direction to reach the desired destination and keeps the ship "on course." The other functions are important but are subordinate to and serve the goals of the dominant function.

In Jungian terms, the dominant function has the largest share of the available psychic energy under its control. In the hierarchy of the functions, the auxiliary, tertiary, and inferior functions have proportionally less energy available that the individual can direct and control.

The Four Attitudes or Orientations

Understanding the way in which the dominant and other functions interrelate in each type requires an explanation of the Extraversion–Introversion (E–I) and Judging–Perceiving (J–P) dichotomies, the two pairs of attitudes or orientations in type theory. This section explains these dichotomies.

Two Kinds of Energy— Extraversion and Introversion

A major portion of Jung's *Psychological Types* (1921/1971) is devoted to the historical development and description of the concepts of extraversion and introversion. These are seen as complementary attitudes or orientations of energy. The nature and extent of differences between extraversion and introversion translate into profoundly different approaches to or orientations toward life.

The Extraverted Attitude (E) In the Extraverted attitude, energy and attention flow out, or are drawn out, to the objects and people in the environment. The individual experiences a desire to act on the environment, to affirm its importance, to increase its effect. Persons habitually taking the Extraverted attitude may develop some or all of the characteristics associated with Extraversion: awareness of and reliance on the environment for stimulation and guidance; an eagerness to interact with the outer world; an action-oriented, sometimes impulsive way of meeting life; openness to new experiences; ease of communication and sociability; and a desire to "talk things out."

The Introverted Attitude (I) In the Introverted attitude, energy is drawn from the environment toward inner experience and reflection. One desires to stay focused on the internal, subjective state, to affirm its value, and to maintain this focus as long as possible. The main interests of the Introverted type are in the world of concepts, ideas, and inner experiences. Persons habitually taking the Introverted attitude may develop some or all of the characteristics associated with Introversion: interest in the clarity of concepts, ideas, and recollected experience; reliance on enduring concepts and experiences more than on transitory external events or fleeting ideas; a thoughtful, contemplative detachment; an enjoyment of solitude and privacy; and a desire to "think things out" before talking about them.

To many laypeople, the term *extraverted* means *sociable*, and *introverted* means *shy*.[5] Jung's concept is different from and much broader than the layperson's view. Seen as different orientations of energy, a preference for Extraversion or Introversion identifies the direction in which a person's energies typically flow, outward or inward. Extraverts are seen as having more energy directed toward the outer world, with correspondingly less energy available for inner activities. Introverts are seen as having more energy directed toward the inner world, with correspondingly less energy available for activities in the outer world. The comfort with and amount of time devoted to each orientation of energy by individuals results in two recognizable variants of normal human personality—Extraverts and Introverts. These types of people have been recognized throughout history and literature, each making major contributions to society. Myers' descriptions of Extraverts and Introverts reflect the complex, multifaceted nature of Jung's conception.

Two Attitudes or Orientations to the Outer World—Judging (J) and Perceiving (P)

No explicit mention is made by Jung regarding a judging versus perceiving attitude[6] or orientation toward the outer world. Katharine Briggs described such a type classification in her unpublished work prior to the publication of Jung's work. She observed that some people habitually use *judgment* in interacting with the outer, extraverted world, being likely to come to conclusions and achieve closure quickly.

These people were identified later by Myers and Briggs as people with a *Judging* attitude. Briggs described other people as habitually interacting with the outer world using *perceiving*, liking to continue gathering information as long as possible before comfortably coming to closure. These people were identified later as having a *Perceiving* attitude. Katharine Briggs' work in conjunction with Jung's incomplete discussion of this area formed the basis for the J–P formulation used in the MBTI.

The J–P dichotomy has two uses. First, in conjunction with the E–I dichotomy, it is used to identify which of the two preferred functions is the leading or dominant function and which is the auxiliary function. Second, it describes identifiable attitudes or orientations to the outer world. The recognition and development of the character of the J–P dichotomy are a major contribution of Briggs and Myers to the theory of psychological types.

The concept of the J–P attitude was derived over a period of several decades, before any MBTI items were written. Myers' observation of different behavioral patterns formed the basis for the J–P distinction. Behaviors characteristic of persons who used either Thinking or Feeling in their outer life (i.e., who extraverted one of the judgment functions) formed the basis for the Judging pole of the J–P dichotomy. Behaviors characteristic of persons who used either Sensing or Intuition in their outer life (i.e., who extraverted a perceiving function) formed the basis of the Perceiving pole of the J–P dichotomy. *One of the most overlooked characteristics of the J–P dichotomy is that it describes the orientation to the outer or extraverted world for every type.* Others readily notice how people behave in the outer world and, as a result, often recognize someone as having a Judging or a Perceiving attitude relatively early on in the acquaintance.

In any new activity, it is appropriate first to use a perceiving function (S or N) to observe or take in the situation; then it is appropriate to use a judging function (T or F) to decide on the appropriate action. Perceiving types typically remain longer in the observing attitude because it is more comfortable and natural for them. Judging types move more quickly through perception in order to reach conclusions and achieve closure, as they are most comfortable and satisfied when a plan has been developed or when a decision has been made.

The Judging Attitude (J) In the Judging attitude, a person is concerned with making decisions, seeking closure, planning operations, or organizing activities. For Thinking Judging (TJ) types, the decisions and plans are more likely to be based on logical analysis; for Feeling Judging (FJ) types, the decisions and plans are more likely to be based on weighing and assessing values. But for both TJ and FJ people, who characteristically live in the Judging (J) attitude, perception tends to be shut off as soon as they have observed enough to make a decision. In contrast, people who prefer the Perceiving attitude will often suspend judgment to take another look, reporting, "We don't know enough yet to make a decision." People who prefer Judging often seem in their outer behavior to be organized, purposeful, and decisive, frequently stating, "Yes, we do have enough information to make this decision."

Procrastination can be the result of perception with a deficit of judgment. Prejudice can come from judgment with a deficit of perception. People new to the MBTI sometimes erroneously assume that Judging types are necessarily *judgmental*. It is important to understand that Judging refers to decision making, the exercise of judgment, and is a valuable and indispensable tool. It is also important to distinguish between a preference for using a Perceiving function in the outer world (P) and *perceptiveness*. Just as J types should not be assumed to be judgmental, P types should not be assumed to be especially discerning.

A source of confusion for many people learning about the MBTI is the fact that *Judging* includes both Thinking and Feeling and *Perceiving* includes both Sensing and Intuition. Figure 3.1 shows this relationship.

The Perceiving Attitude (P) In the Perceiving attitude, a person is attuned to incoming information. For Sensing Perceiving (SP) types the information is more likely to be the immediate realities in the environment, what is happening and is observable. For Intuitive Perceiving (NP) types the information is more likely to be new ideas, interesting patterns, and future possibilities. But for both SP and NP types, the Perceiving attitude is open, curious, and interested. Persons who characteristically live in the Perceiving attitude seem in their outer behavior to be spontaneous, curious, adaptable, and open to what is new and changeable. Their aim is to receive information as long as possible in an effort to miss nothing that might be important.

The Theory of Type Development

An important aspect of Jung's type theory is its focus on the development of personality throughout the life span. There is a hierarchy of functions that describes an individual's personality at any stage of life. This hierarchy of dominant, auxiliary, tertiary, and inferior functions permits and encourages the kind of development and adaptation that is likely to be most useful for an individual at each stage of life.

Type Development During Childhood

Type theory assumes that children are born with a predisposition to prefer some functions to others. Children are most interested in their preferred functions. They are motivated to exercise their dominant function and to a somewhat lesser extent their auxiliary function, becoming more skillful, adept, and *differentiated* in their use. Jung described a *differentiated function* as one that is separate and exists by itself, so that it can operate on its own without being mixed up

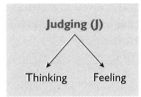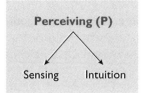

Figure 3.1 The J–P Dichotomy
Source: From *Introduction to Type* (6th ed., p. 6), by I. B. Myers, with L. K. Kirby & K. D. Myers, 1998. Palo Alto, CA: Consulting Psychologists Press. Used with permission.

with or contaminated by any other function (1921/1971). A sense of competence comes from exercising a function well, and with the reinforcement of constant practice these functions become more controlled and trustworthy. The pleasure of using preferred functions generalizes to other activities requiring use of the functions and leads to the surface traits, behaviors, and skills associated with these functions.

While this development of preferred functions is occurring, there is relative neglect of the opposite functions. In this sequence of events, for example, a child who prefers Sensing perception and a child who prefers Intuitive perception will develop along divergent lines. Each will become relatively differentiated in an area in which the other remains undifferentiated. Both channel their interests and energies into activities that give them a chance to use their minds in the ways they prefer, and each acquires a set of surface traits that grows out of the basic preferences.

Type Development During Adolescence and Adulthood

As a child becomes an adolescent and then an adult, continued exercise of the dominant and auxiliary functions promotes further enjoyment, development, and differentiation of them as compared with their opposite inferior and tertiary functions. For example, a person who develops Sensing in a highly differentiated way is likely to become an astute observer of the immediate environment. In the process, the person acquires some of the characteristics assumed to follow from this acute awareness: realism, practicality, and common sense. While paying attention to the specifics of the environment, the person spends less time and energy using Intuition, which is the perceiving function opposite to Sensing. Focusing on the present (S) gives people who prefer the Sensing function less time for focusing on the future (N); focusing on the concrete (S) gives them less energy for focusing on the abstract (N); focusing on practical applications (S) gives them less interest in theoretical issues (N); and focusing on reality (S) gives them less time for focusing on the imaginary or fanciful (N).

Type Development over the Life Span

Type development is seen as a lifelong process of gaining greater command over the functions or powers of perception and judgment. For each type, two of the four functions are assumed to be more interesting and more likely to be consciously developed and used. The two less-preferred functions are assumed to be less interesting and are likely to be relatively neglected. Development comes from striving for excellence in those functions that hold the greatest interest and from becoming at least passable in the other less interesting but essential functions.

In youth and adulthood, the task is to develop the first (*leading,* or *dominant*) and the second (*auxiliary*) functions. The theory assumes that these innate, natural functions are best suited to helping a person find a comfortable and effective place in the world—the task of youth and adulthood. "Specializing" by devoting a great deal of energy to one's dominant and auxiliary functions is therefore appropriate during the first half of life. During midlife, people appear to be naturally motivated toward completing their personalities through gradually adding the previously neglected tertiary and inferior functions to the sphere of operation. In the second half of life, it is appropriate to be a "generalist" rather than a specialist. Development of this kind allows individuals to add new perspectives and experiences that were previously not very fulfilling to them. Giving greater energy and attention to the tertiary and inferior functions involves a corresponding lessening of energy and attention to the dominant and auxiliary functions. However, this does not involve a change in a person's type. *Type theory assumes that type does not change over the life span.* Rather, the expression of type may vary in accordance with different stages of life and different life circumstances.

A very few exceptional persons may reach a stage of development at which they can use each function relatively easily as the situation requires. For most people, however, striving for a comfortable and effective expression of the four mental functions is an interesting and challenging life-long process, with no expectation that a person will arrive at a predetermined level of development.

Influence of the Environment on Type Development

In the type model, *environment* becomes extremely important because it can foster development of each person's natural preferences, or it can discourage them by reinforcing activities that are less satisfying, less comfortable, and less motivating. The latter situation makes it difficult to acquire confidence and skill in one's natural preferences. In fact, environmental interference with type development can distort or suppress a person's natural, innate type. Individuals to whom this occurs may become skillful in using an initially less-preferred function but may also be less content, may feel less competent, or may be out of touch with their own best gifts. The MBTI does not necessarily reveal the extent to which natural development has been fostered or thwarted. Chapters 5 and 6 will discuss some of the strategies for helping individuals identify their true preferences.

Rationale for a Type Development Theory

Some people dislike the idea of a dominant function and prefer to think of themselves as using all the functions equally. Others strive for equal development of the functions, erroneously believing this to be necessary or desirable. Jung said that when energy is shared equally between two opposite mental functions, differentiation cannot occur. Both functions remain undeveloped, which produces an unconscious "primitive mentality" in which neither function can be directed and controlled. When a person tries to attend to two incompatible opposites at the same time, they "jam" each other and no clear signal comes through. For example, a person who is "pulled" equally toward Sensing and Intuition might focus on concrete facts in the present, move quickly to future possibilities, switch to an entirely different set of facts, and so on. Persistent vacillation among perceiving functions would very likely produce confusion and frustration for the individual. At the point at which a decision needs to be made based on available information, Sensing facts and Intuitive possibilities may be indistinguishable from one another. Thus, if either one of a pair of functions is to develop, the other must be shut off most of the time to give the person a chance to gain experience and confidence in the natural, preferred function.

In Jungian typology, therefore, optimum use of the four functions is to be obtained not through equality but rather through selective development of each function in proportion both to its relative importance to the individual and to its useful relationship to the other processes. The general goal of development is to

- Become differentiated with the preferred functions— adequately develop a dominant, most-conscious function used primarily in the preferred attitude, and a balancing and somewhat less conscious auxiliary function used primarily in the less-preferred attitude.
- Eventually admit the least-developed processes to conscious, purposeful use in the service of the dominant process and for selected tasks or for limited periods of time. This use may require the dominant and auxiliary functions to temporarily relinquish control in consciousness so that the third or fourth function can become more accessible.
- Use each of the functions for the tasks for which they are best fitted. For example, a dominant Intuitive type may find that using her inferior Sensing is the most effective way of handling important financial records; a dominant Thinking type may find employees to be less resistant to organizational change when they are given an opportunity to voice personal concerns and issues.

The Universality of Type

The growing evidence regarding the biological basis of psychological type, which is described in detail in Chapter 9, gives credence to Jung's assumption that type is universal, that is, that the personalities of all human beings are structured in accordance with type dichotomies. Support for universality comes from the fact that many translations of the MBTI are being used successfully and many more are being developed. Users in other countries and cultures report excellent results in applying personality type concepts. All four dichotomies and all 16 types are recognized in other countries and cultures. However, the way the opposite preferences in each dichotomy are *expressed* in other cultures may vary considerably from the way they are expressed in U.S. culture. A discussion of this and related issues regarding the universality of type can be found in Chapter 14.

The Dynamic Interaction of the Preferences

When people respond to the items on the MBTI assessment tool, they are not only casting votes for Extraversion (E) or Introversion (I), Sensing (S) or Intuition (N), Thinking (T) or Feeling (F), and Judging (J) or Perceiving (P); they are also providing the information needed to form a hypothesis about their *type dynamics*. Each four-letter type stands for a complex set of dynamic relationships among the functions (S, N, T, and F), the attitudes (E and I), and the attitude or orientation to the outer world (J and P). The letters in any type appear in this order: E or I, S or N, T or F, J or P. All 16 possible combinations of letters occur—ESTJ, ISFP, INFJ, ENTP, and so on.

The Jungian Basis for Type Dynamics

Jung's recognition of the dynamic character of his typology evolved over time, and the amount of detail he provided about its various elements varied considerably. He first (1921/1971) described eight preference types, focusing on the dominant function of each and the attitude (E or I) in which the dominant function was typically used. Jung described but did not go into great detail concerning the need for a secondary function "whose nature is different from, but not antagonistic to, the primary function" (Jung, 1921/1971, p. 406). According to Jung, every type has an "auxiliary function which is in every respect different from the nature of the primary function." From these statements, Myers and Briggs reasoned that the auxiliary function is oriented to the less-preferred attitude. Indeed, there are several references in Jung's writing to the three remaining functions having an opposite attitudinal character. For example, in writing about introverts with thinking dominant (p. 387), Jung commented that the counterbalancing functions (that is, auxiliary, tertiary, and inferior functions) have an extraverted character. Myers and Briggs therefore assumed the following:

- For each type, one function will lead, or be dominant. This is the first function.
- Members of each type will mainly use their first function in their favorite attitude. That is, Extraverts use the first function mainly in the outer world of Extraversion; Introverts use the first function mainly in the introverted world of concepts, ideas, and inner experience.
- In addition to the first, or dominant, function, a second, or auxiliary, function will be developed to provide balance.
- The auxiliary function provides balance between Extraversion and Introversion. For Extraverts, the first, or dominant, function will be extraverted, and the second, or auxiliary, function will typically be used in the inner world. For Introverts, the first, or dominant, function will be introverted, and the second, or auxiliary, function will typically be used in the outer world. *With the auxiliary, or second, function, therefore, a person develops comfort and facility in living in both the outer world and the inner world.*

Notice that in this model, *Extraverts show their first, or best, function to the outside world; Introverts show their second-best function to the outside world, saving their best function for the inner world of ideas.* It follows, therefore, that Introverts are more likely to be underestimated in casual contacts.

The fact that the second function provides balance between Extraversion and Introversion also provides a correction to a common misconception by persons new to type theory. Extraverts may assume that type theory says they never like to be alone, and Introverts may assume that type theory says they never like to be sociable. *Type theory, however, assumes that everyone lives in both the extraverted and introverted worlds to some extent.* Many people attain comfort and competence in both worlds, but for each person, one attitude is preferred over the other. A well-developed Introvert can deal ably with the extraverted world when necessary but works best, most easily, and with less fatigue when concentrating on concepts or inner experience. A similarly well-developed Extravert can deal effectively with concepts or inner experience but works with most interest, satisfaction, and energy externally in action. Good type development fosters the ability to extravert comfortably and to introvert comfortably but also assumes a clear and natural preference for one attitude or the other.

- The auxiliary function also provides balance between perception and judgment. As specified by Jung, if the first function is a perceiving function (S or N), the second function will be a judging function (T or F). Or, if the first function is a judging function (T or F), the second function will be a perceiving function (S or N). *When using the auxiliary function effectively, a person gains command of both perception and judgment,* that is, of taking in information and making decisions.

- The J–P dichotomy, as noted earlier, *points to the function used in the extraverted attitude, for both Extraverts and Introverts.*

- The function opposed to the dominant function is typically the least-developed, or inferior, function. It can also be referred to as the fourth function. The inferior function tends to be used in the less-preferred attitude of Extraversion or Introversion.

- The function opposite to the auxiliary function is the tertiary, or third, function. Several views regarding the attitude typically used by the tertiary function have been proposed. For the purposes of exposition and consistency with the 1985 *Manual,* we will assume that the dominant function operates in the preferred attitude and that the auxiliary, tertiary, and inferior functions all take the opposite, less-preferred attitude.[7] Jungians themselves do not agree about some specifics of Jung's psychological type theory, particularly in relation to the orientation of the auxiliary function as identified by the J–P dichotomy.[8]

These assumptions make it possible to use the type letters to identify the first (dominant), second (auxiliary), third (tertiary), and fourth (inferior) functions and their typical attitudes for each of the 16 types.

Identifying the Dynamics of Each Type

The four letters of type show the preference order (see also Table 3.2).

First letter: preference for the Extraverted (E) or Introverted (I) attitude of energy

Second letter: preference for Sensing (S) or Intuitive (N) perception

Third letter: preference for Thinking (T) or Feeling (F) judgment

Fourth letter: preference for a Judging (J) or Perceiving (P) attitude toward the outer, extraverted world

Remember that for any type, the middle two letters identify the dominant and auxiliary functions. The following section presents a straightforward way to determine the dynamics of type for any four-letter type.

Steps for Identifying the Hierarchy of Functions

Step 1: The first step is to look at the last letter of the type, J or P. It will tell us whether a judging function (T or F) or a perceiving function (S or N) is typically *extraverted* in that type. For example, for ESTJ, the J shows that the judging function is extraverted. The judging function preferred by an ESTJ is *Thinking.* The J in the formula points to Thinking as the extraverted function for ESTJ. As a reminder of this fact, we put a small $_E$ beside the T in ESTJ.

EST$_E$J

Table 3.2   Positions of the Preferences

E–I	S–N	T–F	J–P
Attitudes	Perceiving Functions	Judging Functions	Attitudes
Extraversion or Introversion	Sensing or Intuition	Thinking or Feeling	Judging or Perceiving

Step 2: For the second step, we remember that in type dynamics, one function is extraverted and the other function is introverted. For ESTJ, we know that T is the extraverted function. The remaining middle letter is S, so S must be the introverted function. As a reminder, we put a small $_I$ beside the S.

S$_I$

The type can now be shown as follows:

ES$_I$T$_E$J

Step 3: For the third step, we remember that the first letter tells us which attitude is preferred and thus the attitude in which the type's *dominant function* is used. We therefore look at the *first* letter of the type. We see that for ES$_I$T$_E$J it is E. It tells us that ESTJ *extraverts* the dominant function.

Step 4: The fourth step looks at the function that has an $_E$ beside it. For ES$_I$T$_E$J it is T. We can now match that $_E$ with the first letter, E. This match tells us that the dominant function of ES$_I$T$_E$J is T, Thinking.

Step 5: We identify the auxiliary function by default—it is the other middle letter, S$_I$, Sensing, and the small $_I$ beside it reminds us that it is *introverted.*

To complete the dynamics of ESTJ, we turn our attention to the two type function letters that *do not* appear in the type—N and F. We know that one of these will be the tertiary function and the other the inferior function. Two simple rules are all that is needed: The tertiary function is opposite to the auxiliary function, and the inferior function is opposite to the dominant function. Therefore, for ESTJ:

N (Intuition) is the tertiary function. Following the convention in the 1985 *Manual,* we specify its attitude as introverted, the same as for the auxiliary function.

F (Feeling) is the inferior function. The inferior function takes the attitude opposite to the dominant function. For ES$_I$T$_E$J, *introverted Feeling* is the inferior function.

Example of Identifying the Hierarchy of Functions

The same five steps are used for all types. Here is an illustration for an Introverted type, INFP.

Table 3.3 Priorities and Direction of Functions in Each Type

ISTJ

#1	DOMINANT	S	(I)
#2	AUXILIARY	T	(E)
#3	TERTIARY	F	(E)
#4	inferior	N	(E)

ISFJ

#1	DOMINANT	S	(I)
#2	AUXILIARY	F	(E)
#3	TERTIARY	T	(E)
#4	inferior	N	(E)

INFJ

#1	DOMINANT	N	(I)
#2	AUXILIARY	F	(E)
#3	TERTIARY	T	(E)
#4	inferior	S	(E)

INTJ

#1	DOMINANT	N	(I)
#2	AUXILIARY	T	(E)
#3	TERTIARY	F	(E)
#4	inferior	S	(E)

ISTP

#1	DOMINANT	T	(I)
#2	AUXILIARY	S	(E)
#3	TERTIARY	N	(E)
#4	inferior	F	(E)

ISFP

#1	DOMINANT	F	(I)
#2	AUXILIARY	S	(E)
#3	TERTIARY	N	(E)
#4	inferior	T	(E)

INFP

#1	DOMINANT	F	(I)
#2	AUXILIARY	N	(E)
#3	TERTIARY	S	(E)
#4	inferior	T	(E)

INTP

#1	DOMINANT	T	(I)
#2	AUXILIARY	N	(E)
#3	TERTIARY	S	(E)
#4	inferior	F	(E)

ESTP

#1	DOMINANT	S	(E)
#2	AUXILIARY	T	(I)
#3	TERTIARY	F	(I)
#4	inferior	N	(I)

ESFP

#1	DOMINANT	S	(E)
#2	AUXILIARY	F	(I)
#3	TERTIARY	T	(I)
#4	inferior	N	(I)

ENFP

#1	DOMINANT	N	(E)
#2	AUXILIARY	F	(I)
#3	TERTIARY	T	(I)
#4	inferior	S	(I)

ENTP

#1	DOMINANT	N	(E)
#2	AUXILIARY	T	(I)
#3	TERTIARY	F	(I)
#4	inferior	S	(I)

ESTJ

#1	DOMINANT	T	(E)
#2	AUXILIARY	S	(I)
#3	TERTIARY	N	(I)
#4	inferior	F	(I)

ESFJ

#1	DOMINANT	F	(E)
#2	AUXILIARY	S	(I)
#3	TERTIARY	N	(I)
#4	inferior	T	(I)

ENFJ

#1	DOMINANT	F	(E)
#2	AUXILIARY	N	(I)
#3	TERTIARY	S	(I)
#4	inferior	T	(I)

ENTJ

#1	DOMINANT	T	(E)
#2	AUXILIARY	N	(I)
#3	TERTIARY	S	(I)
#4	inferior	F	(I)

Step 1: Identifying the Function That Is Extraverted The last letter tells us that INFP extraverts the preferred perceiving function, N, so we put a small $_E$ beside the N.

IN$_E$FP

Step 2: Identifying the Function That Is Introverted Put a small $_I$ beside the F (remembering that if one middle letter is extraverted, the remaining one is introverted).

IN$_E$F$_I$P

Step 3: Matching with the First Letter Look at the first letter, I, which tells us that INFP prefers the *Introverted attitude* and therefore *introverts the dominant function.* Feeling is therefore the dominant function because it is the one that is *introverted.*

IN$_E$F$_I$P

Step 4: Identifying the Auxiliary Function Intuition, the other middle letter, is the *auxiliary function,* and it is shown as being *extraverted.*

Step 5: Identifying the Tertiary and Inferior Functions The opposite of *auxiliary Intuition* is *tertiary Sensing;* the attitude is

extraverted, the same as the auxiliary function. The opposite of *dominant introverted Feeling* is *inferior extraverted Thinking.*

Understanding the Dynamics of the Type Description

Once the principles and mechanical steps are grasped, one can figure out the type dynamics for all of the 16 types. Table 3.3 shows the priorities and directions of the four functions for each of the 16 types. When the hierarchy of functions has been determined, the dynamic relationships for a type can be understood. We will use the type ENTP as an example.

ENTP is an Extravert with Intuition (N) as the dominant, extraverted function and Thinking (T) the auxiliary, introverted function. In theory, therefore, ENTPs trust Intuition (#1) most, use it most, develop it most, and shape their lives to give the maximum freedom for pursuing their intuitive goals. They use their Thinking (#2) in pursuit of something challenging to their Intuition but may not let their Thinking (#2) veto anything their Intuition (#1) seriously desires. Being oriented to the challenge of new possibilities (N #1) in the outer world (E), they may often find themselves committed to too many projects. Intuitive types, especially those who extravert their Intuition, typically underestimate the time it takes to bring activities to completion. When the ENTP decides there are too many activities for the available time, the Thinking (#2) function is needed. The ENTP withdraws into the inner world (I), analyzes the costs and consequences of continuing or dropping each activity, and makes a logical judgment (#2) about which projects to drop. With more mature type development, the ENTP may learn to take time to pull back from the exciting challenges (N #1) for action (E) and consider (I) whether the costs permit adding new activities (T #2) *before* taking on new commitments.

The fourth, or inferior, function of ENTP is Sensing (#4). ENTPs need to train themselves not to neglect realities (#4) in the enthusiasm for possibilities (#1). Type theory says that Sensing (#4) and Feeling (#3) develop more slowly for an ENTP. One way to develop Sensing and Feeling is on a project chosen by Intuition (#1). To accomplish the project the ENTP will need to know many facts and be able to deal with many practical details; thus Sensing (#4) comes into play to help Intuition (#1). Further, the project may require working in a team or persuading other people; thus Feeling (#3) also comes in to help Intuition (#1). In good type development, people tend to use their less-preferred functions *in the service of* their preferred functions, rather than out of attraction to the less-familiar functions themselves.

The preceding description of the way ENTPs use their type dynamics should not be taken literally as a hard-and-fast, methodical procedure that all ENTPs follow. Rather, the dynamics of any particular type tend to flow naturally and seamlessly from function to function, usually without the conscious attention of the individual.

Dynamics of Type Reflected in the Type Descriptions

The descriptions of each of the types are built on the same kinds of dynamic principles that were shown in the description of ENTP. The booklets in the *Introduction to Type* series are valuable guides for describing the MBTI types. Notice that in the *Introduction to Type* booklets, descriptions for types with the same dominant function appear on facing pages. It is important to understand that the type descriptions, which may seem like horoscopes to the uninitiated, are firmly based on the dynamics of type theory, supplemented by years of observation of the types and empirical results from research.

Types Are Created by Exercise of Preferences

Under this theory, people create their "type" by the exercise of their preferences with regard to their use of perception and judgment. People who have the same preferences tend to have in common whatever qualities *result* from the exercise of those preferences. The interests, values, needs, and habits of mind that naturally result tend to produce a recognizable kind of person. We can therefore begin to *partly* describe individuals by stating their preferences as ENTP, ESFJ, INFP, or whatever the case may be.

We can also begin intelligently to expect ENTPs to be different from others in ways characteristic of previously known ENTPs. To describe them as belonging to that type (if they agree that it *is* their type) in no way infringes on their right to be what they like. They were exercising that right when they found, consciously or unconsciously, that they liked Extraversion, Intuition, Thinking, and the Perceiving attitude.

In dealing with people, when we keep their type in mind, we are respecting not only their abstract right to develop along lines of their own choosing but also *the importance of qualities they have developed by making that choice.* For example, if, for whatever reason, they have not exercised one or more of their preferences, they may not have developed a type, or at least a type that they can report clearly. Not everyone is a type. Young people in particular may respond to the MBTI tool at a stage when their type is just beginning to emerge in a way they themselves can recognize and report. One purpose of administering the MBTI to young people, including those whose type has not yet fully evolved, is to help familiarize them with the areas with which they may be struggling. Conscious awareness of the opposite poles of each dichotomy may enable them to clarify and gain confidence with an emerging natural preference.[9]

Learning About the Types

Once the principles of type dynamics are understood, the next step is to see how these dynamics play out in each of the 16 types. Perhaps the best way to approach this learning is to adopt a "typological lens" when interacting with others and observing them in their daily lives. Finding consistencies in the attitudes and behaviors of people of the same or similar types that "make typological sense" adds to one's depth of understanding. It can be especially helpful to ask people what they were focusing on in a given situation and how they arrived at a particular conclusion. Their response to such questions may or may not support a typological explanation and is an excellent way to differentiate between behaviors that are and are not legitimately type related. In creating the Indicator, Isabel Myers was confident of people's ability to report accurately about themselves. That same confidence in people's knowledge of themselves can greatly enhance our understanding of the 16 types.

Type theory seems simple, but it is in fact rich and complex. People of the same type differ in many ways. Some within-type differences may reflect habitual ways in which a person expresses aspects of less-preferred functions and attitudes, as indicated in the Step II Expanded Interpretive Report (EIR). One's type may also be affected by social and cultural pressures and by the stage of type development reached. To truly understand type, there is no substitute for a prolonged period of interested skepticism in which you match your observations and knowledge of people with predictions from Jung's theory.

Other strategies for understanding the types are described in the next chapter.

Conclusion

This chapter has placed the MBTI personality inventory in the context of Jung's development of the theory of psychological types, beginning with his attempt to classify people into the two categories of extraverts and introverts, and his later addition of the two pairs of opposite functions (sensing versus intuition and thinking versus feeling) to his descriptive system. Myers and Briggs extended Jung's three-category system to include a fourth pair of attitudes, Judging and Perceiving. The J–P dichotomy describes identifiable external behavior, in addition to enabling the determination of type dynamics. Definitions, descriptions, and examples of the opposite functions and attitudes and their different dynamic interactions were given as illustrations of both the complexity and practical applications implicit in using the MBTI.

Jung's notion of type development and the goals of development over the life span were explained and illustrated, the rationale and method for determining the dynamics of any four-letter type were set out, and an example of how type dynamics emerge in one type was given in detail.

In summary, the MBTI contains four separate dichotomies: E–I, S–N, T–F, and J–P. Two of these, S–N and T–F, describe functions and reflect basic preferences for use of perception and judgment. The other two, E–I and J–P, reflect attitudes or orientations. Together, these functions and orientations influence how a person perceives a situation and decides on a course of action. All of these choices are like forks in the road of human development, offering different paths that lead toward different kinds of excellence. How far different individuals will go, how much excellence they will actually achieve, depends in part upon their energy and aspirations. The kind of excellence toward which they are headed is determined, according to type theory, by the inborn preferences that direct them at each fork in the road.[10]

Understanding the 16 Types   4

When making practical use of type theory and data, it is important to consider what the theory leads us to expect as well as what has been observed in people of that type. The usefulness of feedback to any individuals, groups, and organizations may depend to a large extent upon the interpreter's knowledge of characteristics associated with each of the 16 types. People who are new to type can find that keeping 16 different personalities in mind is rather daunting, as comfortable familiarity with the distinctive qualities of the types requires considerable time and experience. Trying to memorize the characteristics of the 16 types is not helpful and does not lead to an appreciation of the dynamic character of type. Therefore, this chapter provides some approaches to learning about type that will help move practitioners from an initial focus on the four type dichotomies to a familiarity with and understanding of the complex wholes represented in the 16 types.

The goal of this chapter is to enhance understanding of type differences for both new and experienced users of the *Myers-Briggs Type Indicator* personality inventory. The basic groundwork for understanding the 16 types was provided in Chapter 3, which explained the theoretical basis for the dynamic character of the types. This chapter builds on that knowledge in the following ways:

- It facilitates acquisition of knowledge through familiarity with type tables and through precision in the use of type language.
- It provides descriptions of the characteristics of groupings of types that have two preferences in common. These include combinations of the functions, combinations of the attitudes, and attitude-function combinations.
- By focusing first on these "building blocks" of type it is easier to understand and retain the qualities associated with dynamic whole types.
- It describes two-letter type combinations and whole types from three perspectives: the Jung-Myers theory, careful observation by experienced type experts and the self-reports of individuals, and the most current empirical research. The research cited focuses on evidence relevant to the distinctive features of a particular grouping or whole type. The three-pronged approach to type descriptions—theory, observation, research—ensures confidence in our understanding of type similarities and differences in a wide variety of circumstances and application settings.

A wealth of descriptive, anecdotal, and research information is available that describes whole types and the various combinations of type preferences. To facilitate learning, this chapter will first focus on two-letter type groupings and then concentrate on describing the 16 whole types.

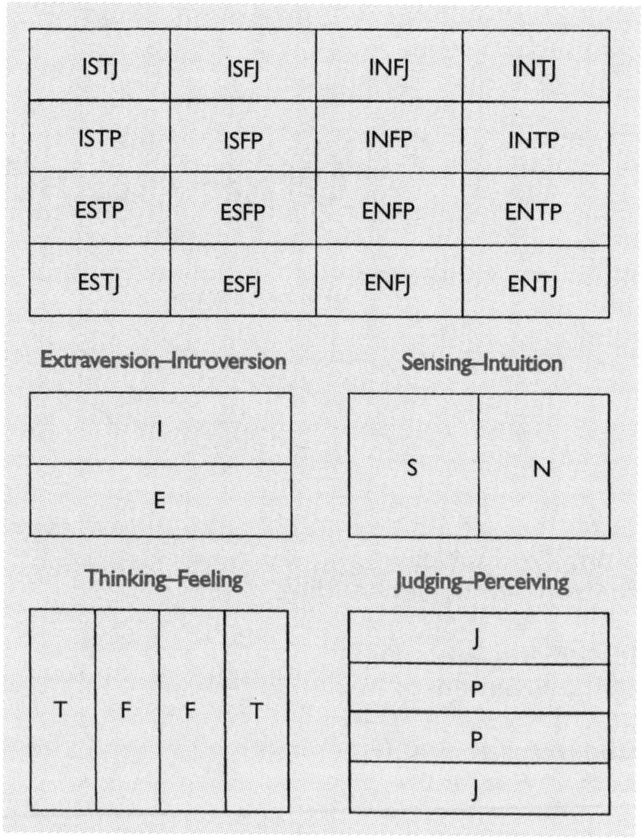

Using Type Tables to Promote Understanding

An excellent way to begin to understand whole types and particular combinations of preferences is to become familiar with the *type table*, which presents the 16 types in a logical relationship. There is much to be learned from type tables; they show the frequencies of types in groups of people that have characteristics in common: for example, the same occupation, college major, avocation, management philosophy, or communication style. A wide variety of variables of interest to researchers and practitioners can be explored using type tables, allowing easy visual observation so that hypotheses can be explored. Statistical analysis of type table data ensures confidence in the meaning inferred from the type frequencies observed. A common statistic used is the *self-selection ratio* (SSR), which compares the percentage of each type in a sample relative to its percentage in an appropriate base comparison group. For a detailed explanation of this statistic, see Chapter 9.

Figure 4.1 Format of Type Tables

Type theory leads us to hypothesize that the groupings of types on particular type tables are the result of choices that are directly or indirectly influenced by type preferences. For example, if an occupation requires attention to detail, system, and order and if that occupation attracts the types who in theory should prefer attention to detail, system, and order—the Sensing Judging types—then the table provides construct validity for type theory as well as useful information for career counselors. If a type table shows that Feeling types are rarely found in a particular high-pressure, product-focused company, this could help a management consultant explain some possible communication issues that are causing problems for the company. Many of the applications chapters in Part V of this manual present information and analyze data in type table form.

Placement of Types on the Type Table

The type table was designed by Isabel B. Myers as a way to highlight similarities and differences of the types by their placement in the table. Familiarity with the placement of types enables quick recognition of which types predominate and which are infrequent in different samples and populations. Figure 4.1 depicts the format of type tables. Note that each type has three letters in common with any adjacent type. The placement of each of the preferences and the rationale given by Myers for placements are described below.

Extraverts (E) and Introverts (I) Introverted types appear in the first and second rows of the type table. Extraverted types appear in rows 3 and 4. Isabel Myers' mnemonic aid for E–I placement is that Introverts are more likely to have their heads *up* in the clouds, and Extraverts are more likely to have their feet *down* on the ground.

Sensing (S) Types and Intuitive (N) Types Sensing types and Intuitive types are positioned on the type table in the same order as in the name of the S–N dichotomy, namely with Sensing on the left and Intuition on the right.

Thinking (T) Types and Feeling (F) Types The Thinking types compose the two outer columns of the table. Feeling types are contained in the two inner columns. Myers chose this placement so that it would be easy to remember by considering that the Feeling types, with their greater need for affiliation, are in the middle columns, surrounded by other types. The more objective Thinking types are in the outer columns, with unpeopled space beside them.

Judging (J) Types and Perceiving (P) Types Note that the decisive Judging types are found in the top and bottom rows, giving boundaries for the flexibility and adaptability of the Perceiving types, who are in the two middle rows.

Summary

Type tables and type groupings present data on the construct validity of the MBTI—that is, evidence that the MBTI accurately reflects Jung's theory and the constructs it includes. Type tables also provide information and insight into the characteristics of the types. One goal of becoming familiar with the type table format is to be able to recognize a sample's characteristics at a glance and thus obtain a great deal of information quickly. As an aid for achieving this goal, Table 4.1, arrayed as a standard type table, shows the contribution that each preference makes to each of the 16 types, regardless of the unique dynamics of each type.

Identifying Groupings of the Preferences

When practitioners use the same terms to mean different things, confusion and misunderstanding inevitably occur. It is therefore important to clarify the terminology used to refer to particular combinations of type preferences in order to achieve consistency in the use of language among MBTI users. This section covers terminology for combinations of Extraversion and Introversion with each of the four functions (E and I with S, N, T, and F), groupings of the four attitudes (E and I with J and P), and combinations of the four mental functions (S and N with T and F).

In the past, terms such as *Extraverted Intuitive types,* or *EN types,* were sometimes used to refer to all types whose four letters included Extraversion and Intuition (ENFJ, ENTJ, ENFP, and ENTP) *or* to refer to the *two* types for whom extraverted Intuition is the dominant function (ENTP, ENFP). The first usage does not take type dynamics into account, while the second meaning of the combination refers to the dynamic character of types. The current emphasis on studying whole types and type dynamics makes clarity in such terminology critical. The terminological conventions described below are used throughout this manual and are included in the Glossary.

Combining Extraversion or Introversion with the Four Functions

Only two types share the same dominant function and attitude. For example, ISFP and INFP are referred to as the *dominant introverted Feeling types.* However, four types share a preference for the same attitude and function. For example, ISFP, ISFJ, INFP, and INFJ share a preference for Introversion and Feeling; we refer to these four types as having a preference for *Introversion with Feeling.*

Confusion can occur when the attitude of Extraversion or Introversion is combined with one of the four functions, Sensing, Intuition, Thinking, or Feeling. Terms such as *dominant introverted Sensing* types and *dominant extraverted Thinking* types are used to identify the dynamic combinations. However, when the four types who prefer both Extraversion and Thinking are present—ESTJ, ENTJ, ESTP, ENTP—the designation *Extraversion with Thinking* is correct. The same convention is used with other combinations of E and I with the other functions.

Combining the Four Attitudes

Combining E and I with J and P gives us practical insights about type dynamics.

Combinations of the two attitudes of energy (E and I) and the two attitudes toward the outer world (J and P) do more than reflect the presence of the two attitudes specified; they identify particular type dynamics. Extraverted judging types (the EJ types, ESTJ, ENTJ, ESFJ, ENFJ) are those whose dominant function is an *extraverted judging* one (ET or EF). Introverted perceiving types (the IP types, ISTP, INTP, ISFP, INFP) are those whose dominant function is an *introverted judging* function (IT or IF). The dominant function of EP types (ESTP, ESFP, ENTP, ENFP) is an *extraverted perceiving* (ES or EN) function, and the IJ types (ISTJ, ISFJ, INTJ, INFJ) have a dominant *introverted perceiving* function (IS or IN). When researchers and practitioners focus on these combinations, attention to their dynamic status can provide practical insights.

Table 4.1   Contributions Made by Each Preference to Each Type

| | Sensing Types | | Intuitive Types | |
	With Thinking	With Feeling	With Feeling	With Thinking
Introverts — Judging Types	**ISTJ** **I** Depth of concentration **S** Reliance on facts **T** Logic and analysis **J** Organization	**ISFJ** **I** Depth of concentration **S** Reliance on facts **F** Warmth and sympathy **J** Organization	**INFJ** **I** Depth of concentration **N** Grasp of possibilities **F** Warmth and sympathy **J** Organization	**INTJ** **I** Depth of concentration **N** Grasp of possibilities **T** Logic and analysis **J** Organization
Introverts — Perceiving Types	**ISTP** **I** Depth of concentration **S** Reliance on facts **T** Logic and analysis **P** Adaptability	**ISFP** **I** Depth of concentration **S** Reliance on facts **F** Warmth and sympathy **P** Adaptability	**INFP** **I** Depth of concentration **N** Grasp of possibilities **F** Warmth and sympathy **P** Adaptability	**INTP** **I** Depth of concentration **N** Grasp of possibilities **T** Logic and analysis **P** Adaptability
Extraverts — Perceiving Types	**ESTP** **E** Breadth of interests **S** Reliance on facts **T** Logic and analysis **P** Adaptability	**ESFP** **E** Breadth of interests **S** Reliance on facts **F** Warmth and sympathy **P** Adaptability	**ENFP** **E** Breadth of interests **N** Grasp of possibilities **F** Warmth and sympathy **P** Adaptability	**ENTP** **E** Breadth of interests **N** Grasp of possibilities **T** Logic and analysis **P** Adaptability
Extraverts — Judging Types	**ESTJ** **E** Breadth of interests **S** Reliance on facts **T** Logic and analysis **J** Organization	**ESFJ** **E** Breadth of interests **S** Reliance on facts **F** Warmth and sympathy **J** Organization	**ENFJ** **E** Breadth of interests **N** Grasp of possibilities **F** Warmth and sympathy **J** Organization	**ENTJ** **E** Breadth of interests **N** Grasp of possibilities **T** Logic and analysis **J** Organization

Combining the Two Kinds of Mental Functions

> Each pairing of mental functions identifies four types. For example, the SF types are ESFJ, ESFP, ISFJ, ISFP.

Combining two mental functions does not imply type dynamics and therefore can have only one referential meaning. Sensing Thinking (ST) types, for example, are only the four types that prefer both Sensing and Thinking; Intuitive Feeling (NF) types are those four types who prefer both Intuition and Feeling. Other two-letter and three-letter combinations may also be studied but do not present terminological difficulties. Table 4.2 shows the terminology used to specify the eight dominant functions (note that these also define the *eight types* specified by Carl G. Jung) and the

eight combinations that combine E or I with each of the four functions.

When presenting data on type tables it is common practice to include information for two-letter combinations of preferences. See Table 7.14 in Chapter 7 as an illustration of such a type table.

Characteristics of Groupings of the Preferences

It is often useful to describe a set of types that have common characteristics. The main problem in grouping types is to restrict the description to the common characteristics found

Table 4.2   Terminology for Describing Combinations of Preferences

Dynamic Combinations		E–I with the Functions	
ESP Types	The two dominant extraverted Sensing types— ESTP and ESFP	ES Types	Extraverts with Sensing The four types—ESTP, ESFP, ESTJ, ESFJ
ISJ Types	The two dominant introverted Sensing types— ISTJ and ISFJ	IS Types	Introverts with Sensing The four types—ISTP, ISFP, ISTJ, ISFJ
ENP Types	The two dominant extraverted Intuitive types— ENTP and ENFP	EN Types	Extraverts with Intuition The four types—ENTP, ENFP, ENFJ, ENTJ
INJ Types	The two dominant introverted Intuitive types— INTJ and INFJ	IN Types	Introverts with Intuition The four types—INTJ, INFJ, INTP, INFP
ETJ Types	The two dominant extraverted Thinking types— ESTJ and ENTJ	ET Types	Extraverts with Thinking The four types—ESTJ, ESTP, ENTJ, ENTP
ITP Types	The two dominant introverted Thinking types— ISTP and INTP	IT Types	Introverts with Thinking The four types—ISTP, ISTJ, INTP, INTJ
EFJ Types	The two dominant extraverted Feeling types— ESFJ and ENFJ	EF Types	Extraverts with Feeling The four types—ESFP, ESFJ, ENFP, ENFJ
IFP Types	The two dominant introverted Feeling types— ISFP and INFP	IF Types	Introverts with Feeling The four types—ISFJ, INFJ, ISFP, INFP

in every type in the group. Characteristics found in only one or two types in a group of four should not be reported as typical of the whole group. This section provides brief descriptions of the characteristics of each group based upon our expectations from type theory and consistent findings of experienced observers. It is important to bear in mind that these descriptions apply to mature, well-developed members of each grouping and may not apply to all people who self-report that type.

Following each description is a table summarizing selected research results relevant to that group of types. The research summaries are divided into four general content areas. Research relevant to personality variables, psychotherapy, health, stress, and coping are shown first because type theory was developed by Jung to address his observations of normal personality differences within the context of his psychotherapeutic practice. Education research appears next, followed by research on type and career variables. Education was an early and continuing focus of Isabel Myers in her own research, as were the implications of type for career choice and career satisfaction. The last content area is organizations, leadership, management, and teams. This is the most recent area to receive research attention.

Readers may note that although a good deal of research has focused on specific type groupings, detailed information for some groupings is much more extensive than for others. The fact that there is little research evidence describing particular groupings may be due to little interest in the grouping by researchers or the scope and focus of the

research, rather than the actual absence of notable characteristics for that grouping. For groupings where there is very little research to report, a brief narrative describing the available research is provided instead of a table.

There is little information available for some type groupings and combinations of preferences, perhaps due to lack of interest on the part of researchers.

The summaries of research contained in all of the tables in this chapter are constrained by the following factors:

- They are dependent on what researchers have chosen to study and what they decided to report in their research articles and therefore may not represent all possible potentially useful information.
- The research reported is limited to compilations of MBTI research results, rather than individual journal articles. For example, previous research as well as the most recent research that emerged from the national sample studies are included in the application chapters of Part V of this manual. Those chapters therefore serve as a research source. The same is true of the chapters in *MBTI Applications* (Hammer, 1996b), another source for the research results in this chapter.
- Only statistically significant results and clearly distinguishing rankings on variables are listed. However, sample sizes and research methods vary considerably. Caution in interpretation and generalization of results is therefore appropriate.

■ The results included are limited to those that could be briefly summarized and easily understood without detailed explanations. Studies that look at more complex type issues are therefore not included.

Source notes follow each table. Readers who wish detailed information about a particular research result should consult the sources cited. Following each table and its source notes is a brief commentary that highlights interesting findings and contrasts some of the results for that combination or type with results found for other relevant preference combinations and types. These comments attempt to place the research within a broader context of societal expectations and biases. Because the comments do not summarize the research results, it is best to review each table *before* reading the comments.

Additional Cautions in Interpreting Research Results

Interesting observations emerge when we look at research for particular type groupings and whole types in the four content areas described above. Most notable is the fact that people with some combinations of two preferences, as well as some whole types that are presented later in the chapter, seem to be associated with "positive" characteristics in one or more content areas while other combinations and types are characterized in a more "negative" way. This is particularly evident in results in the first content area—personality, psychotherapy, health, stress, coping—and the second area—education. These kinds of effects highlight the presence of the *type bias* that results when a single norm is applied to everyone within our society. In such a single-norm approach, some types inevitably are viewed as more competent, emotionally adapted, or successful than are other types whose qualities are not in accord with the cultural notion of the "desirable" individual. For example, test items designed to assess qualities such as self-confidence, optimism, comfort in the outer world, stress tolerance, and good coping skills are likely to overlap in content with characteristics that legitimately reflect a preference for Extraversion or Introversion. This overlap in item content, along with the effects of living in a society that favors an Extraverted over an Introverted use of energy, contributes to some of the negative- and positive-seeming research results reported in some tables. Chapter 10 discusses some of these issues in more detail.

Bias is also evident in the area of education, where there seems to be a prevailing assumption that everyone learns in the same ways and therefore should respond well to the same teaching methods. From a typological perspective there are distinct differences in the ways different types learn. This is apparent in how the types perform on standard educational achievement measures and in such behavioral measures as school dropout rates. Chapter 11 presents the details of such sources of type bias.

Another factor should inhibit overgeneralizing and making inferences about the brief research results shown in the tables. Whereas the descriptions of the typical characteristics of members of the type groupings and whole types reflect mature, well-developed people, research studies very likely include a quite broad spectrum of those same types. We cannot tell from the data shown to what extent this factor may contribute to both the more negative characterizations found in some tables and the more positive outcomes observed.

The discussion of each type grouping begins with the distinctive dynamic feature that the types in each group share. The descriptive phrases shown for each grouping were created by Isabel Myers to identify and help people remember its central distinctive feature.

The Columns of the Type Table: The Four Mental Functions (ST, SF, NF, NT)

Isabel Myers considered the columns of the type table to be the most important of the groupings of the types, particularly where career choices are concerned. These groups focus on the combinations of perception (S and N) with judgment (T and F). The type characteristics are assumed to stem from the preferred use of these mental functions. The pairings of functions have received a great deal of research attention over the years. Function pairings are often viewed as learning styles or cognitive styles. This is an area of interest to educators, career counselors, and organization specialists.

Two column types, NF and NT, are also used to designate two of the four temperaments described by Keirsey and Bates and discussed later in this chapter (Keirsey & Bates, 1978). The focus in describing NF and NT as temperaments is different from the present focus. However, for ease of contrast, the research results that describe NF and NT types in this section are repeated in the section on temperaments.

Table 4.3 compares the column types based on a knowledge of their components. Specific descriptive and research information about each of the four column types follows.

STs: The Practical and Matter-of-Fact Types

ISTJ			
ISTP			
ESTP			
ESTJ			

For the four Sensing Thinking (ST) types, one of the two functions, Sensing or Thinking, is the dominant function, and the other is the auxiliary function.

ST people rely primarily on Sensing for purposes of perception and on Thinking for purposes of judgment. Their main interests focus on facts because facts can be collected

Table 4.3   The Combinations of Perception and Judgment

People who prefer	ST Sensing and Thinking	SF Sensing and Feeling	NF Intuition and Feeling	NT Intuition and Thinking
Focus attention on	Facts	Facts	Possibilities	Possibilities
And handle these with	Nonpersonal analysis	Personal warmth	Personal warmth	Nonpersonal analysis
They tend to become	Practical and matter-of-fact	Sympathetic and friendly	Enthusiastic and insightful	Logical and ingenious
And find scope for their abilities in	Technical areas with facts and objects	Practical help and services for people	Understanding and communication with people	Theoretical and technical developments

and verified directly by the senses—by seeing, hearing, touching, counting, weighing, and measuring. The ST types typically approach their decisions regarding facts using objective analysis because what they trust is Thinking, with its linear and logical process of reasoning from cause to effect, from premise to conclusion. In consequence STs tend to be practical and matter-of-fact. Type theory predicts that STs will be attracted to fields that demand nonpersonal analysis of concrete facts, such as economics, law, surgery, business, accounting, production, and the handling of machines and materials. The frequency with which ST types are found in such fields bears this out. Table 4.4 summarizes relevant research results for ST types.

Most of the results in Table 4.4 seem in accord with an ST approach to the content areas shown. For example, seeking personal counseling is not a "natural" way of solving problems for types who focus on logically assessing the facts of their situation. STs' academic performance, educational and career preferences, and characteristics as leaders, managers, and team members are also consistent with the qualities that would be expected for people who focus on Sensing and Thinking as the preferred ways of perceiving and coming to conclusions. Possible support for the reported disadvantage that Sensing types face from typical academic testing procedures is shown in the overrepresentation of ST types in the Academic Decathlon (a "performance-based" indicator of competence) relative to their frequency as National Merit Finalists (a "test score–based" indicator).

SFs: The Sympathetic and Friendly Types

	ISFJ	
	ISFP	
	ESFP	
	ESFJ	

For Sensing Feeling (SF) types, one of the two functions, Sensing or Feeling, is the dominant function, and the other is the auxiliary function.

SF people, like ST people, rely primarily on Sensing for purposes of perception, but they prefer Feeling for purposes of judgment. They too are mainly interested in facts they can gather directly through the senses, but they approach their decisions with a subjectivity that is based on their personal value system. This subjectivity and the warmth they convey comes from their trust of Feeling, with its power to weigh how much things matter to themselves and others. In contrast to Sensing Thinking types, they are more interested in facts about people than in facts about things.

SFs tend to be sympathetic and friendly. In theory, we would expect them to be attracted to fields where their personal warmth can be effectively applied to concrete situations. The combination of Sensing and Feeling can be valuable in selling tangibles, service-with-a-smile jobs, teaching (especially in the early grades and applied fields), nursing, pediatrics, and other health fields involving direct patient care. The sympathetic and friendly SFs are frequent at all levels of direct patient care. Table 4.5 summarizes relevant research results for SF types.

There is a growing body of research that shows overrepresentation of some Sensing types among people with hypertension and/or heart disease. These findings are presented and discussed in Chapter 10. The specific and intriguing finding in Table 4.5 with regard to SF males can yield many hypotheses that require empirical evidence to support or negate them as possible explanations for the research result. For example, one could conjecture that the qualities of conscientiousness and loyalty that may contribute to SF *overrepresentation* among hypertensives are similar to those that contribute to SF *underrepresentation* in referrals to substance abuse programs. For this and similar findings, however, we must consider the amount and kind of contribution type may make to the diagnosis of hypertension, as well as recognizing that the majority of SF males do not suffer from hypertension.

As was found for the ST group, the education results support often-noted bias toward Intuition in our educational assessment procedures, and both teacher beliefs and approaches in organizational settings highlight differences between the ST qualities shown in Table 4.4 and the SF orientation reflected in this table.

Table 4.4   Research Describing ST Types

Personality, Psychotherapy, Health, Stress, Coping	Underrepresented among students seeking counseling[1]
Education	As teachers, endorsed an external system of belief about discipline for children (children develop as a result of external conditions)[2]
	Performed worse than NF types on a series of academic aptitude tests among middle school students[2]
	Outperformed both NF and NT dental hygiene students[2]
	Second highest in number of reported books read per year[2]
	Overrepresented among Academic Decathlon participants compared with their proportion among National Merit Finalists[2]
	Overrepresented among female school administrators in the People's Republic of China[3]
	Overrepresented among Hawaiian foreign language students at the University of Hawaii[3]
	Ranked lowest among chemical engineering students in passing curriculum[2]
Careers	Lowest of four in "Co-worker cohesion," "Supervisor support," and "Task orientation" as ideal work environment characteristics; higher than NFs and NTs in "Clarity" and "Managerial control"[4]
Organizations, Leadership, Management, Teams	As managers evaluating alternatives, may be predisposed to impose "erroneous regularity and structure" on random events; become more decisive in well-defined and regulated environments[5]
	Are task oriented as change agents[5]
	Recommend behavior modification of people rather than changing tasks when policies fail[5]
	Were the only grouping to use behavior modification to promote change[6]
	Looked at the fewest reports and were the most satisfied information users among MBA students in a study of information use[6]
	Had strongest preference for tabular reports as a source of information[6]
	Showed most risk avoidance; more inclined to take risks when in an environment consistent with their type[6]
	Maintained high interest throughout a production simulation that required learning well-defined, structured procedures[6]
	More accepting of closed climates in a study of type and organizational climate[6]
	Ranked second of four in lowering costs in a computer simulation where goal was to achieve the lowest cost of production[6]

Source: [1]Quenk & Quenk, 1996; [2]DiTiberio, 1996; [3]Kirby & Barger, 1996; [4]See Chapter 12, "Uses of Type in Career Counseling"; [5]Haley, 1997; [6]Walck, 1996.

NFs: The Enthusiastic and Insightful Types

		INFJ
		INFP
		ENFP
		ENFJ

For Intuitive Feeling (NF) types, one of the two functions, Intuition or Feeling, is the dominant function, and the other is the auxiliary function.

People who prefer Intuition for perceiving and Feeling as the way to come to conclusions typically possess the same personal warmth as SF people. However, since they prefer Intuition to Sensing, they focus their interest upon possibilities rather than concrete situations. They are likely to be attracted to new projects, things that have never happened but might be made to happen, or truths that have not yet come to light. NF types are typically interested in the complexities of communication, and their Intuition provides them with an interest in patterns that underlie immediate facts, symbolic meanings, and theoretical relationships. Feeling provides the interest in using these intuitive insights in human relationships.

The personal warmth and commitment with which NF people seek and follow up possibilities tend to make them enthusiastic as well as insightful. They often have a marked gift for the spoken or written word and can communicate both the possibilities they see and the values they attach to those possibilities. They are likely to be attracted to work that involves the unfolding of possibilities, especially possibilities for people, such as in teaching (particularly in the upper grades and college), selling intangibles, counseling,

Table 4.5   Research Describing SF Types

Personality, Psychotherapy, Health, Stress, Coping	Males overrepresented among hypertensive patients[1]
	Underrepresented among new students referred to a substance abuse workshop[2]
Education	As teachers, endorsed interaction of inner and outer forces to account for the development of children, in a study of teachers' beliefs about discipline[3]
	Lowest of four in number of reported books read per year[3]
	Ranked third of four among chemical engineering students ranked highest to lowest in order of passing[4]
Careers	Among dietitians, more satisfied with occupational specialty[5]
	Reported higher intent to leave than NTs in study of "intent to leave current job"[5]
Organizations, Leadership, Management, Teams	Often suggest consultative, group process solutions and put more importance on people-oriented information[6, 4]
	Used transactional analysis almost exclusively compared with other groupings[4]
	Showed most risk tolerance and were more likely to take risk when operating in an environment incompatible with their type[4]
	Ranked first in lowering cost in a computer simulation where goal was to achieve lowest cost of production[4]

Source: [1]Shelton, 1996; [2]Quenk & Quenk, 1996; [3]DiTiberio, 1996; [4]Walck, 1996; [5]Hammer, 1996a; [6]Haley, 1997.

writing, and research. Table 4.6 summarizes research relevant to NF types.

The results listed in Table 4.6 illuminate the quite different approaches of NF types as compared with ST types in all four areas, as well as highlight the influence of Intuition compared with Sensing in these types. Much evidence has been reported showing that the characteristics that emerge from an underlying preference for Intuition combined with a Feeling preference lead to an interest in both providing and receiving psychological services, particularly those that support a person-centered approach. The results in education on academic performance and teaching and learning styles reflect the effects of an Intuitive approach to this area, and the influence of NF is quite apparent in the values and behaviors shown in the career and organizational variables that characterize NF research results. It is interesting to note that NF types were disinterested or did not perform well in areas that called on their less-preferred functions, such as in the production simulation studies.

NTs: The Logical and Ingenious Types

			INTJ
			INTP
			ENTP
			ENTJ

For Intuitive Thinking (NT) types, one of the two functions, Intuition or Thinking, is the dominant function, and the other is the auxiliary function.

Like NF people, NT people prefer Intuition for purposes of perception, but they prefer the objectivity of Thinking for purposes of judgment. They too focus on possibilities, theoretical relationships, and abstract patterns, but they judge these from a nonpersonal, cause-and-effect perspective. They often pursue possibilities that are technical, scientific, theoretical, or executive, where attention to the human issues may be secondary.

NTs tend to be logical and ingenious. They are best in solving problems within their field of special interest, whether scientific research, mathematics, the more intricate aspects of finance, or any sort of pioneering or innovative endeavor in a wide variety of technical or administrative areas. Table 4.7 summarizes relevant research results for NT types.

In this table we can see both the differential influence of T rather than F on some of the research results and some similarities and differences in comparison to the SF table of results. Although some of the over- and underrepresentations shown for NT types make "typological sense," other observations require further study and replication to achieve understanding—for example, the underrepresentation among hypertensives and overrepresentation reported for Type A behavior. Knowledge of the specific samples and methods that generated these results would help, and readers who are particularly interested in this area may wish to review the original studies involved.

The results shown for education, careers, and organizational variables reinforce what was observed for the effects

Table 4.6   Research Describing NF Types

Personality, Psychotherapy, Health, Stress, Coping	Predominate among providers of psychological services[1]
	Overrepresented among client-centered psychologists[1]
	Underrepresented among behavioral psychologists[1]
	Overrepresented among students seeking counseling[1]
	Underrepresented among both male and female chronic pain patients[2]
	Females tended to be married much longer in comparison with female NTs[1]
	Underrepresented among men who had undergone coronary bypass surgery[2]
	ENF physicians had "dealing with patients' emotional difficulties" and "advising/counseling patients" as typical practice activities[3]
Education	As teachers, endorsed an internal system of belief about discipline for children (children develop from an unfolding of potential)[4]
	As middle school students, performed better than ST types on a series of academic aptitude tests[4]
	Reported reading more books than any other combination[4]
	Among Japanese students, were overrepresented among foreign language students at the University of Hawaii[5]
	Ranked second out of four in passing among chemical engineering students[4]
Careers	Reported less job satisfaction with occupational specialty than other types[3]
	Had higher perceptions of the expected utility of possible alternate jobs than SFs in a study of "intent to leave current job"[3]
	Higher than STs and SFs on "Innovation" as ideal work environment characteristic [6]
Organizations, Leadership, Management, Teams	Believe information on people more important than other information[7]
	Least satisfied information users[7]
	Had weakest preference for tabular reports in a study of information use[7]
	More likely to use group- and people-oriented techniques to promote change[7]
	Rely on anecdotes, catchy symbols, vivid imagery to make points[7]
	Use personal evaluations of situations to reduce uncertainty[7]
	May ignore statistical evidence and overestimate their ability to work through plans or implement them[8]
	Took an intermediate position of nominal risk taking; were more likely to take risk when operating in an environment incompatible with their type, in a study of risk tolerance[7]
	Lost interest rapidly and "dropped out" in a production simulation that required learning well-defined, structured procedures[7]
	Ranked third of four in simulated attempt to achieve lowest production costs[7]

Source: [1]Quenk & Quenk, 1996; [2]Shelton, 1996; [3]Hammer, 1996a; [4]DiTiberio, 1996; [5]Kirby & Barger (1996); [6]See Chapter 12, "Uses of Type in Career Counseling"; [7]Walck, 1996; [8]Haley, 1997.

of Intuition compared with Sensing, as well as highlight the NT as compared with NF typological influence—for example, the NT focus on structure and the NF focus on people in management situations.

The Rows of the Type Table: The Four Attitudes (IJ, IP, EP, EJ)

The rows of the type table group the Introverted and Extraverted perceiving types, IJs, whose dominant function is an *introverted* perceiving function, and EPs, whose dominant function is an *extraverted* perceiving function, and the Introverted and Extraverted judging types, IPs, whose dominant

function is an *introverted* judging function, and EJs, whose dominant function is an *extraverted* judging function.

IJs: The Decisive Introverts

ISTJ	ISFJ	INFJ	INTJ

Table 4.7 Research Describing NT Types

Personality, Psychotherapy, Health, Stress, Coping	Overrepresented among students preferring cognitive approaches to psychotherapy; underrepresented for affective approaches[1]
	Females tended have much shorter marriages than female NFs[1]
	Underrepresented among male substance abusers[1]
	Males underrepresented among hypertensive patients[2]
	Overrepresented among those having Type A behavior[2]
	Underrepresented among both male and female chronic pain patients[2]
Education	Endorsed an internal system (children develop from an unfolding of potential) in a study of teachers' beliefs about discipline[3]
	As writing instructors, gave higher grades to students of the same type[3]
	Obtained higher geometry achievement scores among rural high school students[3]
	Reported reading third highest number of books per year[3]
	Overrepresented among top 100 executive educators[3]
	Ranked highest among chemical engineering students in passing curriculum[3]
Careers	Less satisfied with career among secondary marketing education teachers[4]
	Overrepresented among secretaries stating they disliked their work[4]
Organizations, Leadership, Management, Teams	As managers, see patterns in structured data, ignore cases that negate their beliefs, may resort to quick, superficial studies; may persevere in beliefs despite contradictory evidence[5]
	Tend to use survey feedback to promote organizational change[6]
	Sought more quantitative data than NFs in solving an unstructured case study problem[6]
	Found information about organizational structure important in study of information content[6]
	Took an intermediate position of nominal risk taking; more likely to take risk when operating in an environment incompatible with their type, in a study of risk tolerance[6]
	Lost interest rapidly and "dropped out" in a production simulation that required learning well-defined, structured procedures[6]
	Most strongly favored open climates and rejected closed climates, in a study of type and organizational climate[6]
	Ranked last in lowering costs in a computer simulation where goal was to achieve the lowest cost of production[6]

Source: [1]Quenk & Quenk, 1996; [2]Shelton, 1996; [3]DiTiberio, 1996; [4]Hammer, 1996a; [5]Haley, 1997; [6]Walck, 1996.

All four Introverted Judging (IJ) types have a dominant introverted perceiving function and an auxiliary extraverted judging function.

IJs are introspective, persevering, and hard to convince or change, unless compelling data are provided that override a decision or foregone conclusion. IJs can appear resistant to change because they extravert their preferred auxiliary judging function, Thinking or Feeling. This means they state their conclusions rather than providing the data for their conclusions (their introverted, dominant perceiving function). They can therefore appear to others to be adamant and inflexible. However, since their perceiving function is the dominant, most crucial one, they will relinquish a conclusion if provided with new information that contradicts the conclusion, even when it seems to other people that the IJ's decision is firm and intractable. Table 4.8 summarizes relevant research results for IJ types.

One might cautiously infer that the results showing that female IJ types report longer and fewer marriages is a reflection of a likely IJ emphasis on persistence, stability, and permanence in many aspects of life. Readers particularly interested in this area are referred to the relationship studies discussed in Chapter 10.

Particular caution is needed in interpreting the "substance abuse" results in this and other Chapter 4 tables. The majority of data in this area were gathered within substance abuse treatment programs—people who were referred to and/or voluntarily entered treatment. Over- and underrepresentations are best interpreted with this in mind. Actual base rates by type for substance abuse are not available. Therefore, typological results may best reflect the greater or lesser *attraction* of the types or members of particular type groupings to treatment programs, rather than greater or lesser incidence of substance abuse.

Table 4.8   Research Describing IJ Types

Personality, Psychotherapy, Health, Stress, Coping	Females married longer than any other female combination[1]
	Female ITJs married fewest number of times compared with all other female groupings[1]
	More likely to be substance abusers, among the four combinations[1]
	Overrepresented among male substance abusers[1]
	Overrepresented among females in a substance abuse program[1]
	Underrepresented among new college students required to attend substance abuse workshop[1]
Education	Scored higher among college students on an algebra final examination[2]
	Males more likely to persist in engineering school[2]
	Overrepresented among Japanese students of language at the University of Hawaii[3]
	As medical students, scored second lowest of the four on the 16 PF Leadership Scale[4]
Careers	Higher than IPs on "Managerial control" and lower than EPs on "Physical comfort" as ideal work environment characteristics[5]
Organizations, Leadership, Management, Teams	Dislike transition periods in the work setting; tend to withdraw during transitions to process and examine new information; accept and support change only when it fits with their inner understanding[6]
	Least likely to take risk in a study of risk tolerance among top executives[7]

Source: [1]Quenk & Quenk, 1996; [2]DiTiberio, 1996; [3]Kirby & Barger, 1996; [4]Myers & McCaulley, 1985; [5]See Chapter 12, "Uses of Type in Career Counseling"; [6]Barger & Kirby, 1995; [7]Walck, 1996.

It is also interesting that IJ types are *underrepresented* among college students who were showing the kinds of behaviors assumed to reflect actual or potential substance abuse. This same discrepancy between college behaviors and later appearance in substance abuse treatment programs occurs for other type groupings and types, as will be seen in later Chapter 4 tables.

Research results in the areas of education, careers, and organizational variables all seem in accord with expectations considering the qualities associated with the IJ combination.

IPs: The Adaptable Introverts

ISTP	ISFP	INFP	INTP

All four Introverted Perceiving (IP) types have a dominant introverted judging function and an auxiliary extraverted perceiving function.

IPs are introspective, adaptable in little things, and firm on important issues because their dominant judging function is central to their personality. Others may assume that the outer flexibility and adaptability of IPs reflects their internal state as well. Such an assumption is usually unjustified, especially

when important inner judgments are at issue. In such circumstances, the flexibility of the IPs' extraverted auxiliary perceiving function can be overridden by their dominant judging function, Thinking or Feeling. When this occurs, IPs can appear intractable and resistant to change. For new information to be effective in promoting a willingness to change, it must address the logic or values of their dominant judging function or it will be rejected as irrelevant. Table 4.9 summarizes relevant research results for IP types.

At first glance, we might assume that the four IP types—ISTP, ISFP, INTP, and INFP—may be vulnerable to some personal and relationship difficulties, as well as career indecision and dissatisfaction, while valuing work autonomy and adapting well to change in the work setting. However, an understanding of type provides a context within which to realistically assess the probable meaning of some of the results shown. The previously mentioned limitations of substance abuse data need to be considered here. That ITP females report more marriages may be related to their observed tendency to be less satisfied with relationships in general, as discussed in Chapter 10, where it is suggested that different definitions of *satisfaction* may be operating for different types.

The education, career, and organizational variables that seem to distinguish IP types are quite consistent with a highly flexible approach to life. IP types may not be particularly motivated to seek the closure of a career decision, nor by standard notions of "leadership" and "control" of their environment. Career decisiveness and leadership are highly valued in our culture, and therefore IP types tend to stand out as marching to a different drummer. If carefully done

Table 4.9   Research Describing IP Types

Personality, Psychotherapy, Health, Stress, Coping	Female ITPs married most number of times compared with all other female groupings[1]
	Except for ISFPs, more likely to be substance abusers among four combinations[1]
	Overrepresented among male substance abusers[1]
Education	As medical students, scored lowest of the four on the 16 PF Leadership Scale[2]
	Among medical students, said they decided late and, even though in medical school, were not confident about their decision[2]
Careers	Particularly likely to say they did not like their work, in a general study of job satisfaction[3]
	Higher than EJs on "Autonomy" as ideal work environment characteristic; lower than EJs and IJs on "Managerial control"[4]
Organizations, Leadership, Management, Teams	During transitions tend to be flexible and adaptable in small things and respond positively unless change violates inner values and principles—their dominant judging function[5]
	One of two groups least positive about using statistical methods as an information source[6]

Source: [1]Quenk & Quenk, 1996; [2]Myers & McCaulley, 1985; [3]Hammer, 1996a; [4]See Chapter 12, "Uses of Type in Career Counseling"; [5]Barger & Kirby, 1995; [6]Walck, 1996.

substance abuse studies confirm an overrepresentation of these types, perhaps a contributing factor might be the stresses related to living in a manner that is not in accord with prevailing values.

EPs: The Adaptable Extraverts

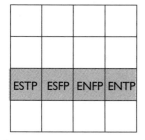

All four Extraverted Perceiving (EP) types have a dominant perceiving function (S or N) that is *extraverted* and a judging function (T or F) that is the introverted auxiliary function.

EPs are active, energetic, and sociable and often seek new experiences. They adapt even more easily to new outer conditions than do the IPs, for whom the extraverted perceiving function has only an auxiliary status. Their dominant extraverted perceiving function leads them to trust and eagerly engage the outer world. They are optimistic about what that outer world has to offer and about their ability to interact with it in a satisfying way. Their optimism may be perceived as excessive risk taking to types who approach the world more cautiously (often the types who introvert their perceiving function—for example, dominant introverted Sensing (ISJ) and dominant introverted Intuitive (INJ) types). EPs embrace new opportunities with optimism, and obstacles are seen as merely temporary setbacks

or challenges to be met. At times, the pull to new experiences or possibilities in the world can override their auxiliary introverted judgment, and they may in fact fail to achieve their optimistic intent. Table 4.10 summarizes relevant research results for EP types.

It makes quite a difference when the dominant function of a type grouping is an extraverted perceiving function rather than an introverted judging one—at least in the kinds of variables reflected in Table 4.10 for EP types, as compared with Table 4.9 for IP types. Remember that both IP and EP types extravert their perceiving function and introvert their judging function, but for IP the extraverted function is the auxiliary one, and for EP it is the dominant function. The EP types appear less frequently in substance abuse groups than the IP types, in spite of the fact that college officials assess them as showing behaviors that reflect or are predictive of substance abuse problems.

In this table, EP types seem to demonstrate the same kind of flexibility and adaptability as the IP types, but their dominant extraverted perceiving function may contribute to their greater tendency to engage in societally valued leadership behavior.

EJs: The Decisive Extraverts

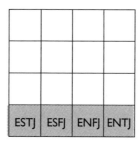

Table 4.10 Research Describing EP Types

Personality, Psychotherapy, Health, Stress, Coping	Underrepresented among male substance abusers[1]
	Underrepresented among females in a substance abuse program[1]
	Overrepresented among new college students required to attend substance abuse workshop[1]
	Underrepresented among men who had undergone coronary bypass surgery[2]
Education	As medical students, scored second highest of the four on the 16 PF Leadership Scale[3]
Careers	Higher than IJs on "Physical comfort" as ideal work environment characteristic; lower than EJs on "Managerial control"[4]
Organizations, Leadership, Management, Teams	Enthusiastically support transitions at work and respond resourcefully to new demands and challenges; may move too quickly for others' comfort; will resist change if not involved in decision-making process[5]
	One of two groups least positive about using statistical methods as an information source[6]

Source: [1]Quenk & Quenk, 1996; [2]Shelton, 1996; [3]Myers & McCaulley, 1985; [4]See Chapter 12, "Uses of Type in Career Counseling"; [5]Barger & Kirby, 1995; [6]Walck, 1996.

All four Extraverted Judging types have a dominant extraverted judging function (T or F) and an auxiliary introverted perceiving function (S or N).

EJs are fast moving, decisive, and confident looking, and they enjoy making things happen. It can be difficult for them to let go of a decision or conclusion because their dominant judging function (Thinking or Feeling) tends to be more persuasive than their auxiliary perceiving function (Sensing or Intuition). They are therefore harder to convince than the IJs, for whom judgment is auxiliary and has less authority in the personality. For EJs, new data are less compelling than the consequences (Thinking or Feeling) of persisting in a possibly faulty decision. They are therefore more likely to change their minds if a likely negative effect of a course of action is pointed out. EJs are seen by others as natural leaders, and they relish that role, as it permits them to exercise their dominant judging function to reach decisions and get things done. Table 4.11 summarizes the research results for EJ types.

A number of the research results in Table 4.11 are opposite to or quite different from those in Table 4.9 for the opposite IP types, particularly in the substance abuse, educational leadership, and career decisiveness areas. Note that most of the characteristics associated with ESTJ, ENTJ, ESFJ, and ENFJ are consistent with qualities valued in our society. In these research results this can be seen especially in their apparent comfort with administration, managerial control, long-range planning, and apparent effectiveness during organizational change.

Combinations of Perception and Orientations to the Outer World: SJ, SP, NP, and NJ

The SJ, SP, NP, and NJ grouping of types identifies types that use the same perceiving function in the same attitude of Extraversion or Introversion, regardless of whether their perceiving function is dominant or auxiliary in their type.

A focus on this grouping allows us to understand the different dynamics involved in *introverting Sensing* (characteristic of the SJ types) as compared with *extraverting Sensing* (characteristic of the SP types); and *extraverting Intuition* (characteristic of the NP types) as compared with *introverting Intuition* (characteristic of the NJ types). A description of the distinctive character of these dynamic processes is included in each of the four sections that describe common dynamic elements. These descriptions are adapted from *Introduction to Type Dynamics and Development* (Myers & Kirby, 1994).

It should be noted that two of the combinations included here, SJ and SP, are also used to describe two of the four temperaments identified by Keirsey and Bates, along with the NF and NT combinations previously discussed. As was the case for SJ and SP, the research evidence for these combinations that is shown in this section is repeated in the discussion of the temperaments.

SJs: The Realistic Decision Makers

ISTJ	ISFJ		
ESTJ	ESFJ		

All four Sensing Judging (SJ) types introvert their Sensing function, regardless of whether it is dominant (ISTJ, ISFJ) or auxiliary (ESTJ, ESFJ), and extravert their preferred judging function, Thinking or Feeling. People find it difficult to describe what is involved when one is introverting any one of the functions. This is particularly true when trying to describe the process of introverting Sensing, which involves

Table 4.11   Research Describing EJ Types

Personality, Psychotherapy, Health, Stress, Coping	Males married longer than any other male type combination[1]
	Underrepresented among female substance abusers[1]
	Underrepresented among male substance abusers[1]
	Underrepresented among male hypertensive patients[2]
Education	Overrepresented among top 100 executive educators[3]
	Overrepresented among freshman dental students[3]
	Overrepresented among female school administrators in the People's Republic of China[3]
	As medical students, scored highest of the four on the 16 PF Leadership Scale[4]
	Among medical students, more often stated they decided on medicine early and were confident they were in the right field[4]
Careers	ESJs had highest career satisfaction among elementary and secondary school teachers[5]
	Facet-specific (facets of the job) results were "keeping busy and doing things for others"[5]
	Overrepresented among those rated high on retirement planning among university faculty and staff planning to retire[5]
	Higher than IPs and EPs on "Managerial control" as ideal work environment characteristic; lower than IPs on "Autonomy"[5]
	In national sample, highest of all types in "Satisfaction with work" and "Satisfaction with company"[6]
Organizations, Leadership, Management, Teams	Readily organize the external environment during change, make quick decisions, gather resources, create structures, move ahead; may have difficulty dealing with ambiguities; may strive to implement structure prematurely[7]

Source: [1]Quenk & Quenk, 1996; [2]Shelton, 1996; [3]DiTiberio, 1996; [4]Myers & McCaulley, 1985; [5]Hammer, 1996a; [6]See Chapter 12, "Uses of Type in Career Counseling"; [7]Barger & Kirby, 1995.

directing one's energy and attention inward in order to remember external reality and events, as well as internal thoughts, feelings, bodily sensations, and memories. The focus is on taking in new information and integrating it into an internal storehouse for retrieval when needed. When introverting Sensing, one's goal is to form a solid, substantial, and accurate understanding of the world and one's place in it.

The effect of introverting Sensing can be seen in the ways that SJ types are typically described. They are seen as seeking order in their environment, as organized, dependable, and conservative. They tend to solve problems by reliance on past experiences, and they dislike ambiguity. People are often unaware of the wealth of factual and experiential data SJs bring to bear in making decisions because their data tend to remain inside their heads. When they are called upon to give evidence and provide the detailed bases for their decisions, other types may feel overwhelmed by the information and see it as unnecessary minutiae. At times, SJs, especially those for whom introverted Sensing is dominant (ISTJ and ISFJ), can run the risk of being distracted from their goals by their focus on collecting the facts that are relevant to the goal at hand. Table 4.12 summarizes relevant research results for SJ types.

As was pointed out for substance abuse data, there are limitations on generalizing hypertension and heart disease data that were collected primarily on samples that appeared

in treatment programs, although evidence from the Consulting Psychologists Press national sample gives some credence to these treatment program results. The "responsible" SJ types are not likely to show behaviors that college officials associate with actual or potential substance abuse. The education results in this table pinpoint the tendency of many types who include a preference for Sensing to excel in performance-based assessments of competence as compared with test-based measures. The remaining results in Table 4.12 appear consistent with what might be expected for people who introvert Sensing and extravert their preferred judging process.

SPs: The Adaptable Realists

ISTP	ISFP		
ESTP	ESFP		

All four Sensing Perceiving types extravert Sensing, regardless of whether it is dominant (ESTP, ESFP) or

Table 4.12   Research Describing SJ Types

Personality, Psychotherapy, Health, Stress, Coping	Overrepresented in both male and female samples of coronary heart disease patients[1]
	Underrepresented among new college students required to attend a substance abuse workshop[2]
Education	Underrepresented among six small private "student-centered" high schools[3]
	Scored lower on the National Teacher Exam than would be predicted by their classroom performance[3]
	Females more likely to persist in school in a large sample of engineering school students[3]
	Overrepresented among female school administrators in the People's Republic of China[3]
	Overrepresented among Chinese and Chinese-Filipino students of language at the University of Hawaii[4]
	More frequent among African American students[4]
Careers	Among elementary school teachers, more satisfied with the supervision they received[5]
	Frequent among pharmacists, medical technologists, and teachers, especially in the lower grades[6]
	Among physicians, had "maintaining consistent and predictable schedule and performing habitual activities" as work setting characteristics[5]
Organizations, Leadership, Management, Teams	Developed significantly fewer possible solutions than NJs and found the fewest figures in the embedded figures test in problem-solving study[7]

Source: [1]Shelton, 1996; [2]Quenk & Quenk, 1996; [3]DiTiberio, 1996; [4]Kirby & Barger, 1996; [5]Hammer, 1996a; [6]Myers and McCaulley, 1985; [7]Walck, 1996.

auxiliary (ISTP, ISFP), and introvert their preferred judging function, Thinking or Feeling. The process of extraverting Sensing involves directing one's energy and attention outwardly, noticing sights, sounds, smells, touch, human reactions—in short, everything present—in great detail and accurately. One's focus is on intensely experiencing what is happening in the present and on seeking stimulation through the variety and vividness of one's sensations. When extraverting Sensing, one's goal is to experience as much as possible by having an unending variety of Sensing experience.

The effects of extraverting Sensing can be seen in the way SP types are described. They tend to seek new experiences in the present moment and are curious about the world around them. They adapt to situations as they arise and are good observers of the immediate situation. SPs are attracted to work that focuses on attending to facts and details in the immediate environment. They are relatively uninterested in the long-range aspects or implications of what they do. They are stimulus-seekers and flourish when they can experience a great deal of external stimulation. Table 4.13 summarizes relevant research results for SP types.

Table 4.13 highlights some of the ways in which some types do not have "equal opportunity" in the educational sphere. ESTP, ESFP, ISTP, and ISFP types tend to be active, hands-on learners, and their particular ways of learning and demonstrating intellectual competence are not accommodated well in standard educational programs and in standard measures of achievement. Like the ST types (Table 4.4), when assessed using a performance measure (the Academic Decathlon) rather than a standardized test

measure, they fare better than would be expected from some of the other data. Results like these encourage recognition that the competence of SP types may often go unrecognized throughout our educational system and that this chronic problem may well influence both their motivation toward and opportunities for receiving the higher education needed for the careers where they appear infrequently.

NPs: The Adaptable Innovators

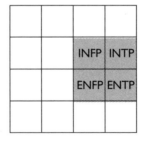

All four Intuitive Perceiving (NP) types extravert Intuition, regardless of whether it is their dominant (ENFP, ENTP) or auxiliary (INFP, INTP) function, and introvert their preferred judging function, Thinking or Feeling. The process of extraverting Intuition involves scanning the outer world for whatever is new—new ideas, new people, or new possibilities—with an aim of changing and reshaping the environment. One's focus is on exploring and experiencing the world in all its potentialities. When extraverting Intuition, one's goal is to find and explore possibilities through new and exciting challenges.

Table 4.13   Research Describing SP Types

Personality, Psychotherapy, Health, Stress, Coping	Overrepresented among male hypertensive patients[1]
Education	Overrepresented among least decided in a study of career decisiveness among undergraduates in education[2]
	Higher percentage of undergraduates failed the Texas Academic Program Test than any other combination[3]
	Notably missing among teachers at all levels of education[3]
	Overrepresented among Academic Decathlon participants compared with their proportion among National Merit Finalists[4]
	Overrepresented among Hawaiian students of language at the University of Hawaii[4]
	More frequent among African American students[4]
Careers	Research not available
Organizations, Leadership, Management, Teams	Maintained high interest throughout a production simulation that required learning well-defined, structured procedures[5]

Source: [1]Shelton, 1996; [2]Hammer, 1996a; [3]DiTiberio, 1996; [4]Kirby & Barger, 1996; [5]Walck, 1996.

Table 4.14   Research Describing NP Types

Personality, Psychotherapy, Health, Stress, Coping	Overrepresented among female substance abusers[1]
	Underrepresented among both male and female chronic pain patients[2]
Education	Overrepresented among six small private "student-centered" high schools[3]
	Outscored SJ types on vocabulary in a study of specific learning tasks[3]
Careers	Facet-specific job satisfaction results for elementary and secondary school teachers mentioned "trying their own methods"[4]
	Had a higher turnover rate compared with SJs in a working environment conducive to SJs[4]
Organizations, Leadership, Management, Teams	Did better than other groupings at embedded figures task[5]

Source: [1]Quenk & Quenk, 1996; [2]Shelton, 1996; [3]DiTiberio, 1996; [4]Hammer, 1996a; [5]Walck, 1996.

The process of extraverting Intuition is reflected in the way NP types are described. They constantly seek the challenge of the unknown and adapt to new possibilities as they arise. They are unconventional, independent spirits who hate to be fenced in. They enjoy seeking new solutions for both old and new problems and like the challenge of the apparently impossible or the very difficult, especially in the realm of possibilities in the world.

Table 4.14 summarizes the few results available for NP types. The results seem consistent with the qualities associated with extraverting a perceiving function. However, a number of hypotheses could be developed regarding differential results for these types as chronic pain patients. Perhaps the same kind of flexibility that may contribute to performance on a task like the embedded figures test also contributes to their lower incidence among chronic pain patients.

NJs: The Visionary Decision Makers

		INFJ	INTJ
		ENFJ	ENTJ

Table 4.15   Research Describing NJ Types

Personality, Psychotherapy, Health, Stress, Coping	Underrepresented among male hypertensive patients[1]
	Overrepresented among those having Type A behavior[1]
Education	Research not available
Careers	Overrepresented among freshman dental students[2]
Organizations, Leadership, Management, Teams	Developed more possible solutions to the Dunker box problem than SJs[3]

Source: [1]Shelton, 1996; [2]DiTiberio, 1996; [3]Walck, 1996.

All four Introverted Judging (IJ) types introvert Intuition, regardless of whether it is their dominant (INFJ, INTJ) or auxiliary (ENFJ, ENTJ) function, and extravert their preferred judging function, Thinking or Feeling. The process of introverting Intuition involves attending to unconscious images and connections to develop new patterns and ways of seeing things. One's focus is on changing and reshaping the environment to bring into being one's inner vision and insight through finding patterns and meaning in the world. When introverting Intuition, one's goal is to develop inner intuitive patterns for understanding the world.

The process of introverting Intuition is reflected in the way NJ types are typically described. They strive to accomplish the goals of their inner vision and are driving, persistent, and determined. They can be charismatic leaders who attract dedicated followers. They have the ability to present their inner vision in a compelling, convincing way by framing it in terms of either long-range logical consequences or long-range impact on important values.

As is apparent from Table 4.15, NJ types seem to be one of the combinations that research and/or researchers find of little interest, as compared to the other three combinations in this grouping. The reported under- and overrepresentations among hypertensive patients and Type A behavior are similar to those observed for NT types (Table 4.7) and are as difficult to interpret without further study.

Combinations of Judgment and Orientations to the Outer World: TJ, TP, FP, and FJ

The grouping of types TJ, TP, FP, and FJ identifies types that use the same judging function in the same attitude of Extraversion or Introversion, regardless of whether their judging function is dominant or auxiliary in their type. A focus on this grouping allows us to understand the different dynamics involved in the processes of *extraverting Thinking* (characteristic of TJ types) as compared with *introverting Thinking* (characteristic of TP types) and *introverting Feeling* (characteristic of FP types) as compared with *extraverting Feeling* (characteristic of FJ types). A discussion of these important differences is included in each of the four sections that describe common dynamic elements.

A notable feature of this grouping is the fact that a table of research results is provided only for the first combination, the TJ types. No table of research results describing TPs, FPs, or FJs is included because very few reports of research were found within the constraints for inclusion of results. The few results available are therefore provided in narrative form only. The fact that research results are reported primarily for the TJ combination in this grouping may reflect the unique qualities that permit them to be described as "executive" types, a status that is generally highly valued in our culture. In contrast, the TPs, FPs, and FJs hold no similar consistently valued position.

TJs: The Logical Decision Makers

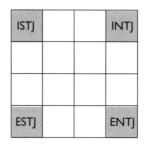

All four Thinking Judging types extravert Thinking, regardless of whether it is the dominant (ESTJ, ENTJ) or auxiliary (ISTJ, INTJ) function, and introvert their preferred perceiving function, Sensing or Intuition. The process of extraverting Thinking involves seeking to bring order to one's external environment, which is accomplished through expressing thoughts and judgments with directness and clarity. One's focus is on critiquing systems, procedures, and ideas so that consequences can be anticipated and acted upon quickly. When extraverting Thinking, one's goal is to create logical order in the external world by making the outer environment rational.

The process of extraverting Thinking is apparent in the way TJ types are described. These occupants of the four corners of the type table are tough-minded, executive, analytical, and instrumental leaders. They readily take on leadership roles in whatever setting they are in, and they

Table 4.16   Research Describing TJ Types

Personality, Psychotherapy, Health, Stress, Coping	Overrepresented among students preferring cognitive approaches to psychotherapy; underrepresented for affective approaches, except for ESTJs[1]
	Underrepresented among male hypertensive patients[2]
	Overrepresented among those having Type A behavior[2]
Education	Overrepresented among freshman dental students[3]
	Overrepresented among female school administrators in the People's Republic of China[3]
	Overrepresented among Chinese, Chinese American, mainland Chinese, and Taiwanese students of language at the University of Hawaii[4]
Careers	Frequent among health care executives[5]
	ETJ types had a more positive sense of well-being than did non-TJ types[5]
Organizations, Leadership, Management, Teams	Most strongly reject T-group norms hypothesized as E, N, F, and P[6]
	NTJs both most successful and most unsuccessful at running high-tech firms in a study of business founders[6]
	STJs more likely to be high performers in a study of high school principals[6]

Source: [1]Quenk & Quenk, 1996; [2]Shelton, 1996; [3]DiTiberio, 1996; [4]Kirby & Barger, 1996; [5]Hammer, 1996a; [6]Walck, 1996.

communicate their confidence in the viability and primacy of focusing on logical outcomes. TJs are seen as confident, in control, and able to implement decisions quickly and effectively. They can easily impose a logical organizational structure in a situation with the goal of effective problem solving. TJs may be seen by others as hypercritical, too quick to judge and act, and tactless in their style of communication, which tends to be direct and to the point. They generally use categorical statements that represent logical conclusions and avoid modifying terms such as *may, tends to,* or *generally.* Table 4.16 summarizes relevant research results for TJ types.

As noted earlier, the TJ combination is the only one of this grouping for which research results are available. The research shown in Table 4.16 is mostly consistent with what we would expect for people who extravert Thinking, for example, in their preference for cognitive rather than affective approaches in psychotherapy. The same results regarding hypertension and Type A behavior that were found for NJ and NT types are reported here. Observations in the areas of education, careers, and organizations present no surprises in this table.

TPs: The Adaptable Thinkers

ISTP		INTP
ESTP		ENTP

All four Thinking Perceiving types introvert Thinking, regardless of whether it is their dominant (ISTP, INTP) or auxiliary (ESTP, ENTP) function, and extravert their preferred perceiving function, Sensing or Intuition. The process of introverting Thinking involves seeking to order one's internal thoughts through developing a logical system for understanding. One's focus is on using reflective observation to critique reality and identify the inconsistencies and irrelevancies often overlooked by others. When introverting Thinking, one's goal is to create logical order by developing rational principles for understanding the world.

The process of introverting Thinking can be observed in the way TP types are described. They are objective, skeptical, observant, and curious, especially about materials, events, or possibilities that have or can be made to fit into consistent and orderly frameworks. They can be effective trouble-shooters with the ability to hone in on the essence of problems and find logical solutions for them. They are able to consider a broad range of facts, details, or ideas in order to come to the most accurate conclusion and are unlikely to rule anything out arbitrarily, regardless of how unorthodox or unlikely it may seem to others. Because their Thinking is introverted, others may have difficulty following the logic in their shifts of focus and changes in direction when they are deeply involved in a project. The internal logic may seem so obvious to a TP that he or she will assume that everyone else sees it too.

With regard to research describing TP types, in the national sample they were found to be overrepresented among new college students referred to a substance abuse workshop (Quenk & Quenk, 1996). As observed for certain other combinations, the "typologically associated" behaviors that college officials believe portend substance abuse are not confirmed among those who actually appear in substance abuse treatment programs. TP types are overrepresented among

Hawaiian students of language at the University of Hawaii and are more frequent among African American students (Kirby & Barger, 1996). In a study of career decisiveness (Hammer, 1996a), they were overrepresented among undergraduate education students who were classified as least decided, a result consistent with TP types' possible pursuit of a career that fulfills both their desire for using dispassionate analysis and their desire for a good deal of flexibility and freedom.

FPs: The Gentle Types

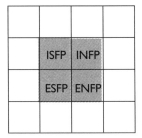

All four Feeling Perceiving (FP) types introvert Feeling, regardless of whether it is the dominant (ISFP, INFP) or auxiliary (ESFP, ENFP) function in their personality. The process of introverting Feeling involves seeking an intense, meaningful, and complex inner life through being attuned to possible contradictions between one's inner values and one's outer life. The focus is on clarifying and maintaining the consistency of one's own values and actions, although their intensity may seldom be expressed to others. When introverting Feeling, one's goal is to identify an inner core of values and establish an external life that is congruent with them.

The process of introverting Feeling is evident in the way FP types are described. They are adaptable, affiliative harmony seekers who are concerned with the human aspects of problems. They often have a knack for enlisting support from others, communicating a sincerity that promotes liking and trust. They welcome others' ideas and genuinely appreciate the contributions people make. Because their Feeling function is introverted, however, others may not be aware of the central values that motivate FPs until one of those values is attacked or disregarded. At such times, the typical flexibility and acceptance of an FP can change to stubborn insistence on doing things the "right" way.

Relevant research for FP types indicates that they were underrepresented among those having Type A behavior (Shelton, 1996). Possible contributing factors are difficult to explore in the absence of additional information.

FJs: The Benevolent Administrators

All four Feeling Judging (FJ) types extravert Feeling, regardless of whether it is the dominant or auxiliary function in their type. The process of extraverting Feeling involves seeking smooth and harmonious relationships with everyone in one's environment through being highly attuned to people's desires and expectations. The focus is on organizing and structuring the environment to meet people's needs and to facilitate the achievement of individual and group goals. When extraverting Feeling, one's goal is to create harmony and cooperation in the external environment and to facilitate others in getting what they need and want. The process of extraverting Feeling is often misjudged as excessive emotionality. When a person is extraverting Feeling, important values are expressed with the goal of ensuring that those values become actualized in the world. Strong affect often accompanies this expression but is secondary to the actualization of personal values.

The process of extraverting Feeling can be seen in the way FJs are described. They are observant about people and their needs and are often expressive leaders. They expend energy trying to make people happy and bringing harmony into relationships. They may be erroneously judged as overly accommodating and even codependent, since their extraversion of Feeling involves bringing harmony into the outer world. In fact, at times they may risk overcommitment to others' welfare, which may prove stressful when they attempt to honor and fulfill all important obligations. FJs are generally quite loyal to others who share important values and goals and may judge those who deviate from those personal values in negative, sometimes harsh ways. Including others and being included is an important value that, when not met, may lead the FJ to experience a sense of failure and hurt feelings.

Available research indicates that FJs were overrepresented among Filipino students in a study comparing language students at the University of Hawaii (Kirby & Barger, 1996) and were also frequently found in the clergy (Myers & McCaulley, 1985). This latter result has been found in numerous studies.

Combinations of Orientation of Energy and Perception: IS, ES, IN, EN

The grouping of IN, EN, IS, and ES is referred to as "the quadrants" because these types make up the four quadrants of the type table. The quadrants combine the functions of perception (Sensing and Intuition) with the Extraverted or Introverted attitude. Note that the types in these quadrants are appropriately described as having Extraversion or Introversion *with* Sensing or Intuition. For example, the four types in the IN quadrant are described as having *Introversion with Intuition* because the grouping does not refer to a dynamic commonality, beyond the fact that Intuition is *either* the dominant or the auxiliary function for these four types. The same style of designation is used for the other three quadrants.

Table 4.17 Research Describing IS Types

Personality, Psychotherapy, Health, Stress, Coping	More likely to be substance abusers[1]
	Overrepresented among male substance abusers[1]
	Overrepresented among females in a substance abuse program[1]
	Underrepresented among new college students referred to a substance abuse workshop[1]
	Overrepresented among members of a cardiac rehabilitation program[2]
	Overrepresented among male hypertensive patients[2]
	Overrepresented among males diagnosed with post-traumatic stress disorder[2]
	In national sample, highest ranked on "Ever had heart disease/hypertension"[3]
Education	Thinking types who were also ISs had higher grades in a study of 2,713 undergraduates[4]
Careers	Research not available
Organizations, Leadership, Management, Teams	Research not available

Source: [1]Quenk & Quenk, 1996; [2]Shelton, 1996; [3]See Chapter 10, "Uses of Type in Counseling and Psychotherapy"; [4]DiTiberio, 1996.

ISs: The Thoughtful Realists

ISTJ	ISFJ		
ISTP	ISFP		

Introverts with Sensing (ISs) like to test ideas to see whether they are supported by facts. They like to deal with what is real and factual in a careful, unhurried way and can become frustrated and irritable when they feel rushed and unable to devote adequate attention to the task at hand. They do not put themselves forward and prefer to stay in the background of projects and activities. Their efforts and accomplishments can easily be overlooked or taken for granted by others. Regardless of whether their Sensing is dominant and introverted (ISTJ, ISFJ) or auxiliary and extraverted (ISTP, ISFP), they are likely to avoid leadership roles and may experience considerable discomfort when forced into such roles. The stress of leading may come to overshadow and diminish their satisfaction with other, enjoyable aspects of their environment. Their quiet and persistent workstyle and dislike of leadership demands may further draw attention away from their quiet but often significant contributions at home and at work. Table 4.17 summarizes relevant research results for IS types.

It seems likely that the kinds of situations that appear to be quite stressful for the four IS types contribute to the results seen in Table 4.17 that show overrepresentations in the areas of substance abuse, as cardiac and hypertensive patients, and in being diagnosed with post-traumatic stress disorder. Bear in mind, however, that the results listed may be limited by the samples available for study. It is particularly noteworthy, therefore, that previously found associations between being an IS type and overrepresentation in cardiac and hypertensive groups were confirmed in the national sample study, whose subjects were not selected for any particular disorder. The implications of this finding are discussed in Chapter 10.

As in previous tables, it is interesting that the IS types are less frequently referred as substance abuse risks in college but based on these data appear more frequently in substance abuse groups. We might conjecture that college officials are attending to the "wrong" signs and behaviors in their attempts to identify at-risk students. It is also possible that IS types are truly not at risk while in school but that the later stresses of adult life and the workplace promote this and other stress-stimulated conditions. The fast-paced, frequently changing, and multiple external demands of today's work environment do not necessarily permit IS types to function in their most comfortable ways. Future research may better pinpoint the complex and likely interacting variables involved.

As four types who are most comfortable when keeping to the background of their environments, it is not surprising that there are few reports of notable characteristics in the areas of education, careers, and organizations.

INs: The Thoughtful Innovators

		INFJ	INTJ
		INFP	INTP

Table 4.18   Research Describing IN Types

Personality, Psychotherapy, Health, Stress, Coping	Overrepresented among students preferring cognitive approaches to psychotherapy; underrepresented for affective approaches[1]
	Underrepresented among behavioral psychologists, except for INTPs[1]
	More likely to be substance abusers[1]
	More likely to be overrepresented among female substance abusers[1]
	Underrepresented among members of a cardiac rehabilitation program[2]
	Underrepresented among male hypertensive patients[2]
Education	Obtained higher grades in courses that were abstract and theoretical in a study of 2,713 undergraduates[3]
	Among middle school students, performed better than ES types on a series of academic aptitude tests[3]
	Among student dental hygienists, performed worse than ES or IS students[3]
	Obtained higher geometry achievement scores among rural high school students[3]
	Overrepresented among academically gifted junior high students[3]
	Males more likely to persist in engineering school[3]
	Achieved higher grades if they were also Feeling types, in a study of 2,713 undergraduates[3]
Careers	Except for INFJs were most dissatisfied of the types with future work opportunities and/or their work[4]
	Among secondary marketing education teachers, were less satisfied[4]
Organizations, Leadership Management, Teams	Research not available

Source: [1]Quenk & Quenk, 1996; [2]Shelton, 1996; [3]DiTiberio, 1996; [4]Hammer, 1996a.

Introverts with Intuition (INs) are introspective and scholarly. They are interested in knowledge for its own sake, as well as ideas, theory, and depth of understanding. They are the least practical of the types, preferring the complexity of theory to the pragmatism of accomplishments in the world. Regardless of whether their Intuition is dominant and introverted (INFJ, INTJ) or auxiliary and extraverted (INFP, INTP), these types enjoy and seek out each other's company, feeling affirmed in their intellectual or philosophical interests and in their disinterest in and sometimes disdain for the practical world that seems to be so attractive to other types. They may be judged by others as too serious and as missing out on many of the activities and experiences available in the outside world. Table 4.18 summarizes relevant research results for IN types.

Like the IS types, the four IN types appear in substance abuse samples. However, unlike the IS types, they are reported as underrepresented among cardiac and hypertensive patients. The national sample studies reported in Chapter 10 generally support these earlier results in that the percentage of the four IN types who report heart disease or hypertension is considerably lower than for the four IS types.

As types who are very serious academically, the results shown in Table 4.18 in the education area are not surprising. The intellectual sphere is often "home" for IN types. It is therefore reasonable that, except for INFJ, they are the types most likely to report one or more ways in which they are dissatisfied with their work lives. Careers and jobs that allow people to devote the majority of their time to intellectual pursuits are relatively uncommon in the modern workplace.

That IN types performed worse as student dental hygienists than ES or IS students highlights the areas in which IN types are competent as well as those where IS and ES types excel. Such a result is certainly in accord with expectations from type theory, as is the lesser satisfaction of INs in teaching marketing.

ESs: The Action-Oriented Realists

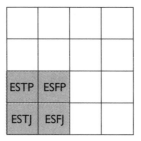

Extraverts with Sensing (ESs) are active, realistic doers and are the most practical of the types. They learn best when useful applications are obvious. They enjoy the material world and devote attention to the appearance of things, both

Table 4.19   Research Describing ES Types

Personality, Psychotherapy, Health, Stress, Coping	Male ESTs married the most number of times of all combinations[1]
	Males less likely to be substance abusers[1]
	Underrepresented among female substance abusers[1]
	Underrepresented among male substance abusers[1]
	Underrepresented among females in a substance abuse program[1]
	Underrepresented among patients in a cardiac rehabilitation program[2]
Education	Obtained higher grades in practical and applied courses in a study of 2,713 undergraduates[3]
	Performed worse than IN types on a series of academic aptitude tests among middle school students[3]
	Overrepresented among female school administrators in the People's Republic of China[3]
	Overrepresented among Hawaiian students of language at the University of Hawaii[4]
	Grades were higher for Thinking types who were also ESs in a study of 2,713 undergraduates[3]
Careers	Among pharmacists had greater overall satisfaction with occupation and greater number of relationships between type preferences and specific job duties[5]
Organizations, Leadership, Management, Teams	Research not available

Source: [1]Quenk & Quenk, 1996; [2]Shelton, 1996; [3]DiTiberio, 1996; [4]Kirby & Barger, 1996; [5]Hammer, 1996a.

aesthetically and from a practical, utilitarian perspective. The pleasure and accomplishment involved in experiencing as much of the world as is possible can be a persistent goal of ESs, and they may go to some effort to seek out particular interesting places, activities, modes of travel, and experiences. Regardless of whether their Sensing is extraverted and dominant (ESTP, ESFP) or introverted and auxiliary (ESTJ, ESFJ), the types in this quadrant typically appear confident of their relationship to the world and all it contains. Table 4.19 summarizes relevant research results for ES types.

There are striking differences between the types in the ES and IS quadrants with regard to substance abuse and cardiac problems. Perhaps the ESs' enthusiasm and optimism about the outer world enables them to welcome life experiences that seem particularly stressful for IS types. Their practicality in the world can also be seen in their greater achievement in practical and applied courses than in academic areas. The results for pharmacists suggest that this field may be particularly fulfilling for types who combine Extraversion with a Sensing preference.

ENs: The Action-Oriented Innovators

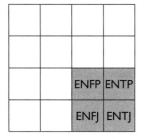

Extraverts with Intuition (ENs) are change agents; they see possibilities as challenges to make something happen. They have wide-ranging interests and like to see new patterns and relationships. Like the types in the ES quadrant, ENs are comfortable with and excited by their interactions with the outer world but are more future oriented in their pursuits and goals. Regardless of whether their Intuition is dominant and extraverted (ENFP, ENTP) or auxiliary and introverted (ENFJ, ENTJ), these four types share a vision of future potentialities in the world, whether for people, structures, institutions, or the general future of human activities.

As found in previous tables, Table 4.20 reveals that college student EN types were seen as at risk for substance abuse but in fact appeared less frequently in one treatment group and were less frequent in a cardiac treatment program. Like the IS types, this grouping has not yielded many reportable results in the areas of careers and organizations. A possible contributing factor is that the four whole types—ENFP, ENTP, ENFJ, and ENTJ—may be quite divergent in their career behavior and organizational pursuits and behaviors.

Combinations of Orientation of Energy and Judgment: ET, EF, IF, and IT

This grouping, like that of E and I with the perceiving functions, does not identify dynamic entities but rather identifies the combination of an attitude *with* a judging function, which may be either the dominant *or* the auxiliary function. None of the four combinations in this grouping yielded many research results, and research is therefore summarized in narrative rather than tabular form.

Table 4.20   Research Describing EN Types

Personality, Psychotherapy, Health, Stress, Coping	Males ENTs married the fewest number of times[1]
	Underrepresented among male substance abusers[1]
	Overrepresented among new college students referred to a substance abuse workshop[1]
	Underrepresented among members of a cardiac rehabilitation program[2]
Education	Grades were higher for Thinking types who were also ENs in a study of 2,713 undergraduates[3]
Careers	Research not available
Organizations, Leadership, Management, Teams	Research not available

Source: [1]Quenk & Quenk, 1996; [2]Shelton, 1996; [3]DiTiberio, 1996.

ETs: The Action-Oriented Thinkers

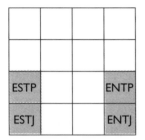

Extraverts with Thinking (ETs) are active and energetic. They are objective and like to make things happen in reasoned, analytical, and logical ways. They expect the same approach from others. Regardless of whether their Thinking is dominant and extraverted (ESTJ, ENTJ) or auxiliary and introverted (ESTP, ENTP), these four types share an expectation that they themselves and those around them should be confident, competent, and effective. ETs can be impatient and annoyed with others' self-doubt, hesitation, and low self-confidence. In consequence, Feeling types in particular may experience ETs as harsh, unsympathetic, and intolerant of others' needs.

Research shows that ETs are overrepresented among female administrators in the People's Republic of China (Kirby & Barger, 1996).

EFs: The Action-Oriented Cooperators

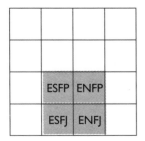

Extraverts with Feeling (EFs) are sociable, friendly, and sympathetic. They like to make things happen for the pleasure or welfare of others. They focus on liking others and being liked and on connecting people with each other. All are sensitive to the nuances of emotion that they pick up from those around them, and they find it hard to function at their best when they are in an environment characterized by frequent conflict and divisiveness. Regardless of whether their Feeling is dominant and extraverted (ESFJ, ENFJ) or auxiliary and introverted (ESFP, ENFP), EF types try to defuse contentious situations or mediate among people who are at odds with each other. The restoration of harmony is not only a strong value for them; it may also be a necessary condition that enables them to remain in any situation.

No relevant research was found for EF types.

IFs: The Reflective Harmonizers

Introverts with Feeling (IFs) are quiet and caring. They have concern for deep and enduring values, as well as for people and the way people feel. Regardless of whether their Feeling is dominant and introverted (ISFP, INFP) or auxiliary and extraverted (ISFJ, INFJ), these types feel things quite intensely and in a manner that can sometimes be puzzling to others. The depth of feeling about individual values can make them appear overly serious and excessively sensitive to their own and others' emotional state. Unlike the EFs, who strive to correct disharmony when they find it, IFs are likely to withdraw from such situations rather than deal directly with the distressing feelings that exist in the situation.

No relevant research was found for IF types.

ITs: The Reflective Reasoners

ISTJ			INTJ
ISTP			INTP

Introverts with Thinking (ITs) are quiet and contemplative. They have concern for basic principles that explain the causes and consequences of events or the workings of things. ITs are the most removed from daily social intercourse and are the slowest to develop social skills. They tend to be indifferent to or dislike small-talk and may find many social interactions unwelcome and stressful. They can be seen as socially awkward or may come across as overly formal and even unfriendly. Regardless of whether their Thinking is introverted and dominant (ISTP, INTP) or auxiliary and extraverted (ISTJ, INTJ), these types are natural and enthusiastic critics of whatever is being presented. The introverted approach they take while evaluating and critiquing contributes to their shared tendency to maintain an impassive facial expression and body language that seems to convey disapproval or disregard of others. As a result, they may be seen, often erroneously, as overly critical, disdainful, or, at best, uninterested in what is going on.

In research, ITs were found to be overrepresented among males diagnosed with post-traumatic stress disorder (Shelton, 1996).

Combinations That Describe the Four Temperaments: SJ, SP, NF, NT

SJ	SJ	NF	NT
SP	SP	NF	NT
SP	SP	NF	NT
SJ	SJ	NF	NT

Two of the combinations of the functions and two of the combinations of perception and orientation to the outer world are used by temperament theorists and researchers to identify the four temperaments—sanguine, choleric, phlegmatic, and melancholic—originally proposed as a descriptive system by the Greek philosopher Hippocrates (460–377 B.C.). These were developed and described in modern form by David Keirsey and Marilyn Bates (1978) and further extended and refined by Linda Berens. The temperaments are identified as Guardian, Artisan, Idealist, and Rationalist. Keirsey and Bates found that selectively combining Intuition with the two judging functions (NF and NT) and Sensing with Myers' two orientations to the outer world (SJ and SP) produced a descriptive personality system similar to the four temperaments Hippocrates described centuries earlier. Modern temperament theorists, therefore, use selected type constructs that are identified by answering the MBTI in order to approximate the constructs specified by temperament theory.

It is important to recognize that temperament theory is not a variant of type theory, nor is type theory a variant of temperament theory.

Type theory and temperament theory are two separate systems for explaining personality that are independent of each other in origin, in the number and kind of basic elements each hypothesizes, and in the way each theory's elements are combined. For example, temperament theory does not require the E–I dichotomy for its explanatory system and does not postulate the dynamic hierarchy and interaction of functions that form the essence of type theory. Temperament theory proposes that four qualitatively different broad categories describe major, fundamental aspects of personality. However, temperament theorists recognize finer distinctions than the four broad categories and ultimately refer to 16 patterns. Type theory proposes 16 categories for completeness, with many more commonalities among the types than are proposed in temperament theory. Both type and temperament theory share a common goal of identifying, describing, and appreciating individual differences in personality that emerge from a set of theoretical constructs.

A number of people who were initially interested in the temperament approach have become familiar with type theory because of the use of selected type constructs to describe the temperaments. Their understanding of the temperaments has been enhanced by knowledge of the 16 types and their dynamic characteristics. Some people who began with type theory have become familiar with temperament theory because of the apparent similarity in constructs. A valuable contribution of temperament theory to type theory is the clarification of the important differences between Extraverted Sensing and Introverted Sensing. To meet the interests of practitioners concerned with both theories, the following section discusses the combinations of type preferences that describe the four temperaments and summarizes relevant research about this theory of personality.

The four temperaments are typically described in terms of their distinctive *core needs and values* and their *talents*. The descriptions that follow focus on these areas.[1]

SJ Temperament: Guardian

The Guardian's core needs are for group membership and responsibility. Guardians need to know they are doing the responsible thing. They value stability, security, and a sense of community. They trust hierarchy and authority and may be surprised when others go against these. Guardians prefer cooperative actions with a focus on standards and norms. Their orientation is to their

Table 4.21   Research Describing SJ Temperament

Personality, Psychotherapy, Health, Stress, Coping	Research not available
Education	Tended to be left brain dominant in a study of brain dominance among technical institute learners[1]
	Scored lower than other three temperaments combined on the Test of Standard Written English but not found to be lower in their grades[1]
	Ranked third among chemical engineering students ranked from highest to lowest order of passing by temperaments[1]
	Underrepresented among six small private "student-centered" high schools[1]
	Scored lower on the National Teacher Exam than would be predicted by their classroom performance[1]
	Females more likely to persist in school in a large sample of engineering school students[1]
	Overrepresented among female school administrators in the People's Republic of China[1]
	Overrepresented among Chinese students and Chinese-Filipino students in study comparing language students at the University of Hawaii[2]
	More frequent among African American students[2]
Careers	Job satisfaction especially high when facets of jobs were theoretically related to their SJ style[3]
	Among elementary school teachers, more satisfied with the supervision they received[3]
	Frequent among pharmacists, medical technologists, and teachers, especially in the lower grades[4]
	Among physicians, had "maintaining consistent and predictable schedule" and "performing habitual activities" as work setting characteristics[3]
Organizations, Leadership, Management, Teams	Developed significantly fewer possible solutions than NJs and found the fewest figures in the embedded figures test in problem-solving study[5]

Note: Some of the research results listed in Tables 4.21–4.24 were previously included in tables of the grouping SJ, SP, NJ, NP and the grouping ST, SF, NT, NF. Research included in those tables was not specifically looking at the temperament grouping but is nevertheless relevant to temperament descriptions.

Source: [1]DiTiberio, 1996; [2]Kirby & Barger, 1996; [3]Hammer, 1996a; [4]Myers & McCaulley, 1985; [5]Walck, 1996.

past experiences, and they like things sequenced and structured. Guardians tend to look for the practical applications of what they are learning. They are usually talented at logistics and at maintaining useful traditions. They masterfully get the right things in the right place at the right time in the right quantity to the right people and not to the wrong people. Guardians know how things have always been done, so they anticipate where things can go wrong. They have a knack for attending to rules, procedures, and protocol. Table 4.21 summarizes relevant research results for the SJ temperament. Note that the research results previously reported for SJ, SP, NF, and NT combinations from a typological perspective are repeated in Tables 4.21–4.24, along with research that specifically studied the four temperaments.

Results in the education area highlight the fact that most educational environments do not recognize the learning style and competencies of people with an SJ temperament. But actual performance rather than standardized test measures gives a more positive picture of their intellectual competence. Results relating to multicultural overrepresentations are addressed in Chapter 14.

Career data for the SJ temperament confirm that careers and work environments that maximize the opportunity to use their preferred approach are more satisfying and that SJs are attracted to careers and work activities that would be predicted from knowledge of their temperament.

SP Temperament: Artisan The Artisan's core needs are to have the freedom to act without hindrance and to see a marked result from action. Artisans highly value aesthetics, whether in nature or in art. Their energies are focused on skillful performance, variety, and stimulation. They tend toward pragmatic, utilitarian actions with a focus on technique. They trust their impulses and have a drive to action. The Artisan's learning style is often concrete, random, and experiential. Artisans enjoy hands-on, applied learning with a fast pace and freedom to explore. They tend to be gifted at employing the available means to accomplish an end. Their creativity is revealed by the variety of solutions they come up with. They are talented at using tools, whether their tools be language, frameworks, paintbrush, or hammer. Artisans tune into immediate sensory information and vary their actions according to the needs of the moment. They are gifted at tactics. They can read the situation at hand, instantly make decisions, and, if needed, take actions to achieve the desired outcome. Table 4.22 summarizes relevant research results for the SP temperament.

It is interesting to speculate about what might contribute to the overrepresentation of SP types among male hypertensives while there is no similar result for the SJ temperament. Perhaps the most likely influence is revealed in the research results listed in the area of education. We saw in Table 4.21 that SJ types are at an educational disadvantage because of

Table 4.22   Research Describing SP Temperament

Personality, Psychotherapy, Health, Stress, Coping	Overrepresented among male hypertensive patients[1]
Education	Tended to be right brain dominant in a study of brain dominance among technical institute learners[1]
	Endorsed none of the strategies that correlate highly with GPA and endorsed five strategies negatively correlated with GPA, among high school students responding to the Coping Strategies Inventory[2]
	Had lower GPA than students of the three other temperaments[2]
	Ranked last among chemical engineering students ranked from highest to lowest order of passing by temperaments[2]
	Overrepresented among least decided in a study of career decisiveness among undergraduates in education[3]
	Higher percentage of undergraduates failed the Texas Academic Program Test than any other combination[2]
	Notably missing among teachers at all levels of education[2]
	Overrepresented among Academic Decathlon participants compared with their proportion among National Merit Finalists[2]
	Overrepresented among Hawaiian students of language at the University of Hawaii[4]
	More frequent among African American students[4]
Careers	Job satisfaction higher when facets of jobs were theoretically related to their SP style[3]
	Had lowest job satisfaction among vocational agricultural teachers[3]
Organizations, Leadership, Management, Teams	Maintained high interest throughout a production simulation that required learning well-defined, structured procedures[5]

Source: [1]Shelton, 1996; [2]DiTiberio, 1996; [3]Hammer, 1996a; [4]Kirby & Barger, 1996; [5]Walck, 1996.

the failure of educational environments to recognize their learning styles and competencies. The data for SP types are even more dramatic, suggesting that our typical educational system is particularly deficient in meeting the educational needs, interests, and learning styles of SP types. It would seem that the very things that are valued and used as criteria of educational success are quite opposite to the style and areas of competency of people with an SP temperament. As noted earlier, performance measures as compared with standardized test measures present a clearer picture of SP achievement. Chapter 11 discusses issues relevant to SP educational performance in some detail.

The few studies in Table 4.22 addressing careers and organizations provide good evidence that when tasks are required that are in accord with an SP temperament approach, these types report success and satisfaction.

NF Temperament: Idealist The Idealist's core needs are for the meaning and significance that come from having a sense of purpose and working toward some greater good. Idealists need to have a unique identity. They value unity, self-actualization, and authenticity. Idealists prefer cooperative interactions with a focus on ethics and morality. They tend to trust their intuitions and impressions first and then seek to find the logic and the data to support them. Given their need for empathic relationships, they learn more easily when they can relate to the instructor and the group. Idealists tend to be gifted at unifying diverse people and helping individuals realize their potential. They build bridges between people

through empathy and clarification of deeper issues. They use these same skills to help people work through difficulties. Thus they can make excellent mediators, helping people and companies solve conflicts through mutual cooperation. If working on a global level, Idealists will be championing a cause. If working on an individual level, they focus on growth and development of the person. Table 4.23 summarizes relevant research results for the NF temperament.

Results in the area of personality and related areas are consistent with expectations of those with an NF temperament, both in their preferences as psychotherapists and interests in being counseled. People with this temperament may deal with stress psychologically rather than through physical reactions, as suggested by their underrepresentation in chronic pain and bypass surgery groups.

In contrast to the SJ and SP temperaments, the NF temperament appears to be more consistent with the teaching and assessment methods of our educational system, and the results in Table 4.23 make sense for those with an NF approach.

The results shown for the career and organizational areas are also in accord with the NF focus on people and their relative disinterest in the technical aspects of their work. Perhaps the results relating to satisfaction and dissatisfaction at work are influenced by the apparent idealism of people with this temperament.

NT Temperament: Rational The Rational's core needs are for mastery of concepts, knowledge, and competence. Rationals want to understand the operating principles of the

Table 4.23   Research Describing NF Temperament

Personality, Psychotherapy, Health, Stress, Coping	Predominate among providers of psychological services[1]
	Overrepresented among client-centered psychologists[1]
	Underrepresented among behavioral psychologists[1]
	Overrepresented among students seeking counseling[1]
	Underrepresented among both male and female chronic pain patients[2]
	Females tended to be married much longer in comparison with female NTs[1]
	Underrepresented among men who had undergone coronary bypass surgery[2]
Education	Tended to be right brain dominant in a study of brain dominance among technical institute learners[3]
	Ranked second among chemical engineering students ranked from highest to lowest order of passing by temperaments[3]
	As teachers, endorsed an internal system of belief about discipline for children (children develop from an unfolding of potential)[3]
	As middle school students, performed better than ST types on a series of academic aptitude tests[3]
	Reported reading more books than any other combination[3]
	Among Japanese students, were overrepresented among foreign language students at the University of Hawaii[4]
	Ranked second out of four in passing among chemical engineering students[3]
Careers	Job satisfaction was especially high when facets of jobs were theoretically related to their NF style[5]
	Reported less job satisfaction with occupational specialty than other types[5]
	Had higher perceptions of the expected utility of possible alternate jobs than SFs in a study of "intent to leave current job"[5]
Organizations, Leadership, Management, Teams	Believe information on people is more important than other information[6]
	Least satisfied information users[6]
	Had weakest preference for tabular reports in a study of information use[6]
	More likely to use group- and people-oriented techniques to promote change[6]
	Rely on anecdotes, catchy symbols, vivid imagery to make points[6]
	Use personal evaluations of situations to reduce uncertainty[6]
	May ignore statistical evidence and overestimate their ability to work through plans or implement them[7]
	Took an intermediate position of nominal risk taking; more likely to take risk when in environment incompatible with own type, in a study of risk tolerance[6]
	Lost interest rapidly and "dropped out" in a production simulation that required learning well-defined, structured procedures[6]
	Ranked third of four in simulated attempt to achieve lowest production costs[6]

Source: [1]Quenk & Quenk, 1996; [2]Shelton, 1996; [3]DiTiberio, 1996; [4]Kirby & Barger, 1996; [5]Hammer, 1996a; [6]Walck, 1996; [7]Haley, 1997.

universe and to learn or even develop theories for everything. They value expertise, logical consistency, concepts, and ideas, and they seek progress. Rationals tend toward pragmatic, utilitarian actions with a technology focus. They trust logic above all else, tend to be skeptical, and highly value precision in language. Their learning style is conceptual, and Rationals want to know the underlying principles that generate the details and facts rather than the details alone. Rationals prefer using their gifts of strategic analysis to approach all situations. They constantly examine the relationship of the means to the overall vision and goal. No strangers to complexity, theories, and models, they like to think of all possible contingencies and develop multiple plans for handling them. They abstractly analyze a situation

and consider previously unthought-of possibilities. Research, analysis, searching for patterns, and developing hypotheses are quite likely to be their natural modi operandi. Table 4.24 summarizes relevant research results for the NT temperament.

Those with an NT temperament seem somewhat similar in their likely way of dealing with stress to those with an NF temperament, in being underrepresented in substance abuse, hypertensive, and chronic pain groups. Perhaps some other coping strategy than a psychological one may be used by people with this temperament. Chapter 10 provides some insights in this regard.

The educational system seems even more favorable for this temperament than for the NF group, as would be

Table 4.24   Research Describing NT Temperament

Personality, Psychotherapy, Health, Stress, Coping	Overrepresented among students preferring cognitive approaches to psychotherapy; underrepresented for affective approaches[1]
	Females tended to have much shorter marriages than female NFs[1]
	Underrepresented among male substance abusers[1]
	Males underrepresented among hypertensive patients[2]
	Overrepresented among those having Type A behavior[2]
	Underrepresented among both male and female chronic pain patients[2]
Education	Ranked highest among chemical engineering students ranked from highest to lowest order of passing by temperaments[3]
	Endorsed an internal system (children develop from an unfolding of potential) in a study of teachers' beliefs about discipline[3]
	As writing instructors, gave higher grades to students of same type[3]
	Obtained higher geometry achievement scores among rural high school students[3]
	Reported reading third highest number of books per year[3]
	Overrepresented among top 100 executive educators[3]
	Ranked highest among chemical engineering students in passing curriculum[3]
Careers	Job satisfaction higher when facets of jobs were theoretically related to their NT style[4]
	Less satisfied with career among secondary marketing education teachers[4]
	Overrepresented among secretaries stating they disliked their work[4]
Organizations, Leadership, Management, Teams	As managers, see patterns in structured data, ignore cases that negate their beliefs, may resort to quick, superficial studies; may persevere in beliefs despite contradictory evidence[5]
	Tend to use survey feedback to promote organizational change[6]
	Sought more quantitative data than NFs in solving unstructured case study[6]
	Found information about organizational structure important in study of information content[6]
	Took an intermediate position of nominal risk taking; more likely to take risk when operating in an environment incompatible with their type, in a study of risk tolerance[6]
	Lost interest rapidly and "dropped out" in a production simulation that required learning well-defined, structured procedures[6]
	Most strongly favored open climates and rejected closed climates, in a study of type and organizational climate[6]
	Ranked last in lowering costs in a computer simulation where goal was to achieve the lowest cost of production[6]

Source: [1]Quenk & Quenk, 1996; [2]Shelton, 1996; [3]DiTiberio, 1996; [4]Hammer, 1996a; [5]Haley, 1997; [6]Walck, 1996.

expected given their interests and kinds of competencies. Both high and low interest areas are revealed in the career and organization results listed in Table 4.24. For example, NTs lost interest in or performed poorly on tasks that required a focus on attending to details in a structured way and in closed rather than open climates.

Characteristics of the 16 Types

Being familiar with the type table and knowing the characteristics of combinations of type preferences and dynamic commonalities are valuable ways of acquiring understanding of the individual differences that are identified through psychological type. However, the unique contribution the MBTI makes to our understanding of personality is through knowledge of the 16 types as complex, dynamic systems. Focusing on whole types enables us to recognize them as broad, complex structures that interact dynamically and develop over the life span. This final section covers the following areas:

- A summary of the dynamics of each type
- A type description (identical to the one presented in the current edition of *Introduction to Type*) for each type
- A summary of research that describes the distinctive characteristics of the type

Table 4.25 is a helpful introduction and overview of the 16 types. It presents the brief descriptions of the types that appear in *Introduction to Type* (Myers, with Kirby & Myers, 1998).

Table 4.25   Characteristics Frequently Associated with Each Type

	Sensing Types		Intuitive Types	
Introverts	**ISTJ** Quiet, serious, earn success by thoroughness and dependability. Practical, matter-of-fact, realistic, and responsible. Decide logically what should be done and work toward it steadily, regardless of distractions. Take pleasure in making everything orderly and organized—their work, their home, their life. Value traditions and loyalty.	**ISFJ** Quiet, friendly, responsible, and conscientious. Committed and steady in meeting their obligations. Thorough, painstaking, and accurate. Loyal, considerate, notice and remember specifics about people who are important to them, concerned with how others feel. Strive to create an orderly and harmonious environment at work and at home.	**INFJ** Seek meaning and connection in ideas, relationships, and material possessions. Want to understand what motivates people and are insightful about others. Conscientious and committed to their firm values. Develop a clear vision about how best to serve the common good. Organized and decisive in implementing their vision.	**INTJ** Have original minds and great drive for implementing their ideas and achieving their goals. Quickly see patterns in external events and develop long-range explanatory perspectives. When committed, organize a job and carry it through. Skeptical and independent, have high standards of competence and performance—for themselves and others.
	ISTP Tolerant and flexible, quiet observers until a problem appears, then act quickly to find workable solutions. Analyze what makes things work and readily get through large amounts of data to isolate the core of practical problems. Interested in cause and effect, organize facts using logical principles, value efficiency.	**ISFP** Quiet, friendly, sensitive, and kind. Enjoy the present moment, what's going on around them. Like to have their own space and to work within their own time frame. Loyal and committed to their values and to people who are important to them. Dislike disagreements and conflicts, do not force their opinions or values on others.	**INFP** Idealistic, loyal to their values and to people who are important to them. Want an external life that is congruent with their values. Curious, quick to see possibilities, can be catalysts for implementing ideas. Seek to understand people and to help them fulfill their potential. Adaptable, flexible, and accepting unless a value is threatened.	**INTP** Seek to develop logical explanations for everything that interests them. Theoretical and abstract, interested more in ideas than in social interaction. Quiet, contained, flexible, and adaptable. Have unusual ability to focus in depth to solve problems in their area of interest. Skeptical, sometimes critical, always analytical.
Extraverts	**ESTP** Flexible and tolerant, they take a pragmatic approach focused on immediate results. Theories and conceptual explanations bore them—they want to act energetically to solve the problem. Focus on the here-and-now, spontaneous, enjoy each moment that they can be active with others. Enjoy material comforts and style. Learn best through doing.	**ESFP** Outgoing, friendly, and accepting. Exuberant lovers of life, people, and material comforts. Enjoy working with others to make things happen. Bring common sense and a realistic approach to their work, and make work fun. Flexible and spontaneous, adapt readily to new people and environments. Learn best by trying a new skill with other people.	**ENFP** Warmly enthusiastic and imaginative. See life as full of possibilities. Make connections between events and information very quickly, and confidently proceed based on the patterns they see. Want a lot of affirmation from others, and readily give appreciation and support. Spontaneous and flexible, often rely on their ability to improvise and their verbal fluency.	**ENTP** Quick, ingenious, stimulating, alert, and outspoken. Resourceful in solving new and challenging problems. Adept at generating conceptual possibilities and then analyzing them strategically. Good at reading other people. Bored by routine, will seldom do the same thing the same way, apt to turn to one new interest after another.
	ESTJ Practical, realistic, matter-of-fact. Decisive, quickly move to implement decisions. Organize projects and people to get things done, focus on getting results in the most efficient way possible. Take care of routine details. Have a clear set of logical standards, systematically follow them and want others to also. Forceful in implementing their plans.	**ESFJ** Warmhearted, conscientious, and cooperative. Want harmony in their environment, work with determination to establish it. Like to work with others to complete tasks accurately and on time. Loyal, follow through even in small matters. Notice what others need in their day-by-day lives and try to provide it. Want to be appreciated for who they are and for what they contribute.	**ENFJ** Warm, empathetic, responsive, and responsible. Highly attuned to the emotions, needs, and motivations of others. Find potential in everyone, want to help others fulfill their potential. May act as catalysts for individual and group growth. Loyal, responsive to praise and criticism. Sociable, facilitate others in a group, and provide inspiring leadership.	**ENTJ** Frank, decisive, assume leadership readily. Quickly see illogical and inefficient procedures and policies, develop and implement comprehensive systems to solve organizational problems. Enjoy long-term planning and goal setting. Usually well informed, well read, enjoy expanding their knowledge and passing it on to others. Forceful in presenting their ideas.

Source: From *Introduction to Type* (6th ed., p. 13), by I. B. Myers, with L. K. Kirby & K. D. Myers, 1998. Palo Alto, CA: Consulting Psychologists Press. Copyright 1998 by Consulting Psychologists Press. Used with permission.

The descriptions and research associated with each of the 16 types follow. Note that the order of presentation is first the eight dominant introverted and extraverted perceiving types, followed by the eight dominant introverted and extraverted judging types.

ISTJ: Introverted Sensing with Extraverted Thinking

Dominant function: S_I

Auxiliary function: T_E

Tertiary function: F_E

Fourth/inferior function: N_E

At Their Best ISTJs have a strong sense of responsibility and great loyalty to the organizations, families, and relationships in their lives. They work with steady energy to fulfill commitments as stated and on time. They go to almost any trouble to complete something they see as necessary but balk at doing anything that doesn't make sense to them.

ISTJs generally prefer to work alone and be accountable for the results; however, they are comfortable working in teams when that is necessary to do the job right, when roles are clearly defined, and when everyone fulfills assigned responsibilities. Competence and responsibility are extremely important to ISTJs, who expect others to be as dutiful and trustworthy as they require themselves to be.

Characteristics of ISTJs ISTJs have a profound respect for facts. They use their Sensing primarily internally, where they have a storehouse of information upon which they draw to understand the present. Thus, they are likely to be

- Practical, sensible, and realistic
- Systematic

ISTJs use Thinking in decision making, taking an objective, logical, and tough-minded approach. Their focus is on the task or system as a whole, rather than on individuals. Thus, ISTJs tend to be

- Logical and analytical
- Detached and reasonable

ISTJs are clear and steadfast in their opinions because they have arrived at them by carefully and thoroughly applying logical criteria based on their experience and knowledge. They believe standard procedures exist because such procedures work. ISTJs will support change only when facts demonstrate such change will bring better results.

How Others May See Them ISTJs are sociable when comfortable in the roles they are playing; however, they generally do not share their wealth of rich Sensing observations and memories except with close friends. Others see their standards and judgments, their desire for structure and schedules, but they may not see their individual, sometimes humorous, private reactions.

It can be hard for ISTJs to see the sense in needs that differ widely from their own; but, once they are convinced that something matters to a person they care about, that need becomes a fact. They then go to great lengths to meet the need, even while continuing to think it doesn't make sense. Others usually see ISTJs as

- Calm, reserved, and serious
- Consistent and orderly
- Valuing traditions

Potential Areas for Growth Sometimes life circumstances have not supported ISTJs in the development and expression of their Thinking and Sensing preferences.

- If they have not developed their Thinking, ISTJs may not have reliable ways of dealing with the world and instead may focus solely on their memories and internal data.
- If they have not developed their Sensing, they may rush into premature judgments and actions without considering new information.

If ISTJs do not find a place where they can use their gifts and be appreciated for their contributions, they usually feel frustrated and may

- Become rigid about time, schedules, and procedures—go "by the book"
- Be critical and judgmental of others
- Find it difficult to delegate—to trust anyone else to do the job right

It is natural for ISTJs to give less attention to their non-preferred Intuitive and Feeling parts. If they neglect these too much, however, they may

- Not see the wider ramifications of current, expedient decisions
- Concentrate on logic so much they don't consider impacts on people
- Fail to respond appropriately to others' needs for connection and intimacy

Under great stress, ISTJs may be unable to use their customary calm, reasonable judgment and get caught up in "catastrophizing"—imagining a host of negative possibilities for themselves and others.

Table 4.26 summarizes relevant research results for ISTJs. The impression one gets from reviewing the health, stress, and coping results in Table 4.26 is that ISTJs respond to life stresses by being overrepresented in substance abuse groups, as heart disease and hypertension patients, in experiencing chronic pain, and in vulnerability to post-traumatic stress disorder, job burnout, and negative affectivity. A similar pattern of stress response is shown for the other dominant introverted Sensing types,

Table 4.26   Research Describing ISTJ

Personality, Psychotherapy, Health, Stress, Coping	Calm, stable, steady, cautious, conventional[1]
	Males among three lowest on two out of three measures of creativity[2]
	Males among three highest on "Soundness"[3]
	Among three male types overrepresented among substance abusers[4]
	Underrepresented among new college students referred for a substance abuse workshop[4]
	One of four male types most common in a substance abuse program[4]
	One of two most overrepresented female types in a substance abuse program[4]
	Overrepresented among men at risk for heart attack—more than three and one-half times the proportion in Myers' high school sample[5]
	Overrepresented among members of a cardiac rehabilitation program[5]
	Males were overrepresented among hypertensive patients[5]
	Overrepresented among men with chronic pain—accounted for 38% of sample studied[5]
	With ISFJs, far outnumber dominant extraverted Sensing types among chronic pain patients[5]
	Both males and females more frequent among chronic pain patients—with the other three dominant Sensing types[5]
	Overrepresented among males diagnosed with post-traumatic stress disorder[5]
	Report highest level of anger and frustration of all the types among those suffering long-term pain[5]
	Overrepresented among experimental psychologists compared with psychologists in general[6]
	In national sample, ranked third highest in "Ever had heart disease or hypertension"[7]
	Ranked fourth highest in "Depersonalization" burnout scale[7]
	Ranked fourth highest in "Negative affectivity"[7]
Education	Adaptively creative learners[8]
	One of the top two types among industrial/technical teachers[8]
	Among the four highest types in college GPA[8]
	Higher on deductive reasoning than dominant Thinking or Feeling types, with other dominant Sensing types[9]
	Among African American college students, most overrepresented of those with a Sensing preference—where S preference was generally overrepresented[9]
	Overrepresented among Hawaiian students in a study comparing language students by ethnic groupings at the University of Hawaii[10]
	Modal type of Chinese, Filipino, and Japanese language students at the University of Hawaii[10]
	More frequent among African Americans[10]
	Academic subjects preferred: math, practical skills[6]
	In national sample "Leisure Activities," overrepresented in "Watching sporting events," underrepresented in "Listening to music," "Writing," and "Appreciating art"[8]

the ISFJs, whose auxiliary function is extraverted Feeling rather than the ISTJ's extraverted Thinking. This discussion therefore is largely applicable to both dominant introverted Sensing types.

What can we conclude from these data and how can practitioners capitalize on such awareness to the benefit of dominant introverted Sensing types? This is not a minor issue, in that ISTJ and ISFJ types represent about 25% of the U.S. population and similar or even larger percentages of the populations of other countries.

First, it is important to keep results such as these in perspective. The large majority of ISTJs and ISFJs are not in substance abuse programs and do not suffer from heart disease, hypertension, chronic pain, job burnout, and the like.

Nor do we know from these data whether a *particular* ISTJ is likely to be characterized by any one or more of the "conditions" cited. What the data suggest is that Introverted Sensing types may be particularly likely to respond to stress in the ways shown in the research table. We can also reasonably hypothesize that their stress response has something to do with the values, motivations, and styles that characterize these types.

Support for this view comes from an examination of the other three research content areas, particularly in career and organizational variables. ISTJs appear to be attracted to, and probably comfortable in, work environments that are efficient, secure, predictable, and conservative, and that permit and promote personal responsibility in

Table 4.26 Research Describing ISTJ continued

Careers	Overrepresented among bank officers and financial managers[11]
	In national sample, highest of all types in liking work environments where "Everything is done by the book" and one of three highest types in liking "Toeing the line"; lowest of all types in liking work environments with "People with different backgrounds"[12]
	In national sample "Organizational Values," placed low value on "Visible autonomy," high value on "Financial security"[12]
	In national sample, dissatisfied with "Promotions" in their job[12]
	Overrepresented among working MBA students compared with national sample[12]
	Overrepresented among both male and female small business owners compared with national sample[12]
	Occupational trends identified: management, administration, law enforcement, accounting[12]
Organizations, Leadership, Management, Teams	Higher on CPI scales So, Sc, Cm, Fm; lower on Do, Cs, Sy, Sp, Wb, To, Ai, Ie, Py, Fx, In, Em[13]
	Higher on Leadership scales (LSI): "Guarded," "Pressuring"[14]
	Departures from SYMLOG Most Effective Profile: underemphasized "Active teamwork toward common goals," "Efficiency, strong impartial management," "Popularity and social success," "Having a good time," "Friendship," "Trust in the goodness of others"; overemphasized "Self-protection, self-interest first," "Conservative and correct ways of doing things" (more than any other type), "Obedience" (more than any other type)[15]
	Rated more negatively after feedback on all leadership items (even though initially rated more positively than most other types) in Naval Academy leadership behavior study where type training was followed by feedback from lower-ranked students[16]

. *Note:* [1]Raters were naive to type when making their ratings; [13]The names of the scales abbreviated in Tables 4.26–4.41 are as follows (brief definitions of these CPI scales can be found in Chapter 13, "Uses of Type in Organizations"): Do = Dominance; Cs = Capacity for Status; Sy = Sociability; Sp = Social Presence; Sa = Self-Acceptance; In = Independence; Em = Empathy; Re = Responsibility; So = Socialization; Sc = Self-Control; Gi = Good Impression; Cm = Communality; Wb = Well-Being; To = Tolerance; Ac = Achievement via Conformance; Ai = Achievement via Independence; Ie = Intellectual Efficiency; Py = Psychological-Mindedness; Fx = Flexibility; F/M = Femininity/Masculinity; [14]Tables 4.26–4.41 report ratings by subordinates of types that were significantly higher or lower on various leadership scales, relative to the other types.

Source: [1]Summary of salient *Adjective Check List* (ACL) data and *Q-Sort* descriptions of 12 of the 16 types. Thorne & Gough, 1991; [2]Highest three and lowest three types on three measures of creativity, calculated separately for males and females. Thorne & Gough, 1991; [3]Highest three and lowest three types on two measures of personal adjustment ("Soundness" and "Efficacy"), which were calculated separately for males and females. Thorne & Gough, 1991; [4]Quenk & Quenk, 1996; [5]Shelton, 1996; [6]Myers & McCaulley, 1985; [7]See Chapter 10, "Uses of Type in Counseling and Psychotherapy"; [8]See Chapter 11, "Uses of Type in Education"; [9]DiTiberio, 1996; [10]Kirby & Barger, 1996; [11]Hammer, 1996a; [12]See Chapter 12, "Uses of Type in Career Counseling"; [13]A study that compared the mean scores of the 16 types on the scales of the *California Psychological Inventory* (CPI) using a sample of 15,102 people who attended leadership development programs at the Center for Creative Leadership. Fleenor, 1997; [14]Results in the same study at the Center for Creative Leadership on the *Leadership Style Indicator* (LSI); [15]A study using SYMLOG (Systematic Multiple-Level Observation of Groups) analysis of 529 subjects from the top three tiers of management. Ratings of SYMLOG values for the 16 types were averaged across all raters. Sundstrom & Busby, 1997; [16]Walck, 1996.

their work lives. The patterns of high and low scores on the *California Psychological Inventory*™ (CPI™) scales are also consistent with these qualities. However, a review of Chapter 13 suggests that stability and personal control in the workplace are increasingly rare. The qualities that are valued, such as teamwork, rapid adaptability to change, flexibility, and the like, are not typically comfortable and natural parts of the ISTJ personality. Dominant introverted Sensing types therefore are particularly vulnerable to experiencing much of their daily life as quite stressful. Even in the personal arena, current trends toward rapid change, geographic mobility, alternative lifestyles, and political and social change may be especially incompatible with the role of Introverted Sensing types as promoters of the continuity and stability of important societal institutions and values.

An understanding of the distinctive style and motivations of Introverted Sensing types can help practitioners in all application areas create effective preventions and interventions both in the workplace and in the personal lives of these types. It is also important to recognize that the other 14 types may be particularly vulnerable to different type-consistent stresses and responses to stress that are less obvious in the particular research studies that have been surveyed.

ISFJ: Introverted Sensing with Extraverted Feeling

Dominant function: S_I

Auxiliary function: F_E

Tertiary function: T_E

Fourth/inferior function: N_E

At Their Best People with ISFJ preferences are dependable and considerate, committed to the people and groups with which they are associated, and faithful in carrying out responsibilities. They work with steady energy to complete jobs fully and on time. They will go to great trouble to do something they see as necessary but dislike being required to do anything that doesn't make sense to them.

ISFJs focus on what people need and want, and they establish orderly procedures to be sure those needs and wants are fulfilled. They take roles and responsibilities seriously and want others to do the same.

Characteristics of ISFJs

ISFJs have a realistic and practical respect for facts. They use their Sensing primarily internally, where they have a wealth of stored information. They remember clearly the details of things that have personal meaning for them, such as tones of voice or facial expression. Thus, ISFJs are likely to be

- Practical and realistic
- Concrete and specific

ISFJs use Feeling to make decisions based on personal values and concern for others. They value harmony and cooperation and work to create them. Thus, they are likely to be

- Cooperative and thoughtful of others
- Kind and sensitive

Their opinions are firm because their decisions are based on careful application of their clear values and their wealth of stored data. ISFJs respect established procedures and authority, believing that these have persisted because they function well. Therefore they will support change only when new data show it will be of practical benefit to people.

How Others May See Them

ISFJs are unassuming and quiet in their interactions, often putting the needs of others—especially family members—ahead of their own. They are uncomfortable with confrontation and will go a long way to accommodate others, though their respect for traditions and people's feelings can lead them to challenge actions they perceive as hurtful or insensitive. People see their values, their desire for structure and closure, their kindness. What others may not see is the wealth of rich, accurate internal Sensing impressions and memories. Others usually see ISFJs as

- Quiet, serious, and conscientious
- Considerate, good caretakers
- Honoring commitments, preserving traditions

Potential Areas for Growth

Sometimes life circumstances have not supported ISFJs in the development and expression of their Feeling and Sensing preferences.

- If they have not developed their Feeling, ISFJs may not have reliable ways of dealing with the world and instead focus solely on their Sensing memories and impressions.
- If they have not developed their Sensing, they may rush into value judgments or taking care of others without considering the realities.

If ISFJs do not find a place where they can use their gifts and be appreciated for their contributions, they usually feel frustrated and may

- Become rigid in supporting hierarchy, authority, and procedures
- Feel unappreciated, resentful—complain a lot
- Be overly focused on immediate impacts of decisions

It is natural for ISFJs to give less attention to their nonpreferred Intuitive and Thinking parts. If they neglect these too much, however, they may

- Not see the wider ramifications of current decisions or procedures
- Find it difficult to assert their needs
- Be uncomfortable applying impersonal criteria to decisions, even when needed

Under great stress, ISFJs can get caught up in "catastrophizing"—imagining a host of negative possibilities. They may then express these without their usual consideration for the impact on people around them.

Table 4.27 summarizes relevant research results for ISFJs. Most of the preceding discussion for ISTJs is applicable to ISFJs, who share dominant introverted Sensing with the ISTJs. Notable differences between ISFJ and ISTJ data are that ISFJs report low levels of assertiveness and are highest in reporting stress associated with health, caring for parents, and balancing home and work, as well as being fourth highest in believing in a higher spiritual power.

The results in the areas of education, careers, and organizations further pinpoint both the similarities and the differences of ISFJs and ISTJs. ISFJs' valuing of stability, loyalty, and structure, and their educational preferences and skills, are consistent with their ISFJ nature. Their focus on harmony, helping others, responsibility, and perseverance makes them particularly vulnerable to stress associated with the rapidly changing workplace, social institutions, and family structure. Their pattern on CPI scales supports their ISFJ approach to life.

ESTP: Extraverted Sensing with Introverted Thinking

Dominant function: S_E

Auxiliary function: T_I

Tertiary function: F_I

Fourth/inferior function: N_I

At Their Best

People with ESTP preferences are energetic, active problem solvers, responding creatively to challenging situations in their environment. They seldom let rules or standard procedures interfere, finding new ways to use existing systems. They develop easy methods to do difficult things and make their work fun. They are flexible, adaptable, inventive, and resourceful, can pull conflicting factions together, and are good team members.

They are popular companions for activities (parties, sports, or work) because of their zest for life and their enjoyment of the moment.

Characteristics of ESTPs

ESTPs are interested in everything going on around them—activities, food, clothes, people, the outdoors, and everything that offers new experiences. Because they learn more from doing than from

Table 4.27 Research Describing ISFJ

Personality, Psychotherapy, Health, Stress, Coping

Trend toward overrepresentation among men married more than two times[1]

One of four most common types among males in a substance abuse program[1]

Overrepresented among females in a substance abuse program[1]

Among substance abusers, are attracted to heroin[1]

Overrepresented among members of a cardiac rehabilitation program[1]

Predominant type among men who had undergone coronary bypass surgery[2]

Overrepresented among female coronary heart disease patients and second most frequent type[2]

With ISTJs, far outnumber dominant extraverted Sensing types with chronic pain[2]

More frequent among both male and female chronic pain patients[2]

One of the four types in college reporting the lowest levels of assertiveness[2]

In national sample, highest in reporting stress associated with "Health," "Caring for aging parents," and "Balancing home and work"[3]

In national sample, ranked third fhighest in "Ever had heart disease or hypertension"[3]

In national sample, ranked fourth highest in "Believing in a higher spiritual power"[3]

Ranked second highest on both "Emotional exhaustion" and "Depersonalization" burnout scales [3]

Ranked third highest in "Negative affectivity"[3]

Education

Males among three lowest on one out of three measures of creativity; females among three lowest on two out of three measures of creativity[4]

Second most frequent type among education majors[5]

As teachers, prefer a basal approach to reading instruction[5]

Rated by psychologists as one of two types least likely to have trouble in school[5]

Rated by faculty as skilled in working with dental patients[5]

Higher on deductive reasoning than dominant Thinking or Feeling types, with other dominant Sensing types[6]

Academic subjects preferred: practical skills[7]

In national sample "Leisure Activities," overrepresented in "Watching TV three hours or more per day," underrepresented in "Playing with computer/video games," "Watching sporting events," "Appreciating art," and "Playing sports"[5]

Careers

Most important features of an ideal job: stable and secure future[8]

Highest of all types in national sample in liking work environment characteristic "Employee loyalty & job security"; one of three highest types in national sample in liking work environment characteristics "Clear structures" and "No expectation for working extra hours"; lowest of all types in liking work environments with "International opportunities"[9]

In national sample, among three types with lowest income[9]

In national sample "Organizational Values," place high value on "Happy family" and low value on "Variety & challenge" and "Visible autonomy"[9]

In national sample, among top four types in valuing "Health" and "Spirituality"[9]

In national sample, dissatisfied with "Promotions," "Stress," and "Salary" in their jobs[9]

Overrepresented among working MBA students compared with national sample[9]

Overrepresented among male small business owners compared with national sample[9]

Occupational trends identified: education, health care, religious settings[9]

Organizations, Leadership, Management, Teams

Higher on CPI scales Sc, Fm; lower on Do, Ai, Cs, Ie, Sy, Py, Sp, Fx, Sa, In, Wb, Em, To[10]

Higher on LSI scales Conservative, Conventional, Guarded, Reserved[11]

Modal type in the organization in study comparing type with internal performance ratings—but ratings were negatively correlated with performance[12]

Showed change on at least four of seven leadership items in Naval Academy leadership behavior study where type training was followed by feedback from lower-ranked students[12]

Note: [10]Brief definitions of these CPI scales can be found in Chapter 13, "Uses of Type in Organizations." See also Table 4.26; [11]Tables 4.26–4.41 report ratings by subordinates of types that were significantly higher or lower on various leadership scales, relative to the other types.

Source: [1]Quenk & Quenk, 1996; [2]Shelton, 1996; [3]See Chapter 10, "Uses of Type in Counseling and Psychotherapy"; [4]Highest three and lowest three types on three measures of creativity, calculated separately for males and females. Thorne & Gough, 1991; [5]See Chapter 11, "Uses of Type in Education"; [6]DiTiberio, 1996; [7]Myers & McCaulley, 1985; [8]Hammer, 1996a; [9]See Chapter 12, "Uses of Type in Career Counseling"; [10]A study that compared the mean scores of the 16 types on the scales of the CPI using a sample of 15,102 people who attended leadership development programs at the Center for Creative Leadership. Fleenor, 1997; [11]Results in the same study at the Center for Creative Leadership on the *Leadership Style Indicator* (LSI); [12]Walck, 1996.

studying or reading, they tend to plunge into things, learning as they go, trusting their ability to respond resourcefully. ESTPs are likely to be

- Observant
- Practical and realistic
- Active, involved in immediate experience

ESTPs make decisions by logical analysis and reasoning and can be tough when the situation calls for toughness. They usually are

- Analytical, rational problem solvers
- Straightforward and assertive

ESTPs are expert at seeing the needs of the moment and reacting quickly to meet them. For the most part, they prefer to deal flexibly with what is, rather than make judgments. They good-naturedly take things as they are and seek satisfying solutions, rather than impose a "should" or "must" of their own.

How Others May See Them ESTPs are strong in the art of living. They love life and immerse themselves in it; others respond to their enthusiasm and good humor. ESTPs are people of action. They usually dislike and avoid theory and written directions. Traditional schools can be difficult for people with these preferences, though ESTPs do well when they see the relevance and are allowed to experiment. Others usually see ESTPs as

- Gregarious, fun-loving, and spontaneous
- Adventurous risk takers
- Pragmatic troubleshooters

Potential Areas for Growth Sometimes life circumstances have not supported ESTPs in the development and expression of their Thinking and Sensing preferences.

- If they have not developed their Thinking, ESTPs will not have a useful way of selecting amongst the barrage of incoming sensory data. They may then have difficulty setting priorities or may make ill-founded decisions.
- If they have not developed their Sensing, they may focus on the Sensing data that are immediately available. Their decisions may then be limited to gratification of their sensual desires, particularly those involving physical challenge and risk.

If ESTPs do not find a place where they can use their gifts and be appreciated for their contributions, they usually feel frustrated and may

- Have trouble accepting structure and meeting deadlines
- Focus entirely on excitement and activity, getting caught up in external activities
- Put enjoying life ahead of important obligations

It is natural for ESTPs to give less attention to their non-preferred Intuitive and Feeling parts. If they neglect these too much, however, they

- May not see the wider ramifications of their actions and decisions
- May forget dates and events that have special meaning to others
- May be unaware of the impact of their actions on others
- May be impatient with discussion or exploration of relationships

Under great stress, ESTPs may have negative fantasies. They may imagine that others do not really care about them, then marshal and distort their Sensing data to provide themselves with "evidence" of this neglect.

Table 4.28 summarizes relevant research results for ESTPs. Some of the possible consequences of extraverting rather than introverting one's dominant Sensing function can be inferred from a review of Table 4.28. ESTPs are rated lower by observers on some measures assumed to reflect psychological adaptation, and in comparison with ISTJs they are less likely to be common in substance abuse and cardiac groups. However, they are frequent in chronic pain groups, like the ISTJs. They seem less subject to the kind of job burnout effects that characterize the dominant Introverted Sensing types, are highest of the types in positive affect, and report satisfaction with their intimate relationships. Note that this type is identified by colleges as candidates for substance abuse training, but in fact ESTPs are less likely to appear in substance abuse treatment programs. Other variables in this content area that do not show up for Introverted Sensing types seem consistent with an ESTP approach to life.

Although the gender difference in measures of creativity is puzzling, the remaining educational results are consistent with expectations for a type whose learning style needs and expression of competence are addressed poorly by our educational system. Note, however, that some of their educational strengths are also indicated. Once in college they tend to remain, perhaps because the broader spectrum of subjects and training methods permits them to meet their educational needs. Chapter 11 discusses educational issues of ESTP and ESFP types in some detail.

The career and organization areas highlight some of the ways ESTPs function in the world of work. They are attracted to type-consistent fields such as marketing and technology, and their confidence and comfort in interacting with the environment are shown in their higher standing on the CPI scales of Dominance, Sociability, Social Presence, and the like. In contrast, they may be judged somewhat negatively for their just as type-consistent lower scores on Responsibility, Self-Control, Tolerance, and other scales.

Some of the characteristics that come naturally and comfortably to ESTPs and their companion dominant extraverted Sensing type, the ESFPs, are well regarded by society, while others can be interpreted as showing immaturity, lack of responsibility, and a lack of seriousness about goals and accomplishments. Much of the data above suggest such societal biases and the ways in which dominant extraverted Sensing types are likely to be misunderstood and misjudged, particularly as students and in the workplace.

Table 4.28   Research Describing ESTP

Personality, Psychotherapy, Health, Stress, Coping	Males among three lowest on "Efficacy"; females among three lowest on "Soundness" and "Efficacy"[1]
	Frequent among college students referred for substance abuse training[2]
	One of three least common types among males in a substance abuse program[2]
	Underrepresented among members of a cardiac rehabilitation program[3]
	More frequent among both male and female chronic pain patients[3]
	Less frequent than dominant introverted Sensing types among female chronic pain patients[3]
	With ISTPs, at highest risk for setbacks due to overdoing among those with long-term pain[3]
	Ranked 15th out of 16 types on using spiritual/philosophical coping resources and 16th out of 16 types on using cognitive coping resources[3]
	One of the four types in college reporting highest levels of assertiveness[3]
	Ranked third lowest in "Emotional exhaustion" and "Depersonalization" burnout scales[4]
	Ranked highest in "Positive affectivity"[4]
	In national sample, ranked fourth highest in satisfaction with "Marriage/intimate relationship"[4]
Education	Males among three lowest on two out of three measures of creativity; females among three highest on one out of three measures of creativity[5]
	Collaborative learners and field dependent learners[6]
	One of two types with lowest overall GPA[6]
	Among the highest in college retention[6]
	With other dominant Sensing types, higher on deductive reasoning than dominant Thinking or Feeling types[7]
	With ISTPs, the modal types of language students at the University of Hawaii[8]
	More frequent among African American high school males compared with Howard University males[8]
	Academic subjects preferred: history, math, practical skills[9]
	In national sample "Leisure Activities," overrepresented in "Playing sports"[6]
Careers	Three top work characteristics favored in national sample: "Variety of tasks," "Independence & achievement," "Clear structure"[9]
	In national sample, among types most dissatisfied with company/organization worked for[9]
	In national sample "Organizational Values," place high value on "Visible autonomy" and low value on "Achievement within system" and "Financial analysis"[9]
	In national sample, among top four types in valuing "Prestige"[9]
	In national sample, dissatisfied with "Promotions," "Opportunity to contribute to society," and "Amount of stress"[9]
	Overrepresented among working MBA students compared with national sample[9]
	Occupational trends identified: marketing, skilled trades, business, law enforcement, applied technology[9]
Organizations, Leadership, Management, Teams	Higher on CPI scales Do, Sy, Sp, Sa, Fx; lower on Re, Sc, To, Ac, Ai, Ie, Py, Fm[10]
	Higher on LSI scale Demanding[11]
	Departures from Most Effective Profile: underemphasize "Active teamwork toward a common goal," "Efficiency, strong impartial management," "Equality," "Responsible idealism and collaborative work"; overemphasize "Self-protection, self-interest first"[12]

Note: [11]Brief definitions of these CPI scales can be found in Chapter 13, "Uses of Type in Organizations." See Table 4.26; [12]Tables 4.26–4.41 report ratings by subordinates of types that were significantly higher or lower on various leadership scales, relative to the other types.

Source: [1]Highest three and lowest three types on two measures of personal adjustment ("Soundness" and "Efficacy"), which were calculated separately for males and females. Thorne & Gough, 1991; [2]Quenk & Quenk, 1996; [3]Shelton, 1996; [4]See Chapter 10, "Uses of Type in Counseling and Psychotherapy"; [5]Highest three and lowest three types on three measures of creativity, calculated separately for males and females. Thorne & Gough, 1991; [6]See Chapter 11, "Uses of Type in Education"; [7]DiTiberio, 1996; [8]Kirby & Barger, 1996; [9]See Chapter 12, "Uses of Type in Career Counseling"; [10]A study that compared the mean scores of the 16 types on the scales of the CPI using a sample of 15,102 people who attended leadership development programs at the Center for Creative Leadership. Fleenor, 1997; [11]Results in the same study at the Center for Creative Leadership on the *Leadership Style Indicator* (LSI); [12]A study using SYMLOG analysis of 529 subjects from the top three tiers of management. Ratings of SYMLOG values for the 16 types were averaged across all raters. Sundstrom & Busby, 1997.

ESFP: Extraverted Sensing with Introverted Feeling

Dominant function: S_E

Auxiliary function: F_I

Tertiary function: T_I

Fourth/inferior function: N_I

At Their Best People with ESFP preferences are exuberant lovers of life. They live in the moment and find enjoyment in people, food, clothes, animals, the natural world, and activities. They seldom let rules interfere with their lives, focusing on meeting human needs in creative ways.

ESFPs are excellent team players, oriented to getting the task done with a maximum amount of fun and a minimum amount of fuss.

Characteristics of ESFPs ESFPs are interested in people and new experiences. Because they learn more from doing than from studying or reading, they tend to plunge into things, learning as they go. They appreciate their possessions and take pleasure in them. ESFPs are likely to be

- Observant
- Practical, realistic, and specific
- Active, involved in immediate experiences

ESFPs make decisions by using their personal values. They use their Feeling judgment internally to make decisions by identifying and empathizing with others. They are good at interpersonal interactions and often play the role of peacemaker. Thus, ESFPs are likely to be

- Generous, optimistic, and persuasive
- Warm, sympathetic, and tactful

ESFPs are keen observers of human behavior. They seem to sense what is happening with other people and respond quickly to their practical needs. They are especially good at mobilizing people to deal with crises.

How Others May See Them ESFPs get a lot of fun out of life and are fun to be with; their exuberance and enthusiasm draw others to them. They are flexible, adaptable, congenial, and easygoing. They seldom plan ahead, trusting their ability to respond in the moment and deal effectively with whatever presents itself. They hate structure and routine and will generally find ways to get around them.

ESFPs tend to learn by doing, by interacting with their environment. They dislike theory and written explanations. Traditional schools can be difficult for ESFPs, though they do well when they see the relevance and are allowed to interact with people or the topics being studied. Others usually see ESFPs as

- Resourceful and supportive
- Gregarious, fun-loving, playful, spontaneous

Potential Areas for Growth Sometimes life circumstances have not supported ESFPs in the development and expression of their Feeling and Sensing preferences.

- If they have not developed their Feeling, ESFPs may get caught up in the interactions of the moment, with no mechanism for weighing, evaluating, or anchoring themselves.
- If they have not developed their Sensing, they may focus on the sensory data available in the moment. Their decisions may then be limited to gratification of their sensual desires, particularly those involving interactions with other people.

If ESFPs do not find a place where they can use their gifts and be appreciated for their contributions, they usually feel frustrated and may

- Become distracted and overly impulsive
- Have trouble accepting and meeting deadlines
- Overpersonalize others' actions and decisions

It is natural for ESFPs to give less attention to their non-preferred Intuitive and Thinking parts. If they neglect these too much, however, they may

- Fail to look at long-term consequences, acting on immediate needs of themselves and others
- Avoid complex or ambiguous situations and people
- Put enjoyment ahead of obligations

Under great stress, ESFPs may feel overwhelmed internally by negative possibilities. They then put energy into developing simplistic global explanations for their negative pictures.

Table 4.29 summarizes relevant research for ESFPs. Many of the results found for ESTPs apply to ESFPs as well, as do the comments that address the results. However, there are also some interesting differences that may be due to the auxiliary introverted Feeling function of ESFPs in contrast to the auxiliary introverted Thinking function of the ESTPs. Gender effects may also be inferred, given the difference in Thinking and Feeling preference incidences for males and females. Thus it is interesting that male ESFPs are among the three highest types on one measure of psychological adjustment (Efficacy) and female ESFPs are among the three lowest, while both male and female ESTPs are judged to be low on these adjustment measures. Since the Efficacy measure was based on ratings by observers who were naive about type theory and the types of their subjects, this result reflects the way in which these type-gender combinations are perceived in our society. Chapter 10 explores this issue. Similarly puzzling type and gender

Table 4.29   Research Describing ESFP

Personality, Psychotherapy, Health, Stress, Coping	Males among three highest on "Efficacy"; females among three lowest on "Efficacy"[1]
	Overrepresented among new college students referred for a substance abuse workshop[2]
	Overrepresented among members of a cardiac rehabilitation program[3]
	Less frequent than dominant introverted Sensing types among female chronic pain patients[3]
	With other three dominant Sensing types, more frequent among both male and female chronic pain patients[3]
	In national sample, ranked 15th out of 16 types on using physical coping resources; 16th out of 16 on using spiritual/philosophical coping resources; highest ranking coping resource was "Emotional"—3rd of the 16 types[3]
	Ranked second lowest on "Emotional exhaustion" and "Depersonalization" burnout scales[4]
	In national sample, second highest in satisfaction with "Marriage/intimate relationship"[4]
Education	Males among three highest on two out of three measures of creativity; females among three lowest on one out of two measures of creativity[5]
	Dependent learners (little intellectual curiosity, look to authority for guidelines) and field dependent learners[6]
	One of two types with lowest overall college GPA[6]
	Among the highest in college retention[6]
	Among highest persisters in college[6]
	Higher on deductive reasoning than dominant Thinking or Feeling types, with other dominant Sensing types[7]
	Academic subjects preferred: history[8]
	In national sample "Leisure Activities," overrepresented in "Watching TV three or more hours per day"; underrepresented in "Reading" and "Working out/exercising"[6]
Careers	Most important features of an ideal job: "A stable and secure future"[9]
	Highest of all types in national sample in liking work environment characteristics "Making the job as simple as possible" and "No expectation for working extra hours"[10]
	In national sample, among types with lowest income and likely to leave the job[10]
	In national sample "Organizational Values," place high value on "Happy family" and low value on "Achievement within system"[10]
	In national sample, among top four types valuing "Home/family," "Health," "Friendships," "Financial security," "Spirituality"[10]
	In national sample, dissatisfied with "Promotions," "Job Security," "Stress," "Salary," and "Accomplishment" and satisfied with "People I work with"[10]
	Underrepresented among working MBA students compared with national sample[10]
	Underrepresented among both male and female small business owners compared with national sample[10]
	Occupational trends identified: health care, teaching, coaching, childcare worker, skilled trades[10]
Organizations, Leadership, Management, Teams	Higher on CPI scale Sy; lower on Sc, Ac, Py[11]
	Higher on LSI scales Changeable, Energetic, Forceful, Initiating, Resourceful[12]
	Showed change on at least four of seven leadership items in Naval Academy leadership behavior study in which type training was followed by feedback from lower-ranked students[13]

Note: [11]Brief definitions of these CPI scales can be found in Chapter 13, "Uses of Type in Organizations." See Table 4.26; [12]Tables 4.26–4.41 report ratings by subordinates of types that were significantly higher or lower on various leadership scales, relative to the other types.

Source: [1]Highest three and lowest three types on two measures of personal adjustment ("Soundness" and "Efficacy"), which were calculated separately for males and females. Thorne & Gough, 1991; [2]Quenk & Quenk, 1996; [3]Shelton, 1996; [4]See Chapter 10, "Uses of Type in Counseling and Psychotherapy"; [5]Highest three and lowest three types on three measures of creativity, calculated separately for males and females. Thorne & Gough, 1991; [6]See Chapter 11, "Uses of Type in Education"; [7]DiTiberio, 1996; [8]Myers & McCaulley, 1985; [9]Hammer, 1996a; [10]See Chapter 12, "Uses of Type in Career Counseling"; [11]A study that compared the mean scores of the 16 types on the scales of the CPI using a sample of 15,102 people who attended leadership development programs at the Center for Creative Leadership. Fleenor, 1997; [12]Results in the same study at the Center for Creative Leadership on the *Leadership Style Indicator* (LSI); [13]Walck, 1996.

results occur for measures of creativity shown in Tables 4.28 and 4.29.

ESFPs report watching TV as a frequent leisure activity, while ESTPs are overrepresented in playing sports. To what extent gender contributes to this remains for further study. There are notable differences in career and organizational results as well. Like ESTPs, ESFPs are higher on the CPI scale Sociability and lower on the Self-Control, Achievement via Conformity, and Psychological-Mindedness scales. However, the overall results in the career and work areas suggest that ESFP career and work values are quite distinct from those of ESTPs, in the ESFP focus on stability, security, and low job stress, and in the kinds of occupations that appeal to those with an ESFP nature.

INTJ: Introverted Intuition with Extraverted Thinking

Dominant function N_I

Auxiliary function: T_E

Tertiary function: F_E

Fourth/inferior function: S_E

At Their Best   People with INTJ preferences have a clear vision of future possibilities coupled with the drive and organization to implement their ideas. They love complex challenges and readily synthesize complicated theoretical and abstract matters. Once they have created their general structure, they devise strategies to achieve their goals. Their global thinking leads them to develop visionary goals and a broad-brush plan for achieving these within large organizational structures.

INTJs value knowledge and expect competence of themselves and others. They especially abhor confusion, mess, and inefficiency.

Characteristics of INTJs   INTJs see things from a global perspective and quickly relate new information to overall patterns. They trust their insightful connections regardless of established authority or popular opinions. Dull routine smothers their creativity. INTJs use their Intuition primarily internally, where they develop complex structures and pictures of the future. They are likely to be

- Insightful, creative synthesizers
- Conceptual, long-range thinkers

INTJs use their Thinking to make logical decisions. They assess everything with a critical eye, quickly identify problems to solve, and are tough and decisive when the situation calls for toughness. INTJs tend to be

- Clear and concise
- Rational, detached, and objectively critical

INTJs are excellent long-range planners and often rise to positions of leadership in groups or organizations. They are independent, trust their own perceptions and judgments more than those of others, and apply their high standards of knowledge and competence most rigorously to themselves.

How Others May See Them   INTJs present a calm, decisive, and assured face to the world, though they may find it difficult to engage in social conversation. They usually don't directly express their most valued and valuable part: their creative insights. Instead, they translate them into logical decisions, opinions, and plans, which they often express clearly. Because of this, others sometimes experience INTJs as intractable, much to the surprise of the INTJ, who is very willing to change an opinion when new evidence emerges. Others usually see INTJs as

- Private, reserved, hard to know, even aloof
- Conceptual, original, and independent

Potential Areas for Growth   Sometimes life circumstances have not supported INTJs in the development and expression of their Thinking and Intuitive preferences.

- If they have not developed their Thinking, INTJs may not have reliable ways to translate their valuable insights into achievable realities.
- If they have not developed their Intuition, they may not take in enough information or take in only that information that fits their insights. Then they may make ill-founded decisions based on limited or idiosyncratic information.

If INTJs do not find a place where they can use their gifts and be appreciated for their contributions, they usually feel frustrated and may

- Become aloof and abrupt, not giving enough information about their internal processing
- Be critical of those who do not see their vision quickly
- Become single-minded and unyielding in pursuing it

It is natural for INTJs to give less attention to their non-preferred Sensing and Feeling parts. If they neglect these too much, however, they may

- Overlook details or facts that do not fit into their Intuitive patterns
- Engage in "intellectual games," quibbling over abstract issues and terms that have little meaning or relevance to others
- Not give enough weight to the impacts of their decisions on individuals
- Fail to give as much praise or intimate connection as others desire

Under extreme stress, INTJs can overindulge in Sensing activities—watching TV reruns, playing cards, overeating—or become overly focused on specific details in their environment that they normally do not notice or usually see as unimportant (housecleaning, organizing cupboards).

Table 4.30 summarizes relevant research results for INTJs. Dominant introverted Intuitive types with extraverted Thinking are mostly quite different from the other dominant Introverted perceiving type with Thinking, the ISTJs. Except for a reported overrepresentation among substance abusers, INTJs are underrepresented among cardiac and hypertensive groups, report low stress in two areas, and are low in the negative affectivity measure (described in Chapter 10). It is interesting that they are the type reporting the highest fear of reinjury of those with long-term pain and are also high on two of the three job burnout scales. As noted in Chapter 10, INTJs present a complex picture in their experience of and response to life stresses.

The education results in Table 4.30 are quite consistent for a type whose interests and abilities are mostly consonant with our educational system and typical measures of intellectual competence. In a general way, the results for INTJs are the mirror image of those for the opposite type, ESFP. The INTJ focus on competence, achievement, creativity, and independence is also evident in the career and organization areas. Although INTJs fulfill many of the positive expectations and values of society, there are some ways in which their qualities may be viewed less positively. They ranked lowest in values around home and family and other relationship-centered areas, and though high on the CPI scales Responsibility and Self-Control, both kinds of achievement measures, and Intellectual Efficiency, they were lower on scales that concern relating to people—Dominance, Sociability, Social Presence, Self-Acceptance, Good Impression, and Empathy. They similarly underemphasize (in the Systematic Multiple-Level Observation of Groups data) some of the more "social" qualities.

INFJ: Introverted Intuition with Extraverted Feeling

Dominant function: N_I

Auxiliary function: F_E

Tertiary function: T_E

Fourth/inferior function: S_E

At Their Best People with INFJ preferences have a gift for intuitively understanding complex meanings and human relationships. They have faith in their insights and find that they often empathically understand the feelings and motivations of people before the others are themselves aware of them. They combine this empathic understanding with the drive and organization to implement global plans for enhancing people's lives.

INFJs have a visionary grasp of human relationships and possibilities, which, when articulated, can elevate and inspire others.

Characteristics of INFJs INFJs seek meaning and connection in their lives and have little use for details unless they fit with their inner vision. They use their Intuition primarily internally, where they develop complex pictures and understandings. INFJs are likely to be

- Insightful, creative, and visionary
- Conceptual, symbolic, and metaphorical
- Idealistic, complex, and deep

INFJs apply personal values and empathize to understand others and make decisions. They are loyal to people and institutions that exemplify their values but have little interest in those that do not. INFJs prefer to lead persuasively by sharing their vision. They are likely to be

- Sensitive, compassionate, and empathic
- Deeply committed to their values

INFJs want meaning and purpose in their work, their relationships, even their material possessions. They are invested in growth and development for themselves and significant others and are willing to consider unconventional paths to achieve these. They value the depth and complexity of their insights and creative gifts as well as those of others. They want to see these insights realized in the world.

How Others May See Them INFJs readily show compassion and caring for others, but they share their internal intuitions only with those they trust. Because they keep this most valued, important part private, others may find them difficult to know. When they try to communicate their internal sense of "knowing," they often express it metaphorically and with complexity. They especially value authenticity and commitment in relationships.

Though INFJs are usually reserved, they don't hesitate to assert themselves when their values are violated. Then they can be persistent and insistent. Others usually experience INFJs as

- Private, even mysterious
- Intense and individualistic

Potential Areas for Growth Sometimes life circumstances have not supported INFJs in the development and expression of their Feeling and Intuitive preferences.

- If they have not developed their Feeling, INFJs may not have reliable ways of making decisions and accomplishing their goals. Then, their valuable insights and creativity stay locked inside.
- If they have not developed their Intuition, they may not take in enough information or take in only what fits with their internal pictures. Then they will make ill-founded decisions based on distorted or limited information.

If INFJs do not find a place where they can use their gifts and be appreciated for their contributions, they usually feel frustrated and may

- Not give others the information they used to arrive at a decision, and thus seem arbitrary

Table 4.30 Research Describing INTJ

Personality, Psychotherapy, Health, Stress, Coping	Discreet, industrious, logical, deliberate, methodical[1]
	Among three male types overrepresented among substance abusers[2]
	Underrepresented among members of a cardiac rehabilitation program[3]
	Had the highest fear of reinjury of all the types among those suffering long-term pain[3]
	Highest rank on coping resources used was spiritual/philosophical—ranked third out of the 16 types[3]
	In national sample, lowest in reporting stress associated with "School" and "Caring for aging parents"[4]
	In national sample, lowest in "Watching TV" as method of coping with stress[4]
	In national sample, ranked third lowest in "Ever had heart disease or hypertension"[4]
	In national sample, ranked highest in saying "No" to belief in a higher spiritual power[4]
	Ranked fourth highest on "Emotional exhaustion" and third highest in "Depersonalization" burnout scales[4]
	Ranked fourth lowest in "Negative affectivity"[4]
Education	One of two types with highest undergraduate GPA[5]
	Among highest persisters in church-related colleges[5]
	Participant learners (learn course content and like to go to class)[5]
	Projected self greatest number of years into the future in essays[5]
	One of two types with highest first semester college GPA[5]
	One of two types most frequent among RAs at a women's college[5]
	Highest GPA among persisters in college[5]
	One of two types most frequent among female student affairs officers[5]
	In national sample "Leisure Activities," overrepresented in "Taking classes, going to school," "Appreciating art," "Playing with computers or video games," "Working out/exercising"; underrepresented in "Watching TV three hours or more per day"[5]
	Higher on deductive reasoning than Feeling types, with other dominant Intuitive types[6]
	Academic subjects preferred: science[7]
Careers	Most important features of an ideal job: creativity and originality[8]
	One of three highest types in liking work environment characteristic "Variety of tasks" as well as highly favoring "Clear structure" and "Independence & achievement"; lowest of all the types in liking work environments characterized by "Making the job as simple as possible"[9]
	In national sample "Organizational Values," place high value on "Financial analysis" and low value on "Business sociability"[9]
	In national sample, among four types valuing "Achievement"[9]
	In national sample, among types with highest income; dissatisfied with "Future work opportunities," "Promotions," and "Job security" in their job[9]
	In national sample, ranked lowest (65.1%) of all types in valuing "Home/family," "Financial security" (50.0%), "Relationships & friendships" (30.8%), and "Community service"[9]
	Overrepresented among working MBA students compared with national sample[9]
	Overrepresented among female small business owners compared with national sample[9]
	Occupational trends identified: scientific or technical fields, computers, law[9]
Organizations, Leadership, Management, Teams	Higher on CPI scales Re, Sc, Ac, Ai, Ie, Py, Fm; lower on Do, Sy, Sp, Sa, Gi, Em[10]
	Higher on LSI scales Adaptable, Analytical, Appreciative, Deliberate, Determined, Fair, Independent, Initiating, Methodical, Organized, Resourceful, Self-Confident, Supportive, Understanding[11]
	Lower than the other TJ types on "Tough-minded, self-oriented assertiveness"[12]
	Departures from SYMLOG Most Effective Profile: underemphasize "Active teamwork toward a common goal," "Efficiency, strong impartial management," "Popularity and social success" (on which they were also significantly lower than ESTJs, ENTPs, and Feeling types), "Protecting less able members," "Having a good time," "Friendship"; seen as overemphasizing "Self-protection, self-interest first," "Conservative, established, correct ways of doing things," "Obedience" (more than any type except ISTJs)[12]

Note: [10]Brief definitions of these CPI scales can be found in Chapter 13, "Uses of Type in Organizations." See Table 4.26; [11]Tables 4.26–4.41 report ratings by subordinates of types that were significantly higher or lower on various leadership scales, relative to the other types.

Source: [1]Summary of salient ACL data and Q-Sort descriptions of 12 of the 16 types. Raters were naive to type when making their ratings. Thorne & Gough, 1991; [2]Quenk & Quenk, 1996; [3]Shelton, 1996; [4]See Chapter 10, "Uses of Type in Counseling and Psychotherapy"; [5]See Chapter 11, "Uses of Type in Education"; [6]DiTiberio, 1996; [7]Myers & McCaulley, 1985; [8]Hammer, 1996a; [9]See Chapter 12, "Uses of Type in Career Counseling"; [10]A study that compared the mean scores of the 16 types on the scales of the CPI using a sample of 15,102 people who attended leadership development programs at the Center for Creative Leadership. Fleenor, 1997; [11]Results in the same study at the Center for Creative Leadership on the *Leadership Style Indicator* (LSI). [12]A study using SYMLOG analysis of 529 subjects from the top three tiers of management. Ratings of SYMLOG values for the 16 types were averaged across all raters. Sundstrom & Busby, 1997.

- Base their judgments on little data, on a sense of "knowing" that has little basis in reality
- Withdraw their energy and insight
- Become resentful and critical

It is natural for INFJs to give less attention to their non-preferred Sensing and Thinking parts. If they neglect these too much, however, they may

- Be unable to verbalize their inner insights in a way that others can understand
- Fail to check their insights against reason and practicality, and end up following a vision that has little possibility of being realized
- Become single-minded in pursuit of a vision

Under great stress, INFJs may become obsessed with data they normally would consider irrelevant or overindulge in Sensing activities such as watching TV reruns, overeating, or buying things that have little meaning for them.

Table 4.31 summarizes relevant research results for INFJs. The difference in auxiliary extraverted Feeling rather than auxiliary extraverted Thinking yields quite striking contrasts in the personality, stresses, values, interests, and career- and job-related variables of INFJs. They are attracted both to the practice of psychotherapy and to benefiting from it as clients. In contrast to the INTJs, they report the highest stress of all the types in areas associated with work, intimate relationships, and school and in areas designated as "other" and report the greatest dissatisfaction with their marriage/intimate relationship.

INFJs are similar to INTJs in being particularly favored in the educational sphere, although their leisure activities focus on introverted activities that are more artistic, in contrast to the INTJs' more "intellectual" pursuits.

Some insight into the patterns revealed in the personality area may be gained by reviewing the research results on careers and the work setting. From the values and interests shown, as well as from their typological character as highly in tune with unconscious communications, one might infer that INFJs are quite sensitive to nuances and undercurrents of feeling in many aspects of their lives. As such, situations that are not particularly stressful for some other types may prove stressful for INFJs. Their dissatisfactions in many areas may be partly due to their possibly idealistic criteria for satisfaction. INFJ males are among the most oblivious to their partner's dissatisfaction in an intimate relationship, and INFJs in general express dissatisfaction with their intimate relationships.

ENTP: Extraverted Intuition with Introverted Thinking

Dominant function: N_E

Auxiliary function: T_I

Tertiary function: F_I

Fourth/inferior function: S_I

At Their Best People with ENTP preferences constantly scan the environment for opportunities and possibilities. They see patterns and connections not obvious to others and at times seem able to see into the future. They are adept at generating conceptual possibilities and then analyzing them strategically.

ENTPs are good at understanding how systems work and are enterprising and resourceful in maneuvering within them to achieve their ends.

Characteristics of ENTPs ENTPs are enthusiastic innovators. Their world is full of possibilities, interesting concepts, and exciting challenges. They are stimulated by difficulties, quickly devising creative responses and plunging into activity, trusting their ability to improvise. They use their Intuition primarily externally and enjoy exercising ingenuity in the world. ENTPs are likely to be

- Creative, imaginative, and clever
- Theoretical, conceptual, and curious

ENTPs use their Thinking primarily internally to analyze situations and their own ideas and to plan. They admire competence, intelligence, precision, and efficiency. ENTPs are usually

- Analytical, logical, rational, and objective
- Assertive and questioning

ENTPs are enterprising, resourceful, active, and energetic. They respond to challenging problems by creating complex and global solutions. They are usually adept at "reading" other people, seeing how to motivate them, and assuming leadership. They can do almost anything that captures their interest.

How Others May See Them ENTPs are spontaneous and adaptable. They find schedules and standard operating procedures confining and work around them whenever possible. They are remarkably insightful about the attitudes of others, and their enthusiasm and energy can mobilize people to support their vision.

Their conversational style is customarily challenging and stimulating because they love to debate ideas. They are fluent conversationalists, mentally quick, and enjoy verbal sparring. When they express their underlying Thinking principles, however, they may speak with an intensity and abruptness that seem to challenge others. Others usually see ENTPs as

- Independent, autonomous, and creative
- Lively, enthusiastic, and energetic
- Assertive and outspoken

Potential Areas for Growth Sometimes life circumstances have not supported ENTPs in the development and expression of their Thinking and Intuitive preferences.

- If they have not developed their Thinking, they may not have reliable ways to evaluate their insights and make

Table 4.31   Research Describing INFJ

Personality, Psychotherapy, Health, Stress, Coping	Sincere, sympathetic, unassuming, submissive, weak[1]
	Males are among the three lowest on "Efficacy"[2]
	Overrepresented among a sample of male therapists[3]
	Among the three male types most "oblivious" to partner's dissatisfaction with the relationship[3]
	With ISTPs, ranked first among all the types in using spiritual/philosophical coping resources[4]
	Overrepresented among clinical psychologists compared with a range of psychologists[5]
	In national sample, highest in reporting stress associated with "Work," "Intimate relationship," "School," and "Other"[6]
	In national sample, highest in coping with stress by "Talking to professional"[6]
	Ranked second lowest in "Positive affectivity" and third lowest in "Negative affectivity"[6]
	In national sample, ranked highest in being dissatisfied with "Marriage/intimate relationship"[6]
Education	One of two types with highest first semester college GPA[7]
	Among top four types in undergraduate GPA[7]
	Among highest college persisters[7]
	Among highest persisters at church-related schools[7]
	In national sample "Leisure Activities," overrepresented in "Writing" and "Appreciating art," underrepresented in "Watching sporting events"[7]
	Higher on deductive reasoning than Feeling types, with other dominant Intuitive types[8]
	With ISTJs, modal type of language students at the University of Hawaii[9]
	Predominated among Japanese Americans in a study of classroom behaviors in children of different ethnic groups[9]
	Academic subjects preferred: art, English, music[5]
Careers	Most important features of an ideal job: "Use of my special abilities"[10]
	Three top work characteristics favored in national sample: "Variety of tasks," "Clear structure," "Independence & achievement"; lowest of all the types in liking work environments with "Opportunities for advancement & high pay but not job security"[11]
	In national sample, among top four types in valuing "Spirituality," "Learning," and "Community service"[11]
	In national sample, dissatisfied with "Promotions" and "Salary" in their work[11]
	In national sample, ranked lowest in valuing "Health" (55.3%), "Financial security" (50.0%), and "Prestige & status" (0%)[11]
	Occupational trends identified: religion, counseling, teaching, arts[11]
Organizations, Leadership, Management, Teams	Higher on CPI scales Ai, Fm; lower on Do, Sy, Sp, Sa, Wb, Gi, In[12]
	Higher on LSI scales Delegating, Dependable, Easygoing, Fair, Guarded, Initiating, Patient, Permissive, Reflective, Reserved, Supportive[13]

Note: [12]Brief definitions of these CPI scales can be found in Chapter 13, "Uses of Type in Organizations." See Table 4.26; [13]Tables 4.26–4.41 report ratings by subordinates of types that were significantly higher or lower on various leadership scales, relative to the other types.

Source: [1]Summary of salient ACL data and Q-Sort descriptions of 12 of the 16 types. Raters were naive to type when making their ratings. Thorne & Gough, 1991; [2]Highest three and lowest three types on two measures of personal adjustment ("Soundness" and "Efficacy"), which were calculated separately for males and females. Thorne & Gough, 1991; [3]Quenk & Quenk, 1996; [4]Shelton, 1996; [5]Myers & McCaulley, 1985; [6]See Chapter 10, "Uses of Type in Counseling and Psychotherapy"; [7]See Chapter 11, "Uses of Type in Education"; [8]DiTiberio, 1996; [9]Kirby & Barger, 1996; [10]Hammer, 1996a; [11]See Chapter 12, "Uses of Type in Career Counseling"; [12]A study that compared the mean scores of the 16 types on the scales of the CPI using a sample of 15,102 people who attended leadership development programs at the Center for Creative Leadership. Fleenor, 1997; [13]Results in the same study at the Center for Creative Leadership on the *Leadership Style Indicator* (LSI).

plans to carry them through. Then they go from enthusiasm to enthusiasm with little actually accomplished.

- If they have not developed their Intuition, they may not take in enough relevant information, resulting in "insights" unrelated to current reality.

·If ENTPs do not find a place where they can use their gifts and be appreciated for their contributions, they usually feel frustrated and may

- Become brash, rude, and abrasive

- Criticize others, especially those who seem to them to be inefficient or incompetent
- Become rebellious and combative
- Become scattered—unable to focus

It is natural for ENTPs to give less attention to their non-preferred Sensing and Feeling parts. If they neglect these too much, however, they may

- Not take care of the details and routine required to implement their insights

■ Not give enough weight to the impact of their ideas and plans on others

■ Be excessively and inappropriately "challenging and stimulating"

Under great stress, ENTPs can be overwhelmed by detail, losing their ability to generate possibilities. Then they focus on a minor or distorted detail, thinking that it is supremely important.

Table 4.32 summarizes relevant research results for ENTPs. The research results for ENTPs seem to fit well with the way they are typically described. Their high activity level, multiple interests, and enthusiasm for exploring the limits of the environment come through in some of the ways they are perceived—males as lowest on the "Soundness" measure of adaptation, females as high on the "Efficacy" measure—in their frequency in remedial at-risk programs as high school students and as violators of college alcohol policies, in their high standing on creativity measures and values in this area, and in their overrepresentation regarding many leisure activities. These are just a few of the results that illustrate the way in which predictable attitudes and behaviors develop through the exercise of type preferences.

Also consistent with an ENTP approach to life is their reported standing on variables related to experiencing and coping with stress. They have the highest mean level of coping resources and are highest in coping with stress by "confronting the problem," report the lowest stress in several life areas, are lowest in reporting heart disease and hypertension, and are low in job burnout measures. These results are consistent with observations suggesting that ENTPs and their companion dominant extraverted Intuitive type, the ENFPs, seem to seek out and function effectively at high levels of stress—at least from the point of view of other types. This suggests that the perception of stress varies markedly across the types. Further discussion of stress variables appears in Chapter 10.

One intriguing result shown in Table 4.32 is the exactly opposite standing of ENTPs (dominant extraverted Intuitive types with auxiliary introverted Thinking) and INTJs (dominant introverted Intuitive types with auxiliary Extraverted Thinking) on "fear of reinjury" among chronic pain patients. INTJs reported the highest fear and ENTPs the lowest. One might speculate about the possible differential role of the inferior function of these types on this very specific behavior.

Results in the education, career, and organization areas further confirm the descriptive characteristics of ENTPs. Their high assertiveness (reported in the personality content area) is readily connected to their independence and initiating results on Leadership scales. They are high on Dominance, Capacity for Status, Sociability, Social Presence, Self-Acceptance, Tolerance, and similar scales that are predictable for their type, and lower on Responsibility, Socialization, Self-Control, Communality, Achievement via Conformity, and Femininity/Masculinity—also not surprising associations.

As we shall see, many of the results found for ENTPs are also characteristic of ENFPs (Table 4.33), the other dominant extraverted Intuitive type.

ENFP: Extraverted Intuition with Introverted Feeling

Dominant function: N_E

Auxiliary function: F_I

Tertiary function: T_I

Fourth/inferior function: S_I

At Their Best For people with ENFP preferences, life is a creative adventure full of exciting possibilities. ENFPs are keenly perceptive about people and insightful about the present and future. They experience a wide range of feelings and intense emotions. They need affirmation from others and readily give appreciation and support.

ENFPs are good at understanding how people and groups work and are persuasive and compelling in pursuing what is important to them. They are adaptable, blooming where they are planted. Their energy and enthusiasm encourage others to bloom as well.

Characteristics of ENFPs ENFPs are innovators, initiating projects and directing great energy into getting them underway. Using Intuition primarily externally, they are stimulated by new people, ideas, and experiences. They find meaning and significance readily and see connections that others don't. They are likely to be

■ Curious, creative, and imaginative

■ Energetic, enthusiastic, and spontaneous

ENFPs value harmony and goodwill. They like to please others and will adapt to others' needs and wishes when possible. ENFPs primarily use Feeling internally, making decisions by applying personal values through identification and empathy with others. ENFPs are likely to be

■ Warm, friendly, and caring

■ Cooperative and supportive

ENFPs have exceptional insight into possibilities in others and the energy and motivation to help actualize them. They feel confident moving ahead based on their insights, and their enthusiasm tends to bring others along with them.

How Others May See Them ENFPs are usually lively, gregarious, and sociable, with a large circle of friends. They are interested in almost everything and bring a zest to life that draws others to them. At the same time, they value depth and authenticity in their close relationships and direct great energy to creating and supporting open and honest communication.

ENFPs hate routine, schedules, and structure and usually manage to avoid them. They are normally verbally fluent, even in extemporaneous situations; however, when their deepest values need expression, they may suddenly be

Table 4.32   Research Describing ENTP

Personality, Psychotherapy, Health, Stress, Coping	Enterprising, friendly, resourceful, headstrong, self-centered[1]
	Males among three lowest on "Soundness"; females among three highest on "Efficacy"[2]
	Overrepresented among female substance abusers[3]
	Overrepresented among those having Type A behavior[4]
	With ENFPs, had highest mean level of coping resources[4]
	Reported lowest fear of reinjury of all the types among a group suffering long-term pain[4]
	One of four types in college reporting the highest levels of assertiveness[4]
	In national sample, lowest in reporting stress associated with "Children," "Intimate relationship," and "Health"[5]
	In national sample, highest in coping with stress by "Confronting the problem"[5]
	In national sample, ranked lowest in "Ever had heart disease/hypertension"[5]
	In national sample, ranked third highest in "Not Sure" re: "Belief in higher spiritual power"[5]
	Ranked fourth lowest on "Emotional exhaustion" and lowest in "Depersonalization" burnout scales[5]
Education	Males among three highest on two out of three measures of creativity; females among three highest on one out of two measures of creativity[6]
	Projected self second-greatest number of years into the future in essays[7]
	Frequent among high school students in remedial at-risk program[7]
	One of two types most frequent among college alcohol policy violators[7]
	In national sample "Leisure Activities," overrepresented in "Taking classes, going to school," "Writing," "Appreciating art," "Playing sports," "Playing with computers or video games"; underrepresented in "Watching TV three hours or more per day"[7]
	With other dominant Intuitive types, were higher on deductive reasoning than Feeling types[8]
	With INTPs, among middle school students, had lower grades than aptitude scores would predict[8]
	More frequent among African American males compared with Howard University males[9]
	Academic subjects preferred: art, science[10]
Careers	Most important features of an ideal job: creativity and originality[11]
	In national sample, highest of all types liking work environment characteristics "Independence & achievement" and "Opportunities for advancement & high pay, but not job security" and including "Variety of tasks" and "Clear structure" among top three characteristics; one of top three types liking "International opportunities" as a characteristic[12]
	In national sample, among those types most dissatisfied with work and among those with highest income[12]
	In "Organizational Values," value "Autonomy" and "Achievement"[12]
	In national sample, dissatisfied with "Promotions," "Opportunity to use talents," and "Salary" in their work[12]
	Overrepresented among working MBA students compared with national sample[12]
	Occupational trends identified: science, management, technology, arts[12]
Organizations, Leadership, Management, Teams	Higher on CPI scales Do, Cs, Sy, Sp, Sa, To, Ai, Ie, Py, Fx, In, Em; lower on Re, So, Sc, Cm, Ac, Fm[13]
	Higher on LSI scales Independent, Initiating[14]
	Departure from SYMLOG Most Effective Leader Profile: seen as underemphasizing "Active teamwork toward a common goal," "Efficiency, strong impartial management," "Collaborative work," "Trust in the goodness of others"; seen as overemphasizing "Self-protection, self-interest first," "Popularity and social success"[15]

Note: [13]Brief definitions of these CPI scales can be found in Chapter 13, "Uses of Type in Organizations." See Table 4.26; [14]Tables 4.26–4.41 report ratings by subordinates of types that were significantly higher or lower on various leadership scales, relative to the other types.

Source: [1]Summary of salient ACL data and Q-Sort descriptions of 12 of the 16 types. Raters were naive to type when making their ratings. Thorne & Gough, 1991; [2]Highest three and lowest three types on two measures of personal adjustment ("Soundness" and "Efficacy"), which were calculated separately for males and females. Thorne & Gough, 1991; [3]Quenk & Quenk, 1996; [4]Shelton, 1996; [5]See Chapter 10, "Uses of Type in Counseling and Psychotherapy"; [6]Highest three and lowest three types on three measures of creativity, calculated separately for males and females. Thorne & Gough, 1991; [7]See Chapter 11, "Uses of Type in Education"; [8]DiTiberio, 1996; [9]Kirby & Barger, 1996; [10]Myers & McCaulley, 1985; [11]Hammer, 1996a; [12]See Chapter 12, "Uses of Type in Career Counseling"; [13]A study that compared the mean scores of the 16 types on the scales of the CPI using a sample of 15,102 people who attended leadership development programs at the Center for Creative Leadership. Fleenor, 1997; [14]Results in the same study at the Center for Creative Leadership on the *Leadership Style Indicator* (LSI); [15]A study using SYMLOG analysis of 529 subjects from the top three tiers of management. Ratings of SYMLOG values for the 16 types were averaged across all raters. Sundstrom & Busby, 1997.

awkward and express their judgments with uncharacteristic intensity. Others usually see ENFPs as

- Personable, perceptive, and persuasive
- Enthusiastic, spontaneous, and versatile
- Giving and seeking affirmation

Potential Areas for Growth   Sometimes life circumstances have not supported ENFPs in the development and expression of their Feeling and Intuitive preferences.

- If they have not developed their Feeling, they may go from enthusiasm to enthusiasm, never committing the energy necessary to actualize their insights, or they may make overly personal decisions.
- If they have not developed their Intuition, they may fail to take in enough information, lack trust in their own insights, be uncertain, and accept others' perceptions too quickly.

If ENFPs do not find a place where they can use their gifts and be appreciated for their contributions, they usually feel frustrated and may

- Become scattered, have trouble focusing, be easily distracted
- Fail to follow through on decisions
- Become rebellious, excessively nonconforming
- Ignore deadlines and procedures

It is natural for ENFPs to give less attention to their non-preferred Sensing and Thinking parts. If they neglect these too much, however, they may

- Not take care of the details and routine required for implementing their inspirations
- Overextend themselves—have trouble saying no to interesting possibilities and people
- Fail to apply reason and logic to assess their inspirations and decisions

Under great stress, ENFPs may become overwhelmed by detail and lose their normal perspective and sense of options. Then they tend to focus on an unimportant or distorted detail, letting it become the central fact of their universe.

Table 4.33 summarizes relevant research results for ENFPs. Not unexpectedly, the results in Table 4.33 are quite similar in many ways to those for ENTPs and are therefore not repeated in detail for ENFPs. This is the case regarding their standing on physical symptoms of stress, being lowest in reporting stress in a number of life areas and having highest reported levels of coping resources. Interesting differences are that one study found ENTPs overrepresented among substance abusers, and they were also frequent types to violate alcohol policy. However, they were not referred more frequently in college to substance abuse workshops. ENFPs, in contrast, were overrepresented in this area in college but did not appear more frequently in actual substance abuse groups—at least based on the available data.

Both ENTPs and ENFPs ranked third highest in not being sure regarding a belief in a higher spiritual power (note that the large majority of every type indicated such belief, as shown in Chapter 10). Different studies also indicate that students of both types may be seen as troubled and/or troublesome at school, with ENTPs likely also to be seen as underachievers—a result in accord with observations by teachers and parents. While both ENTPs and ENFPs indicate art as a preference in academic subjects, ENFPs indicate English and music in contrast to ENTPs' attraction to science. ENFPs also appear to be attracted to careers in education, while this does not appear to be the case for ENTPs. Their occcupational trends also differ except for a shared interest in art, with ENFPs attracted to counseling, teaching, and religion and ENTPs to science, management, and technology.

In the career area, creativity, independence, and variety are important for both dominant extraverted Intuitive types. ENFPs are notable in their valuing of home and family, friendships, and community service—all areas that may reflect their auxiliary Feeling function. ENFPs are found to be underrepresented among working MBA students, while ENTPs are overrepresented in this category.

ISTP: Introverted Thinking with Extraverted Sensing

Dominant function: T_I

Auxiliary function: S_E

Tertiary function: N_E

Fourth/inferior function: F_E

At Their Best   People with ISTP preferences carefully observe what is going on around them. Then, when the need arises, they move quickly to get to the core of a problem and solve it with the greatest efficiency and the least effort. They are interested in how and why things work but find abstract theories uninteresting unless they can quickly apply them. They often function as troubleshooters.

ISTPs resist regimentation and rules, thrive on variety and novelty, and enjoy the challenge of solving a new, concrete, extensive problem.

Characteristics of ISTPs   ISTPs use their Thinking primarily internally to see the essential structure underlying the facts. Their minds seem to work almost like computers, organizing data, reasoning impersonally and objectively. They make rational decisions based on a great deal of concrete data. ISTPs are likely to be

- Detached and objective critics
- Analytical and logical problem solvers

ISTPs are realists, focusing on what is and what can be done with it, rather than on theoretical possibilities. They

Table 4.33   Research Describing ENFP

Personality, Psychotherapy, Health, Stress, Coping	Enthusiastic, outgoing, spontaneous, changeable, impulsive[1]
	Overrepresented among a sample of male therapists[2]
	Overrepresented among new college students referred for a substance abuse workshop[2]
	Underrepresented among female coronary heart disease patients[3]
	Underrepresented among men with chronic pain[3]
	With ESTJs, had highest total coping resource scores of all the types[3]
	With ENTPs, had highest mean level of coping resources[3]
	Ranked first of all 16 types in using social and emotional coping resources, and second in using cognitive resources[3]
	In national sample, lowest in reporting stress associated with "Other"[4]
	In national sample, lowest in coping with stress by "Developing physical symptoms"[4]
	In national sample, ranked fourth lowest in "Ever had heart disease/hypertension"[4]
	In national sample, ranked third highest in "Not Sure" re: "Belief in higher spiritual power"[4]
Education	Males and females among three highest on one measure of creativity[5]
	Highly represented among third- to sixth-grade academically talented students[6]
	Innovatively creative learners[6]
	As teachers, least likely to see student behaviors as serious problems[6]
	Second most frequent among national CASE professor of the year finalists[6]
	Third most frequent among education majors in college[6]
	As teachers, prefer whole language approach to reading instruction[6]
	Rated by psychologists among three types most likely to have trouble in school[6]
	In national sample "Leisure Activities," overrepresented in "Writing," "Appreciating art," "Playing musical instrument," "Listening to music," "Reading"; underrepresented in "Watching TV for leisure" and "Watching TV three hours or more per day"[6]
	Higher on deductive reasoning than Feeling types, with other dominant Intuitive types[7]
	Among African American college students, most underrepresented among those with an Intuition preference (where N was underrepresented)[7]
	Academic subjects preferred: art, English, music[8]
Careers	Most important features of an ideal job: creativity and originality[9]
	In the national sample, lowest of all the types in liking work environments where "Everything is done by the book"; one of three highest types in liking "Independence & achievement," "Teamwork," and "People from different backgrounds"[10]
	In national sample "Organizational Values," place low value on "Achievement within system"[10]
	In national sample, among top four types in valuing "Home/family," "Friendships," "Creativity," "Learning," and "Community service"[10]
	In national sample, dissatisfied with "Promotions" and "Salary"; satisfied with "People I work with" in their work[10]
	In national sample, ranked highest in valuing "Relationships & friendships" (79.5%), and "Being creative" (55.1%)[10]
	Underrepresented among working MBA students compared with national sample[10]
	Underrepresented among male small business owners compared with national sample[10]
	Occupational trends identified: counseling, teaching, religion, arts[10]
Organizations, Leadership, Management, Teams	Higher on CPI scales Do, Cs, Sy, Sp, Sa, To, Ai, Ie, Fx, In, Em; lower on So, Sc, Gi, Cm, Ac[11]
	Higher on LSI scales Appreciative, Easygoing, Energetic, Resourceful, Understanding[12]
	Showed change on at least four of seven leadership items in Naval Academy leadership behavior study in which type training was followed by feedback from lower-ranked students[13]

Note: [11]Brief definitions of these CPI scales can be found in Chapter 13, "Uses of Type in Organizations." See Table 4.26; [12]Tables 4.26–4.41 report ratings by subordinates of types that were significantly higher or lower on various leadership scales, relative to the other types.

Source: [1]Summary of salient ACL data and Q-Sort descriptions of 12 of the 16 types. Raters were naive to type when making their ratings. Thorne & Gough, 1991; [2]Quenk & Quenk, 1996; [3]Shelton, 1996; [4]See Chapter 10, "Uses of Type in Counseling and Psychotherapy"; [5]Highest three and lowest three types on three measures of creativity, calculated separately for males and females. Thorne & Gough, 1991; [6]See Chapter 11, "Uses of Type in Education"; [7]DiTiberio, 1996; [8]Myers & McCaulley, 1985; [9]Hammer, 1996a; [10]See Chapter 12, "Uses of Type in Career Counseling"; [11]A study that compared the mean scores of the 16 types on the scales of the CPI using a sample of 15,102 people who attended leadership development programs at the Center for Creative Leadership. Fleenor, 1997; [12]Results in the same study at the Center for Creative Leadership on the *Leadership Style Indicator* (LSI); [13]Walck, 1996.

are often creative at dealing with the immediate problems and good at hands-on tasks. ISTPs are likely to be

- Practical and realistic
- Factual and pragmatic

ISTPs are expedient and believe in economy of effort—doing only what is needed with the least possible discussion and fuss. Their focus is on getting the desired results.

How Others May See Them ISTPs are egalitarian and generally tolerant of a wide range of behavior—until their ruling logical principles are attacked. At that point, they can surprise others by expressing their firm and clear judgments. ISTPs listen and seem to agree because they are not disagreeing; later, others may find the ISTP was analyzing and making internal judgments.

With their constant scanning for information and focus on results, ISTPs will change course readily if they see another, more efficient way. Because of this, others sometimes have trouble "reading" them. They tend to be quiet and reserved, though they can be quite talkative in areas in which they have a lot of knowledge. Others usually see ISTPs as

- Adaptable, action-oriented risk takers
- Confident, independent, and self-determined

Potential Areas for Growth Sometimes life circumstances have not supported ISTPs in the development and expression of their Sensing and Thinking preferences.

- If they have not developed their Sensing, ISTPs may have no reliable way of getting accurate data about the external world or of translating their thoughts into action.
- If they have not developed their Thinking, they may get caught up in the realities around them and not take time to do the internal logical processing they need to make good decisions. Then their actions may be haphazard responses to immediate needs.

If ISTPs do not find a place where they can use their gifts and be appreciated for their contributions, they usually feel frustrated and may

- Become cynical and negative critics
- Withdraw their attention and energy
- Postpone decisions

It is natural for ISTPs to give less attention to their non-preferred Feeling and Intuitive parts. If they neglect these too much, however, they may

- Overlook others' emotional needs and values
- Not give sufficient weight to the impacts of their decisions on others
- Focus so intently on immediate results that they lose track of the long-term ramifications of their decisions and actions

Under great stress, ISTPs may erupt outwardly in inappropriate displays of emotion. The resulting explosive anger or hurt tearfulness is quite unnerving to others and embarrassing to the usually calm and controlled ISTP.

Table 4.34 summarizes relevant research results for ISTPs. The research summarized in Table 4.34 for ISTPs with regard to stress-related variables bears some obvious similarities to the results shown in Table 4.26 for ISTJs. Bear in mind that ISTP dynamics are dominant introverted Thinking with auxiliary extraverted Sensing, while dynamics for ISTJ are dominant introverted Sensing with auxiliary extraverted Thinking. Thus, although these two types share all but one letter, their dominant and auxiliary functions and the attitudes in which they are habitually used are different. It seems that sharing the three letters creates many similarities in the stress area, while in many other respects the different dynamics of these two types lead to quite different research results in other areas, for example in personality descriptors, academic interests, and career and organization variables.

It is equally interesting to compare the ISTP picture with that presented in Table 4.28 for ESTPs. ISTPs and ESTPs use their preferred functions in the same attitudes—that is, both extravert Sensing and introvert Thinking, but the ISTP has *dominant* introverted Thinking and auxiliary extraverted Sensing, while the ESTP has *dominant* extraverted Sensing and auxiliary introverted Thinking. The effects of their different dynamics are quite dramatic in the stress and coping areas and in other ways as well.

Although it appears that the commonality of letters to ISTJ types rather than type dynamics is operating regarding stress variables, it is also plausible that the underlying reasons for these similar stress responses may be quite different for these two types. The same attitude or behavior is often stimulated and motivated by quite different issues for different types, and the same issues may be expressed quite differently in the attitudes and behaviors of different types. These observations apply to type similarities and differences in general.

ISTPs are reported to be overrepresented in substance abuse, heart disease, and hypertension groups, post-traumatic stress disorder patients, and risk for setbacks due to overdoing among long-term pain patients. They rank low in assertiveness, low in mean level of coping resources, lowest in using social coping resources, and highest in coping with stress by expressing anger and upset, although they were lowest in stress associated with balancing home and work. They also ranked lowest in positive affectivity and appeared in the four most dissatisfied groups with regard to marriage and intimate relationships. What could account for these "negative"-seeming results?

Perhaps of all the types, ISTPs may be the most specific in what they find acceptable and appealing and what makes no "logical" sense to them. Their particular dynamics may thus be associated with resistance to accepting and appreciating points of view divergent from their own. This is consistent with an approach that looks at life through a lens of logical analysis applied to concrete reality.

Table 4.34   Research Describing ISTP

Personality, Psychotherapy, Health, Stress, Coping	Females among the three lowest on "Soundness"[1]
	Overrepresented among males in a substance abuse program[2]
	Overrepresented among men at risk for heart attack[3]
	Overrepresented among members of a cardiac rehabilitation program[3]
	Overrepresented among male hypertensive patients[3]
	Overrepresented among men with chronic pain[3]
	Overrepresented among males with post-traumatic stress disorder[3]
	With INTPs, had lowest mean level of coping resources[3]
	With ESTPs, at highest risk for setbacks due to overdoing among those with long-term pain[3]
	With INFJs, ranked first among all the types in using spiritual/philosophical coping resources[3]
	Ranked lowest of all 16 types in using social coping resources[3]
	One of the four types in college reporting the lowest levels of assertiveness[3]
	In national sample, lowest in reporting stress associated with "Balancing home and work"[4]
	In national sample, highest in coping with stress by "Getting upset and angry and showing it"[4]
	In national sample, ranked second highest in "Ever had heart disease/hypertension"[4]
	In national sample, ranked fourth highest in "No" and highest in "Not Sure" re: "Belief in higher spiritual power"[4]
	Ranked lowest in "Positive affectivity"[4]
	In national sample, ranked fourth most dissatisfied with "Marriage/intimate relationship"[4]
Education	Males among three lowest on one of three measures of creativity; females among three highest on one of two measures of creativity[5]
	Among three types rated by psychologists as most likely to have trouble in school[6]
	Frequent among high school students in remedial at-risk program[6]
	Highly represented among male college scholarship athletes[6]
	Among lowest in college retention[6]
	In national sample "Leisure Activities," overrepresented in "Playing with computers or video games"; underrepresented in "Listening to music" and "Writing"[6]
	Performed lower on deductive reasoning, with other dominant Thinking types[7]
	With ESTPs, modal types of language students at the University of Hawaii[8]
	Academic subjects preferred: math, practical skills[9]
Careers	Most important feature of an ideal job: "A stable and secure future"[10]
	In national sample, highest of all types liking "Independence & achievement" in the work environment, and including in top three desirable characteristics "Clear structure" and "Variety of tasks"[11]
	In national sample "Organization Values," place low value on "Outgoing affiliation" and "Financial analysis"[11]
	In national sample, among top four types in valuing "Autonomy"[11]
	In national sample, dissatisfied with "Promotions" in their work[11]
	Occupational trends identified: skilled trades, technical fields, agriculture, law enforcement, military[11]
Organizations, Leadership, Management, Teams	No CPI scales higher; lower on CPI scales Do, Cs, Sy, Sp, Sa, Wb, Re, To, Gi, Ac, Ai, Ie, Py, In, Em[12]
	Higher on LSI scales Critical, Detached, Guarded, Independent, Resourceful[13]
	Departures from Most Effective Profile: underemphasize "Active teamwork toward a common goal," "Efficiency, strong impartial management," "Having a good time," "Friendship," "Equality"; overemphasize "Self-protection, self-interest first"[14]
	In a study of the influence of type dynamics on ways of dealing with conflict, tended to compromise[15]

Note: [12]Brief definitions of these CPI scales can be found in Chapter 13, "Uses of Type in Organizations." See Table 4.26; [13]Tables 4.26–4.41 report ratings by subordinates of types that were significantly higher or lower on various leadership scales, relative to the other types.

Source: [1]Highest three and lowest three types on two measures of personal adjustment ("Soundness" and "Efficacy"), which were calculated separately for males and females. Thorne & Gough, 1991; [2]Quenk & Quenk, 1996; [3]Shelton, 1996; [4]See Chapter 10, "Uses of Type in Counseling and Psychotherapy"; [5]Highest three and lowest three types on three measures of creativity, calculated separately for males and females. Thorne & Gough, 1991; [6]See Chapter 11, "Uses of Type in Education"; [7]DiTiberio, 1996; [8]Kirby & Barger, 1996; [9]Myers & McCaulley, 1985; [10]Hammer, 1996a; [11]See Chapter 12, "Uses of Type in Career Counseling"; [12]A study that compared the mean scores of the 16 types on the scales of the CPI using a sample of 15,102 people who attended leadership development programs at the Center for Creative Leadership. Fleenor, 1997; [13]Results in the same study at the Center for Creative Leadership on the *Leadership Style Indicator* (LSI); [14]A study using SYMLOG analysis of 529 subjects from the top three tiers of management. Ratings of SYMLOG values for the 16 types were averaged across all raters. Sundstrom & Busby, 1997; [15]Hammer & Huszczo, 1996.

Such an approach is further shown in the specificity of their viewpoint in the education, career, and organization areas. They are highest of the types in valuing independence and achievement in a career; they also highly value autonomy, clear structures, and task variety. As leaders, they appear critical, detached, guarded, independent, and resourceful, and they also do not seem to consider people and relationship factors to be of importance. Further emphasizing the suggestion that this type marches to a quite different drummer than many other types is that they do not come out higher on any CPI scale and are lower on many scales that reflect characteristics that are highly valued in our culture—Dominance, Capacity for Status, Sociability, Social Presence, Self-Acceptance, and Well-Being (these latter two may reflect the effect of others' perception of them). They are also lower on Responsibility, Tolerance, Good Impression, both kinds of achievement, Intellectual Efficiency, Psychological-Mindedness, Independence, and Empathy. It is important to recognize that these "low" positions on scales are quite consistent with a dominant function that emphasizes objectivity and a dispassionate seeking after truth and accuracy.

One research result suggests that ISTPs may have qualities that are not often seen by others. In the study of coping resources, ISTPs were tied with INFJs as the type with the highest rank in using spiritual/philosophical coping resources. That these two quite different types are similar in this regard is intriguing. We might infer that there are aspects of ISTP inner life that few people see. In fact, experience verifies that ISTPs share their most private and intimate thoughts and feelings with a very few, select people. This selectivity likely contributes to the difficulty other types have in understanding, appreciating, and getting close to the essence of the ISTP nature.

INTP: Introverted Thinking with Extraverted Intuition

Dominant function: T_I

Auxiliary function: N_E

Tertiary function: S_E

Fourth/inferior function: F_E

At Their Best People with INTP preferences are independent problem solvers who excel at providing a detached, concise analysis of an idea or situation. They ask the difficult questions, challenging others and themselves to find new logical approaches.

INTPs' best work may emerge when they are allowed to work independently on a problem whose solution requires an approach that runs counter to prevailing wisdom or knowledge. Though they typically work best alone, their incisive critiques and summaries can assist a group in getting to the core of complex problems.

Characteristics of INTPs INTPs use their Thinking primarily internally to find or develop underlying principles and logical structures for understanding and explaining the world. They approach almost everything with skepticism, form their own opinions and standards, and apply these standards rigorously to themselves. They highly value intelligence and competence. INTPs are likely to be

- Logical, analytical, and objectively critical
- Detached and contemplative

INTPs see possibilities and connections beyond the present and obvious. They are curious and seek knowledge for its own sake. They love to theorize and discuss abstractions. INTPs are usually

- Mentally quick, insightful, and ingenious
- Intensely curious about ideas, theories, and what makes things work

INTPs quickly see inconsistencies and illogicality and enjoy taking apart and reworking ideas. They naturally build complex theoretical systems to explain the realities they see. They find it difficult to work on routine tasks but bring great energy, intensity, and focus to researching or analyzing a complex problem that arouses their curiosity.

How Others May See Them INTPs are usually quiet and reserved though they can be talkative in areas in which they are especially knowledgeable. Unless their work requires action, they are more interested in the challenge of finding solutions than in putting solutions to practical use. They prefer not to organize people or situations.

INTPs are tolerant of a wide range of behavior, arguing and raising issues only when they believe it is reasonable to do so. This flexibility disappears, however, when their ruling principles are challenged; then they stop adapting. INTPs prize precision in communication and dislike redundancy or stating the obvious. They want to express the exact truth, but they may make it so complex that others have difficulty understanding. Others usually see INTPs as

- Quiet, contained, calm, and detached observers
- Independent, valuing autonomy

Potential Areas for Growth Sometimes life circumstances have not supported INTPs in the development and expression of their Intuitive and Thinking preferences.

- If they have not developed their Intuition, INTPs may have no reliable way of taking in information and be immersed in their internal logical systems. Then they find it difficult to actualize or even communicate their ideas.
- If they have not developed their Thinking, they may go from insight to insight, never analyzing them with a critical eye or integrating them into a whole.

If INTPs do not find a place where they can use their gifts and be appreciated for their contributions, they usually feel frustrated and may

- Become cynical and negative critics
- Be sarcastic and destructively critical

Table 4.35   Research Describing INTP

Personality, Psychotherapy, Health, Stress, Coping	Candid, ingenious, shrewd, complicated, rebellious[1]
	Females among three lowest on "Soundness"[2]
	Highly represented among college students taking foreign languages[3]
	Rated by psychologists among three types most likely to have trouble in school[3]
	Most frequent among college students referred for alcohol and drug violations[3]
	Among females, more likely to persist in engineering school[3]
	Males were highest on "obliviousness index" (relatively unaware of spouse's dissatisfaction with the relationship)[4]
	One of three types overrepresented among female substance abusers[4]
	Overrepresented among females in a substance abuse program[4]
	Overrepresented among males with post-traumatic stress disorder[5]
	With ISTPs, had lowest mean level of coping resources; ranked 16th out of 16 types on total resources[5]
	Ranked 15th out of the 16 types on using both cognitive and social coping resources, and 16th on using emotional resources[5]
	Underrepresented as clinical psychologists compared with psychologists in general[6]
	In national sample, ranked third highest in "No" and second highest in "Not Sure" re: "Belief in higher spiritual power"[7]
	Ranked fourth lowest in "Positive affectivity"[7]
	In national sample, third highest in dissatisfaction with "Marriage/intimate relationship"[7]
Education	Males among three highest on two of three measures of creativity; females among three highest on one of three measures of creativity[8]
	Performed significantly lower on deductive reasoning, with other dominant Thinking types[9]
	With ENTPs, had lower grades than would be predicted from aptitude scores among middle school students[9]
	Males more likely to persist in school among engineering school students[9]
	Academic subjects preferred: art, science[6]
	In national sample "Leisure Activities," overrepresented in "Appreciating art," "Writing," "Taking classes, going to school," "Playing with computers or video games"[3]

- Isolate themselves and put off action
- Engage in verbal sparring and arguments

It is natural for INTPs to give less attention to their non-preferred Feeling and Sensing parts. If they neglect these too much, however, they may

- Be insensitive to the needs of others for information and emotional connection
- Decide something they or others value is not important because it is "not logical"
- Fail to consider the impact of their ideas or style of expression on others
- Be impractical, forgetting details such as appropriate dress, unpaid bills, physical needs

Under great stress, INTPs may erupt outwardly in inappropriate displays of emotion. The resulting explosive anger or hurt tearfulness is quite unnerving to others and embarrassing to the usually calm and controlled INTP.

Table 4.35 summarizes relevant research results for INTPs. Most of the similarities of INTPs to their companion dominant introverted Thinking type, ISTPs, appear in the area of personality, stress, and coping variables. An interesting difference in this area is the INTP's standing as being highest on the "obliviousness index" that reflects lack of awareness of a partner's dissatisfaction with the relationship, whereas they are similar to the ISTPs in themselves being high in dissatisfaction with their relationship. This result, like others reviewed, may reflect an interesting nuance in understanding the types. That INFJ men are second highest in "obliviousness" (Table 4.31) requires consideration of the likely different perceptions and motivations of INTPs and INFJs, a point made previously in the earlier discussion of ISTPs.

Some similarities and many differences appear in the areas of education, careers, and organizations. INTPs are seen as highly creative, while ISTPs are among the lowest in this regard, and INTPs' educational and recreational interests tend to be more artistic and intellectual than those of ISTPs. Their ideal job includes creativity, originality, and earning a lot of money, as compared with the "stable and secure future" characteristic of ISTPs. Both types

Table 4.35   Research Describing INTP *continued*

Careers	Most important features of an ideal job: creativity and originality; earning a lot of money[10]
	Lowest of all types in liking work environments with "Clear structures & responsibilities," "Employee loyalty & job security," and "Working as part of a team"; one of three highest types liking work environments with "International opportunities" and "Advancement/pay but not job security"; include in top three desirable work environment characteristics "Variety of tasks," "Independence & achievement," and "Clear structures"[11]
	With INFPs, most dissatisfied with work they do, where they work, and future work opportunities, and likely to leave job[11]
	In "Organizational Values," place high value on "Autonomy"[11]
	In national sample, dissatisfied with "Promotions," "Salary," "Job security," "Predictability," and "Working conditions"[11]
	In national sample, ranked highest in valuing "Autonomy, freedom, independence" and lowest in valuing "Religion or spirituality"[11]
	Overrepresented among working MBA students compared with national sample[11]
	Occupational trends identified: scientific/technical fields[11]
Organizations, Leadership, Management, Teams	Higher on CPI scales Ai, Ie, Py, Fx, In; lower on Do, Sy, Sa, Wb, Re, So, Sc, Gi, Cm, Ac[12]
	Higher on LSI scales Dogmatic, Easygoing, Energetic, Fair, Independent, Initiating, Resourceful, Understanding[13]
	Rated higher than the eight other types in study on SYMLOG value "Tough-minded, self-oriented assertiveness" as well as "Rugged, self-oriented individualism" and "Passive rejection of popularity, going it alone" and lower than all but two of the types on "Obedience to the chain of command, complying with authority"[14]
	Departures from SYMLOG Most Effective Profile: seen as underemphasizing "Active teamwork toward a common goal," "Efficiency, strong impartial management," "Popularity and social success" (significantly lower than ESTJs, ENTPs, and Feeling types), "Protecting less able members," "Collaborative work," "Trust in the goodness of others," "Friendship"; seen as overemphasizing "Self-protection, self-interest first," "Self-oriented assertiveness" (more than any other type), "Passive rejection of popularity, going it alone" (more than any other type), "Passive noncooperation with authority"; deviated furthest from organizational culture's notion of teamwork[14]
	In a study of the influence of type dynamics on ways of dealing with conflict, tended to compromise[15]
	On teamwork variables, were found to value self-oriented individualism that may interfere with teamwork[15]

Note: [12]Brief definitions of these CPI scales can be found in Chapter 13, "Uses of Type in Organizations," See Table 4.26; [13]Tables 4.26–4.41 report ratings by subordinates of types that were significantly higher or lower on various leadership scales, relative to the other types.

Source: [1]Summary of salient ACL data and Q-Sort descriptions of 12 of the 16 types. Raters were naive to type when making their ratings. Thorne & Gough, 1991; [2]Highest three and lowest three types on two measures of personal adjustment ("Soundness" and "Efficacy"), which were calculated separately for males and females. Thorne & Gough, 1991; [3]See Chapter 11, "Uses of Type in Education"; [4]Quenk & Quenk, 1996; [5]Shelton, 1996; [6]Myers & McCaulley, 1985; [7]See Chapter 10, "Uses of Type in Counseling and Psychotherapy"; [8]Highest three and lowest three types on three measures of creativity, calculated separately for males and females. Thorne & Gough, 1991; [9]DiTiberio, 1996; [10]Hammer, 1996a; [11]See Chapter 12, "Uses of Type in Career Counseling"; [12]A study that compared the mean scores of the 16 types on the scales of the CPI using a sample of 15,102 people who attended leadership development programs at the Center for Creative Leadership. Fleenor, 1997; [13]Results in the same study at the Center for Creative Leadership on the *Leadership Style Indicator* (LSI); [14]A study using SYMLOG analysis of 529 subjects from the top three tiers of management. Ratings of SYMLOG values for the 16 types were averaged across all raters. Sundstrom & Busby, 1997; [15]Hammer & Huszczo, 1996.

like a variety of tasks at work. INTPs seem quite dissatisfied with many aspects of their work lives, which may be partially related to the high value they place on autonomy, freedom, and independence—qualities that may be difficult to find and maintain in many work environments.

While INTPs show lower scores on some of the same CPI scales as ISTPs, notably the ones reflecting "relationship" issues, unlike the ISTPs they are higher on scales that "fit" their type—Achievement via Independence, Intellectual Efficiency, Psychological-Mindedness, Flexibility, and Independence. They are also understandably lower on Achievement via Conformity. ISTPs are lower on both kinds

of achievement. Other organizational variables reveal many other ways in which the INTP preference for working independently is expressed and viewed by others.

Both the "positive"-appearing and "negative"-appearing research results for INTPs are consistent with the characteristics that we would reasonably expect to develop given INTP dynamics. The results for both ISTPs and INTPs, like those for some of the other Introverted types, put societal values in sharp relief in revealing that the qualities that are most meaningful and motivating for particular types may be devalued and unappreciated in the larger society.

ESTJ: Extraverted Thinking with Introverted Sensing

Dominant function: T_E

Auxiliary function: S_I

Tertiary function: N_I

Fourth/inferior function: F_I

At Their Best People with ESTJ preferences like to organize projects, operations, procedures, and people and then act to get things done. They live by a set of clear standards and beliefs, make a systematic effort to follow these, and expect the same of others. They value competence, efficiency, and results and display them in their work and play.

They enjoy interacting and working with others, as long as the others are responsible about meeting deadlines and completing assigned tasks. They work best in situations where clear, known problems can be solved with proven techniques.

Characteristics of ESTJs ESTJs take an objective approach to problem solving and are tough when the situation requires toughness. They use their Thinking primarily externally to organize their lives and work, and they have little patience with confusion, inefficiency, or halfway measures. ESTJs are likely to be

- Logical, analytical, and objectively critical
- Decisive, clear, and assertive

ESTJs focus on the present—what is real and actual. They apply and adapt relevant past experience to deal with problems, and they prefer jobs where results are immediate, visible, and tangible. ESTJs are likely to be

- Practical, realistic, and matter-of-fact
- Systematic and pragmatic

ESTJs are usually excellent administrators because they understand systems and logistics. They can project the steps needed to accomplish a task, foresee potential problems, assign responsibilities, and marshal resources. They cover all the bases, leave no loose ends, and get things done on time. When they see things are not working, they will plan and act to correct the situation. Otherwise, they prefer proven procedures and systems. Their orientation is to tasks, action, and the bottom line.

How Others May See Them Because they naturally devise systems, procedures, and schedules, others rely on ESTJs to take charge and get things done. Others may also find them overpowering at times because ESTJs are so certain about how things should be. Because they are clear and straightforward in their communication, people seldom have to wonder where they stand.

ESTJs can be quite gregarious and generally enjoy interacting with people, especially around tasks, games, traditions, and family activities. They take relationship roles seriously and fulfill them responsibly. Others usually see ESTJs as

- Conscientious and dependable
- Decisive, outspoken, and self-confident

Potential Areas for Growth Sometimes life circumstances have not supported ESTJs in the development and expression of their Sensing and Thinking preferences.

- If they have not developed their Sensing, ESTJs may decide too quickly before taking in enough information. Then their decisions will reflect their previously formed judgments or biases.
- If they have not developed their Thinking, they may not have a reliable way of evaluating information and thus end up making inconsistent or overly harsh decisions.

If ESTJs do not find a place where they can use their gifts and be appreciated for their contributions, they usually feel frustrated and may

- Become rigid and dogmatic
- Be intrusive, "know-it-all" experts, overpowering others and refusing to listen
- Get picky about details and be impatient with those who do not follow procedures exactly

It is natural for ESTJs to give less attention to their nonpreferred Feeling and Intuitive parts. If they neglect these too much, however, they may

- Apply logic even when emotions and impacts on people need primary consideration
- Fail to respond to others' needs for intimate connection and processing of feelings
- Not always see the wider ramifications of a seemingly simple, direct action

Under great stress, ESTJs may feel alone and unappreciated and be unable to communicate their feeling of distress and despair.

Table 4.36 summarizes relevant research results for ESTJs. Dominant extraverted Thinking types with auxiliary introverted Sensing present quite a different research picture from that of the ISTP dominant *introverted* Thinking types with auxiliary extraverted Sensing. The results show ESTJs to be contented, to be high on coping resources, and to have a positive outlook about themselves and the world. However, some results that reflect stress-related behavior differentiate ESTJs from, for example, ESTPs, in that ESTJs are overrepresented as coronary bypass patients, as showing Type A behavior, among men with chronic pain, and as high in the emotional exhaustion aspect of job burnout. It is interesting that they are overrepresented among men who have been married more than two times and also report high satisfaction with their current marriage or intimate relationship.

Perhaps these somewhat mixed responses to stress are partially a function of some of the other research results

Table 4.36   Research Describing ESTJ

Personality, Psychotherapy, Health, Stress, Coping	Contented, energetic, practical, prejudiced, self-satisfied[1]
	Males among the three highest on "Soundness" and "Efficacy"[2]
	Overrepresented among men who had been married more than two times[3]
	One of three least common types among males in substance abuse program[3]
	Females underrepresented in a substance abuse program[3]
	One of two male types underrepresented in a substance abuse program[3]
	Second most frequent among men who had undergone coronary bypass surgery[4]
	Overrepresented among those having Type A behavior[4]
	Overrepresented among men with chronic pain[4]
	With ENFPs, had highest total coping resource scores of all the types[4]
	With ENTJs, had second-highest mean level of coping resources[4]
	Ranked first of all 16 types in using cognitive coping resources and second in using emotional and social coping resources[4]
	Ranked third highest on "Emotional exhaustion" burnout scale[5]
	Ranked fourth highest in "Positive affectivity" and lowest in "Negative affectivity"[5]
	In national sample, ranked third most satisfied with "Marriage/intimate relationship"[5]
Education	Females among three lowest on two out of two measures of creativity[6]
	One of top two types among industrial/technical teachers[7]
	Among top four types in college GPA[7]
	Most frequent type among school administrators[7]
	One of two types most frequent among top 100 executive educators[7]
	Overrepresented among top 100 executive educators[8]
	Frequently represented among college RAs[7]
	Least likely of the types to report suicidal ideation in college[7]
	Among highest in college retention[7]
	Highly represented among vocational teachers[7]
	In national sample "Leisure Activities," overrepresented in "Playing sports" and "Watching sporting events," underrepresented in "Listening to music"[7]
	Performed lower on deductive reasoning, with other dominant Thinking types[8]
	Academic subjects preferred: math, practical skills[9]

shown in the education, career, and organization areas. ESTJs appear to be ambitious and hardworking, with high standards of competence, personal responsibility, and conformity to clear and well-established structures. Their naturally dominant leadership style may contribute to their confidence in their abilities and optimism about successfully achieving their goals, with an accompanying likelihood of overdoing that can lead to physical and emotional stress reactions.

The other ESTJ research results are in accord with the type characteristics we would expect to emerge from their dynamic focus on applying logical decisions to current data in the external environment. They are seen on the CPI scales as high on Dominance, Sociability, Social Presence, Self-Acceptance, Well-Being, Socialization, Self-Control, Tolerance, Good Impression, Communality, and Achievement via Conformance—all qualities considered desirable in our society. They are lower on Achievement via Independence, Intellectual Efficiency, Psychological-Mindedness,

Flexibility, and Femininity/Masculinity. As we shall see, several of these high and low scales are different for the ESTJ companion type, the ENTJs, who also have dominant extraverted Thinking.

Overall, then, the data for ESTJs suggest that people of this type are seen quite positively in our culture and that their particular characteristics conform readily to a normative notion of success and psychological adaptation.

ENTJ: Extraverted Thinking with Introverted Intuition

The dynamics of ENTJ are as follows:

Dominant function: T_E

Auxiliary function: N_I

Tertiary function: S_I

Fourth/inferior function: F_I

Table 4.36   Research Describing ESTJ *continued*

Careers	Overrepresented among bank officers and financial managers[10]
	Most important features of an ideal job: "A stable and secure future"[10]
	Had highest score on retirement planning in a study of university faculty and staff planning to retire[10]
	Highest of all types in national sample in liking work environments with "Clear structures & responsibilities" and "Working as part of a team"; one of three highest types favoring "Toeing the line" and "Going by the book," and include "Variety of tasks" among top three desirable characteristics[11]
	In national sample "Organizational Values," placed high value on "Achievement within system"[11]
	In national sample, among types most satisfied with their work and working conditions[11]
	In national sample, dissatisfied with "Promotions" in their work[11]
	In national sample, among top four types in valuing "Health," "Financial security," "Achievement," and "Prestige"[11]
	In national sample ranked highest in valuing "Financial security" (76.0%), "Achievement & accomplishment" (69.2%), and "Prestige & status" (14.3%)[11]
	Overrepresented among working MBA students compared with national sample[11]
	Overrepresented among both male and female small business owners compared with national sample[11]
	Occupational trends identified: management, administration, law enforcement[11]
Organizations, Leadership, Management, Teams	Higher on CPI scales Do, Sy, Sp, Sa, Wb, So, Sc, To, Gi, Cm, Ac; lower on Ai, Ie, Py, Fx, Fm[12]
	Higher on LSI scales Dogmatic, Impatient, Impulsive, Initiating, Manipulating, Pressuring[13]
	Departures from SYMLOG Most Effective Profile: underemphasize "Active teamwork toward common goals," "Efficiency, strong impartial management," "Equality," "Responsible idealism, collaborative work," "Trust in the goodness of others"; seen as overemphasizing "Self-protection, self-interest first"[14]
	Most positive about using statistical methods as an information source[15]
	Rated by employees as using an adaptation approach to creativity—the methodical and incremental approach to change[15]
	Showed change on at least four of the seven leadership items in Naval Academy leadership behavior study where type training was followed by feedback from lower-ranked students[15]
	In a study of the influence of type dynamics on ways of dealing with conflict, tended to compete[16]

Note: [12]Brief definitions of these CPI scales can be found in Chapter 13, "Uses of Type in Organizations." See Table 4.26; [13]Tables 4.26–4.41 report ratings by subordinates of types that were significantly higher or lower on various leadership scales, relative to the other types.

Source: [1]Summary of salient ACL data and Q-Sort descriptions of 12 of the 16 types. Raters were naive to type when making their ratings. Thorne & Gough, 1991; [2]Highest three and lowest three types on two measures of personal adjustment ("Soundness" and "Efficacy"), which were calculated separately for males and females. Thorne & Gough, 1991; [3]Quenk & Quenk, 1996; [4]Shelton, 1996; [5]See Chapter 10, "Uses of Type in Counseling and Psychotherapy"; [6]Highest three and lowest three types on three measures of creativity, calculated separately for males and females. Thorne & Gough, 1991; [7]See Chapter 11, "Uses of Type in Education"; [8]DiTiberio, 1996; [9]Myers & McCaulley, 1985; [10]Hammer, 1996a; [11]See Chapter 12, "Uses of Type in Career Counseling"; [12]A study that compared the mean scores of the 16 types on the scales of the CPI using a sample of 15,102 people who attended leadership development programs at the Center for Creative Leadership. Fleenor, 1997; [13]Results in the same study at the Center for Creative Leadership on the *Leadership Style Indicator* (LSI); [14]A study using SYMLOG analysis of 529 subjects from the top three tiers of management. Ratings of SYMLOG values for the 16 types were averaged across all raters. Sundstrom & Busby, 1997; [15]Walck, 1996; [16]Hammer & Huszczo, 1996.

At Their Best People with ENTJ preferences are natural leaders and organization builders. They conceptualize and theorize readily and translate possibilities into plans to achieve short-term and long-term objectives. They readily see illogical and inefficient procedures and feel a strong urge to correct them—to organize people and situations to get them moving in the right direction.

ENTJs are strategic visionaries, adept at planning for the future needs of the people and organizations for which they are responsible.

Characteristics of ENTJs ENTJs use their Thinking primarily externally and are thus natural critics. They set their own standards and are forceful in applying them to others, to organizations, and to themselves. They value intelligence and competence and abhor inefficiency or ignorance. They can be tough when the situation calls for toughness. ENTJs are likely to be

- Analytical, logical, and objectively critical
- Decisive, clear, and assertive

ENTJs are intellectually curious, seek new ideas, and like complex problems. They use their Intuition primarily internally to conceive possibilities and create the insights they use in making decisions and plans. ENTJs are likely to be

- Conceptual and global thinkers
- Innovative theorizers and planners

ENTJs are usually excellent solvers of organizational problems. They are keenly aware of the intricate connections within organizations and are action oriented and strategic—they think ahead, anticipate problems, devise broad plans and systems, and marshal human and material resources to achieve goals. They are generally disinterested in routine maintenance activities, preferring new challenges.

How Others May See Them ENTJs love, and are energized by, stimulating interactions with people. They often challenge people's statements and behaviors, expecting that others will defend them and that, as a result, mutual learning will take place. ENTJs admire and seek out people who are knowledgeable and who stand up to them, say what they think, and argue persuasively.

ENTJs prefer that things be settled and clear, but their love of ideas can pull them into wide-ranging Intuitive exploration and discussions. Their verbal fluency, decisiveness, self-confidence, and urge to organize others can overpower people at times. Others usually see ENTJs as

- Direct, challenging, and decisive
- Objective, fair, and stimulating

Potential Areas for Growth Sometimes life circumstances have not supported ENTJs in the development and expression of their Intuitive and Thinking preferences.

- If they have not developed their Intuition, ENTJs may make decisions too quickly without considering alternatives or exploring possibilities. In this case, their decisiveness can become dictatorial.
- If they have not developed their Thinking, they may not have a reliable way to evaluate their insights and make plans. Then their decision making will be inconsistent and changeable.

If ENTJs do not find a place where they can use their gifts and be appreciated for their contributions, they usually feel frustrated and may

- Become overly impersonal and critical
- Be intrusive and directive—giving orders without listening
- Become abrasive and verbally aggressive

It is natural for ENTJs to give less attention to their nonpreferred Feeling and Sensing parts. If they neglect these too much, however, they may

- Fail to notice or value another's need for personal connection, appreciation, and praise
- Fail to factor into their plans the needs of others for support and processing time
- Overlook specifics and realistic factors that are necessary to carry their plans to completion

Under great stress, ENTJs can be overwhelmed by self-doubt, feel alone and unappreciated, and be unable to express their distress to others.

Table 4.37 summarizes relevant research results for ENTJs. ENTJ research results as displayed in Table 4.37 show some general and specific similarities to the data for ESTJs, as well as quite a few differences that suggest the influence of the different auxiliary functions, Sensing and Intuition. It is quite interesting that there is no overlap in the

adjectives with which the two types are described, with ENTJs seen as ambitious, forceful, optimistic, aggressive, and egotistical and ESTJs described as contented, energetic, practical, prejudiced, and self-satisfied. (See Chapter 9 for a further discussion of the distinctive adjectives with which the types are described.) As is found for other types, ENTJs are overrepresented among college students referred for substance abuse workshops but underrepresented in actual substance abuse treatment programs. It is interesting that ESTJs, while similarly uncommon in substance abuse groups, do not seem to be identified as at risk in college.

ENTJs are ranked high in coping resources and low in reporting stress in several life areas, and unlike ESTJs, who report high job burnout through emotional exhaustion, ENTJs rank lowest on this variable and are similar to ESTJs on positive and negative affectivity.

ENTJs show success in the educational sphere similar to that of ESTJs, though their academic interests are toward English and science, as compared with the ESTJ interest in math and practical skills. In career variables they show also some type-consistent differences from ESTJs, most notably in workplace values and satisfaction, which focus more on future-oriented and independent pursuits than appears to be the case for the ESTJs. Both types share satisfaction with their work and working conditions, and ENTJs are among those with the highest salaries. Both types also tend to deal with conflict by competing.

Perhaps even more clearly than is the case for ESTJs, ENTJ research results highlight what is valued, respected, and desired in our culture. Nevertheless, the data also suggest that some "negative" effects can accompany these highly regarded qualities.

ISFP: Introverted Feeling with Extraverted Sensing

Dominant function: F_I

Auxiliary function: S_E

Tertiary function: N_E

Fourth/inferior function: T_E

At Their Best ISFPs live in the present with a quiet sense of joyfulness; they want time to experience each moment. They prize the freedom to follow their own course, have their own space, and set their own time frame, and they give the same freedom and tolerance to others. They are faithful in fulfilling obligations to people and things that are important to them.

ISFPs take time to develop intimacy with others, but, once they do, those relationships are very important. They express their devotion to others spontaneously in many quiet ways.

Characteristics of ISFPs ISFPs are guided by a strong core of inner values and want their outer life to demonstrate those values. They want their work to be more than just a job; they want to contribute to people's well-being or

Table 4.37   Research Describing ENTJ

Personality, Psychotherapy, Health, Stress, Coping	Ambitious, forceful, optimistic, aggressive, egotistical[1]
	Overrepresented among behavioral psychologists[2]
	Overrepresented among new college students referred for a substance abuse workshop[2]
	One of two types underrepresented among males in a substance abuse program[2]
	Underrepresented in female chemical dependency sample[2]
	Overrepresented among members of a cardiac rehabilitation program[3]
	With ESTJ, had the second-highest mean level of coping resources[3]
	Ranked first of all 16 types in using physical coping resources[3]
	One of the four types in college reporting the highest levels of assertiveness[3]
	In national sample, lowest in reporting stress associated with "Work" and "Finances"[4]
	In national sample, highest in coping with stress by "Trying to think of options"[4]
	In national sample, ranked second highest in "No" and fourth highest in "Not Sure" re: "Belief in higher spiritual power"[4]
	In national sample, ranked lowest on "Emotional exhaustion" burnout scale[4]
	Ranked second highest in "Positive affectivity" and lowest in "Negative affectivity"[4]
Education	Males among three highest on one of three measures of creativity; females among three highest on one out of three measures of creativity[5]
	Most frequent among national CASE professor of the year finalists[6]
	Among top four types in college GPA[6]
	One of two types most frequent among top 100 executive educators[6]
	Overrepresented among top 100 executive educators[7]
	One of two types most frequent among RAs at women's college[6]
	Frequent among college students referred for substance abuse training[6]
	Among highest in college retention[6]
	Highest grades among persisters in college[6]
	One of two types most frequent among female student affairs officers[6]
	In national sample "Leisure Activities," overrepresented in "Working out/exercising"[6]
	Performed lower on deductive reasoning, with other dominant Thinking types[7]
	Academic subjects preferred: English, science[8]

happiness. They don't enjoy routine but will work with energy and dedication when doing something they believe in. ISFPs are likely to be

- Trusting, kind, and considerate
- Sensitive and gentle

ISFPs are acutely aware of the specifics and realities of the present—the people and the world around them. They learn by doing more than by reading or hearing and get involved in day-to-day caretaking activities. ISFPs are likely to be

- Observant
- Realistic, practical, concrete, and factual

ISFPs are attuned to the feelings and needs of others and flexible in responding to them. They often have an affinity for nature and for beauty in all living things—people, plants, and animals. They prize most those who take time

to understand their values and goals and who support them in achieving those goals in their own way.

How Others May See Them   ISFPs are adaptable and flexible unless something that matters strongly to them is endangered; then they stop adapting. They care deeply about people but may show it through doing things for others more than through words.

ISFPs tend to be quiet and unassuming, and their warmth, enthusiasm, and playful humor may not be apparent to people who don't know them well. They prefer to observe and support rather than organize situations; they have little wish to dominate.

ISFPs may be underestimated by others and may also underrate themselves. They often take for granted what they do well and make too much of the contrast between their inner standards and their actual behavior and accomplishments. Others usually see ISFPs as

Table 4.37   Research Describing ENTJ *continued*

Careers	Highest of all types in national sample in liking work environments with "A variety of tasks," "People with different backgrounds," and "International opportunities"; lowest of all the types in liking work environments with "No expectation of extra hours" and "Toeing the line." Include "Independence & achievement" and "Clear structure" among top three desirable characteristics[9]
	In national sample, one of two types most satisfied with work, where they work, and future work opportunities, unlikely to leave job, and among those with highest income[9]
	In national sample "Organizational Values," place high value on "Financial analysis" and low value on "Nurturing affiliation"[9]
	In national sample, among top four types valuing "Home/family," "Achievement," "Creativity," and "Learning"[9]
	Greatest work environment satisfiers are opportunities to use talents and to contribute to society, job security, opportunities for learning and for accomplishment[9]
	In national sample, ranked highest in valuing "Home/family"[9]
	Overrepresented among working MBA students compared with national sample[9]
	Overrepresented among both male and female owners of small businesses compared with national sample[9]
	Occupational trends identified: management, leadership[9]
Organizations, Leadership, Management, Teams	Higher on CPI scales Do, Cs, Sy, Sp, Sa, Wb, Re, So, Em, To, Gi, Ac, Ai, Ie, Py, Fx, In; lower on Fm[10]
	Higher on LSI scales Adaptable, Energetic, Fair, Impersonal, Independent, Initiating, Opinionated, Resourceful[11]
	Departures from SYMLOG Most Effective Profile: underemphasize "Active teamwork toward a common goal," "Efficiency, strong impartial management," "Having a good time," "Protecting less able members," "Equality," "Collaborative work," "Friendship," "Trust in the goodness of others"; overemphasize "Self-protection, self-interest first"[12]
	In a study of the influence of type dynamics on ways of dealing with conflict, tended to compete[13]

Note: [10]Brief definitions of these CPI scales can be found in Chapter 13, "Uses of Type in Organizations." See Table 4.26; [11]Tables 4.26– 4.41 report ratings by subordinates of types that were significantly higher or lower on various leadership scales, relative to the other types.

Source: [1]Summary of salient ACL data and Q-Sort descriptions of 12 of the 16 types. Raters were naive to type when making their ratings. Thorne & Gough, 1991; [2]Quenk & Quenk, 1996; [3]Shelton, 1996; [4]See Chapter 10, "Uses of Type in Counseling and Psychotherapy"; [5]Highest three and lowest three types on three measures of creativity, calculated separately for males and females. Thorne & Gough, 1991; [6]See Chapter 11, "Uses of Type in Education"; [7]DiTiberio, 1996; [8]Myers & McCaulley, 1985; [9]See Chapter 12, "Uses of Type in Career Counseling"; [10]A study that compared the mean scores of the 16 types on the scales of the CPI using a sample of 15,102 people who attended leadership development programs at the Center for Creative Leadership. Fleenor, 1997; [11]Results in the same study at the Center for Creative Leadership on the *Leadership Style Indicator* (LSI); [12]A study using SYMLOG analysis of 529 subjects from the top three tiers of management. Ratings of SYMLOG values for the 16 types were averaged across all raters. Sundstrom & Busby, 1997; [13]Hammer & Huszczo, 1996.

■ Quiet, reserved, and private—hard to know well
■ Spontaneous and tolerant

Potential Areas for Growth   Sometimes life circumstances have not supported ISFPs in the development and expression of their Sensing and Feeling preferences.

■ If they have not developed their Sensing, ISFPs may have no reliable way of getting accurate data about the external world or of actualizing their values. Their decisions will be based on little information and be overly personal.
■ If they have not developed their Feeling, they may get caught up in Sensing realities and not take time to do the internal valuing process by which they make their best decisions. They may avoid decision making, allowing others or circumstances to decide for them.

If ISFPs do not find a place where they can use their gifts and be appreciated for their contributions, they usually feel frustrated and may

■ Withdraw from people and the situation
■ Be excessively self-critical
■ Passively resist structures and rules
■ Feel unappreciated and undervalued

It is natural for ISFPs to give less attention to their non-preferred Thinking and Intuitive parts. If they neglect these too much, however, they may

■ Reject or not take seriously logical systems
■ Feel ill-equipped to deal with complexity
■ Not always see the wider ramifications of their specific, immediate decisions

Under great stress, ISFPs can become uncharacteristically critical of themselves and others, verbalizing harsh and negative judgments.

Table 4.38 summarizes relevant research results for ISFPs. Insight into the meaning of the research results in Table 4.38 for ISFPs comes from the description of this

Table 4.38   Research Describing ISFP

Personality, Psychotherapy, Health, Stress, Coping	Females among three highest on "Soundness" and among three lowest on "Efficacy"[1] Among three male types most "oblivious" to partner's dissatisfaction with the relationship[2] Overrepresented among males in a substance abuse program[2] Third most frequent among female coronary heart disease patients[3] Males overrepresented among hypertensive patients[3] Ranked 15th of 16 types in using emotional coping resources and 16th in using physical coping resources; ranked 15th in total resources[3] One of the four types in college reporting the lowest levels of assertiveness[3] In national sample, highest in reporting stress associated with "Finances" and "Children"[4] In national sample, highest in coping with stress by "Trying to avoid stressful situations," "Getting upset or angry and not showing it," "Sleeping," and "Watching TV"[4] In national sample, ranked highest in "Ever had heart disease/hypertension"[4] Ranked highest on "Emotional exhaustion" and "Depersonalization" burnout scales[4] Ranked second highest in "Negative affectivity"[4]
Education	Males among three lowest on one out of three measures of creativity; females among three highest on one out of three measures of creativity and among three lowest on one out of two measures of creativity[5] Projected self fewest number of years into the future in essays[6] Among lowest in college retention[6] Among highest persisters in college[6] In national sample "Leisure Activities," overrepresented in "Watching TV three or more hours per day" and "Watching TV for leisure"; underrepresented in "Reading," "Working out/exercising," "Writing," "Appreciating art," and "Taking classes, going to school"[6] Lower on deductive reasoning, with other dominant Feeling types[7] Academic subjects preferred: practical skills[8]
Careers	More likely to say they disliked their work, among bank officers and financial managers[9] Lowest of all types in national sample in liking work environments with "A variety of tasks"; one of three highest types in favoring "Loyalty & security," "Making the job as simple as possible," and "No expectation of extra hours"; include among top three desirable work characteristics "Clear structure" and "Independence & achievement"[10] In national sample, among those with lowest income and unlikely to leave job[10] In national sample "Organizational Values," placed high value on "Happy family" and low value on "Variety & challenge"[10] In national sample, greatest dissatisfiers were "Promotions," "Job security," "Salary"[10] In national sample, ranked lowest in valuing "Achievement & accomplishment," "Education & learning," and "Being creative"[10] Underrepresented among working MBA students compared to national sample[10] Underrepresented among both male and female small business owners compared with national sample[10] Occupational trends identified: health care, business, law enforcement[10]
Organizations, Leadership, Management, Teams	Higher on CPI scale Fm; lower on Do, Cs, Sy, Sp, Sa, Wb, Re, To, Gi, Ac, Ai, Ie, Py, In, Em[11] Higher on LSI scale Easygoing[12] In a study of the influence of type dynamics on ways of dealing with conflict, tended to avoid conflict[13]

Note: [11]Brief definitions of these CPI scales can be found in Chapter 13, "Uses of Type in Organizations." See Table 4.26; [12]Tables 4.26–4.41 report ratings by subordinates of types that were significantly higher or lower on various leadership scales, relative to the other types.

Source: [1]Highest three and lowest three types on two measures of personal adjustment ("Soundness" and "Efficacy"), which were calculated separately for males and females. Thorne & Gough, 1991; [2]Quenk & Quenk, 1996; [3]Shelton, 1996; [4]See Chapter 10, "Uses of Type in Counseling and Psychotherapy"; [5]Highest three and lowest three types on three measures of creativity, calculated separately for males and females. Thorne & Gough, 1991; [6]See Chapter 11, "Uses of Type in Education"; [7]DiTiberio, 1996; [8]Myers & McCaulley, 1985; [9]Hammer, 1996a; [10]See Chapter 12, "Uses of Type in Career Counseling"; [11]A study that compared the mean scores of the 16 types on the scales of the CPI using a sample of 15,102 people who attended leadership development programs at the Center for Creative Leadership. Fleenor, 1997; [12]Results in the same study at the Center for Creative Leadership on the *Leadership Style Indicator* (LSI); [13]Hammer & Huszczo, 1996.

type as gentle, unassuming, loyal individuals who tend to minimize their own skills and accomplishments and prefer to be in a supportive rather than a leadership role. That females are among the three highest on the "Soundness" measure of adaptation and among the three lowest on the "Efficacy" measure makes sense when we consider ISFP qualities in relation to the indicative and contraindicative adjectives on these two adjustment measures (see Chapter 10, Tables 10.1 and 10.2, and the accompanying discussion of type and gender biases apparent in these measures).

In light of the makeup of ISFPs, it is not surprising that they are overrepresented in groups with apparent stress-related conditions, such as heart disease and hypertension, and that they, like nearly all the Introverted types, appear in substance abuse groups as well. That ISFPs are quite low in overall coping resources and in using emotional and physical coping resources is to be expected for a type who by their very nature prefer to be in nonstressful situations. This observation is supported by their being highest in coping with stress by trying to avoid it, getting upset and not showing it, sleeping, and watching TV. The results for burnout measures and negative affectivity are also consistent with the ISFP desire for low-key situations.

The education, career, and management results also make sense in this regard. ISFPs projected themselves the fewest number of years into the future. With their orientation to concrete, straightforward experience and accomplishment in the present, it is not surprising that the academic environment may not be interesting, comfortable, and affirming for them. Similarly, few of today's work environments permit working steadily on a limited set of tasks, nor does the workplace in general reward loyalty and security, simplicity of tasks, and not working overtime.

The CPI scales that show them as higher on Femininity/Masculinity (reflecting being sympathetic, warm, modest, and dependent) and lower on Dominance, and various "social," "self-image," and "achievement" measures are also consistent with the natural approach of ISFPs.

The interests, competencies, and contributions of ISFPs may not be readily recognized in a context that tends to value quite different interests and achievements. The fast-paced, rapidly changing workplace may be a particularly likely arena where the quiet persistence, competence, resourcefulness, and talents of ISFPs may go unseen and unrewarded.

INFP: Introverted Feeling with Extraverted Intuition

Dominant function: F_I

Auxiliary function: N_E

Tertiary function: S_E

Fourth/inferior function: T_E

At Their Best People with INFP preferences have an inner core of values that guides their interactions and decisions. They want to be involved in work that contributes to both their own growth and inner development and those of others—to have a purpose beyond their paycheck. They make a priority of clarifying their values and living in congruence with them.

INFPs recognize and honor the emotional and psychological needs of others, even when others may not have recognized or expressed their own needs.

Characteristics of INFPs INFPs primarily use their Feeling preference internally where they make decisions based on their values of self-understanding, individuality, and growth. Living by moral commitments to what they believe in is crucial to INFPs. They are likely to be

- Sensitive, concerned, and caring
- Idealistic and loyal to their ideas

INFPs enjoy reading, discussing, and reflecting on possibilities for positive change in the future. They are curious about ideas and quick to see connections and meanings. INFPs are likely to

- Be curious and creative
- Have long-range vision

INFPs are usually fascinated by opportunities to explore the complexities of human personality—their own and others'. They tend to work in bursts of energy and are capable of great concentration and output when fully engaged in a project. They are generally faithful in fulfilling obligations related to people, work, or ideas to which they are committed, but they can have difficulty performing routine work that has little meaning for them.

How Others May See Them INFPs find structures and rules confining and prefer to work autonomously. They are adaptable and flexible until something violates their inner values. Then they stop adapting. The resulting expression of value judgments can emerge with an intensity that is surprising to others.

INFPs tend to be reserved and selective about sharing their most deeply held values and feelings. They value relationships based on depth, authenticity, true connection, and mutual growth. INFPs prize most those who take time to understand their values and goals. Others usually see INFPs as

- Sensitive, introspective, and complex
- Original and individual
- Sometimes difficult to understand

Potential Areas for Growth Sometimes life circumstances have not supported INFPs in the development and expression of their Intuitive and Feeling preferences.

- If they have not developed their Intuition, INFPs may not have reliable ways to take in information and may fail to notice the realities of situations. Then they make decisions based solely on personal values and find it difficult to translate their values into action.

- If they have not developed their Feeling, they may not take time for the inner valuing process by which they make their best decisions, instead going from one exciting possibility to another and achieving little.

If INFPs do not find a place where they can use their gifts and be appreciated for their contributions, they usually feel frustrated and may

- Have uncharacteristic difficulty expressing themselves verbally
- Withdraw from people and situations
- Not give enough information to others, especially about important values

It is natural for INFPs to give less attention to their non-preferred Thinking and Sensing parts. If they neglect these too much, however, they may

- Become easily discouraged about the contrast between their ideals and accomplishments
- Reject logical reasoning even in situations that require it, asserting the supremacy of their internal viewpoint
- Be impractical and have difficulty estimating the resources required to reach a desired goal

Under great stress, INFPs may begin seriously doubting their own competence and that of others, becoming overly critical and judgmental.

Table 4.39 summarizes relevant research results for INFPs. Several of the research results reported for ISFPs appear for the companion dominant introverted Feeling types, the INFPs. Males are overrepresented in several substance abuse studies. INFPs in general tend to be low in assertiveness and positive affectivity, while being the highest type on the negative affectivity scale. They appear infrequently as working MBA students and as owners of small businesses, have an easygoing leadership style like the ISFPs, and tend to avoid conflict when presented with it.

A number of dissimilarities to ISFPs are also evident in comparing Tables 4.39 and 4.38. Though ISFP males were not very high or low on the "Soundness" and "Efficacy" (they were fourth lowest on "Efficacy") adaptation measures, INFP males were the lowest on both of these measures. INFP males also showed the highest levels of depression and high levels of anger and frustration with chronic pain, although they were underrepresented as chronic pain patients. They also were second lowest in reporting having heart disease or hypertension, perhaps suggesting some selectivity of this type in their stress-related responses.

As a type typically seen as serious, contemplative, and with high ideals, it is not surprising that they are the most likely to report suicidal thoughts in college. In contrast to ISFP college students, and no doubt related to their auxiliary Intuition preference, INFPs' use of leisure time is overrepresented in activities such as writing, appreciating art, reading, and listening to music. INFP career interests and values are also different from those of ISFPs. Creativity is the most important feature of an ideal job, and they are among the three highest in wanting independence and achievement in their work, as well as autonomy. These career characteristics may not be readily available to them, in that they, like INTPs, report the most dissatisfaction with most aspects of their jobs and report the intention of leaving these jobs.

INFPs are higher on the CPI scales Achievement via Independence and Flexibility, and like the ISFPs they are higher on Femininity/Masculinity and lower on Dominance, Sociability, Social Presence, Self-Acceptance, Well-Being, Good Impression, and Achievement via Conformity. Unlike the ISFPs, they are also lower on Socialization, Self-Control, and Communality and are *not* lower on Intellectual Efficiency, Psychological-Mindedness, Independence, and Empathy.

These differences, as well as those relating to educational interests, pinpoint some of the reasons that INFPs may be more readily recognized and appreciated by others than is the case for ISFPs and that may contribute to their more mixed responses to life stresses. Nevertheless, the aspects of living and ways of succeeding that give meaning and satisfaction to INFPs are not necessarily reflected in the kinds of variables shown in Table 4.39. The same appears true for ISFPs and some of the other types whose natural qualities may be somewhat divergent from those of the larger culture.

ESFJ: Extraverted Feeling with Introverted Sensing

Dominant function: F_E

Auxiliary function: S_I

Tertiary function: N_I

Fourth/inferior function: T_I

At Their Best People with ESFJ preferences like to organize people and situations and then work with others to complete tasks accurately and on time. They are conscientious and loyal, following through even in small matters, and they want others to be the same. They value security and stability.

Sociable and outgoing, ESFJs enjoy celebrations and traditions and bring a very personal caring to the workplace and home. They want to be appreciated for themselves and for what they give to others.

Characteristics of ESFJs ESFJs use their Feeling primarily externally and radiate warmth and energy. They are encouraged by approval and hurt by indifference or unkindness. Conflict-filled or tense situations make them uncomfortable, and they work to ensure these don't occur. ESFJs are likely to be

- Warm, sympathetic, and helpful
- Personable, cooperative, and tactful

Table 4.39   Research Describing INFP

Personality, Psychotherapy, Health, Stress, Coping	Artistic, reflective, sensitive, careless, lazy[1]
	Males were lowest on both "Soundness" and "Efficacy"[2]
	Overrepresented among a sample of male therapists[3]
	Males likely to be overrepresented among substance abusers[3]
	Overrepresented among female substance abusers[3]
	Males one of four types most common in a substance abuse program[3]
	One of three types overrepresented among males in a substance abuse program[3]
	Underrepresented among men with chronic pain[4]
	Showed the highest level of depression of the 16 types with chronic pain[4]
	Reported second-highest level of anger and frustration among those suffering long-term pain[4]
	One of the four types in college reporting the lowest levels of assertiveness[4]
	In national sample, ranked second lowest in "Ever had heart disease/hypertension"[5]
	Ranked third lowest in "Positive affectivity" and highest in "Negative affectivity"[5]
	In national sample, ranked second highest in dissatisfaction with "Marriage/intimate relationship"[5]
Education	Have a general advantage in foreign language learning[6]
	Most likely of the types to report suicidal thoughts in college[6]
	One of two types most frequent among college alcohol policy violators[6]
	In national sample "Leisure Activities," overrepresented in "Writing," "Appreciating art," "Reading," and "Listening to music"[6]
	Performed significantly lower on deductive reasoning[7]
	Academic subjects preferred: art, English, music[8]
Careers	Most important features of an ideal job: creativity and originality[9]
	Among three highest types favoring work environments with "Independence & achievement," and include among top three desirable characteristics "Variety of tasks" and "Clear structure"[10]
	In national sample, with INTPs, were dissatisfied with the kind of work they do, where they work, and future work opportunities, and were likely to leave the job[10]
	In national sample "Organizational Values," placed high value on "Nurturing affiliation"[10]
	In national sample, among top four types valuing "Autonomy" and "Creativity"[10]
	In national sample, greatest dissatisfiers in the work environment were "Promotions," "Amount of stress," and "Opportunities for accomplishment"[10]
	Underrepresented among working MBA students compared with national sample[10]
	Underrepresented among both male and female small business owners compared with national sample[10]
	Occupational trends identified: counseling, writing, arts[10]
Organizations, Leadership, Management, Teams	Higher on CPI scales Ai, Fx, Fm; lower on Do, Sy, Sp, Sa, Wb, So, Sc, Gi, Cm, Ac[11]
	Higher on LSI scales Appreciative, Easygoing[12]
	Showed change on at least four of the seven leadership items in Naval Academy leadership behavior study where type training was followed by feedback from lower-ranked students[13]
	Tended to avoid conflict in a study of the influence of type dynamics on ways of dealing with conflict[14]

Note: [11]Brief definitions of these CPI scales can be found in Chapter 13, "Uses of Type in Organizations." See Table 4.26; [12]Tables 4.26–4.41 report ratings by subordinates of types that were significantly higher or lower on various leadership scales, relative to the other types.

Source: [1]Summary of salient ACL data and Q-Sort descriptions of 12 of the 16 types. Raters were naive to type when making their ratings. Thorne & Gough, 1991; [2]Highest three and lowest three types on two measures of personal adjustment ("Soundness" and "Efficacy"), which were calculated separately for males and females. Thorne & Gough, 1991; [3]Quenk & Quenk, 1996; [4]Shelton, 1996; [5]See Chapter 10, "Uses of Type in Counseling and Psychotherapy"; [6]See Chapter 11, "Uses of Type in Education"; [7]DiTiberio, 1996; [8]Myers & McCaulley, 1985; [9]Hammer, 1996a; [10]See Chapter 12, "Uses of Type in Career Counseling"; [11]A study that compared the mean scores of the 16 types on the scales of the CPI using a sample of 15,102 people who attended leadership development programs at the Center for Creative Leadership. Fleenor, 1997; [12]Results in the same study at the Center for Creative Leadership on the *Leadership Style Indicator* (LSI); [13]Walck, 1996; [14]Hammer & Huszczo, 1996.

ESFJs focus on the present and base decisions on experience and facts. Though they enjoy variety, they adapt well to routine and don't like work that demands mastery of abstract ideas or impersonal analysis. They enjoy their possessions and take good care of them. ESFJs are likely to be

- Practical, realistic, and down-to-earth
- Decisive, thorough, and consistent

ESFJs are sensitive to the needs of each individual in their environment and good at providing practical caring. Much of their pleasure and satisfaction comes from the comfort and pleasure of others.

How Others May See Them
ESFJs are energized by interaction with others and genuinely interested in others' lives and concerns. They feel most comfortable in structured situations and enjoy creating order, structure, and schedules. They prefer to do things the traditional and accepted way.

For the sake of harmony, ESFJs will agree with others when they can. However, they also have strong values, which they express clearly and confidently when they think it is appropriate.

ESFJs value family and social ties. They enjoy belonging and are good at celebrations and traditions. Others usually see ESFJs as

- Sociable, outgoing, enthusiastic, and energetic
- Organized and orderly
- Committed to preserving traditions

Potential Areas for Growth
Sometimes life circumstances have not supported ESFJs in the development and expression of their Sensing and Feeling preferences.

- If they have not developed their Sensing, ESFJs may not take in much information before making decisions and jump to conclusions before fully understanding a situation. They may then impose those decisions on everyone around them.
- If they have not developed their Feeling, they may be tentative and uncertain, accepting the judgments of others too quickly.

If ESFJs do not find a place where they can use their gifts and be appreciated for their contributions, they usually feel frustrated and may

- Doubt themselves and focus their attention entirely on satisfying the needs of others
- Worry and feel guilty
- Become controlling in their push for harmony—"we will all get along"
- Become overly sensitive, imagining slights where none were intended

It is natural for ESFJs to give less attention to their non-preferred Thinking and Intuitive parts. If they neglect these too much, however, they may

- Find it difficult to acknowledge and deal with the truth of problems with people or things they care about
- Support those in charge or the standard procedures too uncritically
- Fail to see wider possibilities or alternative ways of doing things

Under great stress, ESFJs may find themselves uncharacteristically critical of others and of themselves. Their negative thoughts and opinions then trouble them greatly.

Table 4.40 summarizes relevant research results for ESFJs. ESFJs, in contrast to ISFPs, have dominant *extraverted* Feeling with auxiliary introverted Sensing rather than dominant *introverted* Feeling with auxiliary extraverted Sensing. This difference in dynamics leads to some striking differences, most notably in the way ESFJs are seen relative to psychological adaptation (males being among the highest on "Soundness" and females among the highest on both "Soundness" [on which female ISFPs were also high] and "Efficacy" [where ISFP females were among the lowest]). ESFJs are underrepresented in substance abuse groups, and unlike many other types they were also underrepresented among new college students referred to a substance abuse workshop. Apparently ESFJ behavior does not raise substance abuse concerns among college officials.

It is curious that one study found males to be underrepresented among men at risk for heart attacks, while another study found women to be the most frequent type with coronary heart disease. Replication and further study of this possible gender difference is called for, especially in light of the other results that suggest that ESFJs have a high mean level of coping resources, rank highly in using spiritual/philosophical resources, and are highest in coping with stress by relying on religion and by talking to someone else. They were second highest in believing in a higher spiritual power and highest in indicating satisfaction with their marriage or intimate relationship.

ESFJs seem to find environments with expectations of "toeing the line" a comfortable place to work. They are attracted to careers in education, health care, and religion, this latter a frequent way of coping with life stress as well. It is interesting that ESFJ desires for clear structure, loyalty, security, and making the job simple may more likely be met in the context of their other ESFJ qualities. ISFPs, who express the same values, may not have the same helpful context to help meet these desires. Perhaps as a result, ESFJs appear quite satisfied with many aspects of their work and do not intend to leave their jobs. Important values for ESFJs are "Health" and "Religion or spirituality," while they were found lowest in valuing "Autonomy, freedom, and independence."

Table 4.40   Research Describing ESFJ

Personality, Psychotherapy, Health, Stress, Coping	Males among three highest on "Soundness"; females among three highest on "Soundness" and "Efficacy"[1]
	Underrepresented among female substance abusers[2]
	Underrepresented among new college students referred for a substance abuse workshop[2]
	Males one of the three least common types in a substance abuse program[2]
	Underrepresented among females in a substance abuse program[2]
	Underrepresented among men at risk for heart attack[3]
	Most frequent type among women with coronary heart disease[3]
	With ENFJs, had the third-highest mean level of coping resources[3]
	With ENFJs, appeared to be at the lowest risk for setbacks due to overdoing among those with long-term pain[3]
	Ranked second in using spiritual/philosophical coping resources[3]
	In national sample, highest in coping with stress by "Talking to someone close" and "Relying on religious beliefs"[4]
	In national sample, ranked second highest in believing in higher spiritual power[4]
	In national sample, ranked highest in satisfaction with "Marriage/intimate relationship"[4]
Education	Males among three lowest on two out of three measures of creativity[5]
	Most frequent type among education majors[6]
	Among highest in college retention[6]
	Most frequent among high school officers in health occupations association[6]
	In national sample "Leisure Activities," underrepresented in "Writing"[6]
	Lower on deductive reasoning, with other dominant Feeling types[7]
	Academic subjects preferred: math, music[8]
Careers	Had highest satisfaction with co-workers in career satisfaction study[9]
	Most important features of an ideal job: service to others[9]
	Highest of all types in national sample in liking work environments with "Toe the line expectations"; among three highest types favoring "Clear structure," "Loyalty and security," and "Making the job as simple as possible"[10]
	In national sample, among those most satisfied with their work and where they work, and unlikely to leave[10]
	In national sample "Organizational Values," place high value on "Happy family," "Outgoing affiliation," and "Business sociability"[10]
	In national sample, among top four types valuing "Home/family," "Health," "Friendships," "Financial security," "Spirituality," "Community service," and "Prestige"[10]
	In national sample, greatest work environment satisfiers were "People I work with," "Amount of responsibility," "Opportunity for societal contribution"[10]
	In national sample, ranked highest in valuing "Health" and "Religion or spirituality" and lowest in valuing "Autonomy, freedom, independence"[10]
	Underrepresented among working MBA students compared with national sample[10]
	Occupational trends identified: education, health care, religion[10]
Organizations, Leadership, Management, Teams	Higher on CPI scales Sy, So, Cm, Ac, Fm; lower on Ai, Ie, Py, Fx, In[11]
	Higher on LSI scales Changeable, Energetic, Forceful, Initiating, Resourceful[12]
	In a study of the influence of type dynamics on ways of dealing with conflict, tended to collaborate[13]

Note: [11]Brief definitions of these CPI scales can be found in Chapter 13, "Uses of Type in Organizations." See Table 4.26; [12]Tables 4.26–4.41 report ratings by subordinates of types that were significantly higher or lower on various leadership scales, relative to the other types.

Source: [1]Highest three and lowest three types on two measures of personal adjustment ("Soundness" and "Efficacy"), which were calculated separately for males and females. Thorne & Gough, 1991; [2]Quenk & Quenk, 1996; [3]Shelton, 1996; [4]See Chapter 10, "Uses of Type in Counseling and Psychotherapy"; [5]Highest three and lowest three types on three measures of creativity, calculated separately for males and females. Thorne & Gough, 1991; [6]See Chapter 11, "Uses of Type in Education"; [7]DiTiberio, 1996; [8]Myers & McCaulley, 1985; [9]Hammer, 1996a; [10]See Chapter 12, "Uses of Type in Career Counseling"; [11]A study that compared the mean scores of the 16 types on the scales of the CPI using a sample of 15,102 people who attended leadership development programs at the Center for Creative Leadership. Fleenor, 1997; [12]Results in the same study at the Center for Creative Leadership on the *Leadership Style Indicator* (LSI); [13]Hammer & Huszczo, 1996.

CPI data for ESFJs show them higher on Sociability, Socialization, Communality, Achievement via Conformity, and Femininity/Masculinity and lower on Achievement via Independence, Intellectual Efficiency, Psychological-Mindedness, Flexibility, and Independence—all results that make sense given the natural approach of ESFJs. They are higher on leadership scales of Changeable, Energetic, Forceful, Initiating, and Resourceful, in contrast to the single leadership scale Easygoing that was reported for ISFPs. ESFJs tend to collaborate in dealing with conflict.

The data suggest that ESFJs embody qualities that are in general highly respected and valued in our culture. This may contribute to their standing on the various stress indicators shown, as well as in their general satisfaction with many aspects of their lives.

ENFJ: Extraverted Feeling with Introverted Intuition

Dominant function: F_E

Auxiliary function: N_I

Tertiary function: S_I

Fourth/inferior function: T_I

At Their Best   People with ENFJ preferences are highly attuned to others, using empathy to quickly understand emotional needs, motivations, and concerns. Their focus is on supporting others and encouraging their growth.

ENFJs are friendly persuaders who can often build consensus among people whose interests and motives are quite diverse. They often act as catalysts, including everyone and drawing out the best in others. They can be inspiring leaders as well as loyal followers.

Characteristics of ENFJs   ENFJs base decisions on personal values. They use their Feeling primarily externally, radiating warmth and energy. They look for and find the best in others and prize harmony and cooperation. They are warmed by approval, responding with energy and devotion, and especially sensitive to criticism or tensions. ENFJs are likely to be

- Warm, compassionate, and supportive
- Loyal and trustworthy

ENFJs see meanings and connections and can be very insightful about others. They are curious about new ideas and stimulated by possibilities for contributing to the good of humanity. ENFJs are likely to

- Be imaginative and creative
- Like variety and new challenges

ENFJs naturally see the potential for growth in others and devote energy to help others achieve it. They are sensitive facilitators. ENFJs take responsibility to organize interactions of colleagues, friends, or family so that all are involved, harmony prevails, and people have fun.

How Others May See Them   ENFJs are energetic, enthusiastic, and very aware of others. Their genuine interest can usually draw out and involve even the most reserved person. They listen to and support others but also have very definite values and opinions of their own, which they will express clearly. ENFJs are energized by people and are socially adept; however, they also have a strong need for authentic, intimate relationships. They bring great enthusiasm and intensity to creating and maintaining these.

ENFJs like their lives to be organized and will work to bring closure to ambiguous relationships or situations. However, if people's needs conflict with schedules and rules, they will put people first. Others usually see ENFJs as

- Sociable, personable, congenial, and gracious
- Expressive, responsive, and persuasive

Potential Areas for Growth   Sometimes life circumstances have not supported ENFJs in the development and expression of their Intuitive and Feeling preferences.

- If they have not developed their Intuition, ENFJs may not see possibilities, making decisions too quickly without taking in enough information or considering factors beyond their own personal values.
- If they have not developed their Feeling, their decisions may be inconsistent and poorly formulated. They may then accept the judgments of others too readily.

If ENFJs do not find a place where they can use their gifts and be appreciated for their contributions, they usually feel frustrated and may

- Worry, feel guilty, and doubt themselves
- Become insistent and controlling in their desire for harmony
- Be overly sensitive to criticism, real or imagined

It is natural for ENFJs to give less attention to their non-preferred Thinking and Sensing parts. If they neglect these too much, however, they may

- Make decisions based solely on personal values when logic is needed also
- Find it difficult to admit to problems or disagreements with people they care about
- Overlook details required to realize their ideals

Under great stress, ENFJs may find themselves suddenly and uncharacteristically critical and fault-finding with others. They generally keep these negative opinions to themselves, but they find such thoughts troubling and upsetting.

Table 4.41 summarizes relevant research results for ENFJs. Like ESFJs, ENFJs seem to be well in accord with societal values and expectations. Male ENFJs are among the highest on the "Efficacy" measure of adaptation rather than the "Soundness" measure observed for ESFJ males, and females are similar to ESFJ females in being high on both measures.

Table 4.41   Research Describing ENFJ

Personality, Psychotherapy, Health, Stress, Coping	Active, pleasant, sociable, demanding, impatient[1]
	Males among three highest on "Efficacy"; females among three highest on "Soundness" and "Efficacy"[2]
	With ESFJs, had the third-highest mean level of coping resources[3]
	With ESFJs, appeared to be at the lowest risk for setbacks due to overdoing among those with long-term pain[3]
	Highest ranks on coping resources used were social and cognitive (ranked third on both among the 16 types); ranked third in total resources of the 16 types[3]
	One of the four types in college reporting the highest levels of assertiveness[3]
	In national sample, highest in coping with stress by "Exercising"[4]
	In national sample, ranked highest in "Belief in a higher spiritual power"[4]
	Ranked fourth lowest on "Depersonalization" burnout scale[4]
	Ranked third highest in "Positive affectivity" and second lowest in "Negative affectivity"[4]
Education	Females among three highest on one out of two measures of creativity[5]
	Rated by psychologists among two types least likely to have trouble in school[6]
	Frequently represented among college RAs[6]
	Most frequent type in ten-year study of college RAs[6]
	Among lowest in college retention[6]
	In national sample "Leisure Activities," overrepresented in "Appreciating art," "Writing," "Listening to music," and "Reading"; underrepresented in "Watching TV three hours or more per day"[6]
	Performed lower on deductive reasoning, with other dominant Feeling types[7]
	Academic subjects preferred: art, English, music[8]
Career	Most important features of an ideal job: "Use of my special abilities"[9]
	Among three highest types in national sample liking work environments with "Variety of tasks," "Teamwork," and "People from different backgrounds"; include in three most desirable characteristics "Independence & achievement"[10]
	In national sample, were among those most satisfied with their work and where they work, but likely to leave the job[10]
	In national sample "Organizational Values," placed high value on "Nurturing affiliation"[10]
	In national sample, among top four types valuing "Friendships," "Learning," "Creativity," and "Community service"[10]
	In national sample, greatest work environment satisfiers are "People I work with," "Opportunities to use talents," "Opportunity to learn," "Job security," "Amount of responsibility," and "Opportunity for societal contribution"; greatest dissatisfiers were "Promotions" and "Salary"[10]
	In national sample, ranked highest in valuing "Education, learning" and "Community service"[10]
	Occupational trends identified: religion, arts[10]
Organizations, Leadership, Management, Teams	Higher on CPI scales Do, Cs, Sy, Sp, Sa, Re, To, Gi, Ac, Ai, Ie, Py, Fx, Em; lower on none[11]
	Higher on LSI scales Appreciative, Compromising, Delegating, Energetic, Fair, Resourceful, Supportive[12]
	Tended to collaborate in a study of the influence of type dynamics on ways of dealing with conflict[13]

Note: [11]Brief definitions of these CPI scales can be found in Chapter 13, "Uses of Type in Organizations." See Table 4.26; [12]Tables 4.26–4.41 report ratings by subordinates of types that were significantly higher or lower on various leadership scales, relative to the other types.

Source: [1]Summary of salient ACL data and Q-Sort descriptions of 12 of the 16 types. Raters were naive to type when making their ratings. Thorne & Gough, 1991; [2]Highest three and lowest three types on two measures of personal adjustment ("Soundness" and "Efficacy"), which were calculated separately for males and females. Thorne & Gough, 1991; [3]Shelton, 1996; [4]See Chapter 10, "Uses of Type in Counseling and Psychotherapy"; [5]Highest three and lowest three types on three measures of creativity, calculated separately for males and females. Thorne & Gough, 1991; [6]See Chapter 11, "Uses of Type in Education"; [7]DiTiberio, 1996; [8]Myers & McCaulley, 1985; [9]Hammer, 1996a; [10]See Chapter 12, "Uses of Type in Career Counseling"; [11]A study that compared the mean scores of the 16 types on the scales of the CPI using a sample of 15,102 people who attended leadership development programs at the Center for Creative Leadership. Fleenor, 1997; [12]Results in the same study at the Center for Creative Leadership on the *Leadership Style Indicator* (LSI); [13]Hammer & Huszczo, 1996.

ENFJs are highest in using social and cognitive coping resources and are similar to ESFJs in being high on coping resources in general. They, too, value religion and spirituality and are the highest in belief in a higher spiritual power.

Many additional qualities and differences from ESFJs are also apparent. ENFJs are low on the "Depersonalization" burnout scale, are high in positive affectivity, and are low in negative affectivity. In addition, females are high on one measure of creativity and are seen as least likely to have trouble in school. Leisure activities that show overrepresentation reflect artistic and intellectual interests, especially in liking writing, in which ESFJs were underrepresented.

Career and organizational results reflect a liking for variety in both tasks and people. They value friendships, learning, creativity, and community service and are among the types most satisfied with their work and where they work. It is therefore interesting that they also report an intention to leave their jobs.

ENFJs are similar to ESFJs on the CPI scales Sociability and Achievement via Conformance. They are reported as higher on Dominance, Capacity for Status, Social Presence, Self-Acceptance, Responsibility, Tolerance, Good Impression, Achievement via Independence, Intellectual Efficiency, Psychological-Mindedness, Flexibility, and Empathy. They are not lower on any CPI scales, unlike ESFJs, who are lower on four of the five on which ENFJs are higher. ENFJ leadership variables differ from those of ESFJs except in being similarly high on Energetic and Resourceful measures. ENFJs are higher on Changeable, Forceful, and Initiating, as compared with the ESFJ high standing on Appreciative, Compromising, Delegating, Fair, and Supportive. Like ESFJs, however, ENFJs tend to compromise in conflict situations.

ENFJs appear from these research data to have many of the people-oriented, cooperative qualities of ESFJs but also appear to enjoy more future-oriented, broad ranging interests that make them seem more ambitious and individualistic in their approach. In contrast to INFPs, whose dominant Feeling function is *introverted* and whose auxiliary Intuition is *extraverted,* ENFJs have desires, competencies, and satisfactions that appear to conform well to what is recognized and valued in the larger culture.

Conclusion

The foregoing descriptions and supporting research show how particular patterns that appear in the type table and the 16 types themselves can be studied and interpreted. The descriptions of two-letter combinations and whole types contained in this chapter are not exhaustive but aim to provide the essential features that make preference combinations and types recognizable and meaningful.

Research results in particular should be viewed as suggestive rather than definitive. The discussions of each research table sometimes include suggestions about the rationale for and implications of research results. It is important to view these suggestions as hypotheses that require careful empirical research and observation. It is equally important to be cautious in generalizing any of the research results to individuals of any type, especially in overinterpreting both "positive"-seeming and "negative"-appearing characteristics. Bear in mind that many of the variables that appear in these research tables are traits with explicit or implicit positive or negative values associated with particular scores. For example, it is clearly "better" to be higher on measures of adaptation than lower, better to be low on the various stress indicators than to be high, better to have many coping resources than few, better to be "creative," obtain high grades, be socially at ease and achievement oriented, and so on.

Readers may have noted that although single preferences and/or combinations of preferences may account for some of the effects reported for each type, the unique combination of effects shown, even given the reporting constraints listed earlier, can best be understood within the context of the dynamic whole type. Practitioners and researchers may find it intriguing that some types who share the same dominant function in the same attitude show quite similar research results, while for others the different auxiliary functions appear to produce marked differences. If this is not an artifact resulting from the particular variables reviewed, it implies even greater complexity and uniqueness to the type system for describing and explaining personality.

Practitioners and researchers might also take note of the observation made in the discussion of ISTPs, where it was suggested that the same behavior can be motivated differently for different types, and that each type may fulfill the same needs and desires through quite different behaviors. It is useful to take this into account when trying to understand type similarities and differences.

One important result of presenting descriptions of the type combinations and types together with observational and research data is that it highlights the fact that for type theory and the MBTI, the whole is greater than the sum of the parts. Researchers can thus be further encouraged to study whole types and type dynamic groupings to yield meaningful and useful results. The conjunction of theory, observational data, and research evidence provides a unique opportunity to look at the breadth and depth of type influences in many areas of human functioning. This approach to type knowledge also affirms the reality of psychological types as dynamic wholes that have an important unifying impact on our individual personalities.

Administration and Interpretation

The two chapters in Part III represent Myers and Briggs' overriding reason for developing the MBTI—the desire to make psychological type theory useful in the lives of individuals and groups. Administering the instrument as recommended and learning to interpret it in the ways intended by its authors are essential to using psychological type for the benefit of the individuals who answer the questionnaire.

Chapter 5, "Administering the MBTI," covers everything that users need to attend to at this critical entry point into the process of providing type results to clients. It covers the who, what, and how of administration by discussing which groups of people are appropriate respondents to the Indicator, how to decide which form of the instrument serves particular purposes, and how to ensure that respondents are free to indicate their preferences most accurately. As you read Chapter 5, you will become aware of the following:

- Type theory leads us to expect young people to be less clear than older people in their preferences.
- Translating the MBTI into other languages is a lengthy and arduous task.
- Careful adherence to administration guidelines can forestall possible misuses of type results.
- There may be special issues associated with administering the MBTI in different settings.
- The MBTI can be administered in several ways, including on-line administration.

Chapter 6, "Interpreting Results of the MBTI and Verifying Type," gives readers both general guidelines and specific recommendations for the most effective ways of explaining type to individuals and groups. In a very real way, all of the information in the manual is in support of accurate interpretations that focus on the value of the MBTI to the client. A major portion of the chapter is devoted to a discussion of ways in which practitioners can help clients verify their type so that it can become beneficial to them in their everyday lives. As you read Chapter 6, you will become aware of the following:

- There are important distinctions between "reported type," "best-fit type," and "true type."
- The percentage of people who agree with their reported type tends to vary depending on the group being studied and the methodology that is used.
- It is important to allow people to self-assess their type before providing them with MBTI results.
- It is important to include some basic information about type dynamics and development in every interpretation session.

- Respondents should be made aware that the MBTI sorts people into qualitatively different categories rather than measuring how much of some trait they have.

Readers of Chapter 6 should be particularly attentive to the recommended language for explaining type to clients. The language guidelines used throughout the manual are designed to discourage the use of jargonlike terms that negatively affect the credibility and professional purposes of the MBTI. The use of certain shorthand terms also encourages stereotyping and a "nothing-but" interpretation of type and type preferences. For example, referring to a person who prefers Feeling as a "Feeler" can be seen to imply that the person exclusively "feels" and never "thinks." Use of such a term also increases the likelihood that the hearer will misinterpret "Feeler" as meaning "a person who is emotional." Readers are encouraged to peruse the Glossary at the end of the manual as a way of becoming aware of terminological usages that lend themselves to stereotyping and misinterpretation.

Administering the MBTI 5

With all self-report instruments, it is important to create an atmosphere that ensures consistency of instructions, conditions, handling of respondent questions, and other administrative variables in order to obtain accurate reports. Particular care is warranted when administering the *Myers-Briggs Type Indicator* personality inventory because it seeks to maximize the respondents' freedom to reveal personality *preferences* rather than skills, abilities, or simple attitudes. In answering each question, respondents must choose between opposite aspects of personality, each of which they use at least some of the time; careful attention to administrative concerns is therefore encouraged. This chapter covers administration guidelines that are applicable in all settings and for all or most respondents. Special administration issues relevant to particular uses of the MBTI assessment tool are discussed in the appropriate application chapters (Chapters 10–14).

Appropriate Populations for Administration

The MBTI varies in the extent to which it is suitable for different kinds of respondents. This section discusses ages appropriate for administration, reading levels required, and translations.

Appropriate Age Groups

The original research for the MBTI measured the responses of a variety of populations from fourth-grade students to mature adults. When using the MBTI with high school students and adults who can read at least at the eighth-grade level, a professional can be reasonably confident of the reported type for individual guidance, provided that the reported type is never used as an established fact but rather is used as a hypothesis for verification.

The MBTI is most appropriate for adults and students ages 14 and over. Be sure to exercise caution in interpreting results with 12- and 13-year-old students; according to theory, type is less developed in young people than in mature individuals. Younger students are likely to have less complete and confident knowledge of themselves and therefore are less able to report about the attitudes and behaviors that underlie their personality preferences. This theoretical assumption is supported by the generally lower reliabilities found for younger respondents (see Chapter 8). However, if you are careful, you can successfully test younger people and provide them with information about their type. Results for younger people may also be used for research that explores type differences in interests or learning styles. You can effectively elicit type for students ages 7 through 12 using the *Murphy-Meisgeier Type Indicator for Children* (MMTIC), for which there is a separate manual (Meisgeier & Murphy, 1987).

Reading Levels Required

The reading level of a set of items can be approximately determined using a variety of approaches (DeVellis, 1991). However, conventional methods for assessing reading difficulty were not designed for test items, particularly an inventory that mixes forced-choice items and word pairs. Syntactic and semantic factors within the items—for example, simple versus complex sentence structure, the fact that each phrase item actually forms two sentences, and the context of the words for the reader—will affect reading levels that are based on formulas of sentence and word length. Thus, you should use common sense when determining the appropriateness of the MBTI for various populations.

The phrase items for Form M were analyzed using the Fry readability formula, which uses the average number of sentences and syllables in 100-word samples to assign approximate grade equivalents to written passages (Fry, 1977). This method yields a reading level of about seventh grade (approximately 12- to 13-year-olds) by treating each item as a single sentence.[1] Remember, however, that reading level is only an approximation and is not a substitute for knowing your clients well enough to assess the suitability of administering the MBTI to them.

Available Translations

Jung's theory is an attempt to describe basic human mental processes that cut across cultural differences. It is therefore reasonable to expect to find evidence of the existence of type and type differences in a wide range of cultures and countries. There are currently 14 commercial translations for which reliability and validity evidence are available and 15 additional translations listed as *research instruments*. Successfully translating the MBTI is a lengthy and arduous task due to the need to take into account cultural and language differences that affect item content and meaning. The procedure essentially requires repeating many of the steps Isabel B. Myers undertook in developing the original MBTI personality inventory. For further information on translations and issues in translating, see Chapter 14 of this manual and Kirby and Barger (1996). Translating into diverse languages is an ongoing process. For information on the status of translations into particular languages, contact the publisher, Consulting Psychologists Press.

Selection of the Appropriate Form

Several forms of the MBTI are available, all of which provide basic four-letter type information. These forms differ in the amount and kind of additional information provided. In selecting a form, consider the purpose of using the MBTI, the time available for testing, and the testing situation. Basic information about the forms appears in Table 5.1. Note that where indicated, computer scoring services and scoring software are available from the publisher.

Form M is now the standard form, replacing Form G. As detailed in Chapter 2, Form M contains the newest items, the most precise scoring procedure, and the most current standardization samples to produce scoring weights. Among other improvements over previous forms, this form was designed to maximize precision of preference identification at the midpoint of each dichotomy and to eliminate the need for separate scoring keys for males and females.

Form M and Form M self-scorable each contain 93 items, all of which are scored for type. Form G contains 126 items, 32 of which are research items not scored for type. The self-scorable version of Form G contains only the 94 items needed to produce type. Self-scorable forms of the Indicator have proven to be the most popular means to

Table 5.1   Forms of the MBTI

Form	Number of Items	Approximate Administration Time	Scoring Method for Four-Letter Type	Primary Uses
M	93	15–25 minutes	Templates or computer	In settings where MBTI can be given in advance
M self-scorable	93	15–25 minutes[1]	Hand-scored by respondent or administrator	Where time and subject availability are issues
G	126	30–40 minutes	Templates or computer	Preceded Form M as standard form
G self-scorable	94	20–30 minutes[1]	Hand-scored by respondent or administrator	Preceded Form M self-scorable
K	131	30–40 minutes	Form G templates or computer	Where EIR subscales will be reviewed later
J	290	75 minutes	Form F templates or computer	Where TDI subscales will be reviewed later

[1]Includes scoring time

Table 5.2   MBTI Profiles and Reports

Form	Report	Content
M or G	Profile	Basic preference information in a two-page report
M or G	Interpretive Report	Profile and interpretive description of reported type
M or G	Interpretive Report for Organizations	Profile and interpretive report that focuses on the individual's type as it is expressed in business and organizational settings
M or G	Team Report	"Team type profile" that describes the functioning of a team with that array of types
M or G	Career Report	Report linking client type with career information and strategies for improving job satisfaction
M or G	Strong & MBTI Career Report	Strong and MBTI results integrated for the client to identify occupations in a comprehensive career development system
K	Expanded Profile	Three-page profile of results on the Expanded Interpretive Report
K	Expanded Interpretive Report	Individualized narrative covering four-letter type, EIR profile and meaning of specific scores, and applications information
J	Type Differentiation Indicator Profile	Results on 27 subscales of the MBTI, including 20 EIR subscales and 7 Comfort-Discomfort scales

obtain results for four-letter type. Most of the items in Form K are used in producing the subscales of the MBTI Step II Expanded Interpretive Report (EIR). Form J is considered the current research form of the MBTI and includes most of the items in other forms. The large pool of items in Form J generates seven subscales in addition to those produced by Form K. These seven subscales in combination with the subscales of the EIR form the Type Differentiation Indicator (TDI). Both the EIR and TDI subscales are available only through computer scoring. For more information, consult the manuals for these scoring methods.

Various profiles and reports are generated by the different forms of the MBTI. Table 5.2 identifies these and shows the form or forms of the MBTI that produce particular profiles and reports.

Gaining Respondent Cooperation

The specific goal in administering the MBTI is to enable repondents to answer the questions in a manner that will reflect their hypothesized "true type" or, more specifically, their verified "best-fit" type. The term *true type* reflects the assumption that every person has an underlying "true" type that may or may not be revealed by a measurement device. As such, the type reported by an individual on the MBTI or in using any other assessment method is always considered to be a hypothesis rather than a "fact." Best-fit type is the type verified by the respondent after participating in an interpretation session with a qualified professional, reading alternative type descriptions, or using other verification procedures. Studies of best-fit type in relation to reported type are discussed in Chapters 2, 6, and 7.

You can maximize accurate assessment of type through the Indicator by attending to several administrative issues both before and during administration. In addition to the general guidelines discussed here, each area of application of the MBTI may have special administration issues. These are discussed in the relevant chapters in Part V.

The MBTI differs from many personality measures in that the results are designed primarily for respondents. However, many people who take the instrument are unaware of its differences from other personality measures. Therefore it is important to explain these differences prior to administration.

The practitioner should strive to create an atmosphere in which individuals are interested in their results, can respond freely to the items, and can feel confident that the results are for their own purposes, not for the benefit of other people. The MBTI items are reasonably transparent, and answers can be falsified. Using the MBTI for purposes such as job selection and advancement is therefore inappropriate, as respondents can easily answer the items so as to appear to be the type favored for a particular job or position within an organization. The MBTI can, however, be successfully included as part of the battery of tools typically used in personnel assessments. In such an application, the individual's type is not released to the manager, and there is a great deal of corroborating information on the individual from other tests, interviews, general employment history, and so forth. Practitioners should also be aware that the responsibility for using an instrument for assessment purposes lies with them as users.

Practitioners are responsible for being familiar with their own state guidelines on using an instrument for assessment purposes and with the intentions and wordings of the Americans with Disabilities Act, Civil Rights Act, Title VII, and other legislation dealing with privacy issues.

To minimize false responses, practitioners should provide respondents at the outset with consistent information about the voluntary nature of the testing process, the nature of the instrument, the purpose for which it is being administered, and the confidentiality of results. Thus potential respondents should be informed of the following:

Taking the MBTI is voluntary. Respondents who are required to take the instrument or who are subject to any form of coercion, such as employer or peer-group pressure to participate in the testing process, are unlikely to provide accurate results. Practitioners can increase respondent cooperation by assuring them that taking the Indicator is voluntary. In addition, the information below can often prove persuasive.

The MBTI does not assess mental or emotional health. The most accurate way of describing the nature of the MBTI is to tell respondents that it looks at naturally varying preferences in the way people take in information and make decisions; it does not reflect intelligence, competence, or mental health. With the proliferation of tests to measure a wide variety of competencies and mental or emotional disorders, respondents may be understandably concerned about what the Indicator will reveal about them. It may therefore be useful to point out to respondents that the MBTI items do not reflect competence or mental health because the items were not designed for these purposes.

The results belong to the respondent. The MBTI is primarily for the benefit of the individual respondent and serves that person's purpose. Purposes can involve applications such as career advisement, learning strategies, couples therapy, and team building. (See application chapters for useful ways of explaining the purposes of the MBTI in each area.) Where the MBTI assessment tool is administered solely for research purposes, researchers might wish to offer respondents personal feedback so they can verify individual results. Such a practice can increase cooperation and allow for more accurate data.

The respondent is the judge of the accuracy of results. A major feature of using the MBTI is the practice of having each respondent verify the accuracy of results. When people know that they will be told the results and invited to confirm or correct the report of their type, their answers are more likely to be genuine.

An individual's MBTI results are confidential. Respondents in a variety of circumstances have legitimate concerns about who will have access to their MBTI results and how such information will be used. Providing assurances that results will not be released without the respondent's permission can alleviate such concerns. Confidentiality can be an especially significant issue when the MBTI is administered in a work environment. See Chapter 13 for detailed recommendations.

Introducing the MBTI

When introducing the *Myers-Briggs Type Indicator* personality inventory, do not call it a *test;* instead refer to it as the MBTI, the Indicator, or the Myers-Briggs personality inventory or questionnaire. Emphasize the fact that the MBTI is designed to indicate equally valuable preferences and does not have right and wrong answers, as do achievement tests.

Some people have trouble finding the right mind-set for answering the MBTI. The setting in which they answer the questions may influence them to report their "work self," "school self," "ideal self," or some other self that is specific to external demands. Preferably, their frame of reference should reflect how they function most naturally, smoothly, and effortlessly, when they are not going "against the grain." Practitioners often use the term *shoes-off self,* but in some settings this expression might be interpreted negatively, for example in the military, where it may mean being lazy.

When asking respondents to take the MBTI, consider the probable type of the individual client or the likely distribution of types in the group. Sensitivity to the following can also increase cooperation:

- Sensing types will want to know that the information will have some practical value.
- Intuitive types will want to see possible future benefits. They may also find the choice between alternatives frustrating; they like the widest possible range of possibilities.
- Thinking types can be expected to be skeptical, since skepticism is an important aspect of their type. It helps to acknowledge the skepticism and suggest they "wait and see."
- Introverted types can be expected to be concerned with privacy issues and whether they may unknowingly reveal sensitive personal information. Administrators can assure them that the MBTI will not reveal anything hidden or negative about them. It will instead organize information they already know about themselves so as to provide an interesting and useful way of understanding themselves and others.

The MBTI is virtually self-administering. All necessary instructions are given on the cover of the question booklets and on the response sheets. In appropriate circumstances, respondents may be given or sent the question booklet and answer sheet for Forms M, G, K, or J to fill out and return for scoring. However, the subsequent verification and interpretation process should not be done through the mail or solely by providing written results without a professional interpreter.

Note that Form M self-scorable and Form G self-scorable are intended for use primarily with groups where administration time is an issue and circumstances do not permit prior administration and scoring. In line with the guidelines for interpretation given in Chapter 6, respondents should not be permitted to self-score the instrument before the interpreter provides them with information about type. Respondents should be encouraged to double-check their scoring to reduce the chance of error.

Regardless of the circumstances in which the MBTI is administered, the following should be reinforced, since many respondents read the instructions on the test booklet in a cursory fashion or not at all:

- Remember there are no right or wrong answers.
- It is best not to think too long about any question; your first response is likely to be most true for you.
- If you cannot decide on a question, skip it.

Guidelines During Administration

When administering the MBTI, these guidelines should be followed:

- Inform the individual that the MBTI has no time limit. Those who are making unusually slow progress, however, may be encouraged to work more rapidly and not study the items at length.
- In administering the MBTI to poor readers or younger children, it may be preferable to read the questions aloud; in reading, the examiner should be sure to sound open-minded and unbiased about both choices.
- When administering forms M, G, K, and J to students below age 17, inform them that many of the questions were originally written for adults and they are not expected to be able to answer every one. However, encourage them to answer all questions if they are able.
- Do not explain questions or meanings of words to respondents. In group testing, do not allow group members to discuss the items.
- When conducting group administration of the MBTI, read the instructions aloud, emphasizing the need for carefully filling in the identifying information. Note that a separate item booklet and answer sheet are provided for template scoring of Form M, so respondents should be careful to match numbers on the answer sheet to the numbers in the item booklet. Computer scoring of Form M requires administration of a single form that incorporates both questions and responses. The self-scorable forms also combine questions and answers in one form. Make sure to use the form that corresponds to the scoring method you plan to use.
- Omissions should be encouraged *only* if respondents do not understand a question or cannot choose an answer because neither choice is more appealing or descriptive of them than the other. The reason for permitting omissions is that no item can reliably contribute useful evidence of type unless choices are understood and the question lies within the respondent's experience. Information about percentages of omissions on Form M can be found in Chapter 7. In actual practice, only about 5% of respondents omit more than two items. However, where there are more than four omissions on the E–I or J–P dichotomy and more than five omissions on the S–N or T–F dichotomy, questions arise about the interpretability of those results. When Form M is computer scored, omissions exceeding these are flagged and a comment recommends caution in interpretation. Practitioners who use scoring templates should check answer sheets that contain more than three omissions overall to determine whether the omissions exceed the limits on any one dichotomy or are spread evenly throughout. Interpretation should proceed cautiously where the number of omissions on any dichotomy is excessive.

- When using the Indicator in work situations, be alert to employee concerns about the demographic question related to employee satisfaction, which is asked so that research on job satisfaction can be carried out. Some respondents may be concerned that the information on satisfaction will be relayed to their superiors. However, if answer sheets are handled with proper attention to issues of confidentiality, this should not be an issue. An explanation of confidentiality procedures should be provided to respondents. But if their concern persists, they can be told to skip that demographic question.

Scoring the MBTI Form M

Form M is the revised version of Form G. The similarities and differences between the two forms are presented in Chapter 2 of this manual. Because of the differences, the results for the two forms may differ as well (see Chapter 7 for data on the statistical relationship between Forms G and M). For the purpose of understanding the scoring for Form M, two differences are worth repeating here:

- Separate scoring for males and females on the T–F dichotomy is not used on Form M.
- Respondents are permitted to mark only one of the two choices provided for each question (there are a number of items on Form G with more than two response choices).

Results for Forms M and G may differ because the two forms are based on different items, scoring weights, and scoring procedures.

Self-scoring, template (hand) scoring, prepaid (mail-in) scoring, and on-site software scoring with the CPP Software System are all available for Form M, as they are for Form G. This section presents the instructions for scoring the self-scorable and template versions of Form M and provides a brief discussion of the software scoring. Users should be aware that templates are also available for scoring prepaid versions of Form M. A set of eight templates, one for each preference, is required.

The prepaid (mail-in) scoring and the on-site software scoring options for Form M use item response theory to derive the person's preferences, type, and preference clarity indexes. These IRT-based procedures yield the most precise classification of a respondent's preferences on the four dichotomies. Both scoring options also allow practitioners to generate their own detailed, computer-scored reports, which are listed in Table 5.2. The kinds of scores available from the mail-in scoring and the software, and a discussion of IRT scoring, are found in Chapter 7. The instructions for scoring Form G and for converting Form G raw scores to preference scores and continuous scores can be found in the 1985 *MBTI Manual*.

Both the template and self-scorable versions of Form M use unit weighting. So, unlike with Form G, there are no separate weights for each item response. Each response is counted as one point. A person's preference on a given scale is therefore the pole of the dichotomy that he or she chose most often. The advantage of using unit weighting is the simplicity of both the interpretation and the scoring, both important considerations when the MBTI is being used in a workshop or group setting when quick results are needed. However, unit weights are not as precise or accurate as the IRT method used with computer scoring because on the template and self-scorable versions, all items are considered to have equal amounts of information. On the computer-scored versions (prepaid mail-ins and on-site software), on the other hand, maximum use is made of all the information available from each item. Items that do a better job of separating people into opposite preferences receive more weight. So, for those who wish the most precise scoring, one of the computer-scored versions is required.

Template Scoring of Form M

Template scoring of Form M is accomplished using four templates, one for each of the E–I, S–N, T–F, J–P dichotomies. Separate scoring keys for males and females are not used with Form M. The T–F template can be used for both sexes. The procedure for scoring is as follows:

1. Place the template over the answer sheet, matching the square openings on the template to the asterisks on both sides of the answer sheet. This will expose the answers marked for E, S, T, or J, whichever template is being used.
2. Count the number of answers showing through the openings in the template to obtain the raw points for E, S, T, or J, whichever template is being used. Write the raw points for this scale in the space provided on the answer sheet.
3. Move the template to the left, matching the square openings on the template to the asterisks on both sides of the answer sheet. This will expose the answers marked for I, N, F, or P, whichever template is being used.
4. Count the number of answers showing through the openings in the template to obtain the raw points for I, N, F, or P, whichever template is being used. Write the raw points in the space provided on the answer sheet. Follow the same procedure for each dichotomy until you have determined all eight raw points.
5. For each individual dichotomy, look at the raw points for each pole and determine which has the larger point value. Write the letter and the number of that preference in the column titled "Preference Clarity Category." If the raw points are equal, write I, N, F or P, depending on the dichotomy, following the tie-breaking method used by Isabel Myers in previous forms of the Indicator (see Chapter 7 for the rationale involved).

Table 5.3   Example of MBTI Form M Template- and Self-Scorable Results

Pole of the Dichotomy	Raw Points	Pole of the Dichotomy	Raw Points	Preference	Preference Clarity
E	20	I	I	E	Very Clear
S	11	N	15	N	Slight
T	18	F	6	T	Moderate
J	19	P	3	J	Clear

6. [*Optional*] If you wish to report back to the respondent additional information about the clarity of his or her preference on each dichotomy, use the conversion table on the template. For that dichotomy, identify the highest raw points and then in the middle column of the table, find the range that contains that raw point value. Read across to the right column and identify the preference clarity category associated with that value. The preference clarity categories are "slight," "moderate," "clear," and "very clear" (see Chapter 6 for how to interpret these categories).

Answering and Scoring the Self-Scorable Form M

The procedure when using the self-scorable form of the MBTI is as follows:

1. Read each question and mark an X in the appropriate box. After all questions have been answered, open the perforation and turn the page.
2. Reading across each row, count the number of marks in each of the boxes in that row. Enter the total in the shaded box to the right of the row. Do this for each row.
3. Next, read down each column and add all the numbers in that column. Enter the total in the box at the bottom of the column. These numbers are the raw points for each preference.
4. For each dichotomy separately, look at the raw points for each pole and determine which has the largest point value. Write the letter of the preference with the largest point value. If the raw points are equal, write I, N, F or P, depending on the dichotomy.
5. [*Optional*] If you wish additional information about the clarity of your preference on each dichotomy, use the conversion table. For each dichotomy, identify the highest raw point value, and then in the first column of the conversion table, find the range that contains this raw point value. Then read across to the second column and identify the preference clarity category ("slight," "moderate," "clear," or "very clear") associated with this value. (See Chapter 6 for how to interpret these categories). If the raw points are equal, just look up that number in the table.

An Example of Template- and Self-Scorable Form M Results

An example of a person's results as they would appear on either the template- or self-scorable versions of Form M appears in Table 5.3, and preference clarity category conversion tables for all four scales appear in Table 5.4. The person whose scores are shown in Table 5.3 answered 20 of the 21 items on the E–I dichotomy in the E direction (there were 20 marks showing through the E part of the template, or there were 20 marks in the E column on the self-scorable), and therefore his raw points for E are 20. Repeating the scoring procedure with either the I portion of the template or the I column on the self-scorable, we find that the point value for I is 1. Because the raw points are 20 for E and 1 for I, the preference letter is E, which is entered on the top line of the results box on the template scoring sheet under "Preference."

Of course, knowing the total number of items on each scale allows you or the respondent to use subtraction to determine the raw points for the other preference on a given dichotomy, once the raw point value for the first preference is known. In this example, knowing that there are 21 items on the E–I scale and then subtracting the 20 raw points for E leaves 1 as the raw point value for I. It is recommended, however, that you also use both portions of the template for each scale, or count down both columns of the self-scorable, as a check on the accuracy of your counts.

The Form M template- and self-scorable versions emphasize the identification of the four preferences that yield a person's type. Determination of preference clarity through the preference clarity category (pcc) is optional when using these forms. The most important aim of emphasizing the preference rather than any estimate of the clarity of the preference is to discourage misinterpretation of the MBTI.

Practitioners and clients who want an estimate of preference clarity for the four dichotomies can use the conversion table shown in Table 5.4. To use this table, the procedure is as follows:

1. Look up the largest of the raw points for that dichotomy. In the example above, the person scored 20 on E and 1 on I.
2. Find the range in the E–I table that contains 20.

Table 5.4   Converting Raw Points to Preference Clarity Categories

Dichotomy	Greatest Raw Points	Preference Clarity Category
E–I	11–13	Slight
	14–16	Moderate
	17–19	Clear
	20–21	Very Clear
S–N	13–15	Slight
	16–20	Moderate
	21–24	Clear
	25–26	Very Clear
T–F	12–14	Slight
	15–18	Moderate
	19–22	Clear
	23–24	Very Clear
J–P	11–13	Slight
	14–16	Moderate
	17–20	Clear
	21–22	Very Clear

Note: Omitting items on a scale may result in the highest raw points on that scale being lower than the range found in this table. In this case, use "slight" as the pcc.

3. Read across to determine which preference clarity category this score represents. In this example, a 20 indicates a "very clear" preference.
4. Follow the same procedure for the preferences shown on each of the remaining three dichotomies.

The reason for deemphasizing scores on the MBTI is that scores are sometimes viewed as reflecting traits that identify greater or lesser proficiency, maturity, or accessibility of a preference.

Make sure clients clearly understand that the focus is on the direction of the preference. The preference clarity categories, like the more precise preference clarity index that results from computer scoring, do not reflect competence, maturity, or ease of access to their preferences. Even the pci, like its predecessor, the preference score, shows only how consistently a person answered the questions in the direction of the preferred pole of a dichotomy.

Using Results for Research Purposes

It is recommended that researchers use one of the computer-scored versions (prepaid mail-in or software) of Form M when the goal is to use scores for research purposes. This will allow the use of the θ scores that result from the IRT scoring, which are the most precise scores available. (It is

not recommended that the pci be used because preference clarity indexes have a more restricted range, which will result in attenuated correlations.) Note that using continuous scores for research is contradictory to the dichotomous nature of the MBTI. It does, however, allow investigators to examine relationships between single MBTI dichotomies and the many traits measured by other instruments using common quantitative statistical procedures. Be cautious in interpreting such results because the correlational method is not consistent with type theory. A preferred alternative to using continuous scores would be to use whole types, the preferences, or the preference clarity categories as independent variables. This would also allow for results from the template- and self-scorable versions of Form M to be used for research. These results can be examined using categorical analyses that are more congruent with type theory. See Chapter 9 for a more thorough discussion of issues associated with analyses of MBTI scores.

Software

The CPP Software System, which uses a Microsoft® Windows® environment, is available under license from the publisher for total on-site management of the MBTI. This system provides three options for MBTI online administration: the items presented to the client on the computer screen; a printed item booklet/answer sheet followed by key-in of the client's responses; an item booklet/answer sheet that can be scanned into the computer on-site.

Once the client's responses have been entered into the computer using one of these three methods, the professional can select the reports desired for immediate printing, for example the MBTI Interpretive Report or the MBTI Career Report. The software provides local customer options for printing.

To facilitate not only the selection and preparation of the appropriate reports but also the management of client information, client information and item responses are collected into a database. In addition, the database will help the professional track the administrations of the MBTI and other assessment tools that are available through the system (e.g., the *Strong Interest Inventory®*, the *California Psychological Inventory*, and the *Fundamental Interpersonal Relations Orientation-Behavior*™ [FIRO-B™]).

The client software module (the part of the software system used by the client when taking the items online) can be networked or installed from a floppy disk for administration of the MBTI at multiple computers. These results can then be transferred to a computer containing the licensed software to produce the appropriate reports and to be included in the database.

Internet Delivery of the MBTI

For electronic administration of the MBTI personality inventory, the CPP Web Administration Site is available under license from the publisher. This delivery system allows the professional to provide clients in remote locations with easy access to assessment via the World Wide Web. The site has been carefully developed to maintain confidentiality of results.

To access the MBTI, clients must receive a password from the professional with whom they are working. Once a client has taken the Inventory, the professional receives automatic notification via e-mail. The professional then downloads the client's responses to his or her own computer and uses the CPP Software System to generate any reports that are available on the system. The professional must then use standard type verification procedures for verifying client type, which can be found in Chapter 6. Other assessments such as the *Strong Interest Inventory* and the FIRO-B are also available through this delivery system.

Guidelines for helping clients verify their reported type appear in Chapter 6. Following these guidelines is important for all practitioners, including those who obtain MBTI results using the Internet.

Each professional with a Web Administration Site receives a unique Web address. He or she can choose to have a personalized introductory page that can include a logo, pertinent business information such as phone and fax numbers, a message to clients, and an e-mail link.

The Web Administration Site provides professionals a safe and efficient option for delivering assessments to clients. The availability of the MBTI and other assessment tools via the World Wide Web means that more clients can benefit from the important information provided through the various individualized reports.

Conclusion

People's assumptions and expectations about the MBTI are likely to be influenced by their previous experiences in answering questionnaires and participating in assessment procedures. The most critical first step in using this instrument is therefore to ensure that clients understand its purposes, how it will be useful to them, and how it differs from other instruments that appear to be similar. Carefully following the administration guidelines in this chapter will increase the likelihood of obtaining accurate results that will benefit the client. A practitioner who understands the rationale underlying the administration guidelines is in the best position to answer client questions and concerns in any situation in which the MBTI is administered. Many of the specific administration issues and possible client concerns are included in appropriate chapters in Part V.

Interpreting Results of the MBTI and Verifying Type

6

This chapter reviews issues in explaining *Myers-Briggs Type Indicator* personality inventory results to clients in any setting and in all areas of application. Special interpretation issues relevant to particular uses of the MBTI are discussed in the appropriate applications chapters (Chapters 10–14). Because MBTI reports are designed to be given directly to respondents, interpretation necessarily includes steps to help respondents verify the accuracy of their results through their own self-knowledge. Bear in mind, however, that whereas professionals may be appropriately skeptical about the capability of any measure to reflect the complexity of personality, laypeople may put too much trust in psychological test data. It is particularly important for interpreters to use strategies that encourage respondents to verify the report against their own experience. The risk of respondents being overly accepting of their results is greater for the Indicator than for instruments that report scores on a continuum because types are reported in letters and descriptions that can give the results a sense of certainty that goes beyond the actual data.

Research Evidence Regarding Reported and Verified Type

A number of researchers have looked at the percentage of respondents who agree with their type reports. Table 6.1 shows the results of four studies of reported and verified type. The studies listed are not strictly comparable because their research designs and the kinds of samples studied varied considerably. Across these studies, perfect agreement on all four letters of type varied from the low of 58%–68% reported by Kummerow to the high of 85% found by Hammer and Yeakley. Reports indicate that agreement on at least three of the four dichotomies is much higher, ranging from Kummerow's 90% to the 99% found by Hammer and Yeakley. The one study of respondents outside the United States involved a sample of 370 participants in type workshops in the United Kingdom. Results for this group were comparable to those for the U.S. samples. Note that in all four studies, Form G was used. Table 9.17 in Chapter 9 provides additional information about reported and best-fit type studies.

Both the Walck and the Hammer and Yeakley studies verify practitioner experience in finding that discrepancies between reported and best-fit type occur most frequently for dichotomies on which initial reported clarity of preference is slight. A slight preference means that the respondent has "split his or her vote," answering about half the items favoring each pole of the dichotomy. Analysis using Cohen's kappa (a measure of the agreement between two ratings) for the Kummerow study and the Hammer and Yeakley study as low and high estimates reveals a range from kappa = .59 as the low estimate to kappa = .79 as the high estimate, where kappa of 0 = no agreement and kappa of 1.00 = perfect agreement. Another way of interpreting the above reported and verified type data is to bear in mind that the expected agreement for any one of the 16 categories by chance alone is only 6.25%. The figures in Table 6.1, therefore, greatly exceed chance expectation.

Although interpreting and verifying type results are important even when respondents report clear preferences, a major task in interpretation is to help respondents with less clear reported preferences arrive at a comfortable and accurate assessment of their type. This is accomplished in an interpretation session mainly through an exploration of how type preferences appear in client behaviors.

Introducing the Interpretation

Interpretation of MBTI results should be a joint process between the professional giving the interpretation and the respondent reacting. The interpreter should never say flatly, "You *are* such and such a type." The statement not only

Table 6.1 Percentage of Respondents Who Agree with Their Type Reports

Source	Agree on 4 Letters	Agree on 3 Letters
Hammer & Yeakley, 1987	85%	99%
Kummerow, 1988	58%–68%	90%–95%
Walck, 1992a	75%	96%
Oxford Psychologists Press, 1993	76%	97%

sounds arbitrary and limiting but also may not be true. MBTI results are, of course, not always right. The reported type should be submitted to the respondent's judgment with statements such as, "This shows how you answered. Does it describe you, or does it fit you?"

As with any self-report instrument, the accuracy of the results depends in part on how willing or able the person is to self-report his or her preferences. If people answering the MBTI inventory feel that they have nothing to gain, they may answer carelessly or even at random. If they fear they have something to lose, they may answer as they assume they should. Many of the administration recommendations in the preceding chapter are ways of maximizing the accuracy of self-report. However, should there be reason to believe that a respondent did not answer candidly, appropriate inquiry might be made.

Essential Points to Make to Clients

It is strongly recommended that respondents self-assess their preferences *prior* to being provided with their MBTI results.

The following eight points are basic information for an initial interpretation session either with individuals or in a group setting. Incorporating them into the feedback plan ensures that a cooperative and collegial tone will be maintained throughout the interpretation and verification process. It is strongly recommended that these points be covered, an explanation of each of the dichotomies be provided, and an opportunity for self-assessment of preferences occur *before* any MBTI results are provided to individuals or groups. This sequence increases understanding, conveys respect for the individual's self-knowledge, and discourages respondents from agreeing too readily with their reported type.

1. No questions, however accurate, can lead to answers that explain all human complexity. The MBTI results give the respondent and the interpreter a hypothesis about an individual's type. As such, the results are a first step toward understanding the respondent's true or best-fit type.
2. Each item in the MBTI requires the respondent to make a choice between two opposite alternatives.

These choices may seem difficult because they all describe activities that are necessary and valuable. Such choices are more difficult than choices between things considered good or bad. It is often useful to describe the process of responding to the MBTI as one of casting votes in four "elections," each with two good candidates.

3. The terms and letters may seem a little strange at first, but the behaviors described by those terms typically are familiar to the respondent.

4. The MBTI is an "indicator," not a test. There are no right or wrong answers. There are also no good or bad, or sick or well, types. All types are valuable.

5. Whatever the type, one *does use* both sides of each dichotomy, though not with equal ease or liking. A useful analogy is that preferences are like handedness. For the most part, people are either right-handed or left-handed. However, people do use both hands, usually reaching first with the preferred hand because it is more comfortable and natural to do so.

6. People typically use and develop more ease and effectiveness with the functions and attitudes they like than with their opposites. However, because this is not always true, one should not assume that having a preference ensures using it skillfully or effectively.

7. Type preferences are important for understanding how people assimilate information and make decisions. They describe processes that will seem familiar to respondents. One value of type is that it helps people use the information they already know about themselves and others in more organized and practical ways.

8. If a reported function, attitude, or whole type does not seem right when MBTI results are provided, respondents can discover and decide for themselves, with help from the interpreter, which preference or which type more accurately describes them.

Explaining the Four Dichotomies

The next step is to explain the nature of the two alternatives that are included in each dichotomy. The following is a recommended procedure for presenting each dichotomy:

1. Define the dichotomy itself by focusing on what it describes. For example: "Extraversion and Introversion deal with how we are energized and how we prefer to use our energy."

2. Define each pole of the dichotomy and give examples relevant to the client's experience or purpose in taking the Indicator. Using language such as the following helps emphasize the important fact that everyone uses both poles of a dichotomy at least some of the time: "When we are extraverting, we are focusing on the outside world of people, the environment, and action. When we are introverting, our attention is on

our internal world of ideas, inner experiences, and reflection."

3. For each dichotomy, discuss the ways in which people who prefer one pole of a dichotomy differ from those who prefer its opposite. For example, "People who prefer Extraversion are likely to be energized by being around people and activities. Extraverts therefore typically seek out situations that permit them to experience and interact with the outside world. People who prefer Introversion are likely to be most energized when they can spend time alone in reflection. Introverts therefore typically seek out situations that permit them to do more introverting than extraverting."

It is helpful to modify the descriptions of the opposite preferences of each dichotomy to accommodate the respondent's type and the time available. Concrete behavioral examples are helpful for bringing the theoretical abstractions into everyday experience, especially when explaining type concepts to Sensing types. Visual aids and illustrative anecdotes that highlight differences are helpful for all types.

Verifying Type

Any type identification method, including an individual's responses to the Indicator, are subject to the errors in understanding and interpretation that are associated with all self-assessment methods. In light of the reliability and validity evidence reported in Chapters 8 and 9, reported type as elicited through the MBTI appears to be the best available personality type estimate for an individual. Nevertheless, the routine use of several corroborating verification methods is recommended in order either to provide maximum assurance that the reported type is correct or to enable identification of a different, better-fitting type. A number of such approaches to verification are described in this section.

An essential first step is to explain each preference in a neutral and unbiased manner and give examples of each pair of opposites that are relevant to the client's interests and life circumstances. When done carefully, this provides an illustration of type differences and is also a first check on the accuracy of the reported type. After each dichotomy has been described, clients should be given an opportunity to assess how they believe they came out in answering the Indicator. This may be accomplished simply by asking them how they think they came out—for example, "How do you think you answered on that one?" An alternative feedback procedure such as that described in *Verifying Your Type Preferences* (Kummerow, 1986) may be used. This is particularly helpful when giving feedback to groups, as it guides respondents through the initial process.

The interpreter may then tell the client which preference was actually reported. (Some respondents may prefer to have their results on the four dichotomies given to them all at once after they have heard about all the dichotomies. The interpreter can ask the respondent which procedure is preferred.) If the client's assessment agrees with reported results, the correctness of the reported preference is tentatively confirmed. When a characteristic is not confirmed, the preference in question should be considered to be in doubt and evaluated further.

In this portion of the feedback process, care should be taken to avoid implying that the client is "wrong" in her or his assessment or that the reported type holds greater weight than the client's self-knowledge. Language such as "You answered indicating the opposite preference of the dichotomy, so we'll have to explore that further" presents the required neutral stance in these circumstances.

Practitioners can choose from among a number of verification aids, depending on the interpreter's level of experience with MBTI interpretation and the needs of the client or client group. The material that follows describes each of these aids.

Brief Descriptions of Each Type

One way of checking the reported type is through the use of the table "Characteristics Frequently Associated with Each Type" on the back of the template scoring profile sheet and also included in *Introduction to Type,* which is discussed below. This table contains short type sketches. People often find it easier to recognize themselves among these miniature portraits than to recognize their preferences one at a time. The booklet *Profile of Your MBTI Results* (Lawrence & Martin, 1996) describes each of the 16 types using a bulleted list of characteristics. Some of the brief descriptions contained in the *Introduction to Type* booklets that are designed for specific groups can also be helpful. These are listed in the next section.

When using the brief type tables for verification, the individual should first read the type description that corresponds to the reported type and then compare this with neighboring type descriptions. Should another type description seem to fit the client as well or better, that type should be respectfully included for consideration as the individual's "best-fit" type.

Using *Introduction to Type*

If people who take the MBTI inventory are to make real use of the results, they need more information than is in the report form and more than they can remember from a verbal explanation. To meet this need, *Introduction to Type* was written to be used as an interpretation and verification tool. When MBTI results are provided to individuals or groups, the task is made simpler if people can further verify their initial assessment of their type by reading one or more of the full type descriptions in *Introduction to Type.* By allowing them to see the type contrasts, this booklet helps respondents "put it all together." Further, practitioners generally agree that people get the most out of type when they have access to *all* 16 type descriptions both during and after verification of their type. It is recommended that all individuals and group members be given a personal copy of *Introduction to Type* or an alternative set of descriptions of all 16 types.

For maximum and continuing type understanding, give each client a full set of type descriptions.

Since the original *Introduction to Type* was written by Isabel Briggs Myers in 1962, it has undergone several revisions. The current version is the sixth edition. It is a guide to understanding MBTI results for respondents in all situations. In addition, versions of the information contained in the booklet are available to address the additional interests of particular groups. These include *Introduction to Type Dynamics and Development* (Myers & Kirby, 1994), *Introduction to Type and Careers* (Hammer, 1993), *Introduction to Type and Teams* (Hirsh, 1998), *Introduction to Type in Organizations* (Hirsh & Kummerow, 1998), *Using Type in Selling* (Brock, 1994), and *Introduction to Type in College* (DiTiberio & Hammer, 1993).

Introduction to Type provides additional information that can be useful in helping a client verify his or her type. The following areas are covered:

- The mutual usefulness of opposite types
- The effects of preferences in work situations
- The effects of different pairings of the preferences
- Type and career choice
- Type and problem solving
- Type and relationships

The full-page type descriptions in *Introduction to Type* are included in Chapter 4. Each describes one type at its best, gives the characteristics of people of that type, describes how others see people of this type, and discusses potential areas for growth within the type. All 16 describe type as exemplified by normal, well-balanced, effective people. In theoretical terms, the descriptions assume adequate development of two processes, the dominant and the auxiliary. However, the section of the type description that discusses potential areas for growth includes information about the possible effects of lack of development of the auxiliary function and the dominant function, as well as a brief description of the natural consequences of devoting less energy to the tertiary and inferior functions.

The facing pages in all versions of *Introduction to Type* give a description of a pair of types with the same dominant process. The pair differ only in their auxiliary process. For example, for the two extraverted Thinking types, the descriptions on the facing pages are ESTJ and ENTJ; both are extraverted Thinking types, but ESTJ has introverted Sensing as the auxiliary process, and ENTJ has introverted Intuition as the auxiliary. Similarly, ISFP and INFP appear on facing pages. Both have introverted Feeling as their dominant function, but for ISFP, extraverted Sensing is the auxiliary, and for INFP, the auxiliary function is extraverted Intuition.

Development of the Type Descriptions

The sixth edition of *Introduction to Type* (ITT) is a revision of the 1993 (fifth) edition, by Linda K. Kirby and Katharine D. Myers. The original (1962) type descriptions, written by Isabel Myers, were firmly grounded in Jung's theory of psychological types, as developed and expanded by Myers and Briggs. Longtime users of the MBTI are aware of major differences in the style, format, and content of the fifth edition as compared to previous versions of the booklet. In developing the type descriptions in this edition, Kirby and Myers preserved the solid theoretical basis provided by Myers. In addition, they capitalized on a wealth of information from their own and others' research, many years of practitioner observations, and the knowledge of people who had expertise about their own and others' types. The revised type descriptions are based on the following resources and procedures:

- Myers' original type descriptions, as well as descriptions published in five different popular works, were reviewed. Statements describing each type were extracted and compiled by type into a questionnaire.
- The questionnaire was administered to groups of five or six people of each type, each of whom had taken the MBTI, received feedback, verified their type, and indicated confidence about their best-fit type—but who had little additional experience using type. About 120 people completed the questionnaire.
- The questionnaire was also sent to about 30 type experts—people who were very experienced and knowledgeable about type in general and about their own type as well.
- The results from both general respondents and type experts were combined with ratings of descriptors used in several research studies conducted by McCarley and Carskadon (1986) and Ruhl and Rodgers (1992). All of these data were compiled to identify descriptors that were ranked "very high," "high," "moderate," and "low."
- The highest-ranked descriptors were used in the ITT descriptions.
- Persons of each type were consulted to ensure that the final descriptors acccurately reflected the characteristics that each type considered to be most important as well as accurate.

These carefully developed type descriptions are further enhanced by the consistency and logic of their presentation. The type descriptions include the type at its best, as characterized by the dominant function and attitude and auxiliary function and attitude, as seen by others, and in terms of potential areas for growth—for example, when either the dominant or auxiliary function is not developed. Each description concludes with a picture of how each type appears in exaggerated form, when there is inadequate access to the tertiary and inferior functions, and when a person of that type is in the grip of the inferior function.

Explaining Type Dynamics and Development

An explanation of the dynamic nature of type theory and the MBTI is typically reserved for a later discussion of type, depending on the time available and the particular application involved. However, if the interpreter will not have a later opportunity to explain type dynamics and development to an individual or group, it is essential that a general explanation of this area be included in the interpretation session. When such a procedure is not included, respondents can easily dismiss their MBTI results as nothing but static and rigid categories or "boxes." Such a misunderstanding will limit a respondent's ability to make practical and effective use of the type information provided. At a minimum, therefore, when the interpreter has only a single opportunity to explain the MBTI, the following aspects of dynamics and development should be covered, at least briefly:

- A four-letter type reflects a dynamic and developmental system for describing personality. Each type typically uses the favorite forms of Perceiving and Judging in specific ways but is also free to use the less-preferred processes as well. A person's type does not change over time; however, people may express their type in somewhat different ways at different times and at different ages and stages of life. One consequence of this is that some people may answer the MBTI questions differently at different life stages.
- Each type has a dominant, or leading, function and tends to use it in the preferred attitude of Extraversion or Introversion. Each type also has an auxiliary, balancing function that tends to be used in the less-preferred attitude of Extraversion or Introversion. The title of each type in *Introduction to Type* identifies the dominant and auxiliary functions. For example, the title for ESTJ is *Extraverted Thinking with Introverted Sensing*. This indicates that for ESTJ types, extraverted Thinking is the dominant function and introverted Sensing is the auxiliary function. The title for INTP is *Introverted Thinking with Extraverted Intuition*, specifying introverted Thinking as the dominant function and extraverted Intuition as the auxiliary function.
- The function that is the polar opposite of the dominant function, called the *inferior function*, tends to be the least developed, least experienced, and least comfortable part of one's type. For example, the inferior function for ESTJ, whose dominant function is extraverted Thinking, is

introverted Feeling, the polar opposite of extraverted Thinking.

- The polar opposite of the auxiliary function is called the *tertiary function*. It tends to be somewhat more accessible and comfortable than the inferior function.
- The dynamics of type, as identified by the dominant, auxiliary, tertiary, and inferior functions, describe the individuality and richness of personality in ways that people can easily recognize and understand. These dynamics are embodied in the type descriptions in *Introduction to Type*.

In addition to covering these basic points, respondents can be directed to the booklet *Introduction to Type Dynamics and Development* (Myers & Kirby, 1994), which presents the dynamic information in a practical and accessible way.

Factors That Influence Accuracy of Self-Report

Each stage of the interpretive process gives information that the respondent can consider and use in evaluating the accuracy of his or her type. In some cases, there is instant recognition of the correctness of the results. For these people, most of the time spent on interpretation will be used in presenting type examples and practical applications. Other individuals have doubts about their type, and the steps described above are designed to bring out new information that may help resolve questions about which is their best-fit type.

Throughout the explanation process, the interpreter should keep in mind possible reasons why the MBTI results may not be an accurate estimate of that person's type. The working assumption of type theory is that each person has innate, or "true," preferences. It is important to be aware of reasons why type preferences may be incorrectly reported. These include the following:

- There may be a lack of differentiation of type. Such a lack occurs more often in young people whose development into a type may still be in the stage of exploration and experimentation. For example, during adolescence there is great value placed on many of the qualities associated with Extraversion. An adolescent who is trying to "fit in" may therefore answer the Indicator as an Extraverted type when in fact Introversion is his or her natural and comfortable preference.
- There may be difficulty in choosing between the expectations of one's parents and one's own preferences. For example, a Sensing type raised in a family in which the parents and siblings prefer Intuition may learn to value Intuitive qualities over Sensing qualities, attempt to develop those qualities, and therefore answer as an Intuitive type on the Indicator.

- The respondent may feel torn between demands of work and his or her own preferences. This source of bias can be greatly minimized through giving careful instructions to respondents when the MBTI is administered.
- The respondent may be in a life crisis and may not be using his or her typical mode of coping. Giving the Indicator when the client is experiencing unusual distress is generally not recommended.
- The MBTI may have been administered in a situation involving authority (e.g., for employment); sometimes respondents answer questions in terms of their perception of that authority's preferences instead of their own.
- The words used to explain the MBTI may have been misunderstood, and the respondent may have rejected the terms because of an assumed negative connotation, as when *Introversion* is interpreted to imply *neurotic* or *shy*, when *Judging* is interpreted to mean *judgmental*, or when *Feeling* is interpreted to mean *overemotional*. When explaining the MBTI, you may need to repeat a discussion of the meanings of these terms in the context of the MBTI.
- The individual may have been influenced by perceived social pressures. Such an effect is most likely to occur with the T–F dichotomy if the respondent equates Thinking with masculinity and Feeling with femininity.
- The respondent may have believed that the type description must fit his or her own characteristics perfectly to be accepted. Carefully explaining, before providing MBTI results, that there are a variety of *individual differences* within any particular type should minimize this effect.
- The respondent may be in a growth period in which previously unused or unappreciated processes are being developed. During such a period, there may be uncertainty about previously trusted processes as the less developed processes become differentiated. For example, during midlife a dominant Feeling type may become fascinated with logically analyzing life problems and correspondingly be less interested in solving problems by maintaining harmony.

All self-report instruments are subject to the kinds of effects described above and to many other effects not intended by those who administer them. Since the MBTI dichotomizes responses, and since the theory postulates "true preferences," the MBTI interpreter should be particularly careful during each stage of the interpretation to help individuals discover for themselves which pole of each dichotomy best fits them.

It is not necessary for the respondent to discover "true preferences" during the introductory session, but it *is* necessary for the interpreter to set the stage for the search. A key tool during interpretation is the full-page type description. Any qualms or demurs should be taken seriously. With experience, an interpreter can judge which of the above steps are necessary for a particular client and which may be omitted; however, the issues and strategies discussed above should be kept in mind during any interpretation.

Interpreting the Preference Clarity Index and Preference Clarity Categories on the MBTI

Quantitative interpretation of MBTI results as an indication that a respondent has "more" or "less" of a preference is incorrect. Such a practice is the most pervasive source of misunderstanding and misinterpretation of the MBTI. Unlike numerical scores on trait instruments that are designed to reflect an "amount" of the trait being measured, the MBTI preference clarity index (pci) is designed to show only how sure the respondent is that she or he prefers one pole of the dichotomy over its opposite. For forms that preceded the current Form M of the Indicator, the term *preference score* was used rather than *preference clarity index*. See Chapter 7 for the rationale for the change in designation and for the details of this index. The number associated with an MBTI preference, whether it is the previous preference score or the current preference clarity index, is most appropriately interpreted as providing information about the likelihood that the preference has been correctly reported. Any questions concerning a preference clarity index should focus on this meaning and be used for joint exploration of the preference at issue.

An alternative to reporting the pci itself is to present the preference clarity category ("slight," "moderate," "clear," "very clear") to the respondent instead. The meanings of these categories are discussed on the next page, but first some cautions are in order.

The preference clarity index is an estimate of relative confidence that a preference has been accurately identified. Any other quantitative interpretation of MBTI results is incorrect and leads to misunderstanding and misinterpretation.

Clarity Does Not Imply Excellence or Type Development

The most frequent error that occurs regarding the numerical portion of MBTI results is assuming that clarity of preference implies excellence; it is incorrect to assume that a person with a preference clarity index of N 30 has a better command of Intuition than a person with N 15. A larger number simply means that the respondent, *when forced to choose,* is more clear about what he or she prefers. While it frequently happens (and it is reasonable to expect) that those who report clear preferences (a) exercise them more and thus (b) are more likely to have developed the skills associated with those preferences and, further, that they (c) are more likely to develop the traits and habits associated with exercise of those skills, this sequence may have been interrupted in any given individual. For example, a person may answer the Indicator to reflect a very clear preference

for Thinking as a way of making decisions. However, for unknown reasons, his or her actual decision making may vacillate unpredictably and inappropriately between Thinking and Feeling, perhaps resulting in generally poor decision making. Another person with the same very clear preference for Thinking may use this preferred process to make generally consistent and satisfying decisions. The preference clarity index for each of these individuals *by itself* does not permit us to determine each individual's inadequacy or excellence in using the Thinking function.

For the same reasons cited regarding "excellence," preference clarity does not imply such concepts as degree of type development, or how "differentiated" a person is, or how well or poorly he or she will perform any given task or succeed or fail in any occupational setting. The use of preference clarity indexes to make such inferences is inappropriate, misleading, and damaging.

Use of the MBTI Step II to Clarify Preferences

The meaning of more and less clear preferences on all the MBTI dichotomies must be interpreted with caution, especially in light of the information available regarding the components or subscales that contribute meaning to each dichotomy. These components are elicited through the scoring of Form K of the MBTI, which yields the Step II Expanded Interpretive Report (EIR) mentioned in Chapter 5. The subscales associated with each MBTI dichotomy do not necessarily identify all the possible components of the underlying type construct, nor are such known and potential components equivalent to the complexity and breadth of Jung's constructs. Rather, each dichotomy not only is hypothesized to be greater than the sum of its identified parts but also is assumed to be influenced by each of the other dichotomies and their particular combination. However, observed patterns of subscale scores within each dichotomy can provide useful information about the clarity of a respondent's preference for one or the other pole of a dichotomy. For example, it is fairly common for respondents to have one or two subscale scores associated with the domain opposite to that of the underlying preference. Thus a person may have an underlying preference for Sensing, yet her Step II pattern of subscales may show her to be habitually using one or more components of Intuition. Such an individual may answer enough items in the Intuitive direction that a low preference clarity index for Sensing may result.

A detailed description of the Step II EIR subscales and their relationship to type preferences is beyond the scope of this manual. A complete description of this scoring system will be available in *Manual for the Step II Expanded Interpretive Report,* which is in press. In interpreting MBTI results, however, it is important to bear in mind that there are several alternative explanations for varying preference clarity indexes. An important possibility is a pattern of using specific components of an underlying preference in a manner that affects one's preference clarity on a dichotomy. The technical features associated with the pci can be found in Chapter 7. The following guidelines for Form M of the Indicator should therefore be viewed in such a context.

Guidelines for Interpreting the Preference Clarity Categories

The guidelines provided here are best used as aids to assist the type verification process. They provide information regarding the confidence one may have that a respondent holds the preference he or she has reported on each dichotomy of the Indicator.

Very Clear Preferences (pci 26–30) Respondents who report very clear preferences (roughly a pci of 26 or more) usually agree that they hold the preferences reported by the MBTI and often most of the characteristics that accompany those preferences. It can be useful to inquire during the interpretation session about how the person uses the less-preferred function or attitude when the situation demands it. For example, one might discuss how a respondent who reports a very clear preference for P meets required deadlines. Do not be surprised to find some respondents who are always on time despite their clear preference for Perceiving.

Clear Preferences (pci 16–25) When an individual's pci is 16 through 25, there is a reasonable probability that the respondent holds and acts on the reported preference and many of the attitudes and skills that accompany it.

Moderate Preferences (pci 6–15) With a preference clarity index of 6 through 15, the respondent may still most often agree with the description of the reported preference, but the interpreter should inquire whether the interpretation fits and should be alert for questions about preference during the explanation. It is quite likely that such an individual makes habitual use of one or more aspects of the opposite pole of the dichotomy and may spontaneously describe such use.

Slight Preferences (pci 1–5) When the preference clarity index is 1 through 5, a change of one or two questions could change the letter designation. The respondent has essentially "split the vote." The interpreter should carefully inquire about whether the reported preference is correct for the person. The interpretation and verification methods described earlier in the chapter will prove helpful here. For some people, less clear preferences reflect discomfort and dissatisfaction in using both domains of a dichotomy. For example, a slight T–F preference may be associated with a report of trouble in knowing whether "to follow my head or my heart." In many cases, however, such a result may be affected by the consistent and comfortable exercise of

Table 6.2 Percentage of Respondents on Form M at Each Level of Preference

Preference Clarity	E–I	S–N	T–F	J–P
Slight	23	21	28	22
Moderate	43	42	42	37
Clear	25	28	21	26
Very Clear	9	9	9	14

Note: N = 3,036. See Appendix for a description of the sample.
Source: National sample.

particular component parts of the T–F dichotomy, as described by Step II subscales. For example, it is not uncommon for a person who prefers Feeling to also reveal a "questioning" approach in decision making (a component of Thinking) rather than an "accommodating" approach (the opposite component of Feeling). Nevertheless, that person still has an underlying preference for the Feeling pole of the Thinking–Feeling dichotomy.

Social demands can also provide different pressures for men and women on the T–F dichotomy. Men are encouraged more toward Thinking activities and women toward Feeling activities. In data reported for Form G in the 1985 *Manual*, one-fifth to one-fourth of males and females showed slight preferences for all dichotomies but T–F. On the T–F dichotomy, two-fifths of males preferring Feeling and females preferring Thinking reported only slight preferences on T–F. In developing Form M, concern for issues around the T–F dichotomy led to the elimination of items that produced different responses for men and women. Items showing significant gender differences were also eliminated in Form M for the three other MBTI dichotomies. Because gender effects appear to be most pervasive for T–F, it is useful to inquire whether less clarity for a respondent indicates clear preferences that seem less clear to the respondent because he or she answered in a socially expected manner, or whether the lesser clarity indicates a conflict between sex role expectations and type preferences.

Interpreters and respondents who do not adequately understand type theory and the MBTI will sometimes interpret less clarity as advantageous, interpreting the "splitting of votes" as indicating good command of both domains. Such an interpretation is theoretically unsound in an approach that emphasizes the adaptive advantages of specialization of mental processes. In addition, there are no research data available that support a notion that "equality" of preferences is advantageous.

As shown in Table 6.2, people with clarity indexes in the "slight" category are not uncommon, ranging from 21% on the S–N dichotomy to 28% on the T–F dichotomy. Although the table does not give a breakdown of clarity of preference by the poles of the dichotomies, analysis indicates a fairly even distribution with the regard to the poles of E–I and T–F dichotomies. The percent of people reporting an E preference who fall in each preference clarity category is about equal to those reporting an I preference, and the same is true for the T–F dichotomy. However, about twice as many people who report a J preference fall into the "clear" and "very clear" categories as compared to those who report a P preference (26.4% versus 13.7%), and about three times as many of those reporting an S preference fall into the "very clear" and "clear" categories as compared to those reporting an N preference (28% versus 9%). Two factors must be considered in attempting to interpret these results. First, the data are based on the national sample, which included more Sensing and Judging types than Intuitive and Perceiving types. Second, the intervals included within the four pci categories are different. The "slight" and "very clear" categories have 5 intervals each (1–5 and 26–30, respectively), while the "moderate" and "clear" categories have 10 intervals each (6–15 and 16–25, respectively). For the practitioner, whether the observed differences in the poles of S–N and J–P are the result of sampling and/or interval influences is not a central concern. The practical implications of client differences in preference clarity are the important area for those who interpret the MBTI. Practitioners who can draw on a wide range of possible "explanations" that might account for different preference clarities will be best prepared to help respondents identify their best-fit type.

Comparative Clarity of Dominant and Auxiliary Functions

The 1985 *Manual* presented data relevant to the hypothesis that the dominant function will reasonably be expected to show greater clarity of preference than the auxiliary function. However, as discussed in Chapter 9, the hypothesis itself may not be an appropriate test of type theory. In addition, subscale patterns revealed in the MBTI Step II may help illuminate sources of differences in clarity for both dominant and auxiliary functions.

Comparison of Phrase Questions and Word-Pair Questions

The preferences for E–I, S–N, T–F, and J–P can be divided into that portion that is obtained from the phrase questions and the portion elicited by word pairs. Computer reports of type results typically provide a preference clarity index for the total of MBTI responses as well as for the phrase question and word-pair question parts. The statement in the 1985 *Manual* that "there is little research dealing with differential responses to Word Pair and Phrase Questions" (Myers & McCaulley, 1985, p. 61) continues to be true at this time of manual revision. The single study reviewed at that time (Nechworth & Carskadon, 1979) has not stimulated additional research on this topic. Inferences about the possible meaning of phrase and word-pair discrepancies are therefore discouraged. In fact, the sections of the profile and narrative that reported scores and types for word-pair and phrase questions separately are no longer provided in the revised computer profile and report.

Conclusion

The interpreter's role is not to determine the accuracy of the MBTI personality inventory. The interpreter's task is to provide ways in which respondents can understand their best and most trustworthy way of functioning. While experience generally shows that clear preferences are likely to be seen as accurate, the interpreter should be prepared for the occasional case in which very clearly reported preferences are the result of the individual's overreaction to doubts about the opposite domain, which may actually be the one the individual prefers. There are also cases in which less clear preferences are subjectively experienced by respondents as clear and consistent. One explanation for this may be the particular pattern the individual may show on component parts of the underlying type dichotomy. As with all psychological instruments, the interpreter should keep in mind that self-report from a limited number of questions, no matter how carefully validated, cannot completely describe any human being. In addition, a small percentage of people may not identify with a psychological type perspective of personality. For these individuals, some other explanatory approach may be more appropriate and meaningful.

Research

Research relevant to the MBTI appears in the three chapters of Part IV, which cover construction, reliability, and validity of the instrument. In addition to the standard information that all test manuals provide in these areas, issues related to the appropriateness of methods and the meaning of results must also be considered in light of Jung's theory upon which the instrument is based. These issues are an important element in all three chapters of Part IV.

Chapter 7, "Construction and Properties of the MBTI," summarizes the lengthy construction efforts of Isabel Briggs Myers that produced Forms A through G of the Indicator. The same theory-based requirements for these forms were addressed in creating Form M, whose items were selected using item response theory. As you read Chapter 7, you will become aware of the following:

- Why all items appear in a forced-choice format and not some other format
- What is meant by a psychological opposite
- How item response theory differs from classical test theory—the approach used in creating previous forms of the MBTI
- The multiple requirements for adding and deleting items in creating Form M
- Why determining the midpoint on each dichotomy is critical
- The characteristics of the national sample used to create Form M

Chapter 8, "Reliability and Measurement Precision," covers the various ways the reliability of the MBTI has been studied. In establishing the reliability of the MBTI, continuous scores on the four scales are used to produce internal consistency and test-retest estimates in a manner that is similar to that used for trait-based instruments. However, the most important aspect of reliability for the MBTI is the consistency of categorical results—whether the respondent is the same type on retest and whether the respondent shows consistent results on different parts of the instrument. Chapter 8 presents reliability evidence from both perspectives. As you read Chapter 8, you will become aware of the following:

- How internal consistency was studied using a "logical split-half" procedure
- The improvement in reliability of Form M over Form G
- How type development influences reliability results in some samples
- Why test-retest categorical agreement can never reach 100%
- The "equivalence" of some item response theory terms to familiar classical test theory terms

In Chapter 9, "Validity," the emphasis is on research on type dynamics and whole types rather than on individual dichotomies, whose validity has been well established. Establishing the validity of each of the dichotomies was a necessary and important aspect of validating the MBTI in earlier years. However, an unfortunate consequence of this focus was the interpretation of the MBTI as reflecting four independent traits—a point of view that was familiar to researchers and for which many statistical techniques were available. Some evidence for the validity of the four dichotomies that was included in the 1985 *Manual* appears in summary form in this chapter, and new data are also presented. The bulk of this chapter, however, consists of evidence that supports the dichotomous nature of the dimensions, the interactive effects specified by type dynamics, and the distinctiveness of whole types. As you read Chapter 9, you will become aware of the following:

- Why discontinuity on a scale supports the existence of a dichotomy
- How the different behaviors of the types is one way to demonstrate validity
- That there are type-consistent relationships to areas such as orientation to time, preference for privacy, anxiety and conformity, and specialty choice in medicine
- Why multiple dependent variables are needed to study whole types
- Two of the ways of studying type dynamics—observer ratings and analysis of variance
- How unique descriptions of whole types by observers provide powerful evidence for the distinctiveness of each type

In reading Part IV, readers may note that the same or similar statements or research data appear in more than one chapter. In addition, some statements and research evidence that are included in the chapters of Part IV may reappear in the applications chapters of Part V. There are several reasons for these repetitions: First, the focus in presenting research may differ in two different chapters—a study that provides validity evidence may also be informative with regard to reliability or to applying the MBTI in a particular setting. Second, some readers of this manual may "dip into" one or another chapter depending on their particular needs and interests rather than reading the chapters in the order in which they appear. They therefore may not have come upon data that are actually relevant to their interests. Third, some information bears repetition simply because it is critical to understanding the MBTI in a variety of contexts.

Construction and Properties of the MBTI

7

The purpose of this chapter is to describe the construction of Form M of the *Myers-Briggs Type Indicator* personality inventory. As discussed in Chapter 2 of this manual, the construction of Form M followed the same general principles as did the construction of the previous forms. The goal was to balance the long tradition of the Indicator with changes suggested by new psychometric approaches. To understand the construction of Form M, therefore, it is important to understand how the previous forms of the Indicator were developed.

The challenges involved in constructing the MBTI derive from the nature of Carl G. Jung's theory of psychological types. These challenges are not typical of most psychological measures because the intent of the Indicator is not to measure people or the traits they are said to "have" or possess, but rather to sort people into groups to which, in theory, they already belong.

All of the forms described in this chapter, including Form M, are designed for Step I of the Indicator, which involves knowing and understanding a person's type. Step I identifies a person's preference on each of four dichotomous scales, E–I, S–N, T–F and J–P. The preferences indicated for these four scales are then combined to yield a four-letter type. As mentioned earlier in this manual, in addition to Step I there are two other scoring methods for the MBTI, called Step II and Step III. Step II yields the four-letter type as well as scores on 20 subscales. Step III adds scores on an additional seven scales, known as the Comfort-Discomfort scales. Construction of Steps II and III are not described in this chapter; the relevant technical material for these steps can be found in their respective manuals (Saunders, 1989, 1987).

As outlined briefly in Chapter 2, the construction of the MBTI was governed by a working hypothesis: that certain valuable differences in normal people result from their preferred ways of using perception and judgment. Consonant with Jung's theory, using the MBTI to determine preferences requires that a person choose between two opposites on each of the four scales. Each scale included in Step I scoring is therefore a dichotomy. The four separate scales designed to determine a respondent's preferences represent the following four dichotomies:

Extraversion or Introversion

Sensing or Intuition

Thinking or Feeling

Judging or Perceiving

The object of the MBTI is to determine the person's preference on each of these four dichotomies so that these results can be reported to the person as a four-letter type. Although the measurement of preferences is currently obtained on four individual scales, the results are meant to be interpreted as whole types. The assumption is that the whole is greater than the sum of the parts. The theoretical rationale for this assumption is presented in Chapter 3 in this manual. The evidence supporting this claim is presented throughout this manual, but particularly in Chapter 9.

History of the Development of Previous MBTI Forms

This section summarizes the development of the MBTI, up to and including Form J of the instrument. Development through Form J occurred in a series of stages, beginning in 1942, continuing to the publication of Form G in 1977, and then culminating in the publication of Form J in 1987. The 1998 revision and the development of Form M will be described in later sections.

The Initial Stage

The initial questions developed by Isabel Briggs Myers and Katharine Briggs to measure Jung's theory were tested first on a small criterion group of about 20 relatives and friends whose type preferences seemed to the authors to be clearly evident from long acquaintance and from a 20-year period of careful observation of behavior. This criterion group was made up exclusively of those persons whose preferences were clear enough to be manifest consistently in observable behavior. This observation convinced the authors that the constellation of behaviors and attitudes described for each type by Jung could be reliably observed. After an initial period of identifying behaviors described by Jung, the authors noted additional behaviors and characteristics. When a behavior seemed to relate to a specific preference, T–F for example, the authors studied its appearance, its antecedents and effects, and its occurrence in persons thought to prefer thinking or feeling. After repeated observations and confirmations or disconfirmations of their hypotheses, they became more sure that (1) certain persons did indeed prefer thinking and (2) specific characteristics were found to be associated with thinking and could be considered derivatives of thinking. Thus, by the time of the initial stages of development of the MBTI, Jung's constructs had been tested and refined by years of observation.

Between 1942 and 1944 a large number of potential MBTI items were written and validated via the initial criterion group. The authors' discussions with respondents also revealed ways to change the items so as to capture the essence of the differences between the types. From these discussions it became clear that the same phrase conveyed quite different meanings to different types.

Forms A and B

Items that survived the initial validation were collected into a set of scales called Form A, and a rearrangement of the same items became Form B. The items were tested on progressively larger samples. These samples were made up mainly of adults because adults were expected to have reached higher levels of type development and to therefore be clearer about their preferences and better able to report them. To remain on a scale, any particular item had to be answered by at least 60% of the people of a given preference with the response that was designed for people of that preference. When using this method, a person's preference was determined by his or her responses to all of the items on that scale.

Form C

Additional item analysis led to the creation of Form C. One criterion for the inclusion of items in Form C was that a question having a high validity for one dichotomy was excluded if it also had a high validity for another dichotomy. For example, an item would be excluded if it correlated well with both the E–I and S–N dichotomies. It was necessary to keep the scales as uncorrelated as possible because otherwise a strong preference for a scale would distort the evidence for another scale. The Form C items were intercorrelated first on 248 adult men and later on 214 adult men. The first intercorrelation had a range of −.17 (E–I x T–F) to .18 (E–I x S–N) with a mean of .11. The second intercorrelation had a range of –.14 (E–I x T–F) to .19 (E–I x S–N) with a mean of .09.

Internal consistency analyses of Forms A and B had made it clear that responses differed in popularity. To allow for unequal popularity and for omissions, responses to items on Form C were weighted. A prediction ratio (see below) was substituted for previous item-test consistency analyses. The ratio showed the probability that the response, if an item were answered at all, would be given in accordance with type. The lower limit to retain an item was a prediction ratio of .60. Form C consisted of items from Forms A and B that survived this analysis, plus one new item and six reworded items.

In 1947 a Form C3 was developed that incorporated item weighting that allowed better differentiation of individuals scoring near 0. Items were weighted as a function of the prediction ratio for the item. The prediction ratio shows the probability that any response is given in accord with total scale score (i.e., the probability that a response designed for Js is given by Judging types and not given by Perceiving types). For each question, then, the (A) answer and the (B) answer have separate prediction ratios. The formula used to calculate the prediction ratio is shown below for both responses to a J–P item.

$$\text{PR for item } J_I = \frac{\text{Percent of J subjects giving } J_I \text{ response}}{\begin{array}{l}(\% \text{ of J subjects giving } J_I \text{ response}) \\ + \ (\% \text{ of P subjects giving } J_I \text{ response})\end{array}}$$

$$\text{PR for item } P_I = \frac{\text{Percent of P subjects giving } P_I \text{ response}}{\begin{array}{l}(\% \text{ of P subjects giving } P_I \text{ response}) \\ + \ (\% \text{ of J subjects giving } P_I \text{ response})\end{array}}$$

These prediction ratios were used to create weights for each response to each item. At this stage the weights were 0 for PR less than .60, 1 for PR .60 to .69, and 2 for PR .70 or greater.

Form D

The years 1956 to 1958 constituted a second major period of development, in preparation for the 1962 publication of the MBTI as a research instrument by Educational Testing Service. Over 200 new items, including word-pair questions, were submitted to a small group of people of known type who were familiar with the Indicator. Items that survived this analysis were submitted to 120 men and women who had taken Form C. The more promising items remaining after item analysis (about 130) were appended to Form C to create an experimental Form D.

When items were evaluated by the small group of people of known type, it was found that some people were more able than others to recognize their own general tendencies. If you ask Introverts, "Under such and such conditions, do you tend to do (A) or (B)?" they are likely to single out the

key word in (A) and the key word in (B), weigh them against each other, and decide which reaction is most like them, in accord with how the questions were designed to be answered. On the other hand, Extraverts respond to this question by harking back to the last time they were in a similar situation and remembering how they behaved. The Extraverts' answer thus reflects behavior on a single occasion surrounded by extraneous contextual factors.

While writing items for Form D, the authors realized that the way to get respondents to concentrate on key words was to give them the key words and nothing else, which formed the word pairs. For example, here are three word pairs:

build   Ⓐ   Ⓑ   invent
benefits   Ⓐ   Ⓑ   blessings
impulse   Ⓐ   Ⓑ   decision

The response to the word pairs indicated that while a number of them had low face-validity, they worked extremely well in separating people into the correct categories. Word pairs also have a number of other advantages over other types of questions, including the following:

- Less distracting
- Less subject to varied interpretation, personal reticence, and conscious or unconscious censorship
- More quickly read and answered, making it possible to have more items without increasing the administration time

The addition of word pairs almost doubled the number of valid items in Form D.

Prior to the 1956–58 development, all analyses were based on administration of the questions to adults. A series of younger-age samplings were then conducted. Younger individuals were presumably less advanced in type development and less clear about their preferences. Each sampling was evaluated to determine the extent to which items became less efficient as samples became younger.

An internal consistency analysis was done with 385 graduate students. As a result, the lower limit of the prediction ratio required for retention of an item was raised from .60 to .63. New items meeting this criterion were added, and weaker items were dropped.

An analysis with undergraduate students showed only slightly lower prediction ratios. The wording of a number of the older items was simplified and used in Forms D0 and D1 with three high school samples. When the simpler wording produced prediction ratios above .63, the revised wordings were adopted in the final experimental form, D2. Reworded items not meeting this criterion were dropped; or, in a few cases, an item was returned to its earlier wording.

In 1957 a large internal consistency analysis of Form D was conducted using a sample of 2,573 Pennsylvania 11th- and 12th-grade males in college preparatory courses and a similar sample of females. In order to prevent a bias in favor of any particular type, a sample of 200 males and 200 females of each type was drawn from this population. Because people of different types differ in their liking for items predictive of their preferences, it was important that weights assigned for types occurring less frequently in the population not be influenced by weightings derived from more frequent types. For types with sufficient numbers, a sample was drawn equally from the upper and the lower half of the students' class. Priority was given to overachievers and underachievers to diminish the difference in intelligence between more and less competent students.

Items were evaluated separately by gender and by type. To correct for differences in type frequency, responses for each type were calculated and averaged by the proportion of that type responding in a particular manner. This procedure was followed in order to give the rarer Introvert types equal weight with the more numerous Extraverts. In addition to the prediction ratios, tetrachoric item-test correlations were computed and used as a check on item selection.

Forms E and F

The surviving items became Forms E and F, which were identical except that Form F contained unscored experimental items. Item weights that had been started in Form C3 were used in these forms and made more stringent. For the first time a tie-breaking formula was adopted, and the preference scores were used instead of percentages to denote the strength of preferences. Form F was used in the large samples collected in preparation for publication by Educational Testing Service in 1962. In the early 1970s Form E was phased out and Form F became the standard form.

Form G

Between 1975 and 1977, almost 20 years after the large-scale data collection in preparation for the publication of Form F, a new standardization of items was carried out. The new analyses seemed appropriate to ensure that cultural changes had not decreased the utility of items and to make some minor modifications that two decades of experience had suggested were desirable. One goal of the restandardization was to investigate at what age schoolchildren could validly take the MBTI.

The new standardization was based on 1,114 males and 1,111 females in grades 4 through 12 in three public schools in Bethesda, Maryland, and in four private schools in the suburbs of Philadelphia, Pennsylvania. The analyses also included a rescoring of a sample of 3,362 University of Florida freshmen tested in 1972 and 1973. A Maryland subsample of 1,101 11th- and 12th-grade students was comparable to the sample used for the original Form F item analyses, consisting largely of college preparatory students of above-average socioeconomic status.

Table 7.1 shows the median item-to-scale correlations for five samples for Form G. The item-test correlations and

Table 7.1   Median Item-Test Correlations for Form G

Sample	N	Median r
Maryland 11th and 12th graders	1,101	.61
10th and 11th graders (two schools)	192	.61
8th and 9th graders (four schools)	360	.58
6th and 7th graders (five schools)	309	.55
4th and 5th graders (four schools)	264	.48

prediction ratios held up well, even for younger students. The utility of items did not diminish, and most items functioned better at the elementary school level than had been anticipated.

As a result of the analyses of the restandardization samples, the scoring weights for the T–F scale were modified for Form F, and a new revision of the MBTI, Form G, was published in 1977. Form G eliminated 38 research items not previously scored for type in Form F, added one new item, and dropped two items that no longer met the criteria for inclusion. Some items were modified to eliminate ambiguity or awkward alternatives. Items were rearranged so that all the scored items preceded unscored items. The rearrangement put the most predictive items at the beginning so that a usable approximation of type could be obtained if the first 50 questions were completed.

When Form G was introduced, Form F was still available, although primarily used as a research form, and the weights for Form F items were therefore changed to match those of Form G. Thus, when scored for type, the 1977 Form F and Form G were essentially interchangeable.

Form G Self-Scorable

The MBTI is often used in workshop settings where it is difficult if not impossible to administer the instrument, collect the answer sheets, and then send them in for computer scoring prior to the workshop. Even if the hand-scoring templates are used, it is time-consuming and often inconvenient to score large numbers of Indicators on-site during a workshop. For these reasons a self-scorable version of Form G was devised.

The first self-scorable form, developed in 1983, was called the Abbreviated Version (Form AV) of the MBTI. It contained the first 50 items from Form G (which best predict to the total scale scores) in a format that permitted self-scoring and provided some interpretive information for the client. Form AV did not provide different weights for men and women on the T–F scale. It was recommended that Form AV be used only for group situations where time pressures preclude administration and scoring of Form G and when maximum type accuracy is less important. A study reported by Kaiser (1981) suggested that these items could act as a "surrogate" for the full set of Form G items. Initial studies of Form AV confirmed this finding and suggested that Form AV was a reasonable short form for Form G. However, a number of later studies of Form AV (Macdaid, 1984b; Most, 1984) suggested that the form was less reliable than Form G.

In response to these findings, Form AV was discontinued and a new self-scorable form of the MBTI was created—the MBTI Form G self-scorable. This form used all 94 of the scored items from the standard Form G. Since it contains exactly the same items and is scored using exactly the same weights as are used to arrive at the four-letter type on the standard Form G, the results from the two instruments are the same. The Form G self-scorable and the standard Form G have the same reliability and validity, since they use the same items and scoring weights.

Step II and Step III

In 1987 an advanced scoring system was developed for the MBTI. An early version of this scoring system was developed decades earlier by Isabel Briggs Myers in collaboration with Mary H. McCaulley but was never published. Myers' original work was expanded upon and published as the *Type Differentiation Indicator* (Saunders, 1987). A new form of the MBTI was created at this time, Form J, which contained all 290 items written by Myers that had survived her previous item analyses. When Form J is scored using this new system, now called Step III, it yields 20 subscales (5 under each of the four dichotomous preference scales) plus 7 scales called Comfort-Discomfort scales.

This was followed in 1989 by a scoring system that produced only the 20 subscales and not the more clinically relevant Comfort-Discomfort scales. This system was originally published as the Expanded Analysis Report (Saunders, 1989). A new form was created at this time, Form K, containing 131 items that were needed to score for type as well as for the 20 subscales and a number of research items. This scoring system is now called Step II.

Issues in the Construction of Previous MBTI Forms

During the development of MBTI forms through Form G, a number of problems were confronted that have implications for understanding the nature of the instrument. These include social desirability, weighting for gender differences, locating the midpoint of the scales, and breaking ties. Some of these problems, like the issue of social desirability, are shared by most psychological and educational tests. Others, such as how to determine the true midpoint of the scales, are unique to the MBTI because of its typological nature. Although these problems are generally handled differently on Form M, they are documented here for users of Form G and because they provide a check on important issues that need to be faced in future development of the instrument.

Social Desirability

All test developers must face the fact that people respond to some items in certain ways not because those responses reflect whatever psychological characteristic the item has been designed to tap but rather because those responses are more popular or socially desirable in the culture. To the extent that this happens, the item becomes more a measure of social desirability than a measure of the characteristic of interest.

Beginning with the development of Form C, the prediction ratio formula described earlier in this chapter was used to control for the social desirability of each item response on the MBTI. The prediction ratio gives the "goodness" of the response, that is, the relationship of the item to all the items for that preference. In order for a response to a question to appear on the scoring keys, the prediction ratio must be .63 or above for a weight of 1, or .72 for a weight of 2, and the item popularity for the opposite preference (i.e., the percentage of individuals with the opposite preference giving that response) must be below .50. In this manner the formula takes social desirability into account.

The denominator of the formula gives a measure of the popularity of the response. If the second term in the denominator of the formula goes above .50, the response has been given by more than half of those for whom that choice was *not* intended; thus it is overpopular (i.e., more socially desirable) and is likely to do more harm than it is worth by displacing people at the center of the scale. A response rejected by the above criteria would be given a 0 weight. Some responses with 0 weight were retained in various forms of the Indicator to provide counters to weighted responses, for other purposes such as their utility on a special scale, or for future use in case the social desirability of the items changes.

For about one-third of the scored questions on Forms F and G, prediction ratios were similar for both responses, and both responses were given the same weight. In another third of the questions, the responses differed somewhat in popularity; in these items, one response was weighted 1 and the other 2, based on the prediction ratio. In the final third of items, one response was much more popular than the other; these questions were given 0 weight for the popular response and 1 or 2 depending on the prediction ratio for the other response.

Items had different response distributions for each of the 16 types; thus a separate analysis was carried out for each type before the first weighted scoring in 1946 and again before publication of Form F. The popularity of each response was tabulated separately for each of the 16 types to guard against extreme variation and to give equal representation to the less frequent types.

Weighting for Gender Differences

Throughout the development of the MBTI, all item analyses were computed separately for males and females. In the first item analysis of 114 males and 110 females (all adults, mostly college graduates), it was discovered that some questions were valid only for one gender. The second item analysis also found gender differences in item validity. In developing Form C, only items that were valid for both genders were retained.

In the early forms separate keys for males and females were used for E–I, S–N, T–F, and J–P. Beginning with Forms E and F the same keys were used for both genders because item analyses showed that for both genders item popularity and prediction ratios were comparable on E–I, S–N, and J–P.

On the T–F scale it was evident that females, even those who in their behavior and attitudes indicated a clear preference for Thinking, had a greater tendency to give certain Feeling responses than did males. The difference was ascribed either to the possibility that certain Feeling responses were more socially desirable for females than for males, or to the effect of social training. Separate weights were assigned to T–F items for each sex, based on the prediction ratios for each item, with checks that the criterion groups were assigned the correct preference.

Numerous studies in the late 1950s and early 1960s confirmed the weightings and the division point on T–F, which tended to produce, among unselected groups of males, a distribution of about 60% T and 40% F. The females' distributions were about one-third T and two-thirds F. From the mid-1960s to the mid-1970s the distributions on the T–F scale showed large changes, while the distributions of the other scales remained stable. A 1972 study of University of Florida freshmen produced only 44% T among males and 30% among females. Almost identical distributions were obtained with the 1975 high school samples used to restandardize the MBTI. In other words, the incidence of Ts had dropped for both males and females.

One might conclude that Ts were a vanishing species at the time of the reweighting or that social/cultural changes have altered the popularity of responses in the Thinking-Feeling domain. The latter interpretation seems compatible with a number of sociological and psychological commentaries, which suggested that Feeling responses might be more acceptable or more popular among young Americans than they were 20 years earlier.

In the restandardization samples for Form G, item-test correlations and prediction ratios were computed, following precisely the same system as in earlier item analyses. No changes were required for the E–I, S–N, and J–P scales. However, Feeling response choices had become more popular and therefore lost some of their weighting. Thinking responses, some of which were formerly penalized for over-popularity, were less popular and therefore gained added weight for that response.

With the restandardized weights used on Form G, the high school male sample contained 61% T and the female sample contained 30% T. This was comparable to the earlier distributions. A rescoring of the University of Florida sample yielded 61% T for males and 30% T for females, also comparable to earlier data.

Omissions

Omissions are permitted in the instructions of the Indicator in the belief that greater validity is achieved by the elimination of doubtful answers. Type can then be indicated by item responses a person is reasonably sure about, uncontaminated by guessing. In practice there typically are few omissions. More than 62% of the respondents in a large Center for Applications of Psychological Type databank sample answered all the questions on Form G, and over 80% had fewer than three omissions.

Research with other psychological measures has established individual differences in response styles, including acquiescence or general willingness to concur. On the MBTI there is no option to say "No" directly because of the forced-choice format, so a person who is unable or unwilling to concur can omit an item. A few people (particularly Introverted Thinking types, who tend not to subscribe unreservedly to any statement short of a mathematical equation) may omit quite a number of responses. Users of Form G answer sheets should examine them for omitted items before scoring. The computer-scored narratives and profiles for Form G contain a section showing the number of omitted items per scale. Inquiry during the interpretation session into the reasons the client omitted specific questions can provide useful verification information.

Locating the Midpoint of the Scales

In developing an indicator based on Jung's theory two additional problems need to be solved. The first problem is whether each dichotomy represents two different kinds of people, each holding to a separate preference. If there are two kinds of people for each scale, is the division point between the groups at the point where the two groups can be most clearly separated?

Jung's theory hypothesizes preferences for opposite inner dispositions that cannot be thwarted without damage to the individual's well-being. Accurately sorting people into the correct category on each of the four dichotomous type constructs is therefore an important goal for the Indicator.

There is a second problem that must be solved. A self-report instrument that aims to accomplish the identification of Jungian types through questions and their resultant scales also has the unique problem of locating the division point, so that the two categories of people are separated with maximum accuracy.

Thus there are two strong reasons why the division point should be as sharp and accurate as possible: (1) to identify the two different groups with maximum accuracy and (2) to use these distinctions to obtain evidence as to whether the preferences are, as postulated by theory, dichotomous.

In Form A, where all items had equal weight, the division point was the point on a given scale at which half the items were answered for each pole. By definition this point was the boundary between people showing one preference and people showing the opposite preference. The only possible check was to see whether the people of known type were correctly classified. From that time on, whenever the scoring was changed by dropping or adding items or by assigning double weight or 0 weight to responses, care was taken not to add more overall weight to one pole of the scale than to the other, lest the distribution of scores shift. Up until the completion of Form C, the people of known type were rescored at each step to make sure that changes would not shift them to the wrong pole.

Throughout the construction of the MBTI assessment tool, numerous steps were taken to deal with the issue of dichotomies and the division points. These included (1) permitting omissions to help avoid the effects of random guessing, (2) allowing for omissions in the scoring formulas, (3) giving lower weightings for overpopular items and higher weightings for the more discriminating responses, and (4) using inclusive groups rather than extreme groups in the item analyses.

Another technique useful in determining the true midpoint is plotting MBTI preferences against an external dependent variable. In order to pinpoint true 0, the dependent variable needs to be sensitive to the slightest indication of a preference, so that at the point where the preference reverses, the plotted line will show a discontinuity in level as well as (or in place of) a disparity in slope. In addition, the sample needs to be very large to stabilize the group means and to make the discontinuity visible and statistically significant. An example of this technique for identifying the division point is illustrated by the measures taken to correct the E–I division point when it became displaced.

Relocating the E–I Division Point Using Grade Point Average

When the scoring for Form F was almost completed, the 0 point on E–I was found to have shifted toward the Extravert pole. The evidence was an unprecedented majority of Introverts when the Pennsylvania High School sample was rescored with the new weights (see the 1985 *Manual*, Appendix B, for a description of this sample). To correct the error, external evidence was needed to find the transition on the dichotomy between the Extraverts and the Introverts.

During the development of Form C, the years-of-college variable had shown a satisfactory discontinuity on E–I. This suggested that, as theory predicts, a preference for Introversion is related to interest and/or performance in academics. This was supported by the high percentage of Introverts in college populations. It therefore seemed reasonable that the intelligence measures for the Pennsylvania High School sample (5,025 males and 4,516 females) and the grade point average (standardized within each class) for the college preparatory courses (3,303 males and 2,511 females) might exhibit discontinuities that would indicate the location of the E–I division point (Myers & McCaulley, 1985).

The Pennsylvania High School sample was rescored with the new E–I division point, and the new location was tested by plotting IQ scores separately for males and females. For males the break, slight but evident because of the large size in the sample, came between the first and second of the groups with the three linked scores. This was the point where the division point for the E–I scale was finally established.

It should be noted that the change in level between E and I was very small in all these analyses, only about .25 standard deviations in grade point average and about 2 points in IQ. For such small differences to be visible, samples of 4,000 to 5,000 are needed.

Breaking Ties

In the early stages of the MBTI's development, equal points for the poles of the same scale were designated by an "x"; thus the type might be designated IxTJ, or ENFx. With Form F, a tie-breaking formula was adopted, on the suggestion of Frederick R. Kling of Educational Testing Service. The formula involves finding the difference between the points for each pole, doubling the difference, and then adding a point if either I, N, F, or P is the larger pole, or subtracting a point if either E, S, T, or J is the larger pole. This tie-breaking formula is also used on Form G.

The logic behind adding a point to the I, N, or P preferences is that these are the less frequent types in the population. If a person is that close to the preference (zero difference), there is probably some environmental response pressure from the "majority" preference. This pressure can result in answers conforming to the majority and contrary to true preferences; thus the person's "true" type is probably I, N, or P. The rationale for tie breaking on the T–F scale was somewhat different. In this culture males more frequently prefer and are socialized toward T; females more frequently prefer and are socialized toward F. On the possibility that the weighting of the scales might have overcorrected for social desirability, tie scores assigned males to T and females to F. However, when the new Form F keys were published in 1978, the scoring was simplified by adding one point to the male Thinking key (i.e., all males get one extra point toward Thinking). This procedure provided insurance against possible overcorrection and allowed the tie-breaking formula to be simplified so that for both males and females one point is subtracted for T and one added for F.

Item Response Theory

The construction of Form M of the MBTI was based on the same assumptions and followed the same general principles that guided construction of the earlier forms of the Indicator. The construction of Form M, however, also involved changes in how items were selected, the method used to score for type, and how the midpoint of the scales was determined. Before describing how these three primary issues were handled in the development of Form M for the 1998 revision, it is necessary to provide an introduction to item response theory (IRT) because IRT was used to accomplish all three of the major construction tasks. As the name implies, IRT is a theory about how item responses are related to the underlying construct in the individual that is presumed to produce those responses.

Item response theory has gained considerable popularity in recent years as a method for developing and evaluating assessment instruments. This is partly due to the fact that it is useful for constructing and evaluating many different kinds of instruments. The most common application has been in designing tests in traditional "ability-based" domains (e.g., achievement, intelligence, aptitude). IRT approaches have also been used in developing tests that do not involve making "right versus wrong" item responses, such as personality tests (Waller & Reise, 1989), interest inventories, and tests designed to help make classification decisions. Embretson (1996) argues that every psychologist should be familiar with IRT since it is the foundation of the "new rules of measurement." A variety of sources (e.g., Drasgow & Hulin, 1990; Hambleton, Swaminathan, & Rogers, 1991; Hulin, Drasgow, & Parsons, 1983) can be consulted for a more thorough discussion of IRT techniques in general. In this section the focus will be on application of IRT to the MBTI. Also see Harvey and Thomas (1996) for a similar discussion as well as for a comparison of IRT, which is based on modern test theory, with classical test theory (CTT) methods of scoring and determining the reliability of the MBTI. In CTT the unit of analysis is the test or scale as a whole; in IRT it is the individual item (Drasgow & Hulin, 1990).

Construction and evaluation of tests based on IRT, therefore, focus on the relationship between a person's "true score" on the psychological characteristic (or *dimension*) in question and the likelihood of making a particular response to an individual test item. For example, how likely is it that a person with a "true" preference for Extraversion will choose the Extraverted response to an item on the E–I scale?

While many different IRT models have been proposed, a highly desirable aspect of current IRT models, as opposed to CTT models, is that they allow for both linear and *nonlinear* relations to exist between the underlying psychological characteristic and the observed item response. This is important for the MBTI because, as will be demonstrated, a nonlinear relationship is both theoretically desirable and empirically accurate. The relationship between the response and the construct can be graphically described using an *item characteristic curve* (ICC). The horizontal axis of an ICC for a particular item shows the varying levels of the psychological characteristic the item is designed to measure. The vertical axis (*pkr*) shows the probability that a person at a given level would respond to the item in the keyed direction.

The scores are called *theta* in IRT terminology and are denoted as θ. Theta corresponds roughly to a nonlinear rescaling of the "true score" of classical test theory (Drasgow & Hulin, 1990). Figure 7.1 shows two hypothetical ICCs. In both cases scores on the far left of the scale represent people with very clear preferences for Extraversion, and scores on the far right of the scale represent people with very clear preferences for Introversion. The right half of the scale, Introversion in the case of the MBTI E–I scale, is called the "keyed" direction. While choice of which pole of the dichotomy is defined as the keyed direction is entirely arbitrary for the purposes of IRT, for the sake of consistency with previous MBTI conventions I, N, F, and P are defined as the keyed direction. So as θ increases from left to right, we would expect higher levels of endorsement of the item in the predicted, or keyed, direction, which is the Introverted direction. In other words, we would expect that people with a clear preference for Introversion would have a much greater chance of giving the Introverted response to an E–I item than would people with a clear preference for Extraversion.

The IRT models that are designed for dichotomously scored items, such as those used on the MBTI, describe each item's characteristics or performance using up to three *parameters*. These parameters define the way in which a person's placement on θ is related to the observed likelihood of endorsing the item in a given direction (e.g., a "correct" response in the case of a right-wrong test item, or a response in the *keyed direction* in the case of a personality or interest inventory item).

The *a* parameter describes an item's degree of *discrimination*. Higher discrimination parameters are associated with items that produce more *information* regarding a person's standing on the characteristic of interest (denoted by θ). In Figure 7.1, the item producing the dashed item characteristic curve has a much higher *a* parameter than the item producing the solid line. The steeper the curve at the particular θ that is most relevant to the purposes of the measurement, the more information is produced and the greater the likelihood of the person responding in the keyed direction to the item. The θ that is most relevant for an MBTI item is described in the next section. For a perfectly flat line, *a* would equal 0, which would indicate *no* information; for such an item, no matter what θ you examined, the likelihood of responding in the keyed direction would be the same.

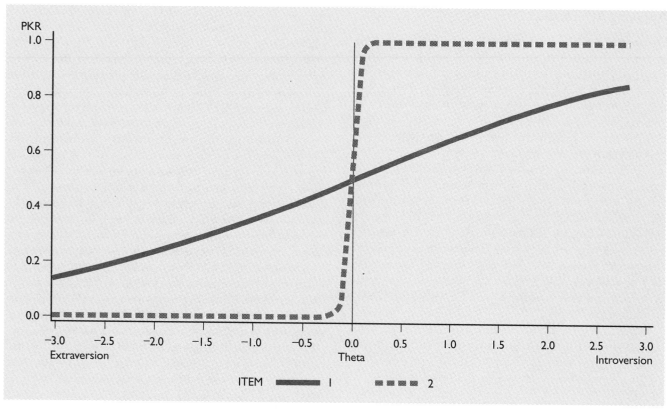

Figure 7.1 Item Characteristic Curves for Two Hypothetical Items

The *b*, or *difficulty*, parameter in IRT quantifies the left-right location of the ICC on the θ scale; items that are more "difficult" will have their ICCs shifted toward the right portion of the horizontal scale, whereas "easier" items will be shifted toward the left. When applied to either right-wrong or inventory-type tests, the main function of the difficulty parameter is in telling us the area on the θ scale at which a given test item produces the maximum amount of information regarding the person's score on the psychological characteristic in question: "Hard" items provide the most information for people who score toward the right end of the θ scale, whereas "easy" items provide maximum information for those who score toward the left end of the θ scale. To place this in MBTI terms, consider an E–I item, where the keyed direction is (arbitrarily) determined to be Introversion. The curve of an E-I item with a high *b* parameter would have its steepest slope not above 0.0, but above a θ that is toward the keyed or Introverted end of the scale. For example, imagine moving the dashed line in Figure 7.1 to the right so that the almost vertical portion of the line would be over the θ at 2.0. This would be an item that provided information about people who are, for example, clear Introverts versus those who are very clear Introverts. Such an item would provide little information about Introverts versus Extraverts because the probability of responding in the keyed direction would be the same for all Extraverts and for Introverts whose θ is less than 2.0.

Finally, the *c*, or *lower asymptote*, parameter defines the baseline for item-endorsement rates that would be expected from individuals who score very far to the left (low) end of the θ scale. In traditional right-wrong tests, a nonzero lower asymptote for the ICC is often attributable to low-ability individuals guessing the correct answer. In tests that do not use right-wrong items, the need for a nonzero lower asymptote can also occur due to such factors as the social desirability (or lack thereof) of a given item response. In MBTI terms an item with a high *c* parameter would mean that even people who are very clear Extraverts have some probability of responding to the item in the Introverted direction.

One of the main strengths of using IRT for test development and evaluation is that it tends to provide a much more detailed view of item functioning than is possible using traditional methods based on CTT. In particular, when using the three-parameter IRT model described above, items can be selected from a pool to form a test that produces the maximum amount of test-level information (which corresponds roughly to the concept of *reliability* in CTT) and discrimination in a prespecified region of the θ scale.

For the MBTI, which employs a cutoff score, items can be selected to produce a scale that demonstrates its maximum discriminating power at, or near, the cutoff point on the scale.

Applying IRT to the MBTI

Although IRT methods were initially developed in the context of ability tests that employed right-wrong items, they are equally applicable to other types of tests (such as personality inventories) that do *not* view item responses in a right-wrong fashion, especially those instruments for which item responses are dichotomous. As is described in more detail by Harvey and Thomas (1996), IRT development and scoring can be readily applied to the MBTI given the fact that each of the four primary MBTI scales is bipolar in nature, with each individual item being scored dichotomously. To apply IRT to the MBTI, one of the responses for each item is designated as the *keyed* response and is associated with θ scores toward the right of the scale. In this case the I, N, F, and P poles were designated as the keyed response for the E–I, S–N, T–F, and J–P scales, respectively. Here, the choice of a keyed pole is arbitrary, serving simply to define the *direction* of the θ scale for each of the MBTI dichotomies.

For example, the hypothetical item denoted by the solid line in Figure 7.1 could be seen as being drawn from the E–I scale (e.g., "easy versus hard to get to know"); in this case, if the I response were designated as the keyed response, all individuals who chose the response "hard to get to know" would be scored as endorsing the item, and those who chose the E response ("easy to get to know") would be scored as not endorsing the item in the keyed direction. Thus for any given θ it is possible to determine the percentage of individuals having that preference that would be expected to produce the I response by examining the location of the ICC above the θ of interest. Thus in the hypothetical solid item in Figure 7.1, in the group of people who share a score of +1.0 (i.e., relatively clear Introverts), we would expect that approximately two-thirds of them (64%) would endorse this hypothetical item in the keyed (I) direction, with the remainder selecting the E-keyed response.

In IRT the θ scale is arbitrary in nature; by convention it is typically expressed as a traditional *z score* (with 0 defining the midpoint, scores below the midpoint being negative, and those above the midpoint being positive). In the context of the MBTI, by selecting the I, N, F, and P poles as the keyed responses, θ scores are analogous to *continuous scores* on each of the four MBTI scales, with positive θ scores defining individuals whose types are I, N, F, and P, and negative θ scores defining individuals whose type lies in the E, S, T, and J direction. (It should be noted, however, that θ scores are not reported to respondents and thus the unwanted connotations resulting from associating a negative number with a preference are avoided.) Categorical MBTI types can therefore be simply assigned by dichotomizing the θ scores; although as a practical matter the θ score cutoff that corresponds to the natural dividing point between types does not necessarily have to fall precisely at $\theta = 0.0$, it does lie in the middle region of the θ scale for each of the four MBTI dimensions. (See the section below about how the midpoint of the scales was in fact adjusted.)

To summarize, although the mechanics of IRT scoring differ quite a bit from the much simpler methods used in CTT, it is a very straightforward matter to apply IRT methods to score the MBTI: Namely, the IRT θ scores correspond directly to the continuous scores that were previously calculated based on the prediction ratio scoring method. These scores can be dichotomized to produce categorical type values in precisely the same way that the earlier PR-based preferences were dichotomized to assign types.

It is also interesting to note that although the PR and IRT methods are derived from different kinds of measurement theories, they tend to agree to a large extent on what constitutes a "good" MBTI item. Generally items whose responses were weighted 2,2 or 1,2 based on the PR method also tend to have high discriminatory power, or information (i.e., they have high values of the *a* parameter, or steep slopes) and also tend to have *b* parameters close to the midpoint of the scale. It is with the other items, those whose responses were not weighted as highly using the PR method, that the two methods tend to disagree the most. A number of these lower-weighted items therefore were not selected for inclusion in the revised Indicator. However, even for items where the agreement is high between the two methods, IRT will generally yield more precise scores.

Model Selection and Fit

Although there are different IRT models available, including one-, two-, and three-parameter models, the three-parameter logistic IRT model was used to select items for the revised MBTI and in the new MBTI scoring system. Each parameter in this model provides useful information about MBTI items. Specifically, the reasons for choosing the three-parameter model are as follows.

First, past research that used IRT methods to examine the MBTI (e.g., Harvey & Murry, 1994; Harvey, Murry, & Markham, 1994; Harvey & Thomas, 1996) has shown quite clearly that the MBTI items do indeed differ with respect to their relationship with the underlying preferences. Some items simply carry more information, or discriminating power, than do other items. In practical terms this is indexed by the *slope* of the ICC for each item. (It was also observed in the PR method by the differential weights associated with the items.) The *a* parameter provides an index of the information provided by each item.

Second, the *b* parameter defines the *location* on the θ scale at which the item provides its maximum information, or discrimination. The above research studies also demonstrated that there is considerable variability across MBTI items with respect to the areas of the preference scale at which they are most informative. For any given MBTI scale it is desirable to have the maximum amount of information occur at the midpoint of the scale. To the extent that this occurs, and to the extent that the midpoint corresponds to the true dichotomy, then the item will be separating people correctly into the two preference categories.

Finally, with respect to the *c* parameter, although past IRT research on the MBTI has suggested that most MBTI items do *not* require a sizable nonzero lower asymptote, a few items do produce ICCs whose lower values do not approximate 0. To accommodate these items a *c* parameter is needed. This parameter is useful in accounting for social desirability or any other factor that would lead people of one preference to have a nonzero likelihood of choosing the response associated with the opposite preference.

Assumptions Underlying the Model

All scoring systems make assumptions, and IRT is not exempt in this regard. As always, it is important to determine, to the extent possible, the degree to which these assumptions are plausible, or consistent with the actual MBTI item responses they are meant to describe and summarize. In the case of IRT scoring, some of the most important assumptions relate to the choice of which IRT model to use. Many of the questions related to model choice were already introduced above: Namely, do the items exhibit differential discrimination (the *a* parameter), does this discrimination occur at different points along the preference scale (the *b* parameter), and are there at least some items with appreciably nonzero lower asymptotes (the *c* parameter)? Research has demonstrated that all of these questions are answered in the affirmative. This research (e.g., Harvey, Murry, & Markham, 1994), which involved fitting the three-parameter model to MBTI item responses, showed quite clearly that considerable variability was present with respect to the estimates of the *a*, *b*, and *c* parameters. The assumption of a three-parameter model is therefore justified.

Another assumption of IRT is that the set of items on a scale is "unidimensional." That is, the item pools for a given scale should be dominated by a single underlying factor. Research that examined the dimensionality of the Form F item pools (e.g., Harvey, Murry, & Stamoulis, 1995) demonstrated that this is indeed the case and that these underlying factors are precisely the ones hypothesized by the MBTI—namely the four preference scales. Subsequent factor analytic studies using the updated Form M item pools have further established the generality of these earlier findings. This is not to say that each of the four MBTI dimensions cannot be broken down into subcategories. Indeed, the factor analysis of the MBTI Research Form, from which the Form M items were selected, demonstrated the existence of 19 subfactors, each of which was related as expected to one of the four preference scales. The existence of such a hierarchical relationship between scales and subscales does not violate the IRT assumption of unidimensionality; MBTI scales are both unidimensional and multifaceted as these are defined

in IRT. This is seen quite clearly in the MBTI Step II and Step III scoring systems.

Another assumption on which IRT is based is that the underlying relationship between the psychological characteristic being measured and the observable responses to the items chosen to measure that characteristic is nonlinear. One of the most compelling arguments in favor of the appropriateness—indeed, the *necessity*—of the three-parameter IRT view of the MBTI can be found in the results obtained using *empirical* ICCs. In this approach an ICC is computed for each item, plotting the *observed* percentage of item endorsements in the keyed direction (vertical axis) against the total number of items endorsed in the keyed direction. Figure 7.2 presents an empirically derived ICC for a strongly discriminating MBTI item; Figure 7.3 presents the empirical ICC for an item with more modest discrimination and a clearly defined nonzero lower asymptote. Because these are empirical ICCs, the horizontal axis represents actual Form G preference scores rather than θ scores.

The results presented in Figure 7.2 make a strong case for the need to use a *nonlinear* model of the relationship between the underlying preference and the observed likelihood of endorsing an item in the keyed direction. There is a very strong s-shaped relationship, with this item providing a large amount of information in the intermediate range of the preference scale and less information (i.e., flatter slope) toward either end of the scale.

The most extreme case of a nonlinear function for an MBTI-like item would be an ICC that assumed the shape of a perfect step function centered exactly over the midpoint of the scale; this would be a case of maximum information and maximum separation between people of opposite preferences on the scale. The dashed line in Figure 7.1 comes very close to representing such an "ideal" item. For an E–I item with such an ICC, *all* of the Introverts would choose the Introverted response and none of the Extraverts would, and vice versa. While some items come close to this limit, it is neither required nor expected that all items assume this form, for two reasons:

First, neither Jung nor Myers believed that everyone was a "type." The fact that even the best of the MBTI items do not conform to the ideal demonstrates the theoretical proposition that for various reasons, including developmental or situational factors, a given person at a given time will have some chance of responding to an item in a direction opposite that of his or her preference.

The second reason why the perfect step function would not be expected is that responses are not equally popular for all types holding that preference, a fact that has been demonstrated in many item analyses conducted over the years. For example, not all Sensing types are equally likely to respond in the Sensing direction to a given Sensing question. For these reasons, desirable items for MBTI scales would be those that showed the general s-shape or pattern but that varied somewhat from the pure step function.

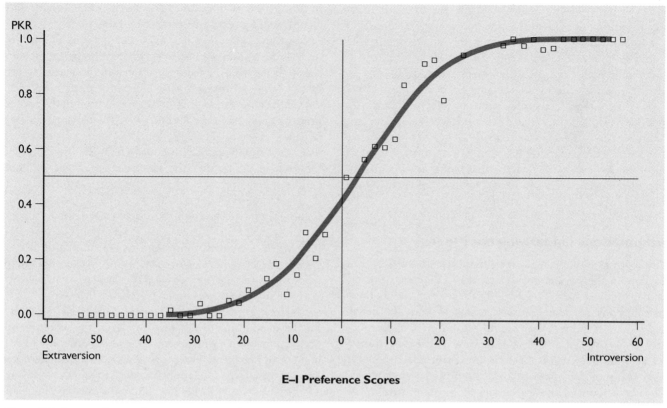

Figure 7.2 Empirical Item Characteristic Curve for an E–I Item with High Discrimination

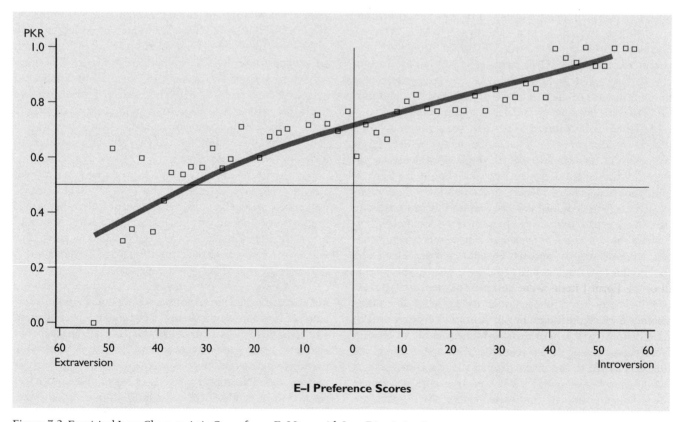

Figure 7.3 Empirical Item Characteristic Curve for an E–I Item with Low Discrimination

Figure 7.2 also shows the very high degree of "fit" of the IRT model to the observed MBTI item responses. The squares in this figure represent the *actual* average rates of item endorsement for respondents grouped according to the number of items endorsed on the scale in the keyed direction (i.e., the square on the farthest right of the figure represents the average of those people who gave the I response to all of the E–I items). The very close correspondence of these values to the overall ICC drawn through these points shows that the IRT model is capable of providing a very good description of "real-world" data.

In summary, the assumptions of IRT are consistent with its use with the MBTI. Having provided a basic introduction to IRT, we turn now to how IRT was used to (1) select items for Form M and (2) score those items.

Selection of Items for Form M

The 1998 revision of the MBTI offered the opportunity to investigate the possibilities of revising, adding, or deleting items from the instrument. To investigate these possibilities, a systematic process was employed to test and select items that would compose a new form of the Indicator: Form M. The five major steps in the item selection process were as follows:

- Step 1: Create an initial item pool
- Step 2: Develop item selection criteria
- Step 3: Construct a research form
- Step 4: Administer the research form to a national sample
- Step 5: Select the final items for the revised MBTI

Step 1: Create an Initial Item Pool

An initial pool of potential items was created from a number of sources. One set of items consisted of all 290 questions contained on Form J of the MBTI. These items comprise all of the items that had survived the years of research and item analysis conducted by Isabel Briggs Myers. Myers had never intended all of these items to be used on the four dichotomous preference scales. Some of the items were created for the purpose of additional scoring methods intended to provide subscale scores—and indeed some of these items are used in the Step II and Step III scoring systems. Although not all of the Form J items were designed to measure type, all were included in creating an initial item pool to determine whether they could function as measures of type as well as fulfill their original function of providing subscale scores.

A second set of items, coincidentally also numbering 290, was added to the initial pool for testing. About 90 of these items were written by two experienced MBTI users, one a clinician and the other a researcher. The other 200 items were created by Thomas (1996b). In most cases these items represented slight revisions of existing MBTI Form J

| Table 7.2 | Item Selection Criteria |

Theoretical Criteria

Theoretically meaningful content

Richness of the item pool

Forced-choice format

Phrase questions and word pairs

Wording for comparable attractiveness

Empirical Criteria

Satisfactory prediction ratios for each response

Satisfactory information at the midpoint of the scale

No significant age or gender differences

Low item-to-scale correlations with nonkeyed scales

items. Revisions included using more up-to-date language in phrase questions or different pairings of words from existing word pairs, or pairing an existing word with a new word. The testing of these new and revised items was undertaken for four reasons:

1. To determine if there were other items that could improve the overall psychometric properties of the MBTI
2. To find new T–F items that did not show gender differences
3. To find new T–F items that might help increase the reliability of this scale
4. To determine the effect of rephrasing certain MBTI items

When writing new items or revising Form J items, the basic procedures outlined by Myers were followed. Some effort was also made to fill potential gaps in the content of a preference domain, although construct coverage was not the primary criterion for an experimental item. Following Myers, item content was deemed to be less important than the ability of the words and form of the sentence to serve as a "stimulus to evoke a type response."

The 290 Form J items combined with the 290 experimental items brought the initial item pool to 580 potential items.

Step 2: Develop Item Selection Criteria

To select the best items from the initial pool of 580 items, a set of criteria was developed by a panel of experts familiar with the history of the instrument and the MBTI research literature. These criteria are listed in Table 7.2. The MBTI Research Advisory Board also played a role in developing and refining the criteria and applying them to the item pool. These criteria were not all developed, nor were they applied, on just one occasion. They evolved through many discussions and many experimental versions of the final revised form. Some of the criteria were applied to the initial item pool as a means of narrowing this pool to a more manageable size. Other criteria then became more important as a means of selecting the final set of items.

As seen in Table 7.2, the item selection criteria can be grouped into two broad categories: theoretical criteria and empirical criteria.

Theoretical Criteria   Theoretical criteria were primarily concerned with ensuring that item content and format were consistent with Jung's and Myers' theories of psychological type in general and specifically with the theory of opposites that underlie type dichotomies. The general guidelines that were followed through all the revisions of the instrument, including Form M, were to write or revise items that accomplished the following:

- Allowed people to self-report their preferences accurately
- Reflected the preferences described by Jung for Extraversion or Introversion (E–I), Sensing or Intuition (S–N), and Thinking or Feeling judgment (T–F)
- Reflected the preference for Judging or Perceiving (J–P), which was created by Isabel Myers to measure the effects of the judging and perceiving attitudes in their Extraverted appearance, so that this information could be used to determine a dominant function
- Reflected the assumption that each pole of the dichotomy is equally valuable

Theoretically Meaningful Content   Before beginning to develop the MBTI, Isabel Myers and Katharine Briggs had thoroughly studied Jung's *Psychological Types* for descriptions of and subtle clues about type preferences and their interactions. They had been carefully observing type for more than two decades and drew on Jungian theory and their observations to generate questions that could be evaluated.

One of the first requirements imposed by the type hypothesis was that justice must be done to quite opposite viewpoints. Each dichotomy requires a choice between equally legitimate alternatives. Thus type questions have no intrinsic good or bad about them and no right or wrong except as a certain answer is right for one respondent and wrong for another having a different type. The questions therefore needed to deal with self-reportable surface contrasts in habits, reactions, and points of view that did not imply inferiority. The respondent should never be placed on the defensive about his or her response, nor should any preference be regarded as superior.

No question could be very extreme, since accuracy was more important near the middle of the distribution than at the ends. It is fairly easy to write items that separate people with very clear preferences on each dichotomy, but this was little help in separating people at the middle of the dichotomy. Similarly, an answer wrongly given by a lot of people near the middle was a hindrance. Since all persons were assigned to one pole or the other on each scale,

discrimination in the center of the scale, where preferences were almost evenly divided, was essential.

Questions were sought not so much for theoretical meaning as for indicating the basic preference that influences the respondent's choice. They were directed to seemingly simple surface behaviors in the hope that they would provide reliable clues to the complex and profound patterns of behavior that could not otherwise be reached in a self-report instrument. The assumption was that preferences themselves are often not consciously formulated, in which case direct questions about them would not be answered accurately. The strategy was to use observable "straws in the wind" to make inferences about the direction of the wind itself. Many of the items, therefore, can be considered "pointers" that indicate a direction of preference. They are not direct measures of the quantity of a trait or of the development or ability of the person who holds that preference.

Since the content of the question was only a stimulus to evoke a type of reaction, some questions seemed to be trivial. The advantage was that they could be asked without impertinence and answered in either direction without strain. As an encouragement to candor, this harmlessness was a great advantage. Sometimes, however, this seeming simplicity backfires when a respondent indignantly decides that nothing significant can come out of such "worthless scraps of information."

It is important to understand that the content areas of the questions were not meant to cover all domains of the preference. Unlike with many educational tests, there was no attempt to precisely specify the domain and then to systematically write items to cover this domain. The intent instead was to identify any clues about preference that would empirically discriminate the groups of people of each preference. The interest in questions was not in the superficial behavior reported but in the evidence the questions could provide about the underlying preferences. Although the primary intent was not coverage of a domain, a range of behaviors thought to indicate each preference was included. For example, the E–I questions touch on Extraverted and Introverted differences in sociability, friendship, and intimacy; detachment or involvement; and outspokenness or reserve. This effort is described in greater detail in the following section.

Richness of the Item Pools   Another theoretical criterion that was used to guide item selection was the need to have the item pools for each scale reflect the richness of that preference domain. Factor analysis was used in two different ways to check for content coverage. Step II scoring of the MBTI is based on a factor analysis of all the items on Form J of the MBTI. As this scoring system demonstrates, each of the four preference domains can be further subdivided in this way into a number of subscales. The Form J items in the pool were mapped onto the 20 subscales from the MBTI Step II to ensure that at least in the initial pool there were items on each of the four preference scales representing each of the subscales associated with that preference. This was done with the realization, however, that the Step II subscales do not in themselves completely define the preference domains. While each of the four dichotomies encompasses more than is represented by the 5 subscales, the subscales do provide at least a minimal criterion by which the richness of the domain can be measured.

A separate factor analysis was conducted of the research form (described below). This analysis also produced a set of subfactors associated with each of the four preference scales. There was a high degree of overlap between the subscales arrived at in this analysis and those defined by the Step II scoring system. The only differences were a result of having used two different item pools and two different samples in the two analyses.

At each step in the item selection process, the items remaining in the pool were compared to these two sets of subscales to ensure that the final scales demonstrated the appropriate richness.

Forced-Choice Format

Questions are presented in forced-choice format primarily because type theory postulates dichotomies. All questions offer choices between the poles of the same dichotomy, E or I, S or N, T or F, J or P. There are no questions that cut across dichotomies. The forced-choice format was required because both poles of a dichotomy are valuable and both are used at different times by everyone. If the items used a different format, many people would correctly respond to both sides of the dichotomy. The goal of the items is to force a series of choices that will determine which of two valuable or useful behaviors or attitudes is preferred by the individual. The forced-choice format also has the advantage of avoiding the bias of acquiescent and social desirability response sets.

A small number of the Form J items in the initial item pool had more than two possible responses. These had been included in previous forms of the Indicator, including Form G, for research purposes to determine which of the responses was more valid. These items were changed by eliminating one or more of the available responses, so that only two responses remained. The responses that were eliminated were those with the lowest weight on Form G. When this criterion did not lead to a clear choice as to which response to eliminate, the response weights from the Step II subscales were used.

Phrase Questions and Word Pairs

MBTI items occur in two different forced-choice formats: phrase questions and word pairs. Originally all questions were phrases followed by a choice. For example, the first question of Form M is

When you go somewhere for the day, would you rather
Ⓐ plan what you will do and when, or
Ⓑ just go?

Word-pair questions were added for Forms E and F. Examples from Form M are:

scheduled Ⓐ Ⓑ unplanned
gentle Ⓐ Ⓑ firm

The instructions for the word pairs are as follows:

Which of these words appeals to you more? Think what the words mean, not how they look or how they sound.

The second sentence in these instructions was added in 1977 with Form G because interviews with persons taking Form F revealed that some persons had answered some of the word pairs on the basis of the sound or the appearance of the words, not their meaning.

Wording for Comparable Attractiveness

Early in the development and testing of questions, the authors discovered that a particular question elicited very different meanings for different types. In writing items, every effort was made to make the responses appeal to the appropriate types—for example, to make the Perceiving response to a J–P item as attractive to people with a Perceiving preference as the Judging response is to those with a Judging preference. The result is that responses may be psychologically rather than logically opposed, a fact that may annoy a number of Thinking types. Item content is less important than that the words and form of the sentence should serve as a "stimulus to evoke a type response." Where the attempt to make choices equally appealing did not succeed on earlier forms, item weighting was adopted (discussed later in detail).

Empirical Criteria

A number of empirical criteria were also used at various stages of the item selection process. The empirical criteria are primarily concerned with ensuring that the items differentiate between people of opposite preferences on each scale and on that scale alone. Both prediction ratios and IRT item parameters were used to select items.

Satisfactory Prediction Ratios for Each Response

A prediction ratio was calculated for each of the responses for the 290 items from Form J and for the 90 items written by the two type experts.

The same cutoff that had been used to select items for Form G was used in the revision process to eliminate items from the initial item pool. Only items with a prediction ratio greater than .62 for at least one of the responses were retained for further analysis.

Satisfactory Information at the Midpoint of the Scale

For each item in the initial item pool the amount of information at the midpoint of the scale was calculated using IRT parameters. For MBTI items, information at the midpoint indicates how well responses to the item separate people into the opposite sides of each dichotomy. Information at the midpoint is the slope of the item characteristic curve at θ = 0 on each scale. No absolute cutoff was used in examining these statistics. The top-performing items on each scale were selected for further testing. See Figure 7.1 for examples of two items with different degrees of information.

No Significant Gender or Age Differences   Form G, like most of the previous forms of the Indictor, uses separate weights for males and females for the T–F scale. The opportunity existed with the 1998 revision to determine whether advanced methodological techniques could be used to select items that would not require separate weighting. Since these techniques can be used to examine item response differences among any grouping of subjects and since the MBTI is administered across a very broad range of ages, three different age groups were examined. The number of minority group members was far too small to justify subgroup analyses for race-based subgroups in the Form M standardization sample. These analyses will be conducted as Form M data on minority samples accumulate.

The analytic technique used to determine whether significant subgroup differences existed in the response to MBTI items was differential item functioning (DIF). The general idea underlying DIF analyses as applied to the MBTI is that people from one subgroup (e.g., males) who have the same overall clarity of preference on a given scale should have essentially the same observed likelihood of endorsing a given item in the keyed direction as individuals who belong to another demographic subgroup (e.g., females). Likewise, at the scale level, the goal would be to have little or no *cumulative* DIF when the items in each of the four MBTI scales are aggregated. Therefore two basic questions were addressed in the DIF analyses: (1) To what degree does each *item* perform similarly across demographic subgroups of MBTI respondents? and (2) To what degree do subgroup differences in responding become evident at the *total number of items endorsed* level?

A DIF analysis was therefore conducted to identify all items in the initial item pool that showed significant gender or age differences. Each item that showed age or gender DIF was examined for content and a decision was made as to whether to retain or drop the item. Earlier research on the items from Forms F and G of the MBTI (Gratias & Harvey, 1998; Harvey, 1997) had shown that DIF is not a serious problem in the MBTI. That is, although some DIF is seen for some individual items, the sizes of the differences are not especially large, and of greater importance, there is only a very small degree of *cumulative* DIF at the scale level. The cumulative DIF is most important because the classification decision (e.g., is this person more likely to have a preference for E or for I?) is made at the scale level. Given that the initial item pool contained new and revised items, new DIF analyses were conducted on the entire pool.

Two approaches were used to quantify DIF. One approach used the Mantel-Haenszel (M-H Δ) technique, popularized by Educational Testing Service, which calculates the degree of difference in observed item-endorsement rates for subgroups of respondents formed by breaking the score estimates into a number of intervals. A major advantage of this method is the existence of widely used rules-of-thumb for gauging the *amount* and *severity* of the observed item-level DIF. A second approach used IRT-based methods that compare the ICCs estimated separately in each subgroup in order to provide a measure of overall DIF at the scale level. In this approach, test-characteristic curves for the demographic subgroups are compared in order to assess the cumulative impact of the DIF on the expected total number of items that would be endorsed in a given direction.

Five items were eliminated from the item pool at this point for gender DIF. For example, the following item from the E–I scale was eliminated because the responses for men and women were significantly different:

Do you usually
Ⓐ show your feelings freely, or
Ⓑ keep your feelings to yourself?

In predicting the likelihood of giving the (B) response to this item, it was more useful to know the respondent's gender (males tended to endorse (B) more than did females) than it was to know the person's E–I preference. Those with a preference for Introversion also were more likely to respond with (B) than were those preferring Extraversion, but the gender difference was more predictive. Since this item functioned differentially for men and women, it was dropped.

Given that Form G uses separate weights for males and females on the T–F scale, it was interesting to discover how few items there were in the pool, from any scale, that exhibited significant DIF. As the example above illustrates, not all of these items were from the T–F scale, either.

For the age group analyses, three age groups were used: under 35, 35 to 50, and over 50. While it would have been desirable to analyze other age groupings as well as or instead of the above, DIF analysis requires large numbers of respondents in each group. The distribution of ages in the sample did not permit other breakdowns.

Items that showed significant DIF by age were examined carefully for content. Some of these items were eliminated because they contained language that high school or college students might have found unfamiliar. Others were retained, however, because in the opinion of the type experts the items might have been tapping some developmental aspects of the preferences. For example, the following Form G word pair was dropped:

party Ⓐ Ⓑ theater

It is likely that the response to this item (overwhelmingly in favor of "party" among the younger group) was due to cultural changes affecting theater attendance rather than to development issues. Four such items were dropped.

Low Item-to-Scale Correlations with Nonkeyed Scales As was done with all previous forms of the Indicator, item-to-scale correlations were calculated for each item to each scale. Items were analyzed on all scales, not only the scale intended. The goal was to select items that made a contribution to only one scale. In some cases, items with high correlations on more than one scale were eliminated. There were, however, a number of items in the item pool in different stages that had high prediction ratios, high information at the midpoint, high correlations with the intended scale, and moderate correlations with a nonintended scale. These were primarily items on the S–N and J–P scales that correlated with the other scale as well as with the intended scale. Since these items met other criteria, both theoretical and empirical, a number of them were retained.

Step 3: Construct a Research Form

Applying the item selection criteria to the initial item pool of 580 items reduced to 264 the number of items for further analysis. A number of different samples were used for the item analyses including college students, adults attending MBTI qualifying workshops, and employed adults in various organizations throughout the United States.

To further reduce the pool, the 264 remaining items were printed on a research form along with two pages of demographic questions that included the following categories:

- "Census data" such as age, education, ethnic group, and income
- Work status
- Satisfaction with work
- Kinds of work performed
- Leisure activities
- Relationship status
- Satisfaction with relationships
- Number of children
- Birth order
- Spirituality
- Health, stress, and coping
- Hours of television watched

Completing the research form were 54 items that make up the *Fundamental Interpersonal Relations Orientation–Behavior* (FIRO-B) instrument. The FIRO-B items were added to provide a source of validity for the MBTI scales and to provide normative and standardization data for the FIRO-B.

Step 4: Administer the Research Form to a National Sample

To provide a new standardization sample for the MBTI item weights, the MBTI Research Form was administered to a sample of adults, 18 years and older, from across the United States. The sampling procedure utilized stratified, single-stage, random-digit dialing of U.S. households with telephones. The targets (i.e., stratification criteria) included percentages of people of age, gender, and ethnic group necessary to match the 1990 U.S. census. A minimum of three attempts was made to contact a respondent at each phone number. To ensure representativeness, the calls were made on weekends and evenings as well as during general business hours on weekdays. When a person answered the phone, trained survey staff briefly described the research study and the respondent was asked to state the ages of the people in the household. If anyone in the household could supply data from a targeted demographic group, the participation of that person was then sought. A payment of one dollar was offered as an incentive to participate in the study.

The survey was conducted over about a two-month period, during which time 16,000 households were screened. Approximately 8,000 households were selected to match the targets, and of these, 4,000 people agreed to participate in the study and were mailed copies of the MBTI Research Form along with a self-addressed, stamped envelope. The return rate for mailed forms was about 80%, yielding a sample of approximately 3,200 respondents.

Step 5: Select the Final Items for the Revised MBTI

An initial factor analysis was conducted on the 264 items making up the Research Form to confirm that the items were loading on the scales as expected. As with almost all other factor analyses of MBTI items, the four MBTI scales emerged as the primary factors. Based on this analysis, 26 items were eliminated because they either did not load on any of the four scales or loaded on a scale different from the one for which they had been keyed based on theory. The dropped items were primarily those that had been keyed to either the S–N or the J–P scales but loaded about equally on both, or loaded slightly higher on the nonkeyed scale.

Two panels of experts, the MBTI Research Advisory Board and another panel of type experts, reviewed the remaining 238 items against the theoretical and empirical criteria described above and shown in Table 7.2. As a result of this process, 93 items were chosen to make up the 1998 MBTI Form M. The characteristics of the final form are shown in a later section of this chapter. First, however, is a discussion of the development of the scoring procedure.

Development of Scoring Procedures for Form M

The 1998 revision also offered the opportunity to test alternative scoring techniques for the MBTI. Two primary methods were chosen for comparison: the prediction ratio method (PR) and a three-parameter item response theory (IRT) model. The PR method was examined because this is the method used to score every form of the MBTI since Form C. A scoring method based on IRT was examined because research had suggested that it might provide better precision around the midpoint of the scales. At least a half-dozen variations of each of these two primary methods were tested. To determine which of these two approaches offered the best method of scoring the MBTI for type, a large-scale best-fit type study was conducted.

Best-Fit Type Study

This study involved a comparison of various methods of scoring sets of MBTI items, using "verified," or "best-fit," type as the criterion. To conduct this study a number of large-scale users of the MBTI were contacted and offered free MBTI forms and feedback reports in exchange for their participation. Over two dozen qualified MBTI users agreed to participate.

Six steps were followed in conducting the true type study:

1. Obtain responses to all 290 Form J items on the MBTI research form from all samples.
2. Conduct an interpretation session with each sample, defining and explaining the MBTI preference scales.
3. Have each person in the group complete a best-fit questionnaire (BFQ) designed to obtain that person's belief about his or her best-fit type.
4. Select items based on criteria unique to the method; i.e., use PR and IRT parameters to select a set of items to be scored to determine type.
5. Score the responses to each set of items using the corresponding PR or IRT scoring methods to arrive at a four-letter type.
6. Compare the type for each person derived from each scoring method to the best-fit type for that person.

Best-fit type was obtained from a best-fit questionnaire that asked the person to identify the preferences on each of the four dichotomous MBTI scales that seemed the best fit with his or her self-understanding. For each of the four preferences, each person also was asked to rate his or her degree of confidence in the estimate of best-fit preference on a 5-point scale ranging from "not at all confident" to "very confident." The best-fit type estimates and confidence ratings were made by each individual after receiving feedback from a qualified interpreter. There was, however, some variation in how the BFQs were administered. Some interpreters asked for the questionnaires to be completed and returned before providing the MBTI results to the person; others returned the MBTI results first and then administered the BFQ.

Over 4,000 Form J answer sheets were distributed, and approximately 2,600 best-fit type questionnaires were returned. After removing cases with missing data, the final sample consisted of $N = 2,116$ people for whom scored MBTI types could be compared to best-fit types. Approximately 56% of the sample was female, and the mean age of the sample was 35 years ($SD = 13.6$). Of those who answered the question asking them to identify the ethnic group with which they identified, 87% indicated White, 8% Black, 3% Hispanic, 1.3% Asian, and 1% Native American.

Two different researchers, one an expert in the PR method and the other in IRT, were given the response data from each Form J for which a BFQ was available along with the gender of the respondent. The researchers were given no other information about the respondents. The MBTI types resulting from the standard Form G scoring procedures, the best-fit types, the best-fit confidence ratings, and all other demographic information were withheld so that the predictions would be independent of any of these data. The researchers each used their own chosen method to select items, to score the responses, and to assign a four-letter "predicted type" to each person in the sample.

As stated, each of the two basic scoring approaches used a somewhat different set of items to arrive at the person's type. This was necessary because both PR and IRT methods are used not only to score but also to select and to weight items to arrive at a preference designation on each scale. Although not common, there were some items that yielded a high prediction ratio for at least one of the responses but provided little information when used in an IRT approach. Because the purpose of this study was to determine which method provided the highest accuracy in predicting best-fit type, each researcher had to be free to choose items that maximized the prediction. It was not useful, therefore, to compare the two methods for the same set of items, since one set would not be optimized for the other approach to scoring.

Using each method, a type was computed for each person in the sample. These data were then sent to a third, independent researcher who compared the two different predicted types with the best-fit type for each person and computed "hit rates." The hit rates are expressed as a percentage of people for whom there is exact agreement between the best-fit type (or preference, when working at the level of individual scales) and the type (or preference) predicted for that person by one of the scoring methods. For example, if one of the scoring methods predicted that a person's type was ENFP and the person had concluded, after hearing the MBTI interpretation, that her best-fit type was in fact ESTP, then this prediction was counted as a "miss" when whole types were being compared. However, when separate comparisons were made of the individual preference scales, these results would yield hits for the E–I and J–P scales and misses for the S–N and T–F scales. Hit rates were computed for the entire sample and for different demographic categories (age, ethnic group, gender) as well as for other breakdowns of the sample, such as type of interpretation received (individual or group) and type of setting (clinical or organizational).

Hit rates were also computed by the confidence level of the best-fit ratings and by preference score ranges.

Eight different versions of the PR method and four different versions of the IRT-based procedure were tested. In each case, regardless of which breakdown of the sample was analyzed, one set of predictions from each method was clearly superior to the others using that same method. Therefore the best prediction from each method was used in the final comparison.

Alternative versions of the PR method included variations in the cutoffs used to select items, in the number of different weights used, in the scores around the midpoint that were used to exclude people from the sample, and in how many responses by people of the opposite preference were allowed before an item was excluded. The best prediction of type using a variation of the PR method used a cutoff of .66, had seven categories of weights, excluded people whose continuous scores ranged from 90 to 110 on each scale, and used a maximum of 40% of the opposite preference who could choose a response and still have the response pass as an acceptable item. Note that although this variation produced the highest best-fit hit rate of all of the PR methods, it differs in all respects from the PR method used with Form G. The four alternatives based on the IRT procedure included varying the cutoffs for IRT item parameters and how the midpoint was adjusted for a given set of parameters.

Results of the Best-Fit Study

The results of the best-fit study are shown in Table 7.3 for the overall sample, for each scale separately, and for males and females separately. One column shows the percentage of agreement between best-fit type and the type as determined by the best of the PR methods. The other column shows the percentage of agreement between best-fit type and the type as determined by the best of the IRT methods. Overall, the best IRT method produced about a 6% higher agreement with best-fit type than did the best of the PR methods. In all other breakdowns the same pattern was observed: IRT produced at least a marginally better percentage of agreement with best-fit type.

Before concluding this section a number of caveats are in order. First, follow-up contacts with most of the interpreters revealed that they had returned the MBTI results to the group before asking the participants to complete the BFQ. This procedure likely biased the hit rates in favor of the PR method, since that is the method that was used to provide the MBTI results received by the participants; it may have been difficult for some people to disagree with the "official-looking" computer-generated results.

Second, the best overall hit rate is fairly low: 64%. Other best-fit studies have yielded a range of 64% to 85%. That the overall accuracy in this study is at the low end of this range is probably due to the fact that many different professionals interpreted the MBTI to a wide variety of groups across a variety of settings. Previous best-fit studies have

Table 7.3 Comparison of Percentage of Agreement with Best-Fit Type for PR- and IRT-Based Scoring Methods

	PR	IRT
Overall	58%	64%
E–I	86.5%	90%
S–N	86%	88%
T–F	85%	86%
J–P	86%	88%
Males	55%	60%
Females	60%	67%

Note: N = 2,116.

used much more homogeneous groups, the same interpreter, and standard interpretation procedures (within-study). More rigorous interpretation standards were sacrificed in this study because large numbers of people were needed to participate so as to yield sufficient numbers of people with slight preference scores, thereby permitting a meaningful analysis. Another factor influencing the hit rate is that the IRT method may not have correctly adjusted the midpoint of some of the scales.

Development of the Form M Self-Scorable and Template-Scorable Versions

As with Form G, a self-scorable version of Form M has been created for use in workshops, classes, and groups when it is inconvenient or impossible to administer Form M prior to the group meeting. A template-scorable version of Form M is also available for those who wish to hand-score their clients' answer sheets. The Form M template- and self-scorable versions both use the same 93 items to arrive at a preference on each of the four scales, as does the standard Form M. However, since IRT can be used only on the computer-scored versions for Form M, an alternative scoring system was developed for the self-scorable and template-based versions.

The goals of choosing an alternative scoring system for the template- and self-scorable versions of Form M were as follows:

- To achieve a high degree of agreement between the results of the self-scorable and template-scorable versions and those that used IRT computer scoring
- To use a system that provides quick scoring to save time in the workshop setting or in hand-scoring by the professional
- To use a scoring method for which hand calculations would be relatively simple so as to reduce the likelihood of making errors in scoring

		Table 7.4

Table 7.4 Percentage of Agreement Between Form M IRT-Scored Versions and Form M Template- and Self-Scorable Versions

Preference	Percentage of Agreement Across All Respondents	Percentage of Agreement After Eliminating Respondents with $\theta \pm .10$ Point from Midpoint of Scale
E	93.8	98.1
I	99.2	99.9
S	99.3	100.0
N	97.6	99.9
T	97.9	100.0
F	98.6	100.0
J	96.8	99.1
P	97.9	99.0

Note: N = 4,692. Percentages shown represent the percentage of people who show the same preference using both the IRT-scored version and the self-scorable version of Form M.

■ To yield results that were easy to interpret and reduced the chance of misinterpretation or overinterpretation of scores

A number of different methods were investigated, all of which showed high convergence with IRT results. A method using unit weighting was adopted since it provided the best match with all of the goals. In this method, the person scoring the instrument simply counts the number of answers given for each pole of each dichotomy. The person's preferences are determined by calculating which pole received the most responses. See Chapter 5 for the exact steps involved in scoring and Chapter 6 for the meaning of the results.

Table 7.4 shows the percentage of agreement between scores derived using the standard Form M IRT scoring program and scores derived from the unit-weighted scoring method used on the template- and self-scorable versions. Agreement for two different samples is shown. The second column includes the entire sample of Form M respondents. In the third column, the sample has been reduced by removing those people whose θ score was plus or minus .10 point from the midpoint of each scale. As the table demonstrates, the correspondence in both samples is extremely high and, as expected, higher in the reduced sample.

The percentage of agreement between results of the IRT scoring system and the unit-weighted scoring system used on the self-scorable and template-scorable versions of Form M is very high.

Scoring the MBTI Using IRT

One of the most significant differences between the traditional PR-based scoring system for MBTI preferences versus the methods typically used in IRT scoring concerns the means by which item responses are used to estimate each person's preference score. Unlike the PR method, IRT methods use a *likelihood-based* approach to scoring.

A fundamental quantity in all of the scoring equations is the expected probability that people with a score of θ will endorse item i in the keyed direction (i.e., choosing the I, N, F, or P answer), which is a joint function of the IRT scoring parameters a, b, and c, plus θ (D is a scaling constant):

$$P_i(\theta) = c_i + (1 - c_i)\ \frac{e^{Da_i(\theta - b_i)}}{1 + e^{Da_i(\theta - b_i)}}$$

A *maximum likelihood* function can be defined based on the expected item-endorsement probability as follows (n = number of items, u = the 1/0 keyed item response):

$$l(u \mid \theta) = \prod_{i=1}^{n} P_i^{u_i} Q_i^{1-u_i}$$

$$\ln l(u \mid \theta) = \sum_{i=1}^{n} [(u_i \ln P_i) + [(1 - u_i)] \ln (1 - P_i)]$$

To obtain the estimate of each person's θ score, the above function is evaluated across a range of possible θ values, and the θ value that produces the "most likely" value for the likelihood function (i.e., highest in absolute value) is used as the estimate of that person's θ score. An example of likelihood functions for two respondents to the MBTI is shown in Figure 7.4. The logic of the IRT scoring procedure is to hypothesize that the person's score could be any value of θ. The likelihood of these hypotheses (i.e., each θ) is then tested using two pieces of data: the person's actual repsonses to each item and all of the information that is known about the characteristics of all of the items. The θ that has the maximum likelihood is then chosen as the best estimate of that person's score. If that score is to the right of the midpoint, then the person's letter is I, N, F, or P, depending on the scale; if the θ score is to the left of the midpoint, then the person's letter is E, S, T, or J. Both of the individuals whose likelihood functions are shown in Figure 7.4 would be classified as having a preference for Introversion because the maximum value (i.e., the highest point) on both functions occurs to the right, or Introverted side, of the midpoint.

Additionally, the *height* of the likelihood function at its maximum point also provides useful information: All other things being equal, higher maximum values are more desirable and are associated with item-response profiles that are more consistent or plausible.

Once an estimate of θ has been established using the maximum likelihood method, a Bayesian approach is used to refine the estimation. The Bayes *expected a posteriori* (EAP) estimate of θ is used.

$$\theta = \frac{\sum_{k=1}^{q} x_k L(x_k) w(x_k)}{\sum_{k=1}^{q} L(x_k) w(x_k)}$$

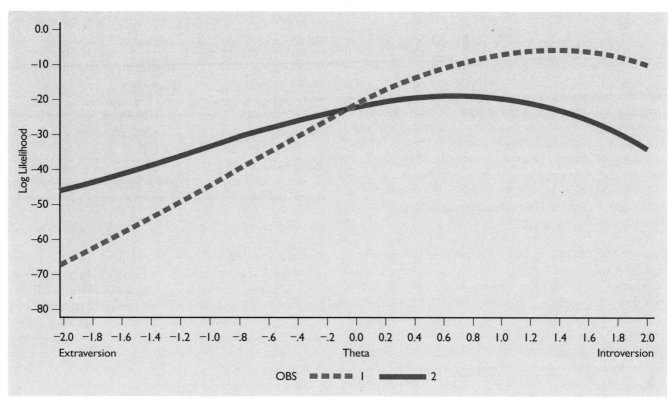

Figure 7.4 Maximum Likelihood Curves for Two Different People

The advantage of using the Bayes EAP scoring method is that the EAP estimate is effectively a *weighted* maximum likelihood estimate of θ, giving more weight to the areas of the assumed θ distribution in which higher numbers of individuals are present and less weight to θ values in less dense portions of the distribution.

Tie-Breaking Procedure

Using IRT scoring, it is very rare for a person's score on any of the four preference scales to land exactly at the θ that defines the midpoint of that scale. Given that the self- and template-scorable versions do not use the more precise IRT scoring, however, ties may be somewhat more common. For all scoring systems, a tie-breaker continues to be used with Form M. All ties are broken in the same direction as with previous forms of the Indicator: I, N, F, or P. When a tie occurs, then the person's preference becomes I, N, F, or P, depending on the scale, and that person's score becomes 1.

The logic behind breaking ties in favor of the N or P preferences is that these are the less frequent types in the population. If a person is that close to the preference (zero difference), there is probably some environmental response pressure from the "majority" preference. This pressure can result in answers conforming to the majority and contrary to true preferences. Thus the person's "true" type is probably N or P.

On the E–I scale, recent estimates of the distribution of preferences in the population (see Tables 7.14 and 7.15; Hammer & Mitchell, 1996) suggest that the proportion of Extraverts and Introverts is about equal. However, the method of breaking ties in the favor of I was retained because in many settings there is still cultural pressure to behave as an Extravert.

On the T–F scale the tie-breaker is in the direction of F for men because men are more socialized to give T responses. For consistency and for continuity with previous methods, the same tie-breaker is used for women, that is, in the direction of F.

Finally, it is important to understand that the decision rules for the tie-breakers should not be overinterpreted. The primary purpose of a tie-breaker is to provide a stimulus for starting a conversation with the respondent about why he or she answered the questions about equally in both directions.

Kinds of Results Available from Form M

Regardless of which version of Form M is used, the goal is to arrive at one of the 16 types, and all versions report the whole type. For respondents who complete the computer-scored versions of Form M, that is, those versions relying on IRT scoring, there are four additional kinds of results available for each scale: a preference letter, a preference clarity index, a preference clarity category, and a continuous score. For the self- and template-scorable versions of Form M, an additional score is available: the raw points for each pole of each dichotomy. Table 7.5 summarizes the kinds of results available for each version of Form M.

Raw Points
Raw points are used only on the self- and template-scorable versions of Form M. Eight raw points are calculated, one for each of the dichotomous preferences (E, I, S, N, T, F, J, P). As described in Chapter 5, these points are calculated by simply summing the number of responses for each pole of each preference scale. Raw points are only an intermediate step used to determine the person's preference on a scale and his or her preference clarity category (see below); they are not meant to be interpreted.

Preference Letter
As with previous versions of the Indicator, the result for each of the four dichotomous scales is reported to the client in the form of a letter, which is a shorthand for which pole of each dichotomy is preferred.

As described earlier in this chapter, the IRT-based scoring procedure yields a score that, in IRT terminology, is called θ. To determine a person's preference on a given scale, the θ for that scale is computed using the IRT three-parameter model. If θ falls to the right of the midpoint of the preference scale, the person's preference is determined to be I, N, F, or P, depending on the scale. If θ falls to the left of the midpoint, the preference is E, S, T or J, depending on the scale.

Preference Clarity Index
The name for the numeral that is associated with a preference on Form M is the *preference clarity index* (pci). This index is analogous to the *preference score* in previous forms of the Indicator. The name was changed to preference clarity index for several reasons:

■ The phrase *preference clarity* better indicates the real meaning of the number.
■ The word *index* is more appropriate for a type indicator since it means "something used or serving to point out; a sign, token, or indication [as in] 'a true index of his character'" and "something that directs attention to some fact or condition" (Random House, 1987).
■ Use of the word *score* had led to misinterpretations of the meaning of the preference score.
■ The word *score* implies a trait approach that is inappropriate for a type indicator.

To calculate the preference clarity index the maximum and minimum θ for each scale were determined using the national sample data. The person's θ score on a given preference scale is divided by the maximum θ for that scale. This ratio is multiplied by 30 and then rounded up to the nearest positive integer. This puts all of the preference clarity indexes on a 1-to-30 scale.

The preference clarity index is thus a ratio showing how consistently the person answered the questions on that scale compared with the maximum possible score achievable on

Table 7.5	Results Available from Form M
Result	**Version**
Whole types	All versions
Preference letters	All versions
Preference clarity index	IRT computer-scored versions (mail-in, Web site, and on-site options)
Raw points	Template- and self-scorable versions
Preference clarity categories	All versions
Continuous scores (θ)	IRT computer-scored versions (mail-in, Web site, and on-site options)

that scale (i.e., the score that would result if the person answered *all* of the items on that scale in the keyed direction). This ratio takes into account the fact that in IRT scoring the MBTI items have different weights, reflecting how well they discriminate between people of opposite preferences. The pci also reflects the fact that the IRT scoring procedure provides a correction for nonlinearity and for social desirability.

This new index solves one of the problems associated with the old preference scores. Because of the manner in which preference scores were calculated, there were widely different ranges across the four scales. For example, the maximum possible preference score for the F preference on Form G was 39 for males, while the maximum possible preference score for the T preference was 65. The same number therefore had different meanings depending on which preference was being considered. The same disparity occurred across scales as well. A score of F 30 on the T–F scale for a male indicated a very clear preference, while a score of E 30 on the E–I scale (where the maximum is 53 for E) indicated only a moderate preference. Standardizing the pci makes interpretation more straightforward.

While the interpretation is made easier by the use of the pci, researchers must be cautioned that its use in correlations may attenuate the results. In any sample, the pci will have less variance than will the continuous scores. Therefore any correlations based on the pci, especially in samples of people with very clear preferences, may be lower than would be the case if continuous scores were used.

Preference Clarity Categories
To aid in interpretation and to lessen the chance that preference scores will be overinterpreted, many of the computer-generated interpretive reports associated with Form G display the preference scores on a grid using bar graphs. The horizontal axis on this grid is labeled using four categories. Starting at the zero point and moving toward the end of the axis in either direction, the labels and the corresponding Form G *preference scores* are as follows: *slight* (1–9), *moderate* (11–19), *clear* (21–39, or 31 for F), and *very clear* (41 or higher, or 31 for F).

Form M employs the same labels in the same order and refers to them as the *preference clarity categories*. The pcc has two different sources: the pci of computer-scored forms and the raw points of template scored and self-scored versions. When using the computer-scored versions of Form M, these categories are associated with pci ranges as follows: *slight* (1–5), *moderate* (6–15), *clear* (16–25), and *very clear* (26–30). When using the template- and self-scorable versions of Form M, these categories are associated with ranges of the raw points for the preferred pole. Since each scale has a different number of items, and therefore a different number of possible raw points, the ranges differ depending on the scale. See Table 5.4 for how to convert raw points into preference clarity categories. This table is printed on the self-scorable form and on the templates used in hand-scoring.

As with Form G, the preference clarity categories are to be treated as heuristics to aid in interpretation, not as cut-off points for decision making. See Chapter 6 for recommendations on how all MBTI results are to be interpreted.

Continuous Scores As with the previous versions of the MBTI, results are also available as continuous scores for use by researchers wishing to correlate MBTI scores with the scores of other instruments or criterion variables. The continuous scores are the values of θ that result from IRT scoring. As such, they are available only for the computer-scored versions of the Indicator.

When researchers desire to correlate MBTI scores with those of other instruments, it is important that they use the θ scores and not the preference clarity indexes. Because a pci is basically a compression of the full range of θ on a given scale, it generally will have less variance than will the corresponding distribution of θ. This means that correlations based on the pci could suffer from restriction of range in certain samples and thus be attenuated.

Determining the Midpoint of the Scales for Form M

To determine the midpoint of each of the scales, additional analyses were conducted. Generally, with an IRT scoring system, the midpoint of the scale occurs at θ = 0.0. However, given that precision around the midpoint is of primary importance for a type instrument, an external criterion was sought. The procedure of using an external criterion to set the division point is consistent with the history of MBTI developments. The criterion used at this point to determine the optimal division point was determined by another best-fit study.

Form M of the MBTI was administered to a number of different samples of adults and students. The individuals were participants in four-day MBTI qualifying workshops or in intensive individual feedback sessions conducted by experienced MBTI trainers. The responses were scored using the IRT item parameters, which yielded a θ for each

Table 7.6	**Percentage of Agreement Between Unadjusted and Adjusted Form M Types and Best-Fit Type**	
Scale	**Agreement of Preference Category Using Unadjusted Midpoint**	**Agreement of Preference Category Using Adjusted Midpoint**
E–I	92%	93%
S–N	92%	94%
T–F	86%	92%
J–P	92%	95%
Overall	72%	78%

Note: N = 157.

person. Each person in each sample also estimated his or her best-fit type. When all of the samples were combined, the total sample contained 157 individuals. For each scale the sample was divided into two categories, one for each of the preferences on that scale. The frequency of the pci was plotted for each category and then placed on the same scale. This allowed for a graphic examination of the effect of various placements of the midpoint for each of the scales.

Prior to any adjustments (i.e., with the midpoint of all scales set at θ = 0.0), the agreement between best-fit type and the type determined by the IRT scoring program was 72%. As shown in Table 7.6, the percentage of agreement using these unadjusted midpoints was 92% for the E–I, S–N, and J–P scales and 86% for the T–F scale.

As shown in Table 7.7, examination of the distributions of unadjusted preference clarity indexes for people of different best-fit preferences revealed a number of "misses," with by far most of the misses being on only one scale. For example, a number of people who declared Feeling as a best-fit preference on the T–F scale had a pci on that scale indicating that they should be classified as a Thinking type. The same condition was observed on the S–N and J–P scales. Consequently it was determined that a slight adjustment to the midpoint of the S–N, T–F, and J–P scales was warranted. The midpoint of the E–I scale was not changed. The adjustments were as follows:

E–I None.

S–N If the unadjusted preference clarity index is between 0 and 1 in the S direction, classify as N.

T–F If the unadjusted preference clarity index is between 0 and 2 in the T direction, classify as F.

J–P If the unadjusted preference clarity index is between 0 and 1 in the J direction, classify as P.

So, for example, if the pci for an individual was J 1, that person would be classified as a P, because in the best-fit sample these people had declared that P was a better fit than was J. A person whose preference and pci were J 2 would still be classified as a J. Another factor considered when

Table 7.7 Agreement on Number of Scales Between Unadjusted and Adjusted Form M and Best-Fit Types

Agreement on	Unadjusted Form M	Adjusted Form M
0 scales	0%	0%
1 scale	1%	0%
2 scales	4%	4%
3 scales	23%	18%
4 scales	72%	78%

Table 7.8 Items per Scale and Item Formats for Form M and Form G

Items per Scale	Form M	Form G
E–I	21	21
S–N	26	26
T–F	24	23
J–P	22	24
Total	93	94
Word pairs	47	45
Phrases	46	49

making the adjustments was to increase the number of people whose best-fit preference matched their Form M preference without creating any more mismatches. The goal was, therefore, absolute gain, *not* net gain. This is why there were no adjustments made to the midpoint of the E–I scale. Moving the midpoint on this scale in either direction would have gained some matches but also created some mismatches.

Another consideration was that the midpoint adjustment not create additional mismatches between Form M and Form G. Therefore, when an adjustment was considered, the Form M preference clarity indexes were plotted against people whose Form G preferences were known in another sample, and the effect of the adjustment on the Form M–Form G match was examined. The adjustments described above created one more match in this comparison and no additional mismatches.

As can be seen in the above discussion, midpoint adjustments were made so as to more accurately classify people whose preference clarity indexes were in the "slight" range. People with preference clarity indexes of 1 or greater on S–N and J–P, and 2 or greater on T–F, were unaffected by the adjustment, and some therefore remained with a reported type that does not match their best-fit type. For example, one person in the sample responded to most of the S–N items on Form M in the N direction but identified S as his best-fit preference on the S–N scale. It was generally true that in the few instances when this occurred it occurred for the same person on more than one scale. In other words, some of the overall "misses" on whole type were due to people who had misses on more than one scale. In three cases where this occurred, the professional interpreters were contacted and asked if they recalled these people and if so to describe them. For all three of these people, the trainers had observed that during the workshop they had used an interpersonal style that made positive interaction with others difficult. One hypothesis, if this anecdotal finding holds up, is that when mismatches occur between best-fit preference and reported preference for which the person has high preference clarity indexes on the mismatched scales, this may be the result of poor type development. Another hypothesis is that there are strong environmental pressures toward certain preferences felt by these

individuals *either* during completion of the instrument *or* during the verification process.

Once the appropriate pci cutoffs were established for each scale on the basis of the best-fit type data, the thetas required to produce those preference clarity indexes were determined and the scoring program was changed accordingly.

Properties of Form M

In this section the properties of Form M are described and in some cases compared to those of Form G. Some statistics on Form G are included here because the comparisons can help in understanding the changes made in moving from Form G to Form M. For a complete reporting of the characteristics of Form G see Myers and McCaulley (1985). Because Form M is now considered the standard form of the Indicator, the emphasis here is on presenting data that describe Form M. Topics covered in this section include comparison of the number of items per scale and of each format for both forms. This is followed by information about the frequency of omissions for Form M as well as a comparison of the types resulting from Form M and Form G. We also look at information relating to the "purity" and independence of the preference scales, including item-to-scale correlations and scale intercorrelations for both forms. The characteristics of the national sample used as the basis of the Form M item selection and scoring procedures are presented. Finally, we discuss an analysis of DIF in Form M by gender and age.

Item Comparison

Form M consists of 93 items, one less than the number of scored items on Form G. Table 7.8 shows the breakdown by scale and by item format for both Form M and Form G. These figures demonstrate that few changes were made in the number of items per scale or in the number of items of different format in moving from Form G to Form M.

Table 7.9   Frequencies of Omissions on Form M

Omissions	n	%	Cum.%
0	2,522	83%	83%
1	283	9%	92%
2	72	2%	95%
3	54	2%	97%
4	33	1%	98%
5	20	1%	98%
6	10	0%	99%
7	7	0%	99%
8	25	1%	100%
9	8	0%	100%
10	1	0%	100%
11	1	0%	100%

Note: N = 3,036. See Appendix for a description of the sample.

Source: National sample.

Another similarity between the two forms is evident in the ordering of the items on Form M. The ordering was designed to correspond to that of Form G as much as possible. All items on Form M that were taken directly from Form G were placed, to the extent possible, in exactly the same position on Form M as they appeared on Form G. When a Form G item was dropped, every attempt was made to place a new or revised item from the same scale in that position on Form M. The ordering of items thus provides a strong sense of continuity for MBTI users and in addition retains many effects of having the items ordered in the manner designed by Myers.

Longtime users of Form G will note that most of the new or revised items that were introduced with Form M occur on the second half of the form. For example, among the first 50 items on Form M are 39 items from Form G. These were the items on Form G that had the greatest power to differentiate people of opposite preferences and were therefore also those items that carried weights of 1 and 2 for their responses. Items in the second half of Form G were more likely to carry weights of 0 and 1, and it was these items that were more often replaced by new or revised items on Form M.

Omissions on Form M

As with Form G, omissions are permitted on Form M in the belief that greater validity is achieved by the elimination of doubtful answers. Type can then be indicated by preferences to the item responses a person is reasonably sure about, uncontaminated by guessing. The IRT scoring program uses all of the information available in producing a type. In practice, there are typically few omissions. Table 7.9 shows the frequency of omissions on Form M. As can be seen in this table, 83% of the respondents answered all of the items and 94% left no more than two blank. A person may leave a large number of blanks on an answer sheet for a number of reasons: a lack of understanding of the vocabulary or sentences due to low reading ability in English; an inability to indicate preferences by responding to MBTI items; or a conscious desire not to reveal oneself, perhaps due to misunderstanding of or lack of trust in the testing environment.

More important than the total number of omissions is the number of omissions per scale. For example, 12 omissions spread evenly across all four scales will cause less of a problem than if all 12 occur on one scale, or two. So that both respondents and interpreters can take this into account during the interpretation process, omissions per scale are reported on most MBTI computer-scored narratives and profiles. In addition, if there are a number of omissions above a certain level per scale, this fact is flagged and a cautionary comment is printed. Specifically, this occurs if there are more than four omissions on the E–I or J–P scale and more than five omissions on the longer S–N and T–F scales. These cutoffs were determined by examining scale reliabilities for people with different levels of omissions.

Relationship Between Form M and Form G Results

A sample of 101 adults from a church congregation in a small Midwestern town were administered both Form G and Form M at the same time. The mean age of the sample was 48 years (*SD* = 18), and the sample was composed of 61% females. The relationship between the two forms is shown in Table 7.10. The overall agreement of whole types was 60% between the two forms, which is somewhat better than what would be expected given the level of agreement on the independent scales (i.e., if we assume that the scales are independent and multiply the percentage of agreement on all four scales, the probability of overall agreement would be 54%). Because a person's whole type is determined by his or her preferences on the four separate scales, the overall agreement between the two forms is somewhat constrained by the level of agreement on the four scales.

It is interesting to note that the lowest agreement is on the S–N scale, which is the longest scale but also the one with the greatest number of Form G items retained on Form M. The sample on which these data are based was predominantly S. Changes for a number of these people who scored around the midpoint on either form may be the cause of the lower level of agreement on this scale.

In conclusion, it should be noted that the level of 60% agreement between Form G and Form M on whole types is actually higher, and in some cases quite a bit higher, than is observed between two administrations of Form G in 10 of the 11 studies reported in the 1985 *MBTI Manual*.

Item-to-Scale Correlations

In the development of the MBTI, item analyses always included both item-to-scale correlations and prediction ratios for each response to all scales, not simply the scale for which the item was designed. Any item that loaded similarly on more than one scale was eliminated. On Form G, biserial correlations computed between the retained items and the scores of other scales had a median absolute correlation range of .07 to .12, as compared to a range of .43 to .55 when correlated with the item's own scale.

The item-to-scale correlations for Form M are shown in Table 7.11. As expected, the median correlations of the Form M items on each scale are considerably higher with their own scale than with the other three scales. The only exception to this trend is the moderate correlation of S–N items with the J–P scale, and vice versa.

Scale Intercorrelations

Intercorrelations of continuous scores for the Form G databank sample and for various Form M samples are shown in Table 7.12. These figures give an estimate of the size of intercorrelations to expect, depending on the distribution of types in a particular research sample. In naturally occurring samples, larger than expected scale intercorrelations can often be attributed to a greater representation than normal of a particular preference. There was also a trend in the Form G analyses (Myers & McCaulley, 1985, Table 9.7) for intercorrelations between J–P and S–N, and J–P and T–F, higher in older age groups.

As expected, the largest correlations in the Form M samples are almost always between S–N and J–P, and some samples also show a relationship between T–F and J–P. The intercorrelation between the S–N and J–P scales for Form M is similar to, if not somewhat higher than, the correlation between these two scales for the Form G databank, although this difference is likely attributable to the heterogeneous nature of the databank sample.

The correlations show that Sensing types are more likely to be J, and Intuitives are more likely to be P. The positive correlations between S–N and J–P probably reflect a fact about the types themselves. Sensing types typically prefer to rely on past experience and dislike unexpected events that require a rapid assessment of new possibilities. A preference for Judging leads to a life that is planned and consistent, decreasing the numbers of such unexpected events. Intuitive types, on the other hand, are attracted to future possibilities and new constructions of events. The Perceiving attitude keeps the door open to an incoming stream of these new possibilities.

Differential Item Functioning

After the 93 items were chosen for Form M, the differential item functioning (DIF) analysis was repeated to once again examine any possible differential effects of items by gender or by age. Although both item- and scale-level analyses were performed, the main focus of these analyses was on the *test-level* DIF results, which directly provide an index of the "bottom line" difference that would be expected on the basis of demographic factors when the MBTI is used in practice. That is, it is relatively common to find that a few

	Table 7.10	Relationship Between Form M and Form G in a Sample of Adults	
Scale	Correlation Between Continuous Scores	Percentage of Agreement in Classification
E–I	.90	90%
S–N	.87	79%
T–F	.89	87%
J–P	.89	87%
Overall Agreement		60%

Note: N = 101. See Appendix for a description of the sample.
Source: Trinity Lutheran Church.

individual items exhibit low to modest levels of DIF at the item level (e.g., Drasgow, 1987); however, such effects typically become a practical concern only to the extent that they exert a significant distorting effect that is visible at the scale level of analysis.

For the item-level DIF results, values of the Mantel-Haenszel (M-H Δ) statistic (an index of both the magnitude and direction of the DIF) that exhibit a significant chi-square and are in excess of 1.5 are viewed as being potentially "significant" in magnitude. With respect to interpreting the individual M-H Δ, the *sign* of each statistic indicates whether the "focal" group (females in the sex-DIF, and young/old individuals in the age-DIF comparisons) scores above or below the "reference" group (males, or middle-aged). Thus negative values for the gender comparison on the J–P scale would indicate that in a group of females and males that are *matched* with respect to clarity of their MBTI preference, females will be less likely to choose the keyed (P) response to the item than will males.

The test-level M-H Δ results for gender and age are graphically summarized in Figures 7.5–7.8 for gender-based DIF and in Figures 7.9–7.12 for age-based DIF. Each of these figures shows *test characteristic curves* (TCC) for each of the comparisons. TCCs are exactly analogous to the item characteristic curves shown earlier, but instead of modeling the probability of responding to a given item in the keyed direction, they show probability of responding in the keyed direction on the entire scale.

In Figures 7.5–7.12 the expected difference between subgroups in terms of *total* numbers of items endorsed in the keyed direction is shown; as an inspection of these results readily indicates, these TCCs are quite close across much of the scale and typically much closer at the type cutoff points. The age-based results are somewhat larger than the gender-based DIF at the points of maximum divergence, which is likely due to the fact that some of the items showing age DIF were retained because they were believed to tap developmental differences that should not be eliminated from the

Table 7.11　Item-to-Scale Correlations for Form M

Items		E–I Scale	S–N Scale	T–F Scale	J–P Scale
E–I items	Median	**.52**	−.11	−.07	−.04
	Minimum	**.43**	−.25	−.17	−.14
	Maximum	**.76**	.03	.05	.01
S–N items	Median	−.10	**.53**	.06	.28
	Minimum	−.15	**.38**	−.17	.10
	Maximum	−.04	**.65**	.25	.39
T–F items	Median	−.06	.05	**.53**	.11
	Minimum	−.13	−.06	**.36**	−.04
	Maximum	.00	.20	**.65**	.21
J–P items	Median	−.05	.30	.10	**.59**
	Minimum	−.14	.12	−.04	**.39**
	Maximum	.03	.46	.31	**.72**

Table 7.12　Intercorrelations of Continuous Scores for Form G and Form M

Sample	N	E–I:S–N	E–I:T–F	E–I:J–P	S–N:T–F	S–N:J–P	T–F:J–P
Form G							
Form G databank	32,671	−.08	−.07	−.07	.13	.38	.21
Form M							
National sample	3,036	−.18	−.12	−.09	.12	.47	.18
CRI sample	154	−.20	−.16	−.07	.08	.49	.20
Trinity Lutheran Church	101	−.24	−.07	−.20	.40	.53	.35
Employee Career Enrichment Program	98	−.04	.03	.07	.12	.49	.32
Test-retest sample	424	−.25	−.17	−.19	.11	.38	.27
Iowa State University	279	−.13	−.18	−.19	.32	.54	.28
Middle TN State University	198	−.06	−.04	−.14	.26	.41	.09
Fairview Health Services	261	−.10	−.10	−.10	−.06	.42	.08

Note: See Appendix for a description of the samples.

instrument. Even at their largest, however, the expected cross-subgroup cumulative differences in item responding represent only a *fraction of a single item response*, suggesting that whatever DIF is present is relatively minor, and/or it effectively "cancels out" across the items in each scale when scale-level scores are estimated.

The results of the M-H Δ analyses at the item level were also quite positive, showing that for the gender and age comparisons no E–I items exceeded the 1.5 cutoff on gender, and only one did in the two columns of age comparisons (i.e., young versus middle-aged and old versus middle-aged); for S–N, no items did; for T–F, only one item exceeded the 1.5 cutoff (on old versus middle-aged); and for J–P, two items

exceeded this minimum cutoff for the gender-DIF analyses. However, if the more stringent cutoff of Δ = 2.0 for targeting potential problem items is used, *no items* from any of these scales can be flagged as producing appreciable levels of DIF when using the M-H Δ technique.

In summary, these results are consistent with earlier DIF studies of the MBTI in showing that there does not appear to be any appreciable cumulative DIF on the basis of age or gender across the four MBTI scales. The fact that the T–F scale, which in the past used a gender-based differential scoring system, exhibited some of the *lowest* levels of DIF in these analyses can be viewed as a compelling argument for doing away with subgroup-based scoring systems for the MBTI.

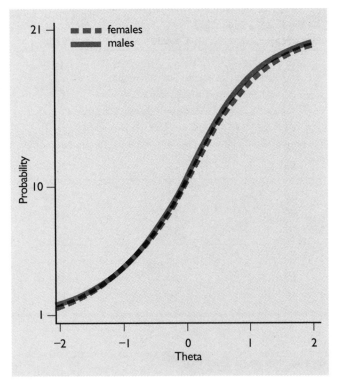

Figure 7.5 E–I Test Characteristic Curves for Men and Women

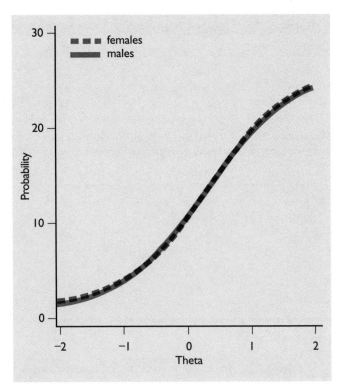

Figure 7.6 S–N Test Characteristic Curves for Men and Women

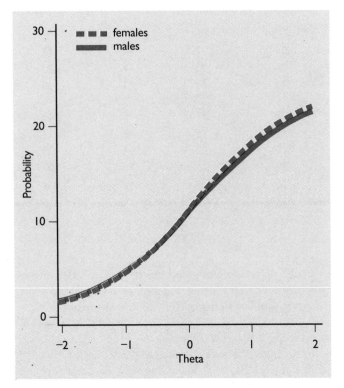

Figure 7.7 T–F Test Characteristic Curves for Men and Women

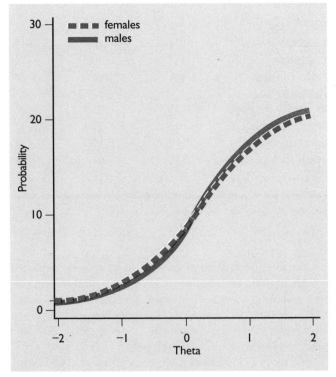

Figure 7.8 J–P Test Characteristic Curves for Men and Women

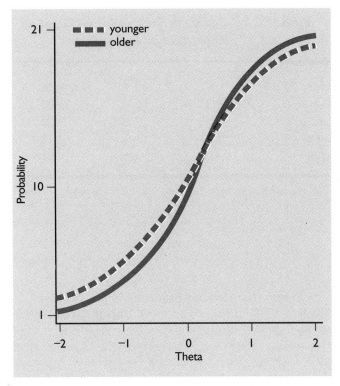

Figure 7.9 E–I Test Characteristic Curves for Older and Younger Respondents

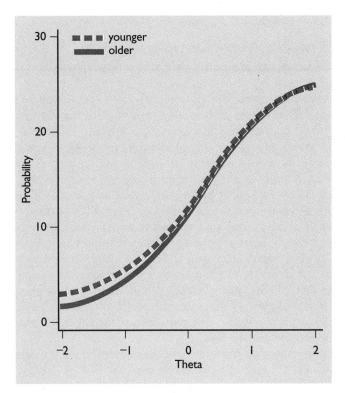

Figure 7.10 S–N Test Characteristic Curves for Older and Younger Respondents

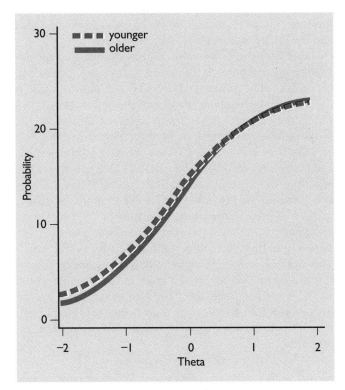

Figure 7.11 T–F Test Characteristic Curves for Older and Younger Respondents

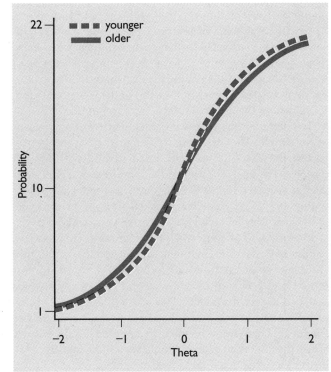

Figure 7.12 J–P Test Characteristic Curves for Older and Younger Respondents

The National Sample and the National Representative Sample

A national sample of adults over age 18 was collected and used for the item analyses for Form M. This was the first time a national sample was used for MBTI item analyses. Results from this sample of about 3,000 people are presented in various places in this chapter and in other chapters. In most places in this manual, where the national sample is referred to, it means this entire data set, with no adjustments made to model the population. (The characteristics of this sample are described in the Appendix.) This is because for most calculations it is more important to have raw data from a large sample. In some instances, however, it was desirable to have a national *representative* sample (NRS), which is described below. The NRS was used when the distribution of types in a sample of interest was being compared to a base population. In these instances, the base population was the NRS.

The raw data from the national sample did not entirely achieve the goal of representing the U.S. adult population because, as with previous attempts to collect a national sample, White women tended to be overrepresented among those who returned the survey forms, and Black men tended to underrespond. While national random phone surveys generally yield an adequate representation of minority group members, this was not the case with the MBTI sampling. Apparently members of minority groups are less likely to complete psychological instruments than they are to complete political or other sociological surveys. Therefore, because the goal was to show the distribution of types in a national *representative* sample (NRS) of the U.S. population, the data from the national sample were recompiled.

Two different methods were used to arrive at a representative sample. After applying the two methods, the type and preference distributions were calculated on both revised samples. The goal of both methods was to have a final sample that matched the 1990 U.S. census on gender and ethnic group. It was not possible to match for age because the national sample included only those 18 years and older.

One method of achieving the target representation was to start with the entire national sample and then randomly eliminate persons from categories that were overrepresented until the number of people in each category matched the census targets. This method resulted in a sample of 1,450 persons. The other method was to weight the results of people from the underrepresented groups in such a way that the final sample would match the census. This method resulted in a total sample of 3,009 persons.

As would be expected, the two methods yielded almost identical distributions of types, with the largest difference being 1.6% for male ISTPs; most other differences were less than 0.5%. Consequently, since the weighted category method resulted in less loss of data, the national sample based on this method is reported here.

Table 7.13	Characteristics of the National Representative Sample		
Group	n	%	% in Census
Males	1,478	49.1%	49.0%
Females	1,531	50.9%	51.0%
White	2,495	83.3%	80.3%
Black	411	13.7%	12.1%
Other	89	3.0%	7.6%

Note: N = 3,009. The sample size for the ethnic data was 2,995, reflecting the fact that 14 of the 3,009 people in the total sample did not indicate their ethnic group. See Appendix for a description of the sample.
Source: National representative sample.

As with the previous national sample (Hammer & Mitchell, 1996), the survey included Hispanic as an alternative in the ethnic identity category. However, the number of Hispanics is not reported with the main ethnic breakdown in the U.S. census. Therefore, solely for the purpose of comparing the demographics in the NRS with census demographics, the same strategy used by Hammer and Mitchell (1996) was used with the current sample. Those indicating Hispanic as their ethnic group in the current national sample were proportionally assigned to the White and Black categories. Note, however, that in the actual sample Hispanics were included and weighted proportionally as a separate group.

Table 7.13 shows how the current national representative sample compares to the census data by gender and ethnic group. The primary difference is that the current national sample contains about half the percentage of people in the "other" ethnic group category. Otherwise the proportions closely match those of the 1990 U.S. census.

Table 7.14 and Table 7.15 show the distribution of types and preferences for males and females in the national representative sample, respectively. The distributions for Blacks and Hispanics are presented in Chapter 14 of this manual.

Prior to this sample, the best estimate of the distribution of types in a national representative sample was the 1996 sample reported by Hammer and Mitchell (1996), which used Form G and employed a rolling norms procedure. In this procedure, data are usually collected sequentially, going from one site to another, until the demographic characteristics of the overall sample (e.g., the percentage of people representing different age groups) matches predetermined target levels.

In the current national representative sample, there are slightly more Introverts than Extraverts among males, while the reverse is true for females. In the 1996 sample, Introverts were slightly more common for both genders. The proportion of Sensing types is between 71% and 75% for both men and women, which is slightly more for the men than in the 1996 sample. There are more Judging than Perceiving types in the new sample, and the percentages are similar to those

Table 7.14 Distribution of Types and Preferences for Males in the National Representative Sample

ISTJ	ISFJ	INFJ	INTJ
242	119	19	49
(16.4%)	(8.1%)	(1.3%)	(3.3%)
■■■■■■■■■■ ■■■■■■	■■■■■■■■	■	■■■

ISTP	ISFP	INFP	INTP
126	112	61	71
(8.5%)	(7.6%)	(4.1%)	(4.8%)
■■■■■■■■■	■■■■■■■■	■■■■	■■■■■

ESTP	ESFP	ENFP	ENTP
83	102	95	59
(5.6%)	(6.9%)	(6.4%)	(4.0%)
■■■■■■	■■■■■■■	■■■■■■	■■■■

ESTJ	ESFJ	ENFJ	ENTJ
165	111	24	40
(11.2%)	(7.5%)	(1.6%)	(2.7%)
■■■■■■■■■■ ■	■■■■■■■■	■■	■■■

E	679	(45.9%)
I	799	(54.1%)
S	1,060	(71.7%)
N	418	(28.3%)
T	835	(56.5%)
F	643	(43.5%)
J	769	(52.0%)
P	709	(48.0%)

Pairs and Temperaments

IJ	429	(29.0%)
IP	370	(25.0%)
EP	339	(22.9%)
EJ	340	(23.0%)
ST	616	(41.7%)
SF	444	(30.0%)
NF	199	(13.5%)
NT	219	(14.8%)
SJ	637	(43.1%)
SP	423	(28.6%)
NP	286	(19.4%)
NJ	132	(8.9%)
TJ	496	(33.6%)
TP	339	(22.9%)
FP	370	(25.0%)
FJ	273	(18.5%)
IN	200	(13.5%)
EN	218	(14.7%)
IS	599	(40.5%)
ES	461	(31.2%)
ET	347	(23.5%)
EF	332	(22.5%)
IF	311	(21.0%)
IT	488	(33.0%)

Note: n = 1,478. See Appendix for a description of the sample.

Source: National representative sample.

in the 1996 sample. The biggest difference between the two samples is in the frequency of Feeling types.

Research with best-fit type with Form G (Harris & Carskadon, 1988; Kummerow, 1988; Walck, 1992b) had suggested that a significant proportion of people, particularly men, who had identified Feeling as their best-fit type were being reported on Form G as having a preference for Thinking. There were two primary hypotheses offered to explain these results. One was that cultural changes occurring since the introduction of the Form G scoring weights (which were themselves a response to prior cultural changes) were causing more pressure to respond in a Thinking manner. The other hypothesis was that the Form G weights had in fact overcorrected for previous changes, particularly for men.

While with Form M there are still more men reporting Thinking and still more women reporting Feeling, the proportions have changed. There are now more people of both genders reporting Feeling—44% of the men and 76% of the women, compared to 31% of the men and 61% of the women in the 1996 Form G sample. The proportion of Thinking–Feeling types among men in the current Form M national sample is closer to the 60–40 split that Myers had targeted than is the Form G proportion. However, the frequency of Feeling among females has also increased.

Conclusion

The history of the development of the MBTI, which spans more than 40 years, is outlined in the first part of this chapter. This brief recounting demonstrates two things about the Indicator. First, every attempt was made during its long history to keep the instrument as true as possible to the theory

Table 7.15   Distribution of Types and Preferences for Females in the National Representative Sample

ISTJ	ISFJ	INFJ	INTJ
106	297	25	13
(6.9%)	(19.4%)	(1.6%)	(0.8%)

ISTP	ISFP	INFP	INTP
36	152	71	27
(2.4%)	(9.9%)	(4.6%)	(1.8%)

ESTP	ESFP	ENFP	ENTP
46	154	148	37
(3.0%)	(10.1%)	(9.7%)	(2.4%)

ESTJ	ESFJ	ENFJ	ENTJ
96	259	50	14
(6.3%)	(16.9%)	(3.3%)	(0.9%)

E	804	(52.5%)
I	727	(47.5%)
S	1,146	(74.9%)
N	385	(25.1%)
T	375	(24.5%)
F	1,156	(75.5%)
J	860	(56.2%)
P	671	(43.8%)

Pairs and Temperaments

IJ	441	(28.8%)
IP	286	(18.7%)
EP	385	(25.1%)
EJ	419	(27.4%)
ST	284	(18.5%)
SF	862	(56.3%)
NF	294	(19.2%)
NT	91	(5.9%)
SJ	758	(49.5%)
SP	388	(25.3%)
NP	283	(18.5%)
NJ	102	(6.7%)
TJ	229	(15.0%)
TP	146	(9.5%)
FP	525	(34.3%)
FJ	631	(41.2%)
IN	136	(8.9%)
EN	249	(16.3%)
IS	591	(38.6%)
ES	555	(36.3%)
ET	193	(12.6%)
EF	611	(39.9%)
IF	545	(35.6%)
IT	182	(11.9%)

Note: n = 1,531. See Appendix for a description of the sample.
Source: National representative sample.

of psychological types. All decisions concerning items, scoring, and validation were driven by the demands of the theory. The goal was to yield an instrument that could be used to reliably sort people into types, not to measure traits.

Since its beginning, the Indicator has undergone constant scrutiny to determine ways to improve it. Changes were made to item wording, item formats, weights, standardization samples, and scoring procedures. All potential changes were measured against two standards—psychometric principles and theoretical congruence. This review of the Indicator's development illustrates why in Chapter 2 of this manual the history of the MBTI is characterized as "A Tradition of Change."

The revision of the MBTI described in this chapter, which culminated in the 93-item Form M, remained true

to this tradition. All decisions were guided by both theoretical and empirical criteria. Item response theory methods, derived from modern test theory, were used to select items that better discriminated between people of opposite preferences. An improvement was made in classification of respondents around the midpoint. A new scoring methodology was introduced using the prediction of best-fit type as the criterion. This same criterion was also used to determine the midpoint of the scales. For the first time, the standardization sample used as a foundation for scoring was based on a national sample of adults. These improvements in the psychometric properties of the Indicator, along with the data presented in the following chapters, suggest that users can continue to rely on the MBTI as a measure of psychological type.

Reliability and Measurement Precision

8

This chapter addresses the reliability of the *Myers-Briggs Type Indicator*, particularly that of the new Form M. Data from the national sample (see Chapter 7 for a description) are presented. The first topic to be examined, internal consistency reliability estimates, includes discussion of two different methods: split-half reliability and coefficient alpha. To permit reliability comparisons with other instruments, we report continuous score reliability estimates for the four preference scales. Sample characteristics that may affect reliabilities are also discussed.

The second topic is test-retest reliability estimates, or replicability of results over time. Again we report continuous score reliability estimates for the four preference scales. However, since MBTI scale scores are assumed to reflect underlying dichotomies, and the major interest of most MBTI users is the consistency of remaining the same type, we also report reliabilities that reflect these hypothesized dichotomies.

The concept of reliability deals not only with estimating internal consistency and replicability over time but also with that part of the variance in reliability estimates that is attributable to the characteristics of respondents. The reliability estimates for the MBTI are expected to vary not only with the statistical procedures adopted but also with characteristics of the respondents such as gender and age. Separate reliabilities are reported for these groups of respondents.

An assumption derived from observations made during the construction of the MBTI instrument is that persons with a good command of perception or judgment (i.e., with good type development) are more likely to be clear about their own preferences. They therefore will report their preferences more consistently. If these assumptions are correct, samples of older persons should have higher reliability estimates than samples of younger persons. Since the quality of perception and judgment is often evidenced by an individual's level of achievement, it is expected that in samples of persons of comparable age levels, those with higher achievement levels will also report their preferences more consistently, and thus these samples will evidence higher reliabilities than samples of their lower-achieving peers. Since the acquisition of good judgment is postulated to be the most difficult to develop, the T–F scale is expected to be particularly vulnerable to deficiencies in type development. Therefore, the lowest reliabilities in less effective samples are expected to occur on the T–F scale.

The third topic in this chapter is measurement precision (and its converse, error) of the new Form M, an approach derived from applying item response theory (IRT; see Chapter 7 for a full explanation of the theory) to the MBTI.

Internal Consistency Reliability Estimates

Internal consistency reliability is concerned with how consistently respondents answer the items on a given scale. The more consistency, the less "noise" in the measurement. One way to examine consistency is to divide the items that compose the scale into parts and then compare the parts with each other. This is usually done through various methods of splitting the scale into halves. Because of the unique nature of the MBTI, however, it is also possible to examine different parts, such as word pairs versus phrase questions. Another way to establish the consistency of the scale is to use coefficient alpha to examine how responses to the items relate to one another.

Split-Half Reliability

One method of determining the internal consistency reliability of a scale is to split the item pool into two halves, compute the internal consistency of each half, and correct the result for the length of the scale. This last step is needed because, at least in the context of classical test theory, longer scales are generally more reliable or consistent.

The usual procedure for determining which items to place in which half is to use random selection from the total set of items on the scale. The characteristics of MBTI items, however, suggested that the items be split using a logical split-half procedure. Each Form M scale was split into halves, taking all available item statistics into consideration and pairing items that most resemble each other. The following variables were considered in splitting the Form M items:

Table 8.1   Internal Consistency (Corrected) of Form G and Form M Continuous Scores Based on Split-Half Correlations

Sample	N	E–I	S–N	T–F	J–P
Form G CAPT Databank	32,671	.82	.84	.83	.86
Form M National Sample	3,036				
Logical Split-Half					
X Half		.90	.92	.91	.92
Y Half		.91	.92	.90	.92
Consecutive Split-Half					
X Half		.91	.92	.89	.92
Y Half		.90	.92	.92	.92
Word Pairs		.91	.93	.92	.94
Phrases		.91	.91	.90	.93

Note: See Appendix for a description of national sample.

- Item format (word pair versus phrase question)
- Item-to-total correlations
- Average value of the IRT b parameter
- Maximum amount of item information (a function of all three IRT parameters)
- Subscale coverage
- Whether the item was an original Form G item or a new or revised item

Another technique, the consecutive items procedure, was also used for splitting items for comparison purposes. In this technique, the first half of the items on the scale formed the X items and the latter half the Y items.

Table 8.1 shows split-half reliabilities of continuous scores for Form M using both the logical split-half and the simple consecutive items procedure for the national sample, both corrected using the Spearman-Brown formula. For comparison, the corrected reliabilities for Form G, based on the logical split-half procedure, are shown for people from the Center for Applications of Psychological Type (CAPT) Form G databank. These correlations demonstrate the improvement in reliabilities in Form M. They also demonstrate that the procedure used to split the items has no effect on the resulting coefficients.

There is an improvement in reliability with Form M.

Although the simple consecutive item procedure is much less time-consuming to perform, it yields almost identical results, perhaps because the ordering of the MBTI items on Form M produces much the same diversity and balance in the two item pools as does the logical procedure. Regardless of the method, the Form M reliabilities in the national sample are quite high.

Table 8.2 Internal Consistency of Form M Continuous Scores Based on Coefficient Alpha

Sample	Gender	N	E–I	S–N	T–F	J–P
National Sample	M, F	2,859	.91	.92	.91	.92
	M	1,330	.91	.93	.90	.93
	F	1,529	.90	.91	.88	.92
Iowa State University	M, F	269	.91	.91	.91	.92
CRI Sample	M, F	140	.89	.93	.91	.94
Trinity	M, F	90	.90	.91	.94	.92
Fairview	M, F	247	.93	.93	.90	.92
	M	37	.93	.93	.91	.93
	F	210	.92	.93	.89	.91
Middle Tennessee State University	M, F	175	.91	.87	.88	.91
	M	76	.91	.87	.86	.88
	F	99	.92	.86	.87	.92
Public Utilities Company	M, F	240	.95	.95	.93	.94
	M	114	.95	.95	.93	.94
	F	126	.95	.95	.93	.94
Ball Foundation	M, F	85	.93	.89	.92	.92
Test Samples (Combined)	M, F	500	.94	.93	.92	.93
	M	200	.93	.93	.91	.93
	F	300	.94	.93	.91	.94
Retest Samples (Combined)	M, F	400	.94	.95	.93	.94
	M	151	.94	.95	.93	.94
	F	259	.94	.94	.93	.94

Note: See Appendix for a description of the samples.

Table 8.3 Internal Consistency Reliability of Form M by Age Group and by Ethnic Group

Age Group	N	E–I	S–N	T–F	J–P
18–21	89	.91	.92	.89	.94
22–25	145	.90	.91	.91	.92
26–30	241	.91	.93	.91	.93
31–40	641	.90	.91	.91	.92
41–50	628	.91	.92	.91	.92
51–60	440	.91	.92	.91	.92
61–70	347	.90	.91	.92	.92
>70	269	.91	.90	.89	.90

Ethnic Group	N	E–I	S–N	T–F	J–P
Adults from National Sample					
African American	120	.88	.87	.84	.91
Latino/Latina/ Hispanic	100	.88	.87	.90	.91
Public Utilities Company	53	.95	.95	.94	.91
College Students					
African American	105	.91	.80	.87	.90
American Indian	17	.96	.86	.87	.91
Asian or Pacific Islander	233	.91	.82	.83	.89
Latino/Latina/ Hispanic	28	.84	.86	.88	.90

Note: See Appendix for a description of the samples.

The items were also split by item format, i.e., into word pairs and phrase questions for each scale. Alpha coefficients were then computed for each. The internal consistencies, corrected for scale length, are also shown in Table 8.1. There were no differences in the reliabilities across the two item formats.

Internal Consistency Coefficients Based on Coefficient Alpha

The internal consistency of the four MBTI scales was also estimated using coefficient alpha, which is the average of all of the item correlations. As the analysis with Form G in the 1985 *MBTI Manual* demonstrated and the present analysis confirms, there is little or no difference between coefficients determined by the split-half and coefficient alpha methods. Table 8.2 shows internal consistency reliabilities estimated by coefficient alpha in the national sample and in a variety of other groups of both college students and adults. There are no differences in reliabilities for males or females in the samples.

The Effect of Sample Characteristics on Reliability

Gender, age, membership in a minority ethnic group, and developmental level can all affect how consistently people respond to a certain set of items. Table 8.2 demonstrated that there are no gender differences in Form M reliabilities. Table 8.3 shows internal consistency reliability coefficients by age group from the national sample and by ethnic groups derived from the national sample and from all of the college student samples collected during the revision. It must be remembered that a reliability coefficient is an index of the consistency of responses made by a particular group at a particular time to a specific set of items designed to measure a psychological construct. The coefficient is therefore limited by the amount of noise or error that derives from two sources. One source is the items themselves. How items are worded, and how consistently they, as a set, tap the construct of interest, will affect reliability. The other source of noise derives from characteristics of the individuals themselves. For example, their age or developmental level may affect how reliably they respond to a certain set of items.

In the broad age range available in this sample, there appear to be few or no differences in reliabilities across age groups. However, the Form G reliabilities reported in the 1985 *MBTI Manual* show lower reliabilities in age groups below 18 years, particularly on the T–F scale. It remains to be seen whether such a pattern will be observed with Form M; the theory would predict that this would be the case. The 1985 *Manual* also suggested that lower reliabilities might be observed in samples of people in midlife. However, as with Form G data reported in the 1985 *Manual*, there was no evidence to support the hypothesis with Form M. The only trend suggested in the Form M age group data in Table 8.3 is that the reliability of the J–P scale may decrease slightly in older samples. The trend is slight, however, and should not be overinterpreted.

The ethnic group data from the adults in Table 8.3 shows that the internal consistency reliabilities for the three ethnic group samples are comparable to those of the overall national sample, with the possible exception of the T–F scale for the African Americans from the national sample, which is somewhat lower. The college student reliabilities show somewhat lower reliabilities for African Americans on the S–N scale and for Asians or Pacific Islanders on the S–N and T–F scales when compared to the reliabilities of the college student samples in Table 8.2.

The 1985 *MBTI Manual* also shows reliability coefficients for Form G for a number of samples that exhibit characteristics related to development that are presumed by theory to affect how people might self-report their preferences. These results can be summarized as follows:

- Underachieving students show much lower consistency in responses than do "overachieving" or high-achieving students. The T–F scale, as predicted, is the most likely to be lower.
- Among high school students, college preparatory students show higher reliabilities than do their classmates who are not in college preparatory courses.
- Students in advanced placement show higher reliabilities than do other groups of students.
- Reliabilities are higher in groups with higher average intelligence as measured by standard intelligence tests. Intelligence scores may be related to MBTI reliability in two ways. First, intelligence can be seen as a result of effective command of perception and judgment; that is, more information is taken in accurately, and better judgments are made. Second, more intelligent students typically have a higher reading level and may have better understanding of the MBTI vocabulary. Greater understanding leads to lower likelihood of random responding and thus greater consistency.
- College and university samples have higher reliabilities than high school samples.

These findings are in accord with type theory. People with a better command of perception and judgment, who are better able to understand the items, and who are more likely to

accurately self-report their preferences will tend to respond more consistently to the items. To the degree that these characteristics are not present in the sample, one should expect lower reliability coefficients. Other than for research purposes, the MBTI should not be used routinely with such groups except as a stimulus for discussion.

Test-Retest Reliability Estimates

Test-retest reliability is an estimate of how stable a characteristic is over time. For the MBTI tool, test-retest reliabilities go beyond the typical computations of correlations for the four continuous scores. Practical questions revolve around the likelihood that on retest a person will come out the same MBTI type; that is, a person will choose the same pole of all four dichotomous domains.

Reliabilities in this section include (a) correlations of continuous scores, (b) the proportion of cases assigned the same letter (direction of preference) on retest, and (c) the proportion of cases reporting the same preferences on retest for all four dichotomies (i.e., the same type), three preferences, two preferences, one preference, or no preferences.

Correlations of Continuous Scores

Before introducing Form M data, data are presented from a test-retest study based on an administration of Form J (Johnson, 1992). These data, not available for the 1985 *MBTI Manual*, are important because of the long period between test and retest. Although the participants were administered Form J in this study, the continuous scores are derived from the same 94 items and weights as used on Form G. These coefficients are shown in Table 8.4. With the exception of the T–F scale for males, the test-retest reliability of the scales is quite good over a two-and-one-half-year period.

Table 8.5 shows test-retest product-moment correlations in three different samples for Form M and, for comparison,

Table 8.4 Test-Retest Correlations of Form J Continuous Scores over a 30-Month Period

	E–I	S–N	T–F	J–P
Males	.78	.85	.57	.83
Females	.81	.80	.70	.81
Total	.79	.83	.62	.82

Note: N = 74.

Source: From "Test-Retest Reliabilities of the *Myers-Briggs Type Indicator* and the *Type Differentiation Indicator* over a 30-Month Period," by D. A. Johnson, 1992, *Journal of Psychological Type, 24.* Copyright 1992 by *Journal of Psychological Type.* Used with permission.

Table 8.5 Test-Retest Correlations of Form G and Form M Continuous Scores

Sample	Interval	N	E–I	S–N	T–F	J–P
Form G						
Meta-analysis	>9 months	559	.70	.68	.59	.63
Meta-analysis	<9 months	1,139	.84	.81	.77	.82
Form M						
VA Commonwealth	4 weeks	116	.94	.90	.83	.90
Public Utilities Company	4 weeks	258	.93	.89	.87	.93
CPP	4 weeks	50	.95	.97	.94	.95
By pci range for combined sample						
1–5		88	.46	.52	.44	.22
6–10		78	.83	.72	.73	.75
11–15		62	.87	.87	.84	.89
16–20		62	.90	.88	.90	.93
21–25		64	.97	.96	.95	.93
26–30		70	.99	.99	.99	.99

Note: Form G data from Harvey (1996) based on Myers and McCaulley (1985). See Appendix for a description of the samples.

Table 8.6 Test-Retest Percentage Agreement of Dichotomies for Form G and Form M

Sample	Interval	N	E–I	S–N	T–F	J–P
Form G						
Meta-analysis	>9 months	1,133	75	76	75	77
Meta-analysis	<9 months	356	82	87	82	83
Form M						
VA Commonwealth	4 weeks	116	87	87	84	88
Public Utilities Company	4 weeks	258	91	92	84	89
CPP	4 weeks	50	96	96	92	96

Note: Form G data from Harvey (1996) based on Myers and McCaulley (1985). See Appendix for a description of the samples.

Agreement of Dichotomies

Table 8.6 shows the test-retest percentages of agreement for the E–I, S–N, T–F, and J–P dichotomies in the three test-retest samples for Form G and Form M. The Form G coefficients are from the meta-analysis by R. J. Harvey (1996). The time intervals in the <9-month Form G studies were five to eight weeks, with one sample of eight months. The intervals in the >9-month category ranged from nine months to six years. The time interval for the Form M studies was four weeks. The agreement across the scales is somewhat higher for Form M, with the T–F scale showing the lowest percentage agreement on both forms. The high agreement in the Consulting Psychologists Press (CPP; publisher of the MBTI) sample probably represents an upper limit to test-retest reliabilities; most of the individuals in this group were very familiar with type theory and had received an MBTI interpretation prior to the study.

One of the studies using Form G that was included in the meta-analysis of test-retest studies deserves specific mention because it helps answer a question often asked by participants in workshops. This was a study of the effect of moods on reliabilities conducted by Howes and Carskadon (1979), who administered the MBTI instrument to introductory psychology student volunteers. Mood changes were effected by asking three groups of students to complete one of three 50-item self-report questionnaires. The mood-elevating form contained positive, optimistic self-statements that most people could honestly agree with; the mood-depressing form contained negatively worded statements; a neutral form contained bland, nonpersonal attitude statements. A post-treatment measure of mood demonstrated that completing these forms had the intended effect on mood. The results showed that mood changes did not significantly affect test-retest MBTI correlations or percentage of agreement on the preference scales.

Another test-retest study is of interest for both historical and theoretical reasons. Isabel B. Myers administered one of

the results of a meta-analysis of test-retest coefficients (divided into two different time intervals) that summarized all of the Form G data from the 1985 *Manual* (Harvey, 1996). For the Form G data, the time intervals represented in the <9-month category are primarily for intervals of one to eight weeks, with one sample using an eight-month interval; for the >9-month category the time intervals ranged from nine months to six years, with the majority at intervals of around two years. The length of time between testings for the Form M data was about one month and should therefore be compared with the Form G <9-month interval.

The test-retest reliabilities of Form M are generally higher than those of Form G.

For both forms the reliability coefficient for T–F is the lowest of the four scales, especially in the student sample, as predicted.

Test-retest reliabilities of continuous scores were also calculated for different ranges of the preference clarity indexes (pci) and are shown in Table 8.5. To attain a sufficient number of people in each range it was necessary to combine all three test-retest samples. In these data there was a clear trend for the stability of the preference clarity indexes to be lower for those people whose original pci was low. This finding for Form M replicates a similar analysis for Form G using categorical data (Myers & McCaulley, 1985).

Table 8.7 Percentage of People with Preferences the Same at Retest (Four Weeks)

Sample	N	Number of Preferences the Same at Retest				
		4	3	2	1	0
VA Commonwealth	116	55	38	4	3	0
Public Utilities Company	258	66	25	8	1	0
CPP	50	80	20	0	0	0
Combined	424	65	28	6	1	0

Note: See Appendix for a description of the samples.

the first forms of the Indicator to the 87 members of the Swarthmore high school class of 1943. At the 50th reunion of this class, Katharine Myers (personal communication) administered Form G to 39 of these same people. Over this 50-year period 8 people (21%) had the same type, 13 (33%) had changed one letter, 16 (41%) had changed two letters, 2 (5%) had changed three letters, and no one in the group had changed all four letters of his or her type. Over a 50-year interval, then, 54% changed either none or just one letter. The level of agreement expected by chance would be 6.25%. These data suggest that personality preferences are fairly stable over long periods of time but that there are some changes. Also note, however, that any changes over time observable in these data are compounded by changes in both the items and the scoring weights of the instrument itself.

Table 8.7 shows the percentages of persons reporting four, three, two, one, or no preferences the same on four-week retest. The chance probability of choosing all four preferences on retest (i.e., coming out the same type) is 6.25%. The actual test-retest probabilities are significantly higher than what would be expected by chance.

While significant improvements over chance have been observed, the test-retest agreement will never reach 100%. One of the factors limiting test-retest agreement over time for whole types (i.e., all four letters the same) is that whole types are arrived at by measuring the four scales separately. As discussed above, responses to the items on each scale are subject to measurement error and to normal fluctuations in the behavior and characteristics of individuals that may affect how they self-report on certain items at certain times. When these factors are aggregated across the four scales, it creates a ceiling on the achievable upper limit of agreement over time. For example, if we consider the categorical test-retest reliabilities of the preference scales for the samples shown in Table 8.6 as independent and multiply them together to arrive at an expectation as to what the agreement for whole types should be over time, the results are 56%, 63%, and 81% for the three samples. These are very close to the actual figures of 55%, 66%, and 80% for the

same samples shown in Table 8.7. To achieve test-retest agreement on whole types over time in, say, the high 80% range, the test-retest reliabilities of the individual scales would all have to be over 96%, which is probably unrealistic for scales that measure such complex and multifaceted constructs as the MBTI preferences, and as it would be for any scale measuring a meaningful psychological construct.

In conclusion, test-retest reliabilities of the MBTI show consistency over time. When subjects report a change in type, it is most likely to occur in only one preference, and in scales where the original preference clarity was low.

Measurement Precision Using the IRT Method

As was noted in Chapter 7 on the construction of Form M, the approach to estimating measurement precision that is taken by IRT is in some ways similar to—but in many ways quite different from—traditional CTT-based methods used to estimate test reliability. Both IRT and CTT view measurement precision as the relative degree to which test scores are free from undesirable, unsystematic sources of variance; tests producing higher levels of precision are viewed as being more *informative* regarding each examinee's true score on the underlying psychological characteristic of interest (in the present case, the preference clarity indexes on each MBTI scale). Both methods likewise define an index that provides a "mirror image" view of precision that is an inverse function of the index of measurement precision; this index is the *standard error,* or SE. Higher standard errors are associated with less precise, less informative tests.

IRT and CTT differ fundamentally, however, regarding the concept of how test precision (or error) should be quantified. In CTT-based approaches, the result is a *single* estimate of the test's reliability for a given group, estimated using a technique such as coefficient alpha, or a test-retest correlation. Estimates based on these techniques were reported in the first part of this chapter.

In contrast, IRT methods begin with the assumption that a single number is *not* adequate to quantify the precision (or degree of error) present in a scale. Instead, the measurement precision of a scale is presumed to be able to vary continuously across the possible range of scores (the θ in IRT terminology, or the preference clarity index in the case of the MBTI). As a consequence, instead of producing a point-estimate of test precision, a scale developed or evaluated using IRT methods provides a graphical *function* that shows the amount of precision that would be expected at any given level of θ. This approach reflects the commonsense notion that scales tend to be more precise for individuals who fall at some levels of θ and less precise for other individuals.

As demonstrated in Chapter 7, this was exactly the goal that Myers set in constructing the MBTI scales. All decisions about item wording, item selection, and setting of the midpoint were made so as to maximize the precision around the *midpoint* of each scale. She was not interested in differentiating between people who demonstrated, for example, a clear versus a very clear preference for Extraversion. Instead, the goal was to make sure, to the extent possible, that people with slight preferences on each side of the midpoint were classified accurately. IRT approaches to precision provide a means to describe and evaluate the precision or error at precisely this point.

CTT-based indexes of measurement precision (i.e., reliability coefficients) will typically be unable to quantify or detect such phenomena. Although it would be possible to calculate reliability coefficients for subgroups of individuals representing different degrees of clarity of preference, the most commonly encountered CTT-based estimates of an instrument's precision simply provide an overall, aggregate estimate of the instrument's precision across the entire range of scale scores. Unfortunately, this global estimate of reliability is likely to overestimate measurement precision at the extremes and underestimate precision in the middle range of scores. Myers was well aware of this limitation of traditional reliability coefficients. Her attempt to overcome this deficiency, and to provide information about precision at the center of the scales, led her to use two kinds of categorical coefficients for estimating reliability, *phi* and tetrachoric, which are used with variables that represent true or artificial dichotomies, respectively. Because *phi* was believed to overstate the reliability of the type categories and tetrachoric to understate the reliability, she was attempting to bracket the "true" reliability. Fortunately, the use of IRT techniques provides a more direct solution to the problem.

The IRT equivalent of the CTT reliability coefficient is the *test information function* (TIF), which shows the amount of precision produced by the test at each possible value of θ; the IRT equivalent of the *standard error of measurement* (SEM) is the *test standard error* (TSE) function, which shows the expected SE that would be found when estimating θ scores from the observed item responses across the full range of possible θ scores. These functions can be graphed, showing clearly how precision and error vary for different scores on the scale.

Figures 8.1–8.4 present the IRT-based TIFs and TSE functions for the Form M item pools (solid line); the corresponding values for the Form G item pools (broken line) are provided in each plot for comparison purposes. As the results clearly demonstrate, the IRT assumption that test precision varies as a function of the particular range of test scores being considered is quite evident. Furthermore, measurement precision tends to be at its highest in the vicinity of the midpoint of each scale, exactly as would be desired for an instrument used to determine dichotomous preferences. Test information functions such as seen in these figures are the result of selecting items like those shown in Figure 7.2 in Chapter 7, that is, items that demonstrate steep slopes around the midpoint of the scale.

Also of interest is the comparison of the height of the TIFs for the Form G versus M item pools. Figures 8.1–8.4 show a direct index of the amount of measurement precision improvement provided by the revised item pools. Likewise, the degree of decrease in the TSE functions provides an index of the reduction in error variance in the θ score estimates. An inspection of the TIFs and TSE functions in Figures 8.1–8.4 shows quite clearly that the Form M items produce appreciable increases in test information and corresponding decreases in SE (especially in the critical region around the θ = 0.0 point, in which the cutoff is located).

This improvement in test precision is always desirable, and it is especially so when a cutoff point is used. That is, any amount of error involved in estimating θ scores near the cutoff point may translate into categorical type misclassifications. Thus, even if the reductions in the SE of estimating θ scores near the cutoff point are relatively modest, potentially important improvements in test-retest categorical type stability—as well as best-fit type agreement rates—may be achieved as a result of the improved measurement seen in the Form M item pools.

Conclusion

The internal consistency of the four MBTI scales is quite high in all samples available to date, whether computed using logical split-half, consecutive item split-half, or coefficient alpha. There has been a substantial improvement in Form M reliabilities over those of Form G, at least in the samples collected so far.

A summary of the Form G data suggests, however, that sample characteristics, particularly those related to type development, may result in variation in reliabilities across groups. Groups composed of people who are believed to have less command over perception and judgment should exhibit lower reliabilities.

Test-retest reliabilities of the MBTI show consistency over time, with levels of agreement much greater than by chance. When subjects report a change in type, it is most likely to occur in only one preference, and in scales where the original preference clarity was low. The test-retest reliabilities of Form M are improved over those of Form G. The reliability coefficient for T–F remains the lowest of the four scales, as expected.

A new method for estimating measurement precision is available with the use of IRT. This method is based on calculating the amount of information that is available from each item that can be used to discriminate people of opposite preferences. The precision of all scales is greater for Form M.

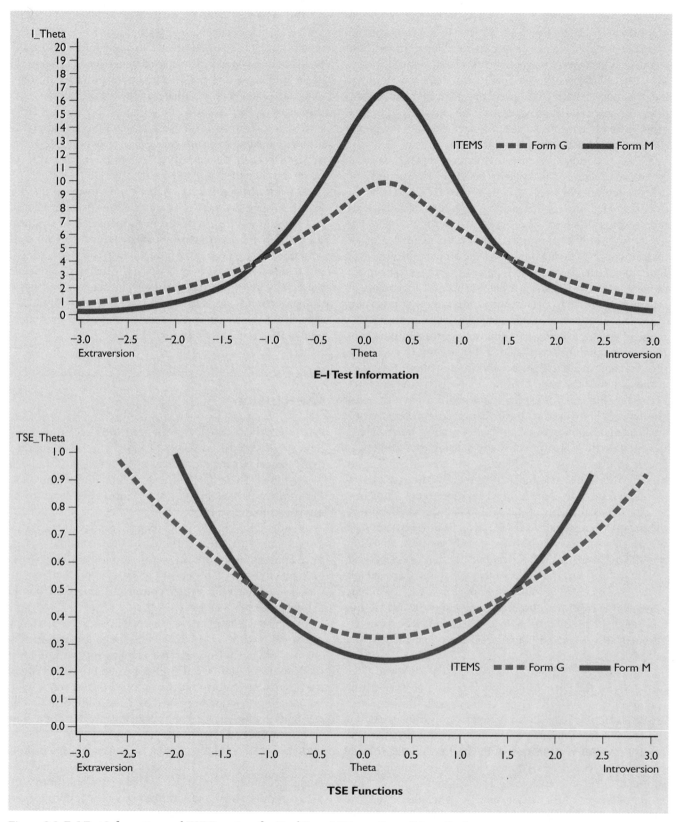

Figure 8.1 E–I Test Information and TSE Functions for Final Form M Versus Form G Item Pools

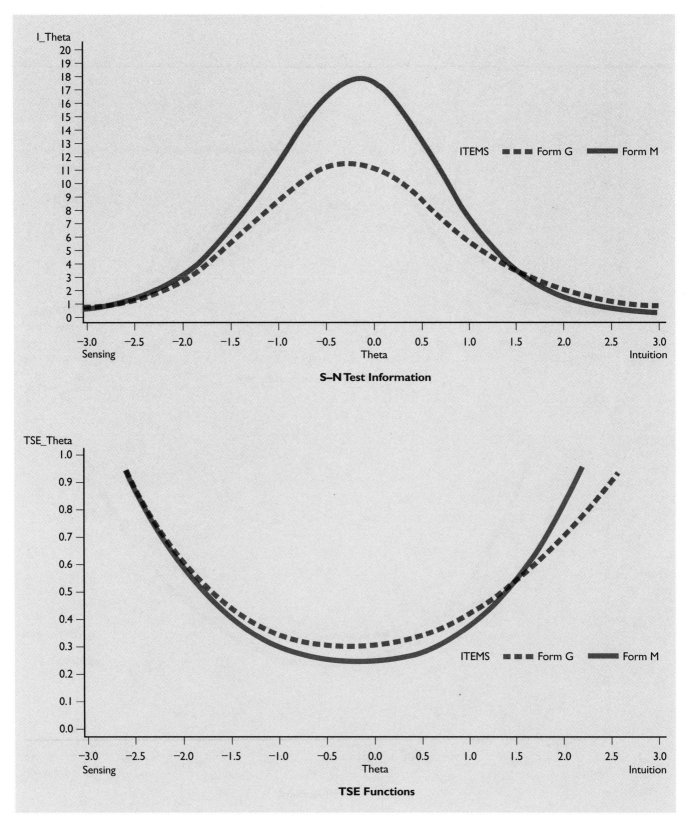

Figure 8.2 S–N Test Information and TSE Functions for Final Form M Versus Form G Item Pools

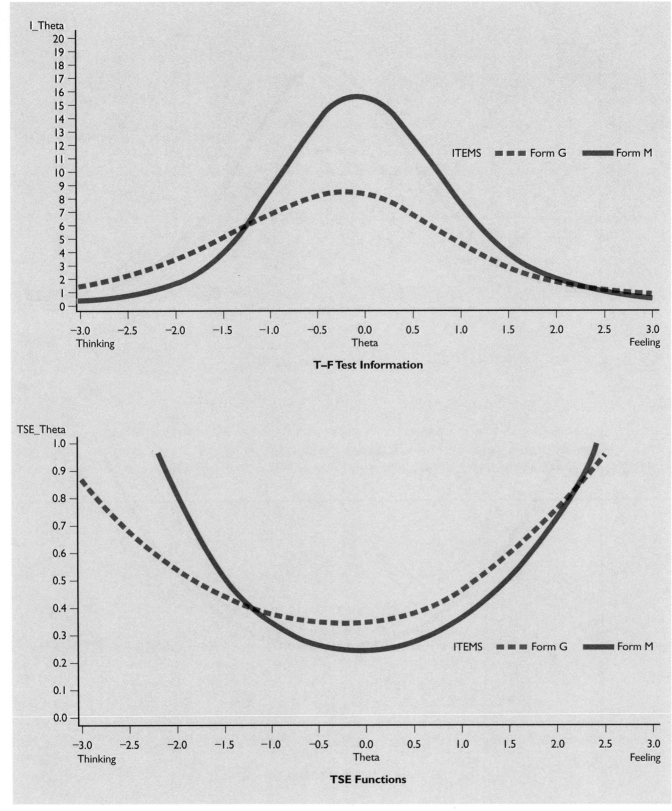

Figure 8.3 T–F Test Information and TSE Functions for Final Form M Versus Form G Item Pools

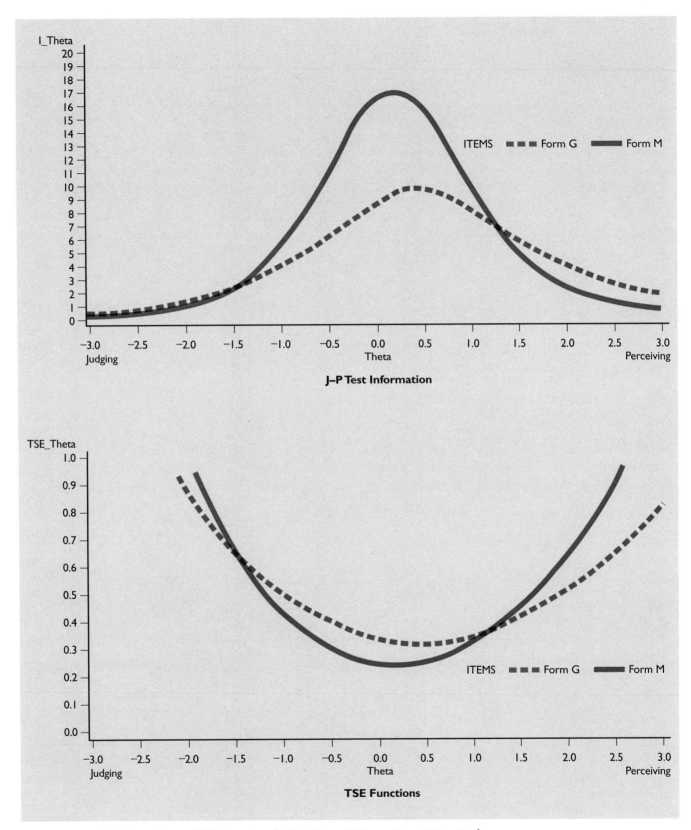

Figure 8.4 J–P Test Information and TSE Functions for Final Form M Versus Form G Item Pools

Validity   9

Because the *Myers-Briggs Type Indicator* personality inventory was designed to implement Carl G. Jung's theory of psychological types, its validity is determined by its ability to demonstrate relationships and outcomes predicted by theory. The theory suggests that persons are, or become, different types, and the MBTI attempts to classify persons according to the type that *they* believe best fits them. The theory postulates that the basic preferences for Sensing or Intuitive perception lead to different interests and that basic preferences for Thinking or Feeling judgment lead to differences in acting on those interests. Motivation, values, and behaviors are seen as surface indicators of the effects of the basic preferences and attitudes. If Jung's theory describes preferences that do exist, and if the MBTI adequately indicates those preferences, then surface behaviors should be in the directions predicted by the theory, with allowances, of course, for measurement error in the instrument, stage of development of the person, and overriding environmental pressures that interfere with expression of type preferences.

There are two broad categories of evidence that can be brought to bear on the issue of the validity of MBTI results. The first category includes evidence for the validity of the separate preference scales that compose the Indicator. This is the level at which measurement takes place with the MBTI. Since the separate preferences are the component parts needed to achieve the goal of helping people identify a whole type, it is important to establish the validity of the separate scales. Evidence falling into this category includes the following:

- Factor analysis of MBTI item pools
- Correlations of MBTI continuous scores for each scale with scores from the scales of other instruments
- Categorical analysis of behaviors believed to be associated with people of different preferences
- Analyses designed to uncover dichotomies
- Analysis of brain activity patterns

The second category of evidence concerns the validity of whole types or of particular combinations of preferences, particularly those combinations that have theoretical importance. The primary goal in using the Indicator is to help a person arrive at a complete four-letter type. It is therefore important to show that each of the 16 types has unique characteristics and that these characteristics are not entirely predictable from knowledge of the separate preferences. According to type theory, there are dynamic relations among the functions and attitudes that make up a person's type that suggest characteristics or behaviors that may not be apparent at a preference-scale level of analysis. Predictions can be made and tested based on the person's dominant and auxiliary functions and the functions that the person extraverts and introverts.

The evidence for this category includes the following:

- Comparison of MBTI reported type with best-fit type
- Analysis of type distributions
- Analysis based on analysis of variance (ANOVA)
- Observations by independent raters
- Analyses involving whole types as the unit of analysis, including attraction and satisfaction in couples, rebelliousness and distress in veterans, and type and time orientation
- Comparisons with factor scores derived from other measures

The application chapters that follow in this manual also contain a wealth of data and analyses that are relevant to the validity of the MBTI at both levels—preferences and whole types. These topics will not be repeated here.

Validity of the Four Preference Scales

Factor Analyses

The factor structure of MBTI item pools provides evidence of the construct validity of the MBTI assessment tool. When examining factor analytic studies it is important to select an item pool that is appropriate for the question being asked. If the research question involves the four preference scales, then the items of interest are only those items that are used to score the four preference scales of the MBTI. These are the 94 items that constitute the Form G or Form F scoring or the 93 items that are used in the new Form M scoring. With the exception of the Form G self-scorable and the new Form M, other forms of the MBTI (i.e., Forms G, K, and J) contain research items, or items used to score for subscales, or both. If these additional items are unwittingly included, as they have been, in a factor analysis designed to test the four-factor structure of the MBTI, the results will, not surprisingly, be other than predicted, as more than four factors are likely to emerge.

Once the appropriate set of items has been selected, the appropriate factor analytic tool must also be used. Two basic kinds of factor analytic studies can be performed: exploratory and confirmatory factor analyses. Exploratory factor analysis is the most widely used, although it provides only limited information about a hypothesized factor structure of a set of items. Although very useful for the purpose of developing hypotheses with respect to the factor structure of an instrument, exploratory factor analysis is not particularly useful in testing the degree to which an already hypothesized structure fits the observed data. Since with the MBTI there is a clearly hypothesized structure based on theory—the four-factor model that represents the four preference scales—confirmatory studies will yield more information about the construct validity of the MBTI. The discussion of these two kinds of factor analyses below relies on the review by Harvey (1996).

Exploratory Factor Analyses   In an exploratory factor analysis of the MBTI, basically two possible outcomes can occur. First, the exploratory analysis can produce a factor structure that appears to be similar to the hypothesized structure. However, because the exploratory factor model is unrestricted in a statistical sense, an infinite number of other equally well-fitting models can also exist that would provide an equally plausible fit to the data. Second, the exploratory analysis could instead produce a factor structure that is different from the predicted structure (e.g., it may contain a different number of factors, or the items may not load on the factors in the predicted fashion).

Several exploratory studies of the MBTI have produced results that are virtually identical to the hypothesized four-factor model: e.g., Harvey, Murry, and Stamoulis (1995); Thompson and Borrello (1986); Tzeng, Outcalt, Boyer, Ware, and Landis (1984). Tischler (1994), analyzing a large sample, found "unusually strong evidence that MBTI items are correlated with (measure) their intended scales; the scales are almost factorially pure" (p. 30).

There have also been two instances reported in the literature where the predicted factor structure was not obtained: Comrey (1983) and Sipps, Alexander, and Friedt (1985). Both of these studies can be questioned regarding one or more of the decisions made when conducting their analyses (e.g., retaining factors based on questionable criteria; forcing an orthogonal rotation on the data; using samples with very low ratios of subjects to items; using the principal components model when it is obvious that MBTI items contain considerable levels of unique variance). The factor structures that emerged from both these studies were tested against the predicted four-factor structure using the more rigorous confirmatory approach, which is discussed in the following section.

Confirmatory Factor Analyses

Confirmatory factor analysis (e.g., James, Mulaik, & Brett, 1982; Jöreskog & Sörbom, 1981) is able to provide a much more definitive test of the plausibility of a hypothesized factor structure than is the exploratory approach. In a confirmatory factor analysis a specific structural model is fitted to the data. If a model fits poorly, then the hypothesized factor structure is disconfirmed. However, as with any model-testing method, even if the hypothesized model fits well, such a finding does not *prove* that the hypothesized model is "correct." There may be other models, not yet tested or even thought of, that demonstrate a similar or even better goodness of fit. Consequently, confirmatory techniques are most powerful when they are used to compare the performance of competing models.

Several confirmatory factor analyses have been conducted on the MBTI. Johnson and Saunders (1990) analyzed the subscales produced by the Step II scoring system of Form J. The results indicated clear support for the plausibility of the predicted hierarchical structure of the instrument (i.e., the subscale-to-overall-preference-scale relationships).

Thompson and Borrello (1989) evaluated the fit of the hypothesized four-factor model, concluding that it fit well in their sample. Neither these researchers nor Johnson and Saunders, however, tested any competing models against which the reported levels of fit could be compared.

Harvey et al. (1995) did test three competing views of the latent structure of the MBTI. The three models were the predicted four-factor model and the two five-factor models developed by Sipps et al. (1985) and Comrey (1983) in their exploratory factor analyses. The results of the Harvey et al. (1995) study provided strong support for the validity of the predicted four-factor model. In contrast, the Sipps et al. and Comrey five-factor models both exhibited severe flaws that suggested that they were fundamentally misspecified (e.g., factor correlations approaching 1.0).

A confirmatory factor analysis was also conducted on Form M, using the data from the national sample ($N = 3,036$; see Chapter 7 for the characteristics of this sample). The software package PRELIS 2 was used to obtain polychoric correlations and asymptotic variance matrices suitable for dichotomous items. The matrices were used by LISREL 8.12 software running the diagonal weighted least squares procedure to estimate the model (Jöreskog & Sörbom, 1981). Also, because the S–N and J–P scales are known to

correlate, the latent variables were allowed to correlate. The adjusted goodness of fit was .949 and the nonnormed fit index was .967. The median of the fitted residuals was −.008. These results indicate an excellent fit to the four-factor model.

In sum, when the exploratory and confirmatory factor analytic results are viewed together, there is strong support for the construct validity of the MBTI. Several large-sample, carefully conducted exploratory studies produced "textbook" four-factor structures that almost exactly matched the hypothesized pattern of loadings (Harvey, 1996). Of even greater importance, several confirmatory studies of both Form G and Form M have unanimously supported the validity of the hypothesized factor structure and in one case conclusively rejected the competing models proposed by Sipps et al. (1985) and Comrey (1983). Although additional confirmatory studies need to be conducted to demonstrate the generalizability of the above findings, there is no question that the results of the factor analytic studies reported over the past 10-year period have been very supportive of the validity of the four-scale structure of the MBTI.

Correlation of MBTI Continuous Scores with Other Scales

A series of tables in this section summarize representative correlations from many different samples with a wide variety of instruments. One set of tables shows correlations based on Form G, while the other set is based on Form M. Many additional correlations for Form G are found in the 1985 *MBTI Manual* (Myers & McCaulley, 1985). Some of the Form G correlations found in the 1985 *MBTI Manual* are repeated here because of their relevance to the construct validity of the preference scales. Correlations with Form G that were not available for the 1985 *Manual* are presented here for the same reason.

In all of these tables, the left-hand columns show the actual product moment correlations of MBTI continuous scores with scales of other tests. Those tables that display Form G correlations use the continuous scores based on placing preference scores on a continuum, as described in the 1985 *Manual*. Those tables that display Form M correlations use theta as the MBTI score. (See Chapter 7 for a definition of theta.)

To make it easier to identify correlates of each preference, the right-hand column in each table designates the letters for preferences where correlations are at least .20 and significant at probabilities of .05 or greater. The .20 cutoff is used simply as a convention, so that by scanning the right-hand columns the reader can quickly identify characteristics associated with each preference and can judge whether these characteristics make sense in light of the expectations of the theory. This has been carried over from the 1985 *Manual* for the sake of consistency. However, the use of this convention means that there are statistically significant correlations shown in the main body of the table that are *not* flagged in the right-hand column because they were <.20. Although small, trends in such correlations may be theoretically as well as statistically significant, and readers are urged to seek these out. For theoretical purposes the direction and trend of the correlations for a given preference scale across a variety of scales and samples is more important than the significance or absolute level of one correlation coefficient in one sample for one scale.

Note that a correlation of at least .20 indicates that at least 4% of the variance is shared among the two variables being correlated. While this may seem like a small portion of variance to those accustomed to evaluating reliability coefficients, it should be noted that these correlations are *validity* coefficients, which in the behavioral sciences are typically much lower. According to Cohen (1988), correlations between variables in personality and social psychology are considered large if they are about $r = .5$, which accounts for only 25% of the shared variance. Correlations of .20 are considered small- to medium-sized effects (Cohen, 1988), which are quite common and meaningful.

Note also that the correlations reported in this chapter are raw (uncorrected) coefficients that may underestimate the true relationship between the latent variables. None of these correlations has been corrected for attenuation or restriction of range. Coefficients that are corrected for attenuation will be higher because the correction takes into account the less than perfect reliability of the two measures involved. Most of the reliability coefficients for the preference scales on Form M are in the .90 range (see Chapter 8) and thus require little correction. Many of the reliability coefficients of the other variables that are displayed in the tables in this chapter are unknown. Given that many of these scales were created only for research purposes or have not been subjected to extensive development, however, it is safe to say that their reliabilities are lower. If these reliabilities were around .60, then the corrected $r = .20$ correlations would be around $r = .27$. Similarly, if the samples used to compute the correlations were restricted in range (i.e., they were relatively homogeneous on the MBTI scale or the other scale), this would also result in lower correlations.

Another point to consider when examining these tables: For the purposes of the theory it is just as important that certain correlations are *not* significant as that other correlations are in the expected directions. For example, Extraversion should be positively correlated with measures of sociability; Thinking should not. The flagged correlation then may not be the most important one for a given hypothesis. For some investigations, overall patterns (both size and direction) may be important, and some of these will be noted below. In addition, a lack of a correlation may be meaningful.

The conventional notation for MBTI correlations, using MBTI continuous scores or thetas, is followed, such that positive correlations are associated with I, N, F, or P, and negative correlations with E, S, T, or J. However, this convention does not apply to either Table 9.1 or Table 9.2 because the researchers who conducted these studies used MBTI preference scores, not continuous scores. In these tables positive correlations are associated with higher scores on the preference at the top of each column.

Correlations of MBTI continuous scores have their limitations as evidence for construct validity. They report only the four preference scales one at a time and do not show the 16 types as dynamic entities. Correlations also have the problem of confounding direction and clarity of preference.

Unless otherwise noted, high scores in the scales reflect the concept named by the author of the scale. For example, if a scale named "Spontaneity" correlates with Perceiving, high scores for spontaneity would be associated with high scores on J–P and there would be a "P" in the right-hand column. Not mentioned in the table but implicit in correlations is the fact that when high spontaneity is associated with Perceiving, low spontaneity is associated with Judging, since J–P is a bipolar scale. Similarly, when a scale is highly associated with Judging, there will be a negative correlation in the J–P column and a "J" in the right-hand column.

Correlations of various instruments thought to be relevant to establishing the validitiy of the MBTI preference scales are found in the tables in this chapter. Tables 9.1 through 9.6 display correlations of the MBTI with other personality instruments.

Table 9.7 shows correlations of the Form M preferences with the General Occupational Themes, the Basic Interest Scales, and the Personal Style Scales of the *Strong Interest Inventory*. The Occupational Scales (OS) are not shown here for space reasons. However, for correlations of Form G with the OS see Hammer and Kummerow (1996). Table 9.8 shows correlations with two additional career-related inventories, the *Career Factors Inventory* (Chartrand, Robbins, & Morrill, 1997) and the *Strong Skills Confidence Inventory* (Betz, Borgen, & Harmon, 1996).

Table 9.9 shows correlations between MBTI continuous scores and scales from two inventories that measure values. Table 9.10 shows correlations of real and ideal work environments based on the Work Environment Scale. Table 9.11 shows correlations with three measures of stress and coping: the *Maslach Burnout Inventory*, the *Coping Resources Inventory*, and the *State-Trait Anxiety Inventory*.

Extraversion   In type theory, Extraversion is an outward attitude in which energy flows toward the environment. This outward turning is manifested in different ways, including the following:

■ *Extraversion* as measured by other instruments: the *16 Personality Factors® Questionnaire* (16PF®), *Millon Index of Personality Styles™*, NEO-PI, and *Jungian Type Survey*

■ *Sense of comfort in the environment*, which is shown in measures named self-acceptance, well-being, autonomy, self-confidence, and stability

■ *Action on the environment*, as shown in correlations with dominance, assertiveness, social boldness, capacity for status, leadership, change, aggression, and exhibition

Table 9.1   Correlation of MBTI Form G Preference Scores and the 16 Personality Factors Questionnaire, Fifth Edition

	E	I	S	N	T	F	J	P
Primary Factors								
Warmth	.41*	−.36*	−.06	−.03	−.32*	.24*	−.15	−.03
Reasoning	−.09	.08	−.18	.27*	.10	−.12	−.03	.02
Emotional Stability	.36*	−.23*	−.12	.09	.09	−.09	−.10	.01
Dominance	.31*	−.23*	−.22	.19	.21	−.20	.01	.04
Liveliness	.48*	−.51*	−.06	−.06	−.03	.09	−.22	.11
Rule Consciousness	−.17	.17	.20	−.20	−.01	.01	.25*	−.37*
Social Boldness	.65*	−.52*	−.16	.19	.17	−.08	−.09	.06
Sensitivity	−.10	.13	−.17	.28*	−.19	.28*	.18	−.13
Vigilance	−.22	.13	.05	−.16	.20	−.12	.12	−.03
Abstractedness	−.15	.06	−.41*	.41*	−.04	.08	−.25*	.31*
Privateness	−.40*	.37*	.18	−.14	.27*	−.23*	.19	−.18
Apprehension	−.32*	.19	.04	.00	−.33*	.27*	.18	−.09
Openness to Change	.06	−.19	−.59*	.54*	−.07	.00	−.29*	.21
Self-Reliance	−.49*	.42*	.06	−.03	.08	−.08	.20	.06
Perfectionism	−.01	.02	.25*	−.23*	.13	−.11	.57*	−.53*
Tension	−.12	.08	−.12	.03	.15	−.03	.01	.10
Global Factors								
Extraversion	.68*	−.61*	−.16	.08	−.18	.19	−.26*	.09
Anxiety	−.38*	.23*	.04	−.08	−.05	.09	.15	−.01
Tough-Mindedness	−.03	.08	.56*	−.56*	.24*	−.26*	.17	−.12
Independence	.39*	−.35*	−.36*	.32*	.22	−.19	−.09	.11
Self-Control	−.13	.17	.38*	−.35*	.08	−.10	.54*	−.57*

Note: N = 119; *p < .05; **p < .01.

Source: From *16PF Fifth Edition Administrator's Guide* (p. 87), by M. Russell and D. Karol, 1994, Champaign, IL: Institute for Personality and Ability Testing, Inc. Copyright 1994 by Institute for Personality and Ability Testing, Inc. Used with permission.

- *Sociability and relatedness to others,* in scales such as outgoing, sociability, social presence, inclusion, affection, warmth, social interaction, social relations, valuing of community, empathy, high interpersonal needs (FIRO Total Needs), and peer cohesion
- *Responsiveness to the environment,* shown in measures such as liveliness and free child
- *Ways of coping* by the use of social and emotional resources
- *Career interests* that relate to general social and enterprising interests and public speaking

Introversion   Introversion in type theory is a neutral term, referring to an inward-turning attitude, one more concerned with inner than outer realities. Unfortunately, in other personality measures Introversion is often associated with scale names that have a negative connotation. To some extent Introverts can be expected to report some anxiety or shyness. In the Introverted attitude the cause of events is sought within the person. In theory Introverts should be less at home in the environment than Extraverts. Some few measures, however, will express the positive qualities of Introverts, such as self-sufficiency on the 16PF. In their career choices, Introverts often select occupations that require sustained attention and interest in concepts and ideas. Constructs related to Introversion include the following:

- *Introversion* as measured by other instruments: *Millon Index of Personality Styles, Jungian Type Survey,* and the internality scale from the *California Psychological Inventory.*
- *Lack of comfort with the environment* in measures such as anxiety, hesitating, retiring, abasement, deference, yielding, and accommodating

Table 9.2   Correlation of MBTI Form G Preference Scores and the *Millon Index of Personality Styles*

	E	I	S	N	T	F	J	P
Enhancing	.40	−.45	−.17	.12	−.02	−.06	.08	−.07
Preserving	−.43	.46	.15	−.10	.06	.00	−.07	.06
Modifying	.43	−.47	−.34	.25	.18	−.24	.08	−.07
Accommodating	−.41	.42	.34	−.21	−.16	.27	−.17	.16
Individuating	.07	−.04	−.06	.10	.45	−.36	−.13	.18
Nurturing	.07	−.13	−.06	.03	−.47	.46	.14	−.14
Extraverting	**.67**	**−.71**	−.39	.26	−.18	.04	.06	−.06
Introverting	**−.63**	**.64**	.24	−.12	.21	−.06	−.11	.12
Sensing	−.18	.17	**.75**	**−.75**	.10	−.10	.24	−.25
Intuiting	.08	−.09	**−.60**	**.60**	−.20	.23	−.24	.25
Thinking	−.05	−.01	.18	−.15	**.62**	**−.57**	.05	−.02
Feeling	−.03	−.01	−.21	.21	**−.62**	**.64**	.00	.00
Systematizing	.12	−.18	−.09	.00	−.05	−.05	**.59**	**−.60**
Innovating	.27	−.29	−.44	.45	.07	−.01	**−.51**	**.55**
Retiring	−.59	.56	.24	−.13	.23	−.07	−.07	.10
Outgoing	.65	−.65	−.39	.29	.04	−.16	−.02	.03
Hesitating	−.55	.60	.18	−.10	.07	.04	−.06	.06
Asserting	−.46	−.52	−.25	.17	.26	−.35	.05	−.03
Dissenting	−.11	.13	.03	.06	.26	−.15	−.39	.44
Conforming	.03	−.10	.30	−.36	.00	−.06	.41	−.44
Yielding	−.46	.47	.21	−.12	−.01	.16	−.11	.13
Controlling	.30	−.30	−.03	.03	.49	−.49	−.14	.15
Complaining	−.20	.24	.15	−.08	.25	−.16	−.26	.28
Agreeing	−.22	.19	.09	−.11	−.57	.57	.27	−.29
Positive Impression	−.07	−.03	.01	.08	−.05	.13	.23	−.16
Negative Impression	−.27	.28	.09	−.02	.05	−.01	−.15	.16

Note: **Bold** indicates scales measuring similar constructs; correlations greater than $r = .25$ are significant at $p < .01$, one-tailed.

Source: From *Millon Index of Personality Styles Manual* (p. 75), by T. Millon, 1994, San Antonio, TX: The Psychological Corporation. Copyright 1994 by Dicandrien, Inc. Used with permission.

- *Need to control external stimulation* in scales such as privateness and preserving
- *Independence from the environment* in measures such as self-reliance and self-control
- *Tendency to be stressed by environmental demands* as evidenced by correlations with burnout scales such as emotional exhaustion and depersonalization
- *Career interests* in the investigative and scientific areas

Sensing Perception   Sensing perception is perception by way of the senses and therefore is concerned with awareness of present realities. Characteristics expected to follow from Sensing perception are realism, common sense, practicality, conservatism, preference for the concrete rather than the abstract, and pleasure in the current moment. Sensing is related to the following:

- *Sensing* as measured by other instruments: *Jungian Type Survey* and *Millon Index of Personality Styles*

- *Taking a practical approach* such as in correlations with tough-mindedness
- *Managing reality* as demonstrated by correlations with scales such as control and order
- *Accepting reality,* as seen in relationships with measures of rule consciousness, accommodating, retiring, self-control, conforming, yielding, socialization, endurance, achievement via conformity, norm-favoring, deference and a valuing of home activities, economic security, and physical comfort
- *Career interests* include conventional, athletics, mathematics, law/politics, organizational management, data management, and office services

Intuitive Perception   Intuition is the perception of possibilities, patterns, symbols, and abstractions. Intuition leads to interest in fields where much of the work is at a symbolic, theoretical, or abstract level, or where it is forging

Table 9.3   Correlation of MBTI Form G Continuous Scores and the *California Psychological Inventory,* Form 434

	Gender	E–I	S–N	T–F	J–P	Summary
Dominance	M	−.50	.02	−.20	−.15	E–T–
	F	−.53	.04	−.17	−.10	E——
Capacity for Status	M	−.42	.23	−.04	.04	EN—
	F	−.43	.24	−.02	.03	EN—
Sociability	M	−.63	.02	−.12	−.02	E—
	F	−.70	.07	−.02	.00	E—
Social Presence	M	−.46	.18	−.14	.19	E—
	F	−.57	.15	.01	.13	E—
Self-Acceptance	M	−.51	.13	−.15	.03	E—
	F	−.58	.13	−.08	.03	E—
Independence	M	−.27	.25	−.23	.07	ENT–
	F	−.30	.26	−.17	.09	EN—
Empathy	M	−.36	.24	.09	.15	EN—
	F	−.56	.23	.05	.23	EN–P
Responsibility	M	−.05	.01	.00	−.32	—J
	F	−.05	.11	−.04	−.14	——
Socialization	M	−.06	−.20	−.05	−.33	–S–J
	F	−.08	−.20	.01	−.29	–S–J
Self-Control	M	.12	−.07	−.03	−.31	—J
	F	.18	−.12	.00	−.24	—J
Good Impression	M	−.15	−.06	−.09	−.34	—J
	F	−.07	−.14	.06	−.25	—J
Communality	M	−.11	−.11	−.08	−.23	—J
	F	−.22	−.16	−.01	−.21	E—J
Well-Being	M	−.21	−.01	−.18	−.19	E—
	F	−.20	.02	−.09	−.11	E—
Tolerance	M	.04	.22	.09	−.01	–N—
	F	−.07	.18	.04	.02	——
Achievement via Conformity	M	−.17	−.10	−.13	−.44	—J
	F	−.14	−.20	−.08	−.44	–S–J
Achievement via Independence	M	.01	.31	−.10	.04	–N—
	F	−.13	.29	−.13	.03	–N—
Intellectual Efficiency	M	−.17	.20	−.19	−.03	–N—
	F	−.29	.25	−.09	.04	EN—
Psychological-Mindedness	M	−.03	.30	−.15	.08	–N—
	F	−.01	.31	−.15	.05	–N—
Flexibility	M	.03	.39	.11	.55	–N–P
	F	−.15	.43	.07	.51	–N–P
Femininity/Masculinity	M	.20	.09	.33	.02	I–F–
	F	.14	.01	.18	−.06	——
Internality	M	.51	−.06	.16	−.02	I—
	F	.54	−.06	.13	−.04	I—
Norm-Favoring	M	−.24	−.30	−.12	−.54	ES–J
	F	−.12	−.29	−.07	−.45	–S–J
Self-Realization	M	−.09	.27	.00	.02	–N—
	F	−.18	.24	.04	.04	–N—
Managerial Potential	M	−.32	.08	−.13	−.21	E—J
	F	−.33	.08	−.10	−.15	E—
Work Orientation	M	−.05	−.08	−.15	−.27	—J
	F	−.08	.00	−.04	−.14	——
Creativity	M	−.06	.53	.09	.52	–N–P
	F	−.28	.53	.00	.43	EN–P
Leadership Potential	M	−.43	−.01	−.23	−.28	E–TJ
	F	−.47	.01	−.15	−.21	E—J

Note: N = 693; 401 males, 292 females; significance levels not reported; summary shows all $r \geq .20$.

Source: From *CPI Manual* (p. 218), by H. Gough and P. Bradley, 1996, Palo Alto, CA: Consulting Psychologists Press. Copyright 1996 by Consulting Psychologists Press. Used with permission.

Table 9.4 Correlation of MBTI Form G Continuous Scores and the NEO-PI

	Gender	E–I	S–N	T–F	J–P	Summary
Neuroticism	M	.16**	−.06	.06	.11	——
	F	.17*	.01	.28*	.04	—F—
Extraversion	M	**−.74***	.10	.19**	.15*	E——
	F	**−.69***	.22**	.10	.20**	EN–P
Openness	M	.03	**.72***	.02	.30	—N–P
	F	−.03	**.69***	−.02	.26	—N–P
Agreeableness	M	−.03	.04	**.44***	−.06	—F—
	F	−.08	.03	**.46***	.05	—F—
Conscientiousness	M	.08	−.15	−.15*	**−.49***	——J
	F	.08	−.10	−.22***	**−.46***	—TJ

Note: N = 468; 267 males, 201 females; *p < .05, **p < .01, ***p < .001. **Bold** indicates scales measuring similar constructs.

Source: From "Reinterpreting the *Myers-Briggs Type Indicator* from the Perspective of the Five-Factor Model of Personality," by R. R. McCrae and P. T. Costa, 1989, *Journal of Personality, 57,* p. 30. Copyright 1989 by Blackwell Publishers. Used with permission.

Table 9.5 Correlation of MBTI Form M Continuous Scores and the FIRO-B

	E–I	S–N	T–F	J–P	Summary
Expressed Inclusion	−.51***	.11***	.17***	.01	E——
Wanted Inclusion	−.36***	.11***	.11***	.04*	E——
Expressed Control	−.23***	.12***	−.20***	.00	E–T—
Wanted Control	.07**	.08***	.21***	.05**	—F—
Expressed Affection	−.47***	.12***	.25***	.00	E–F—
Wanted Affection	−.32***	.07**	.25***	.00	E–F—
Total Inclusion	−.48***	.13***	.15***	.02	E——
Total Control	−.14***	.03	−.01	.04*	——
Total Affection	−.44***	.10***	.28***	.00	E–F—
Total Expressed	−.55***	.16***	.09***	.01	E——
Total Wanted	−.32***	.06**	.25***	.01	E–F—
Total Needs	−.49***	.12***	.20***	.00	E–F—

Note: n = 2,996; *p < .05, **p < .01, ***p < .001. See Appendix for a description of the sample.
Source: National sample.

ground in new areas. Constructs related to Intuition include the following:

- *Intuition* as measured by other instruments: *Jungian Type Survey* and *Millon Index of Personality Styles*
- *Openness to the environment* as demonstrated by correlations with variables such as modifying, sensitivity, openness to change, change, openness, risk taking, flexibility, and variety
- *Thinking abstractly* in relationships with measures of reasoning, abstractedness, and intellectual efficiency and in valuing studying and an academic learning environment
- *Independence* as seen in correlations with scales measuring achievement via independence, free child, and autonomy
- *Career interests* in artistic areas such as music/dramatics, art, applied arts, and writing

Thinking Judgment In theory, Thinking should be associated with analytical, logical, skeptical approaches to problems and to a coolness or distance in interpersonal relationships. Occupations attractive to Thinking types should be those requiring work with material or concepts that are best understood analytically or from a cause-effect framework. Constructs related to Thinking include the following:

- *Thinking* as measured by other instruments: *Jungian Type Survey* and *Millon Index of Personality Styles*
- *Behaviors flowing from logical analysis* as demonstrated by correlations with scales such as asserting, dissenting, complaining, tough-mindedness, expressed control, controlling, and order
- *Behaviors related to thinking and acting independently* as in relationships with measures of independence, autonomy,

Table 9.6 Correlation of MBTI Form M Continuous Scores and the *Adjective Check List*

	E–I	S–N	T–F	J–P	Summary
Achievement	−.20**	−.06	−.30**	−.13*	E–T–
Dominance	−.36**	.01	−.33**	.01	E –T–
Endurance	.03	−.20**	−.34**	−.28**	– ST J
Order	.06	−.24**	−.37**	−.34**	– ST J
Intraception	−.09	.06	.01	−.04	——
Nurturance	−.24**	.07	.32**	.06	E–F–
Affiliation	−.37**	.10	.14*	.14*	E——
Heterosexuality	−.51**	.11	.25**	.17**	E–F–
Exhibition	−.60**	.20**	−.04	.23**	EN–P
Autonomy	−.24**	.19**	−.28**	.18**	E–T–
Aggression	−.28**	.04	−.24**	.04	E–T–
Change	−.39**	.30**	.13*	.42**	EN–P
Succorance	.04	.04	.33**	−.00	—F–
Abasement	.28**	−.03	.33**	−.08	I–F–
Deference	.26**	−.19**	.24**	−.21**	I–FJ
Counseling Readiness	.19**	−.00	.14*	−.13*	——
Self-Control	.44**	−.24**	.02	−.29**	IS–J
Self-Confidence	−.48**	.02	−.15*	.06	E——
Personal Adjustment	−.21**	−.06	.06	.01	E——
Ideal Self	−.24**	.10	−.18**	.03	E——
Creative Personality	−.30**	.22**	−.07	.23**	EN–P
Military Leadership	.01	−.14*	−.22**	−.11	—T–
Masculine Attributes	−.27**	.05	−.25**	.10	E–T–
Feminine Attributes	−.23**	.11	.31**	.08	E–F–
Critical Parent	−.12	.06	−.24**	.00	—T–
Nurturing Parent	−.17**	−.13*	.03	−.11	——
Adult	.01	−.16*	−.35**	−.15*	—T–
Free Child	−.60**	.29**	.04	.33**	EN–P
Adapted Child	.14*	.10	.27**	.08	—F–
Welsh A-1 scale	−.36**	.18**	.19**	.24**	E—P
Welsh A-2 scale	−.10	.35**	.08	.26**	–N–P
Welsh A-3 scale	−.30**	.05	.21**	.10	E–F–
Welsh A-4 scale	−.07	.03	−.22**	−.08	—T–

*Note: n = 247; *p < .05, **p < .01. See Appendix for a description of the sample.*

Source: Iowa State University.

achievement, endurance, risk taking, adult, and valuing work

- *Career interests* in the realistic and investigative areas and in mechanical activities, science, mathematics, law/politics, and data management

Feeling Judgment Feeling judgments are judgments made on the basis of subjective values rather than analysis or logic. Feeling is predicted to be associated with characteristics reflecting care or concern for people; interpersonal warmth; communication through the spoken word, the written word, or the arts; and a trusting rather than a

skeptical approach in making decisions. Correlations include the following:

- *Feeling* as measured by other instruments: *Jungian Type Survey* and *Millon Index of Personality Styles*
- *Concern for others* as demonstrated by correlations with measures of nurturing, warmth, affection, and succorance
- *Adaptability to others* as shown in variables like accommodating, agreeing, agreeableness, sensitivity, abasement, deference, and desire for peer cohesion
- *Career interests* in the social and artistic areas and in activities such as music/dramatics, art, culinary arts, social service, and a people-oriented workstyle

Table 9.7 Correlation of MBTI Form M Continuous Scores and the *Strong Interest Inventory* in Two Samples of College Students

Strong Interest Inventory	E–I	S–N	T–F	J–P	Summary
General Occupational Themes					
Realistic	.08	.01	–.15*	.20**	——P
	–.05	–.06	–.41**	.13	—T–
Investigative	.11	.00	–.16*	–.08	——
	–.10	–.10	–.32**	–.06	—T–
Artistic	.04	.52**	.26**	.25**	–NFP
	–.03	.42**	.11	.04	–N—
Social	–.26**	.16*	.34**	.17**	E–F–
	–.21**	–.17*	.24**	–.18*	E–F–
Enterprising	–.28**	–.05	.03	.01	E——
	–.13	–.22**	–.08	–.10	–S—
Conventional	–.03	–.33**	–.11	–.20**	–S–J
	–.08	–.37**	–.09	–.21**	–S–J
Basic Interest Scales					
Agriculture	–.03	–.07	–.05	.19**	——
	–.14	–.03	–.11	.13	——
Nature	.08	.15*	.06	.22**	——P
	–.06	.12	–.09	.06	——
Military Activities	.01	.05	–.21**	.04	—T–
	–.03	–.01	–.20**	.12	—T–
Athletics	–.13*	–.16*	–.14*	–.01	——
	–.18*	–.25**	–.27**	.02	–ST–
Mechanical Activities	.08	–.01	–.18**	.14*	——
	–.05	–.09	–.43**	.08	—T–
Science	.13*	.05	–.20**	–.07	—T–
	–.05	.03	–.31**	.02	—T–
Mathematics	.04	–.22**	–.21*	–.15*	–ST–
	–.09	–.31**	–.29**	–.14	–ST–
Medical Science	.07	.02	–.02	–.03	——
	–.15*	–.13	–.26**	–.06	—T–
Music/Dramatics	–.02	.43**	.31**	.21**	–NFP
	–.06	.36**	.13	.11	–N—
Art	.07	.48**	.24**	.22**	–NFP
	.00	.41**	.07	.01	–N—
Applied Arts	.10	.48**	.16*	.26**	–N–P
	.02	.34**	–.06	–.01	–N—
Writing	.08	.46**	.13*	.24**	–N–P
	–.06	.43**	.17*	.00	–N—
Culinary Arts	–.16*	.11	.28**	.06	—F–
	–.28**	.00	.14	–.09	E——
Teaching	–.27**	.19**	.21**	.20**	E–FP
	–.17*	–.04	.14	–.15*	——
Social Service	–.25**	.22**	.36**	.15*	ENF–
	–.17*	–.04	.20**	–.11	—F–
Medical Service	–.03	.09	.16*	.07	——
	–.15*	–.18*	–.07	–.11	——
Religious Activities	.04	.15*	.19**	.08	——
	–.15*	–.09	.15*	–.15*	——
Public Speaking	–.28**	.24**	–.11	.12	EN—
	–.21**	–.06	–.14	–.06	E——
Law/Politics	–.16*	.13*	–.25**	–.04	—T–
	–.11	–.18*	–.22**	–.04	—T–

Table 9.7   Correlation of MBTI Form M Continuous Scores and the *Strong Interest Inventory* in Two Samples of College Students *continued*

Strong Interest Inventory	E–I	S–N	T–F	J–P	Summary
Basic Interest Scales (continued)					
Merchandising	–.24**	–.05	.05	.00	E——
	–.09	–.19**	–.01	–.11	——
Sales	–.29**	–.10	–.01	.01	E——
	–.09	–.28**	–.12	–.04	–S—
Organizational Management	–.28**	–.14*	–.09	–.09	E——
	–.16*	–.32**	–.07	–.11	–S—
Data Management	–.00	–.36**	–.28**	–.25**	–STJ
	–.07	–.43**	–.23**	–.23**	–STJ
Computer Activities	.02	–.12	–.14*	–.07	——
	–.05	–.16*	–.14	.00	——
Office Services	–.03	–.29**	–.01	–.18**	–S—
	–.07	–.33**	.03	–.20**	–S–J
Personal Style Scales					
Work Style	–.46**	.07	.37**	.10	E–F–
	–.26**	–.15*	.40**	–.14	E–F–
Learning Environment	–.07	.47**	–.07	.15*	–N—
	–.11	.42**	–.03	.04	–N—
Leadership Style	–.50**	.21**	–.04	.15*	EN—
	–.45**	.06	–.04	.04	E——
Risk Taking/Adventure	–.15*	.21**	–.11	.25**	–N–P
	–.21**	.24**	–.22**	.37**	ENTP

Note: For each scale, top row n = 245 and bottom row n = 197; *p < .05, **p < .01. See Appendix for a description of the samples.

Source: For each scale, top row from Iowa State University and bottom row from Middle Tennessee State University.

Table 9.8   Correlation of MBTI Form M Continuous Scores with the *Skills Confidence Inventory* and the *Career Factors Inventory*

	E–I	S–N	T–F	J–P	Summary
Skills Confidence Inventory					
Realistic	–.06	.12	–.02	.27**	——P
Investigative	.04	.13*	–.23**	.02	—T–
Artistic	–.02	.47**	.17*	.29**	–N–P
Social	–.34**	.19**	.20**	.18**	E–F–
Enterprising	–.37**	.11	–.20**	.13*	E–T–
Conventional	–.01	–.20**	–.26**	–.11	–ST–
Career Factors Inventory					
Career Information	–.07	–.09	.01	–.13	——
Self-Knowledge	.07	–.05	.09	–.20**	——J
Career Choice Anxiety	.20**	–.11	.08	–.13	I——
Indecisiveness	.22**	–.09	.24**	.03	I–F–

Note: Skills Confidence Inventory n = 245, *Career Factors Inventory* n = 197; *p < .05, **p < .01. See Appendix for a description of the samples.

Source: Skills Confidence Inventory from Iowa State University and *Career Factors Inventory* from Middle Tennessee State University.

Table 9.9   Correlation of MBTI Form M Continuous Scores and the *Salience Inventory* and the *Values Scale*

	E–I	S–N	T–F	J–P	Summary
Salience Inventory					
Participation					
Study	−.17	.33**	.05	.21	—N—
Work	−.19	.12	−.19	−.15	——
Community	−.40**	.20	.01	.00	E——
Home	−.21	−.28*	.12	−.10	S——
Leisure	−.11	−.32**	−.05	−.06	–S—
Commitment					
Study	−.11	.36**	−.07	.12	—N—
Work	−.05	.10	−.25*	−.02	—T–
Community	−.41**	.32**	−.03	.08	EN—
Home	−.28*	−.12	.13	.00	E——
Leisure	−.24	−.27*	−.05	−.05	S——
Value Expectations					
Study	−.25*	.40**	−.08	.25*	EN–P
Work	−.21	.13	−.19	.16	——
Community	−.39**	.29*	−.04	.07	EN—
Home	−.36**	−.05	.18	.15	E——
Leisure	−.30*	−.11	.05	.19	E——
Values Scale					
Ability Utilization	−.08	.28**	−.26**	−.01	–NT–
Achievement	−.09	.05	−.12	−.18	——
Advancement	.04	−.08	.03	−.07	——
Aesthetics	−.08	.26**	.20*	.00	–NF–
Altruism	−.17	.33**	.08	.03	–N—
Authority	−.25*	.14	−.31**	.02	E–T–
Autonomy	.05	.34**	−.13	.29**	–N–P
Creativity	−.11	.62**	−.20*	.14	–NT–
Economic Rewards	.18	−.09	.11	−.09	——
Lifestyle	.10	.24*	−.12	.24*	–N–P
Personal Development	.03	.30**	−.05	.07	–N—
Physical Activity	−.08	−.03	.12	.11	——
Prestige	−.03	.02	−.16	−.25**	—J
Risk	−.12	.30**	−.21*	.30**	–NTP
Social Interaction	−.43**	.14	.00	−.05	E——
Social Relations	−.25**	−.06	.11	−.17	E——
Variety	−.11	.33**	.04	.25**	–N–P
Working Conditions	.06	−.13	.19*	−.17	——
Cultural Identity	.12	−.03	.03	−.14	——
Physical Prowess	.03	.02	.01	.10	——
Economic Security	.23*	−.33**	.22*	−.33**	ISFJ

Note: Salience Inventory n = 67, Values Scale n = 110; *p < .05, **p < .01. See Appendix for a description of the sample.

Source: Fairview Health Services.

Table 9.10 Correlation of MBTI Form M Continuous Scores and the *Work Environment Scale*

	E–I	S–N	T–F	J–P	Summary
Ideal					
Involvement	−.20	−.01	.22*	−.03	—F—
Peer Cohesion	−.31**	.12	.39**	.12	E–F—
Supervisor Support	−.27*	.16	.10	−.02	E——
Autonomy	.11	.11	.17	.02	——
Task Orientation	−.21*	.01	.11	−.11	E——
Work Pressure	.17	−.10	−.07	−.17	——
Clarity	−.15	−.14	.20	−.17	——
Control	−.12	−.41**	−.10	−.35**	–S–J
Innovation	−.14	.33**	.17	.07	–N—
Physical Comfort	−.16	.04	.13	.08	——
Real					
Involvement	−.22*	−.01	−.01	.01	E——
Peer Cohesion	−.21*	−.08	−.07	.00	E——
Supervisor Support	−.13	−.13	−.04	.04	——
Autonomy	−.22*	−.19	−.13	−.08	E——
Task Orientation	−.28**	.11	.03	.06	E——
Work Pressure	.01	.23*	.02	.11	–N—
Clarity	−.16	−.13	.04	.02	——
Control	.04	−.03	.10	−.22*	——J
Innovation	−.24*	.00	−.09	−.06	E——
Physical Comfort	−.28**	−.30**	−.23*	−.17	EST–

Note: n = 97; *p < .05, **p < .01. See Appendix for a description of the sample.

Source: Employee Career Enrichment Program, University of Minnesota.

The Judging Attitude The J–P dichotomy is concerned with when a person feels comfortable concluding that evidence is sufficient and a decision can be made. In the Judging attitude a decision is made relatively quickly; in the Perceiving attitude perception continues longer, options are kept open, and adaptability to a changing situation is preferred over following a goal-directed plan.

In theory, characteristics associated with a preference for the Judging attitude are decisiveness, desire for control, order, dependability, and conscientiousness. When Judging is not balanced adequately by Perceiving, Judging may be correlated with prejudice or closed-mindedness. Correlations include the following:

■ *Attempt to create order in the environment* as shown in correlations with scales such as systematizing, perfectionism, and control

■ *Respect for societal mores* as shown in relationships with scales such as order, conforming, rule consciousness, conscientiousness, responsibility, socialization, good impression, self-control, endurance, achievement via conformity, and valuing economic security

■ *Career interests* in the conventional area and in data management and office services activities

The Perceiving Attitude Type theory predicts that the Perceiving attitude will be associated with spontaneity, adaptability, curiosity, and openness to new ideas. If not balanced by Judging, Perceiving may be correlated with undependability. Constructs related to Perceiving include the following:

■ *Openness to the environment,* as shown by relationships with measures of innovation (the opposite of systematizing on the *Millon Index of Personality Styles*), openness to change, abstractedness, openness, flexibility, variety, creativity, change, free child, autonomy, risk taking, and valuing studying

■ *Career interests* in the artistic area and interest in activities related to nature, music/dramatics, art, applied arts, and writing

Table 9.11   Correlations of MBTI Form M Continuous Scores and the *Maslach Burnout Inventory*, the *Coping Resources Inventory*, and the *State-Trait Anxiety Inventory*

	E–I	S–N	T–F	J–P	Summary
Maslach Burnout Inventory					
Emotional Exhaustion	.34**	–.10	–.04	–.09	I——
Depersonalization	.31**	–.17	–.03	–.17	I——
Personal Accomplishment	–.25*	.04	.01	.04	E——
Coping Resources Inventory					
Cognitive	–.34**	.09	–.01	–.03	E——
Social	–.68**	.17*	.17*	.00	E——
Emotional	–.41**	.08	.14	–.12	E——
Spiritual/Philosophical	–.28**	.16	.13	.02	E——
Physical	–.02	.12	–.06	.03	——
Total	–.48*	.16	.12	.00	E——
State-Trait Anxiety Inventory					
State	.32*	–.10	.12	–.30*	I—┘
Trait	.38**	–.06	–.01	–.24	I——

Note: Maslach Burnout Inventory $n = 84$, Coping Resources Inventory $n = 167$, State-Trait Anxiety Inventory $N = 60$; $*p < .05$, $**p < .01$. See Appendix for a description of the samples.

Source: Maslach Burnout Inventory from Fairview Health Services, Coping Resources Inventory from CRI sample, State-Trait Anxiety Inventory from Spielberger (1983).

Comparison of the MBTI and the Jungian Type Survey

The correlations between the MBTI and the *Jungian Type Survey* (JTS), or Gray-Wheelwright (Wheelwright, Wheelwright, & Buehler, 1964), are of special interest to the construct validity of the MBTI because the JTS was developed by two Jungian analysts independently of the MBTI, also with the purpose of identifying Jungian types. Correlations from three different studies are shown in Table 9.12. The sample at the top of the table (Karesh, Pieper, & Holland, 1994) correlated JTS preference scores with MBTI Form G continuous scores. The two samples at the bottom of the table are from the 1985 *MBTI Manual*. The JTS has no scale comparable to J–P.

Despite the relatively positive correlations for the preferences individually, Grant (1965) reported that only 21% of 159 Auburn University students came out the same type on both instruments. Rich (1972) also compared the MBTI and the 15th edition of the JTS on a sample of 98 evening division students in a course on Jung offered at the University of Minnesota. Continuous scores were not used for the analyses; instead, correlations were reported for the sums of MBTI points and the JTS scores. The correlations between the two instruments were E .68 ($p < .01$), I .66 ($p < .01$), S .54 ($p < .01$), N .47 ($p < .01$), T .33 ($p < .01$), and F .23 ($p < .05$). The two instruments appear to be tapping the same constructs.

Evidence for Dichotomies

Jungian theory posits the existence of dichotomies. A promising technique for showing evidence of dichotomies is to plot the means of a dependent variable upon both poles of a preference scale. A dichotomy should show a division point where there is a change in slope or level, or some other disparity, between the two poles of the scale. If possible, the dependent variable should be one in which the two categories of people behave quite differently, even with the barest difference in their scores. It is not easy to identify variables relevant to a given scale that are also relatively free of variance from the other three scales. For example, "gregariousness" is obviously a better variable for testing differences on the E–I scale than on the S–N or J–P scales.

When a disparity can be found, it supports the hypothesis that the scale reflects a dichotomy—that two distinct categories of people, with opposite preferences, have been separated by MBTI scores. It is important to remember, however, that the disparity (and division point) will be clouded by any error variance in the MBTI scales. It is therefore necessary to examine disparities across a number of dependent variables.

When plotting scores of a relevant variable on MBTI scores (which can be continuous scores, preference clarity indexes, or ranges of either type of score), a crucial question is whether the observed disparities in level and/or slope between the two halves of the distribution are consistent

Table 9.12		Correlation of MBTI Continuous Scores (Form G) and the *Jungian Type Survey* in Two Samples		
JTS	N	E–I	S–N	T–F
E	192	–70		
I	192	69		
S	192		–42	–22
N	192		42	21
T	192		03	–34
F	192		–03	35
E–I	47	79		
	42	55		
S–N	47		58	
	42		66	60
T–F	47			66
	42			

Source: Top half of table from "Comparing the MBTI, *Jungian Type Survey,* and the *Singer-Loomis Inventory of Personality,*" by D. M. Karesh, W. A. Pieper, and C. L. Holland, 1994, *Journal of Psychological Type, 30,* pp. 34–35. Copyright 1994 by *Journal of Psychological Type.* Used with permission. Bottom half of table from *Manual: A Guide to the Development and Use of the Myers-Briggs Type Indicator* (p. 210), by I. B. Myers and M. H. McCaulley, 1985, Palo Alto, CA: Consulting Psychologists Press. Copyright 1985 by Consulting Psychologists Press. Used with permission.

with the usual assumption of a continuum or are better explained by the hypothesis of two different populations. If the plots are found to show unusual characteristics that can best be explained as reflecting a dichotomy, then both the theory and the validity of the MBTI would be supported. The conditions for these analyses are as follows:

1. *The basic trend for each half of the distribution should be clearly evident.* The trend should be a function of the relationship between the MBTI preference and the other construct and not a function of the particular sample. Samples of several thousand can, of course, be more finely divided and still yield a stable picture of the distribution slope and level. This provides some insurance against chance variation due to sampling or measurement error. Also, stability is more essential than detail; it is more important to identify the overall stable trend in the data than to focus on how the preference scale should be divided.

2. *Any disparity between the halves should not be "smoothed."* No a priori assumption of a continuum should be imposed on the data by connecting the two halves. Each half of the distribution should be allowed to start at zero as though the other did not exist. The trend of each half can then be determined independently.

3. *A reversal in direction is evidence for dichotomy.* The clearest kind of disparity in slope is a reversal of

direction, for example, a V-shaped or U-shaped line. According to the Jungian hypothesis, each distribution should divide the population into two categories. The slope of the line within each category should reflect the effect of differing clarities of preference. Because the two populations are hypothesized, there is no obligation to harmonize or connect the slopes or lines of the two categories. Between categories, therefore, there can be disparity in any combination of slope, level, and direction.

Examples of U-Shaped Distribution Plots   A series of analyses were made of a sample of 5,025 male Pennsylvania high school students and a sample of 720 male Massachusetts high school students. Each analysis contained six sample groups based on the size of the preference scores (1–17, 19–35, and 37+ on each side of the midpoint). In the Pennsylvania sample, mean IQ scores were computed for each preference score grouping; for the Massachusetts sample, vocabulary scores were used.

Figure 9.1 shows the mean intelligence scores for the male Pennsylvania high school students, divided into six groups of the preference scores for each of the dichotomies, and the mean vocabulary scores for the Massachusetts high school students for the same six groupings for each of the four MBTI scales.

Both the E–I and J–P dichotomies show a trend for clearer preferences (away from the midpoint) to be associated with higher scores. The Perceiving side of the scale is also higher than the Judging side of the scale, which is typical for J–P plots on aptitude/achievement data.

Clear preferences on either Thinking or Feeling are associated with higher scores on both IQ and vocabulary measures. The curve shows greater discrepancy for clear and unclear (near the midpoint) preferences than the curves for E–I and J–P.

The plots for the S–N scale show that this scale does not operate the same on intelligence and vocabulary as do the other scales. Rather than clearer preferences in either pole leading to higher IQ and vocabulary scores, only clearer preferences for Intuition lead to greater scores. This also demonstrates why it is important to choose a variable for each scale that is theoretically appropriate.

Examples of Discontinuities   If Jung was correct about dichotomous populations, and if the MBTI correctly separates the two populations on each preference scale, then a discontinuity around the midpoint of the scale is expected. In order to constitute a discontinuity, there must be a significantly greater rate of change at the point of discontinuity than on either side of that point. It is not sufficient to show that the difference in means or proportions between all contiguous intervals is significant; what is important is evidence for a change in slope or direction somewhere near the hypothesized midpoint of the scale.

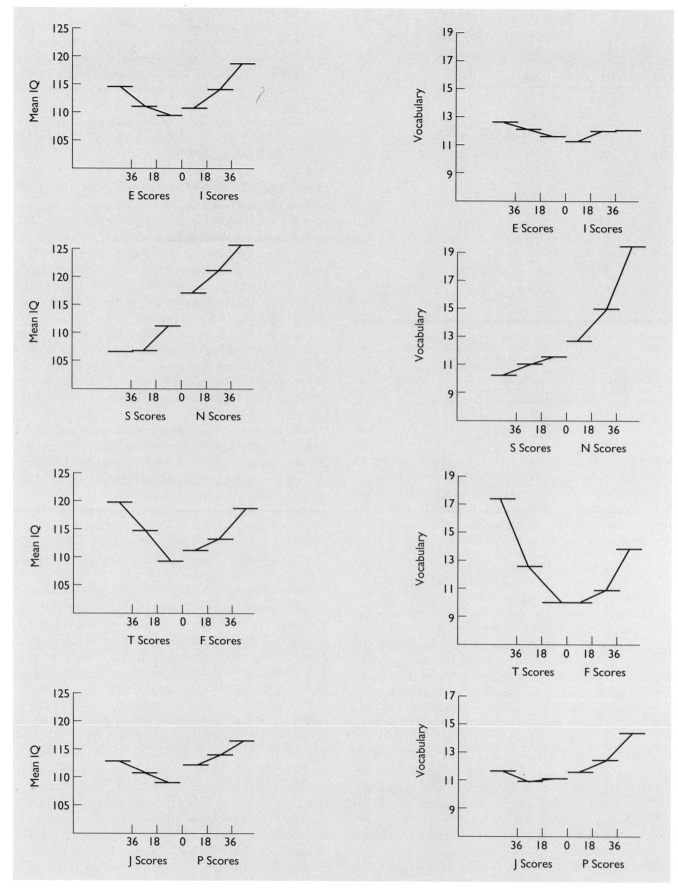

Figure 9.1 Mean Aptitude Scores at Different Levels of Preference Scores for Each of the Dichotomies

Note: Mean intelligence scores are for the male Pennsylvania high school students; mean vocabulary scores are for the Massachusetts high school students.

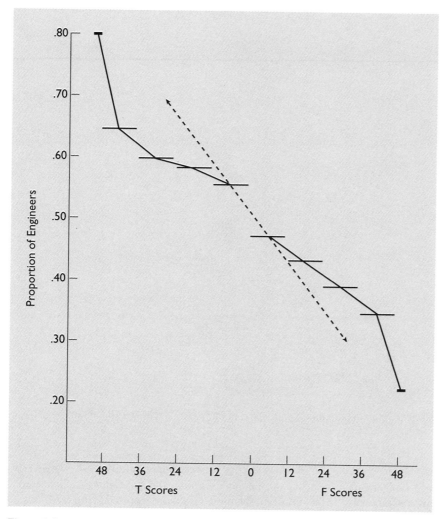

Figure 9.2 Proportion of Engineering Students Who Reported Different Levels of Preference on the T–F Dichotomy

One needs, therefore, evidence for a not-too-steep slope with a significant break at the division point. Because probabilities are influenced by the size of samples, to demonstrate that such a break is significant either the sample must be so large that even a modest discontinuity is significant or the discontinuity must be so large that it is significant even for a modest sample. Each of these alternatives is demonstrated.

Engineering Students and the T–F Scale A comparison of liberal arts and engineering students on the T–F scale is an example of a small difference observable in a large sample and is shown in Figure 9.2. One conspicuous contrast on the T–F scale is between a sample of 2,389 engineering students and 2,177 liberal arts students tested as part of the analyses for Form F. Sixty-eight percent of engineering students preferred Thinking, compared with only 54% of liberal arts students. The liberal arts and engineering samples were combined, making a total sample of 4,566. The proportion of engineers was computed for each 12-point interval along the T–F scale, running both directions from zero.

If the tendency to choose an engineering college is linked to a preference for Thinking or Feeling, then a discontinuity

in the slope should occur at the division point. If the choice of engineering is related only to the clarity of the Thinking or Feeling preference, then the slope should be unbroken. In the analysis of the combined sample, each half of the scale was divided into five intervals of preference scores (1–11, 13–23, 25–35, 37–47, 49+). A *t*-test was used to test for differences between intervals. Of the nine successive differences between adjacent intervals, only the one that fell at the division point was statistically significant ($t = 3.25, p < .001$). The broken line in Figure 9.2 shows the disparity between the steepness at the division point compared to the more gradual slope in the two halves of the distribution. Table 9.13 shows the *t*-value for the difference between each successive interval and the significant *p*-value at the midpoint.

Faculty Ratings of Gregariousness and E–I Preference A comparison of Extraverts and Introverts in "gregariousness" is an example of a large difference in a modest sample and is shown in Figure 9.3. As part of the Educational Testing Service College Student Characteristics Study, Ross (1961) obtained faculty ratings of student characteristics on a seven-point scale. Raters had no knowledge of students'

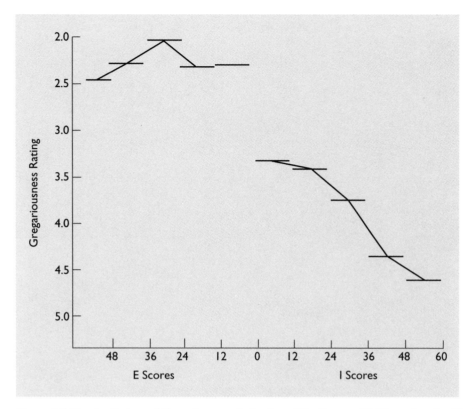

Figure 9.3 Faculty Ratings of Gregariousness in Students Who Reported Different Levels of Preference on the E–I Dichotomy

MBTI results. Ross reported correlations of .50 between the E–I scale and "gregariousness" on a Solitary–Gregarious scale. The sample was a composite of students in four colleges. The subsample of 249 cases shown in Figure 9.3 had a correlation between Extraversion and "gregariousness" of .42. When Extraverts were correlated independently of Introverts, the correlation was only .05. The Introvert correlation independent of Extraverts was −.21. Figure 9.3 indicates that the faculty considered gregariousness a general characteristic of Extraverts, and it was not related to the degree of Extraversion. Introverts of any degree are seen as clearly less gregarious than Extraverts; in addition, Introverts having the clearest preference for Introversion on the MBTI were seen as the least gregarious.

As can be seen in the figure and in Table 9.13, the only significant change between contiguous intervals occurred between the ranges E 1–11 and I 1–11 ($t = 2.80, p < .01$). The change at or near zero is significantly greater than changes between any other positions on the E–I scale. These data support both the existence of a dichotomy on the E–I scale and the correctness of the location of its division point.

Preference for Reading and Differences on the S–N Scale

A comparison of number of books reported read by Sensing and Intuitive types is another example of a large difference in a modest sample. Hicks (1984) described reports of Sensing types and Intuitive types on the number of books reported being read in the past year. Figure 9.4 shows the mean number of books reported being read for persons with different

levels of preference for Sensing or Intuition. The largest difference appears at the midpoint; the clearer the preference for Intuition, the more books are reported being read.

Evidence for Dichotomies in Brain Activity Patterns

Jung, Briggs, and Myers viewed type preferences as inborn dispositions to develop along specific lines. Type may thus be viewed as a basic template that directs and organizes life experiences and contributes to differential responses to similar life events. Jung saw personality as biologically based and concluded that type antithesis must have some kind of biological foundation as well (Jung, 1921/1971). Current methods such as topographic brain mapping and EEG recordings offer hope of uncovering these relationships.

Differences between Extraverts and Introverts have been studied by a number of researchers. Wilson and Languis (1989) discuss an approach to construct validation that involves an attempt to "establish a link between neurocognitive psychophysiological data and psychological type data through the investigation of differences in brain electrical activity patterns . . ." (p. 14). Their first study involved a comparison of those identified by the MBTI as having an Extraverted preference versus those with an Introverted preference. To control for other aspects of type, all other preferences were the same (NTP). Topographic brain mapping data were collected using a protocol based on standard measurement of cortical activity. The research literature on personality differences was used to construct cognitive tasks that were administered during the measurement of evoked potentials.

Table 9.13   t–Values and Significance Between Intervals for Plots Shown in Figures 9.2 and 9.3

Interval	1	2	3	4	5	6	7	8	9
Engineering Study (Figure 9.2)									
t	1.4	1.29	0.74	1.28	3.25	1.55	1.08	0.89	0.69
p					0.001				
Gregariousness Study (Figure 9.3)									
t	0.20	0.64	0.88	0.11	2.80	0.25	0.64	0.104	0.27
p					0.01				

A comparison of the Extraverts and Introverts is shown in Figure 9.5. Significant and consistent differences were found across a number of tests between the Extraverts and Introverts, suggesting that Extraverts demonstrate less cortical arousal than do Introverts. The authors hypothesize that the relatively greater cortical arousal of Introverts leads to their seeking to reduce stimulation from the environment; the authors plan to follow up with larger samples and samples of different preferences.

In other research, Stenberg's (1990) studies of blood flow show higher activity in anterior temporal lobes for Introverts, which may be related to Extraverts being geared to respond and seek excitement in order to avoid underarousal; in contrast, Introverts, who are geared to inspect, may be threatened by overarousal and seek out peaceful pursuits in solitude and tranquility. Evidence from longitudinal studies of temperament (Kagan & Snidman, 1991) focusing on measures of selected limbic sites provide similar support for a physiological basis for Extraversion and Introversion.

Some evidence is also available regarding physiological differences in Sensing and Intuition. Newman (1985), using EEG alpha symmetry ratios, found that Intuitive types as a group showed greater levels of activity in the left hemisphere and Sensing types greater activation in the right hemisphere. Wilson and Languis (1989) reported a similar finding for adults with clear preferences for Extraverted Intuition and Extraverted Sensing; and in preliminary exploratory research, Wilson, Laposky, and Languis (1991) found a pattern of generalized posterior arousal for Intuitive type middle school students.

The growing evidence regarding the biological basis of psychological type gives credence to Jung's assumption that type is universal, that is, that the personalities of all human beings are structured in accord with type dichotomies.

Studies of Behavioral Differences of the Types

Carskadon (1979) reported on 40 psychology undergraduates asked to give a five-minute talk before six judges, with only five minutes' notice. Extraverts stood closer to judges ($p < .05$), had fewer seconds of silence ($p < .01$), and after the talk remembered more names of the judges to whom

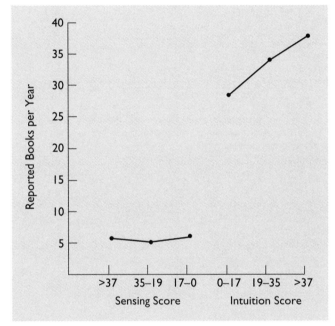

Figure 9.4   Reported Books Read per Year as a Function of Sensing and Intuition Preference Scores

they were introduced at the onset of the experiment ($p < .001$). Thorne (1987) reported communication differences between Extraverts and Introverts by asking undergraduate women to chat with a stranger. Extraverts paired with other Extraverts served as catalysts for mutual sociability. They explored a broader range of topics, looked for a variety of ways they were similar to one another, and discussed more pleasurable topics. Introverts paired with other Introverts tended not to look for common ground with one another beyond their similarity as students, more often hedged in their answers, and had problem-oriented discussions. More moderate conversational patterns occurred when Extraverts were paired with Introverts.

The staff of the Institute for Personality Assessment and Research (IPAR) included behavioral ratings by the staff as part of assessments. Data reported by Gough (1981) and Helson (1975) show significant correlations between rating instruments and MBTI preferences. Ratings are based on the

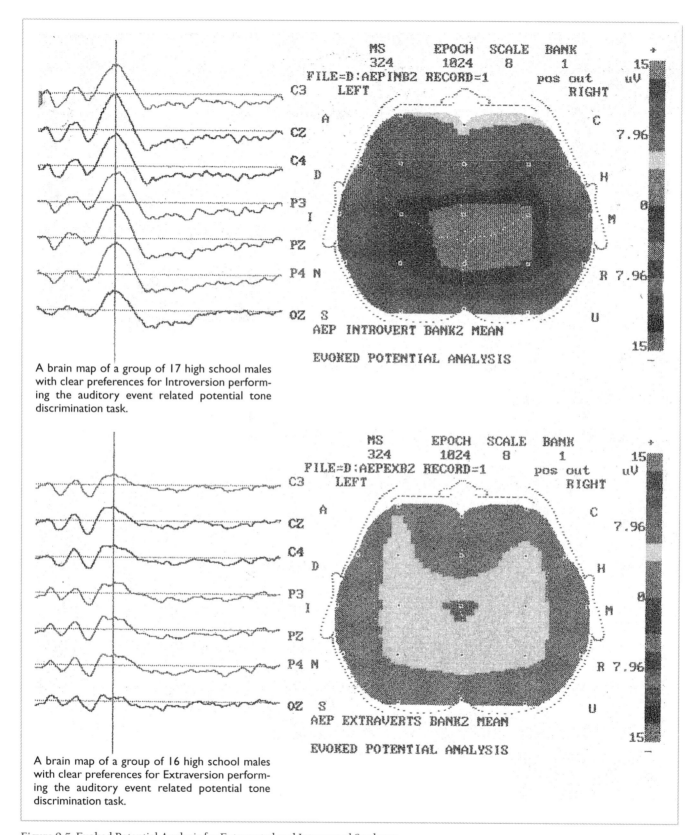

A brain map of a group of 17 high school males with clear preferences for Introversion performing the auditory event related potential tone discrimination task.

A brain map of a group of 16 high school males with clear preferences for Extraversion performing the auditory event related potential tone discrimination task.

Figure 9.5 Evoked Potential Analysis for Extraverted and Introverted Students

Source: Scan generated by M. W. Alcock. Based on "A Topographic Study of Differences in the P300 Between Introverts and Extraverts," M. A. Wilson and M. L. Languis, 1990, *Brain Topography, 2* (4). Used with permission.

Adjective Check List (ACL) (Gough & Heilbrun, 1983) and the *California Q-Sort* (Block, 1978). The ACL was also used by Brooks and Johnson (1979) for self-ratings of undergraduate and graduate students and by Grant (1966) for self-ratings of specific types of college freshmen. Table 9.14 shows the staff ratings reported by Gough (1981) for 244 males and 186 females assessed at IPAR and the self-ratings of 209 students reported by Brooks and Johnson (1979). An important paper by Gough (1965) discusses how data such as these can help provide a conceptual analysis of scale meaning.

The descriptions are consistent with type theory, although some of the male Thinking terms fit male STs better than male NTs. Notice that the observers described the more positive aspects of Thinking in males and the more negative aspects of Thinking in females. They also described the more positive aspects of Feeling in females and the more negative aspects of Feeling in males. These differences may come from the bias of the observers or from the reactions of those observed because they have preferences contrary to cultural stereotypes.

Studies of Creativity

In type theory, creation of something entirely new should be related to a preference for Intuition. Intuition is the mode of perception that is oriented to possibilities and the future and to seeing hitherto unknown patterns. Creativity therefore is expected to be associated primarily with a preference for Intuition and secondarily with a preference for the perceiving attitude, which gives curiosity and receptiveness.

The earliest research with the MBTI and creative people was conducted at IPAR by Donald MacKinnon and his colleagues (Gough, 1976, 1981; Hall & MacKinnon, 1969; Helson, 1965, 1968, 1971, 1975; Helson & Crutchfield, 1970; MacKinnon, 1960, 1962a, 1962b, 1965, 1971). The data below that are not included in these publications were made available by IPAR for this manual.

The IPAR samples of creative people were selected by peer nomination from professions judged to be creative; thus they represent highly creative people in creative fields. It is useful, therefore, to compare the type distributions of highly creative people with one another, with samples of others in creative fields, and with the distribution of types in the general public.

Table 9.15 shows correlations between the MBTI and the *Kirton Adaption and Innovation Inventory* (KAI; Kirton, 1987) in two samples (Fleenor, 1997; Gryskiewicz & Tullar, 1995). The correlations of the MBTI S–N and J–P scales with the total KAI score are similar and demonstrate a relationship between Intuition and Perceiving and the innovation (or, conversely, between Sensing and Judging and the adaptation) style of creativity. The opposite sign of the E–I correlation in the two studies is curious, with sampling error being the most likely explanation, given the disparity in the sample sizes in the two studies.

Type distributions of samples of creative people show their preference for Intuition. The field in which they work makes little difference, although writers tend to be NF and mathematicians and scientists tend to be NT. To be appreciated, the percentage of Intuitive types among creative individuals should be seen in perspective. The frequency of Intuitive types in the general population is roughly estimated at 25%. In the creative samples, all but three of the highly creative men in the four IPAR samples preferred Intuition. Comparison of this distribution with that of the selected college population yields a chi-square statistic of more than 50.00, an occurrence that could happen by chance less than one in a million times.

If Intuition is a key factor in creativity, as theory would predict, then groups rated at different levels of creativity should also differ in the proportion of Intuitive types. In Hall and MacKinnon's (1969) data, architects in the first group were judged by other architects to be highly creative. Those in the second group were working with one of the highly creative architects. The third group was a cross-section sample of members of the American Institute of Architects, matched to the creative architects on age and geographical location. The proportion of Intuitive types decreases significantly between the first, second, and third groups. The contrast between first and third groups yields a chi-square of 17.0 (*p* < .001). Not only does the proportion of Intuitive types increase with level of creativity, but there is also an increase in the Intuition preference score. The mean score for Intuition was 36.2 for the very creative group, 29.6 for their colleagues, and 27.5 for the representative sample of architects.

Where samples differ in level of creativity, less creative samples still have a majority of Intuitive types, but the proportion is lower. It may be also, as with the architects, that the most creative samples not only have more Intuitive types but also express a clearer preference for Intuition. Most samples have a majority of Introverts, though Extraverts and Introverts are more nearly divided in creative samples that are associated with performance. In most of the artistic samples, Feeling types are in the majority; in mathematics and science, Thinking types outnumber feeling types. Isabel B. Myers predicted that creativity would be associated with the open, curious receptivity of the Perceiving attitude. This prediction is mainly upheld. Indeed, in the samples grouped by levels of creativity, greater creativity is associated with a higher proportion of Perceiving types.

Gough (1981) reported a series of samples ranked by an experimental MBTI Creativity Index based on 20 years of creativity research at IPAR. The experimental Creativity Index based on Form G continuous scores is as follows:

MBTI Creativity Index = 3SN + JP − EI − .5TF.

For samples in which an external or internal criterion for creativity was available, the data show that the Creativity Index is significantly and positively correlated with the criterion (Myers & McCaulley, 1985).

Table 9.14   Self-Descriptions and Rater Descriptions Associated with MBTI Preferences

Extraversion	Introversion
Measure	**Measure**
Males	*Males*
ACL[1] Adaptable, alert, appreciative, good-looking, jolly, poised, warm.	ACL[1] Anxious, moody, preoccupied, aloof, apathetic, autocratic, confused, distrustful, evasive, foolish, impatient, indifferent, irritable, pessimistic, self-centered, self-pitying, slow, worrying.
ACL[2] Outgoing (−.30), sociable (−.31), enthusiastic (−.22), optimistic (−.25), talkative (−.28), good-natured (−.26).	ACL[2] Quiet (.24), reserved (.24), aloof (.19), retiring (.20), inhibited (.19), shy (.17).
Q-Sort[2] Emphasizes being with others (−.30), is talkative (−.24), behaves in assertive fashion (−.24), has a rapid personal tempo (−.17), is facially and/or gesturally expressive (−.28).	Q-Sort[2] Keeps people at distance (.28), tends to ruminate and have preoccupying thoughts (.27), reluctant to commit self to definite course of action (.20), tends toward overcontrol of needs (.28), is introspective and concerned with self as an object (.31).
Females	*Females*
ACL[1] Active, kind, adventurous, headstrong, informal, initiative, opportunistic, sharpwitted, zany.	ACL[1] Honest, realistic, calm, complaining, fussy, lazy, methodical, modest, retiring.
ACL[2] Outgoing (−.45), sociable (−.44), enthusiastic (−.49), optimistic (−.25), talkative (−.47), good-natured (−.36).	ACL[2] Quiet (.42), reserved (.40), aloof (.36), retiring (.35), inhibited (.33), shy (.29).
Q-Sort[2] Emphasizes being with others (−.50), is talkative (−.43), behaves in assertive fashion (−.35), has a rapid personal tempo (−.41), is facially and/or gesturally expressive (−.29).	Q-Sort[2] Keeps people at distance (.48), tends to ruminate and have preoccupying thoughts (.30), reluctant to commit self to definite course of action (.41), tends toward overcontrol of needs (.48), is introspective and concerned with self as an object (.17).
Males and Females	*Males and Females*
ACL[1] Interests wide, enthusiastic, forgiving, frank, outgoing, quick, sociable, talkative.	ACL[1] Quiet, reserved, shy, careless, defensive, inhibited, mild, silent, tense, timid, wary, withdrawn.

Sensing	Intuition
Measure	**Measure**
Males	*Males*
ACL[1] Conservative, shy, aggressive.	ACL[1] Adaptable, interests wide, sensitive, complicated, foresighted, idealistic, intelligent, outspoken, reflective, resourceful, sexy, talkative, trusting, unconventional.
ACL[2] Conventional (−.41), conservative (−.38), practical (−.37), interests narrow (−.29), simple (−.28), natural (−.27), contented (−.27), moderate (−.21), commonplace (−.20).	ACL[2] Original (.22), artistic (.20), imaginative (.25), ingenious (.32), complicated (.31), unconventional (.26), reflective (.24), curious (.22), individualistic (.21), interests wide (.20).
Q-Sort[2] Favors conservative values (−.41), judges self and others in conventional terms (−.39), uncomfortable with uncertainty and complexities (−.31), has a clear-cut, internally consistent personality (−.31), subjectively unaware of self-concern, feels satisfied with self (−.29).	Q-Sort[2] Associates to ideas in unusual ways (.43), rebellious and nonconforming (.36), values intellectual/cognitive matters (.25), high degree of intellectual capacity (.24), unpredictable in behaviors and attitudes (.24).
Females	*Females*
ACL[1] Quiet, deliberate, shy, formal.	ACL[1] Forgiving, imaginative, absent-minded, clever, flirtatious, rebellious, resourceful.
ACL[2] Conventional (−.43), conservative (−.35), simple (−.33), interests narrow (−.31), contented (−.16), shallow (−.25), natural (−.23), practical (−.20), moderate (−.18).	ACL[2] Original (.22), artistic (.20), imaginative (.25), ingenious (.22), complicated (.27), unconventional (.20), reflective (.19), curious (.27), individualistic (.31), interests wide (.21).
Q-Sort[2] Favors conservative values (−.39), judges self and others in conventional terms (−.38), uncomfortable with uncertainty and complexities (−.26), has a clear-cut, internally consistent personality (−.22), is subjectively unaware of self-concern, feels satisfied with self (−.20).	Q-Sort[2] Associates to ideas in unusual ways (.36), high degree of intellectual capacity (.32), unpredictable in behavior and attitudes (.32), rebellious and nonconforming (.31), genuinely values intellectual matters (.31).

Table 9.14   Self-Descriptions and Rater Descriptions Associated with MBTI Preferences *continued*

Thinking	Feeling
Measure	**Measure**
Males	*Males*
ACL[1] Alert, logical, assertive.	ACL[1] Curious, interests wide, kind, humorous, unselfish.
ACL[2] Conventional (−.27), conservative (−.25), moderate (−.23), interests narrow (−.21), steady (−.21).	ACL[2] Despondent (.27), artistic (.26), original (.26), interests wide.
Q-Sort[2] Prides self on being objective, rational (−.36), judges self and others in conventional terms (−.29), favors conservative values (−.25).	Q-Sort[2] Enjoys aesthetic impressions (.27), tends to be rebellious (.20), has insight into motive and character (.19).
Females	*Females*
ACL[1] Defensive, hurried.	ACL[1] Sympathetic, soft-hearted, forgiving.
ACL[2] Hard-hearted (−.32), fault-finding (−.30), logical (−.27), ambitious (−.26), opinionated (−.26), severe (−.26), cold (−.25), hostile (−.24).	ACL[2] Trusting (.31), affectionate (.30), pleasant (.30), sympathetic (.26), soft-hearted (.22).
Q-Sort[2] Prides self on being objective (−.32), critical, skeptical, not easily impressed (−.30), basically distrustful of people, questions their motives (−.30).	Q-Sort[2] Has warmth, capacity for close relationships (.35), tends to arouse acceptance in people (.30), is personally charming (.24).

Judgment	Perception
Measure	**Measure**
Males	*Males*
ACL[1] Honest, reasonable, progressive, attractive, hard-hearted.	ACL[1] Forgetful.
ACL[2] Conservative (−.39), conventional (−.29), industrious (−.26), dependable (−.22), organized (−.24).	ACL[2] Disorderly (.28), careless (.30), adventurous (.26), pleasure-seeking (.21), lazy (.29), changeable (.23), restless (.23).
Q-Sort[2] Favors conservative values (−.34), is fastidious (−.28), tends toward overcontrol of needs (−.23), judges self and others in conventional terms (−.32), is moralistic (−.25).	Q-Sort[2] Tends to be rebellious (.40), enjoys sensuous experiences (.32), is unpredictable in behavior and attitudes (.22), is self-indulgent (.18), various needs tend toward relatively direct expression (.24).
Females	*Females*
ACL[1] Cautious, sympathetic, clear-thinking, dependable, cooperative, dignified, industrious, painstaking, practical, precise.	ACL[1] Disorderly, fickle, pleasure-seeking, self-seeking.
ACL[2] Conservative (−.39), conventional (−.37), industrious (−.33), dependable (−.32), organized (−.24).	ACL[2] Disorderly (.25), careless (.29), adventurous (.26), pleasure-seeking (.31), lazy (.22), changeable (.27), restless (.23).
Q-Sort[2] Favors conservative values (−.34), is fastidious (−.37), tends toward overcontrol of needs (−.38), judges self and others in conventional terms (−.25), is moralistic (−.30).	Q-Sort[2] Tends to be rebellious (.32), enjoys sensuous experiences (.32), is unpredictable in behavior and attitudes (.40), is self-indulgent (.44), various needs tend toward relatively direct expression (.25).

Males and Females

ACL[1] Realistic, efficient, stable, moderate, organized, planful, thorough.

Note: Negative correlations are associated with E, S, T, and J; positive correlations with I, N, F, and P.

[1] Brooks & Johnson, 1979. Undergraduate and graduate students (106 male, 103 female) described themselves using the *Adjective Check List* (ACL). All adjectives discriminated significantly between preferences at least at $p < .05$. Listed are the three adjectives with the greatest differentiation plus any others unique to that preference.

[2] Gough, 1981. For the 244 males sample, correlations of .13 are significant at $p < .05$, .16 at $p < .01$, .21 at $p < .001$. For the 186 females sample, correlations of .14 are significant at $p < .05$, .19 at $p < .01$, and .24 at $p < .001$. *Adjective Check Lists* and Q-Sorts are based on observations by at least five staff members.

Table 9.15   Correlation of MBTI Continuous Scores (Form F) and the *Kirton Adaption and Innovation Inventory* in Two Samples

	N	E–I	S–N	T–F	J–P	Summary
Rule/Group Conformity	12,115	–.11	.45	–.01	.40	–N–P
Sufficiency of Originality	12,115	–.30	.47	–.05	.32	EN–P
Efficiency	12,115	–.11	.34	.13	.48	–N–P
Total	12,115	–.23	.54	.01	.49	EN–P
KAI Total	49	.21	.41	–.19	.41	IN–P

Source: Top part of table from "The Relationship Between the MBTI and Measures of Personality and Performance in Management Groups," by J. W. Fleenor, 1997, in *Developing Leaders* (p. 128). Palo Alto, CA: Davies-Black. Copyright 1997 by Davies-Black. Used with permission. Last line from "The Relationship Between Personality Type and Creativity Style Among Managers," by N. D. Gryskiewicz and W. L. Tullar, 1995, *Journal of Psychological Type, 32*, p. 33. Copyright 1995 by *Journal of Psychological Type.* Used with permission.

Gough estimated that in IPAR samples that contain many highly creative people, males with Index scores of 350 or higher can be expected to show creative potential; men with scores of 250 or lower will be less likely to show creative talent. Creativity Index scores calculated from samples not selected as creative, such as the approximately 16,000 males and females in the MBTI databank in 1985, are substantially lower than for the IPAR samples, as would be expected, averaging 239 for males and 233 for females.

A number of other researchers have studied the relationship between the MBTI and creativity. Representative studies can be found in Cropley (1965); Owen (1962); Ruane (1973); Whittemore and Heimann (1965); Burt (1968); Stephens (1975); Erickson, Gantz, and Stephenson (1970); and Gryskiewicz (1982).

Creativity and originality in these studies continue to be associated with Intuition and Perceiving, even in early adolescence. As in the data above, the association with the T–F and E–I dichotomies is less clear, though originality may be more apparent in Extraverts in younger samples.

Other Representative Studies of Differences Between Preferences

This section describes other studies relevant to Jung's theory. Studies related to careers and education are not included here. Carlson and Levy (1973) and Carlson (1980) tested type theory by predicting which types should have the maximum difference on specific variables. They selected these types for experiments testing their hypotheses.

The Carlson and Levy (1973) study tested the relationship between the MBTI and the following:

- Short-term memory using the Digit Span of the *Wechsler Adult Intelligence Scale*® and memory for faces in the *Lightfoot Facial Expression Series.* They found that ITs scored higher than EFs on digit span, and EFs scored higher than ITs on recognizing faces.
- Memory task performance using geometric figures with numbers on the sides and geometric figures with fictitious names on the sides. They found that ITs were higher than EFs in the discrepancy between numbers minus names.
- Person perception using recorded judgments of 20 standardized slides, 2 each for 10 emotions. They found that NPs scored higher than SJs, and females scored higher than males.
- Volunteering for social service using the amount of volunteering of 10 students in a halfway house. They found 7 of 10 volunteers and only 1 of the controls to be ENFP or ENTP.

Carlson (1980) tested the following relationships between the MBTI and other variables:

- Quality of affective memories was tested using blind ratings of critical incidents recalling significant personal experience by judges familiar with type theory. Carlson found that judges correctly identified eight of nine EF types and five of six IT types.
- Interpersonal closeness or distance using the same set of memories as above but rated for presence of individual or interpersonal quality. Carlson found that Introverts gave more individual and Extraverts more interpersonal memories of joy, excitement, and shame.
- Cognitive clarity and vividness of feeling using the same set of memories as above edited to leave only statements of personal experience, also rated blind by a new set of judges. EF memories were rated significantly more vivid in expression than IT memories in joy, excitement, and shame.
- Type differences in personal constructs using judges' blind ratings of concrete or inferential constructs on an abbreviated version of the *Role Construct Repertory Test* (Kelly, 1955). Judges identified inferential constructs on 16 of 20 Intuitive types and 3 of 14 Sensing types. See also Howland (1971) for a similar study.

Orientation to Time   Type theory predicts that Sensing types are more oriented to present events since the present is what can be perceived by the senses. Intuitive types are more attuned to the future, since Intuition is the function that sees possibilities beyond the immediate present. Thinking types are expected to be more concerned with the sequence of time from past through present to future, since Thinking is concerned with cause-effect sequences. Feeling types are expected to be more oriented toward the past, since values are transmitted as the heritage of the past. For each type, the two functions may complement or conflict with one another. For example, SF is concerned with the present moment, but the present moment is colored by past values. Thus one would expect SF types to be relatively more conservative. The NF group, however, can be seen as pulled toward the future by Intuition and toward the past by Feeling. These contrasting forces can be expected to differ in the four NF types as a result of the interplay of the dominant and auxiliary functions and depending on whether these are extraverted or introverted. Time perspective of the Jungian functions is discussed in Mann, Siegler, and Osmond (1968).

There are fewer hypotheses about time and the attitudes, though one would expect Extraverts to be more aware of time changes in the world around them and to see time in more discrete units. Introverts should be more oriented toward ideas that have more continuity and relatively less aware of changes in the world around them. Thus Introverts may be expected to be less accurate in evaluating the time of events.

Isabel Myers hypothesized that Intuitive types are less accurate than Sensing types in projecting how long any given task will require. Seeing possibilities in a sudden flash, Intuitive types would underestimate the time it takes to work out necessary details and to bring the possibility to completion. Organized Judging types can be expected to take time more seriously than spontaneous Perceiving types and to be more effective in meeting deadlines.

Evans (1976) and Yang (1981) supported theoretical connections between Sensing and the present, Intuition and the future, Feeling and the past, and Thinking and no time zone. Studies of type differences in ease of visualizing the future found longer extensions with Intuition and Thinking and shorter ones with Sensing and Feeling (Harrison, 1984; Nightingale, 1973; Seiden, 1970; Smith, 1976).

One would expect Extraverts to experience the world in discrete units of time. This expectation was supported by Seiden (1970), who found that Extraverts related their identity to events or ceremonies that represented change. Extraverts were also more accurate in autokinetic time perception (Veach & Touhey, 1971). Introverts, who are oriented to ideas that are more continuous than external events, see time as more continuous (Seiden, 1970) or oceanic (Knapp & Lapuc, 1965). Nightingale (1973) found that Introverts extend time farther back into the past; Extraverts extend time farther forward into the future.

Organized Judging types can be expected to take time more seriously than spontaneous Perceiving types and to be more effective in meeting deadlines. Evidence for J–P differences in time management appears in a study by Jaffe (1980), in which Sensing, Thinking, and Judging managers were more successful with management by objectives. In student populations there are often significant correlations between Judging and planning and control, which are essential elements of time management. For example, Table 9.16 shows the correlations of MBTI Form G continuous scores with the *Time Management Questionnaire* (Williams, Verble, Price, & Layne, 1995) in a sample of 204 students. The correlation of time management attitudes with Judging is clear. In other

Table 9.16   Correlation of MBTI Continuous Scores (Form G) and the *Time Management Questionnaire*

		E–I	S–N	T–F	J–P	Summary
Short-Range Planning	M	−.24	−.18	.26	−.58	E–FJ
	F	−.14	−.06	−.07	−.46	——J
	M, F	−.18	−.08	.12	−.51	——J
Long-Range Planning	M	−.27	−.31	.09	−.38	ES–J
	F	−.01	−.17	−.05	−.41	——J
	M, F	−.07	−.20	.04	−.42	–S–J
Time Attitudes	M	−.10	−.13	−.22	−.06	——T–
	F	−.01	.15	−.05	−.17	———
	M, F	−.03	.09	−.09	−.14	———
Total Score	M	−.30	−.28	.13	−.56	ES–J
	F	−.10	−.04	−.08	−.48	——J
	M, F	−.15	−.09	.05	−.51	——J

Note: N = 204; 48 males, 156 females.

Source: From "Relationship Between Time-Management Practices and Personality Indices and Types," by R. L. Williams, J. S. Verble, D. E. Price, and B. H. Lane, 1995, *Journal of Psychological Type, 34*, p. 38. Copyright 1995 by *Journal of Psychological Type.* Used with permission.

studies, Judging students took fewer incompletes (Smith, Irey, & McCaulley, 1973), and Judging medical school applicants completed their applications earlier (Kainz & McCaulley, 1975). Sex differences also appear to be important in some samples; Marcus (1976) and Squyres (1980) also found differences in the populations they studied, and in the Williams et al. (1995) study, long-range planning was correlated with Extraversion and Sensing as well as with Judging.

The studies provide support for the predicted differences in the experience and use of time for different MBTI types. There is another important study of type and time orientation by Harrison and Lawrence (1985). However, since this study was primarily concerned with whole types rather than individual preferences, the results are reported in the whole type section of this chapter.

Fantasy and Imagery   Representative studies of fantasy and imagery and MBTI types are Edmunds (1982), Ireland and Kernan-Schloss (1983), O'Haire and Marcia (1980), and Palmiere (1972). These studies found that, as predicted, both fantasy and imagery are of more interest to Intuitive types. In addition, significant differences are found concerning the content and affect of images. The results of these studies can be related to the time orientation studies in that fantasy and imagery can be conceived of as ways of suspending time.

Introversion and the Preference for Privacy   Marshall (1971) studied preference for privacy using a newly developed scale called the *Preference for Privacy Scale* (PPS), which relates to a number of psychological and life behavior measures. The two preferences most closely associated with affiliation on the PPS are Extraversion and Feeling. Grant (1965) found that the four EF types among Auburn students were the only types that stated significantly more often that they dated more than once a week and had no trouble finding dates. The Introverts and especially the IT types were dating less or not at all. The two preferences most closely associated with a need for privacy are Introversion and Thinking.

Marshall's data show a consistent tendency for Introverts to prefer privacy on all the subscales of the PPS, but the most important aspects of privacy for both Introverts and Thinking types are personal space and lack of pressure for self-disclosure. Laypeople sometimes interpret Introversion and Thinking as being associated with a dislike of or a lack of need for people. The data are more consistent with the idea that Introverts and Thinking types enjoy the company of others, as long as they have their needed privacy or are not under great stress.

Optimism and Pessimism Isabel Myers believed that Sensing and Intuition are often related to a pessimistic or optimistic attitude. In a difficult situation, the tendency of Sensing is to assume that what is will not change. Clinicians (e.g., von Franz, 1971) note that types with Sensing dominant often find that when intuitions do occur to them, these are negative and pessimistic. (In the dynamics of type theory, Intuition in a dominant Sensing type would be less conscious and differentiated and therefore less adept at coping with reality problems.) The more optimistic tendency of Intuitive types is to assume that the situation may be difficult now but that some hitherto unseen possibility will turn up.

Extraversion and Introversion can be related to optimism for a different reason. Extraverts in theory are more at home in the world, and thus they may also report themselves as more competent to cope with its demands.

Quenk (1966) looked at type differences as part of a study of fantasy and personal outlook in relation to optimism, pessimism, realism, and anxiety. Responses of the 25 male and 32 female subjects who recorded daydreams for 10 days showed consistent sex differences. Significant MBTI findings were that optimists were more likely to be Extraverts in both sexes; female optimists were more likely to be Intuitive types, and male optimists were more likely to be Thinking types; anxious females were more likely to be Introverts and Intuitive types; anxious males were more likely to be Feeling types. In another aspect of the study, students reporting realistic fantasies were reported to have a clearer preference for Sensing, as would be predicted.

Vaughan and Knapp (1963) reported a study of dimensions of pessimism in which a number of instruments, including the MBTI, were administered to 75 male Wesleyan University undergraduates. Pessimism was significantly associated with Introversion and Thinking, confirming the E–I difference found by Quenk but not the male T–F difference.

Prediction of Specialty Choices in Medicine Isabel Myers' medical sample provides an example of long-term prediction of type differences. She followed her longitudinal sample of 5,355 medical students over a decade from admission to medical school and found specialty choices significantly in the directions predicted by type theory. McCaulley (1977) followed up on the sample a decade later and found that those who changed specialty significantly more often moved to specialties appropriate for their types; the effect was greater for Intuitive types than for Sensing types.

Validity of Whole Types and Type Dynamics

Since the purpose of the Indicator is to help people identify their whole type, validation of the instrument as a measure of the theory requires evidence that the four dichotomies combine in such a way that the whole is greater than the sum of its parts. In other words, characteristics or behavior based either on whole types or on combinations of preferences demonstrating type dynamics should not be explainable based on knowledge of the preferences alone. Because the instrument is based on a complex theory, establishing this kind of validity is more difficult than acquiring evidence for the validity of the four individual scales. This section presents validity evidence for whole types and for combinations of preferences based on type dynamics theory.

Comparison of MBTI Types with Self-Estimates of Type

One way to validate the MBTI assessment tool that avoids some of the problems identified above is to compare MBTI results with self-assessment of type preferences. The chance of picking the correct type is 1 out of 16, or 6.25%. There have been two kinds of studies of best-fit type, differentiated on the basis of how the person's self-assessment of type was determined. One category includes assessments that are based on agreement with written type descriptions of Myers and others. While the focus of some of these studies has actually been on the accuracy of the written type descriptions themselves, the results provide evidence for the existence of the typology to the extent that the type descriptions are based on Jung's and Myers' theories of types and not on collections of sentences derived from definitions of the individual preferences. Comparisons with descriptions written by Myers and her colleagues are particularly important because they were purposely constructed to include statements based on type dynamics theory.

The other category includes a "verification" process that differs by study, although most use brief, nonstandardized descriptions of the individual preferences. Table 9.17 provides a brief summary of the results of all these studies.

Table 9.17   Summary of Studies of Agreement Between Reported and Best-Fit Types

Study	Form	N	Sample	Agreement
Hammer & Yeakley (1987)	G	120	Community Adults	85%
Kummerow (1988)	G	93 M, F	Retail Managers	64%
	G	106 M	Bank Managers	66%
	G	104 F	Bank Managers	58%
Walck (1992b)	G	256	Students	75%
Midpoint Study (1997, cf. Ch. 7)	M	158	Community and Organization Adults	78%
Form M/Form G Study (1998)	M	92	Community Adults	58%
	G	92		53%
Research Form Study (1996, cf. Ch. 7)	M	2,116	Adults and Students	64%
	G	2,116	Adults and Students	58%
Oxford Psychologists Press (1993)	G	370	Adults in Workshops	76%
Qualifying Programs	G	533 M	Adults in Workshops	81%
		989 F	Adults in Workshops	82%
Type Description Studies				
Carskadon (1982)	F or G	129	Students	35% ranked actual type description first
Carskadon & Cook (1982)	F or G	118	Students	50% ranked actual type description first
Ware & Yokomoto (1985)	G	343	Students	62% rated actual type description highest

Carskadon (1982) and Carskadon and Cook (1982) conducted studies of 129 and 118 introductory psychology students, respectively. In each study, students were asked to rank five of Myers' descriptions from *Introduction to Type:* (a) the type reported by the MBTI, (b) the type with the least clear preference reversed, (c) the type with the same functions but E–I and J–P reversed, (d) the type with S–N and T–F reversed, and (e) the type with all four letters different from the reported type. The reported type was ranked first significantly more often than chance for both samples (35% $p < .001$, and 50% $p < .001$).

When choices for the descriptions of the reported type and the type with the closest scale reversed were combined, the percentages of students rating one or the other of these first were 66% for the first study and 75% for the second study. The percentages of students giving first rank to the *opposite* of the reported type were 4% and 13% in the two studies. Students in both studies were significantly ($p < .001$) less likely to select as most accurate the description differing from the reported type on the functions (S–N and T–F) than they were to choose the type differing from the reported type on the attitudes (E–I and J–P). The authors concluded that (a) the idea that type descriptions other than one's reported type might be equally appealing had been refuted and (b) their subjects seemed to feel more confidence or certainty in their preferred functions (S, N, T, or F) and/or more flexibility in their attitudes (E, I, J, or P). These

findings strongly refute any suggestion that respondents interpret MBTI type descriptions as simple horoscopes.

In a similar study, Ware and Yokomoto (1985) asked students to rate (on a scale of 0 to 100%) the accuracy of different type profiles developed by David Keirsey. Unknown to the participants, one of these profiles matched their type as determined by the MBTI, while the others varied in systematic ways. The type description based on their MBTI type was rated highest, at 62%. The description yielding the next highest rating (47%) was the one that resulted from changing the preference letter associated with the person's lowest preference score to its opposite.

We turn now to the methodology whereby the self-assessment is made after receiving an MBTI interpretation from a trained professional. Hammer and Yeakley (1987) studied a sample of 120 adults who had participated in workshops and individual interviews. Results indicated that 85% of the sample produced perfect agreement on all four preferences and that 99% of the sample agreed on at least three of the four. All the individuals who disagreed on one or more preference scales had preference scores of seven points or less on the scale in dispute.

Kummerow (1988) examined the agreement between best-fit type and MBTI reported type in samples of retail managers and male and female bank managers who had participated in an MBTI training program. The procedure followed by the participants in arriving at their self-assessment of type is well documented, making this study a model for other such studies. The agreements with whole type were 64%, 66%, and 58%, respectively. The agreement of three or more letters was 97%, 95%, and 90% for these samples. The T–F scale showed the lowest rate of agreement.

Walck (1992b) asked for self-assessments of type from a sample of 256 undergraduates who participated in an exercise in which (a) a counselor explained type theory, (b) subjects wrote an essay documenting the reasons for their self-assessed choice of type, (c) subjects read Myers (1987), and (d) essays were reviewed and returned to the subjects for clarification as necessary. Identification of whole best-fit types and reported MBTI types agreed for 75% of the subjects; approximately 96% agreed on at least three of the four preferences. Walck also found that over 80% of the disagreements between best-fit type and MBTI-measured type occurred among individuals with "slight" preferences (1–9). Disagreement was most prevalent on the T–F scale.

The agreement between best-fit type and MBTI reported type has been determined for participants attending the MBTI qualifying programs (Hammer, Prehn, & Mitchell, 1994). At the end of each four- or five-day workshop participants are asked to complete a best-fit type questionnaire. The whole type agreement for males is 81% ($N = 533$) and for females 82% ($N = 989$). These findings are especially important because of the size of the samples and because the intensive training experience offers multiple opportunities for participants to assess their best-fit type.

While the results are not shown in Table 9.17 because they focused solely on the T–F scale, Harris and Carskadon (1988) conducted a study of self-assessment accuracy with 339 male and 306 female students. Using the current Form G weights, the agreement between the students' MBTI T–F preference and their self-assessment of the T–F preference was 61% for the males and 79% for the females.

Three self-assessment studies have been conducted with Form M to date. The results are also shown in Table 9.17. In the sample used to set the midpoint of the preference scales, the agreement between best-fit and Form M–based whole types was 78% (see Chapter 7 for a description of this procedure). The large-scale best-fit study used as a basis for determining the optimal scoring procedure yielded a number of estimates of best-fit agreement, some based on item response theory (IRT) methods and others on prediction ratio methods for selecting items and scoring. The best IRT method yielded 64% and the best prediction ratio (PR) method 58% overall agreement. Note that these are probably underestimates of true hit rates because no attempt had been made to optimize the midpoint for either procedure. The third self-assessment study compared Form G and Form M results with best-fit type in a sample of 92 adults from a small rural midwestern town who had no previous exposure to the MBTI. The agreement with best-fit type for Form G was 53% and for Form M was 58%. It is interesting to note that most of the "misses" in this sample occurred in older respondents (in their 70s and 80s).

The results of past best-fit type studies have been generally quite supportive of the construct validity of the MBTI, with whole type agreements ranging from 53% to 85%. Samples of adults that used multiple verification procedures generally have higher agreement. All of the percentage agreements from studies using this methodology are far above the chance value of 6.25%. In the Form G samples the T–F scale showed the lowest agreement.

In the methodology using written type descriptions, the agreement has ranged from 35% to 62%, with the former coming from the study where subjects were required to rank, not rate, descriptions. These figures also are far above the chance value. Even more telling is the fact that in two of these studies the rating of the opposite type description was 4% and 13%.

This percentage agreement in the best-fit studies is even more impressive when agreement on three instead of all four letters of the type is considered; these percentages ranged over 95% in all studies in which this was reported. This is important because in an instrument like the MBTI, where whole type is arrived at using four separate scales, high levels of agreement for whole type require extremely high levels of agreement on each scale. For example, if the best-fit agreement was, say, 90% on each preference scale, and we multiply these percentages as if they were independent probabilities, the expected percentage agreement is only 66%. So agreements in the 70% and 80% ranges indicate a very high degree of validity, in terms of percentage agreement, for the individual MBTI scales.

It is also interesting to note that in the few studies that reported agreement by clarity of preference, almost all of the disagreements occurred on scales for which the person had a preference clarity index in the "slight" range. A number of those people may have reported in that range not because of a lack of measurement precision but because they were genuinely unclear about their preferences. If these people are excluded, the validities are very high indeed.

Another factor affecting the percentage agreement in any best-fit or type description study is the quality (reliability and validity) of the stimulus that is being used to elicit the self-assessment of type. In some cases (e.g., Kummerow, 1988, or the qualifying programs) the procedure has been described quite accurately and it seems likely that the person had every opportunity to discover his or her best-fit type. In some studies, it may be that the MBTI results are actually better predictors of "true" type than are the stimuli being used in the verification process. If the stimuli consist of lists of words, work behavior examples, or personal examples that are idiosyncratic to the interpreter, they may be responsible for much more "noise" in the self-assessment than is present in the assessment accomplished by the standard and tested items of the Indicator. It is also important in conducting such studies that the self-assessments are performed before the people receive their results in a feedback session.

Table 9.18 Type Dynamics Groups for Each Function

Dominant Thinking	Auxiliary Thinking	Dominant Sensing	Auxiliary Sensing
DIT	AIT	DIS	AIS
Introverted (ITP)	*Introverted* (ETP)	*Introverted* (ISJ)	*Introverted* (ESJ)
ISTP	ENTP	ISTJ	ESTJ
INTP	ESTP	ISFJ	ESFJ
DET	AET	DES	AES
Extraverted (ETJ)	*Extraverted* (ITJ)	*Extraverted* (ESP)	*Extraverted* (ISP)
ESTJ	INTJ	ESTP	ISTP
ENTJ	ISTJ	ESFP	ISFP
Dominant Feeling	**Auxiliary Feeling**	**Dominant Intuition**	**Auxiliary Intuition**
DIF	AIF	DIN	AIN
Introverted (IFP)	*Introverted* (EFP)	*Introverted* (INJ)	*Introverted* (ENJ)
ISFP	ENFP	INTJ	ENTJ
INFP	ESFP	INFJ	ENFJ
DEF	AEF	DEN	AEN
Extraverted (EFJ)	*Extraverted* (IFJ)	*Extraverted* (ENP)	*Extraverted* (INP)
ESFJ	INFJ	ENTP	INTP
ENFJ	ISFJ	ENFP	INFP

Preference Scale Interactions

For the purposes of analysis, the four preference scales can be combined in many ways, but two broad categories can be defined. In the first category are those combinations explicitly defined by the theory. These are the combinations of all four preferences that yield a complete type, as well as the combinations of fewer preferences that reflect the dynamic aspects of the types (e.g., dominant extraverted Thinking types).

The second category of preference combinations might be called *elementary interactions*. These are interactions among preferences that can provide evidence for the typological nature of the theory because they represent the elements of whole types. Although these combinations of preferences are not derived specifically from the dynamic aspects of the theory to the extent that significant interactions among preferences can be demonstrated, they are important as building blocks of the theory. Many of these combinations are also of interest in applied situations. The elementary interactions used most frequently involve pairs of preferences, such as ST, SF, NF, and NT, although some combinations of three preferences have also received attention. See Chapter 4 of this manual and Hirsh (1992) for labels given to various letter combinations, descriptions of the characteristics associated with each, and explanations of how they are used by practitioners.

In either case, type theory predicts that the interactions of preferences result in behaviors that cannot be predicted from each preference separately. Because each preference in a given type interacts with all of the other preferences in that type, type theory posits that any combination of two or more preferences will yield behaviors that are more than the sum of the parts. Validity research at this level focuses on demonstrating that various combinations of two-, three-, and four-letter preferences interact to produce behavior that cannot be accounted for by the same preferences considered separately.

Combinations of preferences derived from type dynamics are specific interactions between the E–I and J–P dichotomies that serve to identify the forms (dominant or auxiliary) and attitudes (introverted or extraverted) of the Perceiving and Judging functions. The characteristics associated with the forms and attitudes of the functions transcend the set of general qualities associated with each function. Dominant extraverted Sensing, for example, refers to type characteristics that are qualitatively unique and different from those characteristics shared by all Sensing types. This pattern of interactions creates within each type (a) a hierarchy of development of the four functions and (b) their accessibility to conscious control. Type dynamics give each function within a type its status (as either a dominant, auxiliary, tertiary, or inferior function) and its attitude (introverted or extraverted). Type dynamics for all functions and types are shown in Table 9.18.

Validity research on dynamics involves finding evidence that among and within types the dominant, auxiliary, tertiary, and inferior functions and their attitudes can be distinguished from each other and that the characteristics associated with each are in accord with those predicted by type theory. Because this is a relatively recent area of research, however, it is not always obvious how to translate the predictions of type theory into researchable questions. Future researchers may find additional important questions that have yet to be asked in this area. Nevertheless, some important steps have been taken and are reviewed below.

To understand and critically evaluate some of the evidence that has accumulated at the level of whole types and type dynamics, we must first understand some of the particular problems entailed in validating a theory-based instrument. These problems reveal some subtleties of the theory that tend to be overlooked when type is discussed only at a conceptual level. One of the advantages of using a theory-based instrument like the MBTI, however, is that the interplay between theory and research enriches both.

Issues in Conducting Validity Studies of Preference Interactions

Validity studies of preference interactions, whether they be whole types or type dynamics, raise unique problems that must be understood before results can be interpreted and understood. Many of these problems arise from attempts to apply methodologies developed for and based on trait instruments to the study of typological theories. Among the problems discussed here are the following:

- Use of dependent variables rich enough to validate the multifaceted constructs of type theory
- Use of a criterion with adequate precision
- Dependent variables with sufficient range to differentiate the 16 MBTI types
- Use of appropriate statistical criteria for demonstrating type differences
- Use of multiple dependent variables
- Sample size requirements

Multifaceted Dependent Variables Each of the four dichotomies on which the MBTI assessment tool is based is an example of what Carver has called multifaceted constructs, which he defines as "constructs that are composed of two or more subordinate concepts, each of which can be distinguished conceptually from the others and measured separately, despite being related to each other both logically and empirically" (Carver, 1989, p. 577). Jung's descriptions of the psychological functions and attitudes are a fundamental example of a multifaceted construct. And the research underlying the development of the subscales in the MBTI Step II and Step III scoring systems provides empirical evidence of the multifaceted nature of the preference scales.

When choosing dependent variables to test type theory, therefore, it is important that whenever possible, broad or likewise multifaceted dependent variables be used. Unfortunately, many validation studies emphasize the measurement of singular, unidimensional concepts; consequently, MBTI scales, which are not homogeneous or unitary, are viewed as problematic. Although narrow or unitary measures may, in some instances, or with some analytic strategies, be appropriate criteria to validate the separate dichotomies of the MBTI, they may be misleading when considering interactions of preferences. When a complex, multifaceted independent variable is used to predict a homogeneous dependent variable, it is likely that only certain facets of the complex variable will be related to the simple variable. If this is true, then little of the variance in the dependent measure will be explained. This problem is compounded when a four-way interaction is tested in ANOVA. It is unlikely that all of the many facets of the four complex variables interact with each other in such a way that their interaction will account for a significant percentage of the variance in a single, narrowly defined dependent measure. Narrow, unitary variables simply do not share enough content with MBTI scales to allow for the discovery of interactions among the four dichotomies. To find significant interactions, more complex and multifaceted dependent variables must be used, but these are difficult to find since most instruments used to provide criterion variables are based on unitary variables developed using traditional psychometrics.

Measurement Precision Measurement error always *decreases* one's ability to find meaningful differences between the groups of interest. The inverse of measurement error is precision. All measurement is conducted with some degree of error. Consequently, all observations based on measurements contain a degree of "slack" that yields a certain amount of uncertainty in the results. For example, when comparing the mean of two types on a dependent variable, there is always some error and therefore uncertainty as to what the "real" mean of each type is. The larger the standard error of the dependent variable, the farther apart the group (type) means must be to justify a conclusion that the difference between the types is real and not just a result of chance variation. So when the criterion measures or dependent variables in a type validation study have a large standard error (are imprecise), it is more difficult to find theoretically predicted differences between types. A lot of "background noise" must be overcome before the real differences stand out. Large samples can help reduce standard errors, although in practice it is time-consuming and expensive to obtain sufficiently large samples of all 16 types to reduce standard errors significantly.

Measurement Range Another problem in conducting type validation research results from using variables that yield only a narrow range of possible scores. This problem compounds the difficulties created by imprecise measurement. An extreme example would be to use as a criterion variable a single Likert scale (e.g., a simple 1 to 7 rating scale). If this scale were to be used to compare the means of the 16 types, the maximum possible separation between the means of the types would be less than 0.5 point. If that were the case, to conclude that the 16 means were significantly different from one another the standard deviations (SDs) for each type group would have to be less than 0.2. Given that SDs for Likert scales are typically greater than 1.0, it would be virtually impossible to conclude that the 16 types have scores on that variable that differ significantly from one another.

Analytic Techniques for Demonstrating Type Differences

One technique for examining type validity makes use of analysis of variance (ANOVA), which involves dividing up the variance in a dependent variable and finding out how much of it can be explained by the effects of the independent variables. In these analyses, preferences or combinations of preferences are the independent variables, and some other variable is the dependent variable whose variance is being partitioned. After all of variance in the dependent variable that is attributable to the separate independent variables has been identified, the remaining variance is then examined to determine how much of it can be explained by *interactions* among the independent variables. For example, if all four preferences were used as independent variables in an ANOVA, and the variance attributable to the main effects (the four preference scales) has been determined, the researcher might be interested in examining two-way, three-way, or four-way interactions among the preferences, depending on the research question. If these *interaction effects* are indeed present, then they are evidence that the combinations of preferences are more than the sum of the parts. In MBTI research, such interactions are one way of validating the typological nature of the Indicator.

From a typological perspective, the fundamental unit of analysis is the whole type. For this reason, researchers should consider using whole types as the independent variables in their analyses. It is not necessary to use all 16 types; it depends on what hypothesis is being tested and whether all 16 types would be expected to differ on the specific dependent variable. Such analyses would provide better tests of the theory, regardless of the fact that types are identified by the results on four separate dichotomies. There are precedents in other sciences, however, for identifying larger units of analysis by measuring several characteristics separately. For example, the natural sciences all identify species (i.e., categories) by taking separate measurements or observations on different variables. The measurement of types by separately scoring the four MBTI dichotomies is a direct parallel to how species are identified in biology.

Use of Multiple Dependent Variables   Evidence of the validity of various preference combinations does not require that all 16 types be distinguishable from each other on a single dependent variable, on a single experimental task, or in a single social context. Failure to find significant differences among all 16 types on a given dependent variable does not disconfirm the MBTI as a typology. As the theory states, each type is quite similar to several others: Each type differs from four others by only one letter, from six others by just two letters, and from four others by three letters. Because of this overlap the 16 types should be distinctly different from each other in some ways but like one another in other ways. The parallel between comparing psychological types and comparing species in biology is again evident: Different species of wrens or finches may have similar weights and lengths of beaks yet exhibit distinctive variations in coloring.

To validate type differences, therefore, it is often necessary to employ a *set* of dependent variables and to consider results across the entire set together. As Carlson and Levy point out, "[S]ince any particular situation will invoke only a portion of the typological pattern, critical predictions should be based upon those components of the total type pattern which are intrinsically relevant to the problem at hand" (Carlson & Levy, 1973, p. 563). In other words, because particular variables, tasks, and contexts tend to elicit behaviors that are relevant only to subsets of the four dichotomies, it is unlikely that analysis of a single variable, task, or context will reveal all possible differences among the 16 types.

Sample Size Requirements   The basic unit of analysis in validity research of whole types is the whole type. Because the 16 types are unequally distributed not only in occupational groups but also in the population at large, finding samples that contain a sufficient number of the less frequent types can be difficult. And because the types of people are not known before the data are collected, it is often necessary to collect large numbers of cases in order to get enough people of the less frequent types.

Even in studies that involve fewer than four-way interactions, it is still important to obtain enough people of each type whose preferences contain that interaction. If there are unequal numbers of types, then the findings may primarily reflect the characteristics of the most frequent type in the group. For example, in a study looking at two-way interactions of the E–I and S–N scales, the E–I x S–N interaction includes four groups of types: EN, ES, IN, and IS. The EN group includes ENFP, ENTP, ENFJ, and ENTJ. If the sample of ENs contains 20 ENTPs and 25 ENFPs, but only 4 ENFJs and 5 ENTJs, then whatever conclusions are drawn about ENs will apply primarily to ENTPs and ENFPs. Also, when using ANOVA the interpretation of the interaction is more complicated and requires some additional assumptions if the groups are of unequal size.

Table 9.19   Summary of Significant Main Effects and Interactions Among the Four MBTI Dichotomies Against 73 Dependent Variables

Effects	Number of Significant Results	Average p-Value	Average Percentage of Variance Accounted For	Range of Percentage of Variance Accounted For
Main Effects				
E–I	28	.005	2.42	0.6–9.30
S–N	36	.008	2.88	0.5–10.30
T–F	29	.003	2.55	0.7–9.70
J–P	16	.013	1.32	0.6–4.40
2-Way Interactions				
E–I x S–N	11	.020	.95	0.5–1.80
E–I x T–F	5	.024	.96	0.5–1.80
E–I x J–P	1	.000	2.90	2.90
S–N x T–F	3	.041	.67	0.5–0.8
S–N x J–P	5	.017	.70	0.6–0.90
T–F x J–P	6	.025	.87	0.5–1.10
3-Way Interactions				
E–I x S–N x T–F	3	.013	.93	0.7–1.40
E–I x S–N x J–P	4	.032	.83	0.5–1.10
E–I x T–F x J–P	3	.022	.80	0.6–1.00
S–N x T–F x J–P	3	.028	.83	0.6–1.20
4-Way Interaction				
E–I x S–N x T–F x J–P	3	.009	1.40	0.7–2.20

Note: See Appendix for a description of the sample.

Source: National sample.

Studies of Preference Interactions

Despite the difficulties described above, analysis of national sample data (the characteristics of which are reported in Chapter 7) found evidence of interactions among all possible combinations of the separate preferences. In addition to Form M, data were also collected on additional variables, including work preferences, job satisfaction, and values, all of which were measured with Likert scales. Because missing data varied by dependent variable and respondent, separate samples were drawn for the analysis of each dependent variable. For each of these variables, equal numbers of each type were randomly selected from the respondents who had answered that item. Because some data were missing, these numbers ranged from 29 to 48 for each type. ANOVA was used to test for main effects of the four dichotomous preferences and for all two-way, three-way, and four-way interactions.

Altogether, 73 dependent variables were tested. Table 9.19 reports the number of times each of the main effects and interactions were found to be significant in this set of dependent variables. It also shows the average significance level for each effect, the average percentage of variance accounted for, and the range of percentage of variance accounted for by each main and interaction effect.

The findings reported in this table may be summarized and interpreted as follows:

- Every possible interaction among the four MBTI dichotomies is significant in predicting some of the independent variables in this study. These various interactions among the dichotomies are one piece of evidence for a typology.

- Among the variables tested in this study, the main effects are predictive of more variables and usually account for more variance than do the interactions. Fifty-nine of the study variables were predicted by one or more main effects, while 34 were predicted by one or more interactions. The percentage of variance accounted for ranged from 0.5% to 10.30% for main effects and from 0.5% to 2.90% for the interactions.

- The E–I x J–P interaction predicted the variance of only one of the variables analyzed. All other interactions predicted variance for three or more variables. This is not surprising because according to type theory, the E–I x J–P interaction is the basis for identifying type dynamics groups for the four functions. Consequently, we would expect to find this interaction to be more predictive when tested *within* each function than when tested in a group of all 16 types. (See the section on type dynamics below for a test of within-function interactions of E–I and J–P.)

The results of this study provide particularly convincing evidence that the four MBTI dichotomies cohere as type theory describes. Because there were equal numbers of the 16 types in all of the ANOVA analyses, all of the interactions were statistically independent of the main effects due to the four separate dichotomies. No assumptions had to be made about which effects were primary and needed to be considered first. The finding that all possible interactions were predictive of at least some of the dependent variables in these ANOVAs is clear evidence that the MBTI measures a typology and not just four separate traits.

Studies of Type Dynamics Theory

Validation of type dynamics goes a step beyond asking whether whole types can be distinguished from one another. In studies of type dynamics, the focus is on determining whether particular groups of types, defined by psychological type theory, differ in observable ways. Evidence for the validity of the MBTI as a measure of type dynamics would include results indicating that the status of the functions (e.g., dominant Feeling versus auxiliary Feeling), the attitudes of the functions (e.g., introverted Sensing versus extraverted Sensing), or both (e.g., dominant introverted Intuition versus dominant extraverted Intuition) are different from each other. For example, we might wish to see how extraverted Thinking when it is dominant, as in ESTJs and ENTJs, differs from extraverted Thinking when it serves as the auxiliary function, as in ISTJs and INTJs. We might also seek to find differences between the dominant introverted Intuition of INFJs and INTJs and the dominant extraverted Intuition of ENFPs and ENTPs.

To simplify discussion of these issues, a three-letter code has been constructed that can be used as a shorthand label for all possible combinations of types defined by dynamics theory. The first letter in the code designates the status of the function, the second the attitude in which the function is expressed, and the third the function being considered. Thus, when considering the function of Intuition, there are four type dynamics groups to compare with each other: *d*ominant *i*ntroverted Intuition (DIN); *d*ominant *e*xtraverted Intuition (DEN); *a*uxiliary *i*ntroverted Intuition (AIN); and *a*uxiliary *e*xtraverted Intuition (AEN). To find the type dynamics groups for the other functions, substitute that function's letter as the last letter in the three-letter codes for each type dynamic group.

Three-letter descriptive code

1st letter = Status	2nd letter = Attitude	3rd letter = Function
D = dominant A = auxiliary	I = introverted E = extraverted	S = Sensing N = Intuition T = Thinking F = Feeling

Other comparisons may involve only the dominant versus the auxiliary form of a function. This comparison would be used to determine whether the status of a function explains a difference in behaviors or characteristics associated with certain types. For example, for Intuition the contrast would be between the *DIN + DEN* types and the *AIN + AEN* types. At other times, the comparison may involve only the two different attitudes of the functions to one another; this would be a test of whether attitude alone can explain differences in behaviors or characteristics among certain types. With Intuition, for example, the contrast would be between the *DIN + AIN* and the *DEN + AEN* types. Which comparisons are analyzed depends on what questions are being asked or what hypotheses about type dynamics are being tested. Table 9.18 shows the types composing each type dynamic group for the four functions.

Among the earliest studies to examine differences between the dominant and auxiliary functions were those by Carlyn (1975), McCarley and Carskadon (1983), and Williams and Carskadon (1983). The strategy in all of these studies involved counting the number of people with higher scores on their dominant function than on their auxiliary function. The thinking was that if the dominant function was, as predicted, the most favored, most psychologically salient, or most under conscious control, the score for that function should be higher than for the auxiliary function. However, in all three studies only half or fewer of the people had higher scores for the dominant function than for the auxiliary function.

Myers and McCaulley (1985), using a large database (N = 43,063) of Forms F and G, found that in only about half the cases were the scores on the dominant function higher than those on the auxiliary function. McCrae and Costa (1989), after standardizing the preference scores to adjust for the fact that the S–N continuous score had a greater range than the T–F continuous score, revealed, using a chi-square analysis of 456 cases, no significant association between the largest preference score and the theoretically predicted dominant function. Most recently, Murry, Magidson, and Markham (1997) attempted to find differences between dominant and auxiliary functions. Scoring the MBTI using IRT, they compared mean preference scores of dominant and auxiliary types for each function. They believed IRT scoring would yield a more accurate identification of type preferences. Despite the improvement in scoring, and despite their use of a more rigorous "hybrid" latent trait/latent class model, they were unable to find any support for making a distinction between any of the dominant and auxiliary functions. Although these findings appear to be contrary to the predictions of type theory, it is important to examine the hypotheses tested in these studies and the assumptions that underlie the approaches taken by these authors to testing their hypotheses.

First, all of the analyses described above either tacitly or explicitly assign unintended meaning to high or low preference scores. Even the original hypothesis that drives these analyses—that the person's *score* on the dominant function should be higher than the score on the auxiliary function— is not consistent with current interpretations of the theory (Myers & Kirby, 1994) and is therefore not a good test of type theory. The magnitude of the preference scores used in these studies does *not* indicate development, skill, aptitude, maturity, or excellence in the use of a function. (The same is true of the preference clarity indexes used in Form M.) Yet the meaning ascribed to these scores by the hypothesis and the analyses that derive from it ignores the categorical nature of the preference scales and assumes a quantitative linkage between the properties measured by the MBTI and the scores used to identify type preferences.

Second, the item responses that form the basis for classifying people into different preferences are designed to appeal to people of one preference or the other on a given scale. For example, the "S" response to an S–N item was written to appeal to *all* Sensing types. Measurement at this gross level of the overall preferences does not permit direct inferences about the dominant or auxiliary status of the functions based solely on preference scores.

Quantitative interpretation of preference clarity indexes is not recommended for the Indicator.

Third, by its very nature the dominant form of a function is presumed to be different from its auxiliary form. Myers' method of identifying dominant versus auxiliary functions assumed an interaction between E–I and J–P dichotomies. The impact of this interaction shows up in its effect on the forms and attitudes of the Judging and Perceiving functions.

Interactive effects of the preferences produce something above and beyond the effects of separate preferences.

The characteristics of dominant introverted Feeling, for example, are different and separate from those facets of Feeling that are shared among all Feeling types. Few authors have spelled out such differences explicitly (an exception is Myers & Kirby, 1994). This is one area of type theory that is open for future development. Nevertheless, at present the theory presumes that such differences are real and can be observed. Studies that simply compare scores of the dominant and auxiliary functions ignore these differences.

Fortunately, there are several ways in which differences between dominant and auxiliary forms of the functions can be observed that remain true to the theory. For example, observer ratings of dominant and auxiliary Intuitive types could be examined. Certain characteristics observed by the raters would be predicted to be more frequently associated with people whose Intuition was dominant as compared with those for whom Intuition was auxiliary. The dominant and auxiliary uses of the functions would be expected to differ in some, but not necessarily all, ways. Another approach might be to use ANOVA to compare the mean scores of various groups who share the same function on measures of characteristics that are relevant to that function. Such measures might include vocational interests, values, and attitudes. One study employing each of these approaches to type dynamics is summarized below.

Testing Type Dynamics with Observer Ratings

Although Thorne and Gough (1991) did not explicitly test predictions derived from type dynamics, their data can be analyzed to provide some answers to questions about this aspect of type theory. Their studies involved having naive observers (i.e., the observers did not know the types of the people they were rating) rate Institute of Personality Assessment and Research program participants on a variety of behavioral and psychological measures. The characteristics that the raters ascribed to people who use each function in its dominant and auxiliary forms can then be compared.

Information is not available on all 16 types because Thorne and Gough had sufficient numbers for comparing only 10 types; the tests of type dynamics with respect to Sensing are not available in this data set for some analyses. For Thinking, Feeling, and Intuition, Table 9.20 compares the dominant and auxiliary forms of these functions. There are four columns of data in the table. The numbers in each column were taken from the lists of the 10 "most" and "least" descriptive adjectives used by raters to describe males and females in the sample. In each column, the number before the "/" is the number of adjectives that were shared among types having the dominant and auxiliary forms of each function. This number is an indication of the degree to which raters saw the dominant and auxiliary types as similar. The number after the "/" is the total number of adjectives that raters checked for the dominant and auxiliary types listed in each row of the table. The percentages are the percentages of adjectives that were common to the dominant and auxiliary types being compared in that cell of the table. These percentages range from 0.0 to 13.8, suggesting that independent observers, who did not know the types of the people they were describing, clearly did not see much similarity between types having the dominant versus the auxiliary forms of Thinking, Feeling, or Intuition.

Table 9. 20   Overlap in Number of Adjectives Ascribed to Types Having the Dominant Versus Auxiliary Forms of the Thinking, Feeling, and Intuitive Functions in the IPAR Data

Functions Compared	Least Typical (Males) # Shared Adj/Total # Adj	Most Typical (Males) # Shared Adj/Total # Adj	Least Typical (Females) # Shared Adj/Total # Adj	Most Typical (Females) # Shared Adj/Total # Adj
Dominant Thinking (INTP, ESTJ, ENTJ) Versus Auxiliary Thinking (ENTP, INTJ, ISTJ)	3/55 (5.4%)	3/56 (5.4%)	2/54 (3.7%)	6/56 (10.7%)
Dominant Feeling (INFP, ENFJ) Versus Auxiliary Feeling (ENFP, INFJ)	2/38 (5.3%)	2/37 (5.4%)	0/40 (0.0%)	1/39 (2.6%)
Dominant Intuition (INTJ, INFJ, ENTP, ENFP) Versus Auxiliary Intuition (ENTJ, ENFJ, INTP, INFP)	9/65 (13.8%)	3/75 (4.0%)	5/72 (6.9%)	4/76 (5.3%)

Note: The first number in each ratio is the number of adjectives that were shared among types having both the dominant and auxiliary forms of the function. The second number is the number of different adjectives that were used by raters to describe all of the types listed at the left of each row in the table.

Source: From *Portraits of Type* (pp. 83–100), by A. Thorne and H. Gough, 1991, Palo Alto, CA: Consulting Psychologists Press. Copyright 1991 by Consulting Psychologists Press. Used with permission.

Testing Type Dynamics Using ANOVA   Another method for testing hypotheses derived from type dynamics involves ANOVA. While log linear models are equally appropriate, if not more so, for some data sets, ANOVA is used here because it is likely to be more familiar to a broader spectrum of readers. If anything, ANOVA is apt to be less sensitive in detecting differences. So the results reported below probably understate the differences among type dynamics groups compared with what might have been found with other, less familiar, methods.

In these analyses, the scores of people grouped according to type dynamics for each function should differ on variables that are relevant to their Judging (T–F) and Perceiving (S–N) preferences. For example, if the variable of interest is relevant to Thinking judgments, we would expect to find differences among the type dynamics groups for Thinking. However, we would not necessarily expect to find differences among the Sensing type dynamics groups on the same variables unless those variables were also relevant to the use of Sensing. Given the multifaceted nature of type constructs discussed earlier, however, we should not expect that any single variable will show differences among all type dynamics groupings, even for a single preference such as Thinking: The four Thinking groups, that is, dominant introverted Thinking (DIT), dominant extraverted Thinking (DET), auxiliary introverted Thinking (AIT), and auxiliary extraverted Thinking (AET), are both similar and different. The similarities will affect the scores just as much as the differences will. When a variable is mainly relevant to the attitude in which Thinking is used, then we do not necessarily expect that DIT will differ from AIT, or DET from AET. However, across a diverse collection of variables relevant to the Thinking function, we do expect that all type dynamics groupings will differ in some respects on at least some of the variables.

There are other problems in addition to selecting the proper variables because the requirements for validating the MBTI as a typology are more stringent than for trait-based personality instruments not based on a theory of interactions. Validating type dynamics using ANOVA with a given dependent variable requires the following two conditions: (a) that the E–I x J–P interaction term is significant and (b) that all of the type dynamics groups for each function differ from one another. Both of these conditions are necessary; neither is sufficient by itself.

Evidence for the first condition will be immediately available from the ANOVA results. Evidence for the second condition requires that we demonstrate that the types having different forms and attitudes of the four functions can be distinguished from each other on the same variables for which the E–I x J–P interaction term was significant. For example, consider an analysis that compares people with dominant introverted Thinking (DIT; ISTP and INTP) with those with auxiliary extraverted Thinking (AET; ISTJ and INTJ) on a dependent variable called "importance of friendships." From a trait perspective, the only difference between these types is their preference for Judging or Perceiving. Consequently any differences observed between these groups should be only those attributable to the difference in the J–P preference. Thus in the ANOVA only the J–P main effect would be significant. From a type perspective, however, we seek evidence that the differences between the DIT and AET groups is greater than what can be explained by the J–P preference. If this is true, then in the ANOVA, the E–I x J–P interaction term should be significant among all Thinking types. When extended to all four functions and to all the type dynamics groups within each function, this analysis is a direct test of whether the MBTI accurately measures the status and attitudes of the functions described by type dynamics.

To test these conditions, the data from the national sample were used. National sample data were also collected on work preferences, satisfaction, and values. Equal numbers of each type were randomly selected from the respondents who had answered each item used as a dependent variable. Because some people did not answer all of the non-MBTI questions, the number of people of each type ranged from 29 to 48, depending on which dependent variable was used. This yielded between 58 and 96 people in each type dynamics group (dominant introverted, dominant extraverted, auxiliary introverted, and auxiliary extraverted) for each function, depending on the dependent variable.

For each function, ANOVAs were conducted in two stages. In the first, the E–I and J–P dichotomies were the independent variables. For each function, the interaction between these preferences defines the four possible type dynamics groups (EJ, IJ, EP, and IP). The dependent variables were a series of items asking respondents about their satisfaction with various aspects of their work environments, the importance to them of various life values, and their preference for working in various organizational structures. Responses to these items were on a four-point Likert scale ranging from "Very Satisfied" to "Very Dissatisfied." ANOVAs were run separately for each function on the entire item pool. Items for which the interaction term was significant were identified for further analysis in the second ANOVA.

The second analysis using ANOVAs used the type dynamics groups for each function as the independent variable with four levels. The items for which the interaction terms in the first ANOVA were significant were used as dependent variables in this second phase. The ANOVAs were run separately for each function. Following Toothaker (1991), the GH procedure was used for the multiple comparisons among groups, and alpha was set at .01. For each of the four functions there are four type dynamics groups. Using all possible combinations of these groups yields six possible comparisons among the type dynamics groups for

each function. These comparisons are not independent because a given type dynamics group is involved in more than one comparison. Setting alpha for each comparison at .01 yielded an alpha for the familywise comparisons of .06 for the entire set of comparisons on a given variable.

Table 9.21 presents the results for the Thinking and Feeling groups. Comparisons above the diagonal are for the Thinking groups; those below are for the Feeling groups. Each cell in the table shows the variables on which the following results occurred: (a) in stage one of the analysis, the E–I x J–P interaction term was significant; and (b) in stage two of the analysis, the mean scores of the corresponding type dynamics groups were significantly different, at .01 or beyond. For example, the upper right-hand cell of the table lists the variable "friendships," on which the AET (ISTJ and INTJ) and DIT (ISTP and INTP) groups had significantly different scores. Because the interaction term was significant on this variable, we may conclude that the difference between AET and DIT occurs as a result of the aspects of type that are more than the sum of the parts. Of six comparisons among the Thinking type dynamics groups, three were significant.

The *p*-values for the mean differences are shown in parentheses beside the item number in each cell. Dominant introverted Thinking types (ISTP and INTP), dominant extraverted Thinking types (ESTJ and ENTJ), and auxiliary introverted Thinking types (ESTP and ENTP) all rated relationships and friendships as being more important in their lives than did auxiliary extraverted Thinking types (ISTJ and INTJ). Dominant extraverted Thinking types also rated health as more important than did auxiliary extraverted Thinking types.

Among Feeling groups, dominant extraverted Feeling types (ESFJ and ENFJ) reported a greater frequency of helping, teaching, or counseling activities in their current job compared with auxiliary extraverted Feeling types (ISFJ and INFJ). This was the only variable, and these were the only Feeling groups, that differed significantly on the items used in this study.

Table 9.22 shows results of the same analyses for the Intuition and Sensing type dynamics groups. The cells above the diagonal compare the Sensing groups; those below compare the Intuition groups. One of six comparisons was significant for Sensing type dynamics groups, while two of six were significant among Intuition type dynamics groups. Auxiliary introverted Intuitive types (ENTJ and ENFJ) rated home and family as being more important in their lives than did the dominant introverted Intuitive types (INTJ and INFJ) and the auxiliary extraverted Intuitive types (INTP and INFP). Auxiliary introverted Sensing types (ESTJ and ESFJ) were more satisfied with opportunities for accomplishments at work than were the dominant introverted Sensing types (ISTJ and ISFJ).

Other results from this study shed additional light on the ways in which type dynamics groups are both similar and different. In the first stage there were generally more

Table 9.21 Dependent Variables on Which Thinking and Feeling Type Dynamics Groups Differed Significantly and for Which the ANOVA Interaction Term Was Significant

	DIT ISTP, INTP	DET ESTJ, ENTJ	AIT ESTP, ENTP	AET ISTJ, INTJ	
DIF ISFP INFP	——	(None)	(None)	DIT > AET Friendships (.000)	**DIT** ISTP INTP
DEF ESFJ ENFJ	(None)	——	(None)	DET > AET Health, friendships (.000 & .007)	**DET** ESTJ ENTJ
AIF ESFP ENFP	(None)	(None)	——	AIT > AET Friendships (.000)	**AIT** ESTP ENTP
AEF ISFJ INFJ	(None)	DEF > AEF Social (.004)	(None)	——	**AET** ISTJ INTJ
	DIF ISFP, INFP	**DEF** ESFJ, ENFJ	**AIF** ESFP, ENFP	**AEF** ISFJ, INFJ	

Note: Results for Ts are above the diagonal; results for Fs are below the diagonal. Numbers in ( ) are *p*-values for the multiple comparison test. The type dynamics group to the left of the ">" had the higher score, meaning that group was more satisfied with the aspects of work defined by the item or attached higher importance to it.

DIT = dominant introverted Thinking; AIT = auxiliary introverted Thinking; DIF = dominant introverted Feeling; AIF = auxiliary introverted Feeling; DET = dominant extraverted Thinking; AET = auxiliary extraverted Thinking; DEF = dominant extraverted Feeling; AEF = auxiliary extraverted Feeling.

Key to dependent variables (from the Form M research form): Social: Frequency of helping, teaching, or counseling others in current job; Health: Importance of health in your life; Friendships: Importance of relationships and friendships in your life.

See Appendix for a description of the sample.

Source: National sample.

instances in which the main effects (due to the E–I and J–P dichotomies) were significant compared with the number of significant interactions (E–I x J–P). Of the five variables showing significant interaction effects, four also had significant main effects due to E–I, J–P, or both. This pattern of results tells us that (1) sometimes the differences among type dynamics groups are mainly due to E–I or J–P differences; (2) sometimes the differences among type dynamics groups are mainly due to *interaction* between E–I and J–P; and (3) sometimes the differences among type dynamics groups are due both to the effects of single preferences *and* to the interaction of those preferences.

In the dependent variables examined in this study, the variance explained ranged from 1.1% to 3.3% for the interactions and from 1.0% to 13.4% for the main effects. While none of these percentages is very high, it is important to remember that only a limited set of type preferences and interactions was examined in this study of type dynamics. The single dichotomies were predictive for a greater number of dependent variables in this study. However, based on one study it is not possible to determine whether this finding is because single preferences are predictive of a greater variety of behaviors than are interactions or whether this

study did not include enough of the variables for which the interactions *are* predictive.

Table 9.21 and Table 9.22 show that, for the Thinking–Feeling and Sensing–Intuition dichotomies, respectively, there were one or more variables for which the interaction term was significant *and* for which the mean scores of two or more of the type dynamics groups were also significantly different. However, in several cases the first stage ANOVA identified variables for which the E–I x J–P interaction was significant even though none of the group comparisons was significant. Table 9.23 shows the variables for which the E–I x J–P interaction term was significant in the first-stage ANOVAs for the Thinking and Feeling functions. In addition, it shows which of these variables also had significant *p*-values for one or more of the multiple comparison tests that were run in the second-stage ANOVA. Table 9.24 shows the same results for the Sensing and Intuition functions. What these tables reveal is that for each of the four functions there are significant E–I x J–P interactions. That is, for each of the functions there are characteristics of the type dynamics groups that are more than the sum of the parts.

These two tables, 9.23 and 9.24, also show that significant interactions do not necessarily mean that there are also

Table 9.22   Dependent Variables on Which Sensing and Intuition Type Dynamics Groups Differed Significantly and for Which the ANOVA Interaction Term Was Significant

	DIS ISTJ, ISFJ	DES ESTP, ESFP	AIS ESTJ, ESFJ	AES ISTP, ISFP	
DIN INTJ INFJ	———	(None)	AIS > DIS Accomplishment (.004)	(None)	**DIS** ISTJ ISFJ
DEN ENFP ENTP	(None)	———	(None)	(None)	**DES** ESTP ESFP
AIN ENTJ ENFJ	AIN > DIN Home & Family (.000)	(None)	———	(None)	**AIS** ESTJ ESFJ
AEN INTP INFP	(None)	(None)	AIN > AEN Home & Family (.002)	———	**AES** ISTP ISFP
	DIN INTJ, INFJ	**DEN** ENFP, ENTP	**AIN** ENTJ, ENFJ	**AEN** INTP, INFP	

Note: Results for Ss are above the diagonal; results for Ns are below the diagonal. Numbers in ( ) are *p*-values for the multiple comparison test. The type dynamics group to the left of the ">" had the higher score, meaning that group was more satisfied with the aspects of work defined by the item or attached higher importance to it.

DIS = dominant introverted Sensing; AIS = auxiliary introverted Sensing; DIN = dominant introverted Intuition; AIN = auxiliary introverted Intuition; DES = dominant extraverted Sensing; AES = auxiliary extraverted Sensing; DEN = dominant extraverted Intuition; AEN = auxiliary extraverted Intuition.

Key to Dependent Variables (from the Form M research form): Home & Family: Importance of home and family in your life; Accomplishment: Satisfaction with opportunities for accomplishments at work.

See Appendix for a description of the sample.

Source: National sample.

significant differences between the mean scores of the type dynamics groups. In other words, interactions between the E–I and J–P dichotomies can be present even when the DIT, DET, AIT, and AET groups, for example, cannot be distinguished by their scores on one of the dependent variables.

Such a result is possible because the interaction term represents facets of type that transcend the characteristics described by separate dichotomies. When these "transdichotomous" facets are related to a dependent variable, the result is a statistically significant interaction term in the ANOVA. So when the comparison of mean scores among type dynamics groups shows no significant differences, either the transdichotomous facets of type are similar within all of the type dynamics groups or they are different but have similar effects on the dependent variable. While there is no direct way of knowing which of these is the best explanation, extensive past research with type has suggested that where there are differences in type characteristics, there are different behaviors associated with those characteristics. Thus it seems likely that when the interaction terms are significant but the multiple comparisons are not, the transdichotomous facets of type represented by the interaction are in fact shared among the four type dynamics groups.

This interpretation fits with both type theory and empirical observations of the 16 types. All of the Thinking types, for example, have some characteristics in common even though they also differ in one or more of their other preferences. So at a minimum, what is common to all eight Thinking types (ISTJ, INTJ, ISTP, INTP, ESTP, ENTP, ESTJ, ENTJ) involves the Thinking function. Yet type theory also says that these eight types should differ in how their Thinking is expressed. Thus we should expect to find both commonalities and differences with respect to how these types express their Thinking preference. Because we are dealing with a *typology*, there is no theoretical reason to believe that these commonalities and differences should be attributed only to the separate dichotomies that are either shared or different in the eight Thinking types. In fact, precisely because the MBTI measures a typology, we would expect that some transdichotomous facets of the Thinking function would be shared among the eight Thinking types and some would not. Table 9.21 and Table 9.23, then, show us results that are quite consistent with type theory in this respect.

Other results of this study demonstrate both a statistically significant interaction term in the first-stage ANOVA *and* significant differences among the type dynamics groups

Table 9.23 Dependent Variables for Which the E–I x J–P Interaction Was Significant in Thinking and Feeling Functions

Significant Interactions for Thinking Type Dynamics Groups

Variable	p-Value of Interaction Term
Satisfaction with opportunities for learning at work	.022
Frequency of helping, teaching, or counseling others in current job	.026
Like working in organizations that have a variety of tasks	.038
Importance of health in life	.040*
Importance of relationships and friendships in life	.020*

Significant Interactions for Feeling Type Dynamics Groups

Variable	p-Value of Interaction Term
Frequency of helping, teaching or counseling others in current job	.002*

Note: *Variables for which one or more multiple comparison tests were significant at $p \leq .01$. See Appendix for a description of the sample.

Source: National sample.

Table 9.24 Dependent Variables for Which the E–I x J–P Interaction Was Significant in Sensing and Intuition Functions

Significant Interactions for Sensing Type Dynamics Groups

Variable	p-Value of Interaction Term
Satisfaction with opportunities for promotion at work	.016
Satisfaction with opportunities for accomplishments at work	.028*
Frequency of helping, teaching, or counseling others in current job	.005

Significant Interactions for Intuition Type Dynamics Groups

Variable	p-Value of Interaction Term
Frequency of artistic activities in current job	.025
Frequency of helping, teaching, or counseling others in current job	.010
Like to work in organizations that value independence and achievement	.028*

Note: *Variables for which one or more multiple comparison tests were significant at $p \leq .01$. See Appendix for a description of the sample.

Source: National sample.

in the multiple comparison tests. This result suggests that the effects of dissimilar facets of type on the dependent variable are being observed within the groups that differ. The results for the variable "health" demonstrate this. The E–I x J–P interaction term was significant for Thinking types on this variable. The mean for AET (ISTJ, INTJ) was 3.61, while the mean for DET (ESTJ, ENTJ) was 3.83. The E–I main effect was significant, but because this effect is separate and independent from the significant interaction effect, it does not explain the difference in scores between these groups. From a strictly statistical viewpoint we conclude that there are some characteristics of these types *beyond* the E or I preferences that explain how much importance one attributes to health in one's life. This, then, is an example of a transdichotomous facet of type.

These findings make sense from the theory because Myers used the J–P dichotomy to help identify or point to type dynamics groups. This is not to say that the E–I and J–P combinations bring about or cause type dynamics to appear. In this study the results are not interpreted as the E–I x J–P interaction causing the importance one attaches to health. Rather the interaction points to certain forms and attitudes of Thinking (as defined by type dynamics) that influence how important health is in one's life. In this example, the

statistical interaction term corresponds to the characteristics of auxiliary extraverted Thinking and dominant extraverted Thinking.

In conclusion, Myers explicitly asserted that combinations of E–I and J–P preferences would reflect differences in personality that could not be explained from knowing the preferences separately. And this is precisely what the results in Table 9.23 and Table 9.24 demonstrate. These outcomes thus serve as partial evidence for dynamic and typological aspects measured by the MBTI.

The second requirement for validation of type dynamics was only partially met in this study. Of the six comparisons made for each function, three of the Thinking comparisons, one of the Sensing comparisons, two of the Intuition comparisons, and one of the Feeling comparisons were significant. These results, which provide partial validation for the theory, may be a function of the dependent variables used in each analysis. Table 9.21, for example, reveals that two *different* variables were needed to distinguish DET from AET, DIT from AET, and AET from AIT. Significantly, different variables were required in order to distinguish the type dynamics groups for different functions.

From a typological perspective, this is not surprising, since the MBTI attempts to measure *qualitative* differences in personality. Thus it is unlikely that any single variable would be able to capture all of the important differences among the types. As the results here demonstrate, a diverse set of variables is required even to distinguish type dynamics groups for a single function. Future validation efforts may need to consider a greater variety of qualitatively different variables. Finding appropriate variables is difficult, however, because it demands a knowledge of what behaviors, values, attitudes, or observations are most relevant to the transdichotomous aspects of type dynamics. It is much easier to identify appropriate variables for validating single dichotomies than it is to identify variables that are relevant to the transdichotomous facets of type. It also may be necessary that the items, scales, or instruments used to measure these variables be multifaceted rather than strongly unidimensional.

Finally, the results shown in Table 9.21 and Table 9.22 clearly confirm that the method used to identify type dynamics (i.e., the E–I x J–P interaction) corresponds to facets of type beyond the four simple dichotomies. These facets are present for *all four* functions. So while the results shown in the tables in this section substantiate the typological nature of the MBTI, future validation studies need to explore what additional variables might help fill the gaps.

Studies of Whole Types

Whole type validity involves many different questions that must be answered in ways that may be incompatible within the design of a single study. And some of these questions require large numbers of each type. So within the constraints of time, money, staff, and the available pool of respondents, sometimes validity questions can be addressed only for certain subgroups of types. The study by Otis and Louks (1997) is one example.

Research in this area seeks evidence that whole types can be distinguished from each other on the basis of unique behaviors that are not predictable from knowing the four separate preferences composing them.

For these reasons, validity is achieved cumulatively over many studies addressing different questions.

There are significant complexities and resources needed to compare the 16 types in a single study. For this reason, researchers examining differences among whole types have often been unable to contrast all 16 types. Small sample sizes, limited hypotheses or research questions, and the differential attraction of types to field settings are constraints serving to limit the number of whole types that have been compared. In summary, in the studies below, only the results relevant to differences among whole type are emphasized. Data and questions that address other issues are not discussed, even when they constituted the primary purpose of the study.

Analysis of Type Distributions
Type distributions are the basic method for presenting MBTI data on groups. A type table is sometimes seen as providing merely descriptive information, to be followed by more sophisticated analyses. On the contrary, type tables themselves provide evidence for construct validity. For example, if the type table for a given occupation has significantly more of the types predicted by theory to have interest in, and therefore be more likely to be members of, that occupation, then the type table contributes to construct validity.

The method primarily used to analyze type distributions is the self-selection ratio type table (SRTT) analysis (McCaulley, 1985). This is followed by a chi-square test of the contingency table of interest. SRTT can be used to test how the frequency of a type in an occupation compares with the frequency of that type in a relevant base population; it provides an index of the magnitude of over- or underrepresentation of a given type or preference in a group or occupation. The numerator of the ratio is the percentage of that type in the occupation; the denominator is the percentage of that type in the base population. The ratio will be exactly 1.00 when the type is found in an occupation in exactly the same proportion as it is found in the base population. It will be greater than 1.00 when that type is overrepresented and less than 1.00 when that type is underrepresented. Thus a ratio of 2.00 indicates that about twice as many individuals of that type are found in the occupation as would be expected given the frequency of that type in the base population. Likewise, a ratio of 0.50 indicates that about half as many of that type are found in the occupation as would be expected by chance.

To apply a statistical test to these data a contingency table is created and subjected to a chi-square test. Thus the probability that the frequency of a given type, preference, or any group of preferences occurs by chance can be determined. There are two cautions when using this method, however. One is that in the traditional procedure, comparisons of all 16 types and many different preferences are performed. With this many statistical tests, there is increased risk that some of the significant chi-square values will have occurred by chance. The second caution is that the chi-square statistic itself is very sensitive to sample size. With very large samples, as is often the case with the base population, very small differences can be found to be statistically significant. Users of this technique should then ask whether the results are also practically significant. Examples of analyzing type tables using the SRTT method can be found in Chapters 11 and 12 of this manual and in Hammer (1996a). The *Myers-Briggs Type Indicator Atlas of Type Tables* (Macdaid, McCaulley, & Kainz, 1986) provides hundreds of type tables showing the distribution of types in various occupations.

Another technique, log linear analysis, can also be used to analyze type distributions and draw inferences about construct validity. O'Shea and Mamchur (1989) demonstrate how log linear models can be analyzed to test the predictions of type theory about occupational distributions. McCaulley, Macdaid, and Magidson (1997) have also applied log linear analysis to type distributions and offer a graphical display of the frequency of the types in a sample to the frequency in a base population. One of the advantages of the log linear method is that different models can be fit to the type distribution and then tested statistically. For example, a main effects model would predict that the distributions are a function of the four independent preference scales, with no interaction among them, while a "saturated" model attributes the distributions to the 16 types, that is, to the interaction of the preferences. Another advantage is that when testing various models, the technique controls for the effects of the other type characteristics that are not being tested.

Evidence to support the construct validity of the MBTI based on type table distributions is abundant and compelling, particularly in the area of occupational choice. The preponderance of data show that the distribution of types across occupations generally follows theoretical predictions. These findings have been observed (a) across subgroups within an occupation, (b) across tasks within an organization, and (c) across occupations in a different culture using a translation of the MBTI.

Attraction and Satisfaction Among Couples

Research Question This study by Marioles, Strickert, and Hammer (1996) addressed two questions. The first was whether married and engaged couples are more likely to be of the same or similar type, or whether they are more likely to be of opposite or dissimilar types. The second question asked whether there was any relationship between type and satisfaction with marital or premarital relationships.

Sample and Method The sample consisted of 271 couples being seen in conjoint therapy and 155 couples who were not in therapy. Both of these groups comprised married and premarital couples. Ages ranged from 17 to 79, with an average of 36; duration of marriage ranged from 0 to 47 years, with a mean of 11 years. Eighty-three percent of the sample were Caucasian, 15% were Hispanic, and 2% were Black.

Instruments Form J of the MBTI was used to determine type preferences as well as scores on the 27 subscales of the Type Differentiation Indicator. Relationship satisfaction was measured using the items (rather than the four subscales) of the Dyadic Adjustment Scale (DAS). An attraction ratio (AR) was computed. Analogous to the selection ratio used in career counseling, the AR is the percentage of people of one type who marry a person of another type, divided by the percentage of that other type in the base population. A high AR indicates that the pairing in question occurs more frequently than would be expected given the frequency of that other type in the base population. For example, it is *relatively* difficult to marry an INFP male because there are so few of them in the population. Relationship satisfaction was measured by an item on the TDI answer sheet asking respondents to rate their satisfaction with their current relationship.

Table 9.25 Obliviousness Indexes for Men and Women

	Men			Women	
Type	Index	Rank	Type	Index	Rank
INTP	33	1	ENFJ	13	1
INFJ	31	2	ENFP	12	2
ISFP	22	3	INTJ	11	3.5
ESFP	21	4	ENTP	11	3.5
ENTJ	19	5	ISFJ	10	5
ISTJ	16	6	ESTJ	9	6
ISFJ	14	7	ESFJ	8	7
ESTJ	12	8	ISTJ	7	8
INFP	11	9.5	ESFP	5	9
ENTP	11	9.5	ISFP	4	10
ESFJ	10	11.5	INFJ	0	13.5
ENFJ	10	11.5	ISTP	0	13.5
ESTP	9	13	INFP	0	13.5
ENFP	7	14	INTP	0	13.5
INTJ	0	15.5	ESTP	0	13.5
ISTP	0	15.5	ENTJ	0	13.5

Source: From "Attraction, Satisfaction, and Psychological Types of Couples," by N. S. Marioles, D. P. Strickert, and A. L. Hammer, 1996, *Journal of Psychological Type, 36,* p. 24. Copyright 1996 by *Journal of Psychological Type.* Used with permission.

Results With the exception of ESTJ and ESTP men, and to a lesser extent ISTJ men, the ARs for persons married to someone of the same type were higher for both sexes than were the ARs for persons married to the opposite type. The authors concluded there is little evidence that opposites attract or marry. There seemed to be no type-related pattern to satisfaction ratings. However, the discrepancies between partners' satisfaction ratings suggested the usefulness of an index of satisfaction. This was computed as the difference between the percentage of a given type who say they are satisfied with their relationship and the percentage of that same type who are in relationships where both partners are satisfied. Interviews with couples supported interpreting this ad hoc measure as an index of "obliviousness." A high index value means there was a large percentage of a given type who were satisfied with their relationship when their partner was not.

The obliviousness indexes for each type by sex are shown in Table 9.25. Although not discussed here in the same way it is by the authors, this table provides an opportunity to look for evidence of whole type differences. In evaluating evidence for such differences there are two competing explanations for the rankings shown in the table. If the obliviousness index for each type is produced by type characteristics that are greater than the sum of the separate preferences, then the indexes and the type rankings should be *dissimilar*

Table 9.26 Comparison of Types Most Similar to Those Ranked Highest in Obliviousness for Men and Women

Men			Women		
Type	Index	Rank	Type	Index	Rank
INTP	**33.0**	**1.0**	**ENFJ**	**13.0**	**1.0**
INTJ	0.0	15.5	ENFP	12.0	2.0
INFP	11.0	9.5	ENTJ	0.0	13.5
ISTP	0.0	15.5	ESFJ	8.0	7.0
ENTP	11.0	9.5	INFJ	0.0	13.5
Mean for 4 Similar Types	5.5	12.5	Mean for 4 Similar Types	5.0	9.0

Source: From "Attraction, Satisfaction, and Psychological Types of Couples," by N. S. Marioles, D. P. Strickert, and A. L. Hammer, 1996, *Journal of Psychological Type, 36,* p. 24. Copyright 1996 by *Journal of Psychological Type.* Used with permission.

Table 9.27 Comparison of Types Most Similar to Those Ranked Lowest in Obliviousness for Men and Women

Men			Women		
Type	Index	Rank	Type	Index	Rank
ISTP	**0.0**	**15.5**	**ENTJ**	**0.0**	**13.5**
ISTJ	16.0	6.0	ENTP	11.0	3.5
ISFP	22.0	3.0	ENFJ	13.0	1.0
INTP	33.0	1.0	ESTJ	9.0	6.0
ESTP	9.0	13.0	INTJ	11.0	3.5
Mean for 4 Similar Types	20.0	5.7	Mean for 4 Similar Types	11.0	3.5

Source: From "Attraction, Satisfaction, and Psychological Types of Couples," by N. S. Marioles, D. P. Strickert, and A. L. Hammer, 1996, *Journal of Psychological Type, 36,* p. 24. Copyright 1996 by *Journal of Psychological Type.* Used with permission.

across types having similar preferences. On the other hand, if the obliviousness index for each type is produced only by the summative effects of the separate preferences of the types, then the indexes and the type rankings should be *strongly similar* across types having similar preferences.

The simplest and clearest test of these two competing explanations is to consider the types that are ranked highest and lowest in obliviousness and compare them to similar types that differ by only one letter. Table 9.26 shows such data for the types ranked highest in obliviousness among men and women. Here we see INTPs are the most oblivious among men, with an index of 33 (rank of 1). The four most similar types are INTJ, INFP, ISTP, and ENTP. However, their mean index is only 5.5; their mean rank is 12.5. Although it is normally meaningless to average ranks, in this case the mean rank is being used as an indicator of how close the four similar types are to the highest ranked type.

Among women, ENFJs are the most oblivious, with an index of 13 and a rank of 1. The four most similar types are ENFP, ENTJ, ESFJ, and INFJ. ENFPs are ranked second and have an index that nearly matches that of ENFJs. But as the table shows, the remaining "similar" types are quite dissimilar in their indexes and their ranks. On average, the four most similar types have an index eight points lower than that of ENFJs and are half the list apart from ENFJs in their average rank. Table 9.27 shows the same kind of comparisons for the types with the lowest obliviousness indexes. Here again, the differences between the lowest-ranked types and the types most similar to them are quite evident.

Summary and Interpretation   In summary, then, the ranking patterns we see in these two tables do not appear to be associated with any of the separate type preferences. With the one exception of ENFJ and ENFP women, the types having

the highest and lowest ranks do not share their places with the four types that are most similar to them. Their ranks, then, appear to derive from their unique *typological* characteristics, i.e., from characteristics that are not explainable by the summative effects of the separate preferences.

"Obliviousness" in this study refers to the percentage of a given type who are satisfied with their relationship while their partner is not. In general, more men than women tended to indicate they were satisfied with their relationship when their partner was not. However, there were some major differences by type within the two sexes.

Among men, INTPs and INFJs had the largest percentage who said they were satisfied when their partners were not. Among women, ENFJs and ENFPs were ranked highest in obliviousness. Yet these type rankings were virtually reversed among the sexes. Among women, INTPs and INFJs were among the *least* oblivious. Among men, ENFPs and ENFJs were located near the bottom of the obliviousness rankings. This pattern of results suggests that at least for INTPs and INFJs, and for ENFPs and ENFJs, there may be some major differences between men and women in their experience of intimate relationships.

Moreover, the differences between the highest- (Table 9.26) and lowest- (Table 9.27) ranked types for men and women provide additional evidence that the results are displaying typological effects. First, there appear to be basic sex differences in obliviousness. The mean index for women (averaged across the 16 types, *not* across the total number of women) is 5.6, while that for men is 14.1. This is consistent with Gilligan's observation that women are more attentive to relationship issues than men are (Gilligan, 1982). Second, there are major differences between men and women as to where types are ranked. The two most oblivious types for men (INTP and INFJ) have indexes of 0 for women. The

Table 9.28 Differences Among DSM Diagnoses for the Introverted Types

Axis	Diagnosis	ISTP	INTP	INFJ	ISFJ	INFP	INTJ	ISTJ	ISFP
I	Anxiety Disorder					+			
I	Major Depression						+		
I	PTSD	+							
II	Antisocial	+	+						−
II	Avoidant	+	+		−				
II	Dramatic		−	+	+				−
II	Obsessive	−	−			−		+	
II	Dependent								
II	Odd								

Note: "+" indicates more likely to have the diagnosis and "−" indicates less likely to have the diagnosis than in 400 random samples. The Dramatic cluster includes diagnoses of borderline, cyclothymic, histrionic, and narcissistic personality disorders. The Odd cluster includes diagnoses of paranoid, schizoid, and schizotypal personality disorders.

Source: From "Rebelliousness and Psychological Distress in a Sample of Introverted Veterans," by G. D. Otis and J. L. Louks, 1997, *Journal of Psychological Type, 40,* p. 26. Copyright 1997 by *Journal of Psychological Type.* Used with permission.

three highest-ranked types for women (ENFJ, ENFP, and INTJ) are ranked in the bottom third of the list for men.

The sex difference in the obliviousness indexes is quite strong and clear. However, it does not obscure the equally clear differences as to which types have the highest and lowest obliviousness indexes within each sex. The compatibility between societal sex role expectations and type preferences is a neglected area in type research. Nevertheless there are some relevant clues from at least one study that shed light on these results. Thorne and Gough (1991) found, for example, that independent observers' naive ratings of subjects varied significantly by sex for some types. The differences were most dramatic where stereotypical sex role expectations were most at odds with the characteristics of that type. Their data showed that female INTPs were overwhelmingly described in negative terms by observers who did not know the types of people they rated. Ratings of male INFPs and INFJs were also predominantly negative.

Although other interpretations are possible, the results shown in Table 9.25 suggest that within the same type, sex differences exist in relational awareness. Furthermore, the results in Table 9.26 and in Table 9.27 suggest that these differences derive from characteristics of whole types rather than any additive combination of the separate preferences.

Rebelliousness and Distress in Introverted Veterans

Research Question Otis and Louks (1997) explored the relationship between psychological type and psychological dysfunction.

Sample and Method The sample consisted of 185 male veterans who had been admitted to a Veterans Administration domiciliary and who had requested psychotherapy. The mean age of the study sample was 46.9 years and ages ranged from 30 to 70 years. The majority of the men had multiple

DSM-III-R or DSM-IV Axis I diagnoses; 70% had a diagnosis of substance abuse or dependence. Data were collected at intake assessment, shortly after admission to the domiciliary, and during the early psychotherapy sessions. Except for ENFPs, the sample consisted primarily of Introverts. Only data for the 158 Introverts in the sample were analyzed.

Instruments Data included the Shipley Institute of Living Scale, the original *Minnesota Multiphasic Personality Inventory*™ (MMPI), a clinical interview, and the MBTI Form F or G. A variety of demographic variables were obtained from case records.

Analysis The Wiggins Content Scales of the MMPI were factor analyzed, with two factors emerging, which were named Subjective Distress and Rebelliousness. An ANOVA was performed on subjects' scores on these factors, using age as a covariate and the four MBTI dichotomies as independent variables. A salience analysis of the case record variables was performed in which the mean, median, mode, and variance for each type were compared with those of a large number of random samples taken from the total pool of scores. Depending on what proportion of the random sample scores is higher or lower than that for given types, the results for given types can be interpreted as being significantly different from the scores of the other types in the sample. Due to small sample sizes, some DSM diagnostic categories were collapsed to yield larger groups.

Results The ANOVA using MMPI factor scores as dependent variables showed significant main effects due to T–F and J–P and no significant interaction terms. Differences among the DSM diagnoses for the Introverted types composing the sample are shown in Table 9.28. Among Axis I diagnoses, salience analyses revealed that INFPs were most likely to have anxiety disorder, INTJs to exhibit major depression,

Table 9.29   Differences Among Life History Variables for the Introverted Types

Variable	ISTP	INTP	INFJ	ISFJ	INFP	INTJ	ISTJ	ISFP
Job Length		−	−	+			+	
Never Married	+	−						−
Number of Marriages		+					−	
Length of Marriage				+				
Crime	+	+		−				
Domestic Trouble	+	+						−

Note: "+" means that the type mean was greater than expected and "−" indicates that the type mean was lower than expected on the basis of random sampling distributions.

Source: From "Rebelliousness and Psychological Distress in a Sample of Introverted Veterans," by G. D. Otis and J. L. Louks, 1997, *Journal of Psychological Type, 40,* p. 26. Copyright 1997 by *Journal of Psychological Type.* Used with permission.

and ISTPs to exhibit combat-related post-traumatic stress disorder (PTSD). Among Axis II diagnoses, ITPs were most likely to display antisocial and avoidant personality disorders, and ISTJs were most likely to be designated obsessive-compulsive, while IFJs were most likely to be characterized as "dramatic."

Analysis of life history variables, shown in Table 9.29, found that ITPs were most likely to have been charged with a crime unrelated to substance abuse and to have disciplinary problems at the domiciliary. ISTPs were most likely to have never married, while INTPs and ISFPs were least likely to have never married. INTPs tended to have a greater number of marriages than any other type, while ISTJs had the fewest. ISJs tended to stay in the same job longer than the other types, while INFJs and INTPs had the shortest mean time in their jobs.

Summary and Interpretation   Two things stand out clearly in this study. The first is that the ANOVA found the main effects but none of the interactions to be significant. As mentioned above, ANOVA interaction terms alone are limited in their ability to detect whole type differences. The second major outcome is the finding of distinct differences between whole types in terms of diagnoses and life history variables. A close look at Table 9.28 for diagnoses and Table 9.29 for life history shows that differences between types are not just due to the summative effects of the separate preferences; otherwise, the patterns in the tables would be quite different. Among the patterns revealing whole type differences are the following:

■ INTPs and ISTPs were almost identical in their Axis II profiles and in their crime and domestic trouble histories. Taken by themselves, these findings could be interpreted as the separate effects of the preferences shared between INTPs and ISTPs: Introversion, Thinking, and Perceiving. However, none of the other Introverted, Thinking, or Perceiving types appear to share these effects. Consequently, the outcomes we see with INTPs and ISTPs seem to derive from the interactive combination of these preferences rather than their separate summative effects. It is the interactive combination of the Introverted, Thinking, and Perceiving preferences that creates the unique characteristics that are associated with dominant introverted Thinking. More importantly, these two types are *opposite* in "never married" status, and INTPs had the highest mean number of marriages of any of the types. One might argue that the S–N difference accounts for their opposite scores on "never married." But this interpretation fails because one Sensing type, ISFP, was also least likely to be "never married."

■ INTJs were significantly more likely than any other type to be diagnosed with major depression, while INFPs were most likely to receive the diagnosis of anxiety disorder. These differences are clearly specific to each of these types. None of the other types had significant profiles involving these diagnoses.

■ ISFJs and ISTJs had the two highest means on job length. Two Intuitive types, INFJ and INTP, had the lowest means on this variable. The difference is not just an S–N difference, however, because two other Intuitive types and two other Sensing types were not distinguished from each other on this measure. ISFJs and ISTJs are dominant introverted Sensing types. The job length variable appears to be picking up a significant aspect of this particular pattern of type dynamics. Yet these two types are clearly distinguished from each other by their profiles on Axis II diagnoses and their means on three additional life history variables.

The analyses in this study that relied on quantitative (numerically scored) data really did not reveal much about some of the truly profound differences in how people of different types can exhibit dysfunctional behavior. The important differences among the types were found mainly by looking at the diagnostic categories, which are qualitative measurements. Quantitative measures assume that what is important to know about the person is already contained in a structured measurement tool (such as the MMPI). Qualitative measures, on the other hand, depend on a much more open-ended exploration and discovery process that takes place during an interview by a skilled clinician. The two

Table 9.30	Number of "Most" and "Least" Descriptive Adjectives Uniquely Ascribed to Males of Each Type by IPAR Raters		
	Most Descriptive	Least Descriptive	
Type	# Unique Items	# Unique Items	Total # Unique Items
INFP	8	5	13
INFJ	9	5	14
INTP	9	5	14
INTJ	9	4	13
ISTJ	8	6	14
ENFP	8	6	14
ENFJ	10	8	18
ENTP	10	6	16
ENTJ	7	8	15
ESTJ	8	8	16

Note: The maximum number of unique adjective descriptors for each type is 20.

Source: From *Portraits of Type* (pp. 83–100), by A. Thorne and H. Gough, 1991, Palo Alto, CA: Consulting Psychologists Press. Copyright 1991 by Consulting Psychologists Press. Used with permission.

Table 9.31	Number of "Most" and "Least" Descriptive Adjectives Uniquely Ascribed to Females of Each Type by IPAR Raters		
	Most Descriptive	Least Descriptive	
Type	# Unique Items	# Unique Items	Total # Unique Items
INFP	10	10	20
INFJ	9	9	18
INTP	10	9	19
INTJ	10	8	18
ISTJ	4	9	13
ENFP	8	7	15
ENFJ	9	8	17
ENTP	8	6	14
ENTJ	8	6	14
ESTJ	5	7	12

Note: The maximum number of unique adjective descriptors for each type is 20.

Source: From *Portraits of Type* (pp. 83–100), by A. Thorne and H. Gough, 1991, Palo Alto, CA: Consulting Psychologists Press. Copyright 1991 by Consulting Psychologists Press. Used with permission.

approaches yield very different results, as seen by the fact that Otis and Louks' qualitative descriptions (1997) describe differences between types that were not captured in analyses of their quantitative data. The interested reader is referred to their paper for the rich details of their insights that cannot adequately be conveyed in a brief summary of their work.

Unique Descriptions of Whole Types

Research Question A study by Thorne and Gough (1991) was primarily exploratory and descriptive, with a focus on "the use of the MBTI in studying the interpersonal functioning of effective and creative people."

Sample and Method The sample consisted of 614 people assessed in 12 different assessment programs of one to three days in length held at the Institute of Personality Assessment and Research (IPAR) between 1956 and 1984. The programs involved architects, student writers, research scientists, mathematicians, engineering students, medical school students, law school students, college seniors and sophomores, community residents, and Irish business executives. Ratings of the participants in each program were conducted by 62 women and 127 men of the assessment staff, using a variety of instruments.

Instruments The MBTI Form F was used to identify type. Although data were collected using a large battery of instruments, only data from the Adjective Check List (ACL) are presented here. The ACL consists of 300 adjectives; raters checked each adjective that applied to the person they were assessing. Between 8 and 16 raters independently rated each participant using the ACL. Ratings for assessees were standardized to a base of 10 observers. Ratings for each person on each ACL item thus could range from 0 to 10, and interjudge reliability was .76. None of the raters knew the types of the people they were assessing. Thus their ratings were completely naive with respect to type. This is a crucial point for interpreting the findings summarized below.

Analysis The authors present tables listing the 10 most and 10 least common adjectives associated with the MBTI types. Because the emphasis in this review is on evidence for whole type differences, their data were reanalyzed. From the original tables listing the 10 most and least common adjectives associated with each type, the number of unique adjectives for each type has been counted. These counts are an indicator of the degree to which each type was seen as different by independent observers who did not know the types of the people they were rating. The authors stated they had sufficient numbers to interpret the results for 10 of the 16 types. Data are thus presented for the following types: INFP, INFJ, INTP, INTJ, ISTJ, ENFP, ENFJ, ENTP, ENTJ, and ESTJ.

Results Thorne and Gough's data showed that, as we would expect, types sharing several preferences tended more often to be described with the same adjectives. Types sharing one or no preferences tended to be described with very few of the same adjectives. Table 9.30 and Table 9.31 present the number of unique adjectives used by raters to describe males and females of the 10 types for which sufficient data were available. When examining the last column in Table 9.30 and Table 9.31, it is important to remember that the maximum number of unique adjectives that can be associated with each type in these tables is 20 because Thorne and Gough reported only the 10 most frequently checked adjectives for their "most descriptive" and "least descriptive" categories.

Summary and Interpretation These results show that even types sharing several preferences are seen as noticeably different by independent observers who do not know the types of the people they are describing. These data reveal quite pronounced differences between the types. The minimum number of unique descriptors for a single type ranged from 12 for female ESTJs to a maximum of 20 for INFP females. The average number of unique descriptors for males was 14.7, and for females it was 16.0.

These results are especially significant because they illustrate what is possible when measurement is not constrained by using a narrow scale covering limited content. The ACL offers a great variety of qualitative descriptors that can be used to assess subtle differences in type behavior and is thus able to detect differences spanning an array of diverse qualities. This helps to put the differences between whole types into sharp relief. In fact, while the numbers of unique descriptors shown for each type in the tables is impressive, the differences in *content* of these unique adjectives is even more so. The reader is referred to Thorne and Gough (1991) for a listing of these adjectives for each type.

When observers used the 300-word *Adjective Check List* to describe IPAR program participants, their ratings showed a keen sensitivity to type differences, even though they did not know the types of people they rated. For example, among males, ESTJs were described as practical, frivolous, opportunistic, boastful, tough, outgoing, smug, steady, self-confident, and unscrupulous. Male ENTJs were described as ambitious, planful, responsible, practical, thorough, cowardly, discreet, foresighted, industrious, and reliable. These are the two dominant extraverted Thinking types. In terms of single preferences, they differ only on the S–N dichotomy. Yet among the 10 adjectives most frequently used to describe both types, raters saw them as having only practicality in common. Male INTPs (dominant introverted Thinking) were seen as original, imaginative, complicated, hasty, rebellious, high-strung, individualistic, restless, self-centered, and temperamental. Male INTJs (auxiliary extraverted Thinking) were seen as formal, deliberate, logical, retiring, serious, aloof, methodical, painstaking, thorough, and reserved. Virtually all other pairs of types were described in equally diverse terms. When studies use instruments with a sufficiently broad content, even raters naive to type can clearly see and describe differences among people of different types.

Differences in Observed and Self-Reported Characteristics of Types

Research Question Pearman and Fleenor (1996) designed a study to test whether the 16 types differ significantly from each other on observer ratings and self-report.

Sample and Method The sample consisted of 2,398 managers and leaders who attended programs at the Center for Creative Leadership between 1985 and 1994. Using a large database, 150 persons of each type were randomly selected for analysis, although for two types, only 149 cases were available. Most of the sample were White males between 40 and 55 years old. Their average tenure in a managerial or executive position was eight years. Most were United States citizens, and the majority were from the private economic sector.

Instruments The two instruments used for testing type differences were the *Leadership Style Indicator* (LSI) and the *California Psychological Inventory* (CPI). The CPI yields scores on 20 standardized scales. The LSI contains 48 adjectives used by observers to rate others. The individuals being rated also rated themselves on the same 48 adjectives in the LSI.

Analysis The 20 scales of the CPI were analyzed as dependent variables in ANOVAs, with MBTI type as the independent variable. An ANOVA was also performed using the LSI scales as dependent variables. The *Duncan Multiple Range Test* was used post hoc to determine the ordering of types on the dependent variables.

Results The ANOVAs by type were significant for all CPI scales and for 24 of the LSI scales. However, when type is used as the independent variable in an ANOVA, a significant effect tells us only that the mean for at least one type was significantly different from the means for one or more other types; a significant *F*-test does not necessarily indicate that the means of all 16 types differed from one another. Results of multiple comparison tests were not reported, so there is no way of knowing whether all 16 types were significantly different from every other type on at least one of the CPI or LSI scales. Evidence of such differences is required for validation of whole types.

However, the authors did report a hybrid analysis that incorporated both qualitative and quantitative differences. They compared all 16 types with respect to the scales on which the types scored highest. The result was a profile of the most important scales for each type that revealed how each type is characterized by the CPI or the LSI. The profiles based on each instrument showed that the types all differed from one another. While this kind of analysis does not yield the precision of more sophisticated statistical techniques, its advantage is in avoiding a narrow focus on purely quantitative results that too often obscures important differences in the *qualities* that distinguish the 16 types. (The results of this study are discussed in more detail in Chapter 13 in this manual.)

Summary and Interpretation The self-reported evaluations consistently varied by type. Furthermore, each type could be characterized by a combined CPI and LSI profile that matched the predictions of type theory and Myers' type descriptions. For example, type theory predicts that ETs are likely to be more dominant in social behavior than any other type, and ENTJs had the highest score on dominance. The theory would also predict that ISFPs would score lowest on dominance, which they did. This study also found that all 16 types had scores in the normal *t*-score range on the CPI. From this the authors conclude that the MBTI measures normal and stable personality characteristics for 16 types. Furthermore, within these normal score ranges, all 16 types can be distinguished from one another in ways predicted by type theory.

Type and Time Orientation

Harrison and Lawrence (1985) studied the time orientation of middle school students ($N = 302$). The students were asked to write scenarios about their personal futures, being free to decide how far ahead their description would extend. Based on previous theoretical work by Mann, Siegler, and Osmond (1968, 1971), the authors hypothesized that Intuitive types would be oriented toward the future; Thinking types would have a "linear" perspective incorporating the future, present, and past; Sensing types would be oriented toward the present; and Feeling types would focus more on the past. Using these hypotheses about time orientation, and considering the dominant and auxiliary status of the functions for each type, the authors hypothesized a rank ordering of types based on how long into the future the scenarios of each type were predicted to extend.

Table 9.32 compares the observed with the predicted results. These findings are particularly impressive because the predicted rank ordering of types in the upper half of the table is based on typological criteria, which predicts a different ordering than does the strictly linear or trait criteria used in the bottom half of the table. The differences between the two sets of predicted ranks illustrate that the typological predictions do not reflect a simple additive combination of the S–N and T–F dichotomies. The typological predictions Harrison and Lawrence made rank the types by their dominant functions in combination with the time orientations associated with those functions. This made maximum use of typological information and enabled them to make more precise predictions about rankings of the types.

Table 9.32 Predicted and Observed Ranks of 16 Types by Mean Temporal Extension Scores

Typological Predictions ($r = .98$)[1]

Type[2]	Temporal Orientation[3]	Predicted Rank	Observed Rank
INTJ	*Future* & Linear	1	1
ENTP		2	2
INFJ	*Future* & Past	3	3
ENFP		4	4.5
INTP	Future & *Linear*	5	4.5
ENTJ		6	6
INFP	Future & *Past*	7	7
ENFJ		8	9
ISTP	Present & *Linear*	9	8
ESTJ		10	10
ISTJ	*Present* & Linear	11	12
ESTP		12	14
ISFJ	*Present* & Past	13	11
ESFP		14	13
ISFP	Present & *Past*	15	16
ESFJ		16	15

Trait/Linear Predictions ($r = .88$)[1]

Type[4]	Temporal Orientation	Predicted Rank[5]	Observed Rank
INTJ	Future & Linear	2.5	1
ENTP		2.5	2
INTP	Future & Linear	2.5	4.5
ENTJ		2.5	6
INFJ	Future & Past	6.5	3
ENFP		6.5	4.5
INFP	Future & Past	6.5	7
ENFJ		6.5	9
ISTJ	Present & Linear	10.5	12
ESTP		10.5	14
ISTP	Present & Linear	10.5	8
ESTJ		10.5	10
ISFJ	Present & Past	14.5	11
ESFP		14.5	13
ISFP	Present & Past	14.5	16
ESFJ		14.5	15

Note: [1]Spearman's rho; [2]Dominant type function; [3]Dominant time reference italicized; [4]The most important preference for time orientation is bold; [5]From the trait perspective, NT > NF > ST > SF is the only ranking that can be made; consequently, tied ranks were assigned to the four types within each of these groups.

Source: From "Psychological Type and Time Orientation: Do Middle School Students Differ in Projecting Their Personal Futures?" by D. F. Harrison and G. Lawrence, 1985, *Journal of Psychological Type, 9,* p. 11. Copyright 1985 by *Journal of Psychological Type.* Used with permission.

From the trait perspective only the additive effects of the preferences are important. The S–N dichotomy is *most* salient for time orientation, with Intuitive types predicted to have a longer frame of reference than Sensing types. The T–F dichotomy is second in importance, with Thinking types assumed to have a longer frame of reference than Feeling types. The summative predicted ordering in the second table is therefore NT > NF > ST > SF. From the trait perspective, all Intuitive types are predicted to rank first, followed by all Sensing types. Within the Intuitive and Sensing types, the linear ordering would then rank Thinking types above Feeling types. While the authors did not discuss the rankings predicted by this kind of linear analysis, these rankings are shown in the second part of Table 9.32 for contrast with predictions made by type theory. As illustrated, the linear model lumps the types together in groups of four because it considers only the S–N and T–F preferences in determining ranks.

The correlations of the trait predictions and the typological predictions with the observed rankings were .88 and .98, respectively. Both correlations are significant at $p < .001$. Nevertheless, a visual comparison of the actual and predicted rankings, as well as the difference in the sizes of these coefficients, makes it clear that the typological predictions are much closer to the observed rankings than are the linear predictions. This is because the linear model fails to account for characteristics that are important in understanding a person's orientation to time. These characteristics are accounted for by type theory. More such studies that contrast the two competing explanations—type versus trait—would be invaluable.

Correlations with Factor Scores Derived from Other Measures

Mitchell (1981) reported on data from 475 bank employees at all levels of the organization in a study concerned with the social climate of the organization. Data included FIRO-B (Schutz, 1978), *Strong-Campbell Interest Inventory* (SCII) (Campbell & Hansen, 1981), *Edwards Personality Preference Schedule* (EPPS) (Edwards, 1954), Super's *Work Values Inventory* (WVI) (Super, 1970), and data about job level, type of job, and performance. Factor analysis was used to derive factors from the items of FIRO-B, SCII, EPPS, and WVI. The author describes the factors as *group* phenomena that report value orientations in the group process and the experience of the organization. Factor scores were then created for each person in the sample, and MBTI differences on these factors were identified. Mitchell extended the analyses beyond correlations of the four MBTI preference scales to identification of specific types and type groupings based on the FIRO-B, SCII, EPPS, and WVI. Analysis of variance was used to investigate type differences in factor scores. Note that the MBTI was not included in the original factor analyses. The sample was 55% E, 70% S, 57% T, and 68% J. Mitchell cautioned about generalizing from these data

because of the relatively few Intuitive and Perceiving types. Preferences and types significantly associated with each factor include the following:

- Factor 1: Happy family (harmonious interpersonal relationships with pleasant material surroundings). Highest types were ESFJ, ISFP, ISFJ, and ESFP. Lowest type was ENTP.
- Factor 2: Variety and challenge (latitude to work creatively on intellectually stimulating problems). Highest type was ENTP. Lowest types were ISFJ and ISFP.
- Factor 3: Achievement within the system (orientation toward climbing the corporate ladder). Highest type was ESTJ. Lowest types were ESFP, ESTP, and ENFP. (The highest six types are all Judging types; the lowest six are all Perceiving types.)
- Factor 4: Visible autonomy (free expression of views even when at odds with the social milieu). Highest types were ESTP, INTP, and ENTP. Lowest types were ISTJ and ISFJ.
- Factor 5: Outgoing affiliation (satisfaction in being part of a group). Highest type was ESFJ. Lowest type was ISTP. (Top three types were all EFs; bottom three were all ITs.)
- Factor 6: Business sociability (sociability with a purpose). Highest type was ESFJ. Lowest type was INTJ. (Top four types were all EJs; bottom three were all INs.)
- Factor 7: Financial analysis (scientific and intellectual curiosity about economic and financial matters). Highest types were NTJ types. Lowest types were STP types.
- Factor 8: Nurturing affiliation. Highest types were ENFJ and INFP. Lowest type was ENTJ. (Top seven types were Feeling types; bottom five were Thinking types.)

In the Mitchell study, consistent with theoretical predictions, sociability and concern for others were associated with Extraversion and Feeling; focus on achievement with Judging; and independence, autonomy, and intellectual achievement with Intuition and Perceiving.

MBTI Research Resources

Given space limitations, this manual does not review all of the thousands of research studies conducted with the MBTI. For those interested in additional information on the *Myers-Briggs Type Indicator* that is not covered in this manual, please see *MBTI Applications: A Decade of Research on the Myers-Briggs Type Indicator* (Hammer, 1996b) for a thorough summary of 10 years of research in *seven* areas where the MBTI is frequently used: *career management and counseling; management and leadership; teams; counseling and psychotherapy; education, learning styles and cognitive styles; multicultural applications;* and *health, stress, and coping.* For those interested in more research on the use of the MBTI in organizations and in leadership in particular, see

Developing Leaders: Research and Applications in Psychological Type and Leadership Development (Fitzgerald & Kirby, 1997b). Another excellent source, of course, is the *Journal of Psychological Type*. The Center for Applications of Psychological Type (CAPT) maintains the Isabel Briggs Myers Memorial Library and can provide copies of some research articles. An extensive and regularly updated bibliography of MBTI research is also available from CAPT.

Conclusion

This chapter has examined two kinds of evidence for the validity of the MBTI—evidence for the validity of the four preference scales and evidence for the validity of whole types, including type dynamics. A number of exploratory factor analyses of the MBTI scales have demonstrated very close correspondence with the hypothesized four-factor structure. More rigorous confirmatory factor analyses provide even stronger support for the model. Correlations of the four preferences scales with a wide variety of scales from other instruments support the predictions of type theory regarding the meaning of and the behaviors believed to be associated with the four dichotomies. Evidence for the dichotomous nature of the scales was seen in plots of preference scores against external variables. Analysis of these plots demonstrated that the only significant differences between successive groups of scores were exactly at the midpoint of the scales, which was also where the major changes in direction and slope was observed. An exciting new line of research was presented that uses topograhpic mapping of brain activity patterns and provides strong evidence for the biological basis of the dichotomies. Other studies of behavioral differences, including studies of creativity, differences in orientation to time, fantasy and imagery, desire for privacy, optimism, and anxiety also generally support the theoretical definitions of the scales.

For the first time, evidence has been accumulated to address the question of the validity of whole types and of type dynamics theory. Some of the research presented in this section is based on original analyses of the national sample data collected for this revision. This section reflects the emphasis throughout this manual on whole types and type dynamics. Evidence presented here on type distributions, attraction and satisfaction in couples, reactions to stress, and factor scores derived from other measures suggests that there are characteristics of whole types that are not predictable from knowledge of the individual preferences alone or from simple additive models of the preferences. Descriptions of the types based on self-reports and on ratings by independent observers also show that each of the 16 types can be *uniquely* described with various sets of adjectives and descriptors. A reanalysis of a study of time orientation was also presented that directly compared type theory–based and trait theory–based predictions and showed that the type theory–based predictions were more accurate.

The applications chapters that follow also present research that is relevant to the validity of the individual preference scales and of whole types. Chapter 4 also contains evidence for the validity of the types. Hopefully, the research presented in this chapter and elsewhere in this manual on the validity of whole types and on type dynamics will encourage other researchers to examine these questions.

The Uses of Type

The goal of making psychological type useful in people's lives is realized in each of the five chapters in Part V. The emphasis in all of the chapters is on what is practical and useful, backed up by theoretical consistency and available research evidence. Experienced users will note the addition of two new areas of application, organizations and multicultural settings, to those that appeared in the 1985 *Manual*. Practitioners whose focus is on one particular area of application will find helpful guidelines, many illustrations of ways to use the MBTI in their setting, and selected research evidence that supports such uses.

Readers may note that these chapters sometimes include cross-references to other applications chapters or to chapters in earlier parts of the manual. Material written for a specific application area may be quite relevant in other areas as well. For example, information about learning styles in Chapter 11, "Uses of Type in Education," may be helpful to career counselors (Chapter 12) and management consultants (Chapter 13). Therefore, readers are encouraged to peruse all of the chapters in Part V. Even chapters that may appear from their title and overview to be less interesting or relevant may contain important and generalizable information of use in a variety of applications.

Chapter 10, "Uses of Type in Counseling and Psychotherapy, covers issues relevant to each of the dichotomies as well as to using type dynamics and whole type in addressing the therapeutic process. As you read Chapter 10, you will become aware of the following:

- How neutral and positive type language can enhance psychotherapy
- What different types expect from counseling and how to address those expectations
- How different types are likely to benefit from different kinds of interventions to help them cope with stress
- What issues are of concern in therapy for people of different ages, for couples and families, and for those undergoing treatment for chemical dependency

Chapter 11, "Uses of Type in Education," encompasses all of the information available in this well-studied area of application. As you read Chapter 11, you will become aware of the following:

- How the 16 types differ in their most effective ways of learning
- What academic advantages and disadvantages are associated with some type preferences
- How type preferences relate to preferred writing styles
- How type is influential at all educational levels, from elementary school through university

Chapter 12, "Uses of Type in Career Counseling," presents practical information and recent research relevant to using the MBTI in this important area. As you read this chapter, you will become aware of the following:

- Which occupational trends distinguish the types
- How self-selection ratio type table (SRTT) analysis contributes valuable information to career counselors

- How to avoid using type and career information in a limiting and prescriptive way
- How the same career can prove satisfying to each of the 16 types

Chapter 13, "Uses of Type in Organizations," covers practical considerations and selected relevant research in this increasingly important area of application. As you read this chapter, you will become aware of the following:

- How to introduce and use the dynamic and developmental aspects of type in an organization
- Practical ways of using the MBTI for problem solving, decision making, and conflict resolution
- How the MBTI is effectively used in work teams
- The value of applying a type perspective in leadership development

Chapter 14, "Uses of Type in Multicultural Settings," covers the newest area in which the MBTI is being applied. Multiple issues and a broad range of countries, cultures, and subcultures are included in this area. As a result of both its newness and its breadth, comparatively little definitive research is currently available. As you read Chapter 14, you will become aware of the following:

- When multicultural use of the MBTI is and is not appropriate
- That people of the same type seem to have similar experiences, regardless of the culture in which they live
- That the expression of type preferences in different cultures may be markedly different
- That occupational type tables in different cultures are remarkably similar

Uses of Type in Counseling and Psychotherapy

10

Carl G. Jung based his theory of psychological types primarily on observations of his psychotherapy patients. He repeatedly observed individual differences that seemed to lie outside of the pathological domain; they were not easily attributable to neuroses, character disorders, or other diagnostic categories. Jung also observed these kinds of differences in philosophers, writers, poets, and scientists and found evidence for the universality of his types across cultures, historical eras, and socioeconomic situations. Jung's development and refinement of type theory are described in Chapter 3, and examples of his application of the type approach in psychotherapy appear throughout his many published works. Present-day practitioners who use Jungian typology in counseling and psychotherapy attest to its value, often seeing it as indispensable to their work with clients.

The development of the *Myers-Briggs Type Indicator* personality inventory made type theory more available to psychotherapists and counselors. Indeed, some of the earliest interest in the Indicator was on the part of clinical psychologists. In the 1960s, Mendelsohn and his associates (Mendelsohn, 1966; Mendelsohn & Geller, 1963, 1965, 1967, Mendelsohn & Kirk, 1962) reported on students who sought counseling at the counseling center of the University of California, Berkeley. A 1979 review of the research literature on counseling applications (Carskadon, 1979) reported more than 50 studies. The application of the MBTI to counseling and psychotherapy issues has continued to increase over the years. Recent clinical research literature is reviewed in Quenk and Quenk (1996). For a review of research on the related area of type influences on health, stress, and coping, see Shelton (1996).

The goal of this chapter is to provide counselors and psychotherapists with a practical guide to using the MBTI instrument in the broad variety of settings in which it is appropriate. The chapter is organized so that readers can readily find guidelines relevant to each counseling/psychotherapy issue or specific application. Where available, resources for additional information are suggested. A brief summary of relevant clinical research is included in this chapter.[1]

Advantages of a Typological Approach to Counseling and Psychotherapy

The standard of "normality" against which behavior is judged tends to depend on the prevailing societal and professional view of mental health and psychological adaptation. Jung's observation of consistent, nonpathological individual differences in his patients casts doubt on such a normative view and provides the most compelling reason for taking type into account in psychotherapy and counseling settings. A systematic conception of normal personality differences such as that afforded by psychological type enables mental health practitioners to discriminate between behaviors that are "normal" for one type but may signal difficulties for another type. For example, we would expect an Introverted child to enjoy spending a good deal of time alone but might be concerned when we see the same behavior in a typically active, people-oriented Extraverted child; an ISTJ who is habitually anxious and cautious about taking on new projects would be consistent with her type, while the same behavior in an ENFP would be puzzling; the aggressive behaviors of an ENTJ and an ISFJ would likely have quite different dynamics and motivations.

Understanding what is natural, comfortable, and valued and what is difficult, uncomfortable, and trivial for each of the 16 personality types enables therapists to assess clients from the standpoint of 16 different "norms" of human behavior. When therapists use this approach, clients are more likely to feel appreciated as individuals characterized by legitimate and predictable strengths and frailties. In avoiding comparing clients with a single norm of mental health, practitioners are less likely to make inappropriate diagnoses of pathological conditions. They are also less likely to miss subtle signs of psychological or emotional disturbance. For example, ESTJ and ENTJ clients can often maintain outward composure and efficiency while experiencing extreme internal confusion and distress.

Additional advantages of a typological approach are directly related to using type-based rather than single-norm-based criteria in evaluating and treating clients. A typological approach helps therapists and counselors in the following ways.

Establishing Rapport

Therapists who are aware of type differences listen for them, form tentative hypotheses, and can communicate understanding and acceptance of a client quite early in the interaction. For example, many Introverted clients see their Introversion as "a problem" or even as pathological. A therapist who hears this can clearly explain Introversion as a normal and adaptive energy preference, giving examples and asking the client questions that are likely to accurately reflect the client's feelings and experiences. A couple in marital counseling who in their report of their disagreements appear to differ in the Judging versus Perceiving attitude will *both* feel understood and affirmed when the counselor accurately describes the discomfort each experiences with the other's approach. Experienced practitioners can use such hypotheses about possible type characteristics with regard to all of the preferences, combinations of preferences, and dynamic whole types. Using type knowledge to aid in establishing rapport often occurs before the Indicator has been administered and interpreted, and a practitioner need not use type "language" to talk with clients about type differences. Once the MBTI has been administered and type verified by the client, practitioners can further enhance rapport through continued understanding of the client's type perspective.

Promoting Therapist Neutrality

Practitioners tend to listen to clients' presentation of themselves and their difficulties from a more neutral standpoint when they are aware of the different meanings that may be associated with different type characteristics. They are less likely to interpret a client's style and behavior as disturbed or problematical before evaluating them in the context of the client's type. Counselors are also less likely to view the client's behavior using the bias of their own type. As Jung stated, "The greatest mistake an analyst can make is to assume that his patient has a psychology similar to his own" (1960, p. 259).

Providing a Nonpathological Language for Discussing Problems

The underlying premise of type is that each of the opposite type functions and attitudes is valid, necessary, and useful. The careful use of neutral and positive language in describing the opposite preferences is an effort to convey this notion. People new to type as well as experienced users can attest to the difficulty of avoiding biased and pejorative language in describing one's opposite type or one's less-preferred type characteristics. People often come to counseling because of a long period of disconfirmation by others, dissatisfaction with themselves, and a desire to reduce the distress that limits their lives. A positive way of describing difficulties that are associated with type differences can stimulate increased energy, optimism, and cooperation with the therapy process. This in turn can motivate a client with serious psychological problems to persist in therapy. In contrast, a therapeutic approach that sees the client's type preferences as weaknesses and differences from "normal" behavior can add to the discouragement and hopelessness that may have brought the person to seek help.

Encouraging Change Based on Understanding of Differences

People typically understand others from the point of view of their own type. It is natural for me to assume that my friend's or colleague's motives for an action, what she means by her words, and what she wants me to do in response to her are the same as if I were performing that action, saying those words, or wanting a response. The reality of 16 different types makes such assumptions largely untenable. This is very likely reflected in the frequency with which clients express frustration and despair at their difficulties in living and working effectively with others. Clients who understand type differences gain a useful perspective on the meaning of others' communications and behaviors. With continued guidance from the counselor, they can come closer to understanding the meaning of the words and actions of a person of a different type. For example, an ESFJ client expressed anxiety and concern about losing his job because his quiet and dispassionate INTP supervisor frequently pointed out mistakes and gave praise sparingly. The client believed his supervisor was critical, disapproving, and dissatisfied with his performance. The counselor described and gave the rationale for the natural tendency of a dominant introverted Thinking type to focus on discrepancies rather than on what is going well. The counselor also pointed out that for an ESFJ to be long on criticism and short on praise would indeed indicate disapproval and dissatisfaction with someone's performance. This explanation of the natural differences between INTPs and ESFJs helped the client modify his expectations of his supervisor and made him more resilient and effective in his work situation.

Clients can also be helped to take type into account as a way of accepting and, if desirable, modifying their own behavior and communications. They may benefit by viewing behaviors associated with their own and others' less-preferred sides as expected consequences of specializing in one of each pair of opposites. This can encourage them to appreciate rather than disparage differences. For example, an ISFJ planning a vacation with an ENFP spouse is more likely to compromise about including unscheduled activities if her advance planning and attention to the details of the trip are appreciated by the ENFP as helpful rather than ridiculed as overly controlling and compulsive.

Providing Clients with a Sense of Self-Worth

Counselors have said that what they like most about type is that it gives clients a sense of worth and dignity concerning their own qualities. Clients can be assured at the beginning that finding out about type, one's own and other people's, is a releasing experience, not a restricting one as may have been feared. Finding out about type frees one to recognize one's own natural bent and to trust one's own potential for growth and excellence. There is no obligation or need to be like others, however admirable others may be in their respective ways.

When they see a road toward effectiveness and satisfaction that they can travel by discovering and following their own intrinsically valuable preferences, clients often become more hopeful. As the model is explained, problems and liabilities can be seen as a neglect of less-preferred functions while more-preferred ones were being developed. The stage can be set for looking at the client's problems from the perspective of gaining more effective command over both preferred and nonpreferred functions and attitudes. For example, the Intuitive type can see that the dream of the future is valuable but that present realities may have been overlooked and need more attention. The Sensing type may see that the skills of dealing with present realities are valuable but that including Intuition will open up additional practical options.

Type and the Therapy/ Counseling Process

Psychotherapy and counseling are complex endeavors, and many interacting factors influence the process for both practitioner and client. Issues such as presenting problems, setting where counseling occurs, referral source, allowable number of sessions, therapist theoretical orientation, age of client, and myriad other variables may be involved. The extent to which knowledge and use of the MBTI are appropriate and helpful will vary in relation to this wide range of factors. Experienced therapists, however, report a continuing process of discovering and capitalizing on the insights and richness type provides in their treatment of clients.

This section is designed to provide both new and experienced counselors and psychotherapists with information that they can incorporate and use with clients. Typical counseling issues associated with the individual type preferences are presented first, followed by the more complex and very fruitful area of type dynamics and understanding of each of the 16 types. A third topic is effective communication given the different communication and language styles of clients and therapists.

Counseling Issues Related to Each of the Four Type Dichotomies

The following descriptions are designed to alert counselors to issues frequently associated with each MBTI preference. The information provided can also be useful in helping clients appreciate and use both poles of the dichotomies. This can be especially important for clients whose use of a preferred attitude or function is one-sided or rigid. Such clients can be helped to see the preferences as tools. Part of the counselor's task is helping the client recognize which tool is needed for a given situation. While it is certainly important to affirm the client's natural preferences, helping clients recognize circumstances more suitable to using their less-preferred attitudes and functions can be equally helpful. The safety of the counseling situation can encourage effective use of possibly neglected poles of the dichotomies.

Extraversion and Introversion (E–I) Issues related to the E–I dichotomy focus on the orientation of energy toward the outer world of people, things, and activities (E) or the world of concepts, ideas, and inner experiences (I).

Extraversion Extraverts can be expected to look outward before they look inward for an explanation of the events that occur in their lives. They are more likely to initially blame others or life circumstances for difficulties than to examine their own contributions to problems. Extraverts also tend to

- Gain insight more easily after having an experience. Therefore counseling sessions are likely to be devoted to describing developments of the past week, seeking explanations of past events.
- Become uncomfortable if the counselor is very quiet. They seek active interaction as a verification that they have been heard and may interpret silence and lack of active involvement of the therapist as disapproval and rejection.
- Present such an active, competent face (especially EJ types) that it is easy to miss signs of distress and lack of confidence.
- Do a fair amount of talking as a way of arriving at the "point" of their communication. Counselors should view this not as trivial communication or an attempt to

avoid important issues but rather as the natural "thinking out loud" style of Extraverts.

Some Extraverts seem to use their auxiliary function as well as their dominant function in the Extraverted attitude. This makes them appear to others as "extreme Extraverts" (see the discussion of auxiliary function issues later in this chapter). For Extraverts with this kind of imbalance in their use of energy, the developmental task is balancing their E with their I. They need to learn in small doses to reflect (use I) before acting and to gain greater comfort with solitude and their own company (I). Some Extraverts find they can add Introverted balance to their lives through formal meditation techniques or simply by making sure to include some solitary time in their daily activities. A major value of counseling is to help Extraverts slow down and consider their behavior before they act, and then consider it again after they act.

Introversion Introverts are more likely to look to themselves first for causes of difficulties rather than to others and the environment. They are therefore more intrapunitive than extrapunitive. Introverted clients can be reassured that their instinct to first "blame" themselves for any difficulties is a natural and expected aspect of their Introverted preference. Such a communication can discourage clients from assuming that their self-blaming tendency itself is a personal failing. They will then be more able to consider other people and external circumstances as contributing to misunderstanding and life difficulties. Introverts also tend to

- Gain experience more easily after they have an internal conceptual or experiential framework. Therefore they benefit from comments that help them clarify the concepts or linkages of past experiences that may be behind their own behavior.
- Want to understand what is behind other people's behavior. Such knowledge makes the environment more understandable and therefore safer, so that they can attempt action. Dominant introverted Thinking clients (ISTP and INTP) in particular are often bewildered by others' behavior and misinterpret or overinterpret its meaning.
- Need long pauses during sessions (which may cause discomfort to Extraverted counselors) while they clarify internally what has been said or gain the courage to confide something else to the counselor.
- Benefit from being encouraged to try new Extraverted activities. The therapist can reassure the client that first attempts may be experienced as awkward and uncomfortable but greater ease will come with practice. The goal is for the Introvert to develop a comfortable way of extraverting *as an Introvert* rather than extraverting like an Extravert.

Some Introverted clients introvert both their dominant and auxiliary functions, making them appear as "extreme Introverts." A developmental issue for them is to learn to use their auxiliary function in dealing with people and the Extraverted world. Counselors can encourage this balancing development by suggesting tasks and activities that require the client to extravert the auxiliary and at which he or she is likely to succeed. Continued success often allows the "natural process" to come into play more actively and spontaneously. Introverts benefit from practicing actions and outward expression of opinions.

Sensing and Intuition (S–N)

Issues related to Sensing and Intuition involve the opposite ways clients take in information about the world and what they attend to in their immediate environment.

Sensing In counseling with a Sensing type, issues should be discussed in specific and concrete terms, using frequent examples that are relevant to the client's life experience and circumstances. Sensing clients typically seek counseling for a specific, current problem and tend to be disinterested in a lengthy psychodynamic exploration of their lives. They terminate when that problem is resolved. They may return at some later time to obtain help with another specific issue. Sensing clients are likely to

- See their view of the situation as the only possible one and therefore as permanent or a given. The counselor can broaden the client's perspective by describing practical alternatives for the client to assess.
- See the alternatives proposed as negative. When Intuition is the inferior function (ISJ and ESP types), this will be particularly true. The goal of providing positive possibilities is to teach the client that what is not presently known can be enhancing and not always threatening.
- Benefit from being taught to recognize and appreciate others' intuitions and to put greater trust in their own Intuition when Sensing does not provide adequate answers.

Therapeutic strategies that involve being active can be helpful for grounding Sensing types when their trust in and comfort with reality is shaken. Sensing types are often eager for and obtain great benefit from homework exercises that involve answering specific, factual questions, thinking about and assessing past experiences, and trying out new behaviors. They may be skeptical and uncooperative when an Intuitive counselor suggests interventions that use fantasy and imaging techniques. In such situations, Sensing types who also prefer Feeling may be distressed at "disappointing" the counselor, which can exacerbate feelings of inadequacy.

Intuition Intuitive type clients are likely to use more abstract or symbolic terminology and respond to symbolism and metaphorical allusions from the counselor. They may also make leaps from comments the counselor makes, at times "intuiting" something that is not what the counselor had in mind. Intuitive types tend to be attracted to open-ended and broad-ranging exploration of both their inner and outer

lives and may wish to continue therapy after the initial issues have been resolved. As clients, intuitive types are likely to

- Be so caught up in possibilities that they (1) overlook the facts and the limitations facts impose, (2) assume they already know all the facts, or (3) assume that facts are unimportant. A counselor may need to push Intuitive clients to turn on their Sensing to assess the practical steps needed to turn their possibilities into realities.
- Be independent and see many interesting connections in the process of discussing themselves. Counselors will do well to let them find their own solutions with a minimum of direction.
- Focus on new possibilities and take the position that there must be an answer if they look long enough. This stance can provide hope and optimism in treatment, but a counselor may need to ask whether the client's energy might be better spent on goals for which more immediate possibilities offer needed solutions.

Intuitive type clients enjoy and are often adept at interventions that make use of fantasy and the exploration of psychological connections. They may be resistant to more factual and systematic approaches and disappointed in and critical of counselors who promote them. Such clients may assume that the counselor does not understand the complexity and uniqueness of the client's personality.

Thinking and Feeling (T–F)

Issues related to decision making and the general way of evaluating perceptions and communications involve the difference between Thinking and Feeling.

Thinking A Thinking type is naturally skeptical and critical and can be expected to be so in the counseling session. A counselor therefore should be prepared to back up his or her statements with evidence. Thinking types may also

- Disregard what matters to them (Feeling issues) because "It isn't logical to care so much." At some stage, it is important for them to accept and integrate their values and feelings as valid and deserving of respect. They often do this by including Feeling considerations into their logical, cause-and-effect analyses.
- Not find it useful to be asked to describe feelings. It is also not appropriate to label Thinking types as "defensive" or "intellectualizing" when they have trouble putting feelings into words, or when their words for feelings sound stereotypical or analytical.
- Have issues about discomfort and a sense of inadequacy in social situations, as they tend to take longer than other types to develop comfortable social skills. This is particularly true for dominant introverted Thinking types (ISTP and INTP). Social skills training with easy exercises can be useful when the client sees the logic of learning these skills and when they will enable desired relationships or activities.

Clients who prefer Thinking can benefit from achieving some comfortable ways of expressing approval and appreciation of others. The counselor should be careful not to expect the Thinking type to initially do this with finesse and skill and would do well to recommend low-key, nonemotive approaches. People who prefer Thinking usually have fewer words to describe and discriminate among their own feelings as well as to identify others' expression of feeling. During the process of counseling or psychotherapy, such clients can be helped to identify and make discriminations in this sometimes puzzling area.

Feeling Clients who prefer Feeling benefit from clarifying their values and discussing choices between short-term and long-term goals. They are likely to seek approval and affirmation from the therapist and may be reluctant to state their needs and desires directly. In addition, they may

- Ignore unpleasant facts that conflict with their values. They can profit from *gentle* confrontations with these discrepant facts. At times a counselor's straightforward interpretations can be taken as harsh criticism.
- Become negative and cynical when their goals and values have been undermined or ignored. This is especially detrimental in types in which Feeling is dominant (EFJ and IFP). Finding a new and caring connection or emphasizing good current relationships can be helpful in tempering a cynical attitude.
- Hesitate to state their wishes clearly and assume that other people ought to know their desires without being told. It is useful to point out that Thinking types may not know what matters to another person and it is unkind to make them guess when such information could be provided in a straightforward manner.

Clients who prefer Feeling, especially Feeling Judging types, derive genuine pleasure from helping others create and maintain harmony in their lives. At times, however, they may devote so much energy to other people's needs that they have insufficient time for themselves. Care should be taken not to automatically "diagnose" their behavior as unhealthy or "codependent." It can be a slow process to help Feeling types balance the nurturance that is intrinsic and satisfying for them against legitimate attention to their own desires.

Judging and Perceiving (J–P) Judging and Perceiving are relevant when clients have concerns about organizing and controlling their lives or about adapting and being open to life experiences.

Judging People with a Judging preference bring issues relating to control and authority into sessions. They may be uncomfortable with the therapy process if they perceive it as requiring them to give up control to the therapist. Judging types, especially those who also prefer Sensing, are most comfortable when clear goals and timelines are laid out at the outset of therapy. Clients who prefer Judging are also likely to

- Find adapting to change stressful, especially when their previous strategies have proven ineffective. It can be helpful to have Judging types let go of control for a limited time or in a limited area. The client can "plan" to be flexible.
- Benefit from being taught strategies for using Perception to understand their own or other people's behavior. Judging clients can be taught to ask questions where they think they already have answers. For example, "My son is bad because he . . ." becomes "Why do you suppose he does . . . ?"
- Take the counselor's expressed hypotheses, suggestions, and interpretations as final judgments rather than as the exploration of possibilities. Frequently emphasizing the tentative nature of the counselor's statements is therefore important.

The counselor can help Judging types avoid premature closure by asking them to think about other possibilities and facts that could be relevant and to define a period of time when they "decide not to decide." Judging type clients often feel affirmed by the counselor's recognition of their natural discomfort with lack of closure. They may then be more willing to stay open to their preferred form of perception (Sensing or Intuition) and thus tolerate a delay in final decision making.

Perceiving Types who have a Perceiving preference, especially younger clients, often report problems related to distractibility, procrastination, and difficulty meeting deadlines and organizing their time effectively. In addition, they may

- See even modest structure as unduly restricting, especially if their preference for Perceiving is very clear and consistent. Behavior that can seem irresponsible to others may be seen by the client as a valuable exercise of freedom.
- Benefit from considering the consequences of their approach. Thinking Perceiving clients can learn the use of Judging skills by considering the negative consequences of not coming to closure or being late. Feeling Perceiving clients can consider the harm they may be doing to others by not coming to closure.
- Be able to moderate their approach by examining what happens when they have difficulties with decision making and asking themselves what facilitates or blocks decisions for them. A client can be taught time management or similar Judging skills, but it is usually more useful to mobilize the energy of the decision-making functions, Thinking and Feeling, to understand and overcome blocks to decision making.

People who prefer to extravert the perceiving functions of Sensing or Intuition can be helped to come to closure by being asked to consider how likely it is that they will make the wrong decision given the amount of information they have. For Intuitive Perceiving types overwhelmed with too many options, practice in collecting facts will often eliminate most options as impractical and make their choices manageable. Help in breaking up a large project into smaller, more manageable pieces can also be beneficial.

Counseling Issues Related to Type Dynamics and Development

Type theory leads us to expect greater comfort, confidence, and facility when individuals' most conscious functions, the dominant and auxiliary, are directing their lives. We expect correspondingly greater discomfort, insecurity, and ineptitude when the inexperienced, relatively unconscious tertiary and inferior functions are being used. This expected dynamic is predictable in a system that assumes specialization of opposite pairs of mental functions and attitudes. However, clients who are experiencing psychological and emotional distress may not conform to this hypothesized dynamic picture. The client's type development may be at issue—there may be one or more ways in which the person's type is *undifferentiated*—or there may be no clear and consistent preference for either pole of one or more of the dichotomies. For example, if neither Sensing nor Intuition is the habitual way of perceiving, the person may alternately attend to present data and shift to future possibilities in a haphazard manner; his or her resulting awareness of the world may diverge from that of others in an unpredictable way. This kind of lack of differentiation may significantly contribute to the client's presenting complaints. For further discussion of undifferentiated functions, see Quenk (1985a).

Alternatively (or in addition), nontypological factors may be the major source of the client's difficulties. We can expect general psychological impairment to have an impact on type functioning. Where general impairment seems to be reflected or expressed in inadequate type functioning, the therapist may be able to address the issue from the neutral and affirming perspective of type dynamics. To expand on the example above of a person with an undifferentiated Perceiving function, such a client may be seen as somewhat eccentric and even paranoid because he or she tends to focus on a few concrete facts and move quickly to a global theory that connects those facts in an idiosyncratic way. The therapist can describe such "paranoia" to the client as a difficulty in choosing which kind of perception is most appropriate in a given situation, rather than as a serious "thought disorder." Strategies to help the client notice and differentiate the two kinds of perception can then be adopted as a therapeutic approach. Thus, therapists and counselors who are alert to evidence of dynamic and developmental "signs" can capitalize on this knowledge in formulating and implementing individualized treatment of the client.

Cautions in Making Inferences About Type Dynamics

Therapists and counselors should bear in mind that type theory and the MBTI inventory address individual differences in normal personality functioning, not psychopathological or diagnostic categories as might be elicited in such instruments as the *Minnesota Multiphasic Personality Inventory* (MMPI). Isabel Myers observed that some people were able to use their type more effectively than others, and experience certainly bears this out. Clients seeking counseling and psychotherapy are likely to be less effective in their expression of their type. A knowledgeable practitioner can capitalize on this in treating them. However, the following cautions apply in assessing possible dynamic problems:

- Dynamic and developmental issues can sometimes be hypothesized during the sessions devoted to explaining and verifying the client's type. However, ease or difficulty in verifying a best-fit type are not *by themselves* indicative of the absence or presence of "type-relevant" problems. A more fruitful approach is to attend to possible deviations from the "expected" dynamics of the client's verified or hypothesized type.

- People often experience as "abnormal" the "normal" characteristics of types who are different from themselves, especially when appraising their opposite type. Counselors and therapists need to exercise particular vigilance in this regard. For example, an INTJ therapist must remind herself that the gregariousness and focus on sensual pleasure of an ESFP are natural expressions of type, not evidence of a narcissistic personality disorder; an ENFP counselor should resist viewing his opposite ISTJ client as obsessive-compulsive. Similar cautions apply for all pairs of therapist and client types.

- When a client is the same type as the therapist, the therapist may miss significant dynamic difficulties because what the client describes feels familiar and natural. The therapist may overlook evidence that the client's use of type is ineffective, perhaps viewing the difficulty as situational and external.

Identifying the Dynamics of Type Development

The MBTI provides a therapeutic model that builds on natural strengths before dealing with the weaknesses of less developed aspects of a client's typological makeup. Discovering the client's strengths and reinforcing them is therefore essential. The goal of this section is to help practitioners identify effective use of type as well as signs of possible dynamic and developmental difficulties. Where appropriate, strategies for treatment in dealing with these issues are suggested.

Assessment of the Dominant Function   Since the dominant function in theory gives direction and is the most trustworthy, the counselor should listen for evidence that the dominant function is indeed trusted and giving directions. If the dominant function is Sensing, does the person have a good sense of reality, do practical things well, and enjoy the little pleasures of everyday life? If the dominant function is Intuition, do insights stand up under verification? If the dominant function is Feeling, are values securely in place and can the client live by his or her values comfortably? If the dominant function is Thinking, does the client see consequences clearly and take them into account when governing his or her behavior? The assumption is that relying on well-differentiated, trustworthy functions will lead to more positive outcomes and a greater sense of autonomy for the individual.

Serious consideration should be given to any difficulties an individual is having in the aspects of life related to the dominant function. For example, impracticality in a Sensing type is more serious than impracticality in an Intuitive type since realism should be an essential characteristic of those who prefer Sensing perception. Habitual concern about hurting others' feelings may be a sign of chronic stress in a Thinking type but not in a Feeling type.

Assessment of the Auxiliary Function

Many problems encountered in counseling situations are related to failure to develop the auxiliary function. Isabel Myers' original and revised type descriptions all discuss the consequences of failure to develop the auxiliary function, and sensitivity to these consequences should enter into the interpretive interviews and the conduct of therapy. The developed auxiliary function provides balance between Perception and Judgment and enables expression of both Extraversion and Introversion. Myers with Myers (1980/1995, p. 182) wrote, "In type theory balance does not mean equality of two functions or of two attitudes; instead, it means superior skill in one, supplemented by a helpful but not competitive skill in the other." Some of the effects of failure to develop the auxiliary function are described below:

- Extraverts who habitually extravert both their dominant and auxiliary functions will place so much reliance on the outer world that they will not be in touch with their own inner perception or judgment. For example, according to the theory of type dynamics an ENFP extraverts dominant Intuition and introverts auxiliary Feeling. If he extraverts *both* dominant Intuition and auxiliary Feeling, he may have little ability to judge himself and others from the standpoint of his own inner values. He may therefore rely primarily on others' judgments and be easily influenced by outside circumstances. The therapist can encourage clients who extravert both conscious functions to question the accuracy and relevance of relying on other people's perception or judgment and learn to attend to and value their own "inner voice." Such clients may seek therapy during midlife for issues related to habitual extraverting of the auxiliary function; they may report an emerging feeling that they lack inner substance and have no comfortable sense of themselves.

- Introverts who habitually introvert both their dominant and auxiliary functions will be so caught up in their inner world that they will be ineffective in the outer world. These Introverts may demonstrate the characteristics

usually ascribed to shyness; their one-sided Introversion may result in avoidance of the outer world rather than pleasure in the solitude of their own company. In contrast, well-balanced Introverts relate to the outer world with relative comfort by exercising their auxiliary Extraverted function. One-sided Introversion can be particularly troublesome for young adults striving to succeed in work and in intimate relationships. Indeed, difficulties in these areas often bring such young people to seek help.

- Types with Sensing or Intuition dominant (IJ and EP types) can be so caught up in experiencing life that they fail to direct their activities and come to closure. For example, according to theory an ISTJ has dominant Introverted Sensing and auxiliary Extraverted Thinking. If all or most of her energies are devoted to collecting and storing information, little or none is available to logically organize the information and develop structures for its use in the world. Without an Extraverted auxiliary function, an IJ might look like an exaggeration of a "pack rat," continually collecting either concrete objects (for an ISJ) or more and more theories (in the case of an INJ). An ESFP should theoretically balance dominant extraverted Sensing with auxiliary introverted Feeling. If energy is primarily devoted to stimulation of his five senses, there will be little way for him to select and repeat worthwhile experiences; he is likely to come across as shallow, insincere, and unreliable. In contrast, a more balanced ESFP will use a stable set of inner values to choose which sense experiences are most satisfying and meaningful. Similarly, a balanced ENTP or ENFP will use the Introverted Judging function to choose which exciting projects are worth pursuing and completing, while a less balanced ENP is likely to flit from one exciting idea to another, accomplishing none of them.

- Types with Thinking or Feeling dominant (IP and EJ types) can be so caught up with controlling their worlds that they fail to collect data that would help them understand their experiences. Their judgments and decisions may therefore appear categorical and ill founded because they are in effect using *only* their dominant Judging function without the balance that should be provided by gathering and considering relevant information (Perception). For example, an ENTJ (dominant extraverted Thinking with auxiliary introverted Intuition) should, according to theory, be making judgments about relevant information acquired through Intuition. If little or no data are allowed in, his categorical and extreme judgments will likely come across as overcontrolling and domineering, and he will be seen as judgmental. Similarly, the dominant introverted Feeling of an ISFP, in the absence of auxiliary extraverted Sensing, may result in low self-esteem and hypersensitivity to criticism. The client draws negative, erroneous conclusions about her self-worth because adequate data are not available to her dominant Feeling

Judgment. For further discussion of failure to develop the auxiliary function, see Quenk (1985b).

Assessment of the Tertiary and Inferior Functions

In theory, individuals are least effective and most vulnerable in the areas of their third and fourth functions, especially the fourth, or inferior, function. Counselors new to type theory may take the position that if clients have dominant Feeling, the most helpful counseling strategy is to help them develop their inferior Thinking. This is not the approach taken in developmental counseling, which builds on strengths to get to weakness. The client is encouraged to use the dominant and auxiliary functions to strengthen the less secure and more inexperienced tertiary and inferior functions.

Isabel Myers (Myers & McCaulley, 1985; p. 64) described this in giving the rationale for differential development of type functions. She stated that

> [t]he kind of perception one prefers and the kind of judgment one prefers determine, between them, the directions in which one can develop most fully and effectively with the most satisfaction to oneself. . . . It is sometimes said that both kinds of perception and both kinds of judgment should be developed equally. The answer is that such a dead level of uniformity leaves one with no stable direction for one's life. Each of the four functions has its own objectives, its own fulfillments. The goals of the opposite functions are not compatible. Intuition does not want the same things as sensing. Feeling is not satisfied by what satisfies thinking. One cannot direct one's life effectively toward a desired result until one's best-trusted kind of perception and best-trusted kind of judgment are agreed as to *what* is to be desired.

Individuals are most willing to develop skills in using less-preferred functions when doing so is in the service of their dominant and auxiliary functions. This useful strategy for developing the less-preferred functions helps achieve goals set by the dominant and auxiliary functions. For example, an ENFP in theory would be caught up with new possibilities (dominant Intuition) for people (auxiliary Feeling). It is difficult for an ENFP to deal with matters in a tough-minded fashion (tertiary Thinking) or with attention to practical details (inferior Sensing). If the ENFP is enthusiastic about a project that captures his Intuition and Feeling, Sensing and Thinking will be used in the service of Intuition and Feeling to accomplish the practical aspects of the project. Exercises of this nature are valuable for teaching full use of perception and judgment; they are also a way to help clients identify which functions are easier or more difficult for them.

Experience and maturity can lead to natural development of less-preferred functions. For example, an experienced INTP family practice physician may carefully collect facts and details (tertiary Sensing) and develop a successful "bedside manner" (inferior Feeling) in seeing her patients because doing so serves her dominant Thinking and auxiliary Intuition—which she relies on for arriving at a diagnosis. Experience has also taught her that such an approach encourages patient compliance with treatment.

Counselors can help clients make conscious use of tertiary and inferior functions through practice, not through understanding alone. The counselor can first help clients identify their less-preferred functions and become aware of their level of discomfort with or avoidance of them and then teach them to practice using the functions. Small tasks that may seem inconsequential to outsiders are better for learning to develop functions than are major life decisions. The process of choosing a meal in a restaurant is a better way to practice a new skill than the process of choosing a career. Small tasks are especially important for practicing less-preferred functions, since initial failures can be interesting experiments, not blows to self-esteem. Practical exercises that encourage gaining access to, experiencing, and developing each of the functions can be found in Myers and Kirby (1994).

Eruptions of the Inferior Function

During the course of psychotherapy clients are likely to report concern and distress about episodes of unfamiliar and disturbing thoughts, feelings, and actions. Such reports often conform to eruptions of their unconscious inferior functions. Unconscious energy is most likely to emerge when the client's level of conscious control of dominant and auxiliary functions is lowered. This shift of energy from conscious dominant to unconscious inferior often occurs in response to stress, fatigue, illness, and consciousness-lowering drugs such as alcohol. In terms of type dynamics, it puts the individual in the awkward and distressing position of trying to operate using the least experienced, most undeveloped, most unconscious, and largely ineffectual parts of his or her personality. When a therapist explains the role of the inferior function in normal type dynamics, and describes the predictable form of each inferior function, clients often experience a sense of relief. The predictability of their out-of-character behavior reassures them that they are not in danger of totally losing control of themselves and are not "crazy." The dynamics and descriptions of the eight inferior functions can be found in Quenk (1993, 1996).

Because severe stress often pushes people to seek therapy, clients may not reveal their typical dominant and auxiliary strengths during initial sessions. They may come across as poorly developed, exaggerated versions of their opposite type. Only when the severity of stress has diminished will the therapist recognize the client's more typical type functioning. The presence of unusual stress should be a clue to the practitioner that type may be distorted and that accurate assessment of type will be initially questionable, either through inquiry or through administration of the MBTI.

This section has provided examples of some of the practical applications of type dynamics. For insights into other relevant dynamic issues related to counseling and psychotherapy, see Corlett and Millner (1993), Jones and Sherman (1997), Jung (1923/1971), McCaulley (1990b), Myers and

Kirby (1994), Provost (1993), Quenk (1989), Quenk, A. T. (1985), and Quenk and Quenk (1982).

Capitalizing on Knowledge of Whole Type

Counselors and psychotherapists who incorporate a typological framework into their work can become sensitive to the nuances that differentiate each of the 16 types. They can weave this level of typological awareness into a broad range of therapeutic issues and across a wide spectrum of clients. As experience and knowledge grow, the existence of type differences serves as an implicit assumption that informs the therapist's awareness and appreciation of the individuality of every client. The following comments are examples of just a few of the subtle qualities that emerge as distinctive therapeutic issues for some of the 16 types.

- INFJ clients often admit to the therapist their fear that they are or could easily become "crazy." Their fear is a function of their uncanny ability to "read" the underlying emotions of the individuals and groups of people with whom they interact long before anyone else is aware that such emotions exist.
- ESFP clients acknowledge feeling "not quite grown up" in comparison with other people. This is understandable in light of their focus on sensual experience in the present and their often "fun-loving" approach to life, which does not fit well with the notion of responsibility and attention to long-range goals.
- ISTJ clients, particularly men, tend to agree with a therapist's suggestion that they express love for their children by providing financial security and ensuring that the children behave in an appropriate and responsible manner. These clients can become quite emotional at the therapist's recognition that an ISTJ's family may misinterpret such an expression of love as a need to control and dominate the child.
- ENTP clients may acknowledge with some discomfort that they have an underlying fear that they lack substance and seriousness and that their contributions are not really valued. They may therefore take particular pride in accomplishments that call on less-preferred type characteristics, those that require slow, methodical, and detailed work over an extended period, rather than the more facile, innovative projects that come most easily to them.
- INTP clients, especially women, often report an early awareness of being profoundly different from other children, leading to a hypersensitivity to signs of rejection and to painful memories of being ridiculed and scapegoated as "weird."
- ESTJ and ENTJ clients may view their need for counseling as a "defeat," as personal failure to solve their own life problems. They may project their own sense of incompetence onto the therapist, which can emerge as a challenging, confrontational approach to the counseling/therapy enterprise.

Table 10.1 Indicative and Contraindicative Adjectives on the *Waltz-Gough Efficacy Index*

Indicative Adjectives		Contraindicative Adjectives
active	industrious	anxious
adaptable	initiative	apathetic
alert	persevering	confused
assertive	planful	dependent
capable	realistic	dreamy
clear-thinking	reasonable	immature
confident	reliable	inhibited
courageous	resourceful	irresponsible
curious	responsible	meek
determined	self-confident	quitting
dominant	stable	self-pitying
efficient	versatile	spineless
enterprising		submissive
forceful		weak
independent		withdrawn

Source: From *Portraits of Type* (p. 69), by A. Thorne and H. Gough, 1991, Palo Alto, CA: Consulting Psychologists Press. Copyright 1991 by Consulting Psychologists Press. Used with permission.

Inferences about these and similar distinctive counseling issues for different types can be made from the research of Thorne and Gough (1991). They analyzed extensive observer ratings, self-ratings, and personality measures, such as the *Adjective Check List* and *California Q-Sort,* in relation to the personality types of a variety of subjects who participated in intensive assessment sessions at the Institute for Personality Assessment and Research (IPAR) at the University of California, Berkeley. Two measures of personal adjustment, the *Waltz-Gough Efficacy Index* and the *Marrot Psychological Soundness Index,* were developed from available data and examined in relation to whole types. Importantly, neither the trained psychologists who observed and rated subjects nor the subjects themselves had any knowledge of psychological type. Therefore, the assessments of personal adjustment were made from a general normative view that reflects professional and societal values and expectations. Observer ratings of gender appropriateness were also subject to general notions of adjustment.

The efficacy measure was developed by Waltz and Gough (1984) using items from the *Adjective Check List* data pool. Subjects' scores on efficacy were based on a difference measure of pooled observer ratings on a set of indicative adjectives relative to contraindicative adjectives. Data for 374 males and 249 females in the IPAR sample were analyzed. Table 10.1 lists indicative and contraindicative adjectives.

Comparing the two lists of adjectives provides useful information about what qualities are valued as "efficacious"

Table 10.2 Indicative and Contraindicative Q-Sort Items in the *Marrot Psychological Soundness Index*

Indicative Items	Contraindicative Items
Is a genuinely dependable and responsible person	Feels a lack of personal meaning in life
Behaves in a giving way toward others	Is subtly negativistic; tends to undermine and obstruct or sabotage
Behaves in a sympathetic or considerate manner	Has hostility toward others
Is productive; gets things done	Has a brittle ego-defense system; has a small reserve of integration; would be disorganized and maladaptive when under stress or trauma
Tends to arouse liking and acceptance in people	
Is calm, relaxed in manner	Is basically distrustful of people in general; questions their motivations
Has warmth; has the capacity for close relationships; compassionate	Is self-defeating
Has a clear-cut, internally consistent personality	Is basically anxious
Is cheerful	Feels cheated and victimized by life; self-pitying

Source: From *Portraits of Type* (p. 70), by A. Thorne and H. Gough, 1991, Palo Alto, CA: Consulting Psychologists Press. Copyright 1991 by Consulting Psychologists Press. Used with permission.

in terms of psychological adjustment. Additionally, when we look through a "type lens," it is evident that some types are more likely than others to demonstrate desirable characteristics. EJ types, for example, are readily characterized by many of the adjectives on the indicative list, such as active, assertive, confident, dominant, efficient, forceful, and responsible. IP types, in contrast, may be seen as lacking these qualities and more likely to demonstrate some contraindicative adjectives, such as anxious, inhibited, irresponsible, and withdrawn.

The *Marrot Psychological Soundness Index,* developed in 1981, is based on scoring of Q-sort formulations. Table 10.2 shows the indicative and contraindicative items used to create this index. One can infer that some types, for example, ESTJ or ESFJ, might be more likely to be seen as sound, while other types, for example INFP or INTP, could give the impression of having a deficit of soundness.

Table 10.3 provides the rank order of the 16 types on these two measures of adjustment for males, and Table 10.4 provides the same information for females.

The rank orderings shown in Tables 10.3 and 10.4 are examples of the type and gender biases to which different types in our culture may be subject. Such cultural influences may contribute to or exacerbate the psychological and emotional difficulties that lead people to seek counseling and psychotherapy. Type and gender in combination can have marked effects on how people are assessed by both professional and lay observers. The two highest means for soundness for males are ESTJ and ESFJ; the lowest are INTP and INFP. For females, the highest soundness indexes are ENFJ and ESFJ, and the lowest are INTP and ESTP. Top male scores on efficacy are obtained by ESFP and ESTJ; bottom scorers are INFJ and INFP. For females, top efficacy scores are obtained by ESFJ and ENFJ, and low scorers are

ESTP and ESFP (although sample sizes limit interpretation). Being an ESJ rather than an IP is considered "positive" for males; being an EFJ rather than an ITP is considered "positive" for females.

Client and Counselor Communication Styles

The counseling session offers a laboratory for Isabel Myers' prescription for successful communication. She wrote that "[i]n order to be successful, a communication needs to be listened to without impatience and understood without hostility" (Myers with Myers, 1980/1995).

Clients best understand counseling interventions couched in the their own type language. Sensing language is more concrete; Intuitive language is more abstract and symbolic. Thinking language is more objective and analytical; Feeling language is more personal. With practice and an attentive ear, counselors can use words that help the client feel understood. When introducing a topic to a group, a reference to practical issues (Sensing), new possibilities (Intuition), long-range consequences (Thinking), and help for people (Feeling) will provide motivation for each of the functions.

Sensing types, particularly ISJ types, often describe events with many circumstantial details. Intuitive counselors who immediately see what the client is leading up to can be tempted to interrupt. Interruptions can be seen by the client as a disconfirmation of the client's own style, a lack of understanding or respect.

Intuitive type clients who often use abstract or symbolic terms can lead counselors to erroneously believe they understand the client. The assumption of understanding may rest on the different meanings the client and counselor give to the terms being used. The counselor should

Table 10.3   Rank Order of Types on Two Measures of Adjustment: Males

Type	N	M	SD	Type	N	M	SD
	Soundness				**Efficacy**		
ESTJ	24	108.6	8.7	ESFP	3	320.7	21.2
ESFJ	9	108.2	11.5	ESTJ	25	294.1	46.6
ISTJ	25	107.2	12.0	ENFJ	17	277.5	58.1
ESFP	3	105.0	14.8	ENTJ	32	270.8	53.7
ISTP	10	104.0	17.7	ENTP	23	266.7	40.9
ESTP	7	103.6	9.5	ENFP	33	264.6	42.8
ENFJ	16	102.7	15.5	ISFJ	13	264.2	72.1
ISFJ	13	102.5	20.4	INTP	49	256.9	44.7
ENFP	33	101.9	21.1	ISTJ	27	256.3	56.8
ISFP	9	100.1	23.5	INTJ	53	255.8	52.8
ENTJ	31	99.8	21.9	ESFJ	10	253.8	61.3
INTJ	52	98.8	18.7	ISTP	10	247.9	62.8
INFJ	24	97.5	17.2	ISFP	9	245.3	78.1
ENTP	23	96.0	18.4	ESTP	8	242.5	46.6
INTP	49	94.1	22.5	INFJ	26	240.8	61.1
INFP	33	90.8	23.9	INFP	36	233.5	60.1
	361	99.6	19.2		374	259.1	53.7

Source: From *Portraits of Type* (p. 145), by A. Thorne and H. Gough, 1991, Palo Alto, CA: Consulting Psychologists Press. Copyright 1991 by Consulting Psychologists Press. Used with permission.

investigate whether the meaning he or she attributes to these terms matches the meaning the client wishes to convey.

Communication with Thinking types should begin with the rationale provided by the Thinking type client. New information from the counselor should be given in a logical, concise fashion with clear premises leading to conclusions.

Communication with Feeling types should clearly acknowledge the areas of agreement before raising questions or suggesting alternative courses of action. Feeling types, especially those in distress, are hypersensitive to indications that the counselor may not be on their side.

Yeakley (1982, 1983) developed Communication Style Preferences for each of the types, based on the similarity of functions that are Extraverted. These early studies by Yeakley indicated that high similarity in communication style is significantly associated with effective communication in marriage, in manager-subordinate relationships in business, in the grades teachers give students, in sales to life insurance prospects, and in the types of parishioners ministers attract. Yeakley's 1983 article described "styles of listening" that provide useful suggestions for counselors (p. 22):

■ Listening in the Sensing style means *interpreting* at a very practical level and asking questions such as
What is the speaker saying?

How should the words be decoded?
How should the message be perceived?

■ Listening in the Intuitive style means *understanding* at a much deeper level and asking questions such as
What does the speaker really mean?
What are the assumptions underlying the message?
What are the implications of the message?
What are the possibilities suggested by the message?

■ Listening in the Thinking style means *analyzing* and *organizing* while asking questions such as
What is the structure of the message?
What is the central idea?
What are the main points?
What are the subpoints?
How are the various points related?
Is there adequate evidence to justify each claim?
Is the reasoning logical?
Are the claims true or false?

■ Listening in the Feeling style means *evaluating* and *appreciating* while asking questions such as
What are the values suggested by the message?
Should these values be accepted or rejected?
How do I feel about the message?
How do I feel about the speaker?

Table 10.4   Rank Order of Types on Two Measures of Adjustment: Females

	Soundness				Efficacy		
Type	N	M	SD	Type	N	M	SD
ENFJ	11	116.2	9.8	ESFJ	9	292.0	47.4
ESFJ	9	112.7	11.8	ENFJ	11	291.8	32.7
ISFP	4	110.0	12.1	ENTP	19	286.1	45.3
ESFP	1	105.0	0.0	INTJ	24	272.8	54.2
ISFJ	12	104.5	17.2	ENTJ	14	272.6	41.0
ENFP	29	103.9	17.0	ISTP	2	264.0	11.3
ENTP	19	103.6	12.2	ISTJ	10	251.0	44.5
ENTJ	14	101.1	14.7	ENFP	29	249.6	60.2
ISTJ	10	101.0	13.7	ESTJ	12	246.8	47.6
INFP	47	100.5	19.5	INFP	47	244.3	55.7
ESTJ	12	99.9	22.2	INTP	30	232.2	47.3
INTJ	24	98.7	15.0	ISFJ	12	227.7	38.4
INFJ	15	98.0	20.0	INFJ	15	221.1	51.3
ISTP	2	91.5	29.0	ISFP	4	212.3	66.2
INTP	30	86.7	18.9	ESTP	1	199.0	0.0
ESTP	9	83.0	11.8	ESFP	1	193.0	0.0
	248	100.5	17.3		240	252.5	50.6

Source: From *Portraits of Type* (p. 146), by A. Thorne and H. Gough, 1991, Palo Alto, CA: Consulting Psychologists Press. Copyright 1991 by Consulting Psychologists Press. Used with permission.

Implications of Research on Health, Stress, and Coping with Stress

People often come for counseling and psychotherapy when they have difficulty coping with the stresses of everyday living and working, as well as in dealing with chronic illnesses. Does knowledge of the psychological type of a client help in understanding, assessing, and treating such stress-related complaints? It is reasonable to expect that different types will define, experience, and react to stress in type-consistent ways, may use different kinds of coping strategies in dealing with life problems, and may find different environments more and less hospitable to their natural typological characteristics. The review of research on health, stress, and coping provided by Shelton (1996) supports the differential experiences and responses of the 16 types and groupings of types in these important areas. Relevant results from this review are summarized in the research tables included in Chapter 4.

This section focuses specifically on research results obtained in studies of the 3,000 members of the national sample used to create MBTI Form M, and on recent research with a few other samples and measures that used Form M. The Appendix fully describes the samples used here.

Among other questions, participants in the national sample were asked whether they had ever had heart disease or hypertension, what they found stressful in life, what were their typical ways of coping with stress, and whether they believed in a higher spiritual power. The several previous studies that looked at type and heart disease, as summarized by Shelton (1996), found that across studies, Introverts are more than one and one-half times as frequent in coronary heart disease (CHD) groups than would be expected relative to their proportion in Myers' high school sample.[2] (See 1985 *Manual,* pp. 50–51.) Dominant introverted Sensing types (ISTJ and ISFJ) appear two to three times more frequently as well. Sensing types in general were found to be overrepresented in CHD studies, and SJ types in particular were overrepresented. It is important to note that all of the studies previously reported used subjects who had been diagnosed with CHD and/or were in treatment programs for their illness. Research with the national sample used self-report data from a representative sample that was not in any way selected for presence or absence of heart disease or hypertension. In addition, analyses of these data partialed out age, which could have an effect on results.

Table 10.5 shows the rank order of the 16 types as the percentage of each type who answered "Yes" to the question "Have you ever had heart disease or hypertension?" As shown, the four top-ranking types share a preference for both

Table 10.5	Rank Order of Types Who Answered "Yes" to Ever Having Heart Disease or Hypertension		
Type	**Percentage**	**Type**	**Percentage**
ISFP	27.4	ESTJ	19.4
ISTP	27.2	INTP	18.2
ISTJ	26.6	ENTJ	17.0
ISFJ	24.7	ESTP	15.5
ESFJ	21.8	ENFP	15.4
ESFP	21.0	INTJ	15.4
ENFJ	20.7	INFP	11.7
INFJ	20.4	ENTP	10.7

Note: N = 3,036. See Appendix for a description of the sample.

Source: National sample.

Introversion and Sensing, in agreement with the earlier findings cited above. Five of the top eight types prefer Introversion and three-quarters prefer Sensing. In addition, three-quarters of the top eight prefer Feeling over Thinking. In general, the rankings in this table are in accord with data that reveal specific over- and underrepresentations of types and two-letter combinations of preferences that were found in earlier research. For example, ENFP, INTJ, and INFP, who were underrepresented in the CHD groups in earlier research, occupy the 13th, 14th, and 15th ranks in Table 10.5.

The information in Table 10.5 should alert counselors and therapists to the probability that some types are more prone to develop hypertension or heart disease than others. To the extent that these conditions are a response to the stresses of living, finding ways to reduce stress and encourage effective coping strategies seems an appropriate goal.

With regard to stress, sample members were asked to rate their typical level of stress about work, finances, children, intimate relationship, school, health, caring for aging parents, balancing home and work, and "other." These areas were rated as "very high," "high," "moderate," "low," "very low," or "not applicable." Sample members overall rated all of the areas as moderately stressful, so the focus here is on the more extreme responses—those rating an area as extremely stressful and those rating the area as quite low as a source of stress.

Individual preference effects were studied using log linear comparisons of degree of reported stress for each stress category. The following significant differences were found: Introverts (I) were significantly higher than Extraverts (E) on work stress; types with a Sensing (S) preference were significantly higher than those preferring Intuition (N) on stress associated with health, care for aging parents, and balancing work and home; types who prefer Feeling (F) were significantly higher than those preferring Thinking (T) on the stress of finances, children, health, care for aging parents,

and balancing home and work; types with a Perceiving preference (P) were higher on stress associated with work; types who preferred Judging (J) reported higher stress on health and balancing work and home. Over and beyond these single-preference results, data for whole types suggest some interesting complexities that may be of interest to counselors and psychotherapists. Table 10.6 shows the top-ranked and bottom-ranked types in each stress category.

As can be seen, some areas appear to be particularly stressful for some types but provide minimal stress for others. INFJ is top ranked in four stress categories, and ENTP occupies the bottom rank on three of the nine categories. As an indication of which types appear to be more and less vulnerable to stress areas in general, Table 10.7 shows the number of times each type appears in either the top four "more stressed" group or the bottom four "less stressed" group.

This table suggests that Sensing Feeling types are particularly likely to rate a number of areas stressful and that this is true regardless of their preference for Extraversion or Introversion. Further, ESFPs are among the top ranked in high stress in seven areas, while their companion dominant extraverted Sensing type, ESTP, has no high-stress areas among the top four, and six areas where low stress is reported. Both INTJ and INTP report high stress in some areas and low stress in others, and INTJs are perhaps the most specific in their identification of high- and low-stress areas. The most clearly "less-stressed" types are ESTP, ENTP, and ENTJ; the most clearly stressed are ESFP, ISFJ, and INTP. It is also of note that of the "idealistic" NF types, who might be expected to be especially vulnerable to stress, only INFJs report numerous stress areas.

Although some types appear be more stressed in general than other types, what different types find particularly stressful and nonstressful probably involves a complex interaction among personality, the nature of the stress, and unknown other factors. Counselors and psychotherapists who have worked with clients of different types may find confirmation for their observations in some of these research results. These possible type-by-stressor relationships seem to suggest that the stresses of everyday life have different effects on different types and that some types are more naturally reactive to (or willing to acknowledge) stress than others. Counselors can take this into account when trying to assess the severity of their clients' responses. For example, an ENTP client who reports feeling very stressed in many areas may be of more concern to a therapist than an ISFJ client with the same complaints.

Research also supports the hypothesis that types cope with stress differently and with greater or lesser facility. Earlier work by Hammer (1992) using the *Coping Resources Inventory* revealed that different types reported different kinds of coping resources and also differed in access to coping resources in general. National sample members were asked how they "usually coped with stress" and could mark all the categories that applied. As shown in Table 10.8, a

Table 10.6   Types Reporting Highest and Lowest Mean Levels of Stress in Nine Categories

Category	Types Reporting Higher Stress				Types Reporting Lower Stress			
Work	INFJ	INFP	INTJ	ISTJ	ENTJ	ENFJ	ESFJ	ISFP
Finances	ISFP	ESFP	ENFP	INTJ	ENTJ	ISTP	ESTP	ESTJ
Children	ISFP	ESFP	ISFJ	INTP	ENTP	INTJ	ESTP	ENFP
Intimate relationship	INFJ	ESFP	INTJ	INTP	ENTP	ENFJ	ESTP	ENTJ
School	INFJ	ESFP	INTP	ISFJ	INTJ	ENFP	ENTJ	ESTJ
Health	ISFJ	ESFJ	ISFP	ESFP	ENTP	INTJ	ENTJ	INFP
Caring for aging parents	ISFJ	ESFP	ISFP	ESFJ	INTJ	ESTP	ENTP	INTP
Balancing home and work	ISFJ	INFJ	ESFJ	ENFJ	ISTP	ENTP	INTJ	ESTP
Other	INFJ	INTP	ISFP	ESFP	ENFP	ENTP	ENFJ	ESTP

Note: N = 3,036. Each category rated on a five-point scale; See Appendix for a description of the sample.

Source: National sample.

Table 10.7   Number of Times a Type Is Included in Highest and Lowest Categories

Type	High	Low	Type	High	Low
ISTJ	1	0	ISTP	0	2
ISFJ	5	0	INTP	4	1
ESTP	0	6	ESTJ	0	2
ESFP	7	0	ENTJ	0	5
INTJ	3	5	ISFP	5	1
INFJ	5	0	INFP	1	1
ENTP	0	6	ESFJ	3	1
ENFP	1	3	ENFJ	1	3

Note: N = 3,036. See Appendix for a description of the sample.

Source: National sample.

wide variety of ways of coping with stress were studied. The table shows the top-ranked and bottom-ranked types for each coping method. A comparison of the percentages across categories indicates the relative popularity of different coping methods across types, with "try to think of options" being frequently chosen by all types, and "talk to professional" and "develop physical symptoms" chosen relatively infrequently. Perhaps this latter observation reflects the general percentage of the U.S. population who seek the services of mental health professionals and physicians for perceived stress-stimulated problems.

Although belief in a higher spiritual power is not necessarily related to differential coping with stress, therapists may find it useful to understand their clients' approach to spirituality in order to incorporate this into the therapeutic process. Table 10.9 shows, as might be expected, that the types answered the question "Do you believe in a higher spiritual power?" quite differently. The choices permitted were "yes," "no," and "not sure."

Every type predominantly answered "yes" to this question, as is apparent from the percentages for the "no" and "not sure" categories for the types listed. For example, 64.4% of the INTJ respondents answered "yes," though their percentage of "yes" responses was lowest of all the types. As shown, the four top-ranked types saying "no" or "not sure" all have a preference for Thinking, and with the exception of ISTPs they all prefer Intuition as well. All four top-ranked types saying "yes" prefer Feeling, and three-quarters prefer Extraversion and Judging as well. The clear T–F difference in responding to this question is in accord with the critical approach of Thinking types and the harmony-seeking desire of Feeling types. Therapists might take these natural differences into account in expecting or encouraging different types to use spiritual resources as a way of coping or as a source of satisfaction.

Job burnout as a response to stress has been productively studied using the MBTI instrument, particularly in Garden's 1985 and 1988 research as reviewed in Shelton (1996). Garden found that responses to burnout differed when samples of types who primarily preferred Thinking over Feeling were studied. Specifically, she found that people with a

Table 10.8   Top and Bottom Ranking Types in Methods of Coping with Stress

Coping Method	Highest		Lowest		Coping Method	Highest		Lowest	
Try to avoid	ISFP	59.8	ENTP	26.0	Get upset or angry but	ISFP	36.1	ENTJ	16.7
stressful situations	ESFP	54.5	ENTJ	33.3	don't show it	INFP	34.9	ESTP	20.3
	ESFJ	53.3	ENFP	34.4		ISFJ	34.5	ENFJ	20.7
	ISFJ	53.3	ESTJ	35.2		INTP	34.3	ESTJ	21.1
Confront the problem	ENTP	79.8	ISFP	35.7	Get upset or angry	ISTP	42.9	ENTJ	18.8
	ENTJ	79.2	ISFJ	41.0	and show it	ISFP	39.1	ESTJ	27.7
	ESTJ	73.8	INFP	41.8		ESFP	38.3	INTJ	27.7
	ENFJ	68.3	INFJ	44.9		ENFJ	36.6	INTP	29.3
Talk to someone close	ESFJ	74.1	ISTP	39.0	Develop physical symptoms	ENFP	21.1	ESTP	5.9
	ENFJ	72.0	INTP	45.5		INFJ	20.4	ENTP	7.7
	ESFP	71.1	ISTJ	45.6		ENFJ	19.5	ISTP	7.8
	INFP	63.7	ESTP	45.8		ISFP	16.9	ESTJ	8.6
Talk to professional	INFJ	24.5	ISTP	3.2	Sleep	ISFP	23.3	ESTJ	14.1
	INTJ	16.9	ENTP	6.7		INTJ	23.1	ESTP	15.3
	ENFP	10.9	ESTP	7.6		ESFP	20.6	ENTP	15.4
	INFP	10.3	ESTJ	7.8		ISFJ	20.2	INTP	17.2
Rely on religious beliefs	ESFJ	55.5	INTP	20.2	Exercise	ENFJ	40.2	ISTP	13.0
	INFJ	53.1	ENTP	20.2		ENTJ	35.4	ISFP	16.2
	ENFJ	50.0	INTJ	24.6		ENTP	34.6	ESFP	17.8
	ISFJ	49.4	ENTJ	25.0		INTJ	30.8	ISFJ	20.9
Try to think of options	ENTJ	87.5	ISFP	54.5	Watch television	ISFP	40.6	INTJ	15.4
	INTP	80.8	ISFJ	56.2		ESFP	33.2	ESTP	18.6
	ENTP	79.8	ESFP	62.5		ISTP	31.2	ENFP	20.6
	INTJ	76.9	INFJ	63.3		ISFJ	31.1	ENFJ	20.7

Note: Respondents could mark as many as applied; *p* values for all 2 x 16 chi-squares were significant at .000 to .027 except for "Sleep" category.
See Appendix for a description of the sample.

Source: National sample.

Thinking preference were more likely to seek people out rather than avoid them, as has typically been found for samples drawn from the helping professions, which tend to attract a large proportion of types who prefer Feeling.

The *Maslach Burnout Inventory* (MBI; Maslach, Jackson, & Leiter, 1996) measures the effects of job burnout on individuals. It contains three subscales: Emotional Exhaustion—the depletion of emotional energy, as distinct from physical or mental fatigue; Depersonalization—a response to work that requires personal sensitivity to clients; and Personal Accomplishment—an emphasis on one's effectiveness and success in bringing benefit to clients. The MBI and MBTI Form M were administered to a sample of 82 employees at a large hospital. Table 10.10 shows the mean scores for the three top- and bottom-ranking types for the three MBI scales. Note the apparent vulnerability to "Emotional Exhaustion" and "Depersonalization" forms of burnout of the ISFPs and ISFJs, which is similar to their stress responses as shown in Tables 10.7 and 10.8.

Given the quite small sample size, it is not surprising that nonsignificant results were obtained for an analysis of

Table 10.9   Top-Ranked Types Rating "No," "Not Sure," or "Yes" Regarding Belief in a Higher Spiritual Power

No		Not Sure		Yes	
INTJ	23.1 %	ISTP	19.2 %	ENFJ	91.4 %
ENTJ	14.6 %	INTP	16.2 %	ESFJ	90.2 %
INTP	11.1 %	ENTP	14.6 %	ENFP	89.8 %
ISTP	9.9 %	ENTJ	14.6 %	ISFJ	89.7 %

Note: N = 3,036. See Appendix for a description of the sample.
Source: National sample.

variance using all 16 types and the three MBI scales. However, the same statistic applied to each dichotomy separately yielded significant F values for E–I on "Emotional Exhaustion" ($F = 8.608$, $p = .004$), with Introverts having the higher mean, and "Depersonalization" ($F = 4.146$, $p = .045$), again with Introverts having the higher mean scores. These

0.10   Types with Highest and Lowest Mean Scores on Burnout Scales

l Exhaustion		Depersonalization			Personal Accomplishment	
Low		High	Low		High	Low
ENTJ 11.67		ISFP 11.00	ENTP 2.67		ESTP 46.00	ESTJ 29.00
ESFP 12.00		ISFJ 10.20	ESFP 2.75		ENTP 43.33	ENTJ 33.33
ESTP 14.00		INTJ 8.25	ESTP 3.00		ENFJ 39.83	INTJ 34.75
ENTP 15.33		ISTJ 7.81	ENFJ 5.17		ESFP 39.50	INTP 35.25

ee Appendix for a description of the sample.

Health Services.

0.11   Mean Scores of Highest and Lowest Types on Positive and Negative Affectivity

Affectivity		Negative Affectivity	
	Lowest	Highest	Lowest
ESTP 41.00	ISTP 28.79	INFP 26.60	ENTJ 18.60
ENTJ 40.20	INFJ 29.83	INTJ 20.60	INTJ 20.60
ENFJ 37.75	INFP 30.56	ISFJ 24.97	INFJ 20.67
ESTJ 37.35	INTP 31.00	ISTJ 24.29	ENFJ 20.87

Note: N = 279. See Appendix for a description of the sample.

Source: Iowa State University.

results are in accord with the differential availability of "extraverting energy" of Extraverts and Introverts. Based on these data, however, one's sense of effectiveness appears to be unrelated to energy preference. Analyses for the other three dichotomies did not yield significant results on any of the MBI scales. Studies with larger, more heterogeneous samples may produce more specific results by whole types and groupings of type.

Another study that used Form M explored the *Positive and Negative Affectivity Scales* (Watson, Clark, & Tellegen, 1988) in relation to type. Positive affectivity reflects feelings of happiness, enthusiasm, interest, and inspiration and a general lack of anxiety. Negative affectivity reflects anxiety, fear, distress, and distractedness. A sample of 279 college students at a large Midwestern university were asked to rate their feelings in these areas "during the last three weeks" on a five-point scale varying from "very slightly" to "extremely." Table 10.11 shows the mean scores of the four highest and four lowest types on the two scales.

Analysis of variance of positive and negative affectivity data showed a significant F value ($F = 2.0$, $p = .000$) for positive affectivity, most likely reflecting the tendency of the Extraverted types to score higher than Introverted types, with the possible exception of INTJs. The same statistical procedure for negative affectivity yielded insignificant results. As

suggested in Table 10.11, types in the highest and lowest categories are somewhat inconsistent, and mean differences of high and low groups do not appear to be substantially different. In general, then, these data suggest that although positive affect is more likely to be acknowledged by types who prefer Extraversion, the reporting of negative affect does not differentiate between Extraverted and Introverted types.

Using Type with Different Age Groups

Regardless of whether an assessment tool is used to elicit type, awareness of the reality of type differences is helpful to clinicians who work with clients in all age groups. The breadth of application lends credence to the notion that typology serves as a basic template that influences and interacts with many other factors in an individual's personality. Counselors and psychotherapists are therefore likely to note type influence with clients of any age and who present a wide variety of psychological and emotional problems. This section is designed to advise practitioners and alert them to some of the relevant issues in using type with different age groups.

Issues with Child Clients

Type is most effectively assessed in children using the *Murphy-Meisgeier Type Indicator for Children* (MMTIC), which differs from the MBTI in content, construction, and scoring. For information on type assessment in children, see the manual for this instrument (Meisgeier & Murphy, 1987). Professionals in this area generally advise caution in specifying a type for young and preadolescent children, as there may be wide variations in the developmental process for individual children. Nevertheless, counselors and therapists who treat young children often find that the hypothesized type of a child may be related to the child's presenting problems. For example, some ESTP and ESFP children may be referred for various behavioral disorders, hyperactivity, or attention deficit disorder when in fact the behaviors that stimulated the referral may be well within what is expected for young Extraverted Sensing types, whose natural style is very active, interactive, experiential, and experimental. Awareness of the possible influence of type differences can therefore aid mental health professionals in the diagnostic process. For additional information on the relevance of type in assessing and counseling children, see Murphy (1992, 1997).

Issues with Adolescent Clients

Regardless of the presenting issues that bring adolescent clients to a mental health professional, administration and interpretation of the MBTI can provide immense relief and affirmation for young people who are questioning their acceptability as individuals and members of important peer groups. For example, a 15-year-old INTP who is ambivalent about "fitting in" with her peers can be assured of the reasonable and natural basis for her ambivalence; an ENFP who has been persistently criticized for procrastinating can feel validated by his type description and then encouraged to "go against his grain" by adopting some strategies for meeting deadlines; an INFJ can be reassured that her uncanny knack for knowing the unspoken thoughts and feelings of others is shared by other people of her type; an ESTJ can gain insight into why his friends sometimes are irritated by his attempts to be helpful in group situations.

Psychological type develops over the lifespan. Young people are expected to be less clear about their preferences than mature people, as is evident in the lower reliabilities found when the MBTI is administered to younger groups (see Chapter 8). Some adolescents may have difficulty identifying a best-fit type because of this as well as because their expression of type may be influenced by pressures to "fit in" with the group. Determining a preference for Extraversion or Introversion can be most affected by this. Counselors and therapists who use the MBTI inventory with adolescents should be prepared for questions and doubts from some clients. Other adolescent clients may readily verify a type that fits them well. It is important to convey to unsure clients that this is natural, normal, and predictable and that it is not necessary or important for the client to settle on a type at this stage of life. The counselor can use the client's type information to validate, reassure, and help the adolescent cope with stresses and pressures and better prepare for the future.

Issues with Middle-Aged and Older Clients

As discussed in Chapter 3, Jung's theory predicts differential use and development of type in the second half of life, with greater energy being devoted to exercising the tertiary and inferior functions. There is wide variation in ways of recognizing and expressing less developed functions during midlife and into old age. Many individuals "mellow" into old age, gradually shifting energy and focus from the dominant and auxiliary functions by adding interest in the tertiary and inferior functions. For others, the shift may be more sudden, extreme, and disruptive. These latter older clients are more likely to seek help than those for whom the process is mild and gradual. One can interpret the behavior of many clients who come to therapy with an apparent midlife crisis as the midlife emergence of the third and fourth functions. Clients in this situation may report loss of interest and meaning in what has heretofore been exciting and important, a feeling of being invaded by alien and uncontrollable thoughts and feelings, and a distressing loss of a sense of self. In the most dramatic cases, the individual may leave spouse and family to take up a new partner, or a successful career may become so unsatisfying that the person leaves it to do something entirely different. Therapists sensitive to the characteristics of the inferior function can often interpret the client's experiences in these terms and explore the developmental nature and meaningfulness of these often quite puzzling and distressing experiences. Understanding the meaning and importance of what is happening to them sometimes enables clients to proceed in their development without making major changes in their own and others' lives. For information on the dynamics and development of midlife and older people, see Corlett and Millner (1993), Quenk (1993), and Millner (1998).

Using Type with Couples

Happy and unhappy marriages are found in all type combinations, and type differences and similarities are likely to be only one of several sources of difficulty in a relationship. Regardless of the nature of such other difficulties, a typological approach to couples counseling can enhance the therapeutic process and increase the likelihood of an effective outcome.

Focusing on natural type differences early in the counseling process can be the "neutral ground" that enhances rapport, reassures the couple that the therapist is not likely to "take sides," and provides a nonjudgmental language for discussing sources of irritation and misunderstanding. When interpreting results of the MBTI to a couple, it is useful to let partners guess their preferences as they are discussed and to compare these with the answers given on the Indicator. Both partners can be asked to comment on the accuracy of type descriptions in describing both themselves and their partner and to discuss type characteristics as they affect their relationship.

When couples take the type Indicator "for each other"— that is, when they answer the questions the way they think the partner would (see the section on administration and interpretation later in this chapter)—the therapist can identify probable issues in the couple's difficulties. Particular counseling issues are indicated when couple members recognize that they are different from each other and accurately

Table 10.12   Mutual Usefulness of Opposite Types

Intuitive Types Can Benefit from the Natural Inclination of Sensing Types to	**Sensing Types Can Benefit from the Natural Inclination of Intuitive Types to**
Bring up pertinent facts	Bring up new possibilities
Face the realities of the current situation	Anticipate future trends
Apply experience to solving problems	Apply insight to solving problems
Focus on what needs attention now	Focus on long-term goals

Feeling Types Can Benefit from the Natural Inclination of Thinking Types to	**Thinking Types Can Benefit from the Natural Inclination of Feeling Types to**
Analyze consequences and implications	Forecast how others will react and feel
Hold consistently to a policy	Make needed individual exceptions
Stand firm for important principles	Stand firm for human-centered values
Create rational systems	Organize people and tasks harmoniously
Be fair	Appreciate the Thinking type along with everyone else

Source: From *Introduction to Type* (6th ed., p. 30), by I. B. Myers, 1998, Palo Alto, CA: Consulting Psychologists Press. Copyright 1998 by Consulting Psychologists Press. Used with permission.

assess the nature of their differences by answering the MBTI "correctly" for each other. For such a couple, a typological explanation of the differences they already recognize in each other can be therapeutic. Rather than attributing differences to the partner's "annoying habits," "hang-ups," or "incompetence," the couple can learn to appreciate the nature and reality of their differences as legitimate and interesting.

The task of counseling is very different when the couple believe they are both the same or similar in type (therefore answering for each other "inaccurately"), when in fact they are quite different. When a person believes the partner to be a different type from what he or she actually is, the misperceived partner's communications and behavior are likely to be misunderstood. The misperceiving partner may have a distorted notion of the other's needs and motives. For example, an ENTP husband answered the Indicator for his wife as if she were an ENFP, but she verified her type as ESFJ. Her major complaint in the marriage was that she felt discounted, ignored, and misunderstood by her husband. It became evident during counseling that he did not recognize her central desire for harmony and togetherness. Instead, he assumed that what she really wanted was more freedom to pursue her many interests without interference from him. He was genuinely puzzled when she told him how bad she felt. In another couple, the INFJ husband and his ESFP wife both saw each other as ISTJs; they later recognized that both of their fathers were probably ISTJs. The partners thus projected an exaggerated and distorted ISTJ

personality on each other, each seeing the other as demanding, critical, and controlling. These and similar kinds of discrepancies in the ways couples answer the MBTI for each other can often reveal the nature of the couple's expectations of and projections onto each other.

Differences Related to Each of the Four Dichotomies

Counseling issues vary considerably with the type mix of the couple. Sharing the perspective on the mutual usefulness of opposite types, as shown in Table 10.12 and in *Introduction to Type* (Myers, with Kirby & Myers, 1998), can be a focal point for the couple to gain insight into the validity of their differences and the positive nature of each other's contribution to the relationship. In addition, the following suggest issues and approaches to differences in each of the type dichotomies.

E–I Differences   Issues of sociability (Extraversion) and privacy (Introversion) need to be resolved for couples who differ on this dichotomy. The Extravert needs to have sufficient external stimulation and the Introvert needs sufficient time alone. A first step is getting each partner to recognize the legitimate but different energy needs of the other partner. Such recognition is difficult when either partner is Introverted and expends his or her finite Extraverted energy during the work day. Little Extraverted energy may be left for talking and interacting with the partner or for socializing with others in the evening. An effective recommendation is for the Introvert to have a period of time alone soon after coming home. The couple's agreement to the legitimacy of such brief "alone time" can prove restorative and enable the Introvert to be responsive and sociable.

Couples who differ on Extraversion–Introversion may also have a problem communicating, since the Extraverted partner is more likely to reach decisions by talking them out and getting feedback, while the Introverted partner is more likely to process issues internally, sharing only the final conclusion. This difference leaves the Extraverted partner feeling excluded from an important source of satisfaction—mutual sharing. The Introverted partner may experience the Extraverted partner's insistence on joint problem solving as intrusive and controlling. Explaining their different approaches to processing and sharing information can encourage them to modify their mutual misperception.

S–N Differences   When a couple differs on Sensing and Intuition, misunderstandings can occur because the two people often look at the same event very differently. It is important that they define terms carefully. Intuitive type partners with rapid insights can make Sensing type partners feel slow and mundane. Sensing type partners with a solid sense of reality can cause Intuitive partners to feel impractical and unobservant. Differences of this nature can often be expressed as categorical accusations. A careful explanation of their very different processes of gathering and trusting information can help the couple understand and accept the reality of their differences. The counselor can encourage them to verify their understanding of each other by asking clarifying questions and accepting the answers as valid reflections of the partner's state of mind.

T–F Differences   When a couple differs in Thinking and Feeling, decision-making issues can be a source of difficulty, since one partner will favor a logical, objective approach to arrive at truth and the other will value a personal, subjective approach to arrive at harmony. Thinking types can become irritated when Feeling types appear to ignore the logic of a situation and come to a conclusion that seems illogical; Feeling types often accuse Thinking type partners of being cold, uncaring, and hypercritical. Such misperceptions occur regardless of gender, although gender stereotypes add an additional stressor when addressing Thinking–Feeling differences in relationships.

Differences on this dichotomy are subject to definitional misunderstandings as well as gender stereotypes. Thinking is often confused with intellectual competence and lack of emotion; Feeling is confused with intellectual fuzziness and excessive emotionality. Thinking is assumed to be the special province of men, Feeling of women. Thus when the male prefers Thinking and the female Feeling, there is conformity to what is expected. However, this conformity can encourage both the couple and unaware therapists to assume that gender accounts for what are primarily Thinking–Feeling differences. Research supporting clinical observation regarding type and gender differences can be found in Otis and Quenk (1989) and Demarest (1997). When the male is the Feeling type and the female the Thinking type, confusion and misunderstandings arise because neither partner conforms to expectations. There may be accusations that the woman is unfeminine and the man lacks masculine traits. Helping couples distinguish between genuine gender influences and Thinking–Feeling differences is often a very fruitful therapeutic intervention.

Thinking types can improve relationships by voicing appreciation *before* giving criticism and by making critical comments only when necessary, rather than as a natural, automatic response to the partner and the world at large. Feeling types can improve relationships by stating their wishes clearly, so that the Thinking type does not have to guess about their needs and desires. Feeling types can also avoid having hurt feelings by learning to differentiate between intended critical assessments and comments that sound like personal criticism but are merely impersonal observations from the viewpoint of their Thinking type partner. Couples therapists can be especially helpful by using their type knowledge to "translate" the Thinking language of one partner into the Feeling language of the other, and vice versa. Such "type translations" were first incorporated into psychotherapy by Jung himself. As described by one of his biographers, Barbara Hannah (1976), "[A]fter he had written *Psychological Types* and had considerably more experience of people, Jung was able to speak the 'language' of every type. Just as he took a lot of trouble to learn the languages of his patients (English, French, and so on), so he learned to put things into the language of the psychological type to whom he was talking" (p. 132).

J–P Differences   Issues of order, territory, and lifestyle are typically associated with the Judging–Perceiving dichotomy. Order in the surroundings is often more important to the Judging partner; spontaneity and freedom are more important to the Perceiving partner. How much advance planning is necessary or comfortable for each partner may also be an issue. As a counseling technique, the practitioner might have the couple discuss how they have planned for vacations and what each believes to be the issues in vacation planning. This exercise can be enlightening to couples. Disagreements are also likely to arise about how much data should be collected before making important decisions and taking action. The Perceiving type partner may wish to do an exhaustive search of all the available alternatives before purchasing a new piece of furniture, while the Judging type partner may be ready to decide after seeing only a few items. A counselor can encourage forbearance of each other's styles and suggest ways to compromise to achieve relative comfort for both partners about the timing of decisions.

Table 10.13   Attraction Ratios (AR) for Men and Women Married to Opposite and Like Types

Type of Woman	AR When Married to the Opposite Type	AR When Married to the Same Type	Type of Man	AR When Married to the Opposite Type	AR When Married to the Same Type
ISTJ	0.56	0.53	ISTJ	1.39	0.36
ISTP	0.00	0.00	ISTP	0.00	0.00
ESTP	0.00	0.00	ESTP	3.03	0.00
ESTJ	0.91	0.97	ESTJ	6.06	1.14
ISFJ	0.60	1.49	ISFJ	0.00	1.15
ISFP	0.00	2.17	ISFP	0.00	0.46
ESFP	0.00	4.55	ESFP	0.00	1.67
ESFJ	0.23	3.23	ESFJ	0.00	1.33
INFJ	0.78	6.25	INFJ	0.00	4.17
INFP	1.19	1.67	INFP	0.66	5.26
ENFP	1.28	1.52	ENFP	0.28	1.23
ENFJ	0.00	8.33	ENFJ	0.00	4.76
INTJ	0.00	2.22	INTJ	0.00	3.85
INTP	0.00	3.57	INTP	0.56	4.17
ENTP	0.00	0.00	ENTP	1.23	0.00
ENTJ	0.00	0.00	ENTJ	0.00	0.00

Source: From "Attraction, Satisfaction, and Psychological Types of Couples," by N. S. Marioles, D. P. Strickert, and A. L. Hammer, 1996, *Journal of Psychological Type,* 36, p. 21. Copyright 1996 by *Journal of Psychological Type.* Used with permission.

Type Dynamics in Couples Therapy

The influence of type dynamics (described earlier) is even greater when working with couples than when working with individual clients. Intimate relationships provide a fertile ground for projection of unconscious processes. For example, an INFP–ENTJ couple embody each other's inferior functions. In the normal demands and stresses of everyday life, the INFP husband may easily perceive his ENTJ wife as critical, judgmental, and disapproving, projecting his own inferior extraverted Thinking onto the wife, who is an appropriate "host" for this projection. Similarly, the ENTJ wife can respond by feeling intensely hurt, unloved, and rejected, projecting her own inferior introverted Feeling onto her husband. Couples counselors who are sensitive to these and similar dynamic interactions can help the two people understand their own and each other's often exaggerated reactions. Such awareness can promote mutual acceptance and enhance the intimacy in the relationship.

Couples who share the same type can also face difficulties in relating to each other and to others. Because they share the same blind spots, both may inadvertently neglect important aspects of daily living and avoid incorporating unfamiliar but important alternative perspectives into their lives. A therapist working with such a couple can point out the inevitability of the "missing" points of view in their lives and help them come up with ways of broadening the scope of their activities in useful ways. Another way that like-type couples sometimes handle mutually unappealing tasks is for one partner to take on the responsibility for some of the disliked areas. The reluctantly responsible partner may become resentful and irritable, especially if such efforts go unrecognized or are criticized by the other person. A couples therapist can reduce the strain this causes in the relationship by helping the couple recognize and acknowledge their mutual distastes. They may then be able to divide those tasks more equitably, or at the very least express appreciation to the person who voluntarily "goes against her or his grain."

Research on Type and Couples

Couples often ask how common it is to marry their own type or an opposite type. The 1985 *MBTI Manual* compared data from two samples of couples—Myers with Myers (1980/1995, p. 128) and a sample consisting of combined data from the databank of the Center for Applications of Psychological Type (CAPT). Those data as well as more recent research (Marioles, Strickert, Babcock, Campbell, & Cortner, 1997; Marioles, Strickert, & Hammer, 1996; Sherman, 1981) indicate that people tend to marry similar rather than dissimilar types. For example, Marioles, Strickert, and Hammer (1996) calculated attraction ratios for men and women married to opposite and like types, where higher ratios indicate greater attraction and lower ratios less attraction. Table 10.13 shows the attraction ratios calculated for each type within each gender. The attraction ratio is the percentage of people of one type who marry a person of another type divided by the percentage of that type in the base population. Higher attraction ratios mean that the pairing occurs more frequently than would be expected relative to its occurrence in the base population. Only in three notable instances (ESTJ men married to INFP women, ESTP men married to INFJ women, and ENTP men married to ISFJ women) is there any evidence of opposite types being attracted to each other. Other pairings reflect greater evidence of type similarity.

Marioles et al. (1996) also looked at type and a measure of satisfaction based on self-assessment of the relationship as "very dissatisfied" and "somewhat dissatisfied" (combined) compared with "somewhat satisfied" and "very satisfied" (combined). In examining rankings by the percentage of relationships in which both partners were satisfied, no type-related pattern was found for women. However, the same analysis for men showed a statistically significant higher percentage of male Extraverts in relationships in which both partners were satisfied. It was further observed that INTP men had by far the lowest percentage of relationships in which both partners were satisfied (only 33%), although INTP men themselves reported being satisfied with their relationship. This result led to the development of an obliviousness index—the difference between the percentage of one type who say they are satisfied and the percentage of the same type in the relationships in which both partners are satisfied. The authors hypothesized that the greater the difference in the couple's satisfaction levels, the more "oblivious" is the partner with the higher satisfaction rating. Table 10.14 shows the obliviousness indexes for each type separately by gender. It is interesting to note that INTP men have the highest index of all the types, regardless of gender (33%). ENFJs are highest among female types (13%), though at a much lower percentage than male INTPs.

Another source of data on marital satisfaction comes from the national sample. Subjects in this sample were asked to rate their satisfaction with their marriage or intimate relationship using the same four-point scale as that used in the Marioles et al. (1996) study. The national sample data were analyzed by type but not by gender. Partner satisfaction was not assessed in the national sample study. The two sets of data, therefore, cannot be compared. In addition to rating satisfaction with marriage, subjects in this study were also asked to rate their satisfaction with their friendships and their relationships with family members. Figure 10.1 shows the results for all 16 types in their ratings of the three areas of relationship satisfaction. It is important to note that types who are satisfied or dissatisfied in one relationship area tend to rate the other areas in the same way as well. Perhaps "relationship satisfaction" is a generalized phenomenon that reflects the possibility that different types use different definitions of or criteria for satisfaction. The observation that, in general, types who prefer Extraversion are more satisfied than types who prefer Introversion would tend to support such a conjecture. Introverts may have greater discomfort with and/or "idealized" expectations of relationships in comparison with Extraverts, whose comfort in and greater ease with others may be in operation.

Table 10.14 The Obliviousness Index

Type of Satisfied Person	Percentage of Men of This Type Who Are Satisfied, Whereas the Woman Is Not	Percentage of Women of This Type Who Are Satisfied, Whereas the Man Is Not
ISTJ	16%	7%
ISTP	0%	0%
ESTP	9%	0%
ESTJ	12%	9%
ISFJ	14%	10%
ISFP	22%	4%
ESFP	21%	5%
ESFJ	10%	8%
INFJ	31%	0%
INFP	11%	0%
ENFP	7%	12%
ENFJ	10%	13%
INTJ	0%	11%
INTP	33%	0%
ENTP	11%	11%
ENTJ	19%	0%

Source: From "Attraction, Satisfaction, and Psychological Types of Couples," by N. S. Marioles, D. P. Strickert, and A. L. Hammer, 1996, *Journal of Psychological Type, 36,* p. 24. Copyright 1996 by *Journal of Psychological Type.* Used with permission.

With regard to satisfaction with marriage/initiate relationship, Figure 10.1 shows INFJ, INFP, and INTP types to be the most dissatisfied and ENFJ, ESFP, and ESFJ types to be the most satisfied. INTJ types seem particularly dissatisfied with friendships and relatively more satisfied with their family relationships.

Empirical studies that assess the use of type by therapists in conducting couples therapy are not available. However, the large-scale and multifaceted research of Marioles, Hammer, and their colleagues provides relevant results on attraction, satisfaction, persistence of relationships, and associated variables. For example, their research indicated that the two male types who tended to marry their opposites were ESTJs and ISTJs, and that these two types had also been married most often. Clinical observation and experience seem to support this in that ISTJ–ENFP couples (regardless of gender mix) seem to seek therapy more often than other opposite combinations. However, ESTJ–INFP couples appear relatively infrequently for couples counseling. Perhaps this particular opposite type mix promotes the kind of stability and division of roles and responsibilities that is satisfying for both partners. Another clinical observation is that ISTJ and ESTJ male clients whose wives have initiated a divorce seem to have greater difficulty than other types in adjusting to being single, tend to remarry relatively quickly, and often have several marriages in their history.

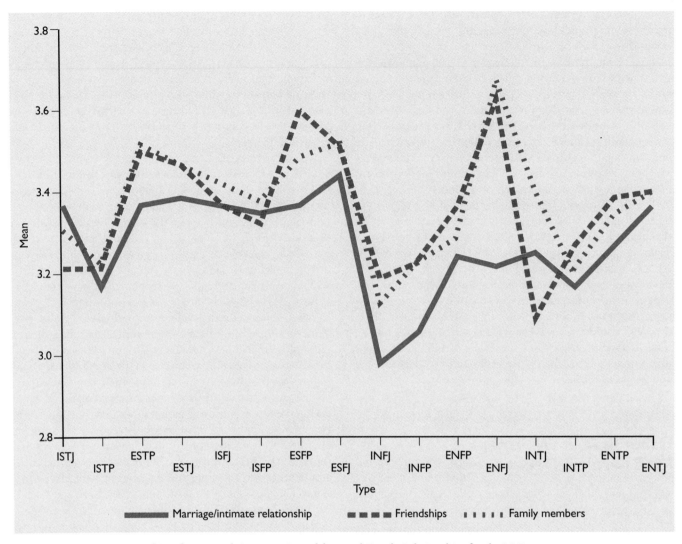

Figure 10.1 Mean Ratings of Satisfaction with Intimate, Friendship, and Family Relationships for the 16 Types

The Marioles-Hammer research project provides insights for couples therapists and reports results about whole type, in addition to differences on the four individual type dichotomies. These ongoing studies also use MBTI Form J and therefore provide information about the 27 subscales scored by that form.

Using Type with Families

Type concepts can be useful in family counseling. The type distribution of the family provides a language for talking about alliances, difficulties in communication, allocation of household tasks, differences over child rearing, and children's career plans.

When working with families, it is particularly relevant to discuss the value of type differences. Any relationship suffers if the oppositeness of preference is treated as an inferiority.

The parent-child relationship suffers severely if a parent tries to make a child into a carbon copy of him- or herself. It is hard on children to find that a parent wishes they were something they definitely are not. Children who are Feeling types may try to distort their type in the desired direction; Thinking types may resist their parent's expectations with hostility. Neither reaction repairs the damage done to the child's self-confidence.

The Judging–Perceiving dichotomy can be important in child-parent relationships. For example, a parent describing a child's behavior in a Judging manner can be shown that his or her every description is full of judgments ("This is wrong." "He shouldn't have done that." "I made a mistake."). Practice in the Perceiving attitude can lead to statements such as, "Why did it look like that to him?" "I wonder if he did it because . . . ?" The essence of the Perceiving attitude is that a topic opens up new questions and creates curiosity for learning more about a situation. Judgment closes the issue; perception opens it up for new discoveries.

Many Judging types benefit from learning to stay longer in the Perceiving mode; many Perceiving types benefit from learning to come to closure.

It can be helpful for the counselor to give parents a perspective on how parenting differs based on the type of the child. It is easier for an orderly, practical Sensing Judging parent to raise a Sensing Judging child who has a desire to conform to structure than it is for that parent to rear an independent Intuitive Perceiving child who finds structure and consistency anathema. Understanding type differences can reduce guilt in the relationship and promote problem solving on the part of both parent and child.

Family therapists report that understanding type often helps all family members modify their perceptions about the meaning and motives behind each other's behaviors. The therapist can suggest ways for family members to better explain themselves and more accurately assess the meaning of each other's communications. Suggestions relevant to using type in families can be found in Meisgeier and Meisgeier (1989) and in Murphy (1992). Ginn (1995) describes the distinct ways in which each of the types functions as a member of a family; the way that type influences different ways of mothering is presented in work by Penley and Stephens (1994).

Using Type in Treatment for Chemical Dependency

It is advisable that a respondent be drug-free for at least 30 days prior to MBTI administration, or that the MBTI be administered at least 30 days after admission to the treatment program, as earlier administration is likely to yield unreliable results and may elicit a client's attempt at coping, albeit unsuccessfully. Chemical- and alcohol-impaired clients are also likely to have a high frequency of low preference clarity indexes when the MBTI is administered during active drug use. When entry into a treatment program is not voluntary and/or a client denies any abuse, inquiry should be made into the client's chemical use pattern during the preceding 30 days, to determine when the MBTI is best administered.

Experienced counselors advise interpreting the MBTI inventory with caution, even after a 30-day drug-free period. As compared with general clients, those with addiction histories may agree too readily with their reported type without carefully assessing its best fit. Such clients can be encouraged to focus on the parts of their description that seem to fit well as a vehicle for helping the counselor in treatment planning. Preliminary analysis of data collected on 500 male and female clients in an alcohol and drug addiction treatment program supports the use of caution in administration and interpretation. The MBTI was administered 30 days after admission and again six months later to these clients. Approximately 80% of them changed on at least one preference on retest, with less

than 20% retaining the same preferences the whole time. These investigators found that clients nearly always reported that their "changed" type was the best fit for them, often describing their earlier type as depicting their way of behaving while addicted. Many clients expressed relief at their newfound freedom to be themselves. However, they also reported that their families and friends showed some difficulty in accepting them in their newly emerged state (Shuck & Manfrin, 1997).

When attempting to determine best-fit type, therapists should be sensitive to such factors as age of onset of drug use. Arrested development of personality can be a consequence of early age of onset of addiction; doubts about type may be present, and helping the client identify his or her natural type may be a gradual and difficult process. Clients with early onset of addiction as well as those with codependency issues may "adopt" the type of the therapist, thus adding to their difficulty in recognizing who they are. Counselors who incorporate their knowledge of type in treating chemically dependent individuals attest that its value lies in helping them better understand their client's psychological makeup and enabling them to tailor interventions to the verified or hypothesized type of the client. Counselors also find it profitable to tailor their language to the client's strengths, as a way of encouraging collaboration in and cooperation with a treatment plan. In one treatment facility where type was routinely collected for both clients and therapists, an attempt was made to "match" clients and therapists in therapy groups. Clients whose types included a preference for Thinking and/or Judging were placed in a group cofacilitated by an INTJ and an ISFJ therapist. Feeling type clients were placed in a group co-led by an INFP and an ENFP, and a Sensing Perceiving therapist requested and was given a group made up of acting-out adolescents. An unusually low dropout rate was found for all three groups. Of particular note was that clients who were mandated to be in treatment voluntarily remained in group treatment longer than was required—a phenomenon that occurred rarely if ever prior to client-therapist "matching" (Shuck & Manfrin, 1997).

Research with addictive populations shows some consistency in finding a preference for Introversion among those who seek treatment for chemical dependency, though generalizing this result to addicted individuals who do not seek treatment is not warranted. For a review of studies of type and chemical dependency, see Quenk and Quenk (1996).

Summary of Clinical Research

This section summarizes the research presented in the 1985 *MBTI Manual* and briefly comments on studies included in the more recent *MBTI Applications* (see Quenk & Quenk, 1996), which covers research available since the manual's publication. Readers are referred to the latter publication for authors, titles, and details of the study results summarized here. The section is organized into major research topics.

Providers and Users of Psychological Services

Type theory can illuminate many of the personality and behavior differences among providers of psychological services, and it raises issues about the delivery of health care. All 16 types are represented by providers of psychological services, and all 16 types become clients, but the distributions of both differ from the general population. In theory, helping people through psychological methods requires more Intuitive than Sensing skills, since Intuition is concerned with perception of patterns, recognition of inferred meanings, and intangible relationships. In a study by Newman (1979), Intuitive types scored significantly higher than Sensing types on ability to identify implied meanings. A study by DiTiberio (1977) found Intuitive types higher for covert feeling messages.

Any career that deals mainly with people tends to attract more Feeling than Thinking types. The 16 studies in the 1985 *MBTI Manual* that looked at characteristics of providers of psychological services confirm this expectation. A higher percentage of therapists/counselors who preferred Feeling over Thinking was found in all but 5 of the 32 samples analyzed separately in the 16 studies. In the 27 studies in which a Feeling preference predominated, the percentages preferring Feeling over Thinking ranged from 52 to 84. The studies covered included samples of counselor trainees (Levell, 1965), secondary school counselors (Terrill, 1970), Veterans Administration therapists (Braun, 1971), counseling supervisees (Beck, 1973), residence hall assistants (Schilling, 1972), doctoral students in the helping professions (Frederick, 1975), counselors of runaway youth (Elliott, 1975), crisis center staff (Galvin, 1976), counseling students (Newman, 1979), APA clinical psychologists (Perry, 1975), psychiatrists and child psychiatrists (McCaulley, 1977), psychotherapists of differing orientations (Levin, 1978), helping professionals of various kinds (McCaulley, 1978), psychologists (Coan, 1979), Canadian student counselors (Casas & Hamlet, 1984), and crisis center volunteers (Macdaid, 1984a).

Across all these studies, Intuition and Feeling tended to predominate. Occupations that require practitioners to deal with large numbers of people tended to have more Extraverts, and there were relatively more Sensing types in the occupations in which counseling is accompanied by more paperwork. Given that the majority of the population prefers Sensing, the fact that most counselors prefer Intuition creates a responsibility for counselors to learn methods for communicating with and treating Sensing type clients.

Differing styles of doing therapy were reported for Sensing and Intuitive type therapists in the more recent studies reviewed in *MBTI Applications* (see Quenk & Quenk, 1996). Differences on the S–N dichotomy were revealed in the assessment of client symptoms and prognosis, the amount and kind of information needed for accurate evaluation of clients, and the use of metaphor. Differences on other dichotomies also provide potentially useful information for therapists in understanding their own styles of doing therapy and insight into ways they can modify their style to better accommodate clients of different types.

The results of some of the recent studies that looked at psychotherapy outcome variables point to possibly complex interrelationships among client and therapist type characteristics and outcome measures such as satisfaction. Therapist-client type similarity appears to affect some kinds of outcomes positively and others in negative or more complicated, nonlinear ways. Some of the earlier results reported by Mendelsohn (1966) seemed to anticipate such results. Relatively small numbers of subjects, types of therapy, different lengths of treatment and treatment settings, and other uncontrolled variables related to clients, therapists, and contexts make comparisons and generalizations from the available studies difficult. However, such results can be useful to practitioners in stimulating awareness of more subtle factors that may be at work in their interactions with clients.

A recent study serves as a model of a carefully conceived, analyzed, and interpreted research effort that capitalizes on an in-depth understanding of type dynamics. Otis and Louks (1997) investigated the hypothesis that psychological dysfunction is expressed differently for different types. They studied a sample of Introverted male veterans using measures of "Rebelliousness" and "Psychological Distress" developed through a factor analysis of the Wiggins Content Scales of the MMPI. They found that INTP and ISTP types were both more likely to score higher than expected on the "Rebelliousness" measure as compared to a random sampling on this dimension, and significantly more likely to be diagnosed with combat-related post-traumatic stress disorder as well as "antisocial" and "avoidant" personality disorders. They were also more likely to have been arrested for a non–substance abuse crime and to have had trouble accommodating to the behavioral constraints imposed by the inpatient treatment facility in which the research was conducted. ISFJs were more likely to score lower on "Rebelliousness," ISFPs had the highest score on "Subjective Distress," and ISFJs and INFJs were more likely to be given one of the "dramatic" diagnoses. INTJ was the only type to stand out with a diagnosis of major depression. The researchers discuss these and other findings in the context of patient histories and as a function of the distinct dynamic qualities of the types.

Professional Orientation

In theory, Extraverts should prefer to focus on environmental issues and to work with larger numbers of individuals and groups. Introverts should prefer to focus on intrapsychic therapy, to work with individuals, and to provide longer-term treatment. Sensing types should prefer to use more applied methods; Intuitive types should prefer more dynamic approaches. Thinking types should prefer more analytical, "tough-minded" approaches, and Feeling types should be drawn to approaches that involve understanding the client's goals and values. Judging types should prefer more directive and controlled kinds of treatment, while Perceiving types should favor methods that emphasize understanding the client. The 1985 *MBTI Manual* reported on several studies that found significant differences ($p < .05$) among counselors of different types. These included Coan (1979), Levin (1978), Perelman (1978), and Witzig (1978).

The studies reported in *MBTI Applications* (see Quenk & Quenk, 1996) confirm those reported earlier in finding type-related factors in preference for treatment models. Practitioners who prefer Thinking tend to apply linear, logical, analytic processes (as in behavioral and cognitive approaches); Feeling types prefer humanistic, affective approaches that emphasize the therapeutic relationship. The Sensing–Intuition and Judging–Perceiving differences found also corresponded to the preferences composing these dichotomies—Judging type counselors like operating in systematic ways, and Perceiving type practitioners prefer more flexibility; those who prefer Intuition like to understand how facts and ideas are interconnected; those who prefer Sensing use more prescribed methods. There appeared to be little if any effect attributable to Extraversion–Introversion differences.

Treatment Strategies

The 1985 *MBTI Manual* noted that "very little work has been conducted on the appropriate treatment method for any given type. However, there is some evidence about the counseling expectations of different types" (p. 73). This same statement appears to be true over 10 years later.

Carskadon (1979) asked college students what qualities they valued in a counselor. Thinking types rated behavioral characteristics higher, and Feeling types rated humanistic characteristics higher. In a study of college students, Weir (1976) found that Feeling types who listened to an audiotape of a counselor demonstrating high unconditional positive regard were significantly more likely to prefer this approach than were other types. A study by Arain (1968) found that among high school students seeking counseling, Thinking types preferred cognitive characteristics in prospective counselors, and Feeling types preferred affective characteristics.

College undergraduates who volunteered for a small group "self-understanding" research project were 84% N (and 51% NF) types (McCary, 1970). In a group of medical students who were asked, "How important is it for the faculty to help you with your own personal development and self-understanding?," ST types reported low interest in self-understanding and NF types reported high interest in self-understanding. The ST types also reported that the faculty placed more emphasis on self-understanding than

they wanted. NF students in the same classes felt that the faculty were neglecting this part of their education (Otis as reported in McCaulley, 1978, p. 188).

The studies by Mendelsohn and his colleagues using students who came to the university counseling center (1962–1967, cited at the beginning of this chapter) found the following significant differences: (1) Compared with their peers, those who preferred Intuition, Thinking, and Perceiving were more likely to be clients of the center; (2) when the students had types similar to those of their counselors, they came for more sessions overall, but they also missed more sessions during treatment; (3) students with types different from their counselors' almost always came for only a few sessions; (4) students who were more like or more unlike their counselors later rated the counseling experience less favorably than did students of middle similarity.

An unpublished study by Grant (1966) compared the type distribution of 114 students with personal problems coming to the counseling center at Auburn University to the distribution of the student body. Types overrepresented in the "problem group" were INFJ, INFP, INTJ, ISFP, ENFP, and ENTP. Students underrepresented were ESTP, ISFJ, ENFJ, ESFJ, ESFP, and ESTJ. INFPs came for more counseling sessions than did other students who sought counseling.

In these few studies, it appears that Intuitive types, who are more interested in psychological approaches to life, are also more likely to seek psychological solutions to their problems. The studies also suggest that there may be a match between the kinds of treatments preferred by clients of a particular type and the kind of treatment offered by practitioners of the same type. The more recent studies reviewed in *MBTI Applications* (see Quenk & Quenk, 1996) confirm this finding. They reveal that just as people who prefer Intuition and Feeling disproportionately become counselors and psychotherapists, so do clients seeking therapy tend more often to be those same types.

Supervision of Counseling and Psychotherapy Students

A number of studies have appeared in the past 10 years that examine type influences on student counselors and therapists in relation to their supervisors as well as specific supervision variables. Type seemed to have little effect on the general satisfaction of supervisees with the supervision experience. However, meaningful outcome measures such as perceived effectiveness of supervision were found to be related to supervisee preference for Thinking or Feeling. A study by Schacht, Howe, and Berman (1989) used scores on the *Barrett-Lennard Relationship Inventory* as a measure of perception of the extent to which former training supervisors were judged as "facilitative" by a sample of clinical and counseling doctoral psychologists who had recently completed their training. The investigators found that, although both Thinking and Feeling types rated highly those supervisors who were high in such areas as "positive regard," "empathy," "unconditionality," and "willingness to be known," Feeling types significantly and consistently rated their most helpful supervisors as higher in "regard" and "empathy" than did Thinking types.

Useful information for counselors and therapists who supervise trainees can be gleaned from studies that focus on the different needs and expectations of student therapists. A study by Swanson and O'Saben (1993) found that Sensing type supervisees expected tangible intervention by supervisors in times of crisis; Extraverted and/or Intuitive type supervisees wanted direct supervision of their therapy sessions; gentle confrontation by the supervisor was desired by supervisees with Introverted and/or Intuitive preferences; and Thinking and/or Perceiving type trainees wanted the supervisor to be willing to engage in struggles and arguments during supervision.

As mentioned by Quenk and Quenk (1996) in their review of the research in this area, there is little if any attention paid to demonstrating whether knowledge of type is useful to supervisors and supervisees in learning to be therapists or in the conduct of psychotherapy. A recent research effort, however, reports on a systematic effort to include training about type in a clinical program. Although the program was a social work curriculum rather than clinical or counseling psychology, the model described could be readily applicable to any effort that trains professionals to treat client populations. Moore, Dietz, and Jenkins (1997) reported on their attempt to incorporate awareness of type by faculty and students throughout the social work curriculum. The MBTI was incorporated into a number of courses with the goal of increasing student self-awareness and appreciation of personality diversity as preparation for their future work with clients. This program extended over an eight-year period. One group of 44 senior social work students were asked to rate the potential utility of the MBTI in social work practice. There was general agreement on its usefulness in helping relationships with clients and co-workers, awareness of personal strengths and limitations, increasing self-awareness, understanding clients and co-workers, and understanding behavioral differences.

The MBTI was one of the instruments used in a counseling project that involved 50 midlife women who described themselves as being in personal and career transition and participated in an eight-week individual and group counseling project (Schadt, 1997). A control group of women on a waiting list for the program were compared on their results on the MBTI as well as on the *Bem Sex Role Inventory,* the *Strong Interest Inventory*, and other scales designed to measure well-being, self-efficacy, and self-esteem. Among the results supporting the effectiveness of the treatment program was the general agreement on the part of study participants—whose type distribution showed higher percentages of E (64%) versus I, N (62%) versus S, F (68%) versus T, and J (68%) versus P—on the value of the MBTI instrument in self-understanding. In addition, a significant correlation was found between subjects' clarity of preference for *either* E or I

and psychosocial well-being ($r = .39$, $p < .05$) and self-esteem ($r = .49$, $p < .01$). Replication of this association and its implications seems warranted.

Administering and Interpreting the MBTI in Counseling and Psychotherapy Settings

In addition to the general issues and guidelines for administration and interpretation covered in Chapters 5 and 6, the following issues are particularly relevant for counseling and psychotherapy clients.

Questions About Administering the MBTI

This section addresses administration issues regarding individual clients, couples, families, and those in addiction treatment programs.

1. **What factors should I consider in the timing of administration?**
   Factors such as presenting complaint, level of stress being experienced, anticipated client interest and receptivity, and reading and comprehension level, among other variables, should be considered in deciding when to administer the MBTI. Some therapists find it helpful to introduce type early in the process; others prefer to wait until they have a sense of the client's type before administering the Indicator. Many therapists decide on the timing of administration based on a variety of client differences. With some clients, giving the Indicator may not be appropriate or helpful at *any* stage of the counseling process. Clients with very serious psychological disturbances may not be able or willing to respond candidly to the Indicator questions. For example, someone diagnosed with obsessive-compulsive disorder may have great difficulty making the choices required on the MBTI, resulting in both increased emotional distress and invalid results. In spite of such caveats, however, a type-aware practitioner can use her or his sensitivity to type issues to help many such clients for whom the usual route of self-reporting on the MBTI may not be an option.

2. **What special approaches are appropriate for couples and families?**
   When using the Indicator with couples and families, administration early in the counseling process, even as "homework" after an initial session, can be useful and advisable, provided there is sufficient confidence that Indicator results will not become just another way for the couple or other family members to attack and disparage each other. When there are signs that the MBTI is likely to be used only for destructive purposes, administration at any time is ill-advised.

Many couples therapists have clients fill out the Indicator twice, once for themselves and a second time the way they believe the partner would answer. Couple members should be discouraged from comparing their responses while answering or before an interpretation session. If Form J or K is being used, it is advisable that Form M be used for the second, "the way your partner would answer," administration. The detailed information provided by the longer form is not useful when the issue is the partners' perceptions of each other's whole type. It is also advisable that the request to fill out the MBTI occur with both people present, rather than at the individual sessions a therapist may schedule in order to obtain individual background information.

3. **Which form should I use?**
The Step I standard Form M, or the earlier Form G, can be used for individuals or couples. Form K or Form J can also be helpful for both individual clients and couples; the individualized information these forms produce may aid both client and therapist in the treatment process. For information about administration and interpretation of these forms, see Saunders (1987, 1989), Kummerow and Quenk (1992), Quenk and Kummerow (1996), and Mitchell with Quenk and Kummerow (1997).

When treating families, the *Murphy-Meisgeier Type Indicator for Children* (MMTIC), briefly discussed in Chapter 5, provides type information for children who range in age from about 7 to 12. However, consideration should be given to administering Form M or Form G to children who are 12 or older.

4. **Where should the MBTI be administered?**
Depending on a variety of situational factors, some counselors prefer to have clients fill out the Indicator within the counseling setting, while others give clients the question booklet and answer sheet to return either by mail or at the next scheduled session. Filling out the MBTI "on site" provides a common setting and ensures return of the materials; having clients respond at home on their own time may encourage more spontaneous responses but also runs the risk of extraneous influences and delay or failure to return materials.

5. **Are there any special cautions I should be aware of?**
In introducing the Indicator to individuals who have come because of psychological difficulties, special attention should be given to possible concerns that it may reveal psychopathology and/or that the client's responses will reveal "unconscious" or other information of a negative nature. It is useful to explain that the purpose of having type information is to enable better understanding of the client's natural and comfortable way of operating and the ways the client may be similar to and different from others. Knowledge of type can also help both client and therapist better understand what is difficult and stressful for the client, how he or she typically reacts to stress, and which coping strategies are likely to be most natural and effective for the individual.

The Indicator should not be administered to clients in an acute state, including those suffering from extreme depression or anxiety, in an ongoing life crisis, or experiencing any type of extreme emotion that is induced by alcohol or drug use. Administration should be delayed until the counselor is confident that the client can respond as his or her "typical" self.

Questions About Interpreting the MBTI and Verifying Type

On rare occasions, a client who has taken the MBTI inventory may be uninterested in knowing the results or the therapist may feel that MBTI information is unlikely to be appropriate or helpful. In general, however, clients are eager to have their results interpreted and interested in the implications of their personality type for counseling and psychotherapy.

1. **What is the first step in interpreting the MBTI to clients?**
When type theory is used in counseling, the first step is to discover the client's true or best-fit preferences. The theory behind the MBTI assumes that preferences are inborn and can become distorted and confused by family and other environmental pressures. Therefore, each stage of interpreting the MBTI results is essentially a testing of the reported or hypothesized type against the respondent's experiences of his or her behavior. Refer to Chapter 6 for ways respondents can use the MBTI to indicate their inherent preferences.

Positive insights can come from an awareness of type distributions in the general population (see the "Uses" chapters in Part V) and of how the client may be different from family and peer groups. The Intuitive type who discovers that everyone else in his or her family of origin prefers Sensing gains a new perspective about having always felt like an outsider. An Extraverted Intuitive type in a career attractive to Introverted Sensing types can realize why work is fatiguing and unsatisfing (see career choice information in Chapter 12).

Clients who have correctly reported their preferences will usually show a sense of release when reading their type descriptions. Such clients will naturally anticipate many of the consequences of their type and will readily discuss the negative aspects of their type in a nondefensive way. They see the negative aspects as simply the opposite side of their strengths.

Isabel Myers believed that environmental pressures were important in determining the likelihood of optimum type development. Causes of distortion of type are described in Chapter 6 and in *Gifts Differing* (Myers with Myers, 1980/1995, pp. 189–192). Both Jung (1921/1971, p. 548) and Myers with Myers (1980/1995, p. 189) wrote that when external influences cause distortion of type, emotional difficulties will follow. Practitioners are therefore advised to exercise caution and carefully check with their clients and with their own observations of their clients for evidence of type distortion. This is particularly important in counseling because a goal of treatment is to identify and strengthen the inherent preferences, not continue and reinforce the distortion.

2. **How do I help my clients determine their best-fit preferences?**

If the client has doubts about the accuracy of the reported preference, be alert to his or her tone when discussing activities. Activities associated with natural preferences are usually described with pleasure or with an offhanded manner, taking them for granted. When clients engage in these activities, they feel motivated and energetic. Activities associated with less-preferred functions are often described in terms of effort, struggle, and discomfort. Engaging in such activities is tiring and can be depressing.

Usually, the client's natural preferences are recognized early in the counseling process, often in the first interpretive session. In some cases, one or more preferences remain in question at the end of the session. Therapist and client can agree to proceed with what is known about the clear preferences while investigating further those that are not clear. For example, if Intuition is clear but there is doubt about whether Thinking or Feeling is preferred, discussion can focus on the implications of preferring Intuition. Between sessions, the client can observe his or her experience during decision making, noting which options occur first and which carry the most weight, and how decisions that turned out to be good or bad were made. This exercise is most useful when the decisions seem relatively minor, such as where to go for dinner or how to schedule a day.

Depending on the purpose of counseling or psychotherapy and how long it is expected to continue, the process of discovering and verifying best-fit type can occur over an extended period of time. Exploring the client's type often becomes an ongoing and natural part of the therapeutic process, with depth of insight and understanding increasing over time. Clarity about a client's type may occur quite late in the process, and in some cases, some measure of doubt may persist.

3. **How can type dynamics be used as an interpretation aid?**

For some clients, doubt about best-fit type involves lack of clarity between Extraversion and Introversion and/or Judging and Perceiving. Because both of these pairs of opposite attitudes are necessary for determining type dynamics (see Chapter 3), doubt about one or the other attitude affects which function is dominant, auxiliary, tertiary, and inferior. Practitioners who are sensitive to type dynamics can listen for or inquire about dynamic differences and use this information to help clients determine their type. For example, if the "doubt" is between ENFP, INFJ, INFP, or ENFJ because the client is unclear about both E–I and J–P, the therapist can look for client characteristics that are associated with either dominant extraverted Intuition (ENFP), dominant introverted Intuition (INFJ), dominant introverted Feeling (INFP), or dominant extraverted Feeling (ENFJ).

Knowledge of typical expressions of the least developed inferior function can also aid interpretation and identification of best-fit type. If a client clearly experiences the inferior function of one type rather than an alternative type, the likelihood is that the opposite of the identified inferior function is the best-fit dominant function. For example, if the doubt is between ESFJ (dominant extraverted Feeling) and ESTJ (dominant extraverted Thinking) and the client reports that under extreme stress he characteristically shows the signs of inferior introverted Thinking (ESFJ) rather than inferior introverted Feeling (ESTJ), serious consideration should be given to ESFJ as the best hypothesis of the client's type. Further exploration of the hypothesis during therapy is likely to provide additional evidence for or against this hypothesis.

Conclusion

This chapter was designed to serve as a practical guide to using the MBTI in a wide variety of settings and with a broad range of clients. The goal was to acquaint readers with a fairly complete picture of the relevance of type to a broad range of areas. Of necessity, the coverage of some topics is brief, but it is intended as suggestive. Readers are encouraged to consult the relevant resources recommended as a way to increase their depth of knowledge. However, the most practical and fruitful way to benefit from type knowledge is through using type with clients, making observations and informal hypotheses, and in general using a "type lens" as an aid to understanding the complexity and individuality of clients seeking help.

Uses of Type in Education   11

Revised by John K. DiTiberio

Educators are faced with the daunting task of preparing students for the rapidly changing demands of the century ahead. Of all the applications of the *Myers-Briggs Type Indicator* personality inventory, perhaps none holds greater promise than education for assisting our efforts to deal with social change in an increasingly pluralistic world.

Throughout her life's work, Isabel B. Myers saw in type theory not only a means for human understanding but also a catalyst for the realization of human potential. While schools and colleges have tended to measure aptitude and accomplishment through the assessment of intelligence, Myers saw things differently. She wrote, "Within limits, type development can substitute for intelligence, because average intelligence, fully utilized through fine type development, will give results far above expectation. However, a serious deficit of type development, especially a deficit of judgment, constitutes a disability for which no amount of intelligence can compensate" (Myers with Myers, 1980/1995, p. 177).

This chapter sheds light on the intersection between type preferences and many traditional benchmarks of success in educational settings, including intelligence (at least as measured by IQ). Education appears to be the application area with the greatest current volume of MBTI research, perhaps because Myers' earliest investigations involved students in school settings. Hence this chapter is structured to provide research data at various levels of education, followed in each case by a discussion of implications for the classroom.

Building upon the comprehensive review of the literature over the past decade found in *MBTI Applications* (Hammer, 1996b), this chapter also includes an updated discussion of some of the early research in education presented in the 1985 *MBTI Manual* (Myers & McCaulley, 1985). Because most of the research to date is on separate dichotomies of the MBTI, a considerable portion of this chapter deals with the four pairs of opposite preferences. Studies of the 16 types in education are highlighted for settings where data are available. Occasionally studies are also cited that refer to the *Murphy-Meisgeier Type Indicator for Children* (MMTIC); the MMTIC manual (Meisgeier & Murphy, 1987) should be consulted regarding its use.

The chapter begins with what we know about the 16 types in education. Because type theory is dynamic, this section includes suggestions for responding to the subtle interaction of MBTI dichotomies within the whole person, not simply the addition of four preferences to one another. For educators, it may be especially instructive to examine patterns for the different types across the life span and thus to acknowledge that for children, adolescents, and adults of the same type, the expression of their preferences must be understood in the context of their type development.

The next section summarizes the research on characteristics of learners, dealing especially with learning styles, cognitive styles, brain patterns, and information processing, with attention to the four MBTI dichotomies one at a time. The characteristics of teachers and patterns of teacher-learner interactions are presented next, including both the benefits and limitations of matching learners with their teachers, supervisors, or settings by type categories.

A section on academic aptitude and performance provides an update of the discussion of early MBTI research in this area, including comparisons with standardized test data. Research findings in mathematics, reading, writing, and foreign language learning highlight the multiple processes employed by different types to produce successful performance. The section pertaining to elementary and secondary education suggests how educators can take type into account in dealing with learning disabilities, behavior disorders, and gifted learners. It also addresses school climate issues as related to the interaction of different types of administrators, teachers, or counselors with students, especially those at risk. College, university, and professional education settings have spawned considerable MBTI research over the decades, and the next section shows how students in higher education can best work to their potential. It is followed by a section on type and cultural differences in education.

The conclusion offers specific suggestions on how to apply Jung's type theory and the MBTI in educational settings. This section describes how to decide whether or not to administer a type indicator, which form of the MBTI is best suited to the age level and educational purposes of the group, ways to maximize the likelihood that individuals will respond to the Indicator according to their "true type," and ethical issues regarding uses of the MBTI in educational contexts. One purpose of this section is to give focus to the increasing enthusiasm for the MBTI as an affirming instrument. Another is to provide appropriate cautions on how to avoid stereotyping or reducing respondents to caricatures. There are already too many unfortunate labels in education.

Working with the 16 Types in Education

The MBTI was designed to indicate not only one's separate preferences on each of four dichotomies but one's whole type as well. Unfortunately, much research on the MBTI in education has solely reported patterns of correlation between a single dichotomy and other variables. To work with individuals as a teacher, counselor, principal, or in other professional roles necessarily requires dealing with a whole person. Thus this section considers the results of studies in which patterns have been observed for the 16 types.

Chapters 3 and 4 are an essential resource for understanding how a person's MBTI profile involves more than a simple addition of four preferences. From a strict linear point of view an ESTJ type and an ESFJ type would appear to have much in common, sharing as they do three of the four preferences. However, the single letter of difference in this case involves the dominant process: Extraverted Thinking versus Extraverted Feeling. Such differences, as will be shown, can have profound implications.

Educators, who are involved in helping to nurture the personal as well as the academic growth of students, can use the theory of good type development to assist in these endeavors. As Chapter 4 suggests, working with an ESFJ student in elementary school requires a different balance between challenge and support than does working with an ESFJ college student or fellow teacher.

Summary of Research on the 16 Types in Education Using Form G of the MBTI

Table 11.1 shows the results from Form G research during the past decade, which produced findings pertaining to one or more of the 16 types. The studies cover a wide range of activities across various levels of education. The results will be discussed by pairs of types sharing the same dominant function in the same attitude.

ISTJ and ISFJ (Dominant Introverted Sensing) ISTJ and ISFJ types share in common a preference for quietly gathering the facts of the situation and carefully storing those facts for later use. For these reasons they are often considered the most reliable of the types. This hard-working orientation to life is represented by the appearance of ISTJs among the top four types in overall undergraduate grades (Schurr & Ruble, 1986) and by ISFJ students being rated by psychologists as among those least likely to have trouble in school (Roberds-Baxter & Baxter, 1994). Their steady-as-you-go orientation to tasks is also reflected in a preference by ISFJ teachers for the basal approach to reading instruction (Lehto, 1990) and in the fact that ISTJ is one of the two most frequent types among industrial technology teachers (Lawrence, 1993). While the concept of creativity is often stereotyped as characteristic of those preferring Intuition, Jacobson (1993) found ISTJs to possess adaptive creativity, as measured by the *Kirton Adaptation and Innovation Inventory*. The difference between ISTJ and ISFJ types is indicated by their different outwardly focused auxiliary processes (Thinking for the former, Feeling for the latter). Given these patterns it is not surprising that ISFJs emerged as the second most frequent type among education majors in college (Grindler & Stratton, 1990) and that they also were rated high by faculty on behavioral skills for dealing with dental patients (Dunning, Lange, & Adams, 1990).

INFJ and INTJ (Dominant Introverted Intuition)

The most quietly imaginative of the types, INFJs and INTJs have consistently appeared near the top in most investigations of academic achievement. Kalsbeek (1987) found them having the highest first semester grades in college, and Woodruff and Clarke (1993) reported them to be the two types with the highest overall college grades. INFJs have been found among the highest persisters in college (Rigley, 1993; Waymire, 1995) and among the top four types in overall grades (Schurr & Ruble, 1986). INTJs had the highest grades among persisters in another study (Anchors, Robbins, & Gershman, 1989) and were among the highest persisters at church-related colleges (Waymire, 1995). At one women's liberal arts college INTJs were among the modal types of resident assistants (Brush, 1989). When junior high school students (ages 12–14) were asked to write about their personal future and to indicate the projected date of their story, INTJs identified the highest mean number of years projected beyond the present (Harrison & Lawrence, 1985); the results reflect the description of Intuition as going beyond the immediate to imagine possibilities. A natural affinity for the academic world would seem to be indicated in the study by Elliott and Sapp (1988), which found INTJs to be Participant learners on the *Grasha-Reichmann Student Learning Styles Questionnaire*; these learners are described as wanting to "learn course content" and "like to go to class" (p. 47).

ESTP and ESFP (Dominant Extraverted Sensing)

From Jung's theory, these types are the least likely to be patient with the demands of traditional academic life, given their preference for experiencing the world directly, actively, and without restriction. Extraverted Sensing draws the individual into the fascinating world of tangible reality, to be heard (with the volume up), touched, smelled, held, and seen up close. They naturally look to the outer world to set the tone for what to do next, as long as the world around them stimulates their senses. Elliott and Sapp (1988) thus found that ESTP college students preferred "collaborative" learning ("liking to work with others") and that ESFPs were "dependent" learners with "little intellectual curiosity" who "look to others for guidelines." (p. 47). Holsworth (1985) found both ESTPs and ESFPs to be "field dependent" on the Group Embedded Figures Test (trusting stimuli presented directly to them, while "field independents" tend to perceive hidden patterns). Perhaps because these types rely on the concrete world around them, unfavorable conditions may sometimes lead them more than any other to do poorly academically, whereas favorable settings allow them to do well. Woodruff and Clarke (1993) found them the two types with the lowest overall grades in college. Anchors and Dana (1989) discovered that they are overrepresented among college students referred for substance abuse training. On the other hand, they were among the highest in another study of college retention (Anchors et al., 1989), and Rigley (1993) found ESFPs among those most likely to persist to graduation.

ENFP and ENTP (Dominant Extraverted Intuition)

These types have been described as the most noticeably enthusiastic regarding new possibilities. With dominant Intuition directed outwardly, they love to challenge existing ideas with fresh and original options and do not like to stick to routine. They therefore present an interesting paradox, since the initiative behind their dominant extraverted Intuition appears to breed success in some arenas and trouble in others. ENFPs were significantly overrepresented among academically talented (labeled as gifted) elementary students (Mills, Moore, & Parker, 1996) but were also rated by psychologists as among the three types most likely to have trouble in school (Roberds-Baxter & Baxter, 1994). ENFPs were found to be creative in innovative ways rather than adaptive ways (Jacobson, 1993). ENTP junior high students (ages 12–14) projected themselves farther into the future than any type except INTJ when asked to write about their personal future (Harrison & Lawrence, 1985). However, ENTPs were also found to be highly represented both among high school students in an off-campus program for at-risk individuals (Hart, 1991) and among alcohol policy violators at one undergraduate college (Barrineau, 1997). They were also overrepresented among those referred for substance abuse training at another university (Anchors & Dana, 1989) and were among the lowest group for retention in college (Anchors et al., 1989). ENFPs were the third most frequent type among education majors (Grindler & Stratton, 1990) and as teachers were found to

Table 11.1   Research on the 16 Types in Education Since 1985 Using Form G

ISTJ	ISFJ	INFJ	INTJ
Adaptively creative learners[18]	Second most frequent type among education majors[12]	One of two types with highest first-semester college grades[19]	Among top two types for undergraduate grades[36]
One of top two types among industrial/technical teachers[21]	As teachers, prefer basal approach to reading instruction[22]	Among top four types for under-graduate grades[33]	Among highest persisters at church-related colleges[35]
Among top four types for college grades[33]	Rated by psychologists as one of two types least likely to have trouble in school[32]	Among top two types for under-graduate grades[36]	Participant learners (learn course content and like to go to class)[11]
	Rated by faculty as skilled in working with dental patients[9]	Among highest college persisters[31]	Projected self greatest number of years in essays on personal future[14]
		Among highest persisters at church-related colleges[35]	One of two types with highest first-semester college grades[19]
			One of two types most frequent among resident assistants at a women's college[6]
			Highest grades among persisters in college[3]
			One of two types most frequent among female student affairs officers[8]

ISTP	ISFP	INFP	INTP
Rated by psychologists among three types most likely to have trouble in school[32]	Projected self fewest number of years in essays on personal future[14]	Have a general advantage in foreign language learning[10]	Highly represented among college students taking foreign languages[27]
Frequent among high school students in remedial at-risk program[15]	Among lowest in college retention[29]	Most likely of the types to report suicidal thoughts in college[20]	Rated by psychologists among three types most likely to have trouble in school[32]
Highly represented among male college scholarship athletes[7]	Among highest persisters in college[31]	One of two types most frequent among college alcohol policy violators[5]	Most frequent among college students referred for alcohol and drug violations[28]
Among lowest in college retention[29]			Among females, more likely to persist in engineering school[24]

prefer the whole language approach to the basal approach in reading instruction (Lehto, 1990). When different types of teachers were asked to review a list of common student misbehaviors, ENFPs were least likely to consider them serious problems in their classrooms (Miner & Hyman, 1988). ENFPs were also the second most frequent type among one year's national finalists for the CASE college professor of the year (Provost, Carson, & Beidler, 1987).

ISTP and INTP (Dominant Introverted Thinking) These types are best known for their quiet analysis of a situation without being distracted by other people. They will work in isolation for long stretches, apparently without the need for breaks or to meet the social requirements of friends or family. It is this value for independence that may be behind the fact that psychologists rated ISTP and INTP as two of the three types (along with ENFP) most likely to have

trouble in school (Roberds-Baxter & Baxter, 1994). ISTPs were also highly represented in an off-campus program for at-risk high school students (Hart, 1991) and among those least likely to persist to graduation at one college (Provost, 1985). Similarly, INTPs were highly represented among college students referred for alcohol and drug violations (Provost, 1991). ISTPs were, however, overrepresented among male scholarship athletes (Chesborough, 1994). INTP females were more likely to persist in engineering school (McCaulley, Macdaid, & Walsh, 1987), and INTPs were overrepresented among college students taking foreign languages (Moody, 1988).

ISFP and INFP (Dominant Introverted Feeling) Among the gentlest of the types, ISFPs and INFPs are quietly, deeply, and personally invested in whatever they do. Because they tend not to volunteer their reactions, others are

Table 11.1   Research on the 16 Types in Education Since 1985 Using Form G *continued*

ESTP	ESFP	ENFP	ENTP
Collaborative learners[11]	Dependent learners[11]	Highly represented among third- to sixth-grade academically talented students[25]	Projected self second furthest number of years in essays on personal future[14]
Field dependent learners[17]	Field dependent learners[17]	Innovatively creative learners[18]	Frequent among high school students in remedial at-risk program[15]
Among two types with lowest overall college grades[36]	Among two types with lowest overall college grades[36]	As teachers, least likely to see student behaviors as serious problems[26]	One of two types most frequent among college alcohol policy violators[5]
Frequent among college students referred for substance abuse training[1]	Among highest in college retention[3]	Second most frequent type among national CASE professor of the year finalists[30]	
Among highest in college retention[3]	Among highest persisters in college[31]	Third most frequent type among education majors in college[12]	
		As teachers, prefer whole language approach to reading instruction[22]	
		Rated by psychologists among three types most likely to have trouble in school[32]	
		Frequent among college students referred for substance abuse training[1]	
		Among lowest in college retention[3]	

ESTJ	ESFJ	ENFJ	ENTJ
One of top two types among industrial/technical teachers[21]	Most frequent type among education majors[12]	Rated by psychologists among two types least likely to have trouble in school[32]	Most frequent type among national CASE professor of the year finalists[30]
Among top four types for college grades[33]	Among highest in college retention[29]	Frequently represented among college resident assistants[2]	Among top four types for college grades[33]
Most frequent type among school administrators[16]	Most frequent type among high school officers in health occupations association[34]	Most frequent type in 10-year study of college resident assistants[13]	One of two types most frequent among top 100 executive educators[23]
One of two types most frequent among top 100 executive educators[23]		Among lowest in college retention[28]	One of two types most frequent among resident assistants at a women's college[6]
Frequently represented among college resident assistants[2]			Frequent among college students referred for substance abuse training[1]
Least likely of the types to report suicidal thoughts in college[20]			Among highest in college retention[29]
Among highest in college retention[29]			Highest grades among persisters in college[3]
Highly represented among vocational teachers[4]			One of two types most frequent among female student affairs officers[8]

Source: [1]Anchors & Dana, 1989; [2]Anchors & Hay, 1990; [3]Anchors, Robbins, & Gershman, 1989; [4]Barrett, 1989; [5]Barrineau, 1997; [6]Brush, 1989; [7]Chesborough, 1994; [8]Daugherty, Randall, & Globetti, 1997; [9]Dunning, Lange, & Adams, 1990; [10]Ehrman & Oxford, 1990; [11]Elliott & Sapp, 1988; [12]Grindler & Stratton, 1990; [13]Hardy-Jones & Watson, 1990; [14]Harrison & Lawrence, 1985; [15]Hart, 1991; [16]Hoffman, 1986; [17]Holsworth, 1985; [18]Jacobson, 1993; [19]Kalsbeek, 1987; [20]Komisin, 1992; [21]Lawrence, 1993; [22]Lehto, 1990; [23]Lueder, 1986; [24]McCaulley, Macdaid, & Walsh, 1987; [25]Mills, Moore, & Parker, 1996; [26]Miner & Hyman, 1988; [27]Moody, 1988; [28]Provost, 1991; [29]Provost, 1985; [30]Provost, Carson, & Beidler, 1987; [31]Rigley, 1993; [32]Roberds-Baxter & Baxter, 1994; [33]Schurr & Ruble, 1986; [34]Walters, Wilmoth, & Pitts, 1988; [35]Waymire, 1995; [36]Woodruff & Clarke, 1993.

often surprised when they discover how much these types have been affected by circumstances. INFPs have been found by research to have a general advantage in foreign language learning (Ehrman & Oxford, 1990) but also to be most likely of the types among college students to have had suicidal thoughts (Komisin, 1992). Another study of college students found INFPs overrepresented among alcohol policy violators (Barrineau, 1997). ISFP junior high students (ages 12–14) projected themselves the fewest number of years into the future among the 16 types when asked to write about their personal future (Harrison & Lawrence, 1985); this reflects the orientation of their dominant Feeling toward present and past loyalties and the value of their auxiliary Sensing for what they can directly witness in the moment. Type theory predicts that ISFPs will be those most dependent on the encouragement of the world around them and the least independently confident of their own abilities. This might help to explain their being among the least persistent in college in one study (Provost, 1985) and among the highest persisters in another (Rigley, 1993).

ESTJ and ENTJ (Dominant Extraverted Thinking) These types like to control all that they can. They are likely to project personal confidence, are forthright, and naturally take command in social or leadership situations. It is therefore not surprising that research continues to confirm ESTJs as most frequent among school administrators (Hoffman, 1986) and that ESTJs and ENTJs were the two types most frequent among the top 100 executive educators (Lueder, 1986). Their take-charge approach to the tangible world leads ESTJs to be the most frequent of the types among industrial and technical teachers (Lawrence, 1993) as well as among vocational teachers (Barrett, 1989). ESTJs were also least likely among college students to have suicidal thoughts (Komisin, 1992). Both ESTJs and ENTJs were among the four types with the highest overall undergraduate grades (Schurr & Ruble, 1986), and both were among the highest for retention in college (Provost, 1985). ENTJs also had the highest grades among persisters in another study (Anchors et al., 1989). At one college ENTJs were overrepresented among students referred for substance abuse training (Anchors & Dana, 1989). But at a women's liberal arts college they were among the two types (with INTJ) most frequent among resident assistants (RAs; Brush, 1989). ESTJs were also overrepresented among RAs in another study (Anchors & Hay, 1990). ENTJs were clearly the most frequent type among one year's national finalists for the CASE college professor of the year (Provost et al., 1987).

ESFJ and ENFJ (Dominant Extraverted Feeling) These are the most friendly and supportive of the types. Their mission in life is to make things easier for others, and they are natural catalysts for group cohesion. ESFJs are thus the most frequent type among education majors in college

(Grindler & Stratton, 1990). They were also found the most frequent type among high school officers in a health occupations association (Walters, Wilmoth, & Pitts, 1988). ENFJs were rated by psychologists as one of the two types (with ISFJ) least likely to have trouble in school (Roberds-Baxter & Baxter, 1994). They were also significantly overrepresented among resident assistants at one university (Anchors & Hay, 1990) and were the most frequent in a 10-year review of patterns among RAs at another (Hardy-Jones & Watson, 1990). With Feeling as a dominant process, these types rely on encouragement and support to do well. Thus, similar to the pattern for ISFPs, we find mixed results in college persistence for ESFJs and ENFJs. In one study (Provost, 1985) ESFJs were among the highest in retention and ENFJs the lowest.

Current Studies of the 16 Types in Education Using Form M of the MBTI

Validation studies of Form M of the MBTI have produced preliminary findings with implications for education, as shown in Table 11.2. It should be noted that subjects came from a wide range of respondents, most of them adults; the results would not necessarily be identical for students. A full discussion of this sample and validation studies of Form M may be found in Chapter 7 and the Appendix.

Table 11.2 shows responses of the 16 types to these questions: "How do you spend your leisure time?"; "How many hours a day do you watch television?"; "How important are each of the following in your life?" The options reported here pertain to school-related activities that tend to be either curricular (e.g., reading, writing, appreciating art) or extracurricular (e.g., playing sports, watching TV, playing with computers or video games). The table indicates those instances in which the percentage of a type endorsing the option was either significantly overrepresented ($I > 1.0$) or underrepresented ($I < 1.0$) compared with the percentage of that type in the sample overall. Because these preliminary studies include instances in which the number of subjects endorsing an option was relatively small, only cases in which the level of statistical significance was either $p < .001$ or $p < .01$ are reported.

Most notable are differences related to a preference for Sensing or Intuition, especially when dominant. ISTJ and ISFJ types stand out largely by their underrepresentation as reporters of almost any kind of leisure pursuit or activity of stated importance in their life. Each indicated only one such activity as favored, along with three (for ISTJ) and six (for ISFJ) as significantly underreported. The reverse finding was true for Extraverted Intuitive types (ENTP, ENFP). Each endorsed six activities for either leisure *or* importance in their life, but in comparison they were underrepresented for either one (for ENTP) or two (for ENFP). Consistent with type theory, these results reflect the relative value for mixing leisure and play with learning for Extraverted Intuitive types, and the contrasting concern for hard work and

Table 11.2   Research on Reports of Leisure Time Preferences Pertaining to Education for the 16 Types Using Form M

ISTJ	ISFJ	INFJ	INTJ
+ Watching sporting events: $I = 1.21$ − Listening to music: $I = 0.83*$ − Writing: $I = 0.52*$ − Appreciating art: $I = 0.49*$	+ Watching TV 3 hrs or more per day: $I = 1.12$ − Education/learning very important: $I = 0.84$ − Achievement/accomplishment very important: $I = 0.80*$ − Playing with computers or video games: $I = 0.74*$ − Watching sport events: $I = 0.69*$ − Appreciating art: $I = 0.58*$ − Playing sports: $I = 0.47*$	+ Writing: $I = 2.64*$ + Appreciating art: $I = 1.87$ − Watching sporting events: $I = 0.45$	+ Taking classes: $I = 2.66*$ + Appreciating art: $I = 1.78$ + Playing with computers or video games: $I = 1.62$ + Working out/exercising: $I = 1.57$ − Watching TV 3 hrs or more per day: $I = 0.58*$
ISTP	**ISFP**	**INFP**	**INTP**
+ Playing with computers or video games: $I = 1.39$ − Listening to music: $I = 0.78*$ − Writing: $I = 0.39$	+ Watching TV 3 or more hrs per day: $I = 1.19*$ + Watching TV for leisure: $I = 1.12$ − Reading: $I = 0.80*$ − Achievement/accomplishment very important: $I = 0.74*$ − Education/learning very important: $I = 0.67*$ − Working out/exercising: $I = 0.66*$ − Writing: $I = 0.52$ − Appreciating art: $I = 0.50*$ − Taking classes: $I = 0.49$	+ Writing: $I = 2.19*$ + Appreciating art: $I = 2.13*$ + Reading: $I = 1.22*$ + Listening to music: $I = 1.20$ − Achievement/accomplishment very important: $I = 0.79$	+ Appreciating art: $I = 2.16*$ + Writing: $I = 2.00*$ + Taking classes, going to school: $I = 1.96$ + Playing with computers or video games: $I = 1.67*$
ESTP	**ESFP**	**ENFP**	**ENTP**
+ Playing sports: $I = 1.79*$	+ Watching TV 3 hrs or more per day: $I = 1.21*$ − Reading: $I = 0.83*$ − Working out/exercising: $I = 0.74$	+ Writing: $I = 2.03*$ + Appreciating art: $I = 1.97*$ + Playing a musical instrument: $I = 1.62*$ + Listening to music: $I = 1.22*$ + Education/learning very important: $I = 1.20$ + Reading: $I = 1.11$ − Watching TV for leisure: $I = 0.89$ − Watching TV 3 hrs or more per day: $I = 0.83$	+ Taking classes: $I = 1.87$ + Writing: $I = 1.74$ + Appreciating art: $I = 1.64$ + Playing sports: $I = 1.56$ + Playing with computers or video games: $I = 1.48$ + Achievement/accomplishment very important: $I = 1.28$ − Watching TV 3 hrs or more per day: $I = 0.76$
ESTJ	**ESFJ**	**ENFJ**	**ENTJ**
+ Playing sports: $I = 1.57*$ + Achievement/accomplishment very important: $I = 1.35*$ + Watching sporting events: $I = 1.20$ − Listening to music: $I = 0.85$	− Writing: $I = 0.62$	+ Appreciating art: $I = 2.01*$ + Writing: $I = 1.89$ + Education/learning very important: $I = 1.54*$ + Listening to music: $I = 1.26$ + Reading: $I = 1.24$ − Watching TV 3 hrs or more per day: $I = 0.66*$	+ Working out/exercising: $I = 1.69$

Note: See Appendix for a full description of the sample. $N = 2,976$ for "Watching TV 3 hrs or more per day"; $N = 2,887$ for "Education/learning very important"; $N = 2,953$ for "Achievement/accomplishment very important"; $N = 3,036$ for all other items. + = Index of attraction (I) indicates significant overrepresentation of the type compared with those from the total sample who endorsed the item; − = Index of attraction (I) indicates significant underrepresentation of the type compared with those from the total sample who endorsed the item. * $p < .001$; all other items $p < .01$. See Appendix for a description of the sample.

Source: National sample.

patient attention to areas of responsibility for Introverted Sensing types.

The kinds of activities either endorsed or not endorsed also confirm type theory. Only NT types (INTJ, INTP, ENTP), who tend to be both conceptual and analytical in focus, listed taking classes and going to school as significantly favored activities, even when responding to questions about leisure; ISFPs did not. Three Intuitive types (ENFP, ENFJ, ENTP) significantly listed education and learning as very important, while two Sensing types (ISFJ, ISFP) did not. Those endorsing writing as a leisure activity included over-representations of all four NF types plus ENTP and INTP, and underrepresentations of ISTJ, ISTP, and ESFJ. Appreciating art was favorably listed for six Intuitive and no Sensing types; on the other hand, three Sensing but no Intuitive types were significantly underrepresented on this item. Only Intuitive types favored reading, listening to music, or playing a musical instrument as leisure activities. Only Sensing types (ISTJ and ESTJ) were overrepresented in watching sporting events. Only SF types (ISFJ, ISFP, ESFP) reported watching three or more hours of television per day, while only Intuitive types (INTJ, ENTP, ENFP, ENFJ) were significantly underrepresented in this activity.

Thinking–Feeling differences accounted for several interesting patterns. Only Thinking types with Extraversion (ESTJ, ENTP) significantly listed achievement and accomplishment as very important, and only Feeling types with Introversion (ISFJ, ISFP, INFP) did not. Playing computer games drew INTP, ISTP, INTJ, and ENTP types; ISFJ types were underrepresented. Playing sports attracted ESTJ, ESTP, and ENTP types, with ISFJ again underrepresented. Working out/exercising was endorsed only by ENTJs and INTJs; it was shunned by ISFPs and ESFPs. It appears that the interest in competition found in many computer games and sports provides the challenge needed by Thinking types, and even the individual challenge of working out or exercising seems to appeal to them as well. For sports, the external activity required also appears to attract Extraverts.

Though these results came from responses to single items on a questionnaire, the patterns confirm what type theory predicts. Educators can learn much from the preferred leisure activities of the 16 types, especially as they highlight traditional characteristics of curricular versus extracurricular activities in school settings.

Implications for the Classroom

"Every type has its good and bad examples," wrote Myers (with Myers, 1980/1995, p. 173). As shown in this section, an understanding of dominant processes and the 16 types can help educators nurture the potential strengths and lessen the likelihood of problems among students. It appears, for example, that in different ways each type may be both open to the encouragement of the academic environment and sometimes also susceptible to the absence of such support.

Dominant Feeling types (ESFJ, ENFJ, ISFP, INFP), according to type theory, work at their best when they care personally about the activity, and conversely they can feel unappreciated or doubt they have much to offer if they lack support. We thus see ISFPs among the highest in persistence in one college and among the lowest in another. At still another college ESFJs were among the highest in retention and their partner ENFJs among the lowest; nationwide, however, both types are in high percentages among education majors. INFPs excel in foreign language learning but as college students report suicidal thoughts more than other types. To deal with students like these, educators can consult type theory to personalize the environment so that dominant Feeling types can especially feel welcomed, regularly encouraged, and challenged in areas in which they have natural strengths.

Dominant Thinking types (ESTJ, ENTJ, ISTP, INTP), according to type theory, are least likely to be influenced by the ups and downs of their surrounding environment since they rely most on decisions made objectively. This tough-mindedness serves them well when they take charge of their environment as student and professional leaders in schools (true especially for ESTJs and ENTJs) or when they engage in careful analysis as in engineering (true especially for ISTPs and INTPs). Problems appear, however, when they do not care enough about the human expectations of their instructors or peers. Thus referrals for substance abuse include disproportionate numbers of ENTJs and INTPs, and school psychologists tend to rate ISTPs and INTPs as having adjustment problems. Again, type theory can help educators provide the kinds of challenges best suited to dominant Thinking types, whether involving work with computers, leadership, or competitive sports.

Dominant Intuitive types (ENTP, ENFP, INTJ, INFJ) seem to have the greatest advantage in education, especially higher education. Their attention to conceptual matters, theory, and broad patterns in complex material suits them well. Thus Introverted Intuitive types (INTJ, INFJ) consistently appear among college students with high grades and the greatest rates of persistence to graduation, and ENFPs are most frequent among academically talented children. Where problems occur, they tend to appear most among Extraverted Intuitive types (ENTP, ENFP), who sometimes are rated by psychologists among those most likely to have trouble in school and who appear among college students referred for alcohol or substance abuse violations. It appears that the need for originality can lead toward creative productivity in some school settings and to trouble-making in others. Again, Jung's theory can help educators to adjust to the needs of each type.

Dominant Sensing types (ESTP, ESFP, ISTJ, ISFJ) vary distinctly in their response to academic life. Furthermore, the remaining four Sensing types, for whom the preference is auxiliary rather than dominant (ESTJ, ESFJ, ISTP, ISFP), similarly differ from one another in education. Those who prefer to use Introverted Sensing, whether dominant (ISTJ, ISFJ) or auxiliary (ESTJ, ESFJ), prefer to record internally the facts of the situation for future reference. This more careful orientation to Sensing appears to lead to high grades for ISTJs and ESTJs, school leadership roles for ESTJs as students or as professionals, and high frequencies of ISFJs and ESFJs among education majors.

On the other hand, those who prefer to use Extraverted Sensing, whether dominant (ESTP, ESFP) or auxiliary (ISTP, ISFP), tend to experience the tangible world more directly, freely, and without structure. Lacking the more organized internal orientation to data of SJ types, they thus are more affected by the ability of the teachers and peers around them to assist with the tasks of learning. Schools and colleges appear less interested in gifts of spontaneity in the experience of the real world. Myers' (1962) early research found that SP types were most prone to drop out of school. The findings reviewed in this section were more mixed. ISFPs were least persistent toward college graduation in one study and most persistent in another. ESTPs and ESFPs had the lowest overall college grades in one study but were among the types most likely to graduate in other studies. ISTPs were rated by school psychologists among those most likely to have trouble in elementary or secondary school and were highly represented in at-risk high school groups, but they reported during interviews by Provost (1985) that they do better in college when not distracted by too many extracurricular activities.

The general lesson from both type theory and the research cited above appears to be that different types need different kinds of support and challenge. A careful understanding of the dominant and auxiliary processes of each type can also suggest different responses to different types when they struggle with school or college contexts. An ESFP facing disciplinary action, for example, is more likely to respond to friendly limit-setting along with active engagement in campus life, while an ISTP in similar trouble needs room to work in isolation without too many social demands.

"The strengths of each type materialize only when the type development is adequate," according to Myers (with Myers, 1980/1995, p. 173). This lesson appears to apply not just to students but to their teachers as well. For example, the study of outstanding college teachers by Provost et al. (1987) reported the general teaching styles of these faculty as well as lessons they had learned over the years about their natural pitfalls. The quotations indicate a confirmation not only of their type preferences but of the theory of type development as well. Students and teachers alike can thus benefit from working first from their natural preferred styles, which then frees up energy to employ less-preferred processes to overcome potential blind spots.

Characteristics of Learners

This section highlights some of the more consistent research findings on each MBTI dichotomy relating to characteristics of learners. The results, summarized in Table 11.3, show how Jung's theory, which underlies the MBTI, can be of powerful use in the classroom. Comprehensive reviews of these studies were conducted by Lawrence (1984) and DiTiberio (1996). What follows is a description of fascinating patterns that have emerged comparing each MBTI dichotomy with aspects of learning styles, cognitive styles, brain patterns, and information processing.

The Extraversion–Introversion Dichotomy

A remarkable series of studies (Wilson & Languis, 1989, 1990) on brain electrical activity found for both adults and adolescents that Extraverts have lower internal arousal than Introverts under all conditions established by the experiment: eyes closed, low-level perceptual tasks, and then higher-level cognitive tasks (see brain map on p. 190). These patterns help us understand the results of other research that shows, consistent with what Jungian theory predicts, that Extraverted students have been found to prefer approaches to learning that are collaborative and that they often depend on the external world for suggestions on how to proceed (Elliott & Sapp, 1988). A number of studies have also found them to lean toward learning styles that involve active experimentation or concrete experience and sometimes both (Gordon, Coscarelli, & Sears, 1986; Hinkle, 1986; Luh, 1991; Penn, 1992). Atman (1993) discovered that Extraverts had a higher sense of goal-directedness and willfulness (described as conation) than Introverts, both as adults and in junior high school settings (ages 12–14). In contrast, Introverted students prefer reflective observation (Hinkle, 1986) and lecture formats (Fourqurean, Meisgeier, & Swank, 1990).

The implications of these findings can be useful for educators. Extraverts work best in action and may be described as stimulus hungry, perhaps due to physiological characteristics of the brain. The hustle-and-bustle that sometimes interrupts the concentration of Introverts may be the needed prompt for Extraverts to engage their minds in learning. Introverts appear to do their best thinking in anticipation rather than on the spot; it now seems clear that this is because their minds are so naturally abuzz with activity that they need to shut out external distractions in order to prepare their ideas. They can and will give an answer to a teacher who demands one immediately but have better second thoughts once they have quiet for concentration. Conversely, Extraverts can and will quietly focus their attention when required, but they will be more inclined to do so if periods of quiet concentration are interspersed with regular doses of active engagement (preferably both spoken and physical) throughout the learning process.

Table 11.3 Characteristics of Learners by Psychological Type

Extraverts	Introverts	Sensing Types	Intuitive Types
Concrete experiential learning style[14, 15, 22, 24]	Reflective observational learning style[15, 23]	Concrete experiential learning style[23]	Abstract conceptual learning style[23]
Active experimental learning style[15, 20, 23, 24]	Visual learners[13]	Learn in several ways[13]	Visual learners[13]
Learn in several ways[13]	Auditory learners[13]	Abstract sequential learning style[9]	Auditory learners[13]
Collaborative learners[11]	Abstract sequential learning style[9]	Concrete sequential learning style[9]	Concrete random learning style[9]
Dependent learners[11]	Participant learners[11]	Collaborative learners[11]	Participant learners[11]
Like projects, simulations, and peer teaching[13]	Like lecture formats[13]	Dependent learners[11]	High conceptual level[5]
External decision makers[14]	Adaptive in creativity[19]	High in fact retention, methodical study, and serialist learning[3]	Holistic learners[3]
Innovative in creativity[19]	Postconventional decision makers[8, 12]	Field dependent[6, 17]	Internal decision makers[14]
High in goal orientation[2]	High internal arousal of brain electrical activity[28, 29]	Left hemisphere learners[3, 16, 18, 27]	Field independent[6, 17]
High academic self-esteem[25]		Adaptive in creativity[19]	Thin boundaries[10]
Connected knowers[7]			Right hemisphere learners[3, 16, 18, 27]
Low internal arousal of brain electrical activity[28, 29]			Innovative in creativity[19]
			Postconventional decision makers[12]
			High in reflective judgment[4]
			High in goal orientation[2]
			High academic self-esteem[25]
			High in academic comfort[1]
			Like self-directed learning[20]

Thinking Types	Feeling Types	Judging Types	Perceiving Types
Abstract conceptual learning style[23]	Concrete experiential learning style[23]	Abstract conceptual learning style[23]	Concrete experiential learning style[23]
Abstract sequential learning style[9]	Abstract random learning style[9]	Like structure and motivation in learning[13]	Active experimental learning style[15]
Participant learners[11]	Dependent learners[11]	Concrete sequential learning style[9]	Like tactile and loud noise learning stimulus[13]
High in fact retention, methodical study, and serialist learning[3]	Holistic learners[3]	Participant learners[11]	Abstract random learning style[9]
Systematic decision makers[14]	Field dependent[6, 17]	High in fact retention, methodical study, and serialist learning[3]	Concrete random learning style[9]
Field independent[6, 17]	Thin boundaries[10]	Like drill and teaching games[13]	Collaborative learners[11]
Left hemisphere learners[3, 26]	Right hemisphere learners[3, 18]	Like independent study[13]	Dependent learners[11]
Adaptive in creativity[19]	Adaptive in creativity[19]	Left hemisphere learners[3, 18, 27]	Holistic learners[3]
Seek self-justice in moral orientation[21]	Seek care and self-care in moral orientation[21]	Adaptive in creativity[19]	Thin boundaries[10]
High in goal orientation among adults[2]	High in goal orientation among junior high students[2]	High in goal orientation[2]	Right hemisphere learners[3, 27]
	Connected knowers[7]	High academic self-esteem[25]	Innovative in creativity[19]
		High academic comfort[1]	Postconventional decision makers[12]

Source: [1]Apostal & Trontvent, 1989; [2]Atman, 1993; [3]Beyler & Schmeck, 1992; [4]Bowen, 1990; [5]Brown & DeCoster, 1991; [6]Canning, 1983; [7]Carter, 1990; [8]Catoe, 1992; [9]Drummond & Stoddard, 1992; [10]Ehrman, 1993; [11]Elliott & Sapp, 1988; [12]Faucett, Morgan, Poling, & Johnson, 1995; [13]Fourqurean, Meisgeier, & Swank, 1990; [14]Gordon, Coscarelli, & Sears, 1986; [15]Hinkle, 1986; [16]Hockersmith, 1986; [17]Holsworth, 1985; [18]Holtzman, 1989; [19]Jacobson, 1993; [20]Johnson, Sample, & Jones, 1988; [21]Liddell, Halpin, & Halpin, 1992; [22]Luh, 1991; [23]Myers & McCaulley, 1985; [24]Penn, 1992; [25]Schaefer, 1994; [26]Shiflett, 1989; [27]Taggart, Kroeck, & Escoffier, 1991; [28]Wilson & Languis, 1989; [29]Wilson & Languis, 1990.

The Sensing–Intuition Dichotomy

The S–N dichotomy has consistently related to distinct differences in the ways students view and respond to education. As examples, Sensing types have been found to like sequential learning (Drummond & Stoddard, 1992) and in general favor both collaborative and dependent learning styles (Elliott & Sapp, 1988). Their approach to creativity tends to be adaptive, while Intuitive types are innovative, on the *Kirton Adaption and Innovation Inventory* (Jacobson, 1993). Sensing types approach learning through fact retention, methodical study, and serialist learning (Beyler & Schmeck, 1992). Sensing was the clearest preference among both students and teachers of vocational education in three studies (Barrett, 1989; Johnson, Zimmerman, & Brooker, 1994; Vollbrecht, 1991). In the 1985 *MBTI Manual,* Myers & McCaulley reported data showing Sensing types as valuing concrete experience on *Kolb's Learning Style Inventory,* while Intuitive types instead valued abstract conceptualization. Several studies have found them to favor the left hemisphere on the *Human Information Processing Survey* (Beyler & Schmeck, 1992; Hockersmith, 1986; Taggart, Kroeck, & Escoffier, 1991), in contrast to Intuitive types, who in the same studies favored the right. A recent review of the literature on brain functioning and type (Power & Lundsten, 1997) confirmed these patterns and called attention not only to hemispheric preference but also to cerebral (favoring Intuition) versus limbic (favoring Sensing) thinking processes as measured by the *Herrmann Brain Dominance Instrument.*

Intuitive types are described as holistic learners (Beyler & Schmeck, 1992), field independent (Holsworth, 1985), and having thin boundaries (Ehrman, 1993). They have been found to score higher than Sensing types on measures of postconventional ethical decision making (Catoe, 1992; Faucett, Morgan, Poling, & Johnson, 1995), reflective judgment (Bowen, 1990), and conation or goal orientation in adults (Atman, 1993). McCaulley and Natter (1974) discovered that a preference for independent study among high school students was found among Intuitive types, a pattern confirmed in a later study of self-directed learning (Johnson, Sample, & Jones, 1988). They were also found to identify with the philosophy of alternative high schools (Steele, 1986). Academic self-esteem (Schaefer, 1994) and academic comfort (Apostal & Trontvent, 1989) have been found to be higher among Intuitive types; however, Hammer and Kummerow (1996) suggested that these kinds of findings reflect academia as it is currently constructed. They called attention to the equally academic value that Sensing types present for practical, hands-on learning.

Many of the battles fought in education over the years may have been representations of a struggle for supremacy between Sensing and Intuition. A back-to-the-basics approach may reflect the cry of students, teachers, or parents who feel inundated by innovations for their own sake. If many of these voices come from Sensing types, it is fully understandable that their natural strengths of methodical, sequential attention to the facts may have been unappreciated. In contrast, the voices of Intuitive types may have been the ones a generation ago calling for independence among learners and innovative approaches to problem solving.

Jung's theory of opposites can help to relieve the polarization, since he wrote so insightfully (1923) about the subtle balance needed between the practical and the imaginative and about the dangers inherent in pitting one too consistently against its opposite. Type theory suggests that Sensing types can and will produce original ideas but usually after first consulting what they know for sure about a topic. They carefully (and more slowly than do Intuitive students) follow each step in sequence. Thus grounded in the real data, they can then produce the kind of big picture that does not lack in detail (as so many of the initial dreams of Intuitive types do). Conversely, Intuitive types can best learn to accumulate necessary facts if their imaginations are first allowed to roam free, without impediment or excessive rules. Once inspired, Intuitive types then have psychological energy left to fill in the missing pieces.

Too often a Sensing student with an Intuitive teacher, or vice versa, may be asked to produce evidence of learning in a manner that feels absolutely backward to them. The research cited in Table 11.3 suggests that Sensing types move first from the particular to the general, and Intuitive types the other way around. Both approaches are useful. Unfortunately neither will emerge in healthy form if authority figures polarize this dichotomy by insisting that one and only one way will work.

The Thinking–Feeling Dichotomy

Thinking types have been found in research to reflect a systematic approach to learning (Gordon et al., 1986). They have also been described as field independent (trusting perceptions of hidden patterns among distracting stimuli), while Feeling types are field dependent (tending instead to follow their perception of the immediate stimuli themselves) (Holsworth, 1985). Beyler and Schmeck (1992) found Thinking types to prefer a fact orientation, methodical study, and serialist learning, and Feeling types to prefer holistic learning. They also found Thinking types to be oriented to the left hemisphere and Feeling types to the right. Shiflett (1989) produced similar findings for Thinking types in terms of brain patterns. Approaches to moral decision making have been found to link Thinking types with concerns for self-justice and Feeling types with care and self-care (Liddell, Halpin, & Halpin, 1992). Thinking types were also found to score highly on goal orientation as adults, but Feeling types scored higher in a study of junior high students (ages 12–14) (Atman, 1993).

An understanding of the Thinking–Feeling dichotomy can shed light on the debate about learner characteristics by gender since it is the only dichotomy of the MBTI to produce consistently different percentages among males and females. While there may certainly be gender differences worthy of note in education, what passes for gender may better be conceptualized as a type difference, as was suggested by Oxford, Nyikos, and Ehrman (1988) in their study of foreign language learners. In a study of separate versus connected knowers, inspired by the writings of researchers in women's studies, Feeling was preferred (along with Extraversion) more often by connected knowers (Carter, 1990).

The research cited in Table 11.3 suggests that Thinking types work best if approached from a systematic perspective, emphasizing independence and a concern for justice. Feeling types, on the other hand, are more motivated if their field dependence is honored, as well as their concern for care. With Thinking type students, teachers may be more effective by presenting logical arguments and reasons behind the assignments; with Feeling types teachers may be more effective if they establish a solidly supportive relationship first and do not shrink away if students seek reassurance in the early stages of learning.

The Judging–Perceiving Dichotomy

Judging types have been found to prefer learning settings with clear structure, motivation, drill, teaching games, and independent study (Fourqurean et al., 1990); sequencing (Drummond & Stoddard, 1992); and fact retention, methodical study, and serialist learning (Beyler & Schmeck, 1992). They are also called "participant" learners, who "want to learn course content and like to go to class" (Elliott & Sapp, 1988, p. 47). Two studies (Beyler & Schmeck, 1992; Taggart et al., 1991) found Judging types oriented to left hemisphere kinds of learning and Perceiving types to the right. Academic self-esteem was higher for Judging types (Schaefer, 1994), as was academic comfort among female Judging types (Apostal & Trontvent, 1989). On the other hand, Perceiving types liked tactile learning and loud noise (Fourqurean et al., 1990) and approaches to learning that are random (Drummond & Stoddard, 1992), both collaborative and dependent (Elliott & Sapp, 1988) and holistic (Beyler & Schmeck, 1992). They were innovative in creativity, while Judging types were adaptive (Jacobson, 1993). Goal orientation was clearest for Judging types, among both adults and junior high students (ages 12–14) (Atman, 1993).

The J–P dichotomy of the MBTI identifies how individuals approach the outer world, with Judging types preferring planfulness and Perceiving types preferring the flexibility to wait and see. As the results in Table 11.3 indicate, Judging types like to know where they are going and when they will get there. They like it when teachers present a plan, and they tend to follow it as given. As we will see in a later section, this probably accounts for their higher grades on the whole. Perceiving types, however, like to

march to different drummers. Compared with Judging type classmates, they need more room to roam without constraints, allowing their natural curiosity to remain alive. The paradox is that since they look to the outer world to stimulate their curiosity they also may look to the outer world to set guidelines for them, whereas Judging types will set their own guidelines if no one does it for them. Thus Judging type teachers (who as we shall see tend to predominate at all levels of education) can benefit all students with their natural sense of closure and organization, but for different reasons. Furthermore, teachers may need to be a bit more patient with the initial response of Perceiving type students, who may not look as outwardly productive as their Judging type classmates until the due date actually arrives. Unless the deadline is imminent (meaning a matter of hours away, not days), there are so many other interesting things to experience and understand that the Perceiving type's motivation to complete a project has not yet taken hold.

In 1985 Myers and McCaulley acknowledged a growing area of MBTI research on how students learn that deals with the complexity of type differences. A key example was the study by Eggins (1979), which investigated aptitude by treatment interaction with 350 sixth-grade students (age 11 or 12) involved in classifying animals into groups. Subjects were randomly assigned to one of three methods: (a) an inductive approach based on Bruner's model, which had the least structure; (b) a didactic approach based on Ausubel's advanced organizer model, designed to relate already familiar facts to new concepts; and (c) a highly structured linear presentation based on Gagne's model, which moved from concrete examples to abstract concepts. Intuitive type students benefited most from Bruner's inductive approach. Sensing types who were also field dependent (as measured by the Group Embedded Figures Test) worked best with Gagne's structured model, while Sensing types who were field independent responded better to Ausubel's approach. SJ and NJ types succeeded with any of the three models, while SP and NP types were significantly affected by the instructional design to which they were assigned. The findings from this study help to set the stage for the next section, which deals with the interaction between learners and teachers.

Conclusion

Educators have long known that learners come in various kinds. Unfortunately, too often they have pointed the finger at some kinds as deficient in comparison with their classmates. The theory and research behind the MBTI shed new light on both the virtues and the potential pitfalls of all types. The data summarized in this section suggest that, especially pertaining to the S–N dichotomy, students and teachers can come to understand better the assumptions and needs associated with different approaches to learning tasks.

Teachers and Teacher-Learner Interactions

Learning goes on in context, and the context usually involves interaction not only with other students but also with instructors. The requirements of the curriculum and especially the characteristics of the teacher play a pivotal role, especially since hierarchy and authority are involved. This section reviews patterns found in MBTI research on teachers, their preferred approaches to teaching, and efforts to match teacher with learner by MBTI profile results. Most of the available studies deal with one dichotomy at a time.

Teaching Style Patterns

The following type patterns of teachers are based on a review of research over a number of years (Lawrence, 1993).

- Teachers who prefer Extraversion like to give students choices and a voice in decisions, are easily attuned to the attention levels of their students, and have classrooms with movement and noise. Introverts instead have quieter and more orderly classrooms and structured learning activities and are more attuned to the ideas they are teaching than to students' attention levels.

- Sensing type teachers tend to emphasize facts, practical information, and concrete skills; keep learning centralized; provide a narrow range of student choices; and start a sequence of questions with a request for facts, seeking a predictable response. Intuitive type teachers instead emphasize concepts, relationships, and implications; provide a wide range of choices for students and encourage their voice in decisions; like to form small groups; expect independence and creative behavior; move freely around the room (especially in elementary or middle school settings); have movement and noise in the classroom; and start their questioning of students with an invitation for synthesis and evaluation.

- Thinking type teachers make few comments about student performance, and when they do, it is from an objective standard. They attend to the class as a whole and invite students in return to attend to what they (the teachers) are doing or saying. Feeling type teachers instead regularly provide both praise and criticism in their words and body language. They like students to spend time on individual work, and they move from student to student to assist them, often attending to more than one student at a time.

- Judging type teachers set and adhere to schedules and have quiet and orderly classrooms. Perceiving type teachers, in contrast, encourage movement around the classroom, independent work, open-ended discussion, and socializing in groups, and allow students to have a voice in decisions.

Lawrence (1993) also reported that when students get off task, they do so differently depending on the type of their teacher. The result is increased activity and noise with Extraverted, Intuitive, and Perceiving type teachers. With Introverted, Sensing, and Judging type teachers, the result is daydreaming, doodling, or withdrawal. Miner & Hyman (1988) found that teachers of different types define student misbehaviors differently. Sensing and Thinking types found student profanity a problem, and Sensing types also saw anything interfering with instruction as misbehavior. Thinking and Judging type teachers identified the most items on a list of possible student behaviors as problems, and ENFPs the fewest. ST type teachers were found by Amis-Reichle (1995) to endorse a belief system that children develop as a result of external conditions around them; NF and NT teachers believed that children develop as a result of internal factors.

Matching Teachers with Learners by Type

Efforts to match teachers with learners by MBTI profiles have met with mixed results at best. A full review of the literature in this area can be found in the education chapter in *MBTI Applications* (DiTiberio, 1996). This review includes 9 studies on matching and learner satisfaction, 6 of them with no statistically significant findings, and 18 other studies on matching and learner outcomes, 9 of them lacking statistical significance plus another with results opposite the hypothesized direction. Most were doctoral dissertations, which perhaps had not been published due to the lack of statistical significance. But the general pattern across many studies deserves consideration.

In the learning styles literature (Guild & Garger, 1985) there is a debate among (a) those who recommend that teachers always attempt to match their style of teaching with the needs of the learner, (b) those who believe that learners of all styles should be challenged to meet the expectations of academic standards, and (c) those who propose a combination of the two. The results of MBTI studies seem to confirm the latter approach. At minimum, it is clear that simple matching by type alone does not guarantee either learner satisfaction or successful outcomes.

It appears that students may need different kinds of instruction at different points in their development. Some studies indeed found that opposite type teachers facilitated significant learning for the students (Donovan, 1994). Others found that matching with same or similar type instructors led to better outcomes (Walter, 1984) or greater student satisfaction (Cooper & Miller, 1991; Lamphere, 1985). One study (Boyd, 1995) found that pairing students with teachers of the same type, while favorable overall, was less favorable than when one MBTI preference was different. In his discussion of research on matching types in education, DiTiberio (1996) commented on four studies of computer-assisted instruction, none of which found significant differences in outcome by type preference. The implication is that students at times need the natural support obtained from a teacher who speaks the same language and at other times may benefit from the challenge of a different type. A careful assessment of the student's needs at any point in time is thus called for, rather than a rote assignment by type. Also one should never assume that MBTI profiles alone, for either student or teacher, will indicate adept performance of behaviors usually associated with type preferences; the MBTI only indicates the preferences themselves.

Furthermore, the MBTI and its positive message about all types sometimes leads to an assumption that the dichotomies are simple to understand and apply. They are not. It is easy to overlook the complexity behind type preferences, as was discovered in a study by Dawson and Guy (1994). They set out to design an interdisciplinary graduate course to appeal to Sensing types, who in earlier literature had been found to favor televised media in learning. The results came out opposite to expectation. What had been overlooked were variables that tended to favor Intuitive type students in spite of the best intentions of the researchers: three written assignments and a final exam in essay format; the content of study focusing on "Adult Years: Continuity and Change"; and interdisciplinary instruction from psychology, sociology, counseling, history, and literature. Furthermore, the authors stated that the televised segments "duplicated neither content nor assigned readings, but expanded and enriched . . ." (p. 39). These findings are similar to those from a study by McCaulley, Godleski, Yokomoto, Harrisberger, and Sloan (1983) with engineering students, wherein Sensing types performed better when homework assignments closely replicated the kinds of questions asked on exams, and Intuitive types performed better when they did not. Indeed, some of the early type research on the value of television and audiovisual aids (Golanty-Koel, 1978) found that Sensing types not only appreciate these media in learning but also benefit from having them repeated.

Intuitive instructors who know type theory often find that when Sensing type students ask them to repeat what has just been said, they mean it literally. Instead, Intuitive types tend to paraphrase, or to say things in other words, which appeals to their own interest in variety and change. Such an approach can frustrate Sensing types, who, especially when under stress in a new subject area, need the reassurance that they got it right, which for them only repetition can bring.

Implications for the Classroom

The very mixed results from MBTI research suggest that matching teacher type with learner type may be too simple a solution. Similarly to Cornett (1983), we may conclude that "style matching can be strongly supported for affective reasons, but overall style matching produces inconsistent achievement outcomes" (p. 41). Barth (1980) also wrote that "when teachers are teaching in ways consonant with their own personal style and professional philosophy, both

they and their students appear to benefit" (p. 15). These comments are consistent both with MBTI research and with type theory, which encourages each individual, whether teacher or student, to approach interactions with others by first drawing on natural strengths, followed then by attention to the needs of different others in the interaction.

Academic Aptitude and Achievement

In the 1985 *MBTI Manual,* Myers and McCaulley presented a comprehensive review of decades of study of MBTI profiles compared with standardized test results. The pattern was clear: Standardized tests, especially in verbal sections, tend to favor Intuitive types. Written language involves symbols representing aspects of reality. It is an entirely different phenomenon to experience reality directly, as Sensing types tend to do naturally: to see, hear, taste, smell, and touch it. Words, phrases, and mathematical formulas are all at least one step removed from the world they are designed to represent.

Standardized Measures of Academic Aptitude

In research on academic aptitude in the past decade (Schurr & Ruble, 1986; Schurr, Ruble, & Henriksen, 1988), verbal scores on the Scholastic Aptitude Test (SAT) tend to be consistently higher for Intuitive types as a group and sometimes also for Introverts and Perceiving types; these patterns essentially replicate earlier findings (McCaulley, 1977; McCaulley & Kainz, 1974). SAT math scores tend to be higher for Thinking types (Gallagher, 1988), a pattern also found in earlier research (McCaulley & Kainz, 1974). Studies using other aptitude instruments present similar findings. With the Iowa Test of Basic Skills (Fourqurean, Meisgeier, & Swank, 1988) and the Comprehensive Test of Basic Skills (Lathey, 1991; St. Germain, 1988), Intuitive type students as a group average higher scores than their Sensing type classmates.

Myers and McCaulley (1985) suggested that while occasional studies show preference for Introversion, Thinking, and Perceiving correlating with academic aptitude, the most consistent patterns are found on the S–N dichotomy. As evidence, Table 11.4 shows the actual means, standard deviations, *t*-values, and significance levels for Sensing and Intuitive types across several samples of aptitude measures. Samples include students from eighth grade (roughly age 13) through medical school. It can be seen that in every study and for every scale or subscale the mean scores were higher for Intuitive types. There were larger differences for scales requiring higher levels of abstract or verbal ability, and smaller differences for tests of more practical skills. Of the 38 scales or subscales studied, 32 were statistically significant. Intuitive types are clearly favored on these kinds of measures.

Requiring a time limit on standardized tests further intensifies the distinction between Sensing and Intuition.

Table 11.4 Mean Aptitude Scores for Sensing and Intuition

Aptitude Measure	Sensing			Intuition			
	N	Mean	SD	N	Mean	SD	t
Junior High School Students							
California Test of Mental Maturity[1]							
Overall IQ	118	101.3	14.2	56	112.2	13.6	4.82***
Florida Eighth Grade Test[2]							
Vocabulary	88	62.0	25.4	65	73.9	25.5	2.84**
Comprehension	87	62.7	25.2	66	72.1	24.8	2.32
Computation	89	60.6	25.8	66	64.5	25.8	.94
Problem Solving	89	64.0	26.5	66	72.6	24.9	2.05*
Everyday Living Math	88	20.0	4.3	66	21.0	4.6	1.36
Everyday Living Reading	89	38.9	5.8	68	40.2	4.9	1.47
Study Skills	89	58.9	25.9	68	68.3	28.8	2.14*
Florida Ninth Grade Test[2]							
Verbal	92	55.0	24.1	71	75.4	21.1	5.63***
Quantitative	92	57.4	27.1	71	74.4	25.9	4.04***
Social Studies	92	50.5	24.0	71	71.8	25.0	5.50***
English	92	52.9	24.2	71	69.9	23.8	4.50***
Mathematics #1	92	56.5	27.2	71	74.7	25.2	4.38***
Mathematics #2	92	61.6	27.8	71	78.1	24.6	3.95***
Science	92	47.8	25.1	71	70.0	25.7	5.54***
Florida Twelfth Grade Placement Test[2]							
Aptitude	48	59.6	26.4	38	75.2	25.7	2.76**
English	48	53.2	27.8	38	71.8	25.5	3.19**
Social Studies	48	49.9	22.8	38	67.1	28.2	3.11**
Reading Index	48	52.3	25.4	38	71.4	25.9	3.43***
Natural Science	48	39.9	23.3	38	64.0	29.9	4.20***
Mathematics	48	61.9	24.5	38	73.6	27.3	2.08*
PSAT[2]							
Verbal	38	39.3	8.3	38	51.4	11.6	5.17***
Mathematics	38	48.6	11.6	39	56.1	14.5	2.49**
Gates Reading Test[2]							
Vocabulary	174	51.1	27.7	124	67.7	27.4	5.11***
Comprehension	174	53.6	27.8	124	67.5	31.2	4.03***
Armed Services Vocational Aptitude Battery[2]							
Electrical	44	37.2	22.7	31	48.4	25.7	1.99
Motor Mechanical	40	35.3	18.4	31	39.7	18.5	1.00
General Mechanical	40	35.4	20.5	31	42.8	16.0	1.64
Clerical/Administrative	40	59.2	16.3	31	71.4	15.9	3.16**
General Technical	40	57.4	16.3	31	70.0	20.9	2.85**
California Test of Mental Maturity[2]							
IQ	271	104.0	15.4	187	112.0	14.8	6.11***
College and University Students							
University of Florida Freshmen and Transfers[3]							
Florida Twelfth Grade Placement Test	1,307	387.2	71.97	1,487	416.9	66.28	11.86***
Scholastic Aptitude Test							
Math	561	544.1	86.84	760	565.7	88.42	4.42***
Verbal	558	495.4	84.03	747	540.4	84.89	9.52***
Medical School Students							
Myers' Longitudinal Study[4]							
Medical School Aptitude Test							
Verbal	1,994	486.6	83.8	2,330	552.3	93.2	24.21***
Quantitative	1,994	506.4	92.2	2,330	538.6	92.0	11.43***
General Information	1,183	483.5	88.3	1,330	539.7	94.7	15.34***
Science	1,992	505.5	86.1	2,329	550.6	90.1	16.75***

Note: *p < .05; **p < .01; ***p < .001.

Source: [1]May, 1972; [2]McCaulley & Natter, 1974; [3]McCaulley & Kainz, 1974; [4]McCaulley, 1977.

Sensing often operates slowly in order to be sure, and Intuition is by definition a kind of perception that involves flashes of insight, hunches, and quick perception through impressions. Neither type particularly enjoys taking standardized aptitude tests such as the SAT or the *Graduate Record Exam* (GRE); Intuitive types are, however, more patient with them. They more quickly get the gist of an abstractly worded sentence stem, record a possible answer by trusting their hunch, and move on to the next question. Sensing types also have hunches but tend not to trust them unless through practice they learn that these "guesses" can help them with timed exercises presenting a wealth of complex material.

Myers and McCaulley (1985) reported data from a number of studies showing 52 correlations between either IQ (a traditional measure of general intelligence), SAT-Verbal (V), SAT-Math (M), *Law Scholastic Aptitude Test* (LSAT), GRE-Verbal (V), or GRE-Quantitative (Q) with each of the MBTI scales. When statistically significant, the correlations were in favor of Introversion, Intuition, Perceiving, and sometimes Thinking, and never in the opposite direction. However, the significant correlation values for E–I and J–P were never above .30 and were infrequently above .20 (5 out of 52 investigations for E–I; 4 out of 52 for J–P). When significant on the T–F dichotomy, 7 out of 52 investigations were above .20. Only the S–N dichotomy stood out: When significant, 23 out of the 52 investigations were above .20, with .47 the highest correlation value reported.

Because of the relatively consistent pattern of significance for both the E–I and S–N dichotomies on aptitude, Myers and McCaulley (1985) further reported mean scores of IN, EN, IS, and ES types for several samples on aptitude. The theoretical prediction that the means would rank in the order of IN > EN > IS > ES was confirmed, a pattern later replicated by Kalsbeek (1987). Myers and McCaulley added a note of caution, however: "It is important not to conclude that ES types are less intelligent than IN types. Scholastic aptitude tests measure the I and N aspects of intelligence particularly valued in academic work; they are not designed to measure the practical, applied intelligence of E and S" (1985, pp. 109–110). Myers (with Myers, 1980/1995) has also wisely noted that "Ns tend to define intelligence as 'quickness of understanding' and . . . S types . . . tend to define intelligence as 'soundness of understanding'" (p. 59). Her profound discussion in those pages suggests that intelligence is a concept that goes well beyond the limited scope of IQ tests or SATs and that Jung's type theory and MBTI research have much to offer to current debates in this area. Back in 1962 Myers wrote of such differences as "habits of mind": "[T]he essential difference between IN and ES which is operative here is a habit of mind which produces, among other results, a characteristic level of interest in activities which suit each type and disinterest in activities which do not" (p. 44). While no studies to date have compared MBTI profiles with measures of multiple intelligence,

the words of Myers and McCaulley suggest that this would be a fruitful line of future investigation.

An early study of college freshmen reported by Myers (1962) called attention to the influence of timed test conditions on S–N differences in academic aptitude. Mean scores on Terman's *Concept Mastery Test* (CMT), an untimed measure of high ranges of vocabulary and verbal reasoning, favored both Introverted and Intuitive types, as in other studies. But the advantage of Intuition was primarily found in students who also preferred Introversion. Myers reported that this was based "in part on the fact that Concept Mastery is untimed, so that the Intuitives' speed is no particular asset, and the Introverts' depth can be fully utilized" (p. 36). These findings were also discussed in Myers and McCaulley (1985).

This study by Myers (1962) is one of several that have highlighted the influence of the clarity of preference on measures of aptitude. Myers and McCaulley (1985) reported that, with the exception of Sensing, as students' preferences became clearer, average IQ scores increased. The pattern held true for Extraversion and Introversion, Thinking and Feeling, and Judging and Perceiving, but only for Intuition on the S–N dichotomy. At all levels of preference, Sensing types scored about the same on IQ. The same pattern regarding the preference score was also reported as it pertained to achievement, with grades remaining relatively the same at all levels of preference for Sensing but tending to increase with clearer preferences for each of the other MBTI polarities.

Grades and Academic Achievement

Studies of type and academic achievement continue to proliferate, but the results appear to be the same as in earlier research: Judging types tend to obtain higher grades than Perceiving types. Apparently the need for closure and an organized approach to external events get results, especially in schools where the predominant teacher type also tends to be Judging. The pattern seems to be the same whether dealing with high school students (Casey, 1986; Kyle, 1985), college freshmen (Kalsbeek, 1987; Pollard, 1989; Provost, 1985), undergraduates in general (Anchors et al., 1989; Schurr & Ruble, 1986; Woodruff & Clarke, 1993), specific majors (Tharp, 1992), or first-year medical students (Neral, 1989). Schurr and Ruble (1988), however, while confirming the preference for Judging, also found different grade patterns in college on other MBTI dichotomies depending on area of study: In abstract and theoretical courses Introverts and Intuitive types obtained higher grades, but in practical and applied courses Extraverts and Sensing types did better. Similarly, Kalsbeek (1987) found that while Introversion, Intuition, and Judging each contributed to first-semester grades, college students' grades in their major fields were influenced only by a preference for Judging.

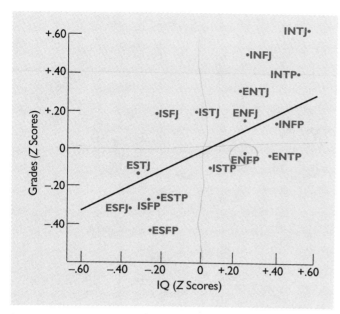

Figure 11.1 Comparison of Intelligence and Grades of the 16 Types in High School

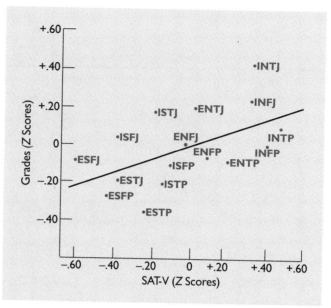

Figure 11.2 Comparison of Aptitude and Achievement of the 16 Types in Liberal Arts

From an early study reported by Myers (1962), Figure 11.1 translates both grades (GPA) and IQ results into standard scores for comparison. She cautioned that to obtain the most accurate portrayal of the natural academic behavior of each type, the plots would have to be done at the high school level before dropout, self-selection, or the decisions of college admission committees have their effect. Thus the mean for each of the 16 types is plotted in this sample of 3,503 college preparatory males from 27 Pennsylvania high schools. The placement of the regression line represents a correlation of .47 between grades and IQ scores.

From this figure, a number of patterns can be observed:

■ Judging types have both higher mean grades and higher mean IQ, and Perceiving types get lower grades than expected for their level of IQ. This pattern may be observed by noting that every Judging type but ESFJ appears above the line, and every Perceiving type but INTP appears below it. Furthermore, for every pairing of types with the first three letters the same, the Judging type has the higher average grades.

■ Intuitive types consistently obtain higher average IQ scores than Sensing types.

■ The three preferences that appear to contribute most to success on these two factors (grades and IQ) are Introversion, Intuition, and Judging.

■ The mean scores for the range of grades extends more than one standard deviation from top (INTJ) to bottom (ESFP). However, a more conservative reading would note that the mean grades for all 16 types fall within a range of *less* than one standard deviation above and below the standard score mean of zero. Thus the advantage of Introversion, Intuition, and Judging is a relative one.

For comparison, Figure 11.2 shows a similar distribution of mean scores for verbal academic aptitude (SAT-V) and grades for liberal arts college students. The range of scores is narrower than for the high school students in Figure 11.1, although Introversion, Intuition, and Judging still appear to be favored among the types performing well on both measures. Myers and McCaulley (1985) also called attention in this figure to the interesting pattern regarding the T–F dichotomy. While Thinking types outscore Feeling types on mean grades for those types appearing in the upper half of the sample, the reverse pattern is found in the lower half. The context of liberal arts seems to draw Thinking types with slightly higher aptitude scores than their Feeling type classmates; but when grades are obtained, the advantage of Thinking is maintained only above the standard score mean of zero, below which Feeling then seems to become a favored preference.

Figures 11.3 and 11.4 provide further results indicating the interaction of academic context with type, aptitude, and performance. As described by Myers and McCaulley (1985), these data show the patterns of 370 medical students using standard scores for both grades and national board scores (in Figure 11.3) and ratings for the same students later in their training by clinical faculty on both medical expertise and enthusiastic involvement in clinical contacts (in Figure 11.4). While ENFJs obtained lower than average grades and board scores, they became far and away the most outstanding performers in the clinical setting in ratings of both medical expertise and enthusiasm. The favorable grades and board scores obtained by INFJ and ISTJ medical students seemed not to help them particularly once involved in clinical rotations, since their ratings by

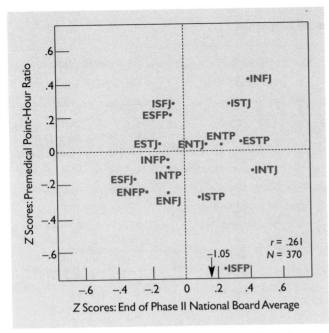

Figure 11.3 Premedical Point-Hour Ratio Compared with the National Board Average at the End of Phase II of Medical School

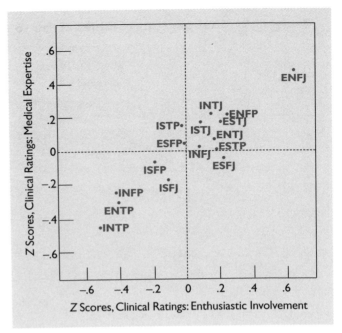

Figure 11.4 Clinical Ratings for Medical Expertise Compared with Clinical Ratings for Enthusiastic Involvement in Medical Students

faculty were barely above average on both dimensions. Six of the eight Extraverted types were rated high for enthusiastic involvement; three of the four NP types (INFP, INTP, ENTP), often known as independent spirits, received low ratings.

These findings are similar to the patterns reported by Schurr, Henriksen, Alcorn, and Dillard (1992), which indicate that standardized measures, which tend to give readings of broad academic aptitude or general knowledge, may not translate into competence in a chosen field of study. They discovered, for example, that both education and nursing students draw a proportionately high number of SJ types. While these types tend to be outscored by Intuitive types on both standardized aptitude and first-year grades, when they persist to graduation they do well and populate the professions of choice.

Tables 11.5 and 11.6 show comparisons of ranks of the 16 types for, respectively, academic aptitude and grades or class standing. These tables include not only the results of early studies reported by Myers and McCaulley (1985) but more recent samples as well. Within each cell of the type table is listed the hypothesized rank based upon Jung's theory of how the various types would be predicted to perform in each domain. For both aptitude (standardized tests) and achievement (grades or class standing), Introversion, Intuition, and, less firmly, Thinking were hypothesized to hold an advantage, as discussed earlier. The open-minded curiosity of Perceiving types leads to a theoretical prediction of their advantage in aptitude; the concern for productivity of Judging types leads to the hypothesis of higher grades.

In specific samples, there was occasionally variation from prediction. However, across the many studies shown in Tables 11.5 and 11.6, type theory appears confirmed. With only a few exceptions IN types consistently obtained ranks, as predicted from theory, as the highest four types for both academic aptitude and grades. The four ES types never obtained a top-four ranking for aptitude and only twice (both involving ESTJ) appeared in the top four ranks for grades. Perceiving types tended to rank higher on aptitude and Judging types on achievement.

Implications for the Classroom

Since the MBTI and Jung's theory hypothesize that type is in part inborn, some rather thorny questions naturally emerge when we examine consistent findings on the aptitude and performance of certain types. It should be noted, however, that even if the MBTI successfully identifies fundamental processes that have an innate component, biology is not destiny. All types can and do behave in varying ways, depending on the requirements of the situation, the opportunity to learn new skills, and the motivation to do so. The data reported on these pages should not be interpreted as an indication of an inherent lack in any type. Instead they should be read as indicating that the preferred starting points for some types may tend to put them at a disadvantage without further intervention, training, support, or challenge. They may also suggest ways to understand the potential biases of educators and psychometricians who design and give weight to standardized assessments of this sort.

Table 11.5 Comparisons of Ranks of the 16 Types by Aptitude

ISTJ (11)	ISFJ (12)	INFJ (4)	INTJ (3)
3 College students SAT-V	4 Auburn males ACT	1 Ball State males SAT-V	1 High school males IQ
5 Univ Florida females SAT-V	6 Engineering students SAT-M	1 Ball State males SAT-M	1 Auburn males ACT
6 Business students SAT-M	7.3 Ball State males SAT-M	1 Ball State females SAT-M	1 Auburn females ACT
6 Auburn males ACT	8 Ball State females SAT-M	2 Auburn males ACT	1 Univ Florida males SAT-V
7 9th–12th graders IQ	8 Auburn females ACT	3 Business students SAT-M	1 Univ Florida females SAT-V
7 Univ Florida males SAT-V	9 Ball State females SAT-V	4 Liberal arts students SAT-V	2 Ball State females SAT-M
9 Auburn females ACT	9 Univ Florida females SAT-V	4 Univ Florida males SAT-V	2 Ball State females SAT-V
9.5 Ball State females SAT-M	10 Medical freshmen MCAT-V	4 Univ Florida females SAT-V	2 9th–12th graders IQ
10 Ball State males SAT-V	11 Ball State males SAT-V	4 Medical freshmen MCAT-V	2 Business students SAT-M
10 High school males IQ	11 High school males IQ	5 High school males IQ	3 Liberal arts students SAT-V
11 Liberal arts students SAT-V	11 Univ Florida males SAT-V	6 9th–12th graders IQ	3 Medical freshmen MCAT-V
12 Ball State males SAT-M	13 College students SAT-V	6 Auburn females ACT	3.5 Ball State males SAT-M
14 Ball State females SAT-V	14 8th graders IQ	7 Ball State females SAT-V	3.5 8th graders IQ
14 Medical freshmen MCAT-V	14 Liberal arts students SAT-V	7 College students SAT-V	5 Ball State males SAT-V
16 8th graders IQ	14 Business students SAT-M	11 8th graders IQ	8 Engineering students SAT-M
16 Engineering Students SAT-M	15 9th–12th graders IQ	12 Engineering students SAT-M	8 College students SAT-V

ISTP (9)	ISFP (10)	INFP (2)	INTP (1)
2 Engineering students SAT-M	2 College students SAT-V	1 Business students SAT-M	1 Ball State females SAT-V
5 Business students SAT-M	7.3 Ball State males SAT-M	1 Medical freshmen MCAT-V	1 Liberal arts students SAT-V
8 9th–12th graders IQ	8 Univ Florida females SAT-V	1 College students SAT-V	1 Engineering students SAT-M
8 Auburn males ACT	9 Ball State males SAT-V	2 Ball State males SAT-V	2 High school males IQ
8 Medical freshmen MCAT-V	9 8th graders IQ	2 Liberal arts students SAT-V	2 Univ Florida females SAT-V
8 College students SAT-V	9 Liberal arts students SAT-V	3 Ball State females SAT-V	2 Univ Florida males SAT-V
9 High school males IQ	9 Univ Florida males SAT-V	3 High school males IQ	2 Medical freshmen MCAT-V
10 Ball State females SAT-V	10 Auburn females ACT	3 9th–12th graders IQ	3 Ball State females SAT-M
10 Liberal arts students SAT-V	11 Ball State females SAT-M	3 Auburn females ACT	3 Ball State males SAT-V
11 Ball State males SAT-M	11.5 Ball State females SAT-V	3 Univ Florida females SAT-V	3.5 Ball State males SAT-M
11 Univ Florida females SAT-V	12 Engineering students SAT-M	3.5 8th graders IQ	4 9th–12th graders IQ
12 Ball State males SAT-V	12 Medical freshmen MCAT-V	4 Ball State females SAT-M	5 College students SAT-V
12 8th graders IQ	13 9th–12th graders IQ	5 Ball State males SAT-M	6 8th graders IQ
12 Univ Florida males SAT-V	13 Business students SAT-M	5 Univ Florida males SAT-V	7 Business students SAT-M
15 Ball State females SAT-M	13 Auburn males ACT	9 Engineering students SAT-M	9 Auburn males ACT
15 Auburn females ACT	14 High school males IQ	16 Auburn males ACT	16 Auburn females ACT

continued

Note: Rank predicted by theory in parentheses; decimals indicate tied rank within the study in question.

Approaches to Reading, Writing, and Foreign Language Learning

As in other areas, quantitative research studies have emerged, especially in the past decade, that call attention to type preferences in the broad arena of literacy: reading, writing, and foreign language learning. In addition, a number of qualitative methods involving observations and interviews with subjects have helped to flesh out how type preferences interact with one's approach to these important tasks.

Quantitative Findings

Traditional research studies employing relatively large samples with measurable outcomes have been reported in the literature. They are summarized here separately for reading, writing, and foreign language learning, in that order.

Reading In studies of reading, the quantitative data are consistent and clear. As in academic aptitude and achievement in general, verbal fluency tends to favor Intuitive types. Studies have investigated the relationship of type with language competence and reading comprehension

Table 11.5 Comparisons of Ranks of the 16 Types by Aptitude *continued*

ESTP (13)	ESFP (14)	ENFP (6)	ENTP (5)
5 College students SAT-V	6 Engineering students SAT-M	2 Ball State males SAT-M	1 8th graders IQ
10 Auburn males ACT	11 Medical freshmen MCAT-V	2 8th graders IQ	1 9th–12th graders IQ
11 9th–12th graders IQ	12 Ball State females SAT-M	4 Ball State males SAT-V	3 Auburn males ACT
11 Business students SAT-M	12 Auburn females ACT	4 Business students SAT-M	3 Univ Florida males SAT-V
11 Auburn females ACT	13 Ball State females SAT-V	4 College students SAT-V	4 Ball State females SAT-V
11.5 Ball State females SAT-V	13 High school males IQ	5 Auburn females ACT	4 High school males IQ
12 Engineering students SAT-M	14 9th–12th graders IQ	6 Liberal arts students SAT-V	4 Engineering students SAT-M
12 High school males IQ	14 Univ Florida males SAT-V	6 Engineering students SAT-M	4 Auburn females ACT
12 Liberal arts students SAT-V	15 Ball State males SAT-V	6 Univ Florida males SAT-V	5 Ball State females SAT-M
13 8th graders IQ	15 Ball State males SAT-M	6 Medical freshmen MCAT-V	5 Liberal arts students SAT-V
13 Univ Florida males SAT-V	15 8th graders IQ	7 High school males IQ	5 Medical freshmen MCAT-V
13 Medical freshmen MCAT-V	15 Liberal arts students SAT-V	7 Univ Florida females SAT-V	6 Ball State males SAT-V
16 Ball State males SAT-V	15 Auburn males ACT	8 Ball State females SAT-V	6 Ball State males SAT-M
16 Ball State males SAT-M	15 Univ Florida females SAT-V	9.5 Ball State females SAT-M	6 Univ Florida females SAT-V
16 Ball State females SAT-M	15 College students SAT-V	14 Auburn males ACT	10 College students SAT-V
16 Univ Florida females SAT-V	16 Business students SAT-M	16 9th–12th graders IQ	12 Business students SAT-M

ESTJ (15)	ESFJ (16)	ENFJ (8)	ENTJ (7)
9 Business students SAT-M	7 Auburn males ACT	3 Engineering students SAT-M	2 Auburn females ACT
10 8th graders IQ	8 8th graders IQ	5.5 Ball State females SAT-V	5 8th graders IQ
10 9th–12th graders IQ	8 Business students SAT-M	6 High school males IQ	5 9th–12th graders IQ
11 Auburn males ACT	12 9th–12th graders IQ	6.5 Ball State females SAT-M	5 Auburn males ACT
13 Ball State males SAT-M	13 Ball State males SAT-V	7 Ball State males SAT-V	5.5 Ball State females SAT-V
13 Liberal arts students SAT-V	13 Auburn females ACT	7 8th graders IQ	6.5 Ball State females SAT-M
13 Univ Florida females SAT-V	14 Ball State females SAT-M	7 Auburn females ACT	7 Liberal arts students SAT-V
14 Ball State males SAT-V	14 Ball State males SAT-M	7 Medical freshmen MCAT-V	7.3 Ball State males SAT-M
14 Engineering students SAT-M	14 Univ Florida females SAT-V	8 Liberal arts students SAT-V	8 Ball State males SAT-V
14 Auburn females ACT	14 College students SAT-V	8 Univ Florida males SAT-V	8 High school males IQ
15 Ball State females SAT-V	15 Engineering students SAT-M	9 9th–12th graders IQ	9 Medical freshmen MCAT-V
15 High school males IQ	15 Medical freshmen MCAT-V	10 Ball State males SAT-M	10 Engineering students SAT-M
15 Univ Florida males SAT-V	16 Ball State females SAT-V	10 Univ Florida females SAT-V	10 Business students SAT-M
16 Ball State females SAT-M	16 High school males IQ	11 College students SAT-V	10 Univ Florida males SAT-V
16 Medical freshmen MCAT-V	16 Liberal arts students SAT-V	12 Auburn males ACT	12 Univ Florida females SAT-V
16 College students SAT-V	16 Univ Florida males SAT-V	15 Business students SAT-M	12 College students SAT-V

Note: Rank predicted by theory in parentheses; decimals indicate tied rank within the study in question.

Source: Auburn University females (*N* = 518): Freshmen at Auburn University (Conary in Myers & McCaulley, 1985); Auburn University males (*N* = 1,191): Freshmen at Auburn University (Conary in Myers & McCaulley, 1985); Ball State University females (*N* = 1,553): Undergraduates at Ball State University (Schurr & Ruble, 1986); Ball State University males (*N* = 1,160): Undergraduates at Ball State University (Schurr & Ruble, 1986); Business students (*N* = 488): Wharton School students (Myers in Myers & McCaulley, 1985); College students (*N* = 611): Humanities students at Scripps College (Dunning in Myers & McCaulley, 1985); 8th graders (*N* = 133): Florida urban and suburban middle school students (Mebane in McCaulley & Kainz, 1976); Engineering students (*N* = 2,188): Freshmen at California Institute of Technology, Cornell, and Massachusetts Institute of Technology (Myers in Myers & McCaulley, 1985); High school males (*N* = 3,503): College preparatory students in suburban Philadelphia (Myers in Myers & McCaulley, 1985); Liberal arts students (*N* = 3,676): Freshmen at Amherst, Brown, Dartmouth, Stanford, and Wesleyan (Myers in Myers & McCaulley, 1985); Medical freshmen (*N* = 4,324): Undesignated medical schools (Myers in McCaulley, 1977); 9th–12th graders (*N* = 458): Florida State University laboratory school students (McCaulley & Natter, 1974); University of Florida females (*N* = 564): Undergraduates at University of Florida (Myers & McCaulley, 1985); University of Florida males (*N* = 741): Undergraduates at University of Florida (Myers & McCaulley, 1985).

Table 11.6   Comparisons of the Ranks of the 16 Types by Grades or Class Standing

ISTJ (9)	ISFJ (10)	INFJ (2)	INTJ (1)
3 Univ Florida females	3 College students	1 Ball State males high school rank	1 Ball State females high school rank
3.5 Liberal arts students	4 Ball State females high school rank	1 Ball State males	1 Ball State females
4 Business students	4.5 Engineering students	1 Business students	1 High school males
4.5 Engineering students	5 Ball State males	1 Auburn females	1 Liberal arts students
5 Ball State females high school rank	5 Univ Florida males	1 Univ Florida females	1 Engineering students
5 High school males	5.5 Ball State males high school rank	1 9th–12th graders	1 Auburn males
6 Auburn males	5.5 Univ Florida females	2 Ball State females high school rank	1 Univ Florida males
7 Ball State males high school rank	6 Ball State females	2 Ball State females	2 Univ Florida females
7 Ball State females	6 High school males	2 High school males	2 Medical freshmen
7 Ball State males	7 Liberal arts students	2 Liberal arts students	3 Business students
7 Univ Florida males	7 Auburn males	2 Engineering students	4 Ball State males
9 Auburn females	9 Business students	2 Auburn males	5 Auburn females
12 College students	11 Medical freshmen	2 College students	5.5 Ball State males high school rank
14 Medical freshmen	13 9th–12th graders	3 Univ Florida males	10 9th–12th graders
16 9th–12th graders	15 Auburn females	3 Medical freshmen	14 College students

ISTP (11)	ISFP (12)	INFP (4)	INTP (3)
6 Business students	3.5 Ball State males high school rank	2 Ball State males high school rank	2 Univ Florida males
7.5 Ball State females high school rank	4 College students	2 Ball State males	3 Ball State females high school rank
8 College students	9 Engineering students	4 Auburn males	3 Ball State females
8 9th–12th graders	9.5 Ball State females high school rank	4 Auburn females	3 High school males
10.5 Ball State females	11 Auburn males	4 Univ Florida males	3 9th–12th graders
11 High school males	12 Ball State females	4 Medical freshmen	5 Liberal arts students
11 Engineering students	12 Liberal arts students	4 9th–12th graders	7 Medical freshmen
12 Univ Florida males	13 Ball State males	5 Ball State females	8 Engineering students
13 Medical freshmen	13 Business students	6 Liberal arts students	10 Business students
13.5 Ball State males high school rank	13 Auburn females	6 College students	10.5 Ball State males high school rank
14 Liberal arts students	13 Univ Florida females	7 Engineering students	11 Univ Florida females
14.5 Auburn males	14 High school males	8 High school males	12 Ball State males
15 Ball State males	15 Univ Florida males	8 Univ Florida females	12 Auburn females
16 Auburn females	15 9th–12th graders	9.5 Ball State females high school rank	13 Auburn males
16 Univ Florida females	16 Medical freshmen	12 Business students	15 College students

Note: Rank predicted by theory in parentheses; decimals indicate tied rank within the study in question.

(Hester, 1990), reported numbers of books read (Hammer, 1985; Hicks, 1984, 1985, 1989; Levine, 1988; Moore & Bayne, 1997), reading comprehension scores on the McGraw-Hill Basic Skills System Reading Test (Thomason, 1983) and the Nelson-Denny Reading Test (Manske, 1988), and proofreading ability (Gordy & Thorne, 1994). In every case Intuitive types had the advantage (except in Hammer's study, where NF types were followed by ST second and NT third in number of books read). These results pertaining to the advantage of Intuition in reading confirm findings from earlier studies reported by Myers and McCaulley (1985).

Specific aspects of reading have drawn findings on other MBTI dichotomies. For example, detail reading favored Introverts and Thinking types, and critical reading favored Judging types (Thomason, 1983). Thinking types performed better in comprehension when reading expository passages and Feeling types when reading narratives (Singer, 1989).

Writing   Type theory also appears to be a natural tool for writing instructors (and for writers themselves). Some of the patterns of preferred writing processes found by quantitative research are as follows:

Table 11.6   Comparisons of the Ranks of the 16 Types by Grades or Class Standing *continued*

ESTP (15)	ESFP (16)	ENFP (8)	ENTP (7)
6 Medical freshmen	10 College students	3 Auburn females	6 9th–12th graders
10.5 Auburn females	10.5 Auburn females	4 Ball State females	8 Medical freshmen
12 Univ Florida females	14 9th–12th graders	7 Univ Florida females	9 Ball State females
12 College students	15 Ball State females high school rank	7 Business students	9 Auburn males
12 9th–12th graders	15 Liberal arts students	7 9th–12th graders	10 Ball State males
13 High school males	15 Engineering students	8 Ball State males high school rank	10 High school males
13 Univ Florida males	15 Univ Florida females	8 Ball State males	10 Univ Florida males
14 Ball State males	15 Medical freshmen	8 Auburn males	10.5 Liberal arts students
14 Engineering students	16 Ball State males high school rank	9 High school males	12 Engineering students
14.5 Auburn males	16 Ball State males	9 Liberal arts students	12.5 Ball State females high school rank
15 Ball State females	16 Ball State females	9 College students	13.5 Ball State males high school rank
15 Ball State males high school rank	16 High school males	11 Univ Florida males	14 Business students
15 Business students	16 Business students	12 Medical freshmen	14 Auburn females
16 Ball State females high school rank	16 Auburn males	13 Engineering students	14 Univ Florida females
16 Liberal arts students	16 Univ Florida males	14 Ball State females high school rank	16 College students

ESTJ (13)	ESFJ (14)	ENFJ (6)	ENTJ (5)
2 9th–12th graders	5.5 Univ Florida females	1 College students	2 Business students
4 College students	8 Business students	1 Medical freshmen	2 Auburn females
5 Business students	8 Auburn females	3 Engineering students	3 Ball State males
6 Auburn females	9 Ball State males	3.5 Ball State males high school rank	3 Auburn males
10 Engineering students	9 Univ Florida males	5 Auburn males	3.5 Liberal arts males
10 Univ Florida females	9 Medical freshmen	6 Ball State males	4 Ball State females
10 Medical freshmen	10.5 Liberal arts students	6 High school males	4 High school males
10.5 Ball State males high school rank	11 Auburn males	7 Auburn females	4 Univ Florida females
10.5 Ball State females	11 College students	7.5 Ball State females high school rank	5 Medical freshmen
11 Ball State females high school rank	11 9th–12th graders	8 Ball State females	5 9th–12th graders
11 Ball State males	12 Ball State females	8 Liberal arts students	6 Ball State females high school rank
11 Auburn males	12 Ball State males high school rank	8 Univ Florida males	6 Engineering students
12 High school males	12.5 Ball State females high school rank	9 Univ Florida females	6 Univ Florida males
13 Liberal arts students	15 High school males	9 9th–12th graders	7 College students
14 Univ Florida males	16 Engineering students	11 Business students	9 Ball State males high school rank

Note: Rank predicted by theory in parentheses; decimals indicate tied rank within the study in question.

Source: Auburn University females (*N* = 518): Freshmen at Auburn University (Conary in Myers & McCaulley, 1985); Auburn University males (*N* = 1,191): Freshmen at Auburn University (Conary in Myers & McCaulley, 1985); Ball State University females (*N* = 1,553): Undergraduates at Ball State University (Schurr & Ruble, 1986); Ball State University males (*N* = 1,160): Undergraduates at Ball State University (Schurr & Ruble, 1986); Business students (*N* = 488): Wharton School students (Myers in Myers & McCaulley, 1985); College students (*N* = 611): Humanities students at Scripps College (Dunning in Myers & McCaulley, 1985); Engineering students (*N* = 2,188): Freshmen at California Institute of Technology, Cornell, and Massachusetts Institute of Technology (Myers in Myers & McCaulley, 1985); High school males (*N* = 3,503): College preparatory students in suburban Philadelphia (Myers in Myers & McCaulley, 1985); Liberal arts students (*N* = 3,676): Freshmen at Amherst, Brown, Dartmouth, Stanford, and Wesleyan (Myers in Myers & McCaulley, 1985); Medical freshmen (*N* = 4,324): Undesignated medical schools (Myers in McCaulley, 1977); 9th–12th graders (*N* = 513): Florida State University laboratory school students (McCaulley & Natter, 1974); University Florida females (*N* = 564): Undergraduates at University of Florida (Myers & McCaulley, 1985); University Florida males (*N* = 741): Undergraduates at University of Florida (Myers & McCaulley, 1985).

- As students, Extraverts prefer to choose their own topics and to read papers aloud for peer response, while Introverts prefer to have the teacher lead the class (Severino, 1989) and score higher than Extraverts both on composition grades and on the Test of Standard Written English (Schurr, Houlette, & Ellen, 1986). Extraverts were also found to send more and longer e-mail messages and replies in a study of computer use (Bail, 1993).

- Sensing types obtain higher ratings as eighth graders (roughly ages 12–13) in expressive writing (Vondran, 1989) and want the teacher to lead the class (Severino, 1989), while Intuitive types prefer to choose their own topics and to read papers aloud (Severino, 1989), use more words per sentence (Carrell & Monroe, 1993), receive high grades on reflective papers and lower grades on reporting (Fisher, 1994), and tend to present an overview with little focus when asked for a summary (Held & Yokomoto, 1983).

- Thinking types obtain higher ratings in persuasive writing as eighth graders (Vondran, 1989). They also make more literary judgments when asked to write an evaluation of material of relatively low quality, while Feeling types instead make self-references while writing about literary material (Price, 1993). Feeling types also use persuasion when asked to write argumentative papers (Fisher, 1994).

- Judging types obtain higher ratings for explanatory essays in eighth grade (Vondran, 1989), and Perceiving types obtain more average and poor ratings in technical writing (Held & Yokomoto, 1983) and use more words per sentence (Carrell & Monroe, 1993; Jensen & DiTiberio, 1989).

Foreign Language Learning In foreign language learning, a number of quantitative studies have indicated that Intuitive and Perceiving types perform well. Moody (1988) found Introverted, Intuitive, Thinking, and Perceiving types most frequent among college students of foreign languages, while Oxford and Ehrman (1988) found Extraverted, Intuitive, and Perceiving types most frequent among foreign language professionals. The highest language aptitude scores in one study were received by Intuitive types (Ehrman, 1995), while Intuitive, Thinking, and Perceiving types obtained high proficiency in reading and speaking foreign languages in two other studies (Ehrman, 1994a; Ehrman & Oxford, 1995). Sensing types were rated among the weakest language learners (Ehrman, 1994b). Gautsch (1993) found that Perceiving types outscored Judging types on measures of language proficiency regardless of the approach to instruction. Ehrman and Oxford (1990) reported a general language learning advantage for Introverted, Intuitive, Feeling, and Perceiving types.

Qualitative Findings

The results of qualitative interviews have indicated differing processes for the various types in foreign language learning, writing, and reading. These kinds of studies remind us of a central tenet of type theory: that all types have the potential for competence but that their preferred processes may put them at a temporary disadvantage until they can find a means (or a mentor) to assist in the transition to the unfamiliar territory of new learning.

For example, Ehrman and Oxford (1990) reported that Sensing types describe language learning as a gradual process, saying that they like to memorize. They find it frustrating to have to "guess" and have a low tolerance for ambiguity. In contrast, Intuitive types tend to be linguistic risk takers and see language learning as often an unconscious process. In another study (Oxford & Ehrman, 1988), Intuitive and Perceiving types reported that they like to search for and communicate meaning (as did Introverts in another study by Ehrman & Oxford in 1989), and Intuitive types liked formal model building and liked to seek out native speakers with whom they could engage in authentic language use. Affective strategies to overcome the fear of using the new language were most helpful to Extraverts and Intuitive types, while Extraverts also liked visualization as an aid to learning. In another study (Ehrman, 1990), NTs were found to be analytical, sometimes to the point of overcomplexity, and liked to build formal models in their learning. In contrast, SFs were not oriented to experimentation, STs preferred specific goals and objectives and a clearly outlined curriculum, and NFs, who cited the fewest actual strategies for language learning, clearly rejected analysis as one of them.

The disparity between the performance of Sensing and Intuitive types in many academic arenas has been narrowed in writing, as reported in several studies. Ferdman and DiTiberio (1996), for example, found that eight fifth-grade students (roughly ages 9–10) who had been identified by their previous teachers as deficient in writing were all Sensing types as indicated by the MMTIC. However, after six months of instruction by the first author, taking type preferences into account, nearly all of these children expressed increased confidence in themselves as writers and were performing accordingly. Many of the successful type-based approaches to writing that had been reported among college students and adults in previous studies (DiTiberio & Jensen, 1995; Jensen & DiTiberio, 1984, 1989) were equally useful for working with elementary students. These kinds of case studies confirm that type preferences, while possibly fundamental in an inborn way, do not have to limit one's potential.

Implications for the Classroom

The general message from research is that effective instruction, at least in the area of language literacy, comes from acknowledging multiple processes. It appears that the

MBTI and Jung's theory provide a useful model for understanding the various activities, stages, and processes that learners go through while acquiring confidence and competence as readers, writers, or speakers of either their native language or a foreign language.

Using Type in Elementary and Secondary Education

This section addresses several current issues in the education of different types of children at the elementary (roughly ages 5–11) and secondary (roughly ages 12–18) levels, with particular focus on gifted students, learning disabilities, and behavior disorders. It is wise to note first that professionals in education, whether classroom teachers or administrators, tend predominantly to prefer Judging at all levels, usually by a ratio of two to one (DiTiberio, 1996; Lawrence, 1993; Myers & McCaulley, 1985). Given the nature of schools as organizations, this is not surprising. There are implications of this finding when attending to different processes in learning, however. Educators need to acknowledge both the virtues and the potential pitfalls of each, including, as one example, Judging and Perceiving approaches alike.

Gifted Students

A recent study dealing with learners identified as academically talented (Mills et al., 1996) found that in using the *Murphy-Meisgeier Type Indicator for Children* (MMTIC) with these students in grades 3 through 6 (roughly ages 8–11), ENFP types were disproportionately represented compared with their frequency in the general population. ENFPs were also more frequent than in an older sample (which used the MBTI) of academically talented students in grades 8 through 10 (roughly ages 13–15). Mills et al. found a slight gender difference, with males appearing more frequently as Extraverted and females as Introverted. Since the same criteria were used to designate these gifted students at the two levels, the authors questioned whether profiles from the MMTIC can faithfully be compared with those from the MBTI. The question clearly deserves further study and echoes Murphy's (1992) suggestion that type in young children should be considered in light of their developmental exploration, not as an established set of "true type" preferences.

Nevertheless, these same preferences for Extraversion, Intuition, Feeling, and Perceiving have been found to characterize gifted learners in other studies, such as the one by Williams (1992) with students aged 7 through 19. Delbridge-Parker and Robinson (1989) found Intuitive, Thinking, and IN types to be predominant among academically gifted junior high students (ages 12–14), and Wittig,

Schurr, & Ruble (1986) found Intuition but also Introversion and Feeling to characterize students in the honors college at a state university. Introversion, Intuition, Thinking, and Perceiving were the most frequent preferences for students attending a national Academic Decathlon competition (Robinson, 1994). These studies confirming Intuition as a process consistently favored among academically gifted students replicate findings reported originally by Myers (1962) for junior high school students.

Because type theory posits potential strengths of all types, results from the MBTI or the MMTIC provide a means for understanding the possible contextual biases that tend to discriminate against otherwise very capable students. Giftedness is often defined in language that mirrors the natural preferences of Intuitive types. However, Robinson's (1994) study produced some interesting contrasts for Sensing types. While in the minority overall among these Academic Decathlon participants, ST and SP types were overrepresented in percentage when compared with samples of National Merit Finalists. The direct activity (for SPs) and competitive atmosphere (for STs) of this medium might draw very capable Sensing types that other means of assessing academic strengths do not. In another interesting study, Chiang (1991) asked gifted learners to rate the effectiveness of their teachers. Extraverted, Sensing, Thinking, and Judging type teachers were given the highest ratings. The rating form, however, listed the following characteristics as options: organization, classroom management, teaching skill, course impact, student participation, and rapport. Open-ended questions pertaining to these successful teachers received the following comments from students: "speaks clearly," "shows energy and excitement," "uses concrete examples," and "presents thought-provoking ideas."

Learning Disabilities and Behavior Disorders

Learning and behavior disorders have been examined in several studies through the lens of type. Conduct-disordered students were found not to vary in type preference from the general population of students, but emotionally disturbed students included higher percentages of Introverted, Thinking, IJ, IP, ST, and IS types (Kelly, 1991). Students labeled with attention deficit disorder (ADD) did not differ by type from the general student body, and subsamples of ADD students with and without hyperactivity also did not vary by type (Meisgeier, Poillion, and Haring, 1994). But ADD students did differ from their teachers in that they included disproportionately higher percentages of Extraverted, Sensing, Feeling, and Perceiving types. Other studies pertaining to learning disabilities produced mixed results, perhaps due to varied criteria for determining these labels. It is clear that these studies deserve replication and that further links should be examined pertaining to a deeper understanding of the intersection of type with learning and behavior disorders in school settings.

Implications for the Classroom

Educators are likely to continue differentiating among students according to categories such as those just highlighted. Both MBTI research and Jung's type theory, however, provide important cautions about the dangers of restrictive labels that favor some students to the neglect of others. It was perhaps with this in mind that Myers entitled her book *Gifts Differing* (with Myers, 1980/1995).

Using Type in Higher Education

Professionals in higher education continue to find a broad range of applications of the MBTI. They include investigations into academic persistence and student retention, extracurricular activities, student leadership, and residence life.

Academic Persistence and Student Retention

Retention in both college and professional education are regular concerns of campus administrators. Type differences seem to relate to how students move successfully through college. For example, a study by Schurr, Ruble, Palomba, Pickerill, and Moore (1997) conducted a follow-up of students 10 years after they entered a midwestern university. A higher overall persistence-to-graduation rate was found for Sensing and Judging types, but as in previous research, preference for Introversion, Intuition, and Judging predicted their entering scores on the Scholastic Aptitude Test (SAT) and their high school rank, and preference for Judging predicted college grades. What was most notable from this study was the fact that persistence to graduation was often the result of an indirect influence of type by way of intermediary factors: Judging through academic and vocational orientations, Sensing through a vocational orientation and choice of an applied major field, and Extraversion with a collegiate orientation, defined as having a loyalty to the college and valuing extracurricular life. The authors concluded that "high levels for some aspects of the total college experience can offset lower levels for other aspects in determining whether students will persist to graduation" (p. 40).

These findings by Schurr et al. (1997) confirm the words of Myers and McCaulley (1985), who wrote that "data on academic achievement report only the end product of these positive or negative learning experiences. Because of the many and conflicting influences on learning, correlations of personality variables with academic achievement are typically low" (p. 102).

The focus of the academic and social context with which students interact seems to be a critical factor, especially in professional education. Often the types of students who are in the minority or whose preferences diverge from the focus of the curriculum tend to drop out. This was found for Feeling, NF, and FP types at the U.S. Naval Academy (Roush, 1989), NF types in engineering (McCaulley, 1990a), and Thinking types in nursing (Kalsbeek, 1987). Other researchers have conversely called attention to those types most likely to succeed or to persist to graduation, whose preferences tend to be congruent with the focus of the major field: ITJ in engineering (Rosati, 1997), TJ in law (Gilchrist, 1991), Sensing, Feeling, and Judging in family medicine and Sensing in obstetrics (Friedman & Slatt, 1988), Judging in dentistry (Erskine, Westerman, & Grandy, 1986), and SJ in nursing (Schurr et al., 1992).

Aside from professional specialties, however, the general atmosphere of higher education also appears to be more conducive to success for some types than for others. Macdaid, Kainz, and McCaulley (1984) analyzed data on attrition in a 10-year follow-up at the University of Florida. ISTJ and ISFJ types had the highest rate of graduation, while ESTP, ENTP, and ISTP types significantly more often had not graduated. FJ types were likely to have graduated early and TP types late; NT types were most likely and ES types least likely to have attended graduate school. Schurr, Ruble, and Henriksen (1989) applied the revised admissions standards at a midwestern university to data on students admitted previously who had successfully made progress through their programs; they found a significant number of Extraverted and SP types among those who would have been denied admission by the new standards. They also called attention to the relatively low SAT scores of SJ types, who, once admitted, persisted beyond expectation toward graduation, in large measure due to their finding applied major fields that channeled their interests and energies.

A promising line of research in higher education settings is represented by the work of Lynch and Sellers (1996). They asked students to indicate the characteristics of their preferred learning environments from descriptions written to reflect ES, IS, EN, and IN patterns. Both adult learners and traditional-age college students tended to prefer environments consistent with their own type preferences. However, overall there was a general preference for ES environments, with IN environments least preferred overall, especially for adult learners.

Extracurricular Activities

Type theory helps us to understand the various kinds of motivations and rewards that facilitate the successful movement of different types through college. It certainly appears to help to have found an area of study congruent with one's type. This may perhaps be due to a greater number of kindred spirits among one's classmates. It also may relate to the expectations of instructors and the curriculum. However, the fact that other types, albeit in smaller numbers, succeed in a particular discipline suggests that nonacademic factors may also be at work, as this section will address.

The Extraversion–Introversion Dichotomy As entering freshmen, Extraverts predicted that they would get involved in campus life, live in coed housing, and participate in Greek activities, while Introverts, who said they anticipated working while in college (Provost & Anchors, 1987), obtained higher grades among persisting students (Anchors et al., 1989). Even though Introverted and Judging types seem to persevere under the academic demands of college, among those who did persist to graduation, Extraverts were shown to have been helped by active involvement in campus life, while Introverts, particularly IP and ISTP types, said they were helped by not being so involved (Provost, 1985). Extraverts also tended to develop a sense of autonomy and purpose and mature interpersonal relationships (Anchors & Robinson, 1992). At their worst, however, Extraverts were found to be frequent among campus judicial offenders (Griffin & Salter, 1993) as well as among those with substance abuse records, as were Intuitive and Perceiving types (Anchors & Dana, 1989; Barrineau, 1997; Provost, 1991).

The Sensing–Intuition Dichotomy Because of the increasingly abstract nature of much of academic life, Sensing and Intuitive types vary greatly in their needs for extracurricular activity. Sensing type students in college were found to be frequent among male scholarship athletes, as were Thinking, Perceiving, and ISTP types (Chesborough, 1994). Sensing types were similarly found to participate in athletics in general (Ruble, Mahan, & Schurr, 1987) and to frequent college basketball games (Schurr, Ruble, & Ellen, 1985; Schurr, Wittig, Ruble, & Ellen, 1988). As entering freshmen, they foresaw marriage as part of the college experience (Provost & Anchors, 1987). Intuitive types, in contrast, valued the increase in individual self-esteem they gained by participating in an outdoor adventure course, as did Feeling and Perceiving types (Taylor, 1990). As entering freshmen, Intuitive types anticipated academic achievement (Provost & Anchors, 1987), perhaps assuming that college would provide the kinds of supports and challenges conducive to their preferred ways of approaching life.

The Thinking–Feeling Dichotomy Thinking types, like Extraverts and Perceiving types, were found frequent among judicial offenders (Griffin & Salter, 1993), and Thinking types were among those with substance abuse records, similar to Extraverted, Intuitive, and Perceiving types (Anchors & Dana, 1989). Thinking types also liked to participate in physical activities such as basketball, track, and cross-country, while Feeling types preferred instead to participate in volleyball, softball, field hockey, and gymnastics, regardless of gender (Wittig, Schurr, Ruble, & Ellen, 1994). At their worst, Feeling type college students, especially INFPs, were found to indicate that they had had suicidal thoughts significantly more often than other types (Komisin, 1992).

The Judging–Perceiving Dichotomy Judging types were found to have higher grades among students who persisted in college (Anchors et al., 1989) and among scholarship athletes in particular (Chesborough, 1994). In contrast, even as they entered college as freshmen, Perceiving types reported that they considered the possibility of dropping out (Provost & Anchors, 1987). Among those on academic probation, EP types were found the most frequent, and TP and INTP types were highest among those with drug violations (Provost, 1991).

Student Leadership and Residence Life

Student leaders, including resident assistants (RAs), tend consistently to prefer Judging, usually in combination with Extraversion and often also with Thinking (Anchors & Hay, 1990; Brush, 1989; Hardy-Jones & Watson, 1990; Petty, 1985). As seen in Table 11.1, ENFJ, ESTJ, and ENTJ types predominate among RAs. These patterns suggest that leadership roles in college settings tend to attract the types of students who like to take charge (Judging) and who bring noticeable energy to the activities they are engaged in (Extraverts).

A number of studies have been completed on the uses of MBTI results as one factor in matching roommates (Carey, Hamilton, & Shanklin, 1985, 1986; Jackson, 1985; Kalsbeek, Rodgers, Marshall, Denny, & Nicholls, 1982; Schroeder & Jackson, 1987). The results have been mixed, at times identifying apparent success and at other times lacking significant findings. One interesting pattern that calls attention to the complexity of matching was seen in Jackson's (1985) study, which reported that identical matches (dominant and auxiliary the same), while successful, were superseded in terms of higher student grades by complementary pairings (dominant the same, auxiliary different). These latter findings are similar to those reported earlier on teacher-student matching by type (Boyd, 1995), whereby matching students with teachers of the same type was less successful than when one MBTI dichotomy was different.

Implications for the Classroom

Type theory and MBTI results have proven to be of use in a wide variety of ways in higher education. Longitudinal studies such as the one by Schurr et al. (1997) reported above shed light on the complex way in which type preferences interact with intervening variables before we can see clear outcomes. Higher education professionals who are concerned about retention of students may consider type theory as one way of understanding the students' diversity of needs.

The traditional ethic of hard work seems suited to some types (Introverted and Judging especially). The fact that college and university administrators tend to favor Judging may tend to reinforce this pattern (DiTiberio, 1996), and these findings have been replicated among female deans and vice presidents of student affairs (Daugherty, Randall, & Globetti, 1997). But other types of students appear to do better with active engagement in campus life (Extraverts). Still others prefer much less extracurricular activity (IP and ISTP especially). Another group appears at risk for academic probation or other disciplinary action unless their need for spontaneous play can be constructively channeled (EP and TP types especially). A knowledge of the strengths as well as the potential pitfalls of each MBTI type can help determine the appropriate balance between challenge and support regarding activity and privacy (E–I), practical involvement and conceptual inspiration (S–N), competition and human connection (T–F), or structure and freedom (J–P).

Type and Cultural Differences in Education

Chapter 15 addresses the widening MBTI literature on cross-cultural differences by type. This section, however, calls attention to studies that point to such differences in educational settings. Issues of diversity are of increasing importance as educators prepare students for the multiple demands of dealing with today's complex world. This section shows how type theory can assist in translating the various "languages" used by different cultural groups in colleges and universities, high schools, and elementary education. Each subsection begins with a brief report of the frequency of types by students' cultural grouping, which is followed by a discussion of the implications for educators.

College and University Settings

In college and university settings, preference for Sensing and Thinking appears to characterize African American students in higher percentages than for Whites (Hill & Clark, 1993; Johnson, 1990; Levy, Murphy, & Carlson, 1972). Samples of Black females especially tend to contain higher percentages of Thinking types (Harrison, 1995; Hill & Clark, 1993). ISTJ was found to be overrepresented and ENFP underrepresented among African Americans (Hill & Clark, 1993). International students coming to American colleges were found by Fu (1992) to report better social and emotional adjustment if they preferred Extraversion; a preference for Thinking was favored by those with better physical health.

These findings suggest either that the overall distribution of types varies across cultural groups or that in order to meet the requirements for entering college, students from minority groups who report preference for the practical (Sensing) and the logical (Thinking) survive the best. Either way, it would help faculty and other higher education professionals, who tend to prefer Intuition, to provide a balance in

their work between their natural value for the imaginative and the abstract on the one hand and real-life applications of learning. While these suggestions were made earlier in the chapter for underserved types in general, the recommendations may have additional implications for cross-cultural understanding.

High School Settings

In high schools (roughly ages 15–18), Ross (1994) found that Extraversion predicted academic achievement among Blacks, contrary to findings for Whites. Melear and Richardson (1994) found higher percentages of Perceiving, EP, SP, and TP types among high school African American males, while May (1992) found higher percentages of SP types among male African Americans in high school but not among females.

Introverted, Intuitive, and Judging types have been found more likely to appear among students in general with high academic achievement at all levels. However, these studies of high school African Americans suggest that educators may benefit from attending to the varied learning styles of different ethnic groups. Serious reflection (Introversion) and structure (Judging) can be balanced, respectively, by opportunities for physical and spoken interaction (Extraversion) and spontaneous playfulness or inquisitiveness (Perceiving).

Elementary and Middle School Settings

Similar findings emerge in elementary (roughly ages 5–11) and middle (roughly ages 11–14) school settings using the *Murphy-Meisgeier Type Indicator for Children* (MMTIC). May (1992) found that SP types predominated among both male and female African Americans in eighth-grade students (roughly age 13): For males 100% were SP, compared with just over 30% among Whites; for females nearly 71% were SP, compared with 50% for Whites. Tobacyk and colleagues reported in one study (Tobacyk, Wells, & Springer, 1988) that Extraversion, Sensing, Feeling, and Judging described students at risk for dropout and in another (Tobacyk, Hearn, & Wells, 1990) that Sensing, Thinking, and Judging described a similar group; nearly all the students in these rural junior high schools (roughly ages 12–14) were African American. Hispanic fourth- and fifth-grade students (roughly ages 9–10) were found by Fourqurean et al. (1990) not to differ from White samples on the four MMTIC dichotomies. However, Rosin (1995) reported that Cree junior high students tended to prefer SP in disproportionate percentages compared with broader samples.

Much has been written about the challenges Sensing types face as they move up the academic ladder (Myers with Myers, 1980/1995). The results of these studies on SP and SJ types across cultural groups call our attention to a further refinement. As especially discussed by Fairhurst and Fairhurst (1995), teachers can provide either concrete structure (SJ) or concrete adaptability (SP). The results may redress a common oversight in instruction not only for different personality types but for students from various cultures as well.

Implications for the Classroom

The issue of diversity in education is illuminated when type differences are taken into account. Variations among students, formerly characterized as the primary result of culture or gender, may also be understood in terms of type. Studies pertaining to type by gender were reported in an earlier section on characteristics of learners, especially relating to the Thinking–Feeling dichotomy. Type theory relieves the pressure to change student characteristics that may be fundamental and intrinsic to the individual. The theory of type development further provides suggestions for how and when to nurture the acquisition of new skills and behaviors by different kinds of students.

It is wise, however, to be careful not to stereotype students by culture, gender, or psychological type. Educators must ultimately deal with individual students, who often vary from others of their ethnic background, gender, or type. Furthermore, students must be provided not only support for their preferred learning styles but also challenge to learn skills that do not come easily and naturally. An appreciation of both differences and developmental needs can help educators to seek an optimum balance.

It is equally dangerous to assume that type theory can account for all differences, including those pertaining to culture or gender. It cannot. As comprehensive as Jung's theory may be, students and their families from various cultures can inform educators about the values they hold, the behaviors they admire, the beliefs they cherish, and their unique ways of viewing and understanding the world.

Administering and Interpreting the MBTI in Educational Settings

Chapters 5 and 6 of this manual should be consulted by anyone intending to administer and interpret the MBTI. They provide standard conditions necessary for the wise and ethical uses of the instrument in most settings. This section addresses issues of particular concern to educators, each framed by a question.

1. **Is it necessary to administer the MBTI or the MMTIC in order to use type concepts in education?**
   No, it is not. Teachers, counselors, coaches, and other educators effectively make use of type theory in a variety of ways without having profiles for the people with whom they interact. The following guidelines can help:
   - Read carefully the descriptions of type dichotomies and the 16 types in sources such as *Gifts Differing* (Myers with Myers, 1980/1995).

- Acknowledge your own preferred ways of gathering information and making decisions while teaching, counseling, coaching, and so forth.
- Notice when students, colleagues, or others with whom you are working do and do not respond as you intended to your presentation, instructions, or expectations.
- Based on your own preferences on the four dichotomies, find a way to translate your intentions into language more understandable by someone with an opposite preference. For example, Sensing teachers may lose the attention of Intuitive students by too carefully repeating every step of an assignment's instructions. If instead they first point to the overall goal of the assignment (the general theme or its purpose), the Intuitive students may be more likely to return to the intermediary steps. Conversely, an Intuitive teacher working with a Sensing student may need to slow down the explanation, carefully repeating each step in the same words as those used before. Usually through a sequential understanding of the parts, the Sensing type is more inclined to understand the end goal of the assignment.
- Be wary of interpreting every behavior of another person as indicating type. Watch instead for general patterns over time in different settings as possible indications of type. Students and teachers alike are sometimes inclined to behave according to their setting's expectations (either real or imagined) in order to accommodate or to learn new skills.

2. **Do I need to take the MBTI myself in order to understand how to use type concepts in education?**
   It certainly helps. The first step in using type theory is to understand how it works for oneself. The MBTI was designed to assist in this process and can provide a reliable hypothesis regarding your type.

3. **Do I need special training before I can use the MBTI?**
   Yes, you do. A college-level course in psychological tests and measurements, or its equivalent, is the minimum prerequisite for purchasing a Level B instrument such as the MBTI. The course should preferably deal directly with the MBTI. If not, it is recommended that you attend one of a number of approved MBTI training programs. You can get a list from the publisher: Consulting Psychologists Press (1-800-624-1765).

4. **What form of the MBTI is best for my educational setting?**
   Reading level is the most important criterion here. MBTI Form M is currently the standard instrument for individuals with a reading level of eighth grade (roughly age 13) and higher. The *Murphy-Meisgeier Type Indicator for Children* (MMTIC) has been designed for students in elementary and middle school settings with a reading level of second grade

(roughly age 7) through seventh grade (roughly age 12). There are also a number of translations of the MBTI into foreign languages such as Spanish, French, German, Korean, and others; see Chapter 14 in this manual and Chapter 8 of *MBTI Applications* (Kirby & Barger, 1996) for suggestions on how to use them.

5. **A colleague told me that there are "short forms" of the MBTI in a number of books that are easy to administer to students. Can't I use one of these?**

Only to help you to read the book. In most cases the authors explicitly state that these checklists or questionnaires are not expected to be reliable or valid assessment tools. Decades of research have instead gone into refining the subtle wording needed to assess a person's type preferences on each dichotomy by way of the MBTI.

6. **What are legitimate uses of the MBTI in working with students?**

The possibilities are many, but they may include the following:

- To assist students to understand themselves and their preferred ways of going about learning, thus enhancing self-confidence
- To help students working with one another to recognize the value of different perspectives and approaches to teamwork
- To help students who face blocks in learning to approach such tasks by first drawing upon their natural strengths, thus saving energy for greater difficulties later on
- To assist fellow teachers, counselors, and other professionals in education to recognize differences among students as potential sources of strength rather than as impediments to learning
- To employ the theory of type development as one way to understand normal transitions through which different types of students (and teachers) tend to proceed

7. **What uses of the MBTI with students should be avoided?**

Simply recognizing that type theory and MBTI results can be misused can alert us to problems such as those indicated below.

- Stereotyping based on MBTI profile results, as in assuming that a person of a certain type always operates in his or her preferred way.
- Emphasizing the pitfalls of a type to the neglect of strengths, as in faulting the slowness of a Sensing type's information-gathering process while ignoring the sureness and confidence that comes from their careful observation, or conversely in faulting the randomness of an Intuitive type's ideas about an assignment while ignoring the inspiration and enthusiasm that comes from their brainstorming.

- Selecting or rejecting students (for example, for group participation or promotion to a higher level) based on type preferences, since type alone does not account for one's potential to contribute well or poorly in a given situation. Lawrence (1993) wisely wrote that to use the MBTI "as a screening device is usually fruitless and often harmful" (p. 92). The harm comes in treating type preferences as barriers rather than possibilities. The fruitlessness may result either from falsification of answers to MBTI questions if the student expects screening is to occur or from factors beyond type that may affect motivation or performance.
- Using type preferences as an excuse or a rationalization for behavior. Perceiving types, for example, often prefer to let impending deadlines motivate their completion of a project. While their preferred process can be respected, all types should be expected to complete the assignment on time according to expectation.
- Using type preferences to manipulate others. Judging types, for example, deserve the opportunity to organize their schedules to get things done. This does not give them the right to expect others to follow suit, unless official responsibilities of their role give them such authority.
- Interpreting the MBTI preference clarity index as indication of degree of ability or lack of it. As Chapter 6 explains in depth, the preference clarity index indicates only the respondent's clarity of preference. Skill, maturity, and development cannot be inferred from scores, either high or low.
- Expecting type to change as the result of either instruction or maturity. As people gain new skills, knowledge, and confidence, they do not change into a different type. They instead become more diverse and well-rounded examples of their inborn type.
- Imposing one's enthusiasm for type theory and the MBTI. Type cannot provide answers for all problems in education, no matter how useful it may be. Even in those arenas where it has been found helpful, other teachers, students, and administrators may have equally useful ways to deal with diversity in their work.

8. **What must I keep in mind while administering the MBTI to students?**

The following factors may either enhance or interfere with your purposes.

- The MBTI works best if completed voluntarily.
- Because teachers, counselors, or other professionals who administer the MBTI hold authority positions, students may respond as they believe they "should"; it is wise to read the instructions to them, which emphasize that there are no right or wrong answers to any of the questions.

- The expectations of the school, the curriculum, or professional standards may invite an "acceptable" choice, thus leading to falsification of one's report of type.
- Because the MBTI looks like a "test," students may assume, on the one hand, that they have to answer every item carefully to get it "right" or, on the other hand, that they must move more quickly than they prefer in order to finish "on time"; the instructions note that respondents should go at their own pace, that there is no time limit, and that they may skip items about which they are not sure.
- Students should be assured that their results will be kept confidential and not shared without their consent, preferably written; once they hear or read the positive language of their own type description, most students are eager to share their profiles, but they should not feel coerced to do so.
- Profile results and feedback on their meaning should always be given face to face by a trained professional, never distributed by mail or through an untrained third party; respondents thus have the opportunity to raise questions about the profile and to validate personally whether it truly reflects their type preferences.
- Students should be encouraged to verify for themselves the degree to which the profile fits them, even if their perceptions seem to contradict what the teacher, the counselor, or classmates think is true for them; other people may have misread prior behavior and thus may have an inaccurate interpretation of the student's type, or the student may need time to digest the feedback before coming to a clearer view of his or her type.
- Sometimes students feel torn between a "school self" and a "home self" or even an "ideal self"; they should be encouraged to explore these various expressions of a broader "best-fit type" (see Chapter 6 for more on that concept).
- Younger students may not always identify with the wording of some items, which may pertain more to adult situations; they should be encouraged to answer as they best understand the situation or to leave the item blank.
- Similarly, if students ask the meaning of a word or phrase they should be encouraged to answer as best they can or to leave it blank; words or phrases should not be explained.
- While generally reliable across most settings, the MBTI, like all self-report instruments, may sometimes be neither reliable nor valid for certain groups, such as those academically at risk or with low reading levels. See Chapter 8 for reliability data on such groups. If the MBTI is used with these individuals, extra time should be devoted to

help them explore their best-fit type beyond the profile results.
- Sometimes educators bring unrealistic expectations to the administration of the MBTI. MBTI results should never be used alone to determine a person's best ways of approaching educational tasks; the influence of factors such as gender, age, culture, personal history, curriculum, current role in the setting, and hierarchy should be considered.
- The conditions for administration and interpretation must be sufficient for the purpose for using the MBTI. One-hour interpretation sessions are never adequate for groups. Interpretive materials should highlight the uses of type in the educational setting appropriate for the respondents. Time for questions, concerns, and skepticism should also be provided. The skill of the person administering and interpreting the MBTI may also contribute to the reliability and usefulness of the results.

9. **Statistically significant research indicates that some types get higher grades or aptitude scores than their opposites. Should I therefore expect less of some types?**

Absolutely not. There are three main reasons why this reasoning is dangerous.

- First, it is risky to generalize from statistically significant research findings to all people of a type. Even though Judging types tend as a group to get higher grades than Perceiving types and Intuitive types higher standardized aptitude scores than Sensing types, you may be working with students whose performance belies the general pattern. There are many individual Perceiving types with the highest possible grades, as well as Sensing types who outperform most of their Intuitive classmates on standardized tests.
- Next, factors in addition to a student's type may contribute to the findings. For example, we know that a majority of teachers from the earliest elementary grades through graduate school faculty prefer Judging; thus high grades for Judging students may result from a more compatible match than for Perceiving students, not from ability alone. Similarly, we know that standardized tests are usually designed by academically minded psychologists, a large proportion of whom are Intuitive types.
- Finally, type theory affirms the potential of all types to perform well in any setting given the motivation and the opportunity to do so.

10. **What resources are most important for using the MBTI in educational settings?**

The materials listed below have been found useful by educators in type concepts and the MBTI. The first list includes aids to interpretation of MBTI profiles. Whenever possible, one of the various forms of *Introduction to Type* should be made available to each respondent. These brief booklets were designed to help individuals make sense out of their MBTI profiles. Those found most appropriate in education are:

- DiTiberio, J. K., & Hammer, A. L. (1993). *Introduction to Type in College*. Palo Alto, CA: Consulting Psychologists Press.
- Hammer, A. L. (1993). *Introduction to Type and Careers*. Palo Alto, CA: Consulting Psychologists Press.
- Hirsh, S. K., & Kummerow, J. M. (1998). *Introduction to Type in Organizations* (3rd ed.). Palo Alto, CA: Consulting Psychologists Press.
- Myers, I. B., with Kirby, L. K., & Myers, K. D. (1998). *Introduction to Type* (6th ed.). Palo Alto, CA: Consulting Psychologists Press.

The following materials are practical aids for introducing type concepts in a variety of ways in school and college settings:

- Meisgeier, C., Murphy, E., & Meisgeier, C. (1989). *A Teacher's Guide to Type*. Palo Alto, CA: Consulting Psychologists Press.
- Provost, J. (1992). *Strategies for Success: Using Type to Do Better in High School and College*. Gainesville, FL: Center for Applications of Psychological Type.
- Van Sant, S., & Payne, D. (1995). *Psychological Type in Schools: Applications for Educators*. Gainesville, FL: Center for Applications of Psychological Type.

The following materials also include practical issues of application but in general provide a thorough discussion of the issues related to type in education:

- Fairhurst, A. M., & Fairhurst, L. L. (1995). *Effective Teaching, Effective Learning: Making the Personality Connection in Your Classroom*. Palo Alto, CA: Davies-Black.
- Lawrence, G. (1993). *People Types and Tiger Stripes*. Gainesville, FL: Center for Applications of Psychological Type.
- Murphy, E. (1992). *The Developing Child: Using Jungian Type to Understand Children*. Palo Alto, CA: Davies-Black.

Conclusion

MBTI research in education has continued to confirm the MBTI's Jungian theoretical constructs. It has also pointed out interactions between individuals of various types with the expectations of their academic environments.

Type theory provides a useful model for conceptualizing the multiple processes that students and teachers employ as they go about the tasks of learning and instruction. The research reviewed in this chapter has suggested how MBTI patterns inform discussion of issues as diverse as instructional approaches to reading, writing, and foreign language, engagement in campus extracurricular activities, interpretation of academic standardized aptitude and achievement results, patterns across both gifted and at-risk students, and the relationship of preferred processes of perception and judgment as defined by Jung to electrical brain activity and to learning and cognitive styles of students as well as teacher behaviors.

Too casual a reading of the type literature in education over the decades can give the impression that the MBTI sorts people into camps of the intellectually capable and those who are not. Indeed, the present review of research has continued to report the affinity of Intuitive types for activities usually associated with academic success: standardized aptitude scores; grades in college, especially in the first year; proficiency measures in reading, writing, foreign language learning, and sometimes mathematics; high percentages among gifted students at all levels; nominations as teacher of the year among college faculty—the list goes on.

It is not enough for educators to point to other chapters of this manual to identify areas of success for Sensing types, such as business careers, some health professions, and the like. What need to be examined intensively are the arenas within academic life where Sensing types thrive and where Intuitive types tend to slack off (even though they often still survive due to flashes of insight through verbal expressiveness). Robinson (1994) found competitive and active aspects of the relatively elite Academic Decathlon competition to appeal to SP types, who in most studies are among those most at risk. Provost (1985) interviewed ISTPs among students who had persisted to successful completion of college and found that *not* being involved in campus social life helped them do well, opposite the finding for other types. These and studies like them need to be replicated so that educators can take seriously the admonition of Myers (Myers with Myers, 1980/1995) that in education, as in all settings, one must deal with variations of giftedness, not simply one kind.

Several research tools can be employed to bring the above effort to fruition. Since type theory is dynamic, further research taking the 16 types into account is clearly called for. The design of Harrison and Lawrence (1985) provides a prototype: Hypotheses were driven by Jungian theory, and responses were solicited from each of the 16 types to the question of study (in this case projections into one's personal future). Other studies have involved intensive qualitative interviews to explore how individuals of a given type respond to educational settings, as done, for example, by Provost, Carson, and Beidler (1987) with outstanding college professors, by Ferdman and DiTiberio (1996) with fifth-grade writers, and by Ehrman (1990) with foreign language professionals.

Some important cautions have been discovered from this review of the MBTI literature. Simplistic applications of MBTI profiles by way of matching teachers with students, for example, produce at best mixed results. Human personality differences appear to be sufficiently complex that variables beyond type must be considered. As the recent study by Schurr et al. (1997) points out, MBTI preferences are best conceptualized as contributing to academic success by interaction with other variables. Thus a strict linear cause-effect approach to MBTI research would appear to produce limited results.

Where possible, MBTI distributions for a sample should be compared with distributions of related groups through selection ratio type table analysis (McCaulley, 1985). The base population for comparison must be carefully selected. But the results can provide perspective on how subjects in the group of concern (ADD children, for example) may be operating in the context of influential others (the types among, for example, their teachers, parents, or classmates). In this regard, type research, especially in education, needs to investigate person-context interactions. When we notice either success or blocks in learning, these results can be viewed not as a direct result of type preferences themselves but as a subtle interaction between the types of our subjects of study and the expectations of those individuals or groups who influence them.

Because of this powerful interplay between nature (what the personality of each student brings to learning) and nurture (the influence of the learning environment), the discussion of type differences in education ultimately pertains to the issue of human growth and development. Whether their efforts are intentional or not, teachers, counselors, and school administrators are involved with the facilitation of not only the academic but also the personal development of students. The words of Myers that began this chapter noted that intelligence, often considered the hallmark of educational expertise, is best accompanied by acceptance and development of type preferences. The chapter similarly concludes with another quotation from Myers (with Myers, 1980/1995, p. 183), which calls attention to the conditions parents must consider to nurture the development of different types of children. Educators in most settings can benefit from her insights:

> Unknowingly parents frequently refuse their children the conditions necessary for good type development: the young introverts who get no peace or privacy, the extraverts shut off from people and activity, the intuitives tied to routine matters of fact, the sensing children required to learn everything through words with nothing to see or handle, the young thinkers who are never given a reason or permitted an argument, the feeling types in a family where nobody cares for harmony, the judging types for whom all decisions are handed down by an excessively decisive parent, and the young perceptives who are never allowed to run and find out.

Uses of Type in Career Counseling 12

Revised by Jean M. Kummerow

The use of the *Myers-Briggs Type Indicator* personality inventory in career counseling to help people find meaningful and productive work was one of Isabel B. Myers' original motivations in the development of the instrument (Saunders, 1991). Career counseling applications were one of the first areas of applied research on type, and the field continues to generate a large number of research studies.

The MBTI assessment tool has been widely used in a variety of career counseling settings including private practice, high schools, community colleges and technical schools, colleges and universities, and organizations. Its use in these settings has been multiple and includes identifying possible job titles to explore, meaningful work environments, compatible interests, and congruous values. Type also contributes to understanding the job search process itself including career exploration, managing change, decision-making strategies, and implementing choices.

The goal of this chapter is to illustrate aspects of using the MBTI with career counseling clients. Its "how-to" focus includes ways to apply research results from both previously reviewed research literature in the 1985 *MBTI Manual* and *MBTI Applications* (1996) and recent research studies. Additional research based on Form M of the MBTI from several samples, including a national one of over 3,000 adult men and women, is incorporated. (For more on the national sample see Chapter 7.) This chapter also highlights relevant career development theory and provides suggestions to practitioners along with case studies that illustrate the usefulness of the MBTI with career counseling clients.

Assumptions Underlying the Use of the MBTI in Career Counseling

Many clients arrive in career counseling with the expectation that the process will be to "give me a couple of tests that will tell me what I should be." They fail to realize there are many factors in occupational choice and satisfaction besides what a few psychological instruments reveal. These factors include physical and mental health, interests, values, personality characteristics, family circumstances, geographic location, job market conditions and trends, education, skills, abilities, cultural/ethnic/gender identification, and so forth. Satisfaction within an occupation includes factors such as the job itself, the organization, pay, supervision, co-workers, and advancement/learning opportunities. To expect the MBTI instrument or any other instrument to provide all of the answers to a career search is improbable and unrealistic. It can be only part of the puzzle in finding one's life's work.

The Changing Nature of Career Counseling Theories

Implicit also in the client's plea for "the answer" is the expectation that career counseling is a matter of matching a person with a job. It is based on the theoretical framework called "trait-and-factor" espoused by Parsons in the early 1900s, which has been the foundation of career counseling for decades (Krumboltz, 1996). If using psychological type within this framework, we would work to match people's types to careers most conducive to that type. However, there are problems inherent in this approach regarding the use of type: People with different types can do the same jobs (perhaps using different approaches), and if everyone were the same type in a job, it is less likely that fresh approaches and innovations would come into that occupation. Furthermore, work environments may differ widely, and thus different types, while doing the same jobs, may be in vastly different workplaces.

Another theoretical framework for career counseling has been called the "person x environment fit theory," which espouses that individuals can take active roles in altering or creating work environments to better fit with their personal preferences (Chartrand, 1991). Thus self-knowledge of type can help one identify what is likely to be satisfying and suggest strategies for changing a work environment to be more conducive to the use of one's own type. It is within this framework that much of this chapter is positioned.

There are a number of other theories in the career counseling field that are included in relevant sections below. Each theory focuses on different aspects of the career counseling process, such as incorporating values, self-efficacy, and interests into the process, and all have much to contribute as a result. Folding psychological type in with these theories helps expand their applicability as well.

The Changing Nature of Work

In addition to the changing views of the theoretical nature of career counseling, the nature of work and career is changing, and hence the essence of career counseling must change also. Arthur and Rousseau (1996) define and redefine the term *career* as follows: "Old Meaning: a course of professional advancement; usage restricted to occupations with formal hierarchical progression, such as managers and professionals. New Meaning: the unfolding sequence of any person's work experiences over time" (pp. 29–30). The old meaning focuses more on what you do, i.e., the job titles you hold, while the new meaning focuses more on who you are and the skills you bring with you from work experience to work experience. Bridges (1994) discusses the importance of identifying and understanding your temperament as one key to prospering in the new world of work. Personalities do carry "implications for the particular roles or situations where the person is likely to work well and be happy" (p. 88). He reminds us too that even within particular fields, different personalities can thrive.

Type is particularly helpful within this new framework of work since its focus is a broad one on the individual. Type also assumes a developmental component so that individuals can adapt to new situations using all parts of their personalities. Counselors can use type to help identify the more satisfying situations and roles, as well as to help individuals adapt to those that seem to be a stretch for them.

The Changing Role of the Career Counselor

Given that the world of work and the view of what's "needed" in career counseling are changing, it only makes sense that the role of the career counselor is changing as well. As Krumboltz (1996) explains,

> Matching an individual to an occupation requires that the occupation have a common and stable set of duties and expectations. At one time, this requirement was quite reasonable. . . . The modern age is changing the old order. Workers are increasingly being expected to accomplish whatever work needs to be accomplished, not merely to fulfill a written job description. . . . Career counselors will have an opportunity to play a major role in helping individuals learn how to cope with the need for new skills and the associated stresses. . . . If career counselors see their job as merely matching individuals to existing occupations, they will rapidly become obsolete because stable occupations as we have known them are on the way out. (pp. 57–58)

Work Environments

In examining the relationship between psychological type and work, the focus on the larger picture of the work environment, including tasks engaged in or avoided and the specific structure of the work environment, seems appropriate. Type preferences are likely to affect activities as well as environments that people find energizing and satisfying.

Table 12.1   Effects of Extraversion–Introversion in Work Situations

Extraverts	Introverts
Like variety and action	Like quiet for concentration
Tend to be faster, dislike complicated procedures (especially ES types)	Tend to be careful with details, dislike sweeping statements (especially IS types)
Are often good at greeting people (especially EF types)	Have trouble remembering names and faces (especially IT types)
Are often impatient with long, slow jobs done alone	Tend not to mind working on one project for a long time alone and uninterrupted
Are interested in the activities of their job, in getting it done, and in how other people do it	Are interested in the details and/or ideas behind their job
Often do not mind the interruption of answering the telephone (especially EF types)	Dislike telephone intrusions and interruptions (especially IT types)
Often act quickly, sometimes without thinking it through	Like to think a lot before they act, sometimes without acting
Like to have people around (especially EF types)	Work contentedly alone (especially IT types)
Usually communicate freely (especially EF types)	Have some problems communicating to others since it's all in their heads (especially IT types)

Table 12.2   Effects of Sensing–Intuition in Work Situations

Sensing Types	Intuitive Types
Like focusing on the here and now and reality	Like focusing on the future and what might be
Rely on standard ways to solve problems and dislike problems in which this approach doesn't work	Like solving new problems in unusual ways and dislike solving routine problems
Like an established order of doing things (especially SJ types)	Dislike doing the same thing repeatedly (especially NP types)
Enjoy using and perfecting skills already learned more than learning new ones	Enjoy learning a new skill more than using it
Work more steadily, with realistic idea of how long it will take (especially ISJ types)	Work in bursts of energy, powered by enthusiasm, with slack periods in between (especially ENP types)
Reach a conclusion step by step (especially ISJ types)	Reach an understanding quickly (especially ENP types)
Are patient with routine details (especially ISJ types)	Are impatient with routine details (especially ENP types)
Are impatient when the situation gets complicated (especially ES types)	Are patient with complex situations (especially IN types)
Are not often inspired and rarely trust the inspiration when they are	Follow their inspirations, good or bad, regardless of the data (especially with inadequate type development)
Seldom make factual errors	Frequently make errors of fact, preferring instead the big picture
Tend to be good at precise work (especially IS types)	Dislike taking time for precision (especially EN types)
Create something new by adapting something that exists	Create something new through a personal insight

Tables 12.1–12.4 identify various likes and dislikes in work situations that Myers and McCaulley (1985) believed were associated with each preference. These are reported for the preferences only, with some combinations of the preferences noted in the tables. Obviously other combinations of the preferences, including whole type combinations, would also affect the desired work situation.

Research also documents the importance of different work environments to different types. The work setting preferences of physicians were reported by Quenk and Albert (1975). Among the findings, Extraverted physicians favored active involvement with the outside world including their patients and their communities. Feeling types emphasized involvement with the people in their lives and practices. Thinking types seemed to concentrate more on the nonpeople aspects of their work such as their continued advancement. Judging types desired to maintain the boundaries in their practices between personal and professional lives.

Research from data using Form M and the *Work Environment Scale* is reported in Chapter 9, "Validity." These data provide information on what is important in an *ideal* work environment (see Table 12.5). The sample consisted of 98 employees in a variety of occupations at a large Midwestern university who attended a session to learn more about themselves. "Co-worker cohesion" (friendly, supportive co-workers) is important in the ideal to Extraverted and Feeling types; this outside focus toward others fits with the theoretical view of Extraversion and Feeling. "Co-worker cohesion" is less important to ST types than to the other function pairings. Perhaps they focus more on the "things" in their work than on the people. "Supervisor support" is more important to the Extraverted types, again with their focus on the outside world, which seems also to include their supervisors to a degree. This support is less important in the ideal work environment for the STs than for the other three function pairings; again, STs may focus less on the people side of how the job is accomplished. "Autonomy" is more important in the ideal to the IPs than to the EJs; later studies in this chapter on values will also show this pattern. "Task orientation" in this sample is more important to the Extraverted than to the Introverted types; this likely fits with their focus on showing the outside world that something has been done. However, "Task orientation" is less important in the ideal to the STs than to other function pairings, a result difficult to explain. By definition

Table 12.3   Effects of Thinking–Feeling in Work Situations

Thinking Types	Feeling Types
Like analysis and putting things into logical order	Like harmony
Can get along without harmony	Efficiency may be badly disrupted by office feud
Tend to be firm minded	Tend to be sympathetic
Do not show emotion readily and are often uncomfortable dealing with people's feelings (especially IT types)	Tend to be very aware of other people and their feelings (especially EF types)
May hurt people's feelings without knowing it	Enjoy pleasing people, even in unimportant things
Tend to decide impersonally, sometimes paying insufficient attention to people's wishes	Often let decisions be influenced by their own or other people's personal likes and dislikes
Need to be treated fairly in accordance with the prevailing standards	Need praise and personal attention
Are able to reprimand people impersonally, although they may not like doing so	Dislike, even avoid, telling people unpleasant things
Are more analytically oriented—respond more easily to people's thoughts (especially IT types)	Are more people oriented—respond more easily to people's values

Table 12.4   Effects of Judging–Perceiving in Work Situations

Judging Types	Perceiving Types
Work best when they can plan their work and follow the plan	Adapt well to changing situations
Like to get things settled and finished	Prefer leaving things open for alterations
May decide things too quickly (especially EJ types)	May unduly postpone decisions (especially IP types)
May dislike to interrupt the project they are on for a more urgent one (especially ISJ types)	May start too many projects and have difficulty finishing them (especially ENP types)
May not notice new things that need to be done in their desire to complete what they are doing	May postpone unpleasant jobs while finding other things more interesting in the moment
Want only the essentials needed to begin their work (especially ESJ types)	Want to know all about a new job (especially INP types)
Tend to be satisfied once they reach a judgment on a thing, situation, or person	Tend to be curious and welcome a new light on a thing, situation, or person

those working in the same setting, some described it as "satisfying and challenging" while others saw the same site as "disappointing and boring."

Work Environments for the National Sample

The national sample was asked how they felt about different work environments with the question, "How would you feel about working in an organization that . . . ?" Twelve different variables were presented, on which they could indicate "Like," "Indifferent," or "Dislike" to as many as they wanted. Table 12.6 ranks these variables and identifies the types with the highest and lowest "Like" percentage responses on each one.

The most important variable in an organizational work environment in this sample was "having clear structures and responsibilities"; nearly 88.6% of the total sample liked that work environment characteristic. ESTJs liked this the most at 96.0% and INTPs, the least, although still 73.7% liked this. The majority of the sample and of every type within that sample also liked having a "variety of tasks," "independence and achievement," "employee loyalty and job security," and "working as part of a team." Of least importance was "everything done by the book," with only 14.9% represented. "Opportunities for advancement and high pay but not job security" was chosen by 28.7% of the sample, and "toe the line" expectations by 35.6% overall.

Table 12.7 presents the five most important work environment characteristics (in descending order) for each type in the national sample. For all Sensing types with the exceptions of ESTP and ESFP, "clear structure" was the most important work environment characteristic. This "clear

STs usually focus on the task to be accomplished and value efficient policies and procedures, something at odds with these results. In this study, SFs desire more clarity in terms of daily work expectations than STs and NTs; this fits with the SF focus on detail and knowing the parameters of their work expectations, along with their desire to fit in with those with whom they work, perhaps by "pleasing" them through doing the work in a way others have delineated. "Managerial control," or using rules to keep people under control, is in the expected directions. Sensing types, more than Intuitive types, would likely want the rules spelled out ahead of time. Judging types, with their desire for structure, would likely desire this more than Perceiving types. "Innovation" is important to Intuitive types, and especially to NFs; change and possibilities are often expressed in Intuition. Pleasant physical surroundings are more important in the ideal to EPs than to IJs; EPs extravert their dominant Perceiving functions and might be more tuned to the external environment than IJs, who introvert their dominant Perceiving functions. Most of these findings fit with what we would expect from type theory and add to our understanding of what makes an ideal work environment for different types.

Depending on what is important to individuals, satisfaction with the work environment may take on different casts. For example, DiMarco (1997) found physical therapy students described the same clinical settings differently depending on their temperament (SJ, SP, NF, NT). Even for

Table 12.5   Ideal Work Environment Characteristics Based on *Work Environment Scale* Subscales Study

Ideal Work Environment Characteristic	Preference	Functions Pairing	Attitudes Pairing
Co-worker Cohesion (friendly, supportive co-workers)	E, F	ST < SF, NF, NT	
Supervisor Support (supportive management)	E	ST < SF, NF, NT	
Autonomy (self-sufficient employees)			IP > EJ
Task Orientation (emphasis on good planning, efficiency, getting job done)	E	ST < SF, NF, NT	
Clarity (employees know what to expect in daily tasks and company policies)		SF > ST, NT	
Managerial Control (use of rules to keep employees under control)	S, J	ST > NF, NT	EJ > IP
		SF > NF	EJ > EP
			IJ > IP
Innovation (variety, change emphasized)	N	NF > ST, SF	
		NF > ST	
Physical Comfort (pleasant physical surroundings)			EP > IJ

Note: Correlations with preferences are >.20. All results are statistically significant at the .05 level or better. Pairs results are based on MANOVAS and post-hoc analyses. See Appendix for a description of the sample.

Source: Employee Career Enrichment Program, University of Minnesota.

Table 12.6   "Liking" of Work Environment Characteristics in the National Sample

Work Environment Characteristic	Average Like %	Highest Like % & Type	Lowest Like % & Type
Clear structures and responsibilities	88.6%	96.0% ESTJ	73.7% INTP
Variety of tasks	86.8%	95.8% ENTJ	77.6% ISFP
Independence and achievements	86.1%	93.2% ENTP	80.3% ISTP
Employee loyalty and job security	79.7%	88.0% ISFJ	53.5% INTP
Work as part of team	78.6%	87.6% ESTJ	61.5% INTP
People with different backgrounds	61.4%	79.2% ENTJ	46.1% ISTJ
Makes jobs simple	47.1%	62.3% ESFP	17.2% INTJ
Does not expect extra hours	45.3%	57.9% ESFP	20.8% ENTJ
International opportunities	36.6%	68.8% ENTJ	22.6% ISFJ
Toe the line expectations	35.6%	43.0% ESFJ	18.8% ENTJ
Opportunities for advancement and high pay but not job security	28.7%	44.7% ENTP	20.8% INFJ
Everything done by the book	14.6%	24.4% ISTJ	4.5% ENFP

Note: See Appendix for a description of the sample.

Source: National sample.

structure" likely provides a grounding in reality for the Sensing types. For the ESTP and ESFP, "clear structure" was either second or third. "Variety of tasks" was the most important work environment characteristic for all Intuitive types with the exception of the INFPs, who put it in second place. "Variety of tasks" may lead to the possibilities often sought by Intuitive types. "Loyalty and security" was among the top five for all types except the NTs, who likely see that work characteristic as less objective and logical than they prefer. They chose instead working with "people with different backgrounds," a characteristic on their top five but on that of no other types. Perhaps "people with different backgrounds" help bring the desired variety and challenge to the work of the NTs.

Overall in this sample it appears that people like to know what it is they are to do and the boundaries for their work but decide their own ways of handling those responsibilities. They also like having some variety and teamwork in an organization that is loyal to them and provides job security. People seem to value some work environment characteristics in similar ways, regardless of type. However, the differences that do emerge seem to fit with type theory.

Table 12.8 lists the four types who *liked* each of the 12 work environment characteristics the most. Remember from Table 12.7 that *all* types like clear structures and responsibilities, variety of tasks, etc. Table 12.8 identifies for each separate work environment characteristic the types

Table 12.7   The Five Most Important Work Environment Characteristics for Each Type in the National Sample

ISTJ	ISFJ	INFJ	INTJ
Clear structure	**Clear structure**	**Variety of tasks**	**Variety of tasks**
Independence and achievement	**Loyalty/security**	**Clear structure**	**Clear structure**
Loyalty/security	**Independence and achievement**	**Independence and achievement**	**Independence and achievement**
Variety of tasks	**Variety of tasks**	Loyalty/security	Teamwork
Teamwork	Teamwork	Teamwork	People from different backgrounds

ISTP	ISFP	INFP	INTP
Clear structure	**Clear structure**	**Independence and achievement**	**Variety of tasks**
Variety of tasks	**Loyalty/security**	**Variety of tasks**	**Independence and achievement**
Independence and achievement	**Independence and achievement**	Clear structure	Clear structure
Loyalty/security	Variety of tasks	Teamwork	Teamwork
Teamwork	Teamwork	Loyalty/security	People from different backgrounds

ESTP	ESFP	ENFP	ENTP
Variety of tasks	**Variety of tasks**	**Variety of tasks**	**Variety of tasks**
Independence and achievement	**Clear structure**	**Independence and achievement**	**Independence and achievement**
Clear structure	**Independence and achievement**	**Teamwork**	Clear structure
Teamwork	**Loyalty/security**	**Clear structure**	Teamwork
Loyalty/security	**Teamwork**	**Loyalty/security**	People from different backgrounds

ESTJ	ESFJ	ENFJ	ENTJ
Clear structure	**Clear structure**	**Variety of tasks**	**Variety of tasks**
Teamwork	**Loyalty/security**	**Independence and achievement**	**Independence and achievement**
Variety of tasks	**Variety of tasks**	**Teamwork**	**Clear structure**
Independence and achievement	**Independence and achievement**	**Clear structure**	**Teamwork**
Loyalty/security	**Teamwork**	Loyalty/security	People from different backgrounds

Note: Those in **boldface** were liked by more than 80% of that type. See Appendix for a description of the sample.

Source: National sample.

liking that characteristic the most. Thus, although "clear structure" was important to every type and among their top five work environment characteristics, it was most important to ISFJ, ISTJ, ESTJ, and ESFJ types. While "toe the line" was not important to any of the types in great numbers, it was relatively more important for ISTJ, ESTJ, ESFJ, and ESFP types. To help place this information in context, those work environment characteristics in bold on Table 12.8 were chosen by over 50% of the types. For example, the 5 types (out of 16) most liking "international opportunities" were INTP, ENTP, ENFP, ENFJ, and ENTJ. Over 50% of the INTPs,

ENTPs, and ENTJs liked this work environment characteristic, while less than 50% of ENFPs and ENFJs chose this as an important work environment characteristic.

The patterns noted on Tables 12.6–12.8 fit with type theory. For example, in theory, "loyalty" is important to SFs, and this is confirmed by the research results. That NTs enjoy challenges seems apparent in their greater desire for "variety of tasks" in their work, "international opportunities," and "advancement without security." In theory, NPs are often independent minded. The research results suggest a number of work environment characteristics that allow that to

**Table 12.8 The Four Types in the National Sample Who Most Liked
Each Work Environment Characteristic**

ISTJ	ISFJ	INFJ	INTJ
Clear structure Toe the line Goes by the book	**Clear structure** **Loyalty/security** **Does not expect extra hours** **Makes job simple** Goes by the book		**Variety of tasks**
ISTP	**ISFP** **Loyalty/security** **Makes job simple** **Does not expect extra hours**	**INFP** **Independence and achievement** **People from different backgrounds**	**INTP** **International opportunities** Advancement/pay, not security
ESTP	**ESFP** **Makes job simple** **Does not expect extra hours** Toe the line	**ENFP** **Independence and achievement** **Teamwork** **People from different backgrounds** International opportunities	**ENTP** **Variety of tasks** **Independence and achievement** **International opportunities** Advancement/pay, not security
ESTJ **Clear structure** **Teamwork** **Loyalty/security** Toe the line Goes by the book	**ESFJ** **Clear structure** **Loyalty/security** **Teamwork** **Makes job simple** Does not expect extra hours Toe the line Goes by the book	**ENFJ** **Variety of tasks** **Independence and achievement** **Teamwork** **People from different backgrounds** International opportunities Advancement/pay, not security	**ENTJ** **Variety of tasks** **People from different backgrounds** **International opportunities** Advancement/pay, not security

Note: The 16 types were ranked from high to low on the percentage responding "like" to each of the 12 work environment characteristics. The four types with the highest percentages are included in the table. Those characteristics in **boldface** were liked by more than 50% of that type. Thus even though no type was attracted to a high degree to "Goes by the book," ISTJ, ESTJ, ESFJ, and ISFJ were attracted more than the other types. See Appendix for a description of the sample.

Source: National sample.

continue, such as liking "independence and achievement," "people from different backgrounds," "international activities," and "advancement and pay without security." SJs, with their focus on "clear structures" and "going by the book," want an orderly work environment rather than forging out on their own, whereas their opposites, the NPs, seem to prefer more variety and change. In theory, Extraverted workers might pay particular attention to their external work environment. Indeed, they seem to have liked more work environment characteristics than did their Introverted colleagues as shown in Table 12.8. The Extraverts also liked "teamwork" relatively more than the Introverts, something we might expect from the theory.

Implications for Practitioners

Type theory and research suggest that type preferences can affect the preferred work environment but also that there are factors that are less type related and that most types have in common. For some clients, especially Sensing ones who like to build on experiences, reviewing their past jobs for understanding what has felt comfortable or uncomfortable in previous work environments may be a helpful beginning point. For other clients, especially Intuitive types, a focus on future possibilities in work environments may be a more interesting start. As clients learn about type, they can use Tables 12.1–12.4 as a focus for the possible environments and work tasks to fit either scenario. Most clients will note that they participate in activities on both sides of the dichotomies. This process helps to illustrate the complexity of type within an individual and also how people often do use both sides.

Tables 12.7–12.8 also emphasize important work environment characteristics for each type based on research results and can serve as resources. Counselors may wish to focus discussions on what seems to be important in the work environment to each type. Other well-known sources of information to clients that cover work setting information include *Introduction to Type* (Myers, with Kirby and Myers, 1998), *Introduction to Type and Careers* (Hammer, 1993), and *Introduction to Type in Organizations* (Hirsh & Kummerow, 1998). The latter publication and *LIFETypes* (Hirsh & Kummerow, 1989) also suggest a "preferred work environment" for each of the 16 types. Clients may find useful the descriptions in *Do What You Are* (Tieger & Barron-Tieger, 1992) on how work fits different types and the suggestions for adapting work tasks to type in *WORKTypes* (Kummerow, Barger, & Kirby, 1997). *Work, Play, and Type* (Provost, 1990) offers suggestions for finding play at work for different types, activities that may help bring work environments more in line with type preferences.

Counselors can stay alert to the work environment factors that seem to be causing strain in the client's work life. A client may be in an environment that does not fit with his or her natural preferences, yet for a variety of reasons prefers not to change environments/jobs. Perhaps the client has

invested a great deal in getting educated/trained in the field, or perhaps he or she is unable to risk a potential loss of income by striking out into a different environment. Hammer (1993) suggests clients might either *alter the job* to fit their personalities or *adapt themselves* to fit the job. Clients may end up doing a bit of both. One of his suggestions is that clients locate or create within the same occupation a particular environment that is more like them or find colleagues with whom they share more similarities. Here are some examples of people who used this strategy:

- An INFJ chemist in a research and development department began working as a liaison between human resources and the scientists to help them better understand one another. He found much in common with those in human resources and was able to increase his job satisfaction.

- An ENFJ computer programmer helped found a support group for programmers at the bank in which he worked. Eventually he moved into training people to work with computer information systems. He found like-minded colleagues, which helped increase his job satisfaction, and then a set of job responsibilities more compatible for his personality.

- An INTJ high school English teacher always took a quick walk by himself at lunchtime and deliberately did not carpool so that he would have quiet, solitary time on the drive home. This slight change of work environment increased his energy and thus his job satisfaction.

- An ESFJ project coordinator found that working among highly technical people was draining her energy and leading to much job dissatisfaction. She wanted more social interaction during her day and more overt signs of appreciation. She kept the same position but transferred her desk into the sales and marketing department. Her colleagues there socialize with her regularly, ask about her family, and often compliment her work. She has decided to stay in the job as a result.

- One ESTP created her own testing and assessment niche in a firm of industrial psychologists. As a consultant on a part-time contract, she also had the flexibility to decide her own schedule, which she found immensely satisfying. She was particularly strong at working with executives who were in a crisis situation in terms of their performance. Her practical, expedient suggestions were just what was needed.

- An ISFP administrative assistant physically changed her work (and her nonwork) environment to better suit her. She was in a space without windows, but she managed to find wallpaper with a huge outdoor scene to make her feel in touch with the outside world. She continually rearranges her office to make things more convenient; SPs often seek an "economy of effort." Her manager gives her complete freedom to set her own priorities, deadlines, and work methods, so when she gets bored with one task, she can immediately jump to another. In her personal life she is a hospice volunteer. When her own mother needed such care, she found hospice workers were like "guardian angels who flew in when we didn't have a clue." She wants to be able to do the same for others now.

Type provides valuable insights into work environment issues. Counselors and clients can use that information to understand the work environment fit and/or misfit, design ways of working within the environment or changing it, or envision a different environment with the goal ultimately to increase job satisfaction.

Occupational Selection

One of the most common and difficult-to-answer questions career counselors face from clients is, "What job should I be in?" The question is difficult in part because it is so narrowly focused. Career counseling emphasizes widening the focus beyond a single job to job clusters and transferable skills, and building skills to find new "jobs" in the future. The U.S. Department of Labor is moving from a task-based approach with its *Dictionary of Occupational Titles* to an Occupational Information Network system to identify skill sets and worker attributes and to encourage people to develop multiple skills (Minnesota Department of Economic Security, 1997). Thus in career counseling the single focus on locating one specific job is too limiting, yet it is also important because it is the perceived need of many of our clients. The process of career counseling includes broadening the focus and teaching clients how to use career development tools in the future.

Even with the concerns discussed above, type remains useful in focusing on both specific jobs and job clusters and potential skill sets. According to type theory, MBTI types would be distributed in occupations consistent with the characteristics of the work environments of those occupations. Occupations may both require and reward specific ways of perceiving information and making decisions on that information; thus different types would be expected to be attracted to different occupations.

Occupational Trends by Type

The focus of this section is on the occupational trends for the eight preferences and the 16 types. Myers and McCaulley (1985, p. 78) note these activities preferred by the eight preferences:

- *Extraverted types:* Work that allows interaction with a succession of people or that has activities outside the office or away from the desk
- *Introverted types:* Work that permits some solitude and time for concentration
- *Sensing types:* Work that requires attention to details and careful observation (such as in applied occupations)

- *Intuitive types:* Work that provides a succession of new problems to be solved (such as in theoretical occupations)
- *Thinking types:* Work that requires logical order, especially with ideas, numbers, or physical objects (such as in occupations with technical/scientific components)
- *Feeling types:* Work that provides service to people and a harmonious and appreciative work environment (such as in occupations emphasizing communications and interpersonal aspects)
- *Judging types:* Work that imposes a need for system and order
- *Perceiving types:* Work that requires adapting to changing situations or where understanding situations is more important than managing them

Occupational trends by type are presented in Table 12.9. The patterns appear more pronounced by the function pairs, or columns of the type table, rather than other combinations; the next section gives further evidence in this regard.

The Importance of the Functions in Job Choice

Data seem to support the trend that the function pairs, ST, SF, NF, and NT, i.e., the columns of the type table, have the most impact on job selection. Hammer and Macdaid (1992a) examined lists of occupational titles for each type and determined the amount of overlap on the occupational lists within pairs of opposite types (see Table 12.10). The overlap ranged from 2% to 14% with the median overlap of 4%. That is, for each pair of opposites only one to seven job titles out of more than 200 occupations appeared among the top 50 occupations for both types. When Hammer and Macdaid compared pairs of types with the same functions (e.g., ST, SF, NF, NT) but different attitudes (IJ, IP, EP, EJ), they found a median overlap of 41%; for those with opposite functions (ST versus NF; SF versus NT) but the same attitudes the mean overlap was only 4% (see Table 12.11). Thus those sharing the same two functions have far more in common in terms of occupational selection than those with opposite function pairs. For example, SFs are more likely to be found in jobs similar to one another and more likely to be in different jobs than NTs.

In general, the function pairs seem to influence career choices in the following manner:

- STs are often found in environments where they can focus on pragmatic ways to use details, such as in business. For example, an ST with a graduate degree in counseling became an expert in psychological testing and its applications.
- SFs like to help people in practical ways, such as in health care and education. An SF with a graduate degree in counseling focused his skills on coaching managers to develop effective working relationships with their staffs.

Table 12.9   Occupational Trends of the 16 Types

ISTJ	**ISFJ**	**INFJ**	**INTJ**
Management	Education	Religion	Scientific or technical fields
Administration	Health care	Counseling	Computers
Law enforcement	Religious settings	Teaching	Law
Accounting		Arts	
or any other occupations where they can use their experiences and attention to detail to get the task done	or any other occupations where they can draw on their experience base to personally help people in a behind-the-scenes manner	or any other occupations where they can facilitate emotional, intellectual, or spiritual development	or any other occupations where they can use their intellectual creativity and technical knowledge to conceptualize, analyze, and get the task done
ISTP	**ISFP**	**INFP**	**INTP**
Skilled trades	Health care	Counseling	Scientific or technical fields
Technical fields	Business	Writing	
Agriculture	Law enforcement	Arts	
Law enforcement			
Military			
or any other occupations where they can use their hands-on, analytical work with data or things	or any other occupations where they can use their gentle, service-related attentiveness to detail.	or any other occupations where they can use their creativity and focus on their values	or any other occupations where they can use their solitary, objective analysis of problems based on their technical expertise
ESTP	**ESFP**	**ENFP**	**ENTP**
Marketing	Health care	Counseling	Science
Skilled trades	Teaching	Teaching	Management
Business	Coaching	Religion	Technology
Law enforcement	Childcare worker	Arts	Arts
Applied technology	Skilled trades		
or any other occupations where they can use their action-oriented focus to attend to the necessary details	or any other occupations where they can use their outgoing nature and enthusiasm to help people with their practical needs	or any other occupations where they can use creativity and communication to help foster the growth of others	or any other occupations where they have the opportunity to take on new challenges continually
ESTJ	**ESFJ**	**ENFJ**	**ENTJ**
Management	Education	Religion	Management
Administration	Health care	Arts	Leadership
Law enforcement	Religion	Teaching	
or any other occupations where they can use logic and organization of the facts to get the task done	or any other occupations where they can use their personal concern to provide service to others	or any other occupations where they can help others with their emotional, intellectual, and spiritual growth	or any other occupations where they can use tough-minded analysis, strategic planning, and organization to get the task done

Source: From *Introduction to Type and Careers* (pp. 16–31), by A. L. Hammer, 1993, Palo Alto, CA: Consulting Psychologists Press. Copyright 1993 by Consulting Psychologists Press. Used with permission.

■ NFs want to help people through working in areas such as religion, counseling, and the arts. An NF with a graduate degree in counseling became a therapist helping people grow, develop, and learn to understand themselves and others better.

■ NTs focus on theoretical frameworks, such as in science, technology, and management, to keep themselves and others challenged. An NT with a graduate degree in counseling used her strategic focus and management skills to become an executive in the human resources area.

Table 12.10	Percent Overlap Between the Top 50 Occupations for Opposite Types
Types	**% Overlap**
ENTJ and ISFP	2
ESTJ and INFP	2
ENFJ and ISTP	4
ESFJ and INTP	4
ENFP and ISTJ	4
ENTP and ISFJ	14
ESFP and INTJ	6
ESTP and INFJ	4
Median	5

Source: From *Career Report Manual* (p. 37), by A. L. Hammer and G. P. Macdaid, 1992, Palo Alto, CA: Consulting Psychologists Press. Copyright 1992 by Consulting Psychologists Press. Used with permission.

Table 12.11	Percent Overlap for Types with Opposite Functions/Same Attitudes Versus Types with Same Functions/Opposite Attitudes
Types	**% Overlap**
ISTJ and INFJ	4
ISTJ and ESTP	36
ESFJ and ENTJ	2
ESFJ and ISFP	32
ENFJ and ESTJ	4
ENFJ and INFP	44
INTJ and ISFJ	4
INTJ and ENTP	52

Source: From *Career Report Manual* (p. 37), by A. L. Hammer and G. P. Macdaid, 1992, Palo Alto, CA: Consulting Psychologists Press. Copyright 1992 by Consulting Psychologists Press. Used with permission.

Keep in mind that all 16 types can and do work in a variety of occupations.

Sources and Examples of Occupational Data

The MBTI research literature has a number of sources of occupational data:

- *Myers-Briggs Type Indicator Atlas of Type Tables* (Macdaid, McCaulley, & Kainz, 1986)
- *Manual: A Guide to the Development and Use of the MBTI,* Appendix D (Myers & McCaulley, 1985)
- *Career Report Manual* (Hammer & Macdaid, 1992a)
- *Journal of Psychological Type* articles
- Various unpublished dissertations
- *Association for Psychological Type Conference Proceedings*

The most comprehensive lists of occupational data sorted by type are published in Appendix D of the 1985 *MBTI Manual* and in the *Career Report Manual* (1992). Each type has a listing of more than 200 occupations chosen most to least frequently by people of that type. The *Atlas of Type Tables* (1986) contains data on hundreds of occupations; each occupation has a separate type table showing the distribution of types within that occupation. These data were gathered between 1971 and 1984. Since these occupational data are available elsewhere, they are not reprinted in this manual.

When reviewing any occupational database, the reader is urged to consider these issues:

- How *representative* is the career sample of current occupational trends in the field? *When* was the sample drawn? Samples from the first three sources above are considered samples of convenience and are relatively old, having been gathered in the 1970s through the mid-1980s. While probably representative of the occupation if the numbers are large and if occupational requirements have

not changed substantially since then, they may reflect also a bias toward people who are interested in psychological type since they have all taken the MBTI. Macdaid (personal communication) reported another possible biasing factor: When occupations were just opening up to women (as was occurring during that time period), the female "pioneers" tended to have EN preferences. Type theory would suggest that ENs would be more likely to move to these new areas with their "let's change it" view of life.

- What is the *gender* makeup of the samples? Most of the occupational samples combine genders. Preliminary research (Macdaid, personal communication) indicates that men and women report similar type distributions in the same occupation if that occupation has been "open" to both men and women. The slight exceptions seem to be on the Thinking–Feeling dichotomy, where more women report Feeling and more men Thinking, although the occupational distributions still lean toward the majority gender in the field. For example, in engineering, the majority of men and women prefer Thinking; however, there are more men than women who prefer Thinking in engineering.

- What are the *educational levels* represented in the occupations? This particularly affects the available lists of occupations for Sensing types, especially the Sensing Perceiving combinations. Those Sensing types with university degrees may notice many occupations shown as most attractive to their type that do not require their level of education; this is likely to be disheartening to some, and the practitioner is urged to put these data into a context. At some point in the future it would be helpful to have occupational lists for each type further divided by educational levels, such as the occupations most frequently chosen by each type with university degrees.

- How *satisfied* are those types with their careers? On the MBTI answer sheet is a question about job satisfaction. In a study by McCaulley, Macdaid, and Granade (1993), of the 66% who answered the question about how much they liked their career, only 2% indicated they "did not." Thus the majority of those in the occupational samples used in the 1985 *MBTI Manual* and in the MBTI Career Report liked their jobs "O.K." or "a lot," and we assume they are generally satisfied. A later section in this chapter examines the occupational satisfaction issue in more detail.
- How *successful* are those types in their career? We have little data to that effect. See Chapter 13 for more background.

To give the reader a sample of what one encounters in studies on careers and type, a synopsis of data on occupational samples from some recent journal articles, conference proceedings, and dissertations is reported in Table 12.12. As can be observed, the type preferences and modal types are what one would likely expect in these various occupational samples.

Hammer (1996a) summarizes the evidence in the "occupational selection" area:

> Evidence to support the proposition that occupational choice is related to the preferences measured by the MBTI is abundant and compelling. The preponderance of data and the contingency table analyses conducted on them show that the distribution of types across occupations generally follows theoretical predictions. Unequal distribution of types consistent with predictions has also been found across groups within an occupation, across tasks within an organization, and across occupations in a different culture using a translation of the MBTI. (p. 37)

Understanding the Numbers in Career Data

In examining the trends in the career data, it is necessary to understand the two kinds of numbers we encounter in the field and the ways those numbers are used:

1. *Absolute frequencies.* These are often presented as percentages and are most useful when reviewing overall labor force trends and attempting to understand the basic characteristics of an occupation.
2. *Self-selection ratios (SSR).* Self-selection ratios or contingency table analyses take into account the relative frequencies of the type in the population as well as in the sample gathered. They are important because type distributions show that each of the 16 types does not contain exactly 6.25% (or a 16th) of the population or of the sample. Thus a ratio, comparing the percentage of each type within a sample group to the percentage existing in the base population, is important because this analysis does take the actual population differences into account. These ratios are meaningful when working with individuals to determine whether the field is relatively more or less attractive to a given

type. Ratios above 1.00 mean that more people of that type are attracted to the occupation than we would expect given their frequency in the base population. Numbers less than 1.00 mean fewer of that type are attracted to the occupation given their frequency in the population. And of course, numbers around 1.00 mean nearly equal frequencies in both the base population and the sample group.

For example, the national sample (a base population) contains more ESTJs (8.7%) than INFPs (4.4%). Yet if we were looking at an occupational sample in which ESTJs and INFPs have similar percentages, such as librarians (Scherdin, 1994), where 7.3% are INFP and 6.1% are ESTJ, we mask these differences. It looks like ESTJs and INFPs find library work equally attractive, at least from these numbers. However, if we compare their frequencies in the sample to the base population frequencies, the INFPs have an SSR = 1.66 and the ESTJs, SSR = .70. Thus the occupation of librarian is more attractive to the INFPs than to the ESTJs. (See Chapter 9, "Validity," for an in-depth discussion of these ratios.)

Sample Question Illustrating SSRs

To further illustrate these concepts, we will explore possible career and educational paths in a business environment. First we start with the national representative sample (the overall sample as well as males and females) as our base population, which is shown in Table 12.13. (Remember the national representative sample was drawn from the national sample to match U.S. census data; see Chapter 7 for more information.)

1. **Which types are attracted to business school?**
   Common sense as well as research suggests "that managers of all types learn to value 'managerial culture,' which can be characterized in type terms as STJ—practical and results-oriented" (Walck, 1996, p. 70). One group valuing this managerial culture is likely to be those pursuing a master's of business administration (MBA). A sample of MBA students, most of whom have work experience (Power & Lundsten, 1997), shows the modal types to be ESTJ and ISTJ, a match with the prediction. Table 12.14 presents the type distribution of this sample of over 1,900 students and compares it with that of the base population, the national representative sample. We can see that this sample of MBA students does draw more STJ types as evidenced both by the frequencies and the ratio above 1. The NTJs, although not as great in numbers and frequencies as the STJs in the sample, have even higher SSRs than the STJs. (Both sets of data are statistically significant.) Thus even more NTs are attracted to the graduate program than STs, given

Table 12.12   Occupational Sample Studies

Occupation	Source	Sample Description	Modal Type	Other Findings
Certified public accountants	Satava, 1996, 1997	N = 439 65% male	ISTJ, ESTJ	National firms had more Extraverts; local firms, more Introverts Extraverts supervised more staff than did Introverts
Dentists and dental specialists	Grandy, Westerman, Ocando, & Erskine, 1996	N = 381 general practice N = 91 specialists Mostly male	ISTJ, ESTJ	No differences in types between general practice and specialists
Fast-growth entrepreneurs; small firm entrepreneurs; small business owners; lower-level managers; managers; executives	Reynierse, 1997	N = 135 to 1,024		72% E = Small firm entrepreneurs 54% I = Fast-growth entrepreneurs 66% S = Lower-level managers 60% N = Small firm entrepreneurs 87% T = Executives 56% F = Small business owners 77% J = Lower-level managers 52% P = Small firm entrepreneurs
High school basketball officials	Scott & Scott, 1996	N = 110 males; wide range of occupations and educational levels	ESTJ	77% = SJ 0% = NP
Hospital nurse managers and staff nurses	Van Ham, 1994	N = 52 nurse managers N = 52 staff nurses		Nurse managers had more T types than staff nurses Staff nurses had more S and F types than a composite sample of women with college degrees
Life insurance agents	Lewis, Tobacyk, Dawson, Jurkus, & Means, 1996	N = 223	ESTJ	74% = E 83% = S 63 % = T 71% = J
Line and staff managers	Reynierse & Harker, 1995	N = 237 line managers N = 190 staff managers		Line versus staff managers: E = 79% versus 53% S = 59% versus 43% T = 90% versus 87% J = 86% versus 67%
Senior student affairs officials on campuses	Daugherty, Randall, & Globetti, 1997	N = 153	INTJ, ENTJ	E = 60% N = 69% T = 57% J = 73% less than 7% were SP types

Table 12.13 Type Distribution of the National Representative Sample (Base Population)

	ISTJ	ISFJ	INFJ	INTJ
	%	%	%	%
Total Population[1]	11.6	13.8	1.5	2.1
Male[2]	16.4	8.1	1.2	3.3
Female[3]	6.9	19.4	1.6	0.9

	ISTP	ISFP	INFP	INTP
	%	%	%	%
Total Population[1]	5.4	8.8	4.4	3.3
Male[2]	8.5	7.6	4.1	4.8
Female[3]	2.3	9.9	4.6	1.7

	ESTP	ESFP	ENFP	ENTP
	%	%	%	%
Total Population[1]	4.3	8.5	8.1	3.2
Male[2]	5.6	6.9	6.4	4.0
Female[3]	3.0	10.1	9.7	2.4

	ESTJ	ESFJ	ENFJ	ENTJ
	%	%	%	%
Total Population[1]	8.7	12.3	2.5	1.8
Male[2]	11.2	7.5	1.6	2.7
Female[3]	6.3	16.9	3.3	0.9

E	1,483	(49.3%)
I	1,526	(50.7%)
S	2,206	(73.3%)
N	803	(26.7%)
T	1,210	(40.2%)
F	1,799	(59.8%)
J	1,629	(54.1%)
P	1,380	(45.9%)

Pairs and Temperaments

IJ	870	(28.9%)
IP	656	(21.8%)
EP	724	(24.1%)
EJ	759	(25.2%)
ST	900	(29.9%)
SF	1,306	(43.4%)
NF	493	(16.4%)
NT	310	(10.3%)
SJ	1,395	(46.4%)
SP	811	(27.0%)
NP	569	(18.9%)
NJ	234	(7.8%)
TJ	725	(24.1%)
TP	485	(16.1%)
FP	895	(29.7%)
FJ	904	(30.0%)
IN	336	(11.2%)
EN	467	(15.5%)
IS	1,190	(39.5%)
ES	1,016	(33.8%)
ET	540	(17.9%)
EF	943	(31.3%)
IF	856	(28.4%)
IT	670	(22.3%)

Note: [1]N = 3,009; [2]N = 1,478; [3]N = 1,531; See Appendix for a description of the samples. For distribution of types and preferences by gender, refer to Tables 7.14 and 7.15.

Source: National representative sample.

their numbers in the base population. Often graduate programs teach theoretical frameworks, something likely attractive to the NT group in theory and seemingly in practice, at least in this sample.

2. **Which types are drawn toward small business ownership?**

A dream for some people is to own their own small business. One way to look at the attraction of a particular type to small business ownership is to compare a sample of small business owners to the national representative sample. In this case we'll use separate data for men (Table 12.15) and women (Table 12.16). The male and female distributions and SSRs are similar. ISTJ and ESTJ are the modal types for both samples, and both have SSRs above 1.00 (with statistical significance at the .001 level), indicating that more of those types are attracted to small business ownership than

we might expect given the base population. However, in both samples, while the INTJs and ENTJs are smaller in numbers, their SSRs are usually higher than those for the STJs, especially in the female sample. Thus even more NTJs are attracted to small business ownership than we might expect given their numbers in the base population. (Note, however, that the male INTJ sample did not reveal statistically significant results and thus needs to be viewed with caution.)

3. **I'm a Feeling type with an MBA, but I don't want to work in a large organization. Might I find other "kindred" spirits in small businesses?**

To put this question in context, consider that there are fewer management jobs now available in organizations due to flattening of the structure, and thus the MBAs may consider small business ownership as an

Table 12.14	Working MBA Students Compared to the National Representative Sample		
ISTJ	**ISFJ**	**INFJ**	**INTJ**
N = 330	N = 63	N = 34	N = 136
17.1%	3.3%	1.8%	7.1%
SSR = 1.48***	SSR = .24***	SSR = 1.21	SSR = 3.43***
ISTP	**ISFP**	**INFP**	**INTP**
N = 81	N = 24	N = 36	N = 117
4.2%	1.3%	1.9%	6.1%
SSR = .78	SSR = .14***	SSR = .43***	SSR = 1.87***
ESTP	**ESFP**	**ENFP**	**ENTP**
N = 119	N = 39	N = 114	N = 195
6.2%	2.0%	5.9%	10.1%
SSR = 1.44**	SSR = .24***	SSR = .73**	SSR = 3.17***
ESTJ	**ESFJ**	**ENFJ**	**ENTJ**
N = 335	N = 91	N = 40	N = 171
17.4%	4.7%	2.1%	8.9%
SSR = 2.01***	SSR = .39***	SSR = .84	SSR = 4.86***

Note: Working MBA students N = 1,925, national representative sample N = 3,009; *p <.05, **p < .01, ***p < .001. See Appendix for a description of the sample.

Source: From "Studies That Compare Type Theory and Left-Brain/Right-Brain Theory," by S. J. Power and L. L. Lundsten, 1997, *Journal of Psychological Type, 43*, p. 25. Copyright 1997 by *Journal of Psychological Type.* Used with permission.

Table 12.15	Male Small Business Owners Sample Compared to Male National Representative Sample		
ISTJ	**ISFJ**	**INFJ**	**INTJ**
N = 112	N = 19	N = 2	N = 23
25.28%	4.29%	.45%	5.19%
SSR = 1.54***	SSR = .53**	SSR = .35	SSR = 1.57
ISTP	**ISFP**	**INFP**	**INTP**
N = 30	N = 6	N = 1	N = 13
6.77%	1.35%	.23%	2.93%
SSR = .79	SSR = .18***	SSR = .05***	SSR = .61
ESTP	**ESFP**	**ENFP**	**ENTP**
N = 30	N = 13	N = 11	N = 20
6.77%	2.93%	2.48%	4.51%
SSR = 1.21	SSR = .43***	SSR = .39**	SSR = 1.13***
ESTJ	**ESFJ**	**ENFJ**	**ENTJ**
N = 107	N = 24	N = 3	N = 29
24.15%	5.42%	.68%	6.55%
SSR = 2.16***	SSR = .72***	SSR = .42	SSR = 2.42***

Note: Male small business owners N = 443, male national representative sample N = 1,478; *p <.05, **p < .01, ***p < .001. See Appendix for a description of the sample.

Source: From *Guide to the Strong and MBTI Entrepreneur Report* (p. 20), by A. L. Hammer, 1997, Palo Alto, CA: Consulting Psychologists Press. Copyright 1997 by Consulting Psychologists Press. Used with permission.

option. We are therefore shifting the base population from the national representative sample to the MBA students in order to understand a possible career path for these students, especially the Feeling type asking the question. Table 12.17 shows this comparison and uses the primarily male small business owner sample. Please note that the small business owner sample used did not typically have MBA degrees; MBAs usually go to work in large organizations (Hammer, 1997). All SF types were relatively more attracted to small business ownership when they were compared with the national representative sample (SSR > 1.00), even though their numbers are small in terms of their workforce trends. However, their results are not statistically significant, and therefore generalizing from them is not recommended. Furthermore, the NF types all have SSRs well below 1.00 with results significant at the .05 or better level,

indicating they are less likely to self-select into small business ownership as a career. For the NTs the index is also below 1.00, indicating the small business career path is less attractive to these MBA students.

In general, these data do not suggest a clearcut career path into small business ownership for the Feeling types, but of course they do not eliminate such a path since that would be an inappropriate way to use psychological type. This Feeling type's career counselor may need to focus on helping this client identify important values and where the client might be able to live out those values, both inside and outside the work environment. For some that work environment may be within a small business and for others in a large organization.

The use of the appropriate base population is an issue when using ratios, and which base is "right" depends on the

Table 12.16	Female Small Business Owners Sample Compared to Female National Sample		
ISTJ	**ISFJ**	**INFJ**	**INTJ**
N = 17	N = 9	N = 1	N = 4
20.73%	10.98%	1.22%	4.88%
SSR = 2.99***	SSR = .57	SSR = .75	SSR = 5.74
ISTP	**ISFP**	**INFP**	**INTP**
N = 5	N = 2	N = 0	N = 2
6.10%	2.44%	0.00%	2.44%
SSR = 2.59	SSR = .25*	SSR = 0.00*	SSR = 1.38
ESTP	**ESFP**	**ENFP**	**ENTP**
N = 2	N = 2	N = 4	N = 5
2.44%	2.44%	4.88%	6.10%
SSR = .81	SSR = .24*	SSR = .50	SSR = 2.52
ESTJ	**ESFJ**	**ENFJ**	**ENTJ**
N = 14	N = 8	N = 1	N = 6
17.07%	9.76%	1.22%	7.32%
SSR = 2.72***	SSR = .58	SSR = .37	SSR = 8.0***

Note: Female small business owners N = 82, female national representative sample N = 1,531; *p <.05, **p < .01, ***p < .001. See Appendix for a description of the sample.

Source: From *Guide to the Strong and MBTI Entrepreneur Report* (p. 18), by A. L. Hammer, 1997, Palo Alto, CA: Consulting Psychologists Press. Copyright 1997 by Consulting Psychologists Press. Used with permission.

Table 12.17	Male Small Business Owners Sample Compared to MBA Students		
ISTJ	**ISFJ**	**INFJ**	**INTJ**
N = 112	N = 19	N = 2	N = 23
25.28%	4.29%	.45%	5.19%
SSR = 1.47***	SSR = 1.31	SSR = .26*	SSR = .73
ISTP	**ISFP**	**INFP**	**INTP**
N = 30	N = 6	N = 1	N = 13
6.77%	1.35%	.23%	2.93%
SSR = 1.61*	SSR = 1.09	SSR = .12*	SSR = .48**
ESTP	**ESFP**	**ENFP**	**ENTP**
N = 30	N = 13	N = 11	N = 20
6.77%	2.93%	2.48%	4.51%
SSR = 1.10	SSR = 1.45	SSR = .42**	SSR = .45***
ESTJ	**ESFJ**	**ENFJ**	**ENTJ**
N = 107	N = 24	N = 3	N = 29
24.15%	5.42%	.68%	6.55%
SSR = 1.39***	SSR = 1.15	SSR = .33*	SSR = .74

Note: Male small business owners N = 443, MBA students N = 1,925; *p <.05, **p < .01, ***p < .001. See Appendix for a description of the sample.

Source: From *Guide to the Strong and MBTI Entrepreneur Report* (p. 20), by A. L. Hammer, 1997, Palo Alto, CA: Consulting Psychologists Press. Copyright 1997 by Consulting Psychologists Press. Used with permission.

question asked. The different base populations used in our examples above gave some contrasting pieces of information. Some types, such as ENTJs, are more drawn toward business school and small business ownership when compared to the general population (the national representative sample); however, comparing the ENTJs to MBA students as the base, they are less drawn toward small business ownership. The opposite case occurs also with some Feeling types; SFs are somewhat attracted toward small business ownership if the base is MBA students (although not to the point of statistical significance); when the base is the national representative sample, they do not appear attracted toward small business ownership.

To put these examples in additional context, the MBA and small business owner samples were based on Form G data, while the national representative sample is from Form M. This may have created some differences. In addition, they are independent samples. In some research, dependent samples would be more appropriate, such as a sample of the types

leaving a particular company compared to the base population of the overall type distribution within that company. Nonetheless, these samples are used to illustrate some points about the use of numbers in career data. SSRs are likely to be helpful with individual cases pondering directions toward which to move. The percentages of types are helpful in understanding some basic characteristics of the occupation or in this case also a particular educational program.

Type Diversity Within an Occupation

At times, while looking at the type trends in an occupation, one can forget the diversity of specialties within an occupation as well as the many different ways people can go about completing tasks even in more narrowly defined jobs. There are niches and specialties within many occupations. The diversity is likely necessary within an occupation to keep the occupation from growing stale and to prevent "group think." When someone has a type different from that of the majority, that individual may even take the role of a "pioneer" by bringing in fresh, new approaches and insights.

Myers (1980/1995) offered data on the specialties of physicians and found that types were likely to specialize in medical fields predicted by type theory. In follow-up work by McCaulley (1977) it was noted that when physicians changed specialties, they more likely went into specialties aligned with their personality preferences. This is presented also as evidence that it is the personality that shapes the occupational path, not the occupational path that shapes the personality. For example, pediatricians did not become ESFJs after entering that specialty, but rather it was their ESFJ preferences that drew them to pediatrics. In other words, according to these data and to type theory, those in the same occupation do not develop a particular personality as a result of their work. The occupation does not cause the personality; rather, personality characteristics may draw people toward certain occupations. Thus, people in the same occupation are likely to share some similar personality characteristics.

The familiar occupation of librarian provides another example of type diversity within an occupation. Stereotypes of librarians suggest they are by preference Introverted, Sensing or Intuitive, Thinking, and Judging.

- ■ Introverted: Concentrate quietly on ideas and information
- ■ Sensing: Look at facts
- ■ Intuitive: Focus on ideas in new ways
- ■ Thinking: Analyze information objectively
- ■ Judging: Follow an organized system to find materials

And, indeed, the individual preferences of I, N, T, and J are in the majority (Scherdin, 1994). Moving to a whole type analysis, the modal type of librarians is ISTJ. Table 12.18 provides a type table of 1,600 librarians who completed the MBTI in 1992. While the percentages between men and women were generally similar on E–I, S–N, and J–P, there were greater differences on T–F, with men 69% T and women 58% T. This illustrates Macdaid's (personal communication) point that even when the majority preference is toward Thinking, women will be less so in their percentages than men because more women are Feeling types in general.

So what happens when people of different personality types do library work? How might they go about their work? Table 12.19 shows a summary by type of some specialties within the library profession and aspects of the job particularly enjoyed by the representative type. This information is anecdotal and provided by librarians interviewed for this chapter.

Each of these 16 individuals works in the same occupation, and each has taken time to be "on the desk" and answer reference questions. They nonetheless have all found areas in which to specialize, and they view some parts of their jobs as more satisfying than others.

Table 12.18   Type Table of Librarians

ISTJ	ISFJ	INFJ	INTJ
N = 265	N = 129	N = 104	N = 184
16.5%	8.1%	6.5%	11.5%
■■■■■■■■■■ ■■■■■■	■■■■■■■■	■■■■■■	■■■■■■■■■■ ■

ISTP	ISFP	INFP	INTP
N = 36	N = 27	N = 116	N = 146
2.3%	1.7%	7.3%	9.1%
■■	■	■■■■■■	■■■■■■

ESTP	ESFP	ENFP	ENTP
N = 18	N = 13	N = 96	N = 94
1.1%	0.8%	6.0%	5.9%
■	■	■■■■■■	■■■■■■

ESTJ	ESFJ	ENFJ	ENTJ
N = 98	N = 66	N = 81	N = 127
6.1%	4.1%	5.1%	7.9%
■■■■■■	■■■■	■■■■■	■■■■■■■■

Note: N = 1,600.

Source: From *Discovering Librarians: Profiles of a Profession*, by M. J. Scherdin, 1994, Association of College and Research Libraries, American Library Association. Used with permission.

Implications for Practitioners

There are clearcut trends in occupational choices by type but also individual differences within occupations. Practitioners can point out both patterns as clients assess jobs for themselves. The function pairs (ST, SF, NT, NF) play the greatest role in occupational choice; therefore, helping clients see how they can access their functions in a job is important.

Career counselors are also urged to encourage their clients to examine potential careers for the possibility of subspecialties or at least ways of changing the mix of activities performed: How can the job and the personality mesh more closely? An example of how clients with different types might find or create special niches within a specific occupation where the likelihood of using their type preferences is higher is seen in Table 12.19 with librarians.

From the data available, practitioners can see patterns and trends in occupational selection by type. However, they should also keep in mind the bigger picture and avoid encouraging clients to go into a career simply because they are the "right" type or discouraging clients from going into a career simply because they are the "wrong" type.

Table 12.19   Sample Specialties Within the Library Profession and Aspects of the Job Enjoyed

ISTJ Cataloguer (public library)	**ISFJ Assistant Public Services Manager (public library)**	**INFJ Reference Librarian (small public library)**	**INTJ Collections and Acquisitions Head (university library)**
Deciding exact subject heading and classification of new works Orderliness of the position Working uninterruptedly in a quiet space	Planning and organizing events with the unofficial title of "project queen" Coordinating staffing needs and organizing training programs to meet those needs Putting out a calendar of events "Bringing both heart and detailed organization" to her work	Coming up with creative ways to meet customers' needs: "I can think of 50 ways to approach their need. I'll make what I have here relate to their topic and show them how it does." Seeing the patrons happy Quiet activities such as paperwork tracking library statistics	Developing and working with policies and procedures and identifying the need for new ones Reviewing curriculum changes and their impact on the library Monitoring the budget and moving monies around to meet needs through paying attention to the big picture
ISTP Automation Specialist (public school system)	**ISFP Archivist (state library)**	**INFP Small Branch Library Manager (public library)**	**INTP Acquisitions Specialist (university library)**
Keeping up with the latest equipment and computer applications Using technology in his work Teaching short courses on computer applications	Surrounding herself with rare books and special documents Finding just what the patrons need to make them happy Camaraderie with other staff	Forming personal relationships with customers and enjoying their idiosyncrasies Being part of the community and touching people's lives Building collaborations: "I see my library as not having any walls, both literally and figuratively"	Analyzing what is needed in the library collection Building high-quality collection through critiquing materials Constantly searching for new knowledge Having a quiet space in which to concentrate deeply
ESTP Technology Specialist (extension division of university)	**ESFP Law Librarian (law firm)**	**ENFP Children's Librarian (public library)**	**ENTP Inter-Library Loan Department Head (public library)**
Trying out and then adapting technologies to the library's needs (as a "techno guinea pig") Preparing and updating Web pages Teaching others how to use the technologies she has learned Being away from her desk	His colleagues and the friendships and teamwork they've developed Variety of requests he gets; "no two days are alike" and even the "law changes weekly" Satisfaction of helping those lawyers find the information they need, although "at times no answer exists and it's hard to figure out when to stop!"	Having a variety of duties and loving them all Having freedom to move from area to area and learning something from each Being creative, such as developing storytime kits for daycare providers	Fielding whatever comes to her and seeing what people are wondering about Determining what piece of the "library puzzle" fits a patron's needs Having a variety of activities Staying on the cutting edge to better help customers
ESTJ Library Services Coordinator (state institution libraries)	**ESFJ Distance Learning Librarian (university library)**	**ENFJ Large Branch Library Manager (public library)**	**ENTJ Library Director (college library)**
Planning how to provide services, thinking through various approaches and the consequences of decisions Taking responsibility and efficiently following through Keeping her technical skills and knowledge up-to-date so she can check the facts quickly	Traveling on-site to teach others basic library skills including searching special indexes, evaluating information they find, and showing them how to order materials on their own Helping students find needed resources, using a personal touch Providing whatever support faculty and students need	Playing a variety of roles such as "hostess, mother, social worker, promoter . . ." Encouraging the process of intellectual development in her patrons Contributing to her staff's own personal and professional development including letting them make mistakes	The information and systems aspects of his job: "Library work can be conceptualized as a flow, which can be done poorly or well, efficiently or inefficiently. It's a series of events to be organized." Making decisions, especially about his own work Staying on task; he's most bothered by personnel issues

Note: This table and accompanying text show possible library specialties and are based solely on interviews with librarians who happen to have these specialties. Special thanks to Karen Kolb, St. Paul (Minnesota) Public Library; M.J. Scherdin, Edgewood College, Madison, Wisconsin; and Donna Breyfogle, University of Manitoba Library, Winnipeg, Canada, for help locating librarians of diverse types. And thanks to all the librarians who responded with information and anecdotes about their work.

Job Satisfaction

Career counseling clients want (a) an occupation that is satisfying or at least more satisfying than the current one and (b) an occupation in which they can perform satisfactorily. The Theory of Work Adjustment (Dawis, 1996) focuses on "the process by which the individual seeks to achieve and maintain correspondence with the environment" (p. 79). When the occupational tasks are congruent between the individual and the environment, more satisfaction is likely to result than when the fit is less positive. The individual and the environment correspond. We would predict that when there is congruency between the individual's psychological type and the task demands of the occupation, more satisfaction is likely to result. Myers and McCaulley (1985) state,

> When there is a mismatch between type and occupation, the client usually reports feeling tired and inadequate. According to type theory, the mismatch causes fatigue because it is more tiring to use less-preferred processes. A mismatch also causes discouragement, because despite the greater expenditure of effort, the work product is less likely to show the quality of products that would be developed if the preferred process were utilized. Tasks that call on preferred and developed processes require less effort for better performance, and give more satisfaction. (p. 78)

Hammer (1996a) provides a summary of the studies of job satisfaction reported in the *Career Report Manual* (Hammer & Macdaid, 1992a) as well as a synopsis of more than a dozen studies on the subject. Among the occupations studied for satisfaction data were bank officers/financial managers, computer professionals, dietitians, elementary and secondary school teachers, intensive care nurses, health care managers and executives, lawyers, managers, occupational therapists, parish pastors, pediatric nurse practitioners, pharmacists, secondary marketing education teachers, secretaries, teachers, and vocational education administrators. Hammer also points out some of the difficulties in looking at satisfaction, such as a restriction in range of data on satisfaction and on unusual classifications of some of the occupational data. He summarizes his literature review as follows:

> When satisfaction is measured globally, its relationship with psychological type is equivocal. However, among those studies that do show a relationship, a pattern seems to emerge. Overall, Introverts and Perceiving types seem less satisfied with their work than do Extraverts and Judging types, although the one study that examined men and women separately suggested that overall results may be misleading if gender is not accounted for. When specific facets or aspects of job satisfaction are employed instead of global measures, the picture becomes clearer. For example, the T–F scale seems to be important in identifying satisfaction with co-workers. Type theory would predict that different types will have different criteria for satisfaction, and this seems to be at least partially supported by the research.
>
> . . .
>
> Studies of person–environment fit . . . suggest that those who are dissatisfied in an occupation tend to be those types who are opposite from the modal type in the occupation. A number of studies have also suggested that those types who are

less frequent or underrepresented in an occupation tend to be less satisfied or have higher intention to leave the occupation than do those types who are more frequent or whose fit with the occupation is judged to be better. (pp. 40–41)

A few additional studies support Hammer's 1996 summary. Murry and Markham (1997) noted that in their sample of employees of a media organization, the INFPs indicated high dissatisfaction and likelihood to leave. Their colleagues with opposite types, ESTJs, indicated high satisfaction and little likelihood to leave. Hammer noted this IP dissatisfaction and EJ satisfaction pattern also.

Hopkins (1997) surveyed 133 members of a professional association on type and concluded that people who felt their job matched their personalities were more satisfied with their jobs than those who did not. SFs were the group least satisfied with their job matches. In personal telephone calls with some subjects, Hopkins (personal communication) noted also that SFs, out of the four function pairs, seemed the most grateful that someone was listening to them and their concerns. In his study, the variables of co-workers, the work itself, and supervision were far more important to job satisfaction than were pay and promotions. His sample was highly educated, high in job tenure, middle-aged, and Caucasian.

Tischler (1996) examined the success of a group of government employees based on their personality fit with their organization. Performing satisfactorily, i.e. success, is often a variable related to satisfaction. He commented that while people may have been drawn to careers and organizations by their personality fits and may remain there and draw comfort and satisfaction partly because of those fits, their success as measured by salary increase and promotions was not significantly related to type. Age, gender, and education were the variables in his sample that did affect success. Thus personality type was not a key factor of success in his sample.

Job Satisfiers and Dissatisfiers in the National Sample

Although there may be many reasons for persons to seek career counseling, one is likely to be dissatisfaction with the current job. In the national sample, data on work satisfaction and dissatisfaction were gathered. Respondents were asked to indicate their responses on a four-point scale of "Very Satisfied," "Somewhat Satisfied," "Somewhat Dissatisfied," or "Very Dissatisfied" on 3 questions related to their overall work (the work, company, and future work opportunities) and 14 questions on aspects of their work. They were also asked to indicate how likely they were to leave their current job within the next year on a scale of "Very Likely," "Somewhat Likely," or "Very Unlikely." Income data were gathered as well. Table 12.20 presents this information for the highest and lowest of the types on the variables related to the overall work satisfaction picture.

The vast majority of people in this sample, over 89%, were at least somewhat satisfied with the kind of work they

Table 12.20   The Types Expressing the Most and Least Work Satisfaction and Likelihood to Leave, and the Highest and Lowest Income Levels in the National Sample

ISTJ	ISFJ	INFJ	INTJ
			Less satisfied with future opportunities
ISTP	**ISFP**	**INFP**	**INTP**
Less satisfied with company	Low income Unlikely to leave	Less satisfied with work Less satisfied with company Less satisfied with future opportunities Likely to leave	Less satisfied with work Less satisfied with company Less satisfied with future opportunities Likely to leave
ESTP	**ESFP**	**ENFP**	**ENTP**
Less satisfied with company	Likely to leave		Less satisfied with work
ESTJ	**ESFJ**	**ENFJ**	**ENTJ**
Satisfied with work Satisfied with company	Satisfied with work Satisfied with company Unlikely to leave	Satisfied with work Satisfied with company Less satisfied with work Likely to leave	Satisfied with work Satisfied with company Satisfied with future opportunities High income Unlikely to leave

Note: All sixteen types were ranked from high to low on each variable. The top (or bottom) four types for each category are listed with these two exceptions: (a) if the gap between the third and fourth types is greater than 3%, only three types are listed; (b) if the gap between any pair of the four top types is greater than 5%, only those types above that gap are listed; e.g., "Satisfied with future opportunities" is listed only for ENTJs. See Appendix for a description of the sample.

Source: National sample.

were doing. The types expressing the most satisfaction with their work were the EJ types. These include the dominant extraverted Feeling types (ENFJ, ESFJ), for whom external harmony is important, and the dominant extraverted Thinking types (ENTJ and ESTJ), for whom taking charge of their external environment is important. In this sample, 77.2% were at least "Somewhat Satisfied" with the organization for which they worked (with ESFJ and ENFJ the most satisfied), and 67.2% were at least "Somewhat Satisfied" with their future work opportunities, with ENTJs clearly the most satisfied with the future. The type with the highest income level was ENTJ, and their polar opposites, ISFP, had the lowest income levels. Those most dissatisfied appeared to be the IP group, especially the INPs who were dissatisfied with their work, their company, and their future work opportunities.

In this sample, an average of 64.7% said they were "Very Unlikely" to leave their jobs within the next year, with those least likely to leave the ENTJ, ESFJ, and ISFP. In contrast, 13.7% of this sample said they were "Very Likely" to leave their jobs within the next year. The types that indicated this most frequently were INTP, INFP, ENFJ, and ESFP. The ENFJ group contains some contrasts; they were among both the most satisfied and the most dissatisfied types with their work. Perhaps ENFJs are not a passive group—they either like their work or they don't, and if they don't, they want to leave it. Their extraverted Feeling seeks harmony in the external environment. Clearly there are individual differences within type, and it would be interesting to further study this ENFJ group in particular to learn more about those differences. By contrast, another dominant Feeling type (but introverted) had a

Table 12.21   Satisfaction/Dissatisfaction with Work Aspects in the National Sample

Work Aspect	Average % of "Very Dissatisfied" Responses	Highest % & Type of "Very Dissatisfied"		Average % of "Very Satisfied" Responses	Highest % & Type of "Very Satisfied"	
Opportunities for promotion	22.3%	32.0%	INTJ	19.6%	35.1%	ENTJ
Salary	15.0%	25.8%	INFJ	19.3%	28.9%	ESTJ
Amount of stress	13.3%	18.9%	INFP	19.8%	29.7%	ESTP
Job security	11.8%	19.7%	INTP	39.0%	56.9%	ENFJ
Opportunities for accomplishment	11.2%	15.3%	INFP	30.8%	51.4%	ENTJ
Opportunities for learning	10.3%	14.4%	ESTP, INFP	36.1%	56.9%	ENFJ
Opportunities to contribute to society	10.3%	16.7%	ESTP	36.3%	54.1%	ENTJ
Predictability/stability of job	10.1%	17.4%	INTP	32.3%	43.5%	ESFJ
Working conditions (hours, vacations, benefits, etc.)	9.5%	15.5%	INTP	38.7%	48.4%	INFJ
Opportunity to use talents or training	9.5%	15.5%	ENTP	38.3%	59.5%	ENTJ
Respect I get	8.9%	13.5%	INFP	36.1%	48.6%	ESFJ
Responsibility	4.4%	8.6%	INTP	41.2%	52.9%	ENFJ
Day-to-day tasks	3.8%	5.9%	ESFP	32.0%	41.7%	ENTJ
People I work with	3.4%	10.0%	INTP	45.9%	60.0%	ENFJ

Note: See Appendix for a description of the sample.

Source: National sample.

different pattern. The ISFPs in the lowest income grouping were among those "unlikely to leave." Perhaps their personal loyalty (dominant introverted Feeling) is more important than their pay and thus they stay at low-paying jobs.

Table 12.21 presents the 14 aspects of work surveyed and provides the sample's average percentage of "Very Dissatisfied" responses along with that of the type most dissatisfied; the same information for the "Very Satisfied" responses is also included. This sample appears most concerned about "opportunities for promotion" (22.3% were "Very Dissatisfied" and 19.6% "Very Satisfied"), with the INTJs most concerned. The ENTJs were the most satisfied of the 16 types on this aspect. This national sample was least concerned about the people they work with (only 3.4% were "Very Dissatisfied," while 45.9% were "Very Satisfied"). The INTPs were the most dissatisfied, while the ENFJs were the most satisfied with their colleagues.

Table 12.22 reports the work aspects that are satisfiers to this sample (over 50% of the type indicated they were "Very Satisfied") and dissatisfiers (over 15% of the type indicated "Very Dissatisfied.") Of the 16 types in this sample, it appears in terms of both overall work satisfaction and particular aspects of work that the ENTJs are the most satisfied (least dissatisfied) and INTPs and INFPs, the most dissatisfied (least satisfied). Perceiving types followed by Introverted types seem to express the most dissatisfaction with aspects of their work. Perhaps the nature of work itself asks them to use their Extraverted and Judging sides more than they would like. The EJ types were least dissatisfied and most satisfied; perhaps

work settings, with their expectations of interaction and closure, more naturally appeal to people of these preferences.

While occupational selection seems most related to the functions (ST, SF, NF, NT), work environment satisfaction seems most affected by the attitudes (IJ, IP, EP, EJ). However, any type can be satisfied in work as well as dissatisfied; these are grouped data and need to be put into the individual contexts.

Turnover

Turnover may result from unsuccessful job performance, changes in the market leading to downsizing, or job dissatisfaction. Vocational research amply supports (a) the prediction of turnover from job dissatisfaction and (b) the fact that people perform better in a job when they are satisfied (Dawis, 1996). In reviewing the literature on type and turnover, the focus has been on job fit/misfit and job dissatisfaction. Hammer (1996a) reviews research from the 1985 *MBTI Manual* and other studies and concludes,

Although few studies have been conducted on turnover, those that are available provide some support for the proposition that types working in environments or jobs that are not a good match for their preferences are more likely to leave or to say they are going to leave than are those whose type provides a better fit for either the tasks or the environment. Future studies examining the relationship of type and turnover should heed Garden's (1989) finding that organizational size may be a mediating variable. One study has suggested that the type of the managers in an organization may also be related to employee turnover. (p. 47)

Table 12.22   The Greatest Dissatisfiers and Satisfiers in the Work Environment

ISTJ	ISFJ	INFJ	INTJ
Dissatisfiers: Promotions **Satisfiers:**	**Dissatisfiers:** Promotions Stress Salary **Satisfiers:**	**Dissatisfiers:** Promotions Salary **Satisfiers:**	**Dissatisfiers:** Promotions Job security **Satisfiers:**
ISTP	**ISFP**	**INFP**	**INTP**
Dissatisfiers: Promotions **Satisfiers:**	**Dissatisfiers:** Promotions Job security Salary **Satisfiers:**	**Dissatisfiers:** Promotions Stress Accomplishment **Satisfiers:**	**Dissatisfiers:** Promotions Salary Job security Predictability Working conditions **Satisfiers:**
ESTP	**ESFP**	**ENFP**	**ENTP**
Dissatisfiers: Promotions Societal contributions Stress **Satisfiers:**	**Dissatisfiers:** Promotions Job security Stress Salary Accomplishment **Satisfiers:** People I work with	**Dissatisfiers:** Promotions Salary **Satisfiers:** People I work with	**Dissatisfiers:** Promotions Salary Use talents **Satisfiers:**
ESTJ	**ESFJ**	**ENFJ**	**ENTJ**
Dissatisfiers: Promotions **Satisfiers:**	**Dissatisfiers:** Promotions **Satisfiers:** People I work with Responsibility Societal contributions	**Dissatisfiers:** Promotions Salary **Satisfiers:** People I work with Opportunity to use talents Learning Job security Responsibility Societal contributions	**Dissatisfiers:** **Satisfiers:** Opportunity to use talents Societal contributions Job security Learning Accomplishment

Note: **Dissatisfier:** Over 15% of the type indicated "Very Dissatisfied"; **Satisfier:** Over 50% of the type indicated "Very Satisfied."
See Appendix for a description of the sample.

Source: National sample.

Garden (1989) studied computer professionals in both large and small companies. Those with I, N, and P preferences expected to leave their employer if it were a larger company; perhaps they sought more autonomy, which is likely to come in a smaller company. Those with S and J preferences said they were more likely to leave smaller companies, perhaps seeking the more detailed regimen of a larger company. Additional studies have not been published since this review by Hammer. Studies reported earlier on "likelihood to leave" are related to the turnover issue, but follow-up would be needed to see if those indicating the desire to leave actually did.

Implications for Practitioners

There are many factors that contribute to career satisfaction and dissatisfaction. Data from the national sample suggest possible areas of concern by type to explore first. However, even when an area of concern is identified, practitioners are urged to find the particular meaning for the individual. For example, although stress is a dissatisfier for many ESTPs and ISFJs, they likely find different things stressful and probably would prefer different methods for handling the stress in their jobs. Some types such as ISFP, ISFJ, and ESFP, who report more dissatisfaction with their salaries and who indeed are the types with the lowest average salaries, may need coaching on how to negotiate for higher salaries or how to groom themselves to take on additional responsibilities for which they might receive higher pay. These types do not typically assert themselves with others. For ENTPs who are also dissatisfied with their salaries but are among the highest paid of the 16 types, the issue and its solution may be something different.

Because the nature of work and the stability of jobs are changing, it is noteworthy that the areas of biggest concern include some that are unlikely to improve. Job security and promotional opportunities are decreasing, while stress is likely to increase. To help clients weather this new world of work, career counseling can help clients focus on their unique talents, some of which the MBTI might help point out; identify methods to teach clients to cope with stress and increase their natural resiliency; and encourage clients to take responsibility for their own career development.

Interests

Interests are also key components in careers. Holland's typology of persons and work environments is a major force in career psychology (Spokane, 1996) and is measured by assessing the interests of individuals. "Individuals seek and remain in congruent environments; and environments recruit, retain and reward congruent people. Congruence is assessed according to the degree of match between the vocational personality of an individual and the environmental type of an occupation or position" (Gottfredson & Holland, 1996, p. 6). Thus, liking the activities associated with one's job and with the people doing the job leads to job satisfaction and tenure.

The tenets of Holland's theory of vocational interests include the idea that both people and environments can be classified into six types: Realistic, Investigative, Artistic, Social, Enterprising, and Conventional (RIASEC); these are often displayed on a hexagon. Figure 12.1 delineates the hexagon and gives brief definitions of each vocational theme. The interests that are most closely related are next to one another on the hexagon, and those that are situated opposite each other are least related. Thus Realistic and Investigative are closely related whereas Realistic and Social are not. Within the Holland codes, people are more likely a combination of types, rather than just one; for example, a counselor may have a Social-Enterprising-Artistic (SEA) code.

There are a number of instruments that measure interests, and several have been correlated with the MBTI. Chapter 9, "Validity," provides information on several studies. Studies on the *Strong Interest Inventory* (*Strong*), the *Kuder Occupational Interest Survey,* the *Opinion, Attitude, and Interest Scales* (OAIS), and the *Vocational Preference Inventory* (VPI) are included in Chapter 11 of the 1985 *MBTI Manual*. A summary and discussion of these studies and additional research also appear in Hammer and Macdaid (1992a) and Hammer (1996a). The latter also includes a summary of a study correlating type with the *Career Occupational Preference System Interest Inventory* (COPS). The most complete data on the relationship of the MBTI to interests is reported in the *Strong and MBTI Career Development Guide* by Hammer and Kummerow (1992 edition for the 1985 *Strong* and 1996 for the 1994 *Strong*).

Hammer and Kummerow (1996) report correlations ranging from 0.00 to .48 between the MBTI preferences and the *Strong* General Occupational Themes, which measure the Holland themes:

- Realistic is moderately correlated with Thinking; its opposite, Social, is moderately correlated with Feeling as well as Extraversion.
- Artistic is moderately correlated with Intuition and Perceiving, as well as Feeling, whereas its opposite, Conventional, is moderately correlated with Sensing and Judging (opposite preferences on the MBTI).
- Enterprising is moderately associated with Extraversion.

Analyzing the correlations between the *Strong* General Occupational Scales and type preferences, Hammer (1996a) noted that the J–P scale showed the lowest and the fewest correlations with *Strong* Occupational Scales. Other publications (Hammer & Macdaid, 1992b) suggest "that this scale is the one least likely to reflect an attraction to a particular occupational field. It more often can be used

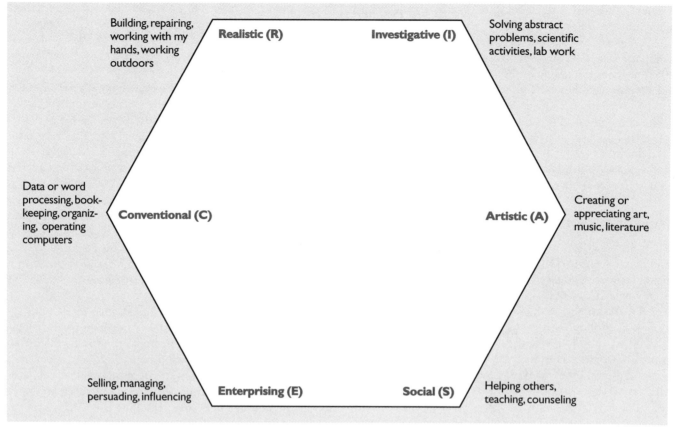

Figure 12.1 Holland's Vocational Types and Brief Definitions

Note: Definitions are from the MBTI research questionnaire (see Chapter 7).

to suggest how an individual might structure his or her job in any field."

Chapter 9 of this manual also contains two samples where *Strong Interest Inventory* data and Form M results are correlated. They confirm the results suggested above. In general, correlations between scales on the *Strong* and the MBTI preferences suggest that the results of the two instruments will, in general, suggest the same directions to clients. However, because the correlations are moderate at best when they exist, they indicate that both instruments (and hence personality and interest data) have unique contributions to make to the career counseling process.

Interests and Self-Efficacy in the National Sample

Social cognitive career theory and research (Lent, Brown, & Hackett, 1996) suggest that "interests are strongly related to one's self-efficacy" (p. 400). What one believes he or she can do often leads to interests in that area. People are likely to pursue and persist in areas where they have confidence in their abilities. To study the variables of self-efficacy or confidence, the performance of various work activities, and interests, the national sample was asked to provide *self-ratings* on the RIASEC themes. The three questions asked were,

1. "How *confident* are you in your ability to perform the following activities," with the choices of "Complete Confidence," "Much Confidence," "Moderate Confidence," "Little Confidence," and "No Confidence."
2. "How often do you *perform* the following activities in your current job," with the choices of "Almost Always," "Sometimes," "Rarely," and "Never."
3. "How much do you *like* to do the following activities (whether or not you are good at it)," with the choices of "Like," "Indifferent," and "Dislike."

In career counseling we would likely concentrate our efforts at least initially on where the client feels he or she has at least moderate confidence in abilities, the activities the client is currently performing, and what the client likes. Table 12.23 presents basic information on this sample in the three categories of information coded by RIASEC responses. This sample liked all the Holland theme activities more than they performed them or had confidence in their abilities, except in the Enterprising area, in which performance and confidence were nearly equal. The most often performed tasks in this group were in the Social area, which is also the most liked area and where these respondents have the most confidence; Conventional was next. The least performed activities were in the Artistic and Investigative areas. In the

Table 12.23 Confidence in Abilities, Performing, and Liking for the RIASEC Codes in the National Sample

Activities	Average % & Range of Types for Confidence in Abilities	Average % & Range of Types for Performing Activities	Average % & Range of Types for Liking Activities
Realistic (R)	50.9%	28.9%	73.3%
	68.6% ESTP–28.6% INFJ	44.0% ISTP–14.2% INFJ	83.9% INTP–63.7% INTJ
Investigative (I)	27.9%	11.7%	33.0%
	64.6% ENTJ–12.2% ISFP	32.2% ENTJ–2.6% ISFP	66.7% ENTJ–16.2% ISFP
Artistic (A)	38.4%	8.0%	57.8%
	62.7% ENFP–23.0% ISTP	18.8% ENTJ–2.0% ENTP	89.8% ENFJ–42.9% ISTP
Social (S)	69.2%	37.0%	79.6%
	95.8% ENTJ–52.0% ISFP	53.9% ENFJ–22.0% INTP	93.8% ENFP–68.6% INTP
Enterprising (E)	37.7%	30.1%	35.5%
	83.0% ENTJ–16.7% ISFP	60.2% ENTJ–18.1% INTP	74.6% ENTJ–18.6% INFJ
Conventional (C)	37.4%	36.2%	39.1%
	61.5% INTJ–22.6% ISFP	58.0% INFJ–23.8% ISFP	50.2% ENFJ–29.1% INFP

Note: See Appendix for a description of the sample.

Source: National sample.

Artistic, Realistic, Social, and Investigative areas, these respondents indicated they liked the activities much more than they performed them. They may wish to devise ways to include more of those activities in their work, if their work is at all flexible in its demands. Or these may be activities that could be included more often in people's nonwork lives.

When looking at the high and low percentages for each Holland code in Table 12.23 and noting the types associated with the endpoints of each range, it is apparent that people of different types like different activities. In some cases they are at the opposite ends from one another in terms of activities liked. For example, of the 16 types, ENTJs liked the Investigative activities the most; ISFPs, their opposite, the least.

Table 12.24 combines three pieces of information:

- The codes of the top four types who had either "Complete" or "Much Confidence" in their abilities in those activities
- The codes of the top four types who "Almost Always" used/performed those activities
- The codes of the top four types who indicated "Like" to the activities

Both genders are combined in this analysis.

These data illustrate the pattern that what one has confidence in, one performs and also likes, at least in this sample. These types and RIASEC themes emerge:

- The NT functions, especially the ENT combination, appear to have the most confidence in that they indicate the highest confidence in two to four activity areas. They often enjoy the challenges of tackling new responsibilities and seem to show the confidence here in their abilities to do so.
- Their polar opposites, the SF functions, do not show as much confidence. In no Holland theme area are they among the top four types with confidence in that area. Perhaps their more natural modesty has kept them from endorsing the extremes of these activities. They may need special encouragement and support when they strike out in new areas since their confidence may be lacking.
- Investigative (abstract problem solving) appears to be a common theme for NTs.
- Artistic is a common theme for NFs. Both typologies emphasize self-expression and communication.
- STs (with the exception of the ESTJs) often endorse the Realistic theme—hands-on, pragmatic activities appeal to STs.
- Both dominant introverted Intuitives (INTJ and INFJ) have confidence in Conventional theme activities, something somewhat unexpected from those who theoretically focus on the big picture. Perhaps it is in the organizing of the data that they have a natural excuse to turn inward and make patterns out of the data.

Table 12.24 Confidence, Performance, and Liking in Abilities for the Highest Ranked RIASEC Themes of the 16 Types in the National Sample

ISTJ		ISFJ		INFJ		INTJ	
Confidence:		Confidence:		Confidence:	AC	Confidence:	IC
Perform:	R	Perform:		Perform:	IAC	Perform:	I
Like:		Like:		Like:	AC	Like:	I

ISTP		ISFP		INFP		INTP	
Confidence:	R	Confidence:		Confidence:	A	Confidence:	RIC
Perform:	R	Perform:		Perform:	C	Perform:	A
Like:	R	Like:		Like:	A	Like:	RIC

ESTP		ESFP		ENFP		ENTP	
Confidence:	RE	Confidence:		Confidence:	AS	Confidence:	RASE
Perform:	R	Perform:	R	Perform:	AS	Perform:	EC
Like:	RE	Like:		Like:	AS	Like:	RIE

ESTJ		ESFJ		ENFJ		ENTJ	
Confidence:	E	Confidence:		Confidence:	AS	Confidence:	ISEC
Perform:	E	Perform:	SE	Perform:	SC	Perform:	IAE
Like:	E	Like:	S	Like:	ASC	Like:	ISEC

Note: Based on the average of the self-ratings by each type. The four types with the highest percentages in each RIASEC cagetory are indicated above. For example, the highest "Confidence" in Realistic abilities was indicated by ISTP, INTP, ESTP, and ENTP. There are these exceptions: (1) only three types were included when the "distance" to the fourth one was >5%, e.g., "Performing" Investigative activities includes only ENTJ, INFJ, and INTJ; (2) five types were included when the "distance" between the fourth and fifth types was within one percentage point, e.g., "Confidence" in Artistic abilities is included for ENFP, ENFJ, INFJ, INFP, and ENTP. See Appendix for a description of the sample.

Source: National sample.

- The INFJs may have some difficulty finding occupations that combine their two opposite codes, Artistic and Conventional; often it is difficult to use diametrically opposed interests in the same occupation. The advent of computer graphics combining both Artistic and Conventional activities may help. Or perhaps there are two subsamples of INFJs here: those who prefer Artistic and those who prefer Conventional activities.

- INFPs have confidence in and like Artistic activities, yet they perform Conventional ones. Performing the opposite activities from what one likes may be creating the tension that leads them to lower levels of job satisfaction overall, as we saw in an earlier section.

- While Conventional correlates to Sensing and Judging at the preference level, it does not do so when we look at the four letters put together into a type. Sensing types do not rate themselves high on Conventional in the three areas of confidence, performance, and liking. Perhaps Sensing types are more cautious in general about rating themselves highly on these, or any, activities. Conventional shows up in some combination in every Intuitive type except for ENFP. Perhaps Intuitive types have performed these activities out of necessity and developed their confidence and liking as a result.

- For the ES types, their performance appears to be related to their dominant functions. Extraverted Sensing types (ESTP and ESFP) perform Realistic activities, perhaps reflecting the hands-on nature of those types. ESTJs (extraverted Thinking dominant) perform Enterprising activities, perhaps reflecting their desire to lead and persuade others. ESFJs (extraverted Feeling dominant) perform Social-Enterprising activities, perhaps reflecting their desire to help and lead people.

A second study of the links between interests, type, and self-efficacy is available on 231 graduate and undergraduate students from a large midwestern university. The study correlates Form M results with the General Occupational Themes as measured by both the *Strong* and the Skills Confidence Inventory (Betz, Borgen, & Harmon, 1996). The latter is a measure of the self-efficacy or confidence an individual has in his or her abilities to perform various activities; skills confidence is measured in each one of the six Holland themes. The MBTI preferences and function pairs (ST, SF, NF, NT) that relate statistically to each General Occupational Theme (GOT) and Skills Confidence scale appear in Figure 12.2. The preferences relate in expected ways to the GOT themes. For example, Realistic, with its focus on

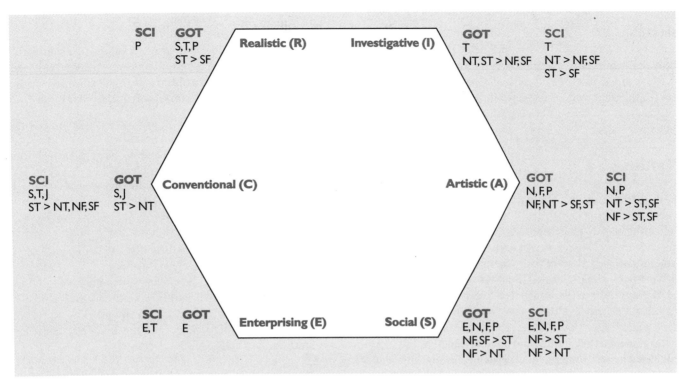

Figure 12.2 MBTI Preferences and Function Pair Differences Associated with RIASEC General Occupational Themes (GOT) and Skills Confidence Inventory (SCI) in a Sample of College Students

Note: All results are statistically significant at the .05 level or better. Pairs results are based on MANOVAS and post-hoc analyses. See Appendix for a description of the sample.

Source: Iowa State University.

hands-on activities, relates to Sensing, Thinking, and Perceiving; Investigative, with its abstract problem solving, relates more closely to Thinking; Artistic, with its self-expression and freedom, to Intuition, Feeling, and Perceiving; Social, with a focus on helping people, to Extraversion, Intuition, Feeling, and Perceiving; and Conventional, with its focus on organization and accuracy, to Sensing and Judging. The function pair pattern results also fit with type theory. A similar pattern emerges for the Skills Confidence Inventory data; what one has confidence in, one tends to like, and vice versa. The relationships reported were statistically significant at least at the .05 level or better and seem to fit with type theory and the previous research.

Implications for Practitioners

Interests generally relate to type in the directions expected, but the size of the relationship is usually moderate to small, especially at the occupational level. Often types that are opposite from one another will have opposite interest patterns as well. Practitioners are urged to use interests to add to the power of personality type, not replace it. An Artistic ESTJ is likely quite different from an Artistic INFP. Both want to be creative yet likely will do so in quite different manners. For example, an Artistic ESTJ found work in the

compensation and benefits area quite creative, while an INFP Artistic used his creativity as an author and university professor. An Enterprising ENFP will lead and persuade in a different manner than an Enterprising ISTJ. One Enterprising ENFP became an attorney specializing in mediating conflicts between small businesses. Her Enterprising ISTJ husband is an executive in a computer company. Each set of information augments the other and increases the practitioner's ability to help clients.

Self-efficacy is another useful concept to explore with clients, and type seems to relate to what clients likely have confidence in performing. It may also provide paths to explore with clients. For example, do the ENTs really have skills in the areas in which they have confidence, or would some reality checking help them? Do the ISFs really lack skills since they report lower self-efficacy when compared to other types, or do they simply need more encouragement to try some activities or to even acknowledge their own skill levels? Self-efficacy data related to interest patterns can suggest areas to focus on first, but as with any instrument they need to be put in the context of the individual.

Kummerow and Hammer (1995) offer a workbook to help clients integrate results from the *Strong* and the MBTI and a guide (Hammer & Kummerow, 1996) to assist practitioners with that integration. *Starting Out, Starting Over* (Peterson,

1995) and *Real People, Real Jobs* (Montross, Leibowitz, and Shinkman, 1995) also look at interests and personality. Grutter (1998a, 1998b, 1998c) has three publications carefully delineating the integration of the two instruments for those wanting to enrich their work lives or make a transition to different roles or responsibilities.

Values

Both theory and research support the importance of work values in making career decisions (Brown, 1996). Options reflecting highly prioritized values are chosen when they are available. Thus career practitioners would do well to understand the values of their clients, since they likely are a driving force in a career decision.

Hammer (1996a) summarized five studies relating type to values or beliefs. Values seem to relate statistically with type preferences in ways that are to be expected, but, as with interests, they do not converge completely. For example, Sensing and Judging often relate to a desire for security and stability, while Intuition and Perceiving often relate to a desire for creativity.

Garden (1997) examined the career paths of 341 software technical professionals in small high-tech companies for motivation profiles and future career directions. In examining the eight preference poles, she found that all valued money and comfort, recognition and autonomy, suggesting that similarities within the profession, not type preferences, made the difference. However, in examining four possible career paths (managerial, technical, challenging project, own company), she found statistically significant type differences. For the larger type cells (>15) she found these patterns:

- Managerial path was chosen most often by ESTJ, ENFJ, ISTJ.
- Technical path was chosen most often by INTJ.
- Challenging project path was chosen *least* often by INFP.
- Own company path was chosen most often by ENTP and INTP.
- ENFPs sorted themselves nearly equally among the four paths.

In a study of a media organization, Murry and Markham (1997) investigated how the collective personality of an organization, based on type, might shape the structure of their espoused values (based on Rokeach's work on values). While the samples in each of the types were not large enough for separate analyses, for the ISTJs and ISFJs there was more of an emphasis on fitting in, predictability, a single culture, and rule orientation. NFs had the most congruence with the top values in this organization, which included an emphasis on quality, team orientation, flexibility and fairness, security of employment, and innovation;

the authors suggest this may be because of the creative nature of this media organization.

Mitchell (1981) also studied work values in a sample of more than 800 employees in a banking organization. See Chapter 9 for more background information on his study. He identified these eight factors as organizational values:

1. *Happy family:* harmonious interpersonal relationships with pleasant material surroundings
2. *Variety and challenge:* latitude to work creatively on intellectually stimulating problems
3. *Achievement within the system:* orientation toward climbing the corporate ladder
4. *Visible autonomy:* free expression of views even when at odds with the social milieu
5. *Outgoing affiliation:* satisfaction in being part of a group
6. *Business sociability:* sociability with a purpose
7. *Financial analysis:* scientific and intellectual curiosity about economic and financial matters
8. *Nurturing affiliation:* developing loyalties, assisting others, and sharing

The types with these as high and low values are listed in Table 12.25.

For the SFs in this sample, "happy family" with harmonious interpersonal relationships was important; by theory SFs value harmony with others. This same value did not appear important to the sample of their opposites, the NTs, who are more likely to value their personal autonomy. In focusing on two opposite types such as ISFJ and ENTP, the same values never appear on both lists. What is important to one is not to the other. The EP group does not seem to be particularly oriented toward climbing the corporate ladder; they are generally free-spirited people, open to the moment. Climbing a corporate ladder likely requires working within a system and planning one's career moves in advance, a style that likely does not appeal to EPs but does to ESTJs.

Values of the National Sample

The national sample was asked to indicate how important 11 values were in their lives on a scale of "Very Important," "Somewhat Important," "Somewhat Unimportant," or "Not Important." Results of responses listed as "Very Important" are shown in Table 12.26.

The values of greatest importance to the entire sample were "home and family," "health," "financial security," "relationships/friendships," and "autonomy, freedom, and independence." Over 50% of nearly every type valued these. Of much less importance to this sample were "community service" and "prestige or status." No type endorsed these as "Very Important" at a rate greater than 25%.

Table 12.27 lists, for each type, the five values most important to that type, as indicated by the average scores on that value. While there is a great deal of similarity between the values for every type, the differences are notable.

Table 12.25 Organizational Values of the 16 Types

ISTJ	ISFJ	INFJ	INTJ
Low: Visible autonomy	**High:** Happy family **Low:** Variety and challenge Visible autonomy		**High:** Financial analysis **Low:** Business sociability
ISTP **Low:** Outgoing affiliation Financial analysis	**ISFP** **High:** Happy family **Low:** Variety and challenge	**INFP** **High:** Nurturing affiliation	**INTP** **High:** Visible autonomy
ESTP **High:** Visible autonomy **Low:** Achievement within system Financial analysis	**ESFP** **High:** Happy family **Low:** Achievement within system	**ENFP** **Low:** Achievement within system	**ENTP** **High:** Variety and challenge Visible autonomy **Low:** Happy family
ESTJ **High:** Achievement within system	**ESFJ** **High:** Happy family Outgoing affiliation Business sociability	**ENFJ** **High:** Nurturing affiliation	**ENTJ** **High:** Financial analysis **Low:** Nurturing affiliation

Source: From *Type and Social Climate in a Large Organization,* by W. D. Mitchell, 1981, unpublished manuscript. Adapted with permission.

Table 12.26 Values of the National Sample Ranked as "Very Important"

Value	Average %	Highest % & Type		Lowest % & Type	
Home and family	84.8%	97.9%	ENTJ	65.1%	INTJ
Health	75.4%	83.8%	ESFJ	55.3%	INFJ
Financial security	67.9%	76.0%	ESTJ	50.0%	INFJ & INTJ
Relationship/friendships	62.6%	79.5%	ENFP	30.8%	INTJ
Autonomy, freedom, independence	60.9%	75.5%	INTP	53.9%	ESFJ
Achievement and accomplishment	51.4%	69.2%	ESTJ	37.8%	ISFP
Religion or spirituality	45.2%	61.6%	ESFJ	22.2%	INTP
Education, learning	41.6%	64.1%	ENFJ	27.7%	ISFP
Being creative	30.8%	55.1%	ENFP	16.3%	ISFP
Community service	11.3%	24.1%	ENFJ	4.8%	INTJ
Prestige or status	7.6%	14.3%	ESTJ	0.0%	INFJ

Note: See Appendix for a description of the sample.

Source: National sample.

Table 12.27 Each Type's Five Most Important Values

ISTJ	ISFJ	INFJ	INTJ
Home/family	Home/family	Home/family	Health
Financial security	Health	Health	Home/family
Health	Financial security	Friendships	Achievement
Autonomy	Friendships	Financial security	Autonomy
Achievement	Autonomy	Autonomy	Financial security

ISTP	ISFP	INFP	INTP
Home/family	Home/family	Home/family	Autonomy
Financial security	Health	Autonomy	Home/family
Health (tie)	Financial security	Health	Health
Autonomy (tie)	Friendships	Friendships	Financial security
Friendships	Autonomy	Financial security	Friendships

ESTP	ESFP	ENFP	ENTP
Home/family	Home/family	Home/family	Home/family
Health	Health	Friendships (tie)	Autonomy
Financial security	Friendships	Health (tie)	Achievement
Friendships	Financial security	Autonomy	Financial security (tie)
Autonomy	Achievement	Financial security	Health (tie)

ESTJ	ESFJ	ENFJ	ENTJ
Home/family	Home/family	Home/family	Home/family
Health	Health	Health	Health
Financial security	Friendships	Friendships	Financial security (tie)
Achievement	Financial security	Financial security	Friendships (tie)
Friendships	Achievement	Learning	Achievement

Note: See Appendix for a description of the sample.

Source: National sample.

- The only two types for whom "home/family" is not first are INTJ and INTP, which given their more individualistic natures makes sense.
- "Health" is among the top three values for every type except ENTPs, who place "home/family," "autonomy," and "achievement" ahead of it. They may be so busy seeking challenges that they pay less attention to their inferior Sensing function and may place a lesser value on health issues.
- "Achievement" is an important value for all the TJ types (ISTJ, INTJ, ESTJ, ENTJ) and for ESFJ, ENTP, and ESFP. "Achievement" is not as important a value to the IP types.
- "Learning" is a very important value only to the ENFJs.
- "Autonomy" is important to all Introverted types plus three of the EP types. It is not as important to the EJ types.

Table 12.28 presents these values in a slightly different format: For each of the 11 values, the four types endorsing the "Very Important" statement the most frequently are included. It appears that the values endorsed most highly by one type are not endorsed as highly by its opposite. For example, one of the top four types valuing "financial security" is ISTJ, not

ENFP; ENTPs are among the top four on "achievement," while their opposites, ISFJs, are not. Feeling types, who make their judgments based on values, endorse twice as many values as important as do the Thinking types. This pattern is particularly pronounced when comparing the four EF types with the four IT types.

Implications for Practitioners

Personality type and values generally converge and diverge in directions expected from type theory. They are also unique pieces of information and warrant inclusion in the career counseling process. People within an occupation are more likely to share similar values than are people across occupational groups. There are also some common values among all types in this sample. Further studies on type and values in other cultures, nationalities, and ethnic groups would be needed to see what indeed is common throughout the world. Practitioners are invited to read Chapter 14 of this manual for more background.

On an individual basis, values may play a large role in careers. Practitioners can use the data presented here as a

Table 12.28   For Each Value, the Four Types Most Often Endorsing "Very Important" in the National Sample

ISTJ	ISFJ	INFJ	INTJ
Financial security	**Health** **Spirituality**	**Spirituality** **Learning** Community service	**Achievement**
ISTP	**ISFP**	**INFP**	**INTP**
Autonomy		**Autonomy** **Creativity**	**Autonomy**
ESTP	**ESFP**	**ENFP**	**ENTP**
Prestige	**Home/family** **Health** **Friendships** **Financial security** **Spirituality** Prestige	**Home/family** **Friendships** **Creativity** **Learning** Community service	**Autonomy** **Achievement**
ESTJ	**ESFJ**	**ENFJ**	**ENTJ**
Health **Financial security** **Achievement** Prestige	**Home/family** **Health** **Friendships** **Financial security** **Spirituality** Community service Prestige	**Friendships** **Learning** **Creativity** Community service	**Home/family** **Achievement** **Learning** **Creativity**

Note: Those in **boldface** were chosen by at least 50% of that type. For each of the 11 values, the 16 types were ranked on the percentage endorsing the "Very Important" response. The four types with the highest percentages for each value appear in the table above. For example, the four types with the highest percentages indicating that "Home/family" is "Very Important" are ESFP, ENFP, ESFJ, and ENTJ. For the value of "Autonomy," the four types highest on that were ISTP, INFP, INTP, and ENTP. See Appendix for a description of the sample.

Source: National sample.

way to compare their clients' reactions with what is typical for their type. The data can serve as reassurance to clients that types may value different things, and that it is good to do so. An ENTP executive with multiple sclerosis was struggling with health and work issues; she couldn't seem to limit her work enough to reduce stress and hence control her illness better. She found it affirming to know that ENTPs do place their autonomy ahead of their health. She was not acting in an unusual way for her type, but in her case it was an unhealthy way. She would need to pay more attention to her health because of her individual condition, while searching for ways to still maintain as much autonomy as possible.

Another ENTP quite surprised himself when he turned down an outstanding job offer because it would mean relocating his high school–age son. He had been pursuing the value of achievement but realized that home/family was most important to him. Indeed, the data confirm that home/family is the most important value to ENTPs (and to all types except INTPs and INTJs). The values data helped him see the bigger picture.

Career Decision Making

At the heart of career counseling is career decision making. Any decision depends on good information and rational judgments, and type theory is based in perception (Sensing and Intuition), which involves gathering data, and in judgment (Thinking or Feeling), which involves making decisions. All major decisions need to involve each function: the Sensing facts, the Intuitive possibilities, the objective analysis of Thinking, and the values focus of Feeling. Also needed are Introverted reflective time and some Extraverted action, as well as a time to stay open with Perceiving and a time to come to a conclusion with Judging. Thus career decision making includes not only the decision itself but also what goes into the decision and its implementation. Type concepts can help clients in all three activities.

Vacccaro (1988) tracked a sample of 210 outplaced managers (mostly male) and noted that on the average it took the Introverted types one month longer to find a new position than it took the Extraverted types at every level of compensation they studied. The Extraverted types are likely to have more contacts or at least make more contacts in the career search process and thus connect more quickly with a new employer. The Introverted types are likely to want to take in information and ponder it, and thus move more slowly and carefully through the job search process.

Hammer (1996a) reviews six studies relating career decision/indecision with type. The studies, mostly of college students, provided evidence that Judging types demonstrate more career decisiveness than Perceiving types. Type theory would predict that Judging types would move toward closure and Perceiving types would move toward gathering options. The data on the other dichotomies, E–I, S–N, and T–F, did not show consistent relationships to career decisiveness.

Freeman (1994) investigated the relationship between career maturity (using the Career Development Inventory) and type (using the MBTI) and found no statistically significant correlations between the two instruments. She suggested that career counselors accept different psychological type preferences as effective processes for making credible career decisions. Type theory would suggest there are a variety of different strategies in making career decisions and that practitioners would do well to be open to them.

Schadt (1997) studied the relationship of type to developmental issues of midlife women including career decision-making self-efficacy. She compared a group of 50 midlife women to a control group of 43 similar women. Overall she found that the career decision-making self-efficacy of the treatment group women increased, although it did not reach statistical significance.

Krumboltz (1992) offers another perspective on career indecision, focusing on the social pressure accompanying the word *indecision*. He believes career indecision is treated almost as a mental disorder by some professional counselors, yet learning how to make a career decision is not necessarily a legitimate activity in U.S. society. He suggests, "Open-mindedness can be viewed as a virtue. Keeping one's options open may be far preferable to stating goals which may or may not be possible of attainment and which could lead to frustration and unhappiness" (p. 244). In his Career Beliefs Inventory (CBI) Krumboltz (1991) identifies 25 scales measuring career beliefs that may keep people from attaining their career goals. In a sample of adults seeking career counseling there were no significant correlations between type and the beliefs blocking career goal achievement as measured on the CBI (Hammer, 1996a). Thus type appears to be independent of behaviors blocking career goal achievement, at least in this research study.

Implications for Practitioners

Since the perceiving (S–N) and judging (T–F) functions are such an important part of career decision making, it is useful to pay attention to how clients are using their functions. The J–P dichotomy based in type dynamic theory focuses on which function is extraverted. J–P itself, like all the dichotomies, contains neutral terms, with neither pole being better or worse. However, the overuse of either one may circumvent the career development process. Judging types may use their thinking or feeling functions to quickly make decisions and perhaps not gather enough information. Implementing the decision may be more difficult as a result. They may find it helpful to caution themselves against quick decisions and take the tack that "my plan is to stay open." Perceiving types may find themselves enjoying the search for options and thus avoid any decision that would close off *any* potentially interesting option. With them a useful tack may be to spend more time looking at what doors remain open with each career decision rather than which doors have been shut.

Introduction to Type and Careers (Hammer, 1993) delineates a career exploration process for each of the 16 types including a preferred method for each type, potential obstacles, and tips. Levin, Krumboltz, and Krumboltz (1995) offer a workbook for integrating MBTI, *Strong*, and Career Beliefs Inventory information. Type dynamics, discussed later in this chapter, also offers suggestions for counselors regarding career exploration including decision making.

Our task in the long run is not just to help people find satisfying jobs and work environments now but also to prepare them for the many career/job searches they will be performing throughout their lives. We need to teach strategies for making decisions, dealing with change, handling stress, and visioning, and for identifying and locating "new jobs" based on the abilities clients possess or on the skills they can learn.

Other Factors Influencing Career Counseling

There are any number of other factors that might influence career counseling, and some of those have been studied in relationship to the MBTI. Ethnicity may be one such factor. In a study of 231 African Americans, Gehringer (1994) found that for five occupational groups there was a similar distribution to occupational groups representative of a national sample. The four occupational samples that differed from the national sample were more heavily ISTJ, the modal type in the African American sample.

Job performance also may be a factor in career development; see Chapter 13 for a review of these issues. Additional personality measures that often describe behaviors on the job, such as the *California Psychological Inventory* (CPI), the *Adjective Check List,* and the *California Q-Sort,* have been reported in Thorne and Gough (1991) as well as the 1985 *MBTI Manual.* Chapter 9 and Chapter 10 of this manual also contain relevant studies.

Four Levels of Type Interpretation in Career Counseling

Hammer (1996a) discusses three levels of type interpretation: static, dynamic, and developmental. A fourth level, behavioral, can be added with the advent of the MBTI Step II (formerly the Expanded Analysis Report). These levels, with relevant applications to career counseling, are discussed below.

Static Level

The static level is the basic and most widely used method when focusing on career counseling. It encompasses a general understanding of each of the dichotomies, combinations of preferences, and the 16 types. People of the same preference, combination of preferences, or whole type share many characteristics in common; individual differences are ignored at this level. This approach is used when career counselors rely solely on type descriptions to understand clients, when clients self-assess, and when trends in job selection by type are calculated with both the frequencies of the particular type within a job and the frequencies compared to a base population.

As John Holland (1994) says, "In general, the strengths of typologies lie in their ability to organize information. In contrast, the weaknesses of typologies lie in their neglect of the processes entailed in change and development" (p. 50). Much of the information presented in this chapter is of the static nature and has been a useful way to organize data about personality and careers. It does not take into account individual uniqueness nor does it allow for change and development. While the static level is well researched and very useful, nonetheless career counselors are urged also to incorporate the other levels and more fully use all of type theory.

Dynamic Level

The dynamic interpretation focuses on the interplay between and among the preferences within the type, specifically how information is perceived and how decisions are made. (See Chapter 3 for more information.) As a review, each type has a dominant or lead function with an auxiliary function for balance. If the dominant function is a perceiving one (Sensing or Intuition), the auxiliary function is a judging one (Thinking or Feeling) and vice versa. This means a person has access to ways of both gathering data and making decisions about these data. Each person also has preferred ways, either Extraverted or Introverted, of expressing the dominant and auxiliary functions, thus enabling the person access to both the internal and external worlds, although one arena will still be the favorite. In terms of type, well-developed people have good balance between Perceiving and Judging and between Extraverting and Introverting; they do not use them equally, but they have conscious access to both sides. Thus they have a preferred means of gathering data and making decisions, as well as personality mechanisms allowing them to both reflect and act. Each type also has a tertiary function and a fourth, or least-preferred, function (also called the inferior), which tend to be less developed and less used. The preferred order of the functions from dominant to inferior is the same for everyone of the same type, but the conscious and appropriate use of the four functions may depend on the person's type development (see the next section).

Using the dynamic approach helps counselors ascertain activities that are likely to be important and interesting to clients. It also helps identify how people are functioning in the use of their type including looking at issues of balance and imbalance. Type dynamics can be used to improve career decision making. For example, dominant extraverted Intuitives (ENTP and ENFP) may find the continual identification of career possibilities very appealing. However, without taking time to turn inward and evaluate these possibilities (i.e., use their introverted judging function), they may find themselves on a perpetual merry-go-round of activity. Dominant introverted Intuitives (INTJ and INFJ) may find themselves endlessly forming internal visions of what's possible for them and may need at times to discuss their visions with others to help access their extraverted decision-making functions. The necessity of accessing both the dominant and auxiliary processes in the appropriate attitudes is important to all clients.

Another way to illustrate the impact of type dynamics in working with clients is based on work incorporating the Risk Taking/Adventure scale of the *Strong Interest Inventory* with type dynamics. Kummerow and Hammer (1995) examined four type combinations in relationship to risk taking: NP, NJ, SP, SJ. Risk taking often involves acting on one's perceptions, hence the preference combinations. Type dynamics, which involve the extraverting or introverting of that perceiving function, make a difference in risk-taking styles.

- NPs extravert their Intuition whether it's dominant or auxiliary; they are out in the world seeing options and possibilities. These types generally are the greatest risk takers (although occasionally they do not see themselves as such). They like finding an interesting possibility and trying it. Kummerow and Hammer (1995) describe the NP style as likely to "jump into new possibilities or move into completely new directions, especially at the conceptual level" (p. 17). They may need help turning inward to their judging function, either Thinking or Feeling, to help them prioritize their possibilities. One ENFP in her mid-20s was caught in a web of possibilities—science museum volunteer coordinator, fundraiser for a children's theater, bookstore manager, social worker for abused women, small business owner growing medicinal plants or perhaps boarding pets, and so forth. She felt she was "leaping like a lunatic" into all these interesting possibilities. It was only when she took time to look at her own priorities and needs that she gained focus.

- The SP by contrast extraverts Sensing, scanning the environment for the most interesting piece of data and then following it. SPs are likely to "take immediate risks if the situation demands it." They prefer "long-term security—home and familiar people are important" (Kummerow & Hammer, 1995). SPs may also need to slow down and introvert to evaluate the most important pieces of data. An ISTP sales representative continually changed jobs, always seeing something better in the next one. As he noted, his résumé looked like Swiss cheese. Every other aspect of his life (home, family) was quite stable. He needed help in analyzing what the next job would really be like (using his introverted Thinking function), not just how it looked at the moment. In addition, he required help identifying the long-term risks and the bigger picture.

- NJs introvert their Intuition. They need to have an internal vision of what's important to them before they will move to action. Sometimes that vision comes easily, sometimes not. They find it nearly impossible to move to action until that vision is in place. Kummerow and Hammer (1995) describe them as willing to "take long-term risks for the sake of strongly held ideals." They prefer "careful analysis and preparation for risks." One ENTJ, recently divorced, said that until she had a vision of what was important to her—that is, keeping her children with

her as much as possible while earning maximum dollars—she felt unable to find a job. With that vision, she could move to action. She found an on-the-road sales job in a resort area for the summer, where she could drive her children along. The calls to customers were short ones, and her children could entertain themselves safely in the car. Each evening was a special time together in a motel.

- SJs introvert their Sensing, and they "will take moderate risks after long thought and preparation." They prefer "to stick with what works" and are "least willing of the combinations to take risks" (Kummerow & Hammer, 1995). One described herself as "staying parked until I'm pushed out." SJs need time to access their memories and experiences as well as to gather more information and ponder it. They like to come up with several plans before proceeding, and all that takes time. One ISTJ was unhappy with his current work situation as an office supervisor. He considered (plan A) transferring to another branch, (plan B) finding a new employer, and (plan C) setting up his own office services business. While he was exploring each of these, plan A worked out and he is now quite happy in his new location.

Hammer and Kummerow (1996) present data indicating that those who introvert a dominant perceiving function (ISFJ, ISTJ, INFJ, and INTJ) score lowest in risk taking on the *Strong* scale. The act of taking in data (whether it's in factual or big picture form) seems to decrease the willingness to take risks. They also noted that for one sample, the FJ types (all of whom extravert Feeling, whether it's dominant or auxiliary) also are lower on risk taking; perhaps the act of harmonizing with one's external environment affects the willingness to take risks.

More illustrations of the impact of type dynamics on career counseling interventions are provided by Heavrin (1998). She presents case studies demonstrating how the dominant and auxiliary can work together well in an INTP client, what happens when the auxiliary is not accessed in an INFJ client, and what occurs with an ENFP when the dominant and auxiliary are both used in the same attitude (Extraverted) instead of opposite E–I attitudes.

Through the inclusion of type dynamics, career counselors can work with clients to round out their information-gathering and decision-making strategies. Practitioners can be alert to when type dynamics are out of balance in their clients and suggest remedies so that clients can access all parts of their personalities.

Developmental Level

The developmental approach to type recognizes that each type has an "ideal" order of development over time: Early in life the dominant function emerges and then the auxiliary, so that by the time one enters the work world, both are accessed and functioning together. The tertiary and finally

Table 12.29   Merging Super's Life-Span Stages with Type Development

Super's Stages/Ages	Super's Career Development Tasks	Hypothesized Type Development Sequence
Growth (4–13)	Becoming aware of the future. Finding ways to develop competencies and to achieve, in order to increase control over one's life.	Dominant (1) function emerges and becomes guiding force in life.
Exploration (14–24)	Crystallizing, specifying, and implementing an occupational choice.	Auxiliary (2) function develops and helps balance dominant.
Establishment (25–44)	Stabilizing, consolidating, and possibly advancing in career(s).	Dominant and auxiliary functions are working together well. Tertiary (3) function may begin to emerge.
Maintenance (45–65)	Holding on (stagnating or plateauing). Keeping up (updating or enriching). Innovating (changing).	Tertiary function may be drawn in to keep those who are holding on from stagnating. For those who are keeping up or innovating, tertiary function may provide new directions and behaviors. Inferior function (4) may emerge in importance and also help provide new directions and behaviors.
Disengagement (over 65)	Deceleration. Retirement planning. Retirement living.	Conscious inclusion and integration of all four functions.

Source: From "The Life-Span, Life-Space Approach to Careers," by D. E. Super, M. L. Savickas, and C. M. Super, 1996, in *Career Choice and Development* (3rd ed.), San Francisco: Jossey-Bass, and *Counseling the Less Preferred MBTI Functions for Career Transition and Disengagement,* by J. Grutter, 1993, paper presented at the Association for Psychological Type Conference, Newport Beach, CA. Used with permission.

the fourth function are often accessed more in midlife and beyond. Integration of all the functions is a natural interest and task in the second half of life. Theoretically, then, there are 16 paths to development depending on the individual's type.

Super's conceptualizations of a life-span approach to career development (Super, Savickas, & Super, 1996) are applicable, and Grutter (1990, 1993) has provided both theory and applications to help us bridge between life-span stages and type development. Table 12.29 provides a summary of this bridging.

As an illustration of these concepts, we will examine the type (and career) development of four EJ friends (ESTJ, ESFJ, ENFJ, ENTJ) who all received graduate degrees in counseling psychology. They are in the maintenance stage of their careers, although the cases will take the reader through the exploration and establishment stages as well (see Tables 12.30–12.33). Those types with the same function pairs (ST, SF, NF, and NT) are likely to notice similar, although not identical, patterns in their work lives. It is also difficult to separate the individual preferences from one another, since type is a dynamic whole; for the sake of the illustrations this was attempted.

These four friends made initial career choices based on their dominant functions, and all have gained comfort using all four functions in their work. The less-preferred functions act to support the dominant and auxiliary ones. They each have two favorite functions they like to rely on the most and with which they feel most at ease, and they also enjoy using their third and fourth functions in their work and in their lives.

For those working with midlife career changers, knowledge of type development concepts is particularly useful. *Navigating Midlife* (Corlett & Millner, 1993) offers much information using typology as a guide to that process. Grutter (1990) offers three case illustrations using type with clients in Super's maintenance stage of their careers. In one of her cases she tracks the career development of an ESFP high school coach and counselor. His tertiary (Thinking) emerged partially with his return to graduate school for a degree in counseling. He became particularly interested in career counseling using computerized programs with high school students, especially those who are at risk. He'll use his Intuition (fourth function) in helping them find possibilities and in helping himself look for new ways to keep current in his field.

Within some clients, counselors may identify that a function has been "skipped" or at least overlooked and encourage the client to try more of its activities. For example, an INFP client spent so much time in childhood and early adulthood developing his analytical side that he missed opportunities to develop his dominant Feeling function.

Table 12.30   One ST's Career and Type Development

ST	For ESTJs
	1: extraverted Thinking (dominant)
	2: introverted Sensing (auxiliary)
	3: Intuition (tertiary)
	4: introverted Feeling (least preferred)

Thinking **Sensing**	This ESTJ began her working career as a secretary and administrative assistant, where she could use her organizing and office skills to efficiently manage the details and work flow. But she always knew she wanted more education and more responsibility.
	Since she knew the university system from growing up in an academic family and since she liked managing, she decided being a dean of students would be a good choice. The graduate program she chose had emphasized student personnel work in the past but became a counseling program, an unexpected turn for her but one she decided to live with. While doing well in graduate school, she nonetheless describes the counseling portion of the training as difficult. Her Intuitive and Feeling functions were being called upon before she was comfortable using them. She did enjoy the academic counseling job she held, especially when she was a coordinator of counselors, where she could use her preferred functions most.
	She went into a research job upon completion of a doctorate in part because she was not geographically mobile due to her husband's position and in part because it fit with her training and personality. Next was a position for more than a decade with a consulting firm conducting job assessments based on testing and interviews. The position was part-time, enabling her to spend time with her two children. Her interests led her to training other professionals about psychological tests and writing practical guides about those tests. Since this was outside the mainstream of her employer's activities, it became increasingly difficult to fit in.
Intuition **Feeling**	She began her own small consulting business to allow herself a variety of work. She finds the training and writing move her toward seeing the big picture and staying current with the theories, as well as recognizing what's really important to the people with whom she works. In her individual work with clients in career counseling, she finds herself more easily tuning in to their emotions and values, something she would have avoided earlier in her practice. While she still enjoys relying most on her Sensing and Thinking, the use of her other functions helps her do her work better.

Table 12.31   One SF's Career and Type Development

SF	For ESFJs
	1: extraverted Feeling (dominant)
	2: introverted Sensing (auxiliary)
	3: Intuition (tertiary)
	4: introverted Thinking (least preferred)

Feeling **Sensing**	This ESFJ grew up in a small midwestern town where being a minister was an exceedingly important job—that's what he decided to do as a way of helping people and as a way of alleviating the guilt he felt after causing a childhood accident. After graduating in English, he entered the seminary and during his internship realized he was in the ministry for the wrong reasons. So he fell back on his plan B and became a high school teacher of English (which is what his mother had done). SFs often choose jobs based on the influence of important people in their lives and for security.
	He felt teaching was a natural activity for him, and he loved it, particularly the grammar and expository writing classes with the "rules" involved; he stayed away from creative writing. He got a master's degree in counseling because he was always being asked for help from his students and friends, and he sought more ways to help them. In addition, his profession required continuing education credits. He found the Thinking aspects of graduate school both intimidating and interesting. But he never planned to leave the classroom. Unfortunately, at the time there was a decline in student enrollment, and he was forced out of a job he had planned to be in all his life. He knew the necessity of the change three years before it happened, so he had plenty of time to prepare.
Intuition	He moved into training and career counseling in a business organization. He has become what he calls a personal coach to hundreds of managers. He is now working inside a large financial company in organizational development work and is quite surprised to find he gets excited about the unpredictable. He never knows which Intuitive direction he will need to go in, but now he enjoys the flow; something will feel right in the moment. He works with people's fears and angers, getting them to face up to their emotions and to their relationship issues. He often consults with problem managers, gathering objective data from others about
Thinking	them. He likes analyzing the data and presenting it in a way that is objective, fair, and shows that he has their best interests at heart. He helps people tell the truth to one another in a kind manner. He has to be creative in coming up with possible ways to work on their problems. His is a very applied approach to helping people, and it incorporates all his functions.
	Like his EJ friends, his personal life has affected his professional life. He is gay, and he found it a relief to let his co-workers know this. However, with his clients, he is concerned some will feel this as an obstacle to working with him and thus has kept it private. His focus has been on the comfort of others, not on himself, in sharing this important part of his life.

Table 12.32   One NF's Career and Type Development

NF	For ENFJs 1: extraverted Feeling (dominant) 2: introverted Intuition (auxiliary) 3: Sensing (tertiary) 4: introverted Thinking (least preferred)
Feeling Intuition **Sensing** **Thinking**	This ENFJ became a nun and a teacher because the nuns provided her the support and self-esteem that was missing from her own family as well as a model for how women could contribute to the world. These extraverted Feeling reasons were her foundation. The specifics of what she did as a nun were less important than the overall ability to influence people's lives for the better (NF). So when the religious order decided she would be a math and chemistry teacher, she did so gladly. She could easily handle all those facts. As a teacher she kept finding herself in a counseling role with student and parental requests for help. She decided she wanted to learn more about counseling and enrolled in graduate school; she liked developing her Thinking side while in school. She left the convent, married, and adopted children. In subsequent jobs as a community college counselor she found herself providing more academic counseling (requiring more ST than she enjoyed) than personal counseling, so she moved to private practice. She has built a practice with eight staff people and provides a variety of services where her NF desire to help people (individuals, couples, groups, fledgling counselors) flourishes. She is always sharpening her skills and keeping current on the Thinking side of her work, and she practices what she preaches to her clients in taking care of the here-and-now aspects (Sensing) of her own life—exercise, nutrition, meditation, leaving her work at work, collegial support, continued learning through reading and workshops, avocational interests, and time alone. She leads a balanced life with her four functions.

Table 12.33   One NT's Career and Type Development

NT	For ENTJs 1: extraverted Thinking (dominant) 2: introverted Intuition (auxiliary) 3: Sensing (tertiary) 4: introverted Feeling (least preferred)
Thinking Intuition **Sensing** **Feeling**	This ENTJ chose her career path logically. She wanted to travel and influence the world, hence a job teaching in the Peace Corps in Asia. She would have change, variety, and many possibilities. Her next job was a logical choice also: While her husband was in graduate school she took a job at the same university as an academic counselor. This confirmed her comfort in the academic life (her father was a professor), and she pursued a graduate degree in counseling. Her subsequent jobs also followed a logical progression from counseling to counselor supervision to training, and they offered her opportunities for change, challenge, and learning (often motivators for NTs). She had a series of jobs but moved from academia and nonprofit organizations into the corporate world after a divorce and the (logical) realization she would have to earn more money to support herself and her children. She has continually progressed to more responsibility and larger management roles where she can concentrate on the big picture and put programs into place that will have a positive effect on the company. She describes how she is compelled to incorporate Sensing and Feeling in her work as well: As a human resources executive she must keep track of many details—she describes it as "tons of factual information"—and she does so in part by hiring the right people for the right job and keeping lots of lists. She finds she must continually get out of her own head and away from what appears rational to her in order to figure out why/how people are reacting from their hearts. Work requires her to always consider the values driving people and relationships. She has found ways to access all four of her functions well.

After a career start in engineering, he realized later that he felt he was missing something (in this case his Feeling function); he tuned into what was important to his values and moved into training, something more in tune with his Feeling values.

At times in clients' lives some functions take on more salience than previously, and the sequence of type development likely identifies which of those functions it is. It may be necessary to help clients integrate their understanding of this process. For example, managers who are Thinking types may in midlife become much more interested in mentoring others and developing a legacy of good relationships; this is their emerging Feeling function, which is either their tertiary or inferior. An INTP researcher moved into management in midlife and found much satisfaction in teaching others research skills. He would stop what he was doing when his staff entered his office and give them his undivided attention as he answered their questions, encouraging their inquiries and gently teaching them skills. Feeling types may find themselves pulled toward more formal and theoretical activities such as schooling which emphasize logical analysis as a way of developing their Thinking sides, or they may find conflict situations interesting instead of something to be avoided. An ENFP found the study of law quite fascinating and enjoyable in midlife; she couldn't believe how much fun it was to analyze a case, an activity she could not have imagined herself undertaking several years earlier. Thus she made a career transition from fund-raiser to law student in midlife. Sensing types may find searching for patterns and studying theories much more engrossing in the second half of their lives. Intuitive types may find that developing a detailed and factual base on a topic of interest holds their attention later in life. Extraverts are often surprised as they age how much they enjoy their introverted time; this would be a natural part of their accessing their Introverted functions. Introverts also report more willingness to extravert in the second half of life regarding the things that are important to them. Fitzgerald (1997) provides additional framing and examples of this process in managers and leaders. *Creative Aging* (Millner, 1998) provides in-depth portraits of the 16 types and their type development.

Behavioral Level (or MBTI Step II)

The MBTI Step II is a scoring method that results in not only the four-letter type but 20 ways, or subscales (5 per dichotomy), in which that type expresses itself. Its results illustrate the unique expression of each type. For example, part of Extraversion is an enjoyment of talking and express-ing one's views. However, it is possible to be an Introvert and also to prefer talking a great deal to others (Expressive). As another example, some Extraverted types prefer one-to-one relationships (Intimate), not opportunities to be in large groups engaging in networking activities (Gregarious).

This level of understanding is very helpful in the career search and decision-making process. It suggests possible strategies and behaviors that are likely to come more easily to the client and those that are more difficult. Even for those who are clear in their preferences, the understanding of the specific behaviors within those preferences is useful. For example, one ISFJ who preferred Receiving (I) realized that to make the necessary contacts in a department she was interested in transferring to she needed to use Initiating (E). Her Step II results helped her understand why those tasks were likely to be difficult but also gave her specific ideas about how Initiating people might go about the task. She made the contacts, found her dream job, and now is using another part of her personality, her Systematic (J) side, to keep her name in front of that department.

For others, understanding of their subscales helps them better incorporate parts of themselves that seem in opposi-tion. For example, decision-making behaviors on the Step II are represented by a combination of scores on two sub-scales: Logical-Empathetic (ideal decision-making strategy) and Reasonable-Compassionate (actual decision-making/

implementation strategy). An ENTJ was experiencing some conflict in her decision making. She was Empathetic (F) in the ideal but Reasonable (T) in her actual style. She would find herself torn between wanting to help people by empathizing and agreeing with them and using her logic to make a decision. Once she understood the conflict she started using the Empathetic (F) to lead her to data to weigh, and relied more on her preferred Thinking side for the actual decision. Decisions are much easier for her now.

Since the focus of this manual is on Step I, readers who are interested in exploring Step II are invited to study these resources: Saunders (1989), Kummerow and Quenk (1992), Quenk and Kummerow (1996), and Mitchell, with Quenk and Kummerow (1997). Step II results are available only from Forms J and K of the MBTI.

Implications for Practitioners

Each level of type interpretation adds to both the client's self-understanding and the practitioner's ability to help the client with career counseling activities. The static level helps with a basic understanding of type characteristics. Type dynamics add an interplay between the preferences, which leads to fuller decision making and more balance within clients' lives. Type development provides a path to development and suggestions of emerging issues for clients along with the hope of continued growth. The MBTI Step II points out the unique ways in which each type is expressed, which offer clues to accessing the behaviors inherent in each subscale pole. All levels can be used interchangeably with clients, and they build on one another.

Administering and Interpreting the MBTI in Career Counseling Settings

Practitioners must first determine if the MBTI is an appro-priate tool to use, and second, administer it properly. Third, they need to spend time verifying type with clients, recog-nizing that how clients answered the Indicator may have been affected by their work activities and may not be the "best-fit" type. General issues and guidelines for adminis-tration and interpretation have been covered in Chapters 5 and 6, and specific issues related to counseling and psy-chotherapy settings are in Chapter 10. The following issues are unique to a career counseling setting.

1. **When should I use the MBTI?**
   In any career counseling practice the practitioner must first determine what information is needed to aid the career counseling process and then which, if any, instruments are to be administered to help pro-vide that information. In part this will depend on the

client's issues and state of mind. Usually a framework for understanding one's personality adds greatly to the career counseling process. Thus in general the MBTI is appropriate to administer to clients who are functioning "normally" and who have at least an eighth-grade reading level. A survey by Graff, Larrimore, Whitehead, and Hopson (1991) identified the MBTI as one of the three most widely used instruments in college settings; the other two were the *Strong Interest Inventory* and the *Self-Directed Search*, both of which are vocational interest assessments. Schadt (1997) noted that the MBTI was the most positively regarded intervention activity in her work with midlife women.

2. **What factors should I consider in timing the administration?**

Any client in crisis needs to have that crisis dealt with before career counseling interventions are appropriate, and the career counselor may or may not have the skill set to handle those situations. Hammer and Kummerow (1996) present a model of appropriate strategies to use with clients based in part on how well clients know themselves and how clearly their vocational interest pattern is formed. For those clients who lack self-awareness and a stable sense of identity and who seem unable to differentiate their interests, therapeutic interventions may be more appropriate than focusing on any career search activities. Those with a clear sense of self but an unfocused interest pattern may need to explore work activities, jobs, and work environments. Those with a differentiated interest pattern but who are unsure of themselves may need short-term support and counseling. This may be the case, for example, immediately following the loss of one's job. Hammer and Kummerow (1996) suggest that it is with those who have a sense of identity and some knowledge of their interests that career counseling is suitable. It is at this point that administering the MBTI is most appropriate.

3. **Which form should I use?**

Either Form M or Form K is appropriate, depending on which "level of interpretation" one desires. Form K provides the MBTI Step II, which allows for addition of a more "behavioral" interpretation. For those with the required clinical training, Form J may be used; it adds Comfort/Discomfort scales.

4. **Are there any particular cautions in administering the MBTI?**

The frame of reference for those taking the MBTI is an important one. In thinking about their careers, some people wonder if it might be best to respond to the MBTI with their work lives in mind. The answer is unequivocally no. If we are attempting to help people find the roles or situations where they are most likely

to work well, then we must concentrate on who they are, not on what they do. It is when people are working with their natural preferences that they are most likely expending the least amount of energy to do the tasks and gaining the most energy from their activities. This does not take away from the reality that people can and do flex with the situations but rather recognizes that each person has a more natural preference in every situation.

5. **What effect does a work frame of reference seem to have on "best-fit" type?**

Several studies have looked at the effects of work on type verification. Kummerow (1988) asked retail store managers who were participants in management development classes to self-assess and to assess their types in work situations (that is, how they were actually doing their work) as well as to verify the type that fit them best overall. She found that the work situations type fit least well in matching the verified type; 57.5% of the sample had identical types between their work situations and verified types. Apparently a number of people were using preferences other than their most natural ones at work.

In a study (Hammer, personal communication) of nearly 1,000 people, about 29% verified a type different from how they came out on the Indicator itself. The sample was made up of those training to use the MBTI professionally, so they were highly attuned to the importance of type verification. Participants who verified a type different from what they reported on the Indicator were asked to indicate which of nine possible reasons affected their results; respondents could choose as many reasons as were applicable. Several work-related reasons were included. These are listed below along with the percentage of those choosing this as an influence on their Indicator results:

- 32.5%: "Aspects of your work that do not 'match' your preferences but which you have mastered, e.g., Introverts who work as trainers may learn and have to use some Extraverted skills to get their job done."

- 22.7%: "Pressures from the culture of the organization in which you work, e.g., Perceivers may feel they 'should' be more planned, systematic, and organized than they prefer to be, and may strive to behave in that way."

- Among the nine possible reasons, the one indicated the most was the one pertaining to "aspects of work."

Thus the research suggests that work may influence the results on the MBTI but also that interpreters can use that information from the work setting to help verify the best-fit type.

6. **How do I help my clients determine their "best-fit" preferences?**

Practitioners can help clients understand influences of work, comprehend the use of all the functions at work, and find a type that best fits the person. A request for information from the client such as "Describe how you use both your Thinking and your Feeling in your work" may elicit a great deal of information, including which function is preferred as well as a reminder that the client does use both. The client may speak of one function being easier to access than the other, of one requiring more (or less) energy, of one being liked more than the other, etc. Through using good counseling skills, counselors can help the client understand what they are saying about the functions and what that means. It is essential in career counseling that practitioners and clients work with verified type. That will give the most comprehensive picture of clients and the kind of work activities from which they are most likely to draw energy and gain satisfaction.

7. **What uses of type in career counseling should be avoided?**

Any approach that stereotypes the person or the occupation is inappropriate. Remember that each person has access to all eight preference domains and that many occupations also require the use of all eight at least some of the time. Using the MBTI to provide the definitive yes or no to a career search would also be inappropriate since so many factors go into career choice besides personality.

Conclusion

The knowledge of type enhances our understanding of clients' preferred work environments, occupational choices, interests, values, satisfactions, self-efficacy, and development.

By itself, each area is useful in career counseling, but with the addition of type each becomes even more meaningful. Career development and career counseling are complex areas, as is type.

Several type-related patterns in this chapter include the following:

- The work environment appears to be more of a focus for the Extraverted types than the Introverted ones.
- In occupational selection, the function pairs (ST, SF, NF, NT) play the largest role in shaping the occupational pattern.
- In work satisfaction, the attitude pairs (EJ, EP, IP, and IJ) play the greatest roles, with the EJs the most satisfied and IPs often the least.
- Values appear somewhat shaped by the differences in Thinking–Feeling, with Feeling types identifying more values of importance to them than Thinking types. Extraverted types also identify more values as important than Introverted types.
- Different types have distinctly different interest patterns from one another. Among the patterns are the NF focus on self-expression and NT focus on abstract problem solving.
- High self-efficacy or confidence in many areas and its link to high interests in those areas describe ENTs.
- Career decisiveness is related to Judging.

That the MBTI personality inventory is useful in helping people find meaningful work where they can be productive has been amply illustrated here. Through using type in all its levels (static, dynamic, developmental, and behavioral) career counselors can help clients explore the external world of work and the internal world of the individual. Through understanding the contributions of type (and its limitations) practitioners can continue to ensure its wise use and help clients use it to make the transition into the new world of work.

Uses of Type in Organizations

13

Contributed by Linda K. Kirby, Nancy J. Barger, and Roger R. Pearman

The primary goal of organizational development today is to create an effective organization that responds quickly and appropriately to changes in the competitive global environment. Research (Denison & Mishra, 1995) and experience demonstrate that the following are crucial components of effective organizations:

- Employee initiative, flexibility, and accountability

- Inclusion of employees in decision making

- A clear sense of organizational and group mission

- Flat and fluid hierarchies

- Flexible and responsive leadership

As this awareness has developed, employee and leader development programs have grown exponentially to try to transform organizations and the ways people work.

As investment in employee development and training has grown, so has use of the *Myers-Briggs Type Indicator* personality inventory, currently exceeding 860,000 administrations per year in organizational settings. Some of this use is for individual career development, but the MBTI is also used as a basic tool in a wide variety of development and training programs focused on organizational effectiveness.

This more general use of the MBTI as a tool in seemingly unrelated training programs has developed because MBTI results, presented within the context of Jungian psychological type theory, have wide applicability to workstyles and interactions. A number of qualities account for the MBTI's usefulness as a basic tool in employee development:

- MBTI results and interpretation focus on how people take in information (perception) and how they prioritize that information to make decisions (judgment)—basic personality facets that underlie most work tasks and training.
- MBTI type enhances people's clarity and comfort with their own workstyles while constructively identifying possible blind spots and areas of vulnerability.
- Type theory and the MBTI give a logical, coherent structure for understanding normal differences among people in a host of other work-related activities: communication styles, teamwork, project management, time management, preferred supervision style and work environment, responses and needs during organizational change, preferred learning styles, and many more.
- Type theory presents a dynamic picture of individual functioning, including recognition of the dominant function as the basis of motivation and identification of customary responses to stress.
- Type theory outlines a model of lifelong individual development, and the MBTI identifies likely paths for development, useful with work groups and in coaching individual leaders and managers.
- The MBTI provides a perspective and data for analyzing organizational culture, management structures, and other organizational systems.
- The MBTI and supporting type resources demonstrate the value added by diversity within the organization or work group. This ethic—the constructive use of differences—is particularly applicable in today's global and diverse organizations.

These powerful potentials of the MBTI and psychological type result when practitioners administer the instrument appropriately, interpret results correctly, lead clients through a process of verifying their type, and add the depth inherent in the dynamic Jungian theory of personality. The theory and construction sections of this manual equip practitioners with the theoretical framework and knowledge of the instrument needed for such in-depth use of type.

The goal of this chapter is to provide specific, practical applications for effective use of the MBTI assessment tool in organizations: to outline and illustrate common organizational uses of the MBTI, suggest appropriate resources, and refer to related research of particular interest to practitioners. When appropriate, the topical sections include considerations related to working with individuals in coaching and development, training with intact work groups, and focusing at the organizational level. Additional sections focus specifically on using the MBTI with teams and in leadership development programs, applications that draw on the uses already described but have special importance in today's organization development work. Though use of the MBTI in career development courses

and counseling in organizations is widespread and significant, this chapter will not directly address this topic; Chapter 12 of this manual is a thorough treatment of information, applications, and research in using the MBTI for career development.

Because the components of human personality indicated by the MBTI underlie so much of human activity, the approaches, exercises, and research suggested in one section are often useful in a slightly modified form for other purposes.

The chapter concludes with a section on administering and interpreting the MBTI in organizations, including suggestions for dealing with common problems that arise in applying the ethical guidelines in organizational settings.

Introducing the MBTI and Psychological Type in Organizations

Gaining acceptance of the MBTI as an organizational tool is easiest when practitioners can present an introductory workshop. However, some organizations require a proposal outlining anticipated use of the MBTI. This section discusses both ways of introducing type into the organization.

Preparing and Presenting MBTI Proposals

Practitioners can begin with hypotheses based on research about type distributions of managers and leaders in organizations. Tables 13.1, 13.2, and 13.3 illustrate patterns of types found in leadership positions in organizations and typical type distributions among people who work in human resources and consulting.

Type tables of large groups of managers and leaders from a wide variety of cultures demonstrate an overrepresentation of Thinking and Judging, compared to general populations (Fitzgerald & Kirby, 1997b). The pattern of TJ managers and leaders is true even in organizations whose goals or work would seem to appeal to people of other types (Craig, Craig, & Sleight, 1988; Hawkins, Williams, & Hawkins, 1990). For example, teaching in elementary schools (children 6 to 12 years) seems to attract an overrepresentation of people preferring Feeling compared to the general population (DiTiberio, 1996), but type tables of principals of those schools show the same TJ pattern as for leaders in other organizations (Macdaid et al., 1986).

Type tables of human resource professionals tend to show higher percentages of Intuition, Feeling, and Perceiving types than appear in type tables of management groups. Types of consultants tend to concentrate in the lower right-hand quadrant of the type table, the four EN types. Practitioners can hypothesize that their own most natural style of gathering information, organizing it, and delivering proposals will need to be modified to speak effectively to organizational leaders and decision makers.

Table 13.1 Type Distribution of Participants in the Center for Creative Leadership's Leadership Development Program in Percentages

ISTJ	ISFJ	INFJ	INTJ
18.2%	3.1%	1.7%	10.5%
ISTP	ISFP	INFP	INTP
3.5%	1.1%	2.5%	6.9%
ESTP	ESFP	ENFP	ENTP
3.4%	1.2%	4.5%	8.0%
ESTJ	ESFJ	ENFJ	ENTJ
16.0%	3.2%	3.0%	13.1%

E	52.5%
I	47.5%
S	49.7%
N	50.3%
T	79.6%
F	20.4%
J	68.9%
P	31.1%
TJ	57.8%
TP	21.8%
FJ	11.0%
FP	9.3%
ST	41.1%
NT	38.5%
NF	11.7%
SF	8.6%
EN	28.6%
IS	25.9%
ES	23.8%
IN	21.6%
Dom T_E	29.1%
Dom S_I	21.3%
Dom N_E	12.5%
Dom N_I	12.2%
Dom T_I	10.4%
Dom F_E	6.2%
Dom S_E	4.6%
Dom F_I	3.6%

Note: N = 26,477.

Source: From "The Relationship Between the MBTI and Measures of Personality and Performance in Management Groups," by J. W. Fleenor, 1997, in *Developing Leaders*, p. 119. Palo Alto, CA: Davies-Black. Copyright 1997 by Davies-Black. Used with permission.

Using Type Knowledge

Knowing the specific types of decision makers is not necessary. Instead, practitioners can use their knowledge of the basic needs associated with each type dichotomy to ensure that proposals address the primary concerns of decision makers:

- E–I: Include time for questions and discussions (E) *and* written information provided ahead of time (I).
- S–N: Include the specifics (who, when, what, how, and how much) along with examples of the MBTI's use in other similar organizations (S) *and* the future vision of how it connects to current problems and could transform the organization (N).
- T–F: Include the logical, objective rationale and cost-benefit analysis (T) *and* the ways in which the MBTI connects to the mission and values of the organization (F).
- J–P: Include suggested structures, plans, and time frames (J) *and* planned flexibility for midcourse changes as new information comes in or the needs change (P).

Using a type perspective also ensures that practitioners have covered the bases in developing their proposal.

Resources

Practitioners can draw on two resources in developing and presenting their proposals: *Using the Myers-Briggs Type Indicator in Organizations* (Hirsh, 1990) and *Type and Change: MBTI Leader's Guide* (Barger & Kirby, 1997a). The first provides a wealth of information about specific uses to illustrate the MBTI's applicability to organizational issues, including lists of benefits of the MBTI to the organization. The second includes a section, "Designing and Presenting a Training Proposal," that focuses on using the MBTI to deal with organizational change, but the process and perspectives discussed apply to presenting the MBTI for other purposes as well.

Introductory Workshops in Organizations

The most effective way to gain acceptance of the MBTI as a tool in organization development is the following:

- Present an introduction to type workshop.
- Return results.
- Verify type.
- Demonstrate applications that add value for the clients while also illustrating the usefulness of the MBTI.

Table 13.2   Type Distribution of Human Resources Personnel

ISTJ	ISFJ	INFJ	INTJ
10.00%	3.95%	2.37%	8.68%
ISTP	**ISFP**	**INFP**	**INTP**
1.84%	0.79%	6.58%	7.11%
ESTP	**ESFP**	**ENFP**	**ENTP**
1.32%	2.89%	9.47%	8.68%
ESTJ	**ESFJ**	**ENFJ**	**ENTJ**
11.84%	5.79%	7.37%	11.32%

E	58.68%
I	41.32%
S	38.42%
N	61.58%
T	60.79%
F	39.21%
J	61.32%
P	38.68%
IJ	25.00%
IP	16.32%
EP	22.37%
EJ	36.32%
ST	25.00%
SF	13.42%
NF	25.79%
NT	35.79%
SJ	31.58%
SP	6.84%
NP	31.84%
NJ	29.74%
TJ	41.84%
TP	18.95%
FP	19.74%
FJ	19.47%
IN	24.74%
EN	36.84%
IS	16.58%
ES	21.84%
ET	33.16%
EF	25.53%
IF	13.68%
IT	27.63%
S_{dom}	18.16%
N_{dom}	29.21%
T_{dom}	32.11%
F_{dom}	20.53%

Note: N = 380.

Source: Data from CAPT databank, April 1998.

The last section of this chapter outlines a group introduction to type and includes resources for practitioners to use during group introductions. It is important for practitioners to allow time to complete all the listed components, including time for verification of best-fit type, for reading full type descriptions, and for applying type to work issues.

Making Type Results Real Applying MBTI information to deal with client issues is the last component of an introductory workshop. This step is crucial: Receiving individual MBTI results can be personally illuminating and affirming but demonstrating the Indicator's use as a tool for solving client problems solidifies clients' understanding of type and helps them begin the process of integrating this perspective into their daily work lives.

Each section in this chapter discusses specific applications to respond to identified client needs. In some organizational situations, the introductory session is for groups of people who do not work together and have not identified common issues. The following are activities that can be used in such settings to reinforce participants' understanding of type and demonstrate how they can apply that understanding to enhance their work lives. The activities are listed in order of the time required, with the briefest applications first and those taking the most time last:

- Ask individuals to pair up with a "talking partner" and take turns telling each other what fits or does not fit in their full type description.
- Form groups of like types (using whole type or dominant functions; see Table 3.3) and ask them to generate

Table 13.3   Type Distribution of Management Analysts and Consultants

ISTJ	ISFJ	INFJ	INTJ
10.00%	2.67%	8.00%	5.33%
ISTP	**ISFP**	**INFP**	**INTP**
2.67%	0.67%	6.67%	6.00%
ESTP	**ESFP**	**ENFP**	**ENTP**
3.33%	1.33%	8.67%	12.00%
ESTJ	**ESFJ**	**ENFJ**	**ENTJ**
9.33%	3.33%	6.67%	13.33%

E	58.00%
I	42.00%
S	33.33%
N	66.67%
T	62.00%
F	38.00%
J	58.67%
P	41.33%
IJ	26.00%
IP	16.00%
EP	25.33%
EJ	32.67%
ST	25.33%
SF	8.00%
NF	30.00%
NT	36.67%
SJ	25.33%
SP	8.00%
NP	33.33%
NJ	33.33%
TJ	38.00%
TP	24.00%
FP	17.33%
FJ	20.67%
IN	26.00%
EN	40.67%
IS	16.00%
ES	17.33%
ET	38.00%
EF	20.00%
IF	18.00%
IT	24.00%
S_{dom}	17.33%
N_{dom}	34.00%
T_{dom}	31.33%
F_{dom}	17.33%

Note: N = 150.

Source: Data from CAPT databank, April 1998.

examples of how they see their type helping them in their work.

- Form groups of like types and ask them to respond briefly to a series of questions about what kinds of information they prefer (S or N), their priorities in making decisions (T or F), their preferences in structuring work tasks (J or P), and when and how they extravert and introvert.
- Form groups of like types and ask them to design together their ideal work environment, with as much detail as possible. Providing a variety of materials—paper, markers, pictures, advertisements, crafts components—allows groups to create interesting and instructive "pictures."

Customizing Introductory Workshops   Just as proposals need to take account of type differences, so do introductory type workshops—and all other organizational training. The research, analysis, and information provided in Chapter 11 of this manual provide what practitioners need to ensure that all of their training is sensitive to type differences in learning styles and will speak effectively to different people. It is particularly important for practitioners to become aware of their own teaching/learning style and ways to modify that style to communicate effectively with people of different types.

Introductory type workshops will also have greater impact when practitioners customize their presentation content, style, and examples to make them clearly relevant to the people and the work of the specific organization. Hahn-Rollins and Mongeon (1988) described an interesting and instructive experience presenting type to Foreign Service officers. They indicated the problems presented by the culture of the group and organization, and reported modifications they made to provide a better fit with the organizational culture. Their process provides a model for taking specific organizational cultures into account in introductory sessions.

Resources   The recommended resource for introductory type workshops is *Introduction to Type* (Myers, with Kirby & Myers, 1998) for each participant. It presents all the information practitioners need to include in the session, provides a structure for participant type verification, describes each of the 16 types in full, outlines several type applications, and gives important guidelines for using type and avoiding misuses. *Introduction to Type in Organizations* (Hirsh & Kummerow, 1998) presents basic type information specifically relevant to organizations. *Using the Myers-Briggs Type Indicator in Organizations* (Hirsh, 1990) provides reproducible masters for overhead presentations in introductory workshops. "Valuing Preferences in the Workplace" (Brock & Kummerow, n.d.) is a handout for participants in introductory workshops and includes a "leader's guide" with suggestions for use in organizations.

Research for Practitioners   Research from the national sample and reports from organization development specialists (Hirsh, 1992a) indicate that people's descriptions of ideal work environments illustrate all the dichotomies identified by the MBTI. This makes the last activity suggested—designing an ideal work environment—an effective way to clarify and apply type with an introductory group.

Table 12.5 in Chapter 12, page 289, presents relationships between MBTI preferences on Form M and subscales on the Work Environment Scale (WES) for a group of university employees. Tables 12.6, 12.7, and 12.8 (on pages 289, 290, and 291, respectively) present research on the preferred work environments identified by whole types in the national sample of adults gathered by Consulting Psychologists Press in its development and testing of Form M items. (See Chapter 7, pages 156–157, and the Appendix for descriptions of this sample and the research).

Practitioners can use this research information to structure and inform their debriefing of the exercise on ideal work environments, allowing them to highlight typical MBTI-related components in the presentations of different type groups.

Summary

Introducing psychological type and the MBTI into organizations can be exciting and rewarding for practitioners, clients, and the organization. Type theory is positive and supportive, the examples and type descriptions fit people, and the possibilities for application and integration into daily life are almost limitless (Brock, 1996). Introducing the MBTI well supports individual workstyles and needs and encourages employee self-confidence, development, flexibility, and autonomy.

On the other hand, if type is introduced briefly and perfunctorily, clients "forget their letters" and don't make use of type knowledge; or when they do use it, they tend to stereotype and label others. An unbiased introduction, with attention to type verification and to the full type descriptions, and some opportunities to apply the information to specific day-to-day work settings provide the best guarantee that clients and the organization will profit from the benefits and avoid the potential pitfalls.

Introducing and Using the Dynamic and Developmental Aspects of Type

Carl G. Jung's theory of personality is dynamic and developmental. The preferences do not exist in isolation but instead interact with each other to form distinctive personality patterns. The resulting psychological types are not static boxes into which people fit—they evolve and become more effective as people learn and develop. Myers and Briggs operationalized Jung's dynamic model in the MBTI, and the influence of each preference on the others underlies the type descriptions in *Introduction to Type* (Myers, with Kirby & Myers, 1998).

The dynamic and developmental components of Jung's theory offer some of the most powerful applications of the MBTI, but this potential is often underused in organizations. Placing type within this Jungian framework also leads clients away from stereotyping and from feeling stereotyped or "boxed in."

Using this deeper interpretive level in conjunction with the MBTI expands its usefulness, providing the basis for the following applications:

- It gives people information about how others experience them by pointing to the function each type uses when interacting with the external world. This clarifies communication styles (Yeakley, 1982, 1983) and is especially helpful for those who prefer Introversion.

- It highlights the role of the dominant function—a central part of individual identity. Research (Hammer, 1996a) and practice (Barger & Kirby, 1995a; Kummerow, Barger, & Kirby, 1997) indicate that identifying a type's dominant function illuminates core values and motivations (for example, see this chapter's section on dealing with organizational change).

- It creates awareness of the need for the balance potentially provided by a person's auxiliary function—balance between perception and judgment and between extraverting and introverting.

- It provides a framework for recognizing type-consistent reactions to everyday stress and consistent but out-of-character reactions to excessive stress.

- It leads people to explore the impacts of midlife developmental periods.

■ It includes a model of lifelong development that can guide self-assessment and identification of developmental goals.

Like MBTI type, these dynamic and developmental perspectives identify areas for individual growth and improvement of interactions among people in a nonjudgmental way.

Presenting Type Dynamics and Development in an Organizational Setting

Every introduction to the MBTI and type needs to include statements about the dynamic nature of type theory: that a psychological type is much more than the adding together of four separate preferences and that each type is a unique combination based on the interactions of the preferences within that type. It is also helpful to state that the preferences indicated by the MBTI are underlying patterns whose expression and development are influenced by a host of environmental factors such as parents and family, education, cultural values, religion, individual life experiences, profession, and so on.

Practitioners can deepen their own understanding of type dynamics and development through reading (Chapters 3 and 4 of this manual; Myers & Kirby, 1994) and observation. Though type tables such as the one in Chapter 3, page 31, provide a quick guide to each type's dynamics, practitioners will feel most comfortable—and will be most effective—when they understand the theory underlying dynamics and can give examples from their own experience.

Clients typically can understand and make use of type dynamics and development with a relatively brief explanation. This explanation can be integrated into a standard "introduction to type" session or presented in a follow-up session.

Integrating Dynamics into the Introduction to Type

Practitioners who include the dynamic picture of type in introductory sessions typically do this by presenting the following points:

■ In MBTI theory, each type has a favorite mental process, called the dominant function. It forms the core identity and direction for the overall personality. In *Gifts Differing* Isabel Myers called it "the general" (Myers with Myers, 1980/1995). Your dominant function will be one of the two middle letters in your four-letter type.

■ That favorite mental process is normally used in your favorite world: the outer world for those who prefer Extraversion, the inner world for those who prefer Introversion. Myers said the extraverted dominant function is like the general who goes out into the field, overseeing and directing everyone. The introverted dominant function is like a general who stays inside the tent, sending out orders.

■ When we talk about types in this way, we use terms such as *an Extraverted Intuitive* type, meaning a type that extraverts its dominant function of Intuition.

■ The other middle letter of the type is called the auxiliary function. It assists the dominant function (Myers likened it to the general's aide-de-camp) by providing balance between perception and judgment and between extraverting and introverting. So if your dominant function is one of the perceiving functions (S or N), your auxiliary function will be T or F, whichever you prefer. This gives people a comfortable way of taking in information and making decisions. And if you prefer Introversion and therefore use your dominant function inside, we would expect you to use your auxiliary helper to deal with the outside world—it's what you normally extravert. This gives people comfortable ways of extraverting and introverting.

The practitioner then focuses on the four-letter type indicated by MBTI results, pointing out that the four letters identify 16 different underlying patterns of perceiving, judging, and directing energy.

Introducing Dynamics and Development in Follow-Up Sessions As mentioned above, even when dynamics will not be directly addressed and described in the introductory session, it is important to include the dynamic context for understanding MBTI results. Then, at a follow-up session, practitioners can refer back to those statements and remind clients that S and N are two different ways of perceiving, T and F two opposite ways of judging. They can then explain dynamics quickly, using the discussion of dynamics in *Introduction to Type* (Myers, with Kirby & Myers, 1998) and making points similar to those listed above.

Using Type Descriptions to Illustrate Dynamics

Whichever way dynamics are introduced, the type descriptions in *Introduction to Type* provide a practical way to illustrate dynamics. Practitioners can use one type description to illustrate how the dynamics play out in a type, or each participant can look at his or her own type description while the professional makes the following points:

First, notice the title of the page: It gives the dominant function in its preferred attitude and then the auxiliary function in its preferred attitude. For example, the title of the first type description is ISTJ—Introverted Sensing with Extraverted Thinking.

Second, notice the "Characteristics" section: The first paragraph defines the dominant function and indicates whether it is normally used inside or is extraverted. The second paragraph describes the auxiliary function in its customary attitude.

Third, the section on "How Others May See Them" captures what this type extraverts (and therefore what others see) and what this type introverts.

The final section of the type descriptions, "Potential Areas for Growth," outlines developmental patterns: what can happen if the dominant and auxiliary functions are not developed and used well, what happens to types under stress, indications of lack of development and use of the nonpreferred functions, and common examples of eruptions of the inferior function.

Applying Type Dynamics and Development

To assist clients in using this information to deepen self-understanding and their understanding of colleagues, practitioners can form dominant-alike groups (types who use the same dominant function in the same attitude) and ask them to discuss questions such as the following:

- What do you extravert? How do you experience that? How do others? What do you introvert? How do you experience that? How do others?
- How does your dominant function find support in your work? How does your auxiliary function provide balance?
- Looking at yourself in childhood, can you see examples of your use and development of the dominant function?

The remaining sections on organizational applications frequently draw on this deeper level of type understanding, and the suggestions for activities there can also be used to illustrate dynamics.

Resources

As indicated above, the brief description of type dynamics in *Introduction to Type,* along with analysis of the type description, is enough for clients to begin to use dynamics. If dynamics are introduced in a follow-up session, this is a good time to use *Introduction to Type in Organizations* (Hirsh & Kummerow, 1998). This booklet provides a review of the basic dichotomies with word lists and includes a section on type dynamics as well as other organizational applications that will be mentioned later in this chapter.

For practitioners and for clients who want to explore further, *Introduction to Type Dynamics and Development* (Myers & Kirby, 1994) gives a deeper explanation of those topics, suggests typical interactions of dominant and auxiliary functions, defines the differences when functions are extraverted and introverted, and gives examples of using dynamics to understand work interactions. The second half of the booklet outlines Jung's developmental model, discusses typical problems or issues that arise for people, explores midlife development, and offers suggestions of ways people can experience preferences that they normally do not use.

Research for Practitioners

Chapter 4 of this manual presents a variety of research studies based on type dynamics. Tables 4.8, 4.9, 4.10, and 4.11, for example, summarize research by the first and last letters of types: IJ, IP, EP, and EJ. Commonalities among these four types that appear in the rows of the type table relate to the dichotomy (S–N or T–F) that they extravert and the

dichotomy that they introvert. For example, the IJ types are the four types who extravert their auxiliary judging function and introvert their dominant perceiving function, and so on.

All research that looks at whole types, as opposed to preferences or preference combinations, also provides information about the dynamic interactions within that type. Such research is summarized in Chapter 4, Tables 4.26–4.41, and in Chapter 9.

Introduction to Type Dynamics and Development (Myers & Kirby, 1994) presents information about the eight dominant functions, including differences related to the auxiliary function. It is based on collections of information from types in workshops. This information is briefly summarized in Table 13.4.

Reading this research and using the findings to observe types will assist practitioners in deepening their understanding of dynamics and in developing examples.

Summary

Organizational clients find the dynamic and developmental framework of type illuminates their own functioning and deepens their understanding of others. Even when dynamics and development are not explicitly introduced to clients, practitioners can use this perspective to expand their own understanding and develop wider and deeper applications of type to work issues.

Improving Communication

One of the most frequent organizational applications of psychological type comes in response to client requests to "help us communicate better" (Sample & Hoffman, 1986). MBTI type includes information about the preferred communication styles of each type and areas of frequent misunderstanding between people of different types. As in the other applications areas, the MBTI both affirms an individual's natural style and identifies ways he or she can modify that style to be more effective.

Following an introduction to type session, clients are able to describe their communication styles and needs in terms of the MBTI preferences. Practitioners can direct clients to "choose one of the preferences about which you feel clear—you recognize this in yourself." Then, forming preference groups based on their choices, the professional can ask the groups, "When someone is trying to communicate something to you, what does this preference—this part of you—want in order to understand and accept the communication?"

To learn more about the kinds of information practitioners can expect, see the "Resources" section that follows. These resources identify work compiled by a number of type professionals that is categorized by preference, preference combinations, and four-letter type.

Table 13.4   The Dominant Function of Each Type

ISTJ	ISFJ	INFJ	INTJ
Respecting and relying on internally stored data about reality and actual events	Respecting and relying on internally stored data about people who are important to them	Relying on clear insights about people and complex pictures of the future	Relying on clear, complex inner pictures of the present and future
ISTP	**ISFP**	**INFP**	**INTP**
Logically organizing vast amounts of specific data about the material world	Living by strong inner values about honoring people and nature	Filtering everything through a coherent core of personal values based on honoring individuals	Logically organizing complex information into global systems to understand the world
ESTP	**ESFP**	**ENFP**	**ENTP**
Delighting in the endless variety of the world and in spontaneously interacting with it	Delighting in the stimulation of interacting with people, embracing the variety of sensing experience	Seeing exciting possibilities for people and pursuing them with energy and enthusiasm	Scanning the environment for options, new and stimulating ideas, exciting possibilities
ESTJ	**ESFJ**	**ENFJ**	**ENTJ**
Decisively, logically, and efficiently structuring the external environment to achieve specific goals	Acting decisively to create an environment that cares for the practical needs of people around them	Providing the structures and encouragement to motivate and energize people to grow	Directing others decisively, structuring the environment to achieve long-term goals

Source: From *Introduction to Type Dynamics and Development*, pp. 8–9, by K. D. Myers and L. K. Kirby, 1994. Palo Alto, CA: Consulting Psychologists Press. Copyright 1994 by Consulting Psychologists Press. Used with permission.

Using This Information

A training session addressing type and communication with people who don't work together can provide individuals in the group with valuable information about why others may misunderstand their communication as well as suggest ways to modify their style. An ENFP, for example, may recognize during the session that co-workers who prefer Sensing have a difficult time "seeing" their vision when the ENFP presents it in enthusiastic, big-picture terms. The ENFP can then ask for assistance from someone in the group with a Sensing preference to learn how to present exciting possibilities in ways that will communicate more effectively with people of different types.

When the group that has generated these communication needs consists of people who work with each other, the information can form the basis for working agreements. See the section "Using Type with Teams" in this chapter for additional suggestions on negotiating working agreements. Collections of such information from employees can also serve a valuable function in management and leadership training or coaching. See the section "Using Type in Coaching Leaders" in this chapter for suggestions.

At the organizational level, understanding people's different communication needs can provide a structure for analyzing and modifying a company's style of communicating with employees and/or with clients. An organization may recognize, for example, that its normal communication style emphasizes the following:

■ **Introversion**
Information generally presented in writing
Little opportunity for discussion except informally
Information restricted—given on a "need-to-know" basis

■ **Intuition**
Information given in general concepts, the "big picture"
Emphasis on the future vision
Little specific direction of how people are to act on a day-to-day basis

■ **Thinking**
Information in the form of logical analysis
Emphasis on the rationale
Little mention of values or impacts on people

■ **Judging**
Information generally presented after decisions have been made
Emphasis on goals, plans, and structures
Little room for flexibility and processing

Once this is recognized, the organization can decide to broaden its systems to include methods that will communicate more effectively to all employees. Organizations that have analyzed their communication using type information have developed some of the following ideas to add to the communication system already in place:

- **Extraversion**

  "Town meetings," with time for questions and/or small group discussions

  Regular informal "brown bag" lunches for leaders and employees

  A variety of face-to-face give-and-take sessions—leaders attending team or department meetings, listening, asking questions, responding

- **Sensing**

  Relating current information to the past

  Fleshing out all vision/mission statements with the realities—what does this mean for the day-to-day work

  Giving the specifics of what is expected of employees

- **Feeling**

  Inviting people to be involved and providing time/support for involvement

  Stating the underlying values of policies

  Acknowledging the impact on employees and working with employees to respond to their concerns

- **Perceiving**

  Communicating *before* final decisions are made, while there's time for process and change

  Building flexibility into plans and schedules

  Demonstrating openness to new information

Practitioners can work with organizational leaders and those in charge of communications to create a type "filter," a checklist to review all communications before they are sent out to ensure that the intended message is heard.

Resources

The type descriptions in *Introduction to Type* (Myers, with Kirby & Myers, 1998) include a brief summary of each type's typical communication style in the section "How Others May See Them." *Introduction to Type in Organizations* (Hirsh & Kummerow, 1998) includes a chart of "Preferred Methods of Communication" related to each of the eight preferences. *Talking in Type* (Kummerow, 1987) is a short handout describing the basic needs of each preference and how to adjust one's conversational style to communicate more effectively.

Additional information useful as background for practitioners or for use with clients who wish to pursue this topic in depth may be found in the following:

WORKTypes (Kummerow, Barger, & Kirby, 1997), especially Chapter 2, includes discussion of communication style by preference, with tips for communicating more

effectively directed to those preferring Extraversion, those preferring Introversion, and so on. A valuable section on mutual misunderstandings examines typical communication styles—and how others may misinterpret them by function pairs (ST, SF, NF, and NT)—and provides suggestions for modifying one's natural styles to communicate more effectively.

Using Type in Selling (Brock, 1994), while focused on that specific application, also includes suggestions for adjusting one's style to the "type mode" another person is using in order to communicate and persuade more effectively.

I'm Not Crazy, I'm Just Not You (Pearman & Albritton, 1997) includes the following information about each four-letter type, collected from questionnaire responses from 48 workshop groups: kinds of information that is attractive to this type; beliefs about communication; and ways this type usually expresses or presents itself. For example, ISTJs are *attracted to* tested and verifiable data that can be analyzed easily; *believe* that precision in detail leads to clarity of thought; and generally *present themselves* in an unassuming manner, preferring to convey information in a calm, careful way.

Pearman and Albritton (1997) also include information by four-letter type about common prejudices or biases in relationship to information, about preconceptions used to evaluate information, and about what they call "hot buttons"—communication styles or content that produces an immediate, negative reaction.

Research for Practitioners

Research supports the usefulness of type in understanding communication patterns and misunderstandings. In two early studies, Yeakley (1982, 1983) found that people who use similar extraverting styles (for example, both extravert their Feeling judgment or both extravert their Intuition) report more satisfying and effective communication with each other than do those with differing extraverting styles. His conclusion provides a useful summary for practitioners:

> People use all four of the communication styles—sensing, intuition, thinking, and feeling—but not with equal preference, skill, or effectiveness. Each of the 16 psychological types has a unique pattern. . . . Two people must use the same communication style at the same time in order to communicate effectively. This often requires some communication adjustment on the part of one or both of the individuals involved. (1983, p. 5)

Thorne (1987) found significant differences in the topics of discussion and the ability to reach common ground when types were similar and when they were different. Hermon (1993) reported significant differences in preferred communication style by type preference based on research with 108 adults (primarily construction workers and technicians). Table 13. 5 summarizes Hermon's statistically significant findings.

Table 13.5   Communication Strategies and Needs: Significant Relationships with MBTI Preferences

Extraversion	Introversion
Want to focus on a wide range of topics	Want to focus on one problem
Sensing	**Intuition**
Want practical, realistic messages	Want imaginative, creative messages
Want well-thought-out, detailed plans	Want challenges and possibilities
Thinking	**Feeling**
No significant relationships	No significant relationships
Judging	**Perceiving**
Want supervisor who "doesn't surprise them"	Want supervisor who is "spontaneous"
Want detailed action plans "with time tables"	Want "spontaneous" and "flexible" plans
Want focus on "completing planned projects"	Want projects to be flexible and open to modification

Source: From "Communication Strategies of Psychological Type," by M. V. Hermon, 1993, in *APT X Conference Proceedings,* p. 92. Kansas City, MO: Association for Psychological Type. Reprinted with permission.

Brock (1995) presented a summary of communication style preferences based on information gathered from workshop participants. It appears in Table 13.6.

Dealing with Conflict

Conflicts develop for a host of reasons unrelated to psychological type: differences in culture, race, gender, and ethnic identification; differences in religion, social views, politics, personal commitments, and other important identifying values; differences in background, personal life events, education, and other shaping experiences; and competitive pressures within work. Because psychological type explains important differences in communication style, information gathering and giving, decision making, and structuring the environment, however, type-related differences often lead or contribute to normal conflicts between colleagues. Experienced practitioners have found that MBTI type differences sometimes play a role in conflicts that may seem to be about other things. In this case, untangling the type-related parts of the conflict and working to resolve them can provide a cooperative base for moving ahead to deal with other, unrelated issues.

This section addresses integrating type with conflict resolution models, common sources of conflict between people with opposite preferences, and using type to provide bridges for resolving conflicts that are not specifically about

type differences. It concludes with suggested resources and references to research.

Integrating Type with a Conflict Resolution Model

Psychologists and sociologists have developed models that provide a structure for resolving conflicts (Kilmann & Thomas, 1975). All of these models suggest ways to avoid or get beyond a win/lose approach to conflict, where one side is "right" and the other is clearly "wrong."

Practitioners' use of any such models in resolving conflicts will be strengthened by integrating type:

- It identifies and affirms an individual's natural style of dealing with conflict.
- It makes clear that others will have a very different style that is equally right for them.
- It supports modifying natural styles to interact more effectively.

This ethic of the MBTI—the constructive use of differences—provides a framework and perspective for using any conflict resolution approach.

Identifying Type-Related Conflicts

The challenge for practitioners is recognizing when conflicts include type-related elements and then leading clients through a process of negotiating so that people get what is

Table 13.6   Behavioral Cues During Communication

Talk It Out *Extraverts*	Think It Through *Introverts*
Rapid speech	Pause in answering or giving information
Interrupt	
Louder volume to voice	Quieter voice volume
Appear to think aloud	Shorter sentences, not run on

Specifics *Sensing Types*	The Big Picture *Intuitive Types*
Ask for step-by-step information or instruction	Ask for the purpose of an action
Ask "what" and "how" questions	Look for possibilities
	Ask "why" questions
Use precise descriptions	Talk in general terms

Logical Implications *Thinking Types*	Impact on People *Feeling Types*
Appear to be testing you or your knowledge	Strive for harmony in the interaction
Weigh the objective evidence	May talk about what they value
Are unimpressed that others have decided in favor	Ask how others have acted or resolved the situation
Conversations follow a pattern of checking logic: "if this, then that"	Matters to them whether others have been taken into account

Joy of Closure *Judging Types*	Joy of Processing *Perceiving Types*
Impatient with overly long descriptions, procedures	Seem to want "space" to make own decisions
The tone is "hurry up—I want to make this decision"	The tone is "let's explore," what are some more factors to consider
May decide prematurely	May decide at the last moment
Enjoy closure	Enjoy processing

Source: From *Four Part Framework* (Rev. ed.), by S. A. Brock, 1995, Minneapolis, MN: Brock Associates. Copyright 1987 by S. A. Brock. Adapted with permission.

important to them in a conflict situation. The following are brief descriptions of conflicts frequently experienced by co-workers who differ on a particular type dichotomy. These descriptions can be a beginning point for practitioners to sharpen their skills in identifying type-related components of conflicts.

Extraversion–Introversion Conflicts here frequently relate to two areas: (1) quick versus more measured pacing and (2) breadth/changeability of topics versus focus.

The natural pace of those who prefer Extraversion is rapid. They develop their ideas by talking about them. As they talk, their thoughts become clearer to them; consequently they often change direction during the course of discussions.

Those who prefer Introversion usually want to process internally and need some talk-free time and space to do so. The thinking-out-loud process of those preferring Extraversion can interfere with their thinking-inside process. Additionally, when people preferring Introversion tune back into the conversation, they may find the discussion has shifted to a different topic.

The opposites on this dichotomy often experience conflict, with Extraverts labeling the Introverts as "withholding" or "not interested," while Introverts experience Extraverts as "invasive." And each may think the other is "avoiding the topic."

Sensing–Intuition Two conflicts that frequently develop related to differences in this dichotomy are (1) agreement on what the problem is and (2) a focus on experience versus a focus on theories.

For Sensing types, the problem or conflict is defined by what actually happened, usually concrete events: "John is late for our meetings 90% of the time." Intuitive types are more likely to see specific behavior as part of a pattern that they think is the real problem: "John has difficulty dealing with authority figures." For Intuitive types, taking some action to ensure that John arrives on time to meetings doesn't deal with the "real" problem. For Sensing types, "difficulty with authority figures" has little meaning and no solution.

When conflicts or problems arise, Sensing types tend to reflect on their experience and trust what they know has worked before in similar situations. Intuitive types are more likely to find theoretical explanations and solutions persuasive: A new book or new interpretation seems more attractive and more likely to achieve long-term results.

Sensing types and Intuitive types sometimes end up in a conflict where each thinks the other "just doesn't get it" (the problem), with Sensing types seeing Intuitive types as unrealistic or "off the wall" and Intuitive types seeing Sensing types as "shooting down" their ideas.

Thinking–Feeling Two frequent conflicts related to this dichotomy are (1) searching for the "right" answer versus exploration of people's ideas and (2) choosing the logical alternative and applying it to everyone versus finding individual solutions that work for people.

Thinking types tend to believe that if a problem can be defined accurately and the relevant evidence gathered, there will be a correct solution, and that's what people should do. Feeling types are much more likely to think that "truth" is not cut and dried: What's right for one may be wrong for another. The "solution" will be found by gathering many perspectives and finding the answer that fits best for everyone.

For Thinking types, the answer that is correct is generally the one supported by logic and reason—the "objective" perspective, with personal considerations and emotions separated out. For Feeling types, personal considerations identify the solution: The best answer is found through empathizing with those involved and finding ways to support them.

Thinking types may experience the decision-making process of Feeling types as irrational, inconsistent, and illogical. Feeling types may experience the decision making of Thinking types as cold and uncaring.

Judging–Perceiving Two of the normal conflicts related to this dichotomy are (1) the need for structure versus the need for flexibility and (2) the desire for closure versus the desire for openness (waiting).

Judging types want clear goals; then they create plans, structures, and time frames to achieve them. Perceiving types typically want clear goals and a deadline; then they want to be trusted to meet them in their own ways.

Judging types want decisions and closure. Ambiguity, delayed decisions, reopening decisions, and changing goals are extremely uncomfortable to them. Perceiving types, on the other hand, want decisions to grow out of the process. Making a decision because "it's time," or because the Judging type wants one, often feels forced, premature, and likely to be the wrong decision to Perceiving types. They have faith in their own internal sense of timing and trust that when the right time comes, they will know: "*Now* is the time; *now* I know what we should do."

Judging types often have trouble trusting that Perceiving types will come through in a timely way, that decisions will be made and action will be taken. Perceiving types often feel hemmed in, limited, and restricted by Judging types.

These are not the only type-related conflicts that practitioners may see in work settings, but they are some of the most common. As practitioners watch work interactions through a type lens, they will be able to identify such conflicts more confidently.

The Advantages of Recognizing Type in Conflicts The benefits of recognizing these components in conflicts is that the type perspective tends to depersonalize disagreements. Colleagues shift from seeing each other as wrong, or willfully obstructive, to recognizing that each is operating out of a valid perspective that needs to be heard and honored in the resolution of the conflict. Conflict resolution becomes much easier when both parties invest in the constructive use of differences.

Using Type as a Bridge in Dealing with Other Conflicts

Practitioners have found type is one way to forge common ground in conflict situations that are unrelated to type differences. Recognizing type differences may be useful in the following kinds of situations:

- Two departments merge, but old loyalties remain.

- A team is formed, with people representing different parts of the organization and having very different priorities and approaches.
- Colleagues from different cultural, racial, ethnic, or educational backgrounds find they have difficulty developing the trust necessary to work together effectively.
- An organization acquires another company and integrates employees, but finds that the organizational cultural differences are getting in the way of anticipated benefits.

In all of these examples, very real differences in culture, styles, and values need to be negotiated. This works best when the people involved can find commonalities as well as differences, which are often all too clear. One way of doing this is to work with them to find their "common ground" (Weisbord, 1992): the goals they share for their work, their desire for congenial and supportive colleagues, their commitment to the organization's success, and so on.

Using the MBTI with such groups can provide common ground on an individual level: People with very different cultural values and styles—organizational or national—find it easy to talk about their type preference similarities (Kirby & Barger, 1996). They frequently find similar attitudes toward school, authority, working on teams, collegial relationships, communication styles, and a number of other type-related behaviors and values. These personal connections developed through use of the MBTI can provide respect and trust between type-alike people as they work to negotiate their differences.

The following example illustrates such a use of type, in this case to bridge differences in national cultures and behaviors. An international communications company reorganized to gain greater efficiency. This process resulted in the forming of a team composed of research and development specialists in Sidney, Australia, and Denver, Colorado. They did much of their "team" work at long distance, using e-mail, fax, and phone. But the time came when they needed to get together, and the Australians came to Denver to work for several months. Problems immediately surfaced that seemed to be about gender, sex discrimination, social and political value differences, and race. The American team was headed by a woman (not unheard of in this U.S. company). The Australians were unaccustomed to women in leadership roles in technical fields and tended to go to her male assistant for information and direction. And they made jokes that were offensive to all of the U.S. women on the team. Meanwhile, the Australians continued to be annoyed that the Americans seemed to know little about Australia, including never being able to get the time/date difference right.

A desperate call to a practitioner who had done numerous workshops with the U.S. members of this team resulted in a workshop using type and culture concepts to look at similarities and differences. Participants first had an introduction to type and worked in type-alike groups to identify common strengths and weaknesses, type-related values and behaviors, and so on.

Then they were grouped by culture—Australia and U.S.—and asked to answer a number of questions about their countries. Finally, Australians and Americans were put together to exchange information about cultural values and behaviors.

The commonalities identified in the type-alike groups and the bonding around "you do it that way too?" carried over into the cross-cultural discussions. Participants had developed respect as they worked together in the type groups and were willing to listen to the information about cultural differences. Interestingly, the "worst" offender with racial- and gender-stereotyping jokes turned out to be the same type as the African-American woman team leader. They had an energizing discussion in their type-alike group about all the ways people had misunderstood them and, though the racial and gender differences didn't disappear, they were able to discuss them in an atmosphere of mutual respect.

Practitioners must never ignore or minimize very real differences in the perspectives and experiences of people of different organizational, cultural, or racial backgrounds; but type can be a bridge—a tool for finding commonality among very different people—and can create an atmosphere where those other differences can be discussed with mutual respect and appreciation.

Using Type in Diversity Training

The context and ethics of the MBTI assessment tool support and encourage diversity: recognizing normal, in-born differences between people; respecting people's right to be who they are and to contribute in the ways that are appropriate for them; appreciating "gifts differing" (the title of Isabel Myers' 1980 book explaining psychological type); and negotiating so that each person gets what he or she needs. The MBTI's support of the "constructive use of differences" has led some practitioners to use the MBTI as part of diversity training programs (Lund, 1995).

There are few published resources and little research on uses of the MBTI in diversity training. Until such information is available, practitioners are urged to proceed with caution. The ethical principles related to the MBTI assume that clients can report their natural preferences, claim their unique personality patterns, assert their right to be different, and negotiate for mutual respect and support of differences. These assumptions do not describe the reality for many co-cultural groups in the United States and other countries, where the dominant culture has defined cultural values, appropriate behaviors and personalities, and so on.

MBTI type cannot be used to gloss over or minimize the diversity issues of clients from cultures that historically have been oppressed. For example, those preferring Introversion in the United States customarily report that they have grown up facing biases about their natural Introverted behaviors and pressures to be someone they are not.

Research evidence (Chapter 9; Myers & McCaulley, 1985) confirms that many natural introverted behaviors are portrayed by other psychological instruments in very negative ways. And observers' interpretations of Introverted behaviors can be largely negative (Thorne & Gough, 1991). These experiences may help those preferring Introversion to develop understanding and sympathy toward others who have been mislabeled and discriminated against by their culture; but the experience of those preferring Introversion does *not* in any direct way compare to the experience of oppressed groups, especially people of color.

At the same time, practitioners report that type is a bridge in crossing cultures and that workshop participants from very different racial, national, and ethnic backgrounds talk readily about their type similarities (Kirby & Barger, 1996). Used with caution and sensitivity, the MBTI may play a role in identifying commonalities as a part of diversity training.

When Type Should *Not* Be Used in Conflict Resolution

Van Sant (personal communication, 1998) suggests that, while type is invaluable in conflict resolution, there are times when it can get in the way and be counterproductive. Type should not be used, for example, when one party wants to talk type implications and the other does not. The intensity of conflicts can be greatly increased if one of the parties uses type concepts in a way that stereotypes or "explains away" the other's perspective.

Van Sant's experience suggests that type may also not be helpful when it becomes a way of intellectualizing a conflict to avoid acknowledging and validating the emotions experienced by the parties in the conflict.

Resources

Several of the type resources already mentioned provide information that will assist practitioners in recognizing type-related conflicts: *Introduction to Type* (1998), *Introduction to Type in Organizations* (1998), *I'm Not Crazy, I'm Just Not You* (1997), and others. Van Sant and Payne (1995) focus on using type in education, but their chapter on "Conflict Resolution" has much wider applicability. It includes discussions of frequent conflict areas related to type preference differences; outlines approaches to solving conflicts typical of the function pairs (ST, SF, NT, and NF); and provides suggestions, tips, and a process for resolving conflicts with different types.

Research for Practitioners

Early research on psychological type and conflict (Kilmann & Thomas, 1975; Mills, Robey, & Smith, 1985) found, in general, that Thinking types tended to be assertive and competitive in conflict situations, Feeling types favored cooperation and accommodation, and those preferring Introversion avoided conflict.

Table 13.7   Preferred Conflict Styles of Types

Dominant Extraverted Thinking (ETJs)	
Males	Compete
Females	Compromise
Dominant Introverted Thinking (ITPs)	Compromise
Auxiliary Extraverted Thinking (ITJs)	Compromise
Auxiliary Introverted Thinking (ETPs)	Compromise
Dominant Extraverted Feeling (EFJs)	Collaborate
Dominant Introverted Feeling (IFPs)	Accommodate
Auxiliary Extraverted Feeling (IFJs)	Accommodate
Auxiliary Introverted Feeling (EFPs)	Accommodate

Source: From "Myers-Briggs Type Indicator and Conflict-Handling Intention: An Interactive Approach," by T. Q. Percival, V. Smitheram, and M. Kelly, 1992, *Journal of Psychological Type, 23*, p. 14. Copyright 1992 by *Journal of Psychological Type*. Used with permission.

Percival, Smitheram, and Kelly's (1992) study administered the *Thomas-Kilmann Conflict Mode Instrument* (MODE) and the MBTI to 340 adults. Comparisons by preference found relationships similar to those in the earlier studies. When they used type dynamics, however, they found even more significant relationships. As they stated, "using the interactive combinations of scales [dynamics] produced a replicable, consistent, and interpretable pattern of results" (p. 10). For example, dominant extraverted Thinking type males identified "Compete" as their preferred strategy for dealing with conflicts, while dominant introverted Thinking types identified "Compromise." Dominant extraverted Feeling types identified "Collaborate" as their preferred strategy, while the other Feeling types preferred "Accommodate." Their findings are summarized in Table 13.7.

Enhancing Problem Solving and Decision Making

The theory of psychological type suggests that the best decisions include using all the perspectives identified by the MBTI functions (Sensing, Intuition, Thinking, and Feeling), and experience with groups in organizations confirms this. Isabel Myers first outlined using the four functions in decision making, and type experts working in a number of different applications areas have developed materials to teach this model (see "Resources" section).

The type decision-making model is straightforward and can be taught very quickly after people have been introduced to type. The best way to put it to work for clients is to lead them through analyzing one of their recent real decisions, helping them recognize what they included in their decision making and what may have been left out from a type perspective. During this process, both individuals and groups get insightful glimpses into the areas they usually ignore.

The following are typical results of analyzing group decisions when one of the functions has been ignored.

When people do not include the Sensing perspective in decision making, they may

- Be short on data and solve the wrong problem
- Ignore information from the past that would be helpful
- Forget to assess the impacts on day-to-day tasks
- Be off on time frames and structure needed for implementation

Fitzgerald (1992) reported working with a research and development team consisting primarily of people who preferred Intuition and Thinking. As she worked with them on their decision making, they recognized that they had consistently sabotaged their own work by failing to accurately assess the time required to implement projects and failing to factor in the actual resources available—all this in spite of several experiences where these failings had created problems for them.

When people do not include the Intuitive perspective in decision making, they may

- Be limited by what has been tried before
- Ignore information about options being tried by other organizations or groups
- Forget to see the interactions that will occur when the plan is implemented
- Find short-term solutions

Clancy (1997) reported that the CEO of an engineering company proposed restructuring managers' roles to flatten the organization and empower employees. He saw this as necessary because increasing demands on managers would soon make their job responsibilities overwhelming. The line managers, who were primarily Sensing types, rejected the plan because "we're doing OK—if it ain't broke, don't fix it." A year later, as their job responsibilities had grown, many of the managers saw the wisdom of the CEO's foresight.

When people do not include the Thinking perspective in decision making, they may

- Fail to assess the logical consequences of each alternative
- Respond primarily to the needs of the people in the immediate situation
- Be overly influenced by the views of trusted people
- Develop solutions that are inconsistent with previous decisions or organizational policies

The volunteer board of a nonprofit career development center consisting primarily of Feeling types found that their decision making was not working well for the center: They had failed to raise client fees when they needed to and had approved expenditures for good and valuable activities for which they did not really have the funds. In assessing the decision making that had led them into this financial hole, they recognized that their meetings focused on trying to accommodate the views of all the board members and that they had persuaded themselves that "good" programs would result in increased clients and would pay their own way.

When people do not include the Feeling perspective in decision making, they may

- Be limited by failing to get information from the people who are involved
- Ignore the impacts on people's life and work
- Forget to evaluate the decision by organizational or group values
- Develop solutions that are logical but impossible to actually achieve

After an introduction to type workshop, the leadership team of a medical center, consisting entirely of Thinking types, exclaimed, "We wish we'd had this before we announced our latest reorganization. We planned everything so meticulously. The reorganization was state of the art, and our rationale was brilliant. But we forgot the people. When we announced it, we really got sandbagged."

Using the Information

Once a group has analyzed the members' usual decision-making style, it can do as the medical center leadership team above did: The team produced a chart for the wall of the conference room that listed the four functions and questions commonly associated with the functions. They put "Feeling judgment" and the questions related to that in red letters and committed to each other that they would review each decision with the chart before finalizing. Kendall and Carr (1997) report using a similar approach in their "Looking Glass" courses, which use management simulations to improve leadership and decision making.

The Missing Feeling Function

The function most frequently ignored in decision making in Western organizations (Fitzgerald & Kirby, 1997b) is Feeling judgment. Research on managers and leaders of organizations reports an overrepresentation of Thinking types in proportion both to the overall population and to reports of the Thinking–Feeling distributions within organizations.

The cultural values of organizations tend to support Thinking approaches to decision making: Be objective, detached, hard headed; put emotions and loyalty aside; follow the logic wherever it leads. The results of such one-sided decision making can create serious problems (Noer, 1993; Molpus, 1997).

Resources

Isabel Myers described using the perspectives provided by each of the four functions to improve decision making (Myers, 1980/1995, especially pp. 194–196). Others have developed and refined her ideas into decision-making models:

Gordon Lawrence's (n.d.) "Zig-Zag Process for Problem Solving" and Katharine Myers' (n.d.) "Decision Making and Type" are handouts that outline the process of using the four functions in decision making. "Type and Problem Solving" in *Introduction to Type* (Myers, with Kirby & Myers, 1998) provides similar information in a somewhat different form, and "Problem-Solving Process Using Type Preferences" in *Introduction to Type in Organizations* (Hirsh & Kummerow, 1998) also suggests ways to use Myers' approach.

All of these provide the basic perspectives needed to get a group started. The members' own experiences will likely lead them to develop questions appropriate for their setting.

Research for Practitioners

The research on decision-making styles and type is not as clear as that on communication styles (Walck, 1996), with situational factors playing a very significant role in the way decisions are made. Huitt (1992) provides an outline of the steps in problem solving and suggests ways that type may relate to each step. Haley and Pini (1994) reported on their observations of groups of managers in Italy and Mexico engaged in problem-solving exercises. The researchers summarized their observations in terms of combinations of the functions, ST, SF, NT, and NF, and reported them in three areas: input bias (information sought and used), output bias (basis for generating alternatives), and operational bias (basis for decisions). Their results are summarized in Table 13.8.

Reviewing Walck's summary and other research on type and decision making points to a problem in type research that was identified by Yeakley (1982, 1983) when he reviewed the research on communication styles: Because type is dynamic, attempting to find correlations and relationships between one MBTI preference dichotomy and some aspect of decision making may lead to frustration.

For example, though all eight types that prefer Feeling will share some definable characteristics, the other three preferences will interact with the Feeling judgment in various ways to create eight distinctive ways Feeling judgment is used. Similarly, though ENTJs and ENFJs differ on only one preference, ENTJs extravert their dominant Thinking function and will make decisions very differently from ENFJs, who extravert their dominant Feeling function. And dominant introverted Thinking types (ISTP and INTP) report using very different decision-making processes from those characteristic of dominant extraverted Thinking types.

Decision making is a complex process. Jung's theory of human personality describes people's basic styles of taking

Table 13.8   MBTI Function Pairs and Decision Making

	ST	NT	SF	NF
Input bias (Information sought and used)	Specific facts (may ignore patterns)	Systematic patterns (may ignore specifics that differ from model)	The opinions of specific people (may ignore hard data)	Symbols, imagery, and metaphors (may ignore practical data)
Output bias (Basis for generating alternatives)	Problem-solving models that have worked in the past	Data that confirm their conceptual pattern	Options supported by important people	Analogies and novel ideas
Operational bias (Basis for decisions)	Regularity, structure, and "fit" with standard practices	Logical categorization based on their conceptual pattern	What people in the situation need or want	Associations from similar experiences or their vision of the future

Source: From "Blazing International Trails in Strategic Decision-Making Research," by C. V. Haley and R. Pini, 1994, in *Proceedings of the Myers-Briggs Type Indicator and Leadership: An International Research Conference*, p. 22. College Park, MD: National Leadership Institute.

in information and making decisions; expanding individuals' natural styles through use of the MBTI will lead to considering a broader range of information and to applying principles and values more consciously in decision making.

Planning, Implementing, and Managing Organizational Change

After decades of fairly stable organizational structures, the 1990s saw an increasing wave of organizational change, and experts predict that this is just the beginning. The combination of advances in information technology and globalizing of markets creates a radically different economic environment from the one that prevailed in industrialized countries in the post–World War II decades. The result is a revolution in organizational structures, in the ways people work, and in the meaning of work.

Organizational Change Experts

This revolution in the ways people work and organizations are structured has spawned a host of analyses, blueprints, and guides to effective organizational change. In type terms, almost all of these are NT blueprints: They give the rational analysis and the big picture, usually leaving out the specifics (S) of exactly what this will look like and how to get from here to there. They also tend to ignore the Feeling perspective of what people need to survive and prosper in the new organization. Both William Bridges (1992b, 1994) and David Noer (1993) focused their organizational change work on the people of the organization.

Even when these change experts recognize the impacts on people, they typically have not taken into account the normal differences in how people respond to organizational change, what they need to accept and support change, and the particular strengths and weaknesses they may bring to the current organizational environment. (Bridges, 1994, is the partial exception: in the career development section of *JobShift* he includes a brief temperament discussion.)

In type terms, most attention to "the people" during organizational change seems to be a recommendation that everyone act like ENTPs (For example, see Pritchett, n.d.):

- E: Look outward to the market, network with people, take quick action.
- N: See the big picture, have vision, use "out-of-the-box" thinking.
- T: Recognize that the past is gone, move ahead in a detached and rational way to fit yourself into the future.
- P: Be flexible, change directions quickly, give up the need for structure.

In some ways, this makes sense: The advice is that every employee become an entrepreneur, take charge of his or her own work life; and, indeed, type distributions of entrepreneurs tend to show an overrepresentation of NTPs (Reynierse, 1997). From a type perspective of normal differences and the value of all types, however, this exhortation to, in effect, change one's type is not very useful. When most organizational change programs do not achieve the desired results and the primary reason found is "the people," the MBTI can make an important contribution.

Using Type to Facilitate Organizational Change

Whatever change model or restructuring plan an organization decides to use, the success of each step in the process depends upon the energy, flexibility, creativity, and commitment of the people in the organization. To be successful, the planning, implementing, and managing of change needs to

Table 13.9   What Each Preference Needs During Organizational Change

Extraversion	Introversion
Time to talk about what is going on	Time alone to reflect on what is going on
Involvement—something to do	To be asked what they think about things
Communication, communication, communication	Thought-out, written communication and one-on-one discussions
To be heard—to have a voice	Time to think through their positions before discussions or meetings
Action, getting on with it, keeping up the pace	Time to assimilate changes before taking action

Sensing	Intuition
Real data—why is change occurring?	The overall rationale—the global realities
Specifics and details about what exactly is to change	A general plan or direction to play around with and develop
Connections between the planned changes and the past	Chances to paint a picture of the future—to create a vision that works for them
Realistic pictures of the future that make the plans real	Options—a general direction, but not too much structure
Clear guidelines on expectations, roles, and responsibilities—or the opportunity to design them	Opportunities to participate in designing the future, to influence the changes

Thinking	Feeling
The logic—why?	Recognition of the impacts on people
What systemic changes will there be? Why?	How will people's needs be dealt with?
Clarity in the decision making and the planning	Inclusion of themselves and others in the planning and implementing of change
What are the goals? What will be the structure?	What values underlie the changes? Are they the right ones?
Demonstration that leadership is competent	Demonstration that leadership cares
Fairness and equitability in the changes	Appreciation and support

Judging	Perceiving
A clear, concise plan of action	An open-ended plan
Defined outcomes, clear goals	The general parameters
A time frame, with each stage spelled out	Flexibility, with lots of options
A clear statement of priorities	Information and the opportunity to gather more
No more surprises!	Loosen up, don't panic, trust the process
Completion—get the change in place	Room to adjust goals and plans as the process continues

Source: From *The Challenge of Change in Organizations*, pp. 22–37, by N. J. Barger and L. K. Kirby, 1995. Palo Alto, CA: Davies-Black. Copyright 1995 by Davies-Black. Used with permission.

include providing what people need to make fundamental transitions in their lives. As in other applications, MBTI type provides a rational structure for understanding those needs and points to ways they can be met.

Barger and Kirby (1995a) integrated type and William Bridges' (1980, 1992b) model of stages of transitions in workshops for leaders and employees in organizations undergoing change. They report results from 2,000 workshop participants responding to the question, "What does this preference need during a time of change?" Table 13.9 summarizes the responses by preference. This kind of information—gathered from employees in the organization—can provide a checklist for leaders.

Information and Inclusion

Type also provides guidance for responding to the common, shared concerns of people during change. People report two overriding needs: the desire to be included in the process in some way and a hunger for information. Practitioners working with organizations during change can draw on the section on communication to ensure that all the types receive the kinds of information they need to accept and support changes; but the stress of change means that people's needs for information increase. Even communication that is well balanced to meet the needs of different types is probably not enough. William Bridges' (1992b)

Table 13.10   Thinking–Feeling During the Grieving Process

Thinking	Feeling
Strengths in dealing with losses and endings	*Strengths in dealing with losses and endings*
exhibit calmness	expect to experience emotions
step back, apply detached logic	are attuned to others' emotional experience
take charge	seek support
"cut loose" and move on	offer support—are good listeners and sympathizers
problem-solve	will take time to process emotional issues
Problem areas in dealing with grieving	*Problem areas in dealing with grieving*
have difficulty accessing their own emotions and grieving	can get stuck in negative emotions
feel overwhelmed and powerless when they experience their own strong emotions	experience everyone's pain, can be distracted by their own and others' emotions
are impatient and uncomfortable with others' emotions	find it difficult to see beyond the immediate personal turmoil
can be overwhelmed by unprocessed emotions	overdo supportive role

Source: From *The Challenge of Change in Organizations*, pp. 87–90, by N. J. Barger and L. K. Kirby, 1995. Palo Alto, CA: Davies-Black. Copyright 1995 by Davies-Black. Used with permission.

term is *over-communicate*, and that's a good guide: Do more of all the different ways of communicating.

All types want to be included in decisions being made that affect their lives in fundamental ways. One of the primary reasons for problems that arise during organizational change is that, typically, a small group of leaders or a task force has analyzed the present, explored the options, and then made a decision. They announce this exciting reorganization or restructuring only to find most others in the organization raising doubts, critiquing, feeling anxious, and losing motivation. For all those who were not part of the process, the change feels imposed on them, and it's natural to resist.

Thinking types can be included by presenting current ideas and alternatives *during the process* of deciding, asking for their analytical critique, and then paying attention to it. For Feeling types, inclusion generally can be achieved similarly, but the questions they want to pursue are the following: How will this affect the people of the organization? What will we do to support people during the change? What kinds of values are held by those making the decisions? Do I trust them?

For those responsible for leading organizational change, including people in these ways often seems too time-consuming and confusing—all those different questions and ideas! This can be particularly challenging to that majority of leaders whose type includes Thinking and Judging. TJs like to make decisions by gathering relevant information and choosing the most logical alternative. They then want to state goals and a plan and move ahead to implement.

However, Thinking–Judging types also highly value being effective and competent. When they understand that their most comfortable style is one that will likely create

resistance and simply won't work—however logical it is on paper—they can move efficiently to inform and include.

Resources

William Bridges' *Managing Transitions* (1992b) persuasively describes the stages people and groups go through during transitions. His recognition of the need to grieve about what is being lost and his description of the confusions of the "neutral zone" are particularly helpful, and he includes a lot of information about supporting people through this process.

Bridges' model of transition stages provided the structure for Barger and Kirby's *The Challenge of Change in Organizations* (1995), which integrates the responses and needs of different types during each stage. Their findings about the Thinking–Feeling dichotomy and Bridges' "endings" are summarized in Table 13.10. Because they found that each type has its own pattern in responding to organizational change, Barger and Kirby include one-page summaries for each of the 16 types, with information about what each type contributes, what each finds difficult, and typical ways each resists change.

Barger and Kirby (1997a, 1997b) also wrote *MBTI Type and Change* and *MBTI Type and Change Participant's Guide*, a structured program with reproducible masters for using the MBTI with people in organizations undergoing change. Topics include developing a metaphor for change; MBTI type preferences and change; dealing with the impact of organizational change; dealing with loss and grieving; and restoring identity and meaning. Along with workshop agendas, scripts, and exercises on these topics, the guide also gives directions for adapting the programs to specific organizations and situations.

Sandra Hirsh's (1992a) *MBTI Team Building Program* includes a section on helping teams deal with organizational change, focusing on the four quadrants of the type table: IS, ES, IN, and EN. Her approach described there, with reproducible masters and a team participant guide, has wider applicability and can be used throughout the organization.

WORKTypes (Kummerow, Barger, & Kirby, 1997) provides suggestions for individual employees in a chapter on managing change, while Barger & Kirby's organizational change chapter in *Developing Leaders* (1997c) focuses on leaders of different types.

Research for Practitioners

Walck (1996) summarized studies of leaders during change. Several correlated MBTI preferences with the *Kirton Adaption and Innovation Inventory* (KAI). They generally found significant correlations between "Innovation" on the KAI and preferences for Intuition and Perceiving on the MBTI; conversely, "Adaptation" correlated with MBTI preferences for Sensing and Judging.

Such research—like much of the current expert advice on organizational change—needs to be interpreted with care by practitioners. The bias of change experts is for "transformational" change, and NPs are most likely to exhibit characteristics associated with this. However, transformational change programs have a high rate of failure, perhaps in part because of the missing type perspectives.

Clancy's (1997) analysis of STJs during organizational change provides a crucial perspective for recognizing these types' contributions to change and their style of leading change programs. Her chapter addresses the "conventional wisdom in the type community" (p. 415)—that STJs have the most difficulty dealing with organizational change—by listing STJ behaviors that are interpreted by others as "resistance" and then explaining their basis and purpose for STJs. She also identifies what STJs need in order to support organizational change programs.

Because STJs comprise so great a part of the workforce in most organizations, and because much of the research implies that Intuitives deal better with change, practitioners need to have the context and information provided by Clancy in interpreting and using this research. MBTI practitioners dealing with changing organizations note that all types will "resist" change if they are not informed and included. All types will struggle in making needed changes if their needs are not met by the organization.

Summary

Helping organizations and employees deal with ongoing change may be the organizational development specialist's greatest challenge. Integrating MBTI type knowledge and perspectives into change programs has proven invaluable—to individual employees and leaders and to the organization.

Recognizing and Managing Stress

Stress is an integral and perhaps inevitable part of organizational life. Organizations place multiple, sometimes contradictory, and often rapidly changing demands on all personnel. The variety and continuity of stressors in the workplace provide a "living laboratory" for recognizing the distinctive ways in which people of each of the 16 types experience and react to stress. Individuals at all levels of the organization can benefit from understanding how they, their co-workers, their supervisors, and those they supervise deal with the stresses of the work environment. Such knowledge encourages type-appropriate ways of managing stress. Stress management has obvious benefits in increased work output, fewer sick days due to stress-related illnesses, decreased employee burnout and job turnover, and other benefits that result from greater employee comfort and satisfaction.

There are two relevant areas in exploring organizational stress in relation to psychological type. The first refers to the particular work situations that each type finds especially stressful and the second to the ways each type tends to react to such stress. Both the sources of stress for each type and the responses to stress are predictable from type theory. Because the theory is based on the different amounts of energy each type has available for different kind of activities, we can observe the effects of these energy differences for each dichotomy as well as at the level of whole types. The next section focuses on stress issues for each dichotomy.

The MBTI Dichotomies

People tend to be energized when using their preferences and fatigued when using their less preferred functions and attitudes. Energy depletion, in addition to the dissatisfaction of doing things that don't "come naturally," is an obvious way to cause stress. For example, Introverts are likely to feel energized when left alone to complete a project, while Extraverts may find this stressful and fatiguing. People who prefer Sensing find carefully checking the facts of a report to be satisfying while those who prefer Intuition would likely find this activity tiring and unmotivating. Providing frequent positive feedback to employees will feel natural and satisfying for a person who prefers Feeling but unnecessary, awkward, and draining to many Thinking types. Working within a set structure is often stressful for people with a Perceiving attitude, while it is comfortable and satisfying for those with a Judging attitude.

Table 13.11 shows the kinds of activities that are likely to be stressful for people having each preference. The table is an adaptation of material presented in *WORKTypes* (Kummerow, Barger, & Kirby, 1997).

As can be inferred from Table 13.11, stress depends on the point of view of each type or type preference. The likely

Table 13.11   Typical Work Stressors for Each of the Eight MBTI Preferences

Stressors for Extraverts	Stressors for Introverts
working alone	working with others
having to communicate mainly by e-mail	talking on the phone a lot
lengthy work periods with no interruptions	interacting with others frequently
having to reflect before taking action	having to act quickly without reflection
having to focus in depth on one thing	too many concurrent tasks and demands
getting feedback in writing only	getting frequent verbal feedback

Stressors for Sensing Types	Stressors for Intuitive Types
attending to own and others' insights	having to attend to realities
having to do old things in new ways	having to do things the proven way
having to give an overview without details	having to attend to details
looking for the meaning in the facts	checking the accuracy of facts
focusing on possibilities	needing to focus on past experience
too many complexities	being required to be practical

Stressors for Thinking Types	Stressors for Feeling Types
using personal experience to assess situations	analyzing situations objectively
adjusting to individual differences and needs	setting criteria and standards
noticing and appreciating what is positive	critiquing and focusing on flaws
focusing on processes and people	focusing on tasks only
using empathy and personal values to make decisions	being expected to use logic alone to make decisions
having others react to questioning as divisive	asking questions that feel divisive

Stressors for Judging Types	Stressors for Perceiving Types
waiting for structure to emerge from process	having to organize selves' and others' planning
being expected to use "inner timing"	working within time frames and deadlines
too much flexibility around time frames and deadlines	others' distrust of last-minute energy
having to marshal energy at the last minute	having to finish and move on
staying open to reevaluations of tasks	developing contingency plans
dealing with surprises	being required to plan ahead

Source: From *WORK Types*, pp. 198–199, by J. M. Kummerow, N. J. Barger, and L. K. Kirby, 1997. New York: Warner Books. Copyright 1997 by J. M. Kummerow, N. J. Barger, and L. K. Kirby. Used with permission.

reaction to overdoing a less-preferred function or attitude is to show one or more of the following: irritability, resistance, low motivation, short temper, discouragement, self-blame and blaming of others. A natural solution to this kind of stress is to avoid tasks and situations that create it. However, avoiding stressful tasks and situations is not always possible. For those situations, an adaptive and effective approach is to recognize, accept, and moderate the context within which the stress occurs. Managers, team leaders, and people throughout the organization can use the relatively straightforward differences in Table 13.11 to modify their demands and expectations of themselves and others.

A simple and effective approach when one must work out of one's opposite preferences (as is often the case) is to acknowledge to oneself and/or appropriate others that the activity is "typologically stressful," anticipate that it is likely to trigger a "typologically predictable" stress reaction, and try to arrange at least a minimum amount of time for activities that replenish and reenergize preferred functions and attitudes. For example, an Introvert who anticipates with dread a week filled with lengthy daily meetings might plan her lunch hours alone in the park; a Feeling type who has to spend the week doing employee performance reviews might take extra time giving positive feedback to others.

Dynamic Types

What each type finds especially stressful in the workplace and typical reactions to stress are understandable and predictable from a knowledge of the characteristics of the dominant function of each type. Both theory and experience show that in general, what each type finds particularly stressful are activities and perspectives that disregard the core needs and values of the dominant function and force attention to the opposite, inferior, function. For example, ESTPs (dominant extraverted Sensing) will likely be stressed by having to spend a week working alone on a long-term strategic plan, an activity that requires use of their inferior introverted Intuition. ISFJs (dominant introverted Sensing) might find it stressful to be given a leadership role in a rapidly changing department.

Theory and experience also show that the types respond differently to moderate, short-term stress as compared to more extreme and long-lasting stress. The typical response to moderate stress is exaggeration of the dominant function—an overdoing of our natural reliance on the most comfortable and developed part of our personality. Barger and Kirby (1995a) describe each dominant function as it appears at its best as well as in exaggerated form. For example, dominant extraverted Intuitives (ENTP, ENFP), who by nature form global pictures and are fast paced, under moderate stress become obsessed with the links between things and spin out of control. Dominant extraverted Thinking types (ESTJ, ENTJ), who are naturally cool-headed and analytical, become coldly detached when in an exaggerated state and try to dominate others by criticizing them. The same principle applies to the dominant function of the other types.

More extreme and persistent stress is likely to call forth out-of-character reactions for each of the types. From a dynamic point of view, the exaggerated use of energy of the dominant function creates an imbalance that produces an equal but opposite expression of energy from the least developed, least experienced, and most uncontrollable function—the opposite, inferior, function. For example, an ESFJ (dominant extraverted Feeling) experiencing extreme stress may "change" from a congenial, helpful person who strives to affirm others to one who is bitingly critical, negative, and sarcastic. An INTP (dominant introverted Thinking) under great stress is likely to lose contact with her typical objectivity and detachment and become focused entirely on whether people like and appreciate her as a person.

Consult the resources in this section for publications that provide detailed discussions of the type-related triggers to stress and typical responses to and expressions of both moderate and more extreme stress.

The Advantages of Recognizing Stress in the Workplace

Type theory and the MBTI provide a rationale for individual responses to stress in the workplace, promote understanding of the sources and nature of what proves stressful for people, and encourage a helpful perspective for assessing and dealing with individuals, groups of individuals, and organizations under stress. Barger and Kirby (1995a) focused on the kind of stress that accompanies change and transition in organizations. They provide information and recommendations for dealing with change that are based on what is stressful for each type during change and what each type needs to make necessary changes as comfortably as possible. When people in organizations understand the dynamic character of each type, they are generally less surprised, angry, anxious, and frustrated by their own and others' reaction to organizational stress. Acceptance, understanding, tolerance, and a cooperative outlook become possible. At the very least, the ability to recognize the predictability of exaggerated and out-of-character reactions puts the assessment of such stress-stimulated behavior in perspective. People's exaggerated and out-of-character responses are then less likely to be seen as serious problems or permanent personality aberrations.

Resources

The Challenge of Change in Organizations (Barger & Kirby, 1995a) provides a wealth of material on types and their reactions to the stress of change and transition in today's organizational climate. Many examples and case studies are provided. *WORKTypes* (Kummerow, Barger, & Kirby, 1997) discusses stress as experienced by each type with examples illustrating stress responses. *Beside Ourselves: Our Hidden Personality in Everyday Life* (Quenk, 1993) gives the rationale for the eruption of the inferior function in response to more extreme and long-term stress and provides many examples and case studies of individual types as well as the interactions of types in personal and work relationships. In addition, a concise presentation of material about the inferior functions appears in the booklet *In the Grip* (Quenk, 1996), which is part of the *Introduction to Type* series. Also helpful is *Work It Out: Clues for Solving People Problems at Work* (Hirsh with Kise, 1996), which provides examples of the effects of the inferior function on different types in work situations.

Research for Practitioners

Recent research on type and stress-related physical condition, psychological issues, and coping behavior is covered in detail in Chapter 10 and summarized and discussed in tables 4.4–4.41 in Chapter 4. A detailed review of earlier research on health, stress, and coping appears in Shelton (1996). Of particular interest is research pinpointing the number and kinds of resources the types report in dealing with stress, as well as evidence that different types are affected differently by the environment. Hammer (summarized in Shelton, 1996) used the Coping Resource Inventory (CRI) to study type differences in a sample that included MBA students, residence hall workers, stress management program clients, and pain patients. The CRI measures cognitive, social, emotional, spiritual/philosophical,

Table 13.12   Ranking of Resources for Each Type

ISTJ (12)	**ISFJ (7)**	**INFJ (4)**	**INTJ (11)**
Cognitive (10)	Spiritual/Philosophical (4)	Spiritual/Philosophical (1)	Spiritual/Philosophical (3)
Spiritual/Philosophical (10)	Cognitive (5)	Cognitive (4)	Cognitive (7)
Social (11)	Social (5)	Physical (5)	Emotional (11)
Physical (11)	Physical (7)	Social (8)	Physical (13)
Emotional (13)	Emotional (10)	Emotional (9)	Social (14)

ISTP (9)	**ISFP (15)**	**INFP (13)**	**INTP (16)**
Spiritual/Philosophical (1)	Social (10)	Physical (9)	Physical (12)
Cognitive (4)	Spiritual/Philosophical (12)	Social (12)	Spiritual/Philosophical (14)
Physical (5)	Cognitive (14)	Cognitive (13)	Cognitive (15)
Social (16)	Emotional (15)	Spiritual/Philosophical (13)	Social (15)
Emotional (9)	Physical (16)	Emotional (14)	Emotional (16)

ESTP (14)	**ESFP (10)**	**ENFP (1)**	**ENTP (8)**
Physical (8)	Emotional (3)	Social (1)	Physical (6)
Emotional (12)	Social (6)	Emotional (1)	Emotional (6)
Social (13)	Cognitive (9)	Cognitive (2)	Social (9)
Spiritual/Philosophical (15)	Physical (15)	Physical (4)	Spiritual/Philosophical (9)
Cognitive (16)	Spiritual/Philosophical (16)	Spiritual/Philosophical (7)	Cognitive (11)

ESTJ (2)	**ESFJ (5)**	**ENFJ (3)**	**ENTJ (6)**
Cognitive (1)	Spiritual/Philosophical (2)	Social (3)	Physical (1)
Emotional (2)	Social (4)	Cognitive (3)	Cognitive (6)
Social (2)	Emotional (7)	Emotional (4)	Social (7)
Physical (3)	Cognitive (8)	Spiritual/Philosophical (5)	Spiritual/Philosophical (8)
Spiritual/Philosophical (11)	Physical (10)	Physical (14)	Emotional (8)

Note: Numbers in parentheses after each resource indicate where each type ranked on that resource compared to other types; numbers in parentheses after each type indicate the ranking of that type on total resources.

Source: From *MBTI Applications: A Decade of Research on the Myers-Briggs Type Indicator* (p.206), A. L. Hammer, editor, 1996. Palo Alto, CA: Consulting Psychologists Press. Copyright 1996 by Consulting Psychologists Press. Used with permission.

and physical coping resources. The types found to have the highest total resources were ENFP and ESTJ, and the type with the lowest score was INTP. Each type showed a different order of typical use of each of the five coping resources. For example, social resources had the top rank and physical resources the bottom rank for ENFJs; emotional was the top rank and spiritual/philosophical the bottom rank for ESFPs.

It can be quite helpful to be sensitive to the different ways that each type copes with stress. Just as each of us is likely to evaluate others' behavior from the point of view of our own type, so are we likely to assume that others cope with stress in the same way we do. When this happens, well-meaning efforts to help someone deal with stress can backfire and create even more stress for the individual. For example, suggesting to an ENFJ that he join an athletic club and work out every day would not be consistent with the low ranking of physical coping resources for ENFJs. Of

course, individual differences within a type might show that a particular ENFJ does in fact use such a coping resource. Table 13.12 shows the rankings of resources for each type, each type's rank as compared to all other types, and the ranking of each type on total resources.

The association of type preferences with different kinds of stressful stimuli was explored by Short and Grasha (1995) in a sample of managers. They looked at sources of stress, coping strategies, and personality moderator variables in relation to MBTI continuous scores. They found that sensation-seeking, assertiveness, and "social hardiness" were significantly associated with Extraversion; social stress was associated with Introversion; Thinking was correlated with Type A behavior, assertiveness, and perceptions of problem-solving skills; Judging was related to effective time management and Perceiving to sensation-seeking. As a result of a number of different analyses of their data, these researchers concluded that the E–I dichotomy was the best predictor of stress and coping and was also related to perceptions of stress. In addition, they found that results for the other dichotomies were limited to perceptions of coping rather than to stress itself. These findings with regard to the relation of Extraversion and Introversion to stress and coping variables are in accord with the findings of Hammer described earlier, as well as with a variety of results reported in Chapter 10 and summarized in Chapter 4.

Using the MBTI with Teams

Teams, teamwork, and team building are central concerns for practitioners working with organizations. Hammer and Huszczo (1996) reported that a survey of companies by the New York Stock Exchange in 1982 found that more than 80% of companies use teams for at least some parts of their work, and the use of teams has increased rapidly in the last few years (Wellins, Byham, & Wilson, 1991; Katzenbach & Smith, 1993).

The practitioner's job in working with teams is to facilitate their working together effectively, and the MBTI has proven to be a valuable tool in meeting this challenge. Myers and McCaulley pioneered the first use of the MBTI as a tool to increase team effectiveness in their work with health care teams in 1974 (Myers, 1974). Though type practitioners have developed a wide variety of new activities, exercises, and resource materials, the basic assumptions underlying using the MBTI with teams remain the same: Knowledge of individual differences will help teams identify the particular talents and gifts that each member brings to his or her task; and this knowledge can help reduce conflict by reframing potential sources of misunderstanding as natural individual differences.

Guidelines for Using Type with Teams

The general guidelines for using the MBTI in organizations (see section "Administering and Interpreting" at the end of this chapter) apply, and there are some additional ones that are especially helpful in working with teams:

- Introduce type and the MBTI with a specific goal, preferably to deal with a problem the team has identified: improve communication, enhance problem solving, team development, etc.
- As much as possible, place type and the MBTI within the context of everyday work. For example, after describing a preference, practitioners can ask the team to brainstorm ways the behaviors associated with this preference would contribute to teamwork.
- Use the MBTI early on in working with a team, rather than introducing it after conflicts have developed. When a team is struggling to agree on budgets, division of tasks, reporting, or other such issues, introducing the

MBTI to help address the conflict can lead to team members using type as an excuse or to stereotype people: "You're an S; *you* do the budget."
- Introduce type dynamics and development early on in your work with a team. Understanding one's own and others' dominant function assists in identifying core values and motivations; it gets at the heart of what people find rewarding and energizing at work. The recognition of what types extravert and introvert is crucial in team communication. This deeper level of type is invaluable to teams.
- Lead the team in a team type analysis: What preferences predominate in the group? Which are missing? What are the dominant functions? How may the distributions affect working together? For example, a team consisting of an ESTJ, an ENTJ, an ENFJ, an INTP, and an ISFP has all dominant Judging types. Recognizing this may lead the team to form agreements around gathering enough information before rushing to judgment. Likewise, a team consisting primarily of dominant Perceiving types may recognize that members need to push themselves to make decisions in a timely way, before they have all the information everyone would like to have.
- Provide information to the team about research findings on type and team effectiveness (see "Research for Practitioners" at the end of this section). Is there a variety of type perspectives? If not, how can the team integrate those other perspectives into its work?
- When disagreements or conflicts emerge, encourage team members to step back and ask themselves if type differences are playing a role. Even if they decide they are not, the mutual exploration can form the basis for dealing with the issues.

Negotiating Working Agreements

Traditionally, people in organizations worked within hierarchical structures, responsible to a superior for getting "their job" completed. Working on teams can produce exciting synergies and collegial support; it also raises issues of loss of autonomy, accountability to colleagues, the requirement of frequent communication, and group problem solving. Negotiating working agreements among team members is a crucial step in assisting people in learning to work together.

Practitioners can use type in negotiating working agreements. The first step is to generate what each team member needs to be able to contribute his or her best work.

Using Type Preference Dichotomies   Negotiating agreements works well at the type preference level when the team is introduced to type: What do those who prefer Extraversion need to be able to make a contribution to this team? Those who prefer Introversion? And so on through all the preferences.

The team can then proceed to negotiate around those identified needs. For example, a team can discuss how to plan and conduct meetings to provide what both Extraverts and Introverts need and therefore get the best that each has to offer:

- Do they need to allow more question and discussion time in the meetings so those who prefer Extraversion can process out loud?
- How far ahead do they need to send out agendas so those who prefer Introversion have time to reflect before having to respond?
- How can they ensure that those who prefer Introversion will have space in the meeting to share their thoughts?

Teams with both Sensing and Intuitive types sometimes designate a time in meetings for each kind of information: "Now it's time for Sensing information"; "now it's time for Intuitive connections and patterns." This ensures that people with each preference have encouragement to participate and that the group will get both kinds of perspectives.

The guiding value for the group is the constructive use of differences—the recognition that, for the team to get the benefit of what each member has to offer, it needs to allow time, space, and encouragement for the differences.

Using Type Dynamics Exploring ways to work together effectively can go to even deeper levels by using dynamics and/or the four-letter type. An initial way of exploring differences is to ask team members, individually or with others of the same type, "How do you define *team?*" Typically, basic definitions of what a team is and does reveal very clear type-related differences: E and F types usually define teams in terms of interactions and communication; F types usually mention collegiality and support; T types typically focus on tasks, effectiveness, and efficiency; and so on. This activity can lead to very profitable discussions of team members' expectations of each other.

Another activity that frequently produces valuable information for team members is asking individuals or team members of the same type to respond to questions such as the following: What does our type contribute to our team? What may our type overdo and overlook? What does our type need to do our best work? What annoys our type? After hearing from everyone on the team, members can explore what they can do to get the benefit of the contributions and to help out in each other's weaker areas.

When Team Members Don't Give the "Right" Answers

Practitioners sometimes worry that asking team members for such information by preference or by type may not produce the "right" answers; that is, they may not say what the research or type theory predicts they will say. There are a couple of ways to think about this that are reassuring.

First, when people have had a good introduction to type and an opportunity to verify their own type preferences, they are almost always able to apply the information to describe themselves at work. When people have verified their type but state that they are different from the description in a number of ways, it gives practitioners the opportunity to repeat a principle that needs repeating: Type does not explain everything. Every individual is unique, and while type may identify some underlying patterns, the ways in which those have been used and developed vary widely from person to person. Though type predicts group behavior (see Chapter 9 for a lot of evidence about this), it cannot confidently predict specific behaviors of any individual in every situation. Practitioners will be true to type theory when they respond by saying something like, "So this is the way you personally express your preference for Extraversion, and it sounds as though it's somewhat different from the ways others may express that same preference."

Second, even if an individual gives information that doesn't relate to type, it does relate to that individual and therefore is valuable to team members. Type's identification and affirmation of natural, normal differences among people often supports individuals in articulating individual needs. Team activities such as those described provide structure and encouragement for team members to ask for what they need—whether it's type related or not.

Making Decisions

Few employees have been taught processes for making decisions as a group. The type decision-making model described in an earlier section of this chapter is very helpful for teams and can provide a structure for discussion and deciding. It can also be quickly expanded to provide a structure based on type preference:

E: Share information and discuss.

I: Reflect and then talk.

S: Identify facts and realities.

N: Generate possibilities.

T: Analyze by likely outcomes.

F: Evaluate by values and relationships.

J: Make a plan.

P: Be open to changing the plan.

The ethic and perspective is the same as with other type discussions: Decisions will be stronger if all the perspectives are included.

Using a Team Type Analysis

Psychological type describes individual personality, and this needs to be explicitly recognized when discussing "team type." Used with this caution, however, analysis of team members' types and the ways they may characterize the group can provide a valuable tool for analyzing where the team is effective and where it can improve.

Looking at preference distributions or at a team type table, for example, allows practitioners to raise questions about the internal working of the team: How do you deal with the Sensing–Intuition differences in the group? Do your plans have enough flexibility for your Perceiving types?

It can also lead to profitable discussions about external relationships—with supervisors or interacting with other teams: With our team preference for Introversion, do we give enough information, often enough, for those outside the team?

The issue of team type similarity or difference is important to explore with the group. The research on type and teams (see "Research for Practitioners" in this section) indicates that teams consisting of individuals with similar communication styles work together more easily and may arrive at decisions more quickly. Teams with differing communication styles take more time to make decisions but may produce outcomes of better quality.

Type Is Not an Appropriate Tool for Selection to Teams

Neither the team nor practitioners should use MBTI results to select team members. This is because the MBTI was designed to assist people in identifying their psychological type preferences. It was *not* designed to indicate how well an individual uses preferences, the skills a person has developed related to type preferences, or other skills related to nonpreferred areas.

The crucial question for the team and practitioner is, given our type distributions, how can we make the best use of each team member and our type knowledge to be as effective as possible?

It is not unusual on small teams to find that members have a lot of type similarity and therefore may be missing some of the benefits of diverse perspectives. The question to pursue with teams with type similarity is, How can we include other perspectives?

When team members have a lot of type differences, it may be reassuring to them to know that, if they can learn to use their differences, they can function very effectively.

Other Team Relationship Issues

The other primary team relationship issue practitioners are asked to address is building team spirit, and practitioners have a number of group development tools—unrelated to type—that contribute to this goal. Integrating the MBTI and type into team-building sessions can enhance the impact and value of these other activities as it affirms differences in the ways people participate and respond.

One type activity that can build knowledge and trust on teams is using Jung's developmental model to generate one-on-one or group discussions: What function(s) have you been called on to use in the workplace? What kinds of feedback from managers or peers have you received about your

use of these? When you think about using a different side of yourself, what concerns you? In development, it is important to be able to draw on all parts of oneself. Which MBTI functions present the greatest challenge to you as you think about using them? *Introduction to Type Dynamics and Development* (Myers & Kirby, 1994) includes questions for exploring one's own development, and with modification these can provide opportunities for team members to see each other in different ways, to expand their knowledge and understanding of each other, and to develop trust.

Team Leaders

Most teams have someone who is the coach or leader, and exploring the impact of the leader's type preferences is a valuable team exercise. If leaders are comfortable with this approach, they can point out portions of their type description that seem particularly important or characteristic of them. They can use their type description and that of other team members to discuss issues in communication, feedback, appreciation, and other topics of importance to the group.

Resources

It's important to start with *Introduction to Type* (Myers, with Kirby & Myers, 1998) and individual type verification. The demands of the team and team tasks can influence the way people respond to the Indicator and their own self-estimate of their type, so it's doubly important to focus on individual clarity about type first.

Sandra Hirsh's (1998) *Introduction to Type and Teams* is a useful booklet for working with teams. Hirsh's (1992a, 1992b) *MBTI Team Building Program Leader's Resource Guide* and *Team Member's Guide* provide reproducible masters and activities for teams. Topics include planning team-building sessions, analyzing a team using type, communication styles, work environments, organizational change, organizational culture, and stress and type.

Other resources mentioned earlier in this chapter also have specific sections on teams or information that can be used with teams: *Introduction to Type in Organizations* (Hirsh & Kummerow, 1998), *WORKTypes* (Kummerow, Barger, & Kirby, 1997), and *Work It Out* (Hirsh & Kise, 1996).

Research for Practitioners

Hammer and Huszczo (1996) summarized and analyzed extensive research on type and teams. This information is very useful to practitioners and will be interesting to most team members. The following is a brief summary of some of their conclusions, based on their analysis of the research.

Conflict Styles Differences in preferred styles of dealing with conflict (see section in this chapter) are very relevant to team functioning and can be explored with excellent results.

Extraversion–Introversion Several studies correlating FIRO-B results and CPI results with type preferences indicate

Table 13.13   Summary of Other Studies Using the Team as the Unit of Analysis

Study	Results
Blaylock, 1983	Diverse groups performed significantly better and more consistently than similar groups; no difference on perceptions of conflict or compatibility.
Webster & Howard, 1989	Diversity positively correlated with performance.
Scholl, 1975	Diverse groups had lower quality of presentation on production task (grammatical, theoretical, and literary qualities of the written product), but better performance on a structured problem-solving task; regardless of task, similar groups took significantly less time; some evidence that outcomes are task dependent.
McCary, 1970	No differences were found between similar and diverse groups on self-concept or trait anxiety; there was a curvilinear relationship (inverted U) between time and state anxiety for the diverse group.
Metts, 1995	E–I, S–N, and J–P diversity and T–F similarity related to higher quality; diversity on J–P was associated with a number of outcome measures, while similarity on this dichotomy was associated with higher ratings on process variables; the set of four MBTI diversity measures was the best predictor of the teams' own ratings of their overall quality; signs of regression coefficients indicated that the ratings of team quality were related primarily to similarity on the T–F dichotomy and diversity on the J–P dichotomy.
Kandell, 1991	Diverse-type groups performed significantly better than similar-type groups; working as a group resulted in a "synergy" that increased performance over the sum of individuals' performance; a significant interaction effect demonstrating that group synergy was greater for the diverse than for the similar groups.
Futrell, 1992	Correlations between heterogeneity and production and quality were low and nonsignificant; the partial correlation of J–P with production was significant.
Brocato, 1985	Type-similar teams worked more quickly than type-diverse teams; no differences in effectiveness on a structured task; on an ambiguous task, the product of the type-diverse teams was rated as being of significantly higher quality.

Source: From *MBTI Applications: A Decade of Research on the Myers-Briggs Type Indicator* (p. 92), A. L. Hammer (Ed.), 1996. Palo Alto, CA: Consulting Psychologists Press. Copyright 1996 by Consulting Psychologists Press. Adapted with permission.

that the Extraversion–Introversion dichotomy is extremely important in understanding team interactions. Many of the values and behaviors identified in literature on teams as important to team functioning correlate with Extraversion on the MBTI. Hammer and Huszczo ask if teams are fully utilizing Introversion.

Similarity and Difference in Team Communication Styles

Hammer and Huszczo reported results of several studies analyzing similarities and differences among team members. The studies that may be of most interest to team members and practitioners take the following approach: Using intact work teams, researchers determine the type of each individual on the team, compute a "similarity index," and then correlate the index with various measures of process and outcomes.

For example, Hammer and Huszczo reported on studies using the *Team Communication Adjustment Index* (TCAI), a tool that identifies communication styles and is consistent with type theory. Their analysis and summary of these studies is presented in Table 13.13.

In brief, they found the following:

Teams with similar communication styles
- Perform their tasks more quickly
- Experience less conflict

- Like each other more
- Listen to one another more

Teams with diverse communication styles
- Are more effective
- Produce better outcomes
- May take more time

Team Leaders Surveying the research in this area, Hammer and Huszczo concluded that MBTI preferences were predictors of values related to leader-member interactions and satisfaction:

- Managers or leaders with MBTI preferences for E and F were generally rated higher on teamwork variables.
- Managers or leaders with NTP preferences, especially INTP, were found to value self-oriented individualism, a value that research on teams indicates interferes with teamwork.
- Leaders who were different in type from the team, especially on the Thinking–Feeling dichotomy, were rated by team members as more effective than leaders who were the same as the team.
- In a study of participative management, all types were able to learn the needed skills, but Feeling types were more able to use the participative leadership style.

Summary

Because the MBTI focuses on self-understanding, understanding others, and appreciation of differences, it is a valuable tool in working with teams. Integrating the MBTI into team interactions, agreements, communication, and decision making provides a language and a structure for creating teams that adds value for team members and for the organization.

Using the MBTI in Leadership Development and Coaching

Leadership development, management training, coaching executives—by whatever name, this is one of the fastest growing areas in organizational development activity. *Consulting Psychology Journal* (Kilburg, 1996) published a special edition on executive coaching; leadership institutes are presenting entire conferences focusing on executive coaching; large organizations such as the Center for Creative Leadership have succeeded remarkably, focusing entirely on management and leadership development; and the question of effective leadership has produced a massive volume of literature.

The analyses of effective leadership and recommendations can be overwhelming to managers and leaders. This chapter will not survey the literature on leadership (for this, see Fitzgerald, 1997a), but professionals who work in leadership development need to do so and find ways to make the information manageable and relevant to those with whom they work. Assuming the professional's expertise in leadership, this section focuses on appropriate and beneficial ways to use the MBTI in leadership development activities.

Use of the MBTI in Leadership Development

According to Fitzgerald (1997b), "The *Myers-Briggs Type Indicator* (MBTI) has become a key resource in leadership development and is widely used in leadership development training and executive coaching" (p. 311). One of the largest sources of data on managers, leaders, and leadership development is the Center for Creative Leadership, which has used the MBTI and psychological type with its participants in group and individual work since 1982.

Fitzgerald (1997b) also pointed out the limitations of the ways the MBTI is used by most professionals in this area by defining "three levels of use" (p. 311): level 1, which uses the type dichotomies; level 2, which introduces and uses type dynamics; and level 3, which uses the type development model. Type dynamics and development have been largely untapped in leadership development work and offer powerful potentials for increasing leader effectiveness and growth.

All of the earlier sections in this chapter offer information that can be readily applied to using the MBTI in leadership development: improving communication, dealing with conflicts, enhancing problem solving and decision making, dealing with organizational change, managing stress, and using the MBTI with teams. Placed in the leadership context, these all provide valuable information for leaders and practical applications for professionals working with them. This chapter will focus primarily on what Fitzgerald terms levels 2 and 3: using type dynamics and development with leaders.

Thinking–Judging Leadership Styles

The overrepresentation of managers who prefer the combination of Thinking and Judging on the MBTI is well documented in a wide variety of studies and in data from a wide variety of cultures (Reynierse, 1997; Fleenor, 1997; Kirby, 1997; Fitzgerald & Kirby, 1997b). Kirby suggested the following explanation:

> The structure and values of organizations seem to have favored the logical and decisive behaviors most comfortable to those preferring Thinking and Judging, but that are less natural or comfortable to the three other comparable combinations of preferences—Feeling and Judging, Feeling and Perceiving, and Thinking and Perceiving. Because Thinking and Judging types are so prevalent in organizational leadership, it may be that Thinking and Judging behaviors have become the accepted definition of what it means to lead, and, therefore, people displaying these behaviors are seen as "leadership material." Other styles of leading may then not be seen as "leadership" because they do not fit the standard definition. (Kirby, 1997, p. 18)

The Challenges This Presents Whatever the causes for this phenomenon, professionals working in leadership development will usually find themselves interacting with a majority of TJs. The challenge for practitioners is to understand and support the natural style and developed skills of TJ leaders while assisting them in seeing the benefits of modifying those skills and that style.

The corollary to the preponderance of TJs in management is that managers with different combinations of preferences normally will have developed a number of skills and behaviors related to Thinking and Judging. With such TJ skills encouraged and supported by their environment, they may not have valued or developed their own natural style of leadership. According to type theory, people are most effective when they have developed their own natural style and then learned to use nonpreferred areas as appropriate. For some leaders who are not TJs, this development of their natural way of leading may not have occurred, as the organizational cultures in which they have worked and succeeded may not have supported such development.

Thinking–Judging Strengths and Weaknesses as Leaders

Research and practice (Barger & Kirby, 1995a) have identified a number of components of TJ leadership style. It is important to remember that these are characteristics of groups of TJs, and individual leaders with those preferences may vary on any number of these qualities and behaviors.

Strengths in leadership associated with Thinking–Judging:

- Focus on creating logical order and structures in the organization and its processes
- Focus on achieving organizational goals
- Use logical reasoning to quickly analyze problems
- Are decisive—make decisions quickly and with confidence
- Move to implement decisions quickly and with confidence
- Emphasize efficiency
- Value competence, set high standards for themselves and others

They may give less attention and energy to, and therefore be less skilled in, some other behaviors that contribute to effective managing and leading.

Weaknesses in leadership associated with Thinking–Judging:

- Creating logical structures that unintentionally limit others' flexibility, creativity, and perspectives
- Emphasizing efficiency *over* inclusion and consultation—failing to involve others in analysis and decision making
- Moving so quickly to decisions that they don't allow the amount of process time others need
- Being so decisive and confident that they make decisions before they have gathered enough information
- Focusing so strongly on achieving goals that they refuse to reopen decisions based on new information
- Placing such value on their own high standards that they fail to recognize alternative standards and positive contributions from others that are different from theirs

Fortunately, much of the current leadership literature includes recognition of the need to develop some of the behaviors that are not naturally part of the TJ style, and many organizational development programs identify skills more naturally related to Feeling and Perceiving preferences as necessary for effective leadership in changing organizations. Thinking–Judging leaders highly value being competent and effective. Using the MBTI allows practitioners to affirm their competence and effectiveness while helping them identify areas where they can improve.

Emphasizing Process, Inclusion, and Flexibility

One of the hardest tasks for Thinking managers, especially those who combine Thinking with Extraversion, is recognizing the process and inclusion needs of others and finding ways to support those. Using type can help identify others' needs for process and inclusion. Thinking types will be particularly receptive to this information if it comes from a respected colleague, someone whose leadership abilities they recognize and who can express these needs in terms of his or her own natural style.

Another effective vehicle for communicating these needs to leaders is using other instruments to provide practical, specific feedback about their style and its impacts. A variety of 360-degree feedback instruments can serve this purpose (Van Velsor & Fleenor, 1997; Fleenor, 1997), giving leaders specific information related to their effectiveness or lack of effectiveness. Practitioners can also make use of information from the *Leadership Styles Inventory* (LSI) and the CPI (Pearman & Fleenor, 1996; Fleenor, 1997), and *Systematic Multiple-Level Observation of Groups* (SYMLOG; Sundstrom & Busby, 1997) in identifying common strengths and weaknesses in leadership by type.

The information provided by looking at other instruments enables practitioners to appreciate some of the nuances that make whole dynamic types different from one another. For example, Table 13.14 presents type data in relation to the 20 CPI Folk Concept Scales. The table shows the types whose mean score was significantly higher or lower than the total sample mean on each scale. Because the sample size was large (15,102 participants in Center for Creative Leadership training programs), only mean differences significant at p < .001 are shown. In interpreting these data, it is important to bear in mind that scores on the CPI scales for all types represent variations within the normal range of each scale. The meaning of high and low scores is shown in the table to discourage misunderstanding of some of the scale names. Note, for example, that although a number of scales seem to differentiate between types preferring Extraversion and those preferring Introversion, there are Extraverted and Introverted types that *don't* appear with the other types with the same attitude. One can thus explore some of the subtle differences in the way a person's whole type differently affects the behavior encompassed by a particular CPI scale. Note that these same CPI data are presented for each type in Chapter 4, Tables 4.26–4.41, and are also discussed in Chapter 9 as evidence of the validity of whole type.

Research from the national sample correlating the *Emotion Quotient Inventory* (EQI) with MBTI results may also provide useful feedback. The small sample size (N = 139) supported only a correlational analysis in relation to the four dichotomies. Results are reported below.

- Extraversion was found to correlate (*p* values significant at <.001) with the following EQI scales:
  Assertiveness
  Emotionality
  Empathy
  Flexibility
  Happiness
  Interpersonal Relations
  Optimism
  Self-Actualization
  Self-Regulation
  Total Adaptability
  Total Emotion Quotient Index
  General Mood
  Total Interpersonal
  Total Stress Management

Table 13.14   Higher and Lower Scoring Types on the 20 Folk Concept Scales of the CPI

Kind of Measure, Scale Name, Meaning of Higher and Lower Scores		High Types	Low Types
Poise, Self-Assurance, Interpersonal Proclivities Scales			
Dominance (Do)	*Higher:* confident, assertive, dominant, task oriented *Lower:* cautious, quiet, hesitant to take initiative	ESTP; ENFP; ENTP; ESTJ; ENFJ; ENTJ	ISTJ; ISFJ; INFJ; INTJ; ISTP; ISFP; INFP; INTP
Capacity for Status (Cs)	*Higher:* ambitious, wants to be success, many interests *Lower:* unsure of self, dislikes direct competition, uncomfortable with uncertainty or complexity	ENFP; ENTP; ENFJ; ENTJ	ISTJ; ISFJ; ISTP; ISFP
Sociability (Sy)	*Higher:* sociable, likes to be with people, outgoing *Lower:* shy, often inhibited, prefers to stay in background in social situations	ESTP; ESFP; ENFP; ENTP; ESTJ; ESFJ; ENFJ; ENTJ	ISTJ; ISFJ; INFJ; INTJ; ISTP; ISFP; INFP; INTP
Social Presence (Sp)	*Higher:* self-assured, spontaneous, versatile, verbally fluent, pleasure-seeking *Lower:* reserved, hesitant to express own views, self-denying	ESTP; ENFP; ENTP; ESTJ; ENFJ; ENTJ	ISTJ; ISFJ; INFJ; INTJ; ISTP; ISFP; INFP
Self-Acceptance (Sa)	*Higher:* has good opinion of self, sees self as talented, personally attractive, talkative *Lower:* self-doubting, readily assumes blame, often thinks others are better, gives in easily	ESTP; ENFP; ENTP; ESTJ; ENFJ; ENTJ	ISFJ; INFJ; INTJ; ISTP; ISFP; INFP; INTP
Independence (In)	*Higher:* self-sufficient, resourceful, detached, persistent to goals regardless of others' agreement *Lower:* lacks self-confidence, seeks support, tries to avoid conflict, difficulty making decisions	INTP; ENFP; ENTP	ISTJ; ISFJ; INFJ; ISTP; ISFP; ESFJ
Empathy (Em)	*Higher:* comfortable about self, well accepted by others, perceptive of social nuances and others' feelings, optimistic *Lower:* unempathetic, skeptical about others' intentions, defensive, limited range of interests	ENFP; ENTP; ENFJ; ENTJ	ISTJ; ISFJ; INTJ; ISTP; ISFP
Normative Orientation and Values Scales			
Responsibility (Re)	*Higher:* responsible, reliable, ethically perceptive, serious about duties and obligations *Lower:* self-indulgent, undisciplined, careless, indifferent to personal obligations	INTJ; ENFJ; ENTJ	ISTP; ISFP; INTP; ESTP; ENTP
Socialization (So)	*Higher:* conscientious, well-organized, easily conforms to rules, seldom gets in trouble *Lower:* resists rules, dislikes conforming, rebellious, gets in trouble, has unconventional views	ISTJ; ESFJ; ENTJ	ENFP; ENTP
Self-Control (Sc)	*Higher:* tries to control emotions and temper, suppresses hostile and erotic feelings, prides self on self-discipline *Lower:* has strong feelings and emotions and makes little effort to hide them, problems with undercontrol and impulsivity, likes new experiences	ISTJ	INFP; ISTP; ESFP; ENFP; ENTP
Good Impression (Gi)	*Higher:* wants to make good impression, tries to please, is conventional, formal, and conservative *Lower:* insists on being self even if causes friction, dissatisfied in many situations, often complains, easily annoyed and irritated	ESTJ; ENFJ; ENTJ	INFJ; INTJ; ISTP; ISFP; INFP; INTP; ENFP
Communality (Cm)	*Higher:* fits in easily, reasonable, sees self as average person, makes little effort to change things *Lower:* sees self as different, not conventional or conforming, changeable and moody	ISTJ; ESTJ; ESFJ	INFP; INTP; ENFP; ENTP

Table 13.14   Higher and Lower Scoring Types on the 20 Folk Concept Scales of the CPI *continued*

Kind of Measure, Scale Name, Meaning of Higher and Lower Scores			High Types	Low Types
Normative Orientation and Values Scales				
Well-being (Wb)	Higher:	feels self in good physical and mental health, optimistic about future, cheerful	ESTJ; ENTJ	ISTJ; ISFJ; INFJ; ISTP; ISFP; INFP; INTP
	Lower:	concerned about health or personal problems, tends to complain about unfair treatment or is pessimistic		
Tolerance (To)	Higher:	tolerant of others' beliefs and values even when different from own, fair-minded, reasonable, tactful	ENFP; ENTP; ESTJ; ENTJ	ISTJ; ISFJ; ISTP; ISFP; ESTP
	Lower:	distrustful, fault-finding, extrapunitive, often has hostile or vindictive feelings		
Cognitive and Intellectual Functioning Scales				
Achievement via Conformance (Ac)	Higher:	has strong will to do well, likes working in setting with clear definitions of tasks and expectations, efficient, well-organized	INTJ; ESTJ; ESFJ; ENTJ	ISTP; ISFP; INFP; INTP; ESTP; ESFP; ENFP; ENTP
	Lower:	difficulty working in setting with strict rules and regulations, easily distracted, tends to stop working when things do not go well		
Achievement via Independence (Ai)	Higher:	has strong drive to do well, likes working in settings that encourage freedom and individual initiative, clear thinking, intelligent	INFJ; INTJ; INFP; INTP; ENFP; ENTP; ENFJ; ENTJ	ISTJ; ISFJ; ISTP; ISFP; ESTP; ESTJ; ESFJ
	Lower:	has difficulty doing best work in vague and poorly defined settings that lack precise specifications, limited interests in intellectual/ cognitive endeavors		
Intellectual Efficiency (Ie)	Higher:	efficient in use of intellectual abilities, keeps on task where others might give up, insightful, resourceful	INTJ; INTP; ENFP; ENTP; ENFJ; ENTJ	ISTJ; ISFJ; ISTP; ISFP; ESTP; ESTJ; ESFJ
	Lower:	has hard time starting on cognitive tasks and seeing through to completion, has difficulty expressing ideas		
Role and Personal Style Scales				
Psychological-Mindedness (Py)	Higher:	insightful, perceptive, understands others' feelings but not necessarily supportive, nurturant	INTJ; INTP; ENFJ; ENTJ	ISTJ; ISFJ; ISTP; ISFP; ESTP; ESFP; ESTJ; ESFJ
	Lower:	more interested in the practical and concrete than abstract, attends more to what people do than how they think or feel		
Flexibility (Fx)	Higher:	flexible; likes change and variety; easily bored by routine, everyday experience; may be impatient; clever, imaginative	INFP; INTP; ESTP; ENFP; ENTP; ENFJ; ENTJ	ISTJ; ISFJ; ESTJ; ESFJ
	Lower:	not changeable; likes steady pace and well-organized, predictable situations; conventional and conservative		
Femininity/ Masculinity (F/M)	Higher:	among males, seen as high-strung, sensitive, esthetically reactive; females seen as sympathetic, warm, modest, dependent	ISTJ; ISFJ; INFJ; INTJ; ISFP; INFP; ESFJ	ENTP; ESTJ; ENTJ
	Lower:	decisive, action-oriented, shows initiative, not easily subdued, unsentimental, tough-minded		

Note: Types shown had means that were significantly higher or lower than the sample mean at $p < .001$. Means for all types fall within the normal range.

Source: From "The Relationship Between the MBTI and Measures of Personality and Performance in Management Groups," by J. W. Fleenor, 1997, in *Developing Leaders,* p. 126. Palo Alto, CA: Davies-Black. Copyright 1997 by Davies-Black. Adapted with permission.

■ No EQI scales were correlated with the MBTI S–N dichotomy.

■ Assertiveness ($p < .003$), Independence ($p < .005$), Stress Management ($p < .040$), and Total Adaptability ($p < .054$) were correlated with Thinking.

■ Empathy ($p < .001$), Interpersonal ($p < .009$), Problem Solving ($p < .044$), Social Responsibility ($p < .000$) and Total Interpersonal ($p < .000$) were correlated with Feeling.

■ Impulse Control ($p < .003$), Problem Solving ($p < .002$), Reality Testing ($p < .007$), and Total Stress Management ($p < .030$) were correlated with Judging.

The need for added flexibility, for rethinking decisions and making midcourse corrections, and for learning to operate without fixed structures can be amply illustrated through any of the literature on organizational change. This recognition will be most effective if Thinking–Judging types can be led to reflect on some of their own decisions that produced unanticipated results and to analyze how the results might have been positively affected by having more flexible and changeable plans.

Once these needs are recognized, Thinking types want logical explanations and practical information about how to develop new skills. Within this context they will respond quickly to learn active listening, ways to acknowledge the contributions of others, how to give positive feedback, and so on.

It's important to emphasize with clients that these new skills will add positive dimensions to skills already developed, not change them into a different kind of person, and that they need to continue to be authentic in their leadership.

Other Leadership Styles

Similar steps can be followed in working with TP, FJ, and FP leaders. In these cases, professionals may also want to explore where and how these leaders have been able to develop their own natural strengths. If these strengths have not been supported, working together to identify their benefits to the organization and avenues for using them can be very profitable in the leaders' development and confidence.

Coaching Individuals

All of the information above can be used in coaching individuals. One effective approach is to use this information early on in the coaching relationship, as part of building the trust necessary for effective coaching. Professionals can lead clients through a process of identifying client leadership strengths related to type and then can work with the client to examine differences between that and the professional's own type-related strengths. Coach and client can then negotiate around their differences using questions such as these: What is important to you in our relationship? What behaviors on my part will respect and honor what's important to you? Which of my strengths would you like to know more about? Will you help me learn more about some of your specific strengths? The process must of course remain focused on the client, rather than the practitioner.

Using this approach encourages a climate of mutual respect and trust while assisting leaders in analyzing their own style. It also models appreciation and negotiation of differences, valuable components of leadership.

Using Type Dynamics

Using the TJ, TP, FJ, and FP combinations in the beginning with leaders is very effective: The applications and the value of the information and process are readily apparent. Because these combinations include the J–P dichotomy, this approach leads naturally into explaining type dynamics (see the earlier section in this chapter "Introducing and Using the Dynamic and Developmental Aspects of Type").

Using type dynamics with leaders provides the following benefits (Fitzgerald & Kirby, 1997a):

1. *It clarifies the relationship between a leader's inner processing and outward functioning.* Because leaders must operate so much in the Extraverted world, they, as well as their followers, may fail to recognize and appreciate their Introverted parts. This can be particularly important for leaders who prefer Introversion and therefore use their dominant function internally, but it's also important for those who prefer Extraversion.

    For example, ENTJ leaders may customarily interact with colleagues and subordinates in ways appropriate and consistent with their dominant extraverted Thinking. They may fail to make others aware of their internal Intuitive processing and give others the impression that they are "all judgment," no information.

2. *It provides a basis for analyzing the relationship between a leader's perception and judgment.* Which function is dominant? Is the auxiliary function well developed? Does it provide the balance that will produce the most effective leadership?

    For example, ESTJ leaders may recognize that their drive for achieving goals efficiently may sometimes lead them to spend too little time consulting their introverted Sensing auxiliary—especially in fast-paced environments requiring quick decisions and actions.

3. *It can increase leaders' self-understanding and their recognition of the impacts they have on their followers.* For example, INFP leaders can recognize that their most important part—their central core of values by which they evaluate everything—seldom gets expressed as they use their auxiliary extraverted Intuition to perform effectively as a leader. The part that is most important to INFPs—their introverted Feeling—is often not known to followers, who can find the leader difficult to understand and feel puzzled about how to meet the leader's expectations. This recognition can lead to explorations of ways INFPs can communicate these personal values effectively to those they lead.

4. *It suggests specific target areas for developing additional leadership skills and some strategies for beginning.* For example, ISTJ leaders may recognize and appreciate the leadership skills exhibited by those who naturally extravert Feeling judgment. Examination of common characteristics of Extraverted Feeling types can provide practical goals for ISTJ development.

5. *It gives a structure for understanding some of the impacts of stress on leadership style.* For example,

ENFJ leaders may recognize that, under stress, they tend to exaggerate their dominant extraverted Feeling to the point of great annoyance to others (see section "Managing Stress" earlier in this chapter). They may focus on finding consensus and harmony when it's time to move on and may be intrusive in their insistence on "helping" others. Recognizing these stress-related behaviors is the first step in learning to deal more effectively with the stresses faced by all leaders.

Using Type Development with Leaders

Type development adds another dimension to leadership development, offering rewards in personal understanding and development as well as growth as a leader. Jung's developmental model, described in Chapter 3 of this manual, can be communicated quickly to leaders and then offers the following opportunities for leadership and personal development:

■ Analyzing development of the dominant and auxiliary functions: How have individuals used these preferred areas? Where in their work and personal life have they found encouragement and support for their development and use? Can they identify areas in their current and future work life where they can effectively apply these?

■ Evaluating their balance—between Extraversion and Introversion and between perception and judgment: Have they developed effective ways of being in the world and drawing on inner resources? Do they have reliable, trustworthy ways of taking in information and of making decisions? Has the press of family, culture, work, or other environmental factors led to a lack of development in one of their preferred areas?

■ Exploring the possibilities of midlife development: What is midlife? How do different types experience it? What issues does it present for leaders? What opportunities does it open up?

■ Discussing maturity and wisdom: What does it mean to have mature judgment? Who have you known whom you considered wise? What characteristics do you associate with that? What positive qualities are described by Jung's concept of individuation? How can you move toward those qualities?

Perhaps because so many leaders in organizations in the 1990s are in some stage of midlife, exploring these kinds of issues leads to exciting discoveries. It can also be reassuring to those who have been struggling to understand their own changes in interest and energy. The developmental model assists them in seeing that these are not puzzling individual weaknesses or confusing symptoms but instead a natural development that can produce beneficial results.

Guidelines for Using Type Dynamics and Development with Leaders

Fitzgerald (1997b) and Fitzgerald & Kirby (1997a) offer suggestions for using dynamics and development in leadership development and executive coaching. The following is a brief summary:

■ Analyze the impact of the function that is *extraverted*. For example, leaders who extravert Thinking may need to hear the impact their logical dissection of problems can have on others and explore ways to provide more positive feedback.

■ Analyze the impact of the function that is *introverted*. For example, leaders who introvert their perceiving function may want to learn how to give others the information they have inside that has guided their Extraverted decisions.

■ Explore the relative emphasis on perception versus judgment. For example, leaders who prefer Judging may want to develop ways to feel comfortable putting off decisions while more information is gathered; those who prefer Perceiving may need to develop comfort in sometimes making decisions without perfect information.

■ Explore the relative emphasis on the outer world, extraverting, versus the inner world, introverting. For example, leaders may find that the fast pace and demands of their environment have resulted in their not giving their Introverted part an opportunity to play a role. Whether that is their perceiving function or their judging function, they will be missing some of their own important strengths if they have not found time and space for their Introversion to play a role.

■ Contrast leaders' type dynamics with those of colleagues or subordinates. For example, exploring what each extraverts and introverts can illuminate long-standing misunderstandings and provide new ways for them to connect.

■ Explore the impacts of leaders' tertiary and inferior functions. For example, have Sensing leaders learned to use and trust their Intuition when that is appropriate? Have Thinking leaders learned to listen to their Feeling?

■ Give opportunities to discuss leaders' inferior functions, especially ways in which it may function as their Achilles heel. For example, are there some things they always overlook? Are there some areas where they never seem to learn from experience?

■ Discuss emergence of the nonpreferred functions at midlife and beyond. For example, for a dominant extraverted Intuitive, what does emerging introverted Sensing look like?

■ Analyze leaders' environments and demands in terms of current and potential use of their strengths and opportunities for development. For example, can a dominant

Feeling type find areas at work to contribute the strengths of that function?

Jung's concept of lifelong growth is extremely appealing to clients. For many, it opens up exciting opportunities personally and professionally. Fitzgerald's chapter (1997b) on using type development with leaders is subtitled "Integrating Reality and Vision, Mind and Heart." The subtitle describes what leaders need to be more effective.

Resources

The recommended resource for introducing type is *Introduction to Type* (Myers, with Kirby & Myers, 1998). Using this booklet keeps the initial focus where it needs to be: identifying leaders' type apart from their work and the roles they play. *Introduction to Type in Organizations* (Hirsh & Kummerow, 1998) provides type descriptions that relate specifically to work and include each type's normal leadership style. *Introduction to Type Dynamics and Development* (Myers & Kirby, 1994) provides the basis for using dynamics and development with leaders, including information that will be helpful in all the suggested applications above.

Hardwired Leadership (Pearman, 1998) provides insights into personality style and shows how to enhance your leadership style to increase personal and work effectiveness and transform group efforts into meaningful results.

Developing Leaders (Fitzgerald & Kirby, 1997b) includes an introduction to the MBTI and discussion of the impacts of MBTI types of leaders (Chapter 1); an analysis of the MBTI and leadership development, including a survey of the literature on leadership (Chapter 2); a chapter on using type dynamics with leaders and another on using type development; and seven specific applications chapters, including using the MBTI with management simulations, using the MBTI Step II with managers, STJs and organizational change, and strategies for improving leaders' communication.

WORK Types (Kummerow, Barger, & Kirby, 1997) includes a chapter on leadership that examines TJ, TP, FJ, and FP leadership styles and offers advice for leaders on improving decision making. Barr and Barr (1994) integrate the MBTI into their *Leadership Development: Maturity and Power,* providing descriptions, analysis, and development activities.

Research for Practitioners

The research literature on the MBTI and management/leadership is extensive and can be overwhelming—to practitioners as well as their clients. Walck has published three surveys and analyses of research in this area: "Psychological Type and Management Research: A Review" (1992); "Management and Leadership" (1996); and "Using the MBTI in Management and Leadership: A Review of the Literature" (1997). Each of these has extensive references to literature and will provide a useful starting point for practitioners to identify research findings that will be relevant in their work.

Using the MBTI with Other Instruments Most leadership development programs and coaching interactions involve use of more than one instrument for providing feedback to leaders. This is appropriate: Different instruments are designed to identify a variety of characteristics and behaviors important to leaders, and use of instruments looking at different aspects adds value for leaders.

It is important for professionals to assist leaders in integrating this information (Fleenor, 1997). In using the MBTI with other instruments, practitioners need to explore research studies relating the MBTI to those other instruments and be prepared to give concise information to clients that will assist them in making use of the information, rather than being overwhelmed by sometimes conflicting data. *Developing Leaders* (Fitzgerald & Kirby, 1997b) includes six chapters reporting research using the MBTI with leaders, including the relationship between the MBTI and several 360-degree feedback instruments and other measures of leadership. It also includes a model for using two instruments together in Schnell and Hammer, "Integrating the FIRO-B with the MBTI: Relationships, Case Examples, and Interpretation Strategies." The *Journal of Psychological Type* is the other primary source for reports of studies on the MBTI and other instruments. Practitioners are urged to consult these resources to assist their use of the MBTI with other instruments, as well as to expand their understanding of common effects of the MBTI preferences in management styles and behaviors.

Using Type in Analyzing Organizations

Psychological type describes individual personality structures; therefore application of type categories to groups such as teams, organizations, and cultures must always proceed with caution, and practitioners cannot assume that knowledge of a particular type's dynamics can be transferred directly to the dynamics of groups.

With that caveat, type can play a useful part in analyzing organizations and providing valuable information about organizational culture and presses on individuals in the organizational environment. The concept of environmental press (Brehm & Kassin, 1993) states that, at some point, groups have enough uniform behaviors, attitudes, and values that group members are expected to conform. Applied to organizations, it is similar to the more familiar concept of organizational cultures that, like other cultures, identify appropriate behavior, manners, dress, values, and so on.

Analyzing Organizational Character

William Bridges (1992a) developed an approach to analyzing the "character of organizations" using Jungian type categories and the type dichotomies of the MBTI. He is careful to point out that simply adding together the number of people with each type preference to determine which are in the majority does not indicate an organization's character (a position supported by comparing type distributions in national samples to analyses of cultural values). Instead, he describes organizational values and behavior related to each of the preferences. Extraverted organizations, for example, are oriented to the market, allow access to decision making, and act quickly, whereas Introverted organizations are oriented toward their internal culture and technology, restrict access to decision making, and respond only after careful study. Bridges also describes the 16 types of "organizational character" and then examines how organizational character affects the ways in which organizations respond to change, growth, and development.

Groups or individuals who have been introduced to type usually enjoy and are quick to use type understanding to characterize their organization, though they may have trouble agreeing on one or more of the preferences. Practitioners can take advantage of these spontaneous connections clients make by structuring an activity analyzing the organization's character. Groups can then identify what opportunities the organization may be missing, difficulties the organization may experience, and so on. They can also profitably discuss the ways the character of the organization may affect employees, especially those who have type preferences different from those supported by organizational values and behavior.

Analyzing Organizational Type Distributions

A different, but related, use of type for organizational analysis involves collecting data about type distributions in different functions or levels of the organization. Though individual type results cannot be shared, grouped data such as type distributions can, with clients' permission, be used to create type tables of different functions. This information can then be used in a variety of ways to help the organization and individuals within it.

For example, Barger (personal communication, 1995) reported using the MBTI with a company that designed, built, and sold houses. Serious conflicts arose between the sales agents and the construction crews, and Barger was asked to negotiate what had become an explosive situation. Because she had used the MBTI with both groups, she was able to identify significant type differences: The sales agents were primarily ENPs and had identified their work in those terms. The construction supervisors were predominantly ISTJs and had related those type preferences to their group. As in the example earlier in this chapter, in "Using Type as a Bridge in Dealing with Other Conflicts," beginning with analysis of group type differences immediately depersonalized a number of the hottest issues and created a climate in the groups that allowed them to negotiate other important issues.

Pearman (1993) reported another use of type distribution information that can be very helpful to organizations:

comparing type distributions of different levels. In working with supervisors, managers, and executives of a multinational manufacturing organization, Pearman collected type data about each group and a group designated by the company as "future managers." He used self-selection ratios to determine types that were over- and underrepresented in higher levels of management, compared to their presence in the lower-level groups. The primary type-related pattern he found indicated that Intuitive types were significantly more likely to be promoted to higher levels of responsibility than were Sensing types. Pearman presented his analysis to the executive management group and led them through an examination and revision of hiring and promotion policies and practices.

Resources

Bridges' (1992a) *The Character of Organizations* is the only thorough attempt to apply MBTI type to organizations. Rytting, Ware, and Prince (1994) reported a study of 348 successful moderate-size companies in the service sector, about half of which were family owned. They compared data on the MBTI type of the chief executive officer of a company and the company's "character" using Bridges' (1992a) Organizational Character Index. The most significant relationship they found was that companies headed by types that extravert their Thinking process were rated as more Extraverted than companies whose leaders introvert their Thinking process. These relationships were independent of whether CEOs preferred Extraversion or Introversion, leading the authors to conclude that introversion of the Thinking process may lead employees to feel excluded from decision making.

Reynierse (1993, 1997), Reynierse and Harker (1995), and Oswick and Mahoney (1993) provide various kinds of analysis of type distributions at different levels of organizational leadership. Their studies can guide practitioners who wish to use this approach to assist organizations in examining their hiring and promotion practices.

Administering and Interpreting the MBTI in Organizations

Chapters 5 and 6 in this manual provide general guidelines for administering and interpreting the *Myers-Briggs Type Indicator* personality inventory. Professionals using the MBTI in organizations need to develop policies and procedures to ensure that those guidelines will be followed by the organizations with which they are working. This includes anticipating potential problems created by organizational cultures and practices in general, as well as identifying factors within specific organizations that could affect working within the guidelines.

This section addresses issues that commonly arise in relationship to administering and interpreting the MBTI in organizations and offers solutions experienced practitioners have developed to respond to those concerns.

Questions About Administering the MBTI

The questions in this section deal with three essential guidelines for practitioners administering the MBTI in organizational settings:

- Respondents to the Indicator must know the purpose for which the MBTI is being used.
- Completing the Indicator must be voluntary.
- Results are confidential and belong to the individual.

Practitioners can develop clear policies and practices to ensure that each of these guidelines is understood and followed by organizational clients.

1. **What are valid uses for the MBTI in organizational settings?**

   Type information should be used to enhance individual and group satisfaction rather than to restrict or limit individual or group functioning. This chapter has outlined a number of appropriate organizational uses of the Indicator: increasing self-understanding, enhancing group interactions, improving individual and group effectiveness at work, and providing an ethical context and tools for dealing with identified problems.

   People in organizations contracting for administration and interpretation of the MBTI sometimes plan to use the results in inappropriate ways, usually because they misunderstand the meaning of psychological type and the correct interpretation of MBTI results. This confusion arises because they are familiar with trait measures, which give information about people's skills, knowledge, or behaviors—for example, the *Management Skills Profile*, the FIRO-B, the *California Psychological Inventory*, the *Kirton Adaptation Innovation Inventory*, and so on. Trait measures yield results that allow organizations to assess an individual's skills, performance, and behaviors in specific areas. Insofar as the traits measured relate directly to the job and the instrument used is reliable and valid, results may be appropriate indicators of an individual's suitability for hiring, promotion, or selection for particular jobs and teams.

The MBTI is not a measure of traits; MBTI results do not indicate intelligence, knowledge, or skills.

   The MBTI is a type-sorting instrument designed to indicate underlying patterns in personalities. When research is conducted on groups who share one or more preferences, there are frequently correlations with specific scales on trait measures; this indicates that, for many people, acting on their type preferences leads to predictable patterns in behavior, values, and motivations. Such research does *not* indicate whether individuals in these type groups use the behaviors with skill, whether their values are fully considered and consciously direct their actions, whether they are well-developed individuals, or whether they enjoy performing certain activities. And the research groups data that may or may not apply to specific individuals.

It is inappropriate to use the MBTI for hiring, promotion, or selection. Results on the Indicator simply do not give information that will be helpful in these functions.

   If a manager or group needs a person with well-developed skills that frequently relate to a particular MBTI preference, they need to use in their decision making past performance with similar tasks or trait measures that indicate whether individuals have those skills and use them well. Deciding that a certain position requires a Sensing type, for example, and selecting a person who reports Sensing on the MBTI for that position is unfair to Intuitive individuals who have developed Sensing skills and is liable to result in disappointing results for the manager and group.

   Practitioners need to be clear about the meaning of MBTI results and be able to identify appropriate and inappropriate uses confidently. Chapters 1, 2, and 3 in this manual discuss the differences between results on trait measures and type-sorting instruments more fully and can assist practitioners in developing their own knowledge and confidence. If they have additional questions, practitioners can consult the publisher of the MBTI or the ethical guidelines of professional organizations such as the Association for Psychological Type, the American Counseling Association, the American Psychological Association, or other groups concerned with appropriate uses of psychological instruments.

   Experienced MBTI practitioners have found it helpful not only to clarify these issues with organizational clients but also to include in a letter of agreement their understanding of the purposes for using the MBTI. This section includes suggested contents for a letter of agreement that can help practitioners ensure their clients use MBTI results appropriately.

2. **How can an organization ensure that individuals are taking the MBTI voluntarily?**

   This can be a difficult issue in organizations. In addition to simply communicating the requirement, practitioners need to find ways to implement it when a manager's or a team's decision may bring pressure, and individuals may find it difficult to assert their own reluctance or opposition. Ideally, practitioners can conduct interviews with group members before administering the MBTI. This step allows practitioners to ensure that clients know that taking the MBTI is voluntary, to inform them about the general nature of MBTI results, to clarify how results will and will not be used, and to prepare ahead of time to deal with issues of authority, trust, and group interactions.

Regardless of whether individual interviews are possible, in conversation with the contracting individual or group practitioners can ask a number of questions to ensure voluntary completion of the MBTI:

- How was the decision made to use the MBTI?
- Were group members involved in the decision-making process?
- What information do group members have about the MBTI and its appropriate uses?
- Do the leader and contracting person understand that each individual may decide whether to complete the Indicator?
- What consequences do they see if one or more individuals in the group choose not to complete the MBTI?
- Are the leader and group prepared to accept each individual's decision and, if necessary, defend it?
- What questions do they have?

If practitioners have clarified the leader's and group's position on voluntary participation to their satisfaction but have not had an opportunity to speak with each individual, they can include in a letter to each respondent the principle that taking the MBTI is voluntary along with an invitation to contact the practitioner with any concerns or issues. This section includes suggested contents for a cover letter to accompany MBTI booklets and answer sheets.

Practitioners occasionally find that one or more members of a group choose not to complete the MBTI. This may relate to an individual's previous experience with other instruments; to previous experience of poor interpretations or uses of the MBTI; to personal issues with the leader, group, or organization; to concerns about protecting privacy; or to group trust issues. If possible, practitioners should speak directly with such individuals to clarify their issues and respond supportively and informatively. If the issue is trust within the group, the practitioner may decide that that issue needs to be dealt with first, before the MBTI is used. In a group in which distrust abounds, the MBTI is not likely to be useful.

If, even after supportive clarification, a group member chooses not to complete the Indicator, practitioners need to have ways to support that decision.

Suggestions for dealing with reluctant participants are included later in this chapter.

3. How can practitioners ensure that MBTI results remain confidential?

Practitioners need to clarify how the MBTI will be distributed to respondents, how answer sheets will be returned, and where the results will be stored. In organizations, MBTI booklets and answer sheets usually are distributed by mail or in a group meeting prior to the MBTI interpretation session. When practitioners are not administering the MBTI face-to-face, as is most often the case, they need to include a cover letter for each participant to accompany the booklet and answer sheet, with instructions for returning the materials to the practitioner.

MBTI results are returned only to the respondent, and results should not be included in an organization's files. Practitioners may keep individuals' results (often useful for follow-up sessions) and should store them in a secure location.

The information presented later in this section on dealing with reluctant participants discusses protecting confidentiality during interpretation sessions.

4. Are there special administration issues when using the self-scorable Form M in organizations?

Practitioners who wish to use the self-scorable form need to include about 30 minutes to introduce the form and have clients complete the Indicator during the session. This needs to be done *before* explaining Jung's theory, defining the preferences, and giving examples. After all participants have completed the Indicator, the practitioner should direct clients to set the form aside while they listen to an introduction and interpretation of type (see outline of an introductory session in this section).

At the point in the introductory session where MBTI results are normally returned, the practitioner will need to lead clients through scoring their own answer sheets, using careful step-by-step instructions to minimize errors in scoring.

Finally, the practitioner should instruct participants to tear out the questions and scoring page and hand them in. This is essential to protect these restricted materials and to ensure that participants do not use the self-scorable with colleagues or friends who are not attending the session.

Self-scorable forms should not, in general, be mailed to participants. Even with very clear instructions, some participants are likely to score their Indicator before the session and therefore enter the session "knowing" their type, which is likely to bias both their self-estimate and their decision on their best-fit type.

5. What should be included in a letter of agreement with the contracting group or person?

Administration issues can be dealt with most effectively by using contracts or letters of understanding prior to administration and by providing a cover letter to accompany each MBTI question booklet and answer sheet. The following issues need to be first clarified in conversation with the contracting person and then included in a letter of agreement:

- The appropriate purpose for using the MBTI
- The voluntary nature of completing the Indicator
- The confidentiality of results—they are for the respondent and will be shared only by the respondent
- The procedures that will be used in administering, returning, and scoring the Indicator
- The places where results will be stored (and not stored)
- Provisions for return of results to participants who do not attend the session
- The requirement that all restricted materials (e.g., question booklets and answer sheets) be returned to the qualified practitioner

It may be useful to include a phrase such as "in accordance with the ethical principles of (professional organization)," which gives the context for the agreements.

6. **What should be included in the cover letter to participants?**

When the MBTI will be distributed through the mail or by anyone other than the practitioner, a letter including the following information needs to accompany each booklet and answer sheet :

- A brief description of the MBTI (for example, "The MBTI is a self-report inventory focusing on how people prefer to take in information, arrive at decisions, and orient themselves to the world.")
- The appropriate purposes for which the MBTI will be used
- The requirement that completing the Indicator is voluntary
- The confidentiality of results (they will be given only to the respondent)
- The provision of a face-to-face interpretation for each respondent
- A brief statement of directions (for example, "Read and follow the directions on the front of the question booklet.")
- Information about returning the question booklet and answer sheet
- The practitioner's name, address, and phone number, with an invitation to call with questions or concerns

Summary

The nature of organizational life—with its time pressures, focus on results, and explicit or implicit authority relationships—makes clarification of the issues discussed in this section particularly important for obtaining valid results on the Indicator in an organizational setting. This is doubly true when the supervisor, manager, or leader of the group is

participating in the session. Ensuring correct administration is a practical matter as well as an ethical one: individual results are more likely to be reliable and valid when guidelines for administration are carefully implemented.

Questions About Interpreting the MBTI

The general guidelines for providing an interpretation of the MBTI and returning results are thoroughly outlined in Chapter 6 of this manual. This section will address implementing the steps in organizational settings, focusing on group interpretations and feedback.

1. **What do practitioners need to present before returning MBTI results?**

Interpretation sessions typically include the following *before MBTI results are returned to clients:*

- Distribution of *Introduction to Type* to each participant for use during the session and for supplemental reading or activities
- Brief background relating the MBTI to Jung, Myers, and Briggs, including Myers' purpose: to make Jung's theory of human functioning of practical use to people
- A definition and illustration of what the MBTI is indicating—underlying preferences, as opposed to characteristics such as traits
- Clarification that everyone uses all of the preference domains identified by the MBTI—psychological type is about people's most natural way of doing something, their "home base"
- A clear statement about the value of each of the preferences identified by type and examples related to work that illustrate their value
- Unbiased descriptions of each dichotomy: basic definitions and a relevant example of each preference
- Explicit acknowledgment that people may be different when they are "at home" and when they are in environments involving authority or other kinds of external pressures (The goal of the introductory session is to help clients assess who they are outside of the roles they play.)
- An opportunity for clients to "self-estimate" their type (This process can be as simple as making a check mark next to the preferences they select after looking at the descriptions in *Introduction to Type*.)
- Explanation or a visual representation of what clients' MBTI results will look like and appropriate interpretations of the preference clarity index (Refer to *Introduction to Type,* which provides a structure for this.)

There are a couple of important reasons for doing all this before returning results. First, the MBTI is different from most psychological inventories, which are trait measures indicating to what extent people possess or display certain behaviors. Organizational clients are typically familiar with trait measures and how the results are interpreted. As a type sorter, the MBTI provides fundamentally different information, and clients need to understand that before seeing "how they came out" (see Chapter 1, pages 4–5, and Chapter 2, page 11, for a more complete discussion of the crucial distinctions between trait and type pictures of personality).

Second, results on all psychometric instruments are estimates or hypotheses based on how an individual responded to questions at a particular time and place, and this is true for MBTI results. Clients, however, tend to be accustomed to believing in numbers—they are "hard" evidence. Practitioners need to support clients in using their own judgment, in assessing their results on the instrument based on their knowledge of themselves. Presenting the information listed above and asking clients to self-estimate their type gives them the information they need and explicit encouragement to process their MBTI results rather than accepting or rejecting them.

2. **How should MBTI results be returned in group settings?**

After following these steps, practitioners have a number of options for reporting MBTI results to each individual. Computer scoring of Form M answer sheets uses item response theory (IRT) scoring, which gives the most accurate estimate of type and provides a variety of optional computer-generated reports. Report options are listed in Table 5.2, page 107, and in the publisher's catalogue. Computer-scoring software is also available.

From the practitioner's viewpoint, the primary limitation of computer-generated MBTI reports is that they give information about each client's *reported* type (results on the MBTI). Researchers report that about 25% of clients disagree with their MBTI results on one or more of the four dichotomies, with indications that the percentage may be higher for those who take the MBTI in a work setting (see Table 6.1, page 116). If computer reports are used, practitioners need to provide a process that will allow each individual to receive a computer report of his or her chosen best-fit type.

Form M can also be scored by the practitioner using scoring templates, and a self-scorable Form M is available. If practitioners choose these scoring options, they can purchase from the publisher forms for reporting MBTI results. A brief report of individual results, coupled with use of *Introduction to Type,* provides all the information included in the computer reports and gives both brief and full descriptions of all 16 types.

Whichever scoring and reporting option a practitioner chooses, care should be taken to protect confidentiality of individual results as they are returned.

3. **How can practitioners assist clients in deciding on their best-fit type in group settings?**

After defining the MBTI preferences, ask clients to combine the four letters they selected while listening to the interpretation. This provides one hypothesis—their self-estimate based on their understanding of themselves, their understanding of what the MBTI is designed to indicate, and the professional's expertise in explaining the type dichotomies. Then return their MBTI results and tell them this is a second hypothesis, based on how they responded to the Indicator questions.

If their two hypotheses agree, clients can go directly to their full type description to verify that this is the best fit for them. If their hypotheses disagree on one or more preferences, practitioners can direct them to use the steps outlined in the "Verifying Your Type" section in *Introduction to Type.* Using the steps and the language there—and ensuring that there is time for it in the session—will provide participants with the opportunity to find the type that fits best for them.

Practitioners should provide a variety of relevant resources in addition to the 16 type descriptions; for example, *Introduction to Type in Organizations* (Hirsh & Kummerow, 1998), *Introduction to Type and Teams* (Hirsh, 1998), or any of the applications resources listed in this chapter provide additional information that can assist clients in deciding on their own best-fit type.

4. **What else needs to be included in an introductory session?**

As indicated in this chapter's section on introducing the MBTI into organizations, introductory sessions need to include opportunities for clients to apply type to their work lives. The activities suggested in this chapter and in the resource materials listed allow clients to expand their understanding of type, to confirm their own preferences, and to recognize the value of using type in interacting with colleagues.

Questions About Other Special Concerns

Even with careful attention to administration and interpretation guidelines, practitioners using the MBTI in organizations can face a number of potentially difficult ethical issues. The most frequent problem areas identified by consultants are the following:

- Interpretation and misinterpretation of the numerical portion of MBTI results
- Ensuring individual confidentiality in group sessions
- Stereotyping of types and bias for or against certain types or preferences
- Copyright violations and use of restricted materials by nonqualified individuals

This section suggests ways to respond appropriately to each of these issues.

1. **How can practitioners ensure that numerical scores are interpreted correctly?**

Numerical scores need to be presented by their name: the preference clarity index. The number that accompanies each letter indicates how clearly and consistently clients "voted" for one of the opposites on a particular dichotomy. These numbers do not indicate "how much" of this preference domain an individual possesses nor how skilled a person may be in using the preference.

High numbers indicate that, when forced to choose, the client consistently chose one pole of the dichotomy over the other. Low numbers indicate that, when forced to choose, the client "split the vote."

It is helpful to tell clients that the MBTI is a "sorter" rather than a measuring instrument. The goal is to sort respondents into the "correct-for-them" category. The MBTI was not designed to indicate strength, skill, or frequency of behaviors.

It can also be helpful to explicitly state that MBTI results do not fall on a normal curve, as do results from most of the instruments with which clients are familiar. When an instrument's results fall on a normal curve, there is a "normal" or "average" range and there are varying degrees of extreme scores with appropriate interpretations. The MBTI does not have norms about where individuals "should come out"; the only standard of judgment for results is the individual's own decision about which pole of a type dichotomy best defines his or her own most natural way of functioning.

2. **How can practitioners ensure individual confidentiality in group settings? How can practitioners deal with reluctant participants who do not complete the MBTI or who decline to share their type with colleagues?**

Practitioners, leaders, and colleagues may all agree with the ethical principles that taking the MBTI is voluntary and that results belong to the individual; however, they can feel puzzled about how to support these principles when using the MBTI in work groups. As indicated in the section on administration, careful preparation and the use of a cover letter to accompany booklets and answer sheets will normally identify people who are unwilling to take the Indicator or who have concerns about sharing their type preferences during the group session. With this information, practitioners can plan their MBTI sessions to ensure that using the Indicator does not put individuals on the spot or add to a climate of distrust.

Members of an intact work group who choose not to take the Indicator need to attend the introductory session: all group or team members need to receive the same information and materials about the MBTI.

They can participate in the "handedness" exercise, receive a copy of the materials provided, listen to definitions and examples of the preferences, and make a self-estimate.

When group members engage in activities related to their decisions about their types, however, it is wisest to provide the non-MBTI taker with a role such as "observer." Practitioners can prepare a simple observer assignment ahead of time; for example: "Observe the process and interactions of each group and be prepared to tell us about one similarity and one difference you observed." This gives those who do not want to take the MBTI a real role to play and ensures that their reluctance will not interfere with the group's ability to develop an understanding of type and application of the concepts.

The same observer role can be offered more generally to the group for those who are unsure of or undecided about one or more of their preferences. This allows those who are not ready to identify their type to participate in the group and learn from their colleagues.

3. **How can practitioners deal with bias and stereotyping?**

In some organizational settings, psychological type and the MBTI have been introduced in ways that lead to stereotyping of individuals and types. People who are targets of such categorizing naturally resent it and often reject type and the MBTI. Such an outcome of an organization development activity obviously does a disservice to the organization and clients, as well as to the MBTI and type theory.

Organizational type practitioners can avoid such misuses of the MBTI by committing to two complementary strategies: (a) developing their own type understanding, including recognizing and finding ways to mitigate the inevitable biases that accompany their own type preferences; and (b) dealing explicitly with bias and stereotyping as part of their introduction to type sessions and any additional work using type.

The MBTI practitioners' responsibility is to present type in an unbiased way, using cogent, relevant examples of the usefulness of the different preferences within the organizational environment. Following this, practitioners need to present the four-letter types as dynamic categories and tendencies. They need to emphasize that every successful adult has developed a variety of behaviors and skills in areas that are not their preferred ones, and that this development, coupled with recognition of one's natural styles, can be a positive contribution to work.

4. **What can help practitioners understand their own biases?**

To present an unbiased explanation of type, practitioners need to understand their own type and how it may affect their presentations. They also need to become aware of their own natural biases related to type. The following professional development actions assist practitioners in meeting these responsibilities:

- *Clarify your own type:* What is your type? Your dominant function? Your auxiliary function? What does your type contribute to your work? Where do your type preferences sometimes get in your way? What is your preferred communication style? How do others experience you as a communicator? A decision maker?

- *Clarify your understanding of the differences between trait-measuring and type-sorting instruments:* What do the numbers accompanying the preference letter (the preference clarity index) mean? What are some everyday examples you can use to quickly explain the differences to your clients?

- *Practice describing the preferences to people of different types and ask for feedback:* Are you describing your nonpreferred areas based on your own use of those areas, or have you gathered information that enables you to describe them as they are experienced and used by people who have those preferences? Do you have colleagues knowledgeable about the MBTI with preferences different from yours? Can you provide mutual feedback?

5. **How can practitioners create a more positive response by participants during the introduction to type session?**

Because psychological type deals with common everyday behaviors, clients sometimes bring their pet peeves and biases into type discussions, often in the form of "humor." *Introduction to Type* includes three sections that practitioners can use to create a more positive response:

- "Constructive Use of Differences" directly addresses typical biases by type dichotomies. Practitioners can discuss these with the group and ask for examples of such biases that they have heard in their organization.

- "Mutual Usefulness of Opposite Types" lists positive ways people with opposite preferences can provide balance to one's perspective. Again, practitioners can review this with clients and ask them for examples of when they have supported or been supported in these ways.

- "Things to Remember About Type" summarizes important points about appropriate and inappropriate use of MBTI results and type.

Practitioners also can reframe biased comments from group members. For example, a client who exclaims, "I'm an Intuitive; I don't do details," can be asked if it would be more correct to say the following: "It's easier for me to grasp and remember details when I have the overall concept fully developed." A client who states that "P stands for Procrastinating" can be reminded that all types may procrastinate, and that the Judging–Perceiving dichotomy is about whether

an individual prefers to structure and schedule the decision-making process or leave it open for additional information—both of which are valuable ways to proceed. *WORKTypes* (Kummerow, Barger, & Kirby, 1997) includes in the chapter on teams a section focusing on type bias, reframing, and tips for dealing with type bias that can be very helpful for practitioners and the groups with which they work.

6. **How can practitioners protect restricted materials and honor copyrights?**

Ensuring that restricted materials are used only by qualified professionals is an important part of practitioners' ethical responsibility. MBTI question booklets and answer sheets need to be collected, including those portions of the self-scorable form. If answer sheets are returned for scoring without the question booklet, the practitioner should contact the individuals directly to retrieve the question booklet. Organizations that use the MBTI with employees regularly may stock question booklets and answer sheets. In this case, the practitioner needs to ensure that the individual responsible for storing and distributing the MBTI understands all steps in administration and return of materials. It is generally best to have such steps in writing.

Copying of copyrighted materials is, of course, illegal. Practitioners need to model respect for copyright, as well as explicitly refusing to "loan" materials to clients for copying. The occasional photocopied answer sheet that has been completed by a client should be returned to the individual unscored, with the offer of an opportunity to complete the Indicator using an original answer sheet.

Conclusion

Used appropriately, the *Myers-Briggs Type Indicator* and Jungian psychological type provide a wealth of positive organizational applications:

- Developing self-understanding
- Increasing appreciation for colleagues
- Improving communication
- Dealing with conflicts
- Enhancing problem solving and decision making
- Planning, implementing, and managing organizational change
- Recognizing and managing stress

Four decades of research support a wide variety of applications and provide resources for practitioners and clients.

Used with work groups and teams or with individuals in developmental activities, the MBTI has proven a practical, positive tool for organizational development.

Uses of Type in Multicultural Settings 14

Contributed by Linda K. Kirby and Nancy J. Barger

CHAPTER OVERVIEW

Isabel Briggs Myers and Katharine Briggs hypothesized, as did Carl G. Jung, that the theory of psychological type identified significant underlying patterns of functioning that are common to all people (Myers with Myers, 1980/1995). In the 1985 *Manual,* Myers and McCaulley stated this hypothesis in their only direct comment on type and culture:

> Jung's theory is concerned with perception and judgment, which are information gathering and decision making, or taking in the stimulus and making the response. Because most behavior is concerned with perception or with judgment, type differences can be expected to occur across a very broad range of life events. Jung believed he was describing mental processes common to the entire human species. To the extent that he was correct, type differences should be consistent across cultures. (p. 223)

Myers and McCaulley then cited three research studies—two with African American students in the United States and one in Japan—that supported the validity of Jung's psychological type theory and of the *Myers-Briggs Type Indicator* personality inventory with those groups (Carlson & Levy, 1973; Myers, 1977; Ohsawa, 1975, 1981).

The years since publication of the 1985 *Manual* have seen rapid expansion of the use of psychological type and of the MBTI personality inventory in international and multicultural settings. "Multicultural Applications" in *MBTI Applications* (Kirby & Barger, 1996) summarizes dozens of articles by researchers and practitioners using the MBTI in non-U.S. cultures. This chapter will refer to some of that research and to interviews with practitioners and researchers using the MBTI in international and multicultural settings, as well as to the authors' experience.[1] Those who desire more complete information on the research should refer to the summaries in Kirby and Barger.

Multicultural and international practitioners use the MBTI in a wide variety of ways—in fact, in all of the ways discussed in the chapters in Part V, "Uses of Type." This chapter will *not* focus on particular applications such as multicultural counseling or organizational development but instead will discuss the broader core issues important to practitioners who want to use the *Myers-Briggs Type Indicator* with groups and individuals who are culturally different from those with whom the MBTI was developed and tested.

Type and Culture

Social and cultural anthropologists have developed dozens of definitions of culture. One that seems clear and straightforward is provided by Geert Hofstede (1991) of the Institute for Research on Intercultural Cooperation: Culture is learned "patterns of thinking, feeling, and acting," or, using Hofstede's analogy to computers, the "software of the mind" (pp. 4–5). In his definition, Hofstede distinguishes *culture* from those parts of human functioning that are genetic and common to all, which he refers to as the "operating system" of the human mind. Hofstede's diagram of human personality, shown in Figure 14.1, outlines these components.

Jung, Myers, and Briggs believed that psychological type provides a basic structure similar to Hofstede's "operating system." For them, the patterns of psychological type are a universal component of human nature. In their view of human functioning, type preferences would fit in the base of Hofstede's diagram and, along with culture, shape each human personality.

Social and cultural anthropologists have not, for the most part, accepted or even explored this Jungian hypothesis.[2] The focus of cultural study and theory has been on the seemingly endless variety of ways in which human beings have organized themselves—on culturally derived differences in assumptions, values, morals, laws, customs, and behavior. On the other hand, psychologists, counselors, and organizational development specialists using psychological type and the MBTI have produced a significant amount of information about the applicability and usefulness of psychological type in a wide variety of cultures. Their experience and research generally support the universality of psychological type patterns.

Those who would use the MBTI in multicultural settings need to be knowledgeable about and respectful of both the *differences in people related to culture* and the *similarities related to psychological type patterns.*

Much more research, such as Wilson and Languis' (1989) study of brain wave pattern differences and the studies reported in Kirby and Barger (1996), is needed to demonstrate the common mental patterns that psychological type

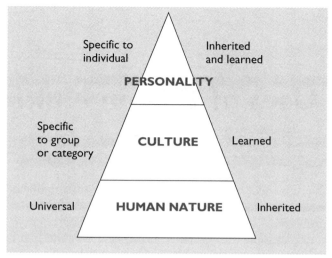

Figure 14.1 Three Levels of Uniqueness in Human Mental Programming

Source: From *Cultures and Organizations: Software of the Mind*, p. 6, by G. Hofstede, 1991. Copyright 1991 by McGraw-Hill. Used with permission.

hypothesizes; but current research and practice with psychological type and the MBTI are sufficient to proceed with the hypothesis that clients in different cultures can recognize and make use of psychological type explanations. While proceeding, practitioners need to recognize the significant influence of culture on the ways different people experience and express psychological type patterns.

Using the MBTI Personality Inventory in Multicultural Settings

Although psychological type may describe universal human characteristics, using any personality instrument with groups culturally different from those with whom it was developed raises questions about appropriateness of the instrument for the target population and about interpretation of results. The remainder of this chapter examines questions related to use of the instrument.

The basic question for practitioners who want to use the MBTI in other cultures is this: Will the MBTI assist their clients in identifying their Jungian type preferences? The items on the Indicator ask respondents to choose between everyday surface behaviors that Myers believed indicate the deeper, underlying patterns of type. The kinds of behaviors she used are affected by cultural values and norms. The MBTI was developed and tested primarily with middle-class, White Americans, and research reports significant evidence for the Inventory's reliability and validity when it is used with people who are culturally similar to them (Hammer, 1996b; Myers & McCaulley, 1985; see also Chapters 8 and 9 of this manual). Will those same questions work to indicate type in groups with different cultural values and norms? Is there comparable evidence for the reliability and validity of the MBTI in cultures other than that of middle-class, White Americans?

Reliability and Validity of the MBTI in Other Cultures

The selection of items and the calculation of item weights for the new Form M of the MBTI included a much more representative sampling of U.S. co-cultural groups than those used to develop and standardize the inventory's earlier forms. Currently available studies of the reliability and validity of the MBTI in other cultures are based on Form G. This research, reported in Kirby and Barger (1996), includes significant evidence for the reliability and validity of the MBTI in a variety of other groups with different cultural characteristics.

For example, hundreds of studies of the validity of the MBTI conducted in predominantly English-speaking cultures report results very similar to those of validity studies conducted in the United States. These include reports of students' type preferences and major fields of study (Casas, 1990; Borham & Watts, 1994); comparisons of type distributions of school administrators in Canada (Anderson, 1992) with those in the United States; differences in type distributions in United Kingdom organizations with those in different cultures (Oswick, Mahoney, & Stein, 1994); comparisons of type distributions of police officers in Australia, the United Kingdom, and the United States (Lidgard & Bates, 1988); and others.

Dozens of studies of the MBTI in more diverse cultures also provide validity evidence. Among others, Call and Sotillo (1993) compared results on the *Group Embedded Figures Test* and type for U.S. students and students from Spanish-speaking countries; Yao (1993) analyzed types of female school administrators in the People's Republic of China; Lim (1994) reported results of using the MBTI with Singaporean high school students; Van Rooyen (1994) compared results of South African female managers on the *Kirton Adaption and Innovation Inventory* and the MBTI to results obtained in similar U.S. studies; and numerous practitioners described their use of the MBTI with diverse groups in the United States (Huitt, 1989; Jones, Ukishima, Sakamoto, Tanouye, & Giron, 1995; Levy & Ostrowski, 1983; Simmons & Barrineau, 1994).

A recent study with two groups of Whites in South Africa provided additional support for the validity of the MBTI in that country (Zietsmann, 1996). One group consisted of 804 White adult high school graduates; the other of 1,943 "reasonably representative of the white South African population with a very diverse sampling of professions, industries, and status levels" (p. 186). Using factor analysis of the responses, Zietsmann found *the meaning of the MBTI items and scales is substantially the same for South African subjects as it is for U.S. subjects* (p. 186; italics in original). No comparable study has yet been completed with their sample of Black South Africans.

The great majority of multicultural and international MBTI studies report results comparable to those found in similar studies in the United States and support the validity of the MBTI instrument when used appropriately in those cultures.

Cultural Groups for Whom the MBTI May Not Be Appropriate

Some practitioners have found that the MBTI personality inventory may *not* work to identify type preferences in cultures in which group or communal identity is a central value. Hofstede refers to such cultures as *collectivist* and defines them as "societies in which the interest of the group prevails over the interest of the individual" (1991, p. 50).

The MBTI has been used successfully in many cultures in which group social values are important: Latin American countries such as Mexico and Brazil, Asian nations such as China and Korea, and African countries such as Nigeria and South Africa. However, when a culture combines values about the centrality of group identity with the experience of oppression, as is true for many indigenous cultures, the MBTI may be less appropriate.

For example, Jopie De Beer (1997), a South African psychologist, reported on a database of almost 6,500 South Africans including 930 Blacks. She expressed this concern about use of the MBTI within Black South African culture:

> Group solidarity amongst the indigenous people of Africa and in particular South Africa is often referred to as UBUNTU (umuntu ngumuntu ngabantu—or, a person only becomes a person through other people). UBUNTU is characterized by the following values: solidarity, cooperation, hospitality, tolerance, joyful service, harmony, dignity, compassion, consensus, trust, compromise, accommodation, caring about others, and readiness to "go the extra mile." (p. 12)

Colin Hopkirk (personal communication, 1997) reported similar questions about using the MBTI with New Zealand Maori who remain primarily within their native culture. He gave the following explanation of the cultural values that may make the MBTI inappropriate for this group: "[T]hey perceive and experience themselves first as a part of the whole creation, second as part of the hapu (tribe) of which they are the product, third as part of the whanau (extended family) from which they descend, and only last as a distinct individual personality."

Collectivist values may make it difficult for individuals within these cultures to respond to the MBTI for at least two reasons:

1. The centrality and importance of group identity and cultural norms may make it difficult for individuals to identify and report their natural individual preferences. Practitioners who use the MBTI in organizational settings within the United States find that an

organization's cultural norms influence people's ability to report their natural type preferences (Kummerow, 1988), and we would expect that broader cultural norms would also influence an individual's desire and ability to use the instrument to indicate his or her underlying preferences.

2. The ways in which type preferences are expressed within these cultures may be significantly different from the ways in which those preferences are generally described from the perspective of an individualistic culture. In a culture that expects and values regular family/group interaction, for example, Introversion may not be expressed by finding time alone. Instead, individuals preferring Introversion may have found other ways—acceptable in their culture—to support their need for internal processing time. Therefore, the items on the MBTI may not tap in to the ways individuals in that culture experience and express their psychological type preferences. For more information on this, see the section in this chapter on interpreting the MBTI.

In spite of these anticipated difficulties, Hopkirk (personal communication, 1997) stated that, in his experience, Maori who are bicultural "seem to accept the MBTI and often find it sensible and useful." Likewise, De Beer made the following observation about using the MBTI with South African Whites, Afrikaaners, and Blacks: "We have not really had major problems with people responding to the indicator. . . . [W]e have been surprised at how easily most cultures seem to understand the items" (De Beer, personal communication, 1997).

That the MBTI personality inventory may not work to identify psychological type in some collectivist cultures does not, of course, necessarily invalidate Jung's hypothesis that these individuals have psychological type preferences. It does encourage caution when using the MBTI in such settings.

In deciding whether the MBTI is appropriate for clients from collectivist cultures, practitioners need to assess degrees of acculturation. Clients whose primary cultural reference is their collectivist culture may find taking the MBTI unhelpful or even offensive, while those who are bicultural or whose primary reference is the majority culture are less likely to experience such difficulties.

Practitioners who have questions about the cultural appropriateness of using the MBTI with particular groups or individuals should consult resources such as the following:

- Rollock and Terrell (1996), *Multicultural Issues in Assessment: Toward An Inclusive Model*
- Sue (1998), *Multicultural Counseling Competencies: Individual and Organizational Development*
- American Psychological Association (1990), *Guidelines for Providers of Psychological Services to Ethnic, Linguistic and Culturally Diverse Populations*

- Dana (1993), *Multicultural Assessment Perspective for Professional Psychology*
- Brislin (1990), *Applied Cross-Cultural Psychology*

These works discuss acculturation and other important issues related to using psychological instruments in cultures different from those within which they were developed.

A slightly different question was raised by practitioners who use the MBTI in an organizational setting in the American Southwest. Their Native American (primarily Navaho and Hopi) clients willingly complete the Indicator and seem to find it useful for understanding communication and team functioning; however, these practitioners question its usefulness for increasing self-understanding for these clients. Their Native cultures include traditional ways for members to discover the meaning of their lives and to understand how their individual existence fits within the history and tradition of the family and tribe. It may be that the culturally identified ways for developing self-understanding for individuals in these cultures will work better and be more appropriate than the MBTI and psychological type theory (K. Salazar and G. Sanchez, personal communication, 1997).

On the other hand, Mary E. Loomis, a Jungian analyst and coauthor of the *Singer-Loomis Inventory,* used Native American concepts such as the medicine wheel, the Powers of the Four Directions, and the Star Maiden Circle as analogies for Jung's psychological type theory in her *Dancing the Wheel of Psychological Types* (1991). In her view, the two approaches to human functioning are complementary.

A more thorough understanding of cultural values in indigenous and collectivist cultures may allow MBTI practitioners to develop culturally congruent ways to present Jung's theory of human functioning.

Cultural Differences in the Expression of Psychological Type: Extraversion and Introversion

The following anecdote was reported by two members of the Association for Psychological Type, a professional association for users of psychological type, whose membership is primarily from North America. The story illustrates an important issue in using the MBTI with cultures other than one's own.

When we first attended a psychological type conference in Great Britain in 1991, we observed to colleagues at the end of the first evening, "You don't seem to have any ENFPs at this conference." They assured us that, as in the United States, ENFPs were well represented in the British Association for Psychological Type and many were present at the conference. We commented that, from our U.S. experience, we couldn't identify ENFPs—or those preferring Extraversion more generally—because they were not exhibiting the characteristics we associated with Extraversion in the United States. The response of our British colleagues was that they found it similarly difficult to identify those preferring Introversion in the United States because U.S.

Introverts exhibited behavior that in the United Kingdom was associated with Extraversion: sociability, comfort with small talk, disclosure of personal information, energetic and fast-paced conversation, and so forth.

Some practitioners and researchers have looked to type distributions in different cultures to explain differences in behavior, believing, for example, that there must be more people preferring Introversion in Britain than in the United States. However, the 1997 normative type sample studies conducted in the United Kingdom and the United States produced very similar percentages of people preferring Extraversion and Introversion—about 50%–50% in each case (see Table 14.1 on p. 379). The difference noted in individual behavior in group settings or with strangers is not due to differences in type preference distribution between the United Kingdom and the United States but instead is due to the ways cultural norms and expectations affect expression of type.

Each culture defines appropriate ways to express particular preferences.

Because culture influences the ways type is expressed, practitioners may need to modify their type definitions, and especially the behaviors they associate with type preferences in their examples, to communicate type effectively in another culture. The preferred way to do this is to interview individuals or groups about how they experience and express their type preferences within their culture. Evidence from interviews with people of different types in a variety of cultures supports both the existence of the underlying type patterns and differences in the ways they are experienced and expressed in different cultures (Barger & Kirby, 1993, 1995b; Intravisit, 1986).

Cultural Differences in the Expression of Psychological Type: Sensing and Judging

To date, almost every culture for which there are type data reports a predominance of Sensing Judging types, and the great majority report STJ as the modal type in the culture (Casas, 1990). Because of the prevalence of this type combination in different cultures and because of the nature of this preference combination, STJ expression of type provides a particular cautionary example for practitioners using type in cultures other than their own.

In De Beer's analysis (1997) of type preferences in South Africa, she stated that South African type experts shared a "common assumption that the indigenous black people are probably more Feeling than Thinking," based on the UBUNTU values characteristic of Black South African culture and observations of the behavior of Black South Africans. Yet the South African database of 6,452 people reports ESTJ and ISTJ as the most common types for Black South Africans, as well as for Whites. Among the 5,000 White South Africans,

these two types accounted for almost 39% of the group, while 67.6% of the 930 Black South Africans reported these types. De Beer believed that, based on her own work in verifying type results with Black South Africans, the STJ predominance shown in the database is correct. This seeming contradiction can be explained when one carefully examines the underlying dynamic of STJ types, rather than applying behavioral standards from other cultures.

The combination of preferences for Sensing, Thinking, and Judging produces a type that introverts Sensing and extraverts Thinking in Jung's dynamic picture of types. (Kirby and Barger addressed the behavioral implications of introverted Sensing in depth in "Multicultural Applications," *MBTI Applications,* 1996.) A culture-neutral description of STJs pictures them as factual, reality-based types: They take reality as a given and internalize the history, traditions, and customs of their culture as "the way things are." They enjoy belonging to a group and feel great loyalty toward that group's past, present, and future. Preserving culture and traditions is a primary value.

Because of this underlying pattern, the observable behavior of STJs is likely to clearly fit the cultural values of the group to which they belong. When their culture values "solidarity, cooperation, hospitality, tolerance, joyful service, harmony, dignity, compassion, consensus, trust, compromise, accommodation, caring about others, and readiness to 'go the extra mile'" (De Beer, 1997, p. 12), as Black South African culture does, STJs are likely to display behaviors congruent with those values. To American eyes, this behavior may appear very different from expectations of STJ behavior based on U.S. cultural experience.

Interpretations of type-related behavior formed through work with middle-class U.S. clients may distort or compromise understanding of type in other cultures. What is needed is a thorough understanding of the underlying type pattern and then exploration of how that pattern may be expressed within a particular culture.

Summary

Using any psychological instrument in a culture different from that in which it was developed and tested requires caution and respect for diversity; however, MBTI researchers and practitioners in a wide variety of cultures report results very similar to those found by researchers and practitioners using the MBTI in the United States. Current evidence supports use of the MBTI in most multicultural settings.

In cultures with value systems that can be described as collectivist, the MBTI may not be appropriate. Practitioners should carefully consider its value and assess whether psychological type is a useful tool for self-understanding for these clients.

When using the MBTI in multicultural or international settings, practitioners need to be aware that cultural values are likely to affect the ways in which individuals express their type preferences. Examples of behavioral patterns based on U.S. samples may need to be modified or changed to reflect the ways cultural norms have influenced clients' type-related behavioral habits.

Practical Concerns About Multicultural Use of the MBTI

Most of the studies reported above and in the research summaries in *MBTI Applications* (Kirby and Barger, 1996) used Form G (sometimes with minor spelling changes; for example, *organise* instead of *organize*). The use of the standard Form G or Form M with clients from other cultures requires attention to some practical issues related to client reading level, age, and language. The suggestions in Chapter 6, "Administration," about reading level and age need to be applied to multicultural clients in ways that fit for the culture. Additionally, the sometimes colloquial and idiomatic language of the Indicator may create difficulties for some clients with English as a second language (ESL).

Reading Levels

Clients taking the MBTI personality inventory need to have a reading level of seventh grade (approximately 12- to 13-year-olds) or above, based on U.S. reading norms. In the United States, eighth graders are usually about 13 years old and have completed seven or eight years of schooling. Practitioners are encouraged to find ways to check their clients' reading levels in English. Wederspahn and Barger (1988) reported a thorough study using Form G with well-educated Filipinos. Based on this, they recommended a TOEFL (Test of English as a Foreign Language) level of 500 as a minimum, but there are no official guidelines or comparable research studies on this question.

Age Levels

The MBTI is appropriate for adults and young people 15 years of age or older. Caution is recommended for use with younger clients (ages 12 to 14), and it is not recommended for use with children below 12 years old except for research purposes. Reliabilities for younger clients are typically slightly lower (though still acceptable) than those for adults, which Myers and McCaulley (1985) suggested may relate to issues of type development in younger respondents.

The *Murphy-Meisgeier Type Indicator for Children* (MMTIC) is recommended for children approximately 7 to 13 years old. The MMTIC consists of questions about everyday experiences common to children in the United States, such as Item #8: "You like to have: A. Lots of friends; B. A few close friends." The *MMTIC Manual* (Meisgeier & Murphy, 1987) states that the reading level for their instrument is 2.0 using a modified Fry system, and, with the exception of one or two items, the experiences drawn upon in the items are at least potentially common to children attending school in a wide variety of cultures.

Language Issues

When the MBTI is used with clients for whom English is not the native language, some special considerations arise, and it is appropriate to check understanding before deciding to use the Indicator. According to the study by Wederspahn and Barger (1988), even when non–native English speakers had sufficient command of English to understand the words in the MBTI Form G, the use of idioms in some items created problems for their Filipino clients: "A speaker of English as a second language (ESL) may know all the words in the idiom 'someone who has both feet on the ground' without understanding the meaning of the phrase (practical/realistic), which is crucial to making a meaningful choice on this item" (p. 12).

Many of the "low frequency vocabulary items" in Form G that created problems for Wederspahn and Barger's Filipino clients have been eliminated in Form M. A few remain because they are good items in the United States, but they may be problematic for all but very advanced speakers of English. The following are words or phrases on Form M that were difficult for Wederspahn and Barger's clients and that practitioners may wish to check with their ESL clients:

ingenious

cramp (does a schedule cramp you?)

hearty

cherish

Some of the idioms in Form G that Wederspahn and Barger found particularly troublesome to ESL speakers have also been removed, but a few remain and, again, should be checked with clients for understanding:

a good mixer

leave you cold

to be tied down

plunge in

go with the flow

The word pairs can create special problems, even for advanced speakers of English, because these items require respondents to choose between different possible definitions of the words and to understand the connotations in the United States. Wederspahn and Barger asked their clients how they defined *touching* (half of word pair #33, Form M: "convincing–touching"). Their clients responded, "making physical contact with the fingers," a correct dictionary definition but not one likely to help respondents indicate their preference for Thinking or Feeling as the item intends. When Barger used Form G with a group of ESL managers of a Southeast Asian oil company (with clients from five different Southeast Asian cultures), she found that they were comfortable with their overall results, but they did ask about the meaning of the word *compassion,* which occurs in three Form M questions: word pair #40, "compassion–foresight"; word pair #53, "compassionate–logical"; and phrase question #87, "Which is a higher compliment, to be called (A) competent, or (B) compassionate?"

P. A. Schmidt (personal communication, 1997), who works in Arab countries in the Middle East, reported client difficulties with the same items and words reported by Wederspahn and Barger. She indicated that she deals frankly with the language concerns of her ESL clients by saying something like this:

> You may encounter some idioms with which you are not familiar, or you may find some words for which you are not sure of the meaning. That is perfectly OK; it's normal for people who fill out the American English version of the MBTI. Just do the best you can in answering the questions and skip any you don't understand. You'll have the opportunity in this class to listen to information about the type preferences and choose your own best-fit type. Your results from the Indicator will be part of that process, but you can "correct your answers," so to speak, as you decide on your own preferences.

Summary

Practitioners who have questions about their clients' ability to understand the meaning of MBTI items are advised to explore these issues with their clients before using the Indicator. Many ESL clients—especially those working in organizational settings—will be familiar with American idioms, and the number of questions affected by language concerns is small. In general, ESL clients find most items easy to answer, and, with attention to reading level, age, and possible language issues, both practitioner and client can feel confident of the validity of their overall results on the MBTI.

Translations of the MBTI

While the MBTI has achieved satisfactory results in a wide variety of cultures, a validated translation of the Indicator in the client's native language is generally the preferred choice. The following sixteen translations have sufficient reliability and validity evidence to be sold commercially:

Anglicized English

Australian English

Bahasa Malay

Chinese

Danish

Dutch

European French

French Canadian

German

Italian

Korean

Norwegian

Portuguese

Spanish

Spanish/Castellano

Swedish

Translations into additional languages are currently listed as "research instruments" and are typically being tested for reliability and validity. Practitioners wanting information about commercially available translations and about those currently being developed and tested should contact Consulting Psychologists Press.

Challenges Faced by Translators of the MBTI

Eduardo Casas, recipient of the Isabel Briggs Myers Memorial Research Award in 1991 for his French translation of the MBTI, has done more than any other person to clarify what is required to develop a valid translation of the MBTI (Casas, 1990). The process and principles Casas identified were parallel in all essentials to those used by Isabel Myers in her original construction of the instrument as outlined in Chapter 9 of the 1985 *Manual.*

Some of the challenges faced by translators of the MBTI are outlined below.

Conceptual Challenges   Translators must strive to find behaviors and attitudes related to type preferences that are appropriate for their culture. The UBUNTU values characteristic of South African Blacks described earlier, for example, include many concepts typically used in Western cultures to describe the Feeling function. If these are *cultural* values followed by most people in this culture, how can a translator find concepts and words that distinguish between Thinking and Feeling for this group?

Linguistic Challenges   According to De Beer (personal communication, 1997), the Zulu language has very few words that convey the concept of the Intuition function, creating a challenge for developing a valid translation of the Sensing–Intuition dichotomy into that language. Sim and Kim (1993) reported difficulty in translating idiomatic expressions such as "cramp you."

Cultural Value Challenges   Sim and Kim (1993) reported that they needed to rewrite some MBTI Form G items when they developed their Korean translation because "the Korean culture does not favor the expression of emotions and feelings" (p. 19). Some of these Form G items that did not work with their Korean sample remain on Form M:

thinking   Ⓐ   Ⓑ   feeling

hearty   Ⓐ   Ⓑ   quiet

Summary

Translators who have successfully faced these challenges and followed the steps in item development, analysis, testing, and weighting used by Isabel Myers in her original construction of the MBTI have developed reliable and valid translations. And they have found what Eduardo Casas (1995) called "experiential validity" as they have used these versions—that is, their translations "work" for respondents. If such a translation of the MBTI is available in the client's native language, practitioners should choose the translation.

Multicultural Scoring Issues

Myers described item weighting as the way the MBTI accounts for the social desirability of items (Myers & McCaulley, 1985). In cultures with values different from those of Americans, one would expect that the social desirability of some items will be different, and therefore those items should be weighted differently to provide clients with the most accurate results.

Weighting of Items in Translations of the MBTI

Developing a valid translation of the Indicator includes testing the translation on a representative sample group and collecting the data needed to assign appropriate item weights. Casas (1990), for example, found that the corresponding French words for the Introverted options on Form G item #31, "quiet" (Form M item #32); Form G item #37, "reserved" (Form M item #38); and Form G item #40, "calm" (not on Form M), did not discriminate between Introverts and Extraverts in his representative sample groups of Francophone Canadians. Either the words used in the translation were inadequate, or cultural values in the French Canadian population supported the choice of these words by both Introverts and Extraverts. Because they do not discriminate, these options carry a weight of 0 in Casas' French translation.

Item Weights in Other Cultures

Differences in social desirability affect responses to the standard MBTI as well as to translations of the MBTI. Casas (1990) calculated prediction ratios on MBTI items for a representative sample of Anglophone Canadian students, for example, and found that some items received prediction ratios sufficiently different from those of Americans that the weighting for those items would be different in Canada. Form G word-pair question #31, "hearty–quiet" (Form M item #32) discriminates between those preferring Extraversion and those preferring Introversion in the United States. For the native English speakers in Casas' Canadian sample, however, "quiet" was the overwhelming choice, and therefore the weighting of scores on this item would be different.

Oxford Psychologists Press (Kendall & McHenry, 1998) conducted research on 196 of Isabel Myers' MBTI Form J items using a census-based national representative sample of adults (N = 1,634) in the United Kingdom. Based on this study, Betsy Kendall and Robert McHenry of Oxford Psychologists Press created a research version of the MBTI with item weights based on the U.K. sample responses. They then conducted best-fit type studies using Form G and their research version. The result of this comprehensive project was publication of the European English MBTI Step I: 87 forced-choice items (63 Form G items plus 24 Form J items) scored using U.K. item weights. Their best-fit type studies indicate a significant increase in best-fit results for U.K. clients (from 63% on Form G to 72% on the European English MBTI Step I), with the largest increase occurring on the Extraversion–Introversion dichotomy.

Bathurst (personal communication, 1997) developed experimental item weights based on MBTI responses in samples of convenience in New Zealand. His analysis indicates that, based on his sample groups, about 43% of the MBTI items would receive weights different from those assigned on the U.S. Form G scoring keys. When Bathurst compared overall MBTI results using U.S. and culture-specific scoring weights, however, MBTI type changed only slightly, with most of the changes occurring on dichotomies on which clients had low preference scores.

Psychometrics Canada Ltd., MBTI distributor in Canada, and Australian Psychologists Press, MBTI distributor in Australia, are conducting research using representative samples in their cultures (Danielle Poirier, personal communication, 1997; David Freeman, personal communication, 1997). These studies may result in culture-specific scoring weights. When such culturally adjusted scoring is not available, U.S. scoring keys can be used, with additional time and energy directed toward helping clients verify type results, especially for those with results near the midpoint.

Summary

Ideally, practitioners would be able to choose MBTI scoring options for multicultural clients that use item weights based on the social desirability of items in their culture. Practically, these are not widely available at the present time. Fortunately, using scoring weights developed with U.S. samples does not appear to present a significant problem for multicultural clients.

Research conducted by Consulting Psychologists Press to create Form M resulted in replacing 45% of the Form G items (often with minor wording changes). A number of items that achieved satisfactory prediction ratios in the United States in the mid-1970s, when Form G was created, did not meet the item selection criteria discussed in Chapter 7. Form M has not yet been tested with multicultural populations, but its reliabilities are higher than those for Form G with diverse U.S. populations, as is its reporting of best-fit type. Future research will indicate whether this new form also provides better results in multicultural settings.

Administering and Interpreting the MBTI in Multicultural Settings

The primary goal during *administration* is creating a climate that allows clients to report their true or best-fit type preferences when they respond to the MBTI items. The primary goal during *interpretation* is to assist clients in processing their MBTI results to decide on their best-fit type. The standard instructions, outlined in Chapters 5 and 6, provide clear guidelines for practitioners. However, achieving these goals with clients from other cultures may require additional care.

Questions About Administration

Administering the MBTI in the U.S. is relatively straightforward: the "directions" for answering the MBTI questions communicate clearly with most clients, and the guidelines in Chapter 5 of this manual provide the additional information practitioners may need to respond to client questions. However, some who use the MBTI in different cultures report administration issues that the multicultural practitioner will want to consider.

1. **Can I use the standard instructions when administering the MBTI to clients in other cultures?**

   Yes, with some modifications or additions. Most multicultural practitioners use the standard instructions, but some also report developing instructions that communicate more effectively with their clients or spending extra time on parts of the instructions that may pose problems within their culture.

   For example, trainers at Oxford Psychologists Press (the U.K. distributor of the MBTI) have found (Kendall, personal communication, 1997) that the phrase "shoes-off self," suggested in the 1985 *Manual* to convey the desired frame of mind for completing the Indicator, does not communicate well to their clients. They communicate the concept of "your natural self" in other ways.

   Practitioners working with some Asian cultures (Park, 1996) report that the standard instruction "there are no right or wrong answers" requires additional explanation for their clients, who are accustomed to receiving test results that compare them favorably or unfavorably with others.

2. **Do cultural values raise particular issues I need to consider when administering the MBTI in other cultures?**

   Yes, and these will vary as cultures differ. For example, in cultures in which position and age confer authority, special care needs to be taken about who is giving the Indicator or who may be participating in a group setting to ensure that clients feel comfortable responding from their individual perspectives.

   A cultural norm of agreeableness, or at least of not questioning, may also affect clients' ability to report their own preferences. Practitioners using the MBTI in some Arab cultures report (Schmidt, personal communication, 1997) that these cultures favor "people acting in a way that pleases and never offends." Schmidt has found it particularly important to emphasize during administration that results are confidential and that the MBTI will be most helpful to everyone if respondents report what they really prefer.

   Cultures classified as "collectivist," in which group identity is more important than individual identity, may present special problems. De Beer (personal communication, 1997) and her colleagues are experimenting with providing the following context for administration with indigenous people, who may find it difficult to respond outside of group norms: "We know you are a person well accepted by your community. Would you, however, in doing this questionnaire, go deep inside yourself to tell us who you know yourself to be, to tell us about your uniqueness."

3. **What can I do to give clients from cultural minority groups the best opportunity to get MBTI results that are valid for them?**

   De Beer (personal communication, 1997) expressed her concerns about using the Indicator with clients whose race, gender, or ethnicity place them in a minority or disadvantaged position within their larger culture. De Beer raised the issue in relationship to Black South Africans, but the question has also been asked about reported type of African Americans (Battle, 1989, 1994) and of other U.S. co-cultural groups (Salazar & Sanchez, personal communication, 1997). DiTiberio, Harrison, Sim, and Kim (1995) suggested that cultural values about gender and work roles affect women's ability to report their preference for Thinking or Feeling in several cultures. And in some cultures, religious affiliation or sexual orientation may create similar problems.

   Clients who belong to a minority or disadvantaged group within their larger culture have often developed an adaptive "coping" personality style that they use in interacting with the dominant culture. The concern is that they may be inclined to report that developed style rather than their actual underlying type preferences.

   Practitioners can address these issues directly during administration. Information such as the following may be helpful to these clients:

   > Most people have developed a lot of different behaviors related to work and family roles they play or relationships they have. For some, the environment has required them to develop a coping personality style that is different in significant ways from who they might prefer to be. The purpose in taking the MBTI is to get at your own individual preferences—apart from the roles you play, the skills you've gained, or the coping behaviors you've developed. As you respond to the Indicator, try to answer as you would truly prefer—who you are outside of the expectations of others. Remember, your results will belong to you and are for your use. You will share them with others only if you wish to.

Questions About Interpreting the MBTI and Verifying Type

The MBTI personality inventory has value for clients when it provides additional self-understanding and when that knowledge can be used to improve their appreciation for and interactions with others who are different from them. The interpretation and verification of MBTI results is the necessary starting point for this learning. For this process of understanding and applying type to be effective, practitioners interpreting the MBTI in cultures other than their own need to be especially sensitive about cultural differences in training and learning styles and in the ways type may be experienced and expressed in the particular culture. Assisting clients in making type useful in their lives requires interpreting type in ways that fit culturally for them.

1. **What kinds of general issues do I need to consider when structuring the feedback session for multicultural clients?**

    The general principle is that practitioners need to be sensitive to cultural customs and norms related to training, learning, and appropriate behavior. In cultures in which psychological testing is not customary and/or where training programs are unusual, practitioners need to be especially sensitive about creating a safe environment for interpretation and verification—in group and individual feedback. For group interpretation, this includes understanding power and authority relationships within the culture and taking care about who will participate.

    When using the MBTI in a culture other than their own, practitioners need to anticipate that participant behavior may differ from their usual experience and prepare themselves by seeking information about training and learning styles within that culture. For example, in some cultures, asking questions of the presenter and interjecting comments is considered impolite or aggressive behavior.

    Hofstede's (1980) landmark study based on his survey of 116,000 employees of a large multinational firm in 50 countries identified two cultural differences that may especially influence client expectations and behavior related to receiving MBTI feedback. Hofstede defined these as follows: "power distance," the degree to which a culture recognizes and respects authority relationships or, conversely, emphasizes equality of power; and "uncertainty avoidance," the degree to which a culture values stability and rules to ensure stability or, conversely, encourages diversity of ideas and behavior. These two cultural differences will particularly affect the ways in which participants view their behavior within a group and their relationship to a group leader.

2. **Are there some specific issues related to practitioner style that I need to take into account when planning an MBTI feedback session?**

    Yes. MBTI practitioners in other cultures report that clients in some cultures find the "American" style of training very fast paced and energetic. In fact, one group of Finnish clients (Barger, personal communication, 1995) referred to their American trainers as "like actors." In general, experience giving MBTI feedback in a variety of cultures seems to support modification of the pacing of the session, with clients requesting a slower pace than the rapid style characteristic of many U.S. trainers (Kendall, personal communication, 1997; Fitzgerald, personal communication, 1997). U.S. trainers have found that giving participants regular pauses for individual reflection or for discussions with a partner seem helpful in these settings, and time for these kinds of activities needs to be built in when planning the session.

    Some cultures may require an altogether different approach to the feedback process from that familiar in the United States and other Western countries. De Beer (personal communication, 1997) reported that, when interpreting to professionals in South Africa, practitioners typically follow the general outline of sessions in the United States. However, indigenous people in rural areas in South Africa prefer to hear about type concepts "in the form of a meeting called an *indaba*," perhaps facilitated by a church group. Interested people, led by the eldest of the community, have a discussion at a leisurely pace about, for example, Introversion. Then, the next week, they have a discussion about Extraversion, and so on.

    Taking account of the expectations and needs of clients when structuring feedback sessions requires both a willingness to adapt one's normal approach and some information about the clients. Cultural anthropologists have produced a massive literature on other cultures that can assist trainers.

3. **What resources are available to allow me to develop my knowledge of these issues in another culture?**

    The following are some resources that we have found particularly helpful for the trainer crossing cultures:

    Understanding Culture's Influence on Behavior (Brislin, 1993) provides a basic summary of this issue in language accessible to those outside of cultural anthropology.

    Intercultural Communication: A Reader (Samovar & Porter, 1991) identifies sensitive issues and provides a wealth of information for communicating effectively across cultural differences.

    Culture's Consequences: International Differences in Work-Related Values (Hofstede, 1980) presents Hofstede's analysis of his survey of cultural differences in 116,000 employees of a single multinational firm in 50 different countries; many of these differences suggest ways to adapt training/presentation styles.

Cultures and Organizations: Software of the Mind (Hofstede, 1991) especially focuses on cultural differences related to work.

International Dimensions of Organizational Behavior (Adler, 1991) also addresses the influence of cultural differences within business organizations.

These are considered "culture-general" approaches (Brislin, Cushner, Cherrie, & Yong, 1986), that is, for the most part, they deal with general issues related to working in a different culture or communicating with people in another culture. For "culture-specific" information, we recommend beginning with a "Culturgram," which can be obtained from the David M. Kennedy Center for International Studies at Brigham Young University. Culturgrams provide the practitioner with brief summaries of basic information about more than 100 different cultures.

4. **Do I need to adjust my basic presentation of type information when working with multicultural clients?**

Yes. Practitioners using the MBTI cross-culturally have found that they need to modify their normal presentation because of a couple of important differences: The specific examples or stories they use to illustrate type preference differences may not be familiar or may not be perceived in the same ways in different cultures; and type preferences may be experienced and expressed differently in another culture from the way they are within the practitioner's own culture. Each of these differences requires developing ways to present type concepts and definitions that fit for the group to whom the practitioner is interpreting.

Of course, adapting MBTI feedback to clients is a basic practitioner skill. Working within their own culture, practitioners use type explanations and examples differently when they are interpreting to a family, for example, than when they are interpreting the same material to a work group. When interpreting within a country or culture different from one's own, this practitioner skill needs to be used consistently.

Some of the needed modifications are fairly obvious. For example, illustrations of Sensing–Intuition differences commonly used in the United States— approaches to budgeting, descriptions of time, ways of balancing checking accounts, and the like—frequently do not succeed in illustrating this difference in non-Western cultures.

Somewhat less obvious but even more important necessary modifications come from the influence of cultural values and norms on the ways in which type

preferences are experienced by individuals and expressed in behavior in different cultures. Earlier sections of this chapter described differences in behavior associated with Extraversion and Introversion in the United States and in the United Kingdom, and differences in the normal, type-related behaviors displayed by STJ types in different cultures. Practitioners using the MBTI in other cultures routinely report such behavioral differences. For example, Schmidt (personal communication, 1997) has found that some behaviors typically seen as related to the judging function of Feeling in the United States are, amongst her Saudi Arabian clients, the cultural norm: valuing harmony and making decisions based on the effects of those decisions on other people. Her descriptions and examples of the Thinking and Feeling functions have had to be adjusted to communicate the differences effectively to these clients.

Preparing by doing research on the values and norms of the culture within which one will be interpreting the MBTI is respectful and essential. Of even greater value, perhaps, is an attitude of exploration with clients. Experienced type practitioners have learned that their best examples come from listening to people of a particular type describe themselves; this is doubly true when working with clients from a culture different from the practitioner's own.

5. **What kinds of type descriptions and supporting materials are available for working with multicultural groups in verifying type?**

Type descriptions and supporting materials are a basic practitioner tool for verifying type. Research with Form G in the United States has shown that clients agree with their reported type about 75% of the time, and when they disagree it is generally on one dichotomy on which they had a low preference score (Myers & McCaulley, 1985). Comparisons of MBTI results and clients' decisions about best-fit type from four other English-speaking countries show similar results (Kirby & Barger, 1996). Best-fit type agreement information about Form M in other cultures is not yet available.

Even if the MBTI identified type preferences this well in all cultures, 20% to 25% of clients would disagree with at least one preference reported. A full type description is the preferred tool for verifying client results and for clarifying a preference that the client questions. The overwhelming majority of type descriptions and supporting materials such as *Introduction to Type* were first published in the United States and draw on the authors' experiences with type as expressed by Americans. In spite of the American perspective inevitably present in these, practitioners in other countries report that the type descriptions in

Introduction to Type communicate well to their clients (Kendall, personal communication, 1997; D. Freeman, personal communication, 1997; P. Cauvin, personal communication, 1997).

Additionally, some type descriptions and supporting materials based on the ways type is expressed in a particular culture have been developed or are in process. The best source of information about culturally appropriate type descriptions and supporting materials is the distributor(s) of the MBTI personality inventory in the country with which the practitioner is working. The Consulting Psychologists Press catalog lists international distributors and contact information.

Summary

For effective multicultural administration of the MBTI, practitioners not only need to be familiar with the standard instructions but also need to consider cultural values that may make it difficult for clients to respond according to those instructions. Practitioners are advised to clarify these issues through private interviews with individual clients, asking about their reactions to the instructions. And it is particularly important to emphasize the customary instruction: If you do not understand an item, just omit it and continue. Clients are likely to get more accurate results if they have omitted items in which the meaning is not clear to them, in which they feel a conflict between the options, or in which they are uncomfortable choosing.

MBTI interpretation and verification of results is the context in which type becomes of value to the client. For this process of understanding and personal application to be effective, practitioners using the MBTI in cultures other than their own need to be especially sensitive to differences in training and learning styles and to differences in the ways type may be experienced and expressed relative to cultural values.

Multicultural Type Distribution Samples

Clients in multicultural settings want to know if the MBTI has been used with cultural groups such as theirs and, if it has, what kinds of type distributions seem characteristic (De Beer, personal communication, 1997; Kendall, personal communication, 1997). Practitioners currently have two basic sources for information on type research and practice in various cultures. The research services of the Center for Applications of Psychological Type (CAPT) in Gainesville, Florida, include a database that will produce type tables from different cultures and lists of articles, dissertations,

and conference papers related to type in various cultures. Also, the chapter "Multicultural Applications" in *MBTI Applications* (Kirby & Barger, 1996) is a summary of published research on type in different cultures.

Most of the information available about type and culture is in the form of type tables of MBTI results in different cultures. Fortunately, that is often the kind of information clients request. Using type tables to illustrate group type distributions requires caution on the part of the practitioner for several reasons.

- A number of factors are known to affect reported type on the MBTI:
  - *Age*—Younger groups more often report higher percentages of Extraversion and Perceiving than do comparable older groups.
  - *Education level*—Groups with higher levels of education report higher percentages of Introversion than do groups with less education completed.
  - *Occupation or field of study*—Occupations, specific jobs within occupations, and chosen fields of study tend to attract people of similar types.
  - *Gender*—Males report higher percentages of preference for Thinking than do females.
- All of the type tables of large groups, including those in this chapter, are based on reported type, rather than verified or best-fit type.

The following cautions are recommended for practitioners in using type tables to hypothesize about national distributions.

1. Carefully assess the group to identify any factors known to affect reported type that may be present in the group. Never assume that because the number of people is large, the group must therefore be representative of the larger culture.
2. Recognize that reported type may be affected by a number of other group or individual factors, including cultural values. We would expect that 20%–25% of a large group would, through the verification process, choose a different type as their "best fit" than the one they reported on the MBTI.

National Norming Samples of Type

One of the most frequently asked questions during type interpretations is, What is the distribution of type preferences in this country or culture? The 1985 *MBTI Manual* included several estimates of the distribution of types in the U.S.: Isabel Myers' Pennsylvania high school students, the MBTI databank at the Center for Applications of Psychological Type, and a study conducted by SRI International on American Values and Life Styles (VALS; Myers & McCaulley, 1985, pp. 45–51). A national sample was analyzed by Hammer and Mitchell (1996). Each of these samples is an

Table 14.1   National Normative Samples of Adults

	ISTJ	ISFJ	INFJ	INTJ
U.S.				
National Representative[1]	11.6%	13.8%	1.5%	2.1%
African Americans[2]	15.0%	12.7%	1.4%	1.9%
Hispanics[3]	11.5%	11.2%	0.0%	.48%
U.K.[4]	13.7%	12.7%	1.7%	1.4%

	ISTP	ISFP	INFP	INTP
U.S.				
National Representative[1]	5.4%	8.8%	4.4%	3.3%
African Americans[2]	5.8%	10.0%	2.5%	3.6%
Hispanics[3]	6.8%	8.6%	1.8%	1.8%
U.K.[4]	6.4%	6.1%	3.2%	2.4%

	ESTP	ESFP	ENFP	ENTP
U.S.				
National Representative[1]	4.3%	8.5%	8.1%	3.2%
African Americans[2]	6.1%	9.7%	8.9%	1.4%
Hispanics[3]	5.6%	10.3%	7.7%	1.8%
U.K.[4]	5.8%	8.7%	6.3%	2.8%

	ESTJ	ESFJ	ENFJ	ENTJ
U.S.				
National Representative[1]	8.7%	12.3%	2.5%	1.8%
African Americans[2]	8.9%	8.6%	1.1%	2.5%
Hispanics[3]	9.4%	18.0%	1.8%	2.9%
U.K.[4]	10.4%	12.6%	2.8%	2.9%

Note: [1]N = 3,009; See Appendix for a description of the sample; [2]n = 363; See Appendix for a description of the sample; [3]n = 340; See Appendix for a description of the sample; [4]n = 1,634; Adults in the United Kingdom, MBTI Step I (European English) reported type.

Source: [1]National representative sample; [2]Subsample of national representative sample; [3]Subsample of national representative sample; [4]Kendall & McHenry, 1998.

estimate of U.S. distributions because the studies include factors known to affect MBTI results: age and development (high school sample), education and occupation (CAPT databank), and response/return rate (VALS and Hammer & Mitchell), with the latter two studies most closely resembling a normative sample.

In 1996 and 1997, Consulting Psychologists Press sponsored a national normative sampling of MBTI results as part of the research for the new MBTI Form M. Table 14.1 displays the results of this weighted national sample, reporting separately on African Americans and Hispanics included within the larger national representative sample. During the same period, Oxford Psychologists Press sponsored a similar normative sampling of MBTI Form G results in the United Kingdom. This U.K. type distribution is also displayed in Table 14.1.

The most notable pattern in all the normative samples (VALS, CPP's Form M sample, and OPP's Form G sample) is the predominance of ISJ and ESJ types, the four types that, in type dynamics terms, introvert their Sensing function. These four types total 44%–52% of the people in each of the samples. When using such data, practitioners need to remember the cautions listed above, including that these samples are based on reported type, rather than best-fit type.

Type Tables by Age and Education Level

Researchers have produced several studies of type distributions in groups that may be presumed to be somewhat comparable, and such samples may provide tentative projections of national type distributions. Tables 14.2 and 14.3 show examples of such research.

Table 14.2   Multicultural Type Distribution Samples of High School Students

	ISTJ	ISFJ	INFJ	INTJ
Pennsylvania[1]	6.92%	6.82%	1.79%	2.62%
Australia[2]	8.6%	3.85%	1.27%	2.05%
New Zealand[3]	16.9%	17.5%	2.4%	1.8%
Singapore[4]	17.0%	6.8%	3.1%	4.3%
	ISTP	**ISFP**	**INFP**	**INTP**
Pennsylvania[1]	4.16%	5.40%	3.89%	3.54%
Australia[2]	5.16%	3.68%	3.23%	3.82%
New Zealand[3]	6.0%	6.6%	4.2%	2.7%
Singapore[4]	6.8%	3.2%	3.6%	4.8%
	ESTP	**ESFP**	**ENFP**	**ENTP**
Pennsylvania[1]	6.52%	9.37%	7.60%	4.89%
Australia[2]	8.54%	9.04%	10.11%	6.73%
New Zealand[3]	4.5%	3.9%	5.7%	2.7%
Singapore[4]	7.3%	3.3%	5.5%	5.3%
	ESTJ	**ESFJ**	**ENFJ**	**ENTJ**
Pennsylvania[1]	14.97%	13.97%	3.61%	3.93%
Australia[2]	17.25%	10.11%	3.23%	3.85%
New Zealand[3]	10.9%	8.2%	3.0%	2.7%
Singapore[4]	15.9%	6.0%	2.7%	5.6%

Note: [1]N = 9,320; [2]N = 3,373; [3]N = 993; [4]N = 1,733.

Source: [1]Myers & McCaulley, 1985; [2]Macdaid, McCaulley, & Kainz, 1986; [3]Bathurst, 1995; [4]Lim, 1994.

Again, practitioners need to remember that these samples reflect reported type in the sample groups and that student groups in different cultures may vary significantly in socioeconomic background.

Multicultural Databases

Organizations in several different countries have MBTI type databases that comprise comparable groups: educated, professional adults who have participated in type training programs in organizational and religious settings. Table 14.4 shows type distributions reported by these organizations.

Though the samples presented here are roughly comparable, practitioners need to remember that these are samples of convenience and should not be assumed to indicate national type distributions.

Type Tables by Occupational Group

Data about type distributions within occupations are available for many more cultures, and they demonstrate patterns that allow greater interpretation. Samples of occupational groups consistently show similar type distribution patterns

in a wide variety of cultures. Table 14.5 uses the example of managers in organizations in different cultures.

Type distribution information about managers in various cultures consistently reports an overrepresentation of the Thinking Judging combination. Practitioners and clients can use this information to explore issues such as the organizational values that lead to the selection of Thinking Judging types for managerial positions or the effects on organizations of having a particular type perspective so dominant in management (Fitzgerald & Kirby, 1997b). Type distributions of teachers, religious workers, psychologists, police officers, and other occupational groups also tend to show similarities across cultures and may be used to explore similar issues.

Summary

Practitioners who use the MBTI multiculturally need to prepare themselves for client questions about use of the MBTI and psychological type in their culture and in similar cultures. They also need to be prepared to respond to questions about type distributions. Fortunately, such information is available from a number of sources referred to in this chapter.

Table 14.3   Multicultural Type Distribution Samples of University Students

	ISTJ	ISFJ	INFJ	INTJ
U.S.				
Traditional Age Males[1]	12.48%	5.44%	2.65%	5.40%
Traditional Age Females[2]	6.86%	11.47%	3.79%	2.16%
Canadian				
Ontario Francophones[3]	18.7%	8.8%	3.9%	8.8%
Anglophone Canadians[4]	10.3%	5.5%	5.4%	5.6%
French[5]	15.3%	3.9%	1.6%	4.3%
	ISTP	**ISFP**	**INFP**	**INTP**
U.S.				
Traditional Age Males[1]	6.81%	4.09%	5.32%	6.63%
Traditional Age Females[2]	2.45%	5.74%	5.67%	2.09%
Canadian				
Ontario Francophones[3]	6.1%	3.9%	6.2%	6.0%
Anglophone Canadians[4]	3.3%	3.3%	9.3%	7.9%
French[5]	13.0%	6.6%	8.2%	13.8%
	ESTP	**ESFP**	**ENFP**	**ENTP**
U.S.				
Traditional Age Males[1]	6.72%	4.41%	6.26%	6.77%
Traditional Age Females[2]	2.81%	8.33%	11.74%	3.50%
Canadian				
Ontario Francophones[3]	4.6%	1.7%	4.7%	4.1%
Anglophone Canadians[4]	3.9%	3.4%	10.0%	5.8%
French[5]	8.9%	3.7%	4.3%	8.3%
	ESTJ	**ESFJ**	**ENFJ**	**ENTJ**
U.S.				
Traditional Age Males[1]	12.81%	5.46%	2.98%	5.78%
Traditional Age Females[2]	8.68%	15.05%	6.42%	3.23%
Canadian				
Ontario Francophones[3]	10.4%	5.9%	2.3%	4.1%
Anglophone Canadians[4]	7.4%	7.3%	6.7%	4.9%
French[5]	4.3%	0.9%	0.4%	2.4%

Note: [1]N = 12,637; [2]N = 14,519; [3]N = 1,024; [4]N = 913; [5]N = 672.

Source: [1]Data from the *CAPT-MBTI Atlas,* 1986. Gainesville, FL: Center for Applications of Psychological Type. Data from one of a series of tables from the CAPT-MBTI Data Bank of MBTI records submitted to CAPT for computer scoring between 1971 and December 1982. The subjects were males who, at the time of testing, were between 18 and 25 years of age inclusive, enrolled in school and attending college. This sample was drawn from 55,971 Form F records and 32,671 Form G records. These two databanks comprised 56% females and 44% males. Education level completed was 6% some grade school, 30% high school diploma, 25% some college, 18% bachelor's degree, 11% master's degree, 3% doctoral or postdoctoral work, and 6% unknown. Age group percentages were 11% under 18, 29% 18 to 20, 12% 21 to 24, 10% 25 to 29, 16% 30 to 39, 10% 40 to 49, 5% 50 to 59, 2% 60 plus, and 5% unknown; [2]Data from the *CAPT-MBTI Atlas,* 1986. Gainesville, FL: Center for Applications of Psychological Type. See footnote 1; [3]Casas, 1990; [4]Casas, 1990; [5]Casas, 1990.

Table 14.4   Selected Multicultural Database Samples

	ISTJ	ISFJ	INFJ	INTJ
U.S.				
Males[1]	15.45%	4.42%	2.63%	7.28%
Females[2]	9.77%	10.30%	4.77%	4.00%
Canada				
Francophone[3]	20.71%	6.57%	1.93%	6.08%
Anglophone[4]	15.78%	8.53%	3.97%	8.37%
New Zealand[5]	14.1%	10.4%	5.0%	5.8%
South Africa[6]	19.9%	6.04%	2.31%	6.28%
Korea[7]	21.57%	8.18%	2.4%	5.48%

	ISTP	ISFP	INFP	INTP
U.S.				
Males[1]	6.07%	3.00%	4.76%	7.05%
Females[2]	2.67%	4.27%	6.32%	3.20%
Canada				
Francophone[3]	6.23%	3.52%	4.88%	5.9%
Anglophone[4]	4.35%	3.26%	5.35%	6.07%
New Zealand[5]	4.8%	4.4%	7.6%	5.5%
South Africa[6]	3.25%	1.72%	2.45%	3.95%
Korea[7]	7.84%	6.51%	3.67%	3.31%

	ESTP	ESFP	ENFP	ENTP
U.S.				
Males[1]	5.90%	3.12%	5.38%	6.86%
Females[2]	2.78%	5.73%	9.80%	4.11%
Canada				
Francophone[3]	4.44%	2.90%	6.71%	5.94%
Anglophone[4]	3.44%	2.05%	5.96%	5.33%
New Zealand[5]	4.2%	3.6%	7.6%	5.0%
South Africa[6]	3.8%	2.05%	3.64%	5.6%
Korea[7]	5.34%	5.37%	3.04%	2.19%

	ESTJ	ESFJ	ENFJ	ENTJ
U.S.				
Males[1]	14.01%	4.39%	2.74%	6.93%
Females[2]	10.07%	10.66%	6.38%	5.17%
Canada				
Francophone[3]	15.02%	3.57%	1.50%	4.01%
Anglophone[4]	11.12%	5.46%	3.91%	7.05%
New Zealand[5]	8.2%	5.6%	3.6%	4.8%
South Africa[6]	23.22%	4.9%	2.23%	8.66%
Korea[7]	14.22%	5.60%	1.84%	3.45%

Note: [1]$N = 15,791$; [2]$N = 16,880$; [3]$N = 2,071$; [4]$N = 12,280$; [5]$N = 11,868$; [6]$N = 6,452$; [7]$N = 13,308$.

Source: [1]Data from the *CAPT-MBTI Atlas*, 1986. Gainesville, FL: Center for Applications of Psychological Type. Data from one of a series of tables from the CAPT-MBTI Data Bank of MBTI records submitted to CAPT for computer scoring between March 1978 and December 1982. This sample was a subset of the Form G databank of 32,956 used in the occupation analyses. Education level completed in this databank was 6% some grade school, 42% high school diploma, 25% some college, 12% bachelor's degree, 8% master's degree, 4% doctoral or postdoctoral work, and 3% unknown. Age group percentages were 14% under 18, 40% 18 to 20, 11% 21 to 24, 7% 25 to 29, 11% 30 to 39, 7% 40 to 49, 4% 50 to 59, 1% 60 plus, and 5% unknown. Used with permission; [2]Data from the *CAPT-MBTI Atlas*, 1986. Gainesville, FL: Center for Applications of Psychological Type. Data from one of a series of tables from the CAPT-MBTI Data Bank of MBTI records submitted to CAPT for computer scoring between March 1978 and December 1982. This sample was a subset of the Form G databank of 32,956 used in the occupation analyses. Education level completed in this databank was 6% some grade school, 35% high school diploma, 24% some college, 17% bachelor's degree, 11% master's degree, 2% doctoral or postdoctoral work, and 5% unknown. Age group percentages were 13% under 18, 27% 18 to 20, 8% 21 to 24, 9% 25 to 29, 18% 30 to 39, 10% 40 to 49, 6% 50 to 59, 2% 60 plus, and 7% unknown. Used with permission; [3]Park, 1996; [4]Park, 1996; [5]Bathurst, 1995; [6]Zietsmann, 1996; [7]Sim & Kim, 1993.

Table 14.5   Multicultural Type Distribution Samples of Managers

	ISTJ	ISFJ	INFJ	INTJ
U.S.[1]	17.0%	3.4%	1.9%	10.0%
Canada[2]	21.9%	2.9%	1.6%	11.8%
Mexico[3]	28.9%	0.3%	0.3%	8.3%
Japan				
Top Managers[4]	7.1%	7.1%	1.8%	12.5%
CEOs[5]	5.9%	4.2%	1.7%	16.1%
England[6]	23.8%	6.5%	2.4%	6.5%
Latin America[7]	28.6%	1.5%	0.0%	7.3%

	ISTP	ISFP	INFP	INTP
U.S.[1]	3.4%	1.2%	2.7%	6.6%
Canada[2]	4.6%	1.2%	2.4%	8.3%
Mexico[3]	4.2%	0.1%	0.1%	3.2%
Japan				
Top Managers[4]	0.0%	3.6%	0.0%	3.6%
CEOs[5]	0.8%	1.7%	0.0%	2.5%
England[6]	4.4%	1.2%	3.1%	2.9%
Latin America[7]	2.8%	0.0%	1.0%	1.0%

	ESTP	ESFP	ENFP	ENTP
U.S.[1]	3.2%	1.4%	5.1%	8.1%
Canada[2]	3.9%	1.0%	3.6%	6.7%
Mexico[3]	4.5%	0.3%	0.1%	4.1%
Japan				
Top Managers[4]	10.7%	5.4%	7.1%	3.6%
CEOs[5]	8.5%	5.9%	4.2%	2.5%
England[6]	3.9%	1.2%	2.9%	4.2%
Latin America[7]	4.4%	0.5%	1.5%	1.9%

	ESTJ	ESFJ	ENFJ	ENTJ
U.S.[1]	15.8%	3.6%	3.4%	13.1%
Canada[2]	15.5%	1.9%	2.5%	10.0%
Mexico[3]	36.3%	0.3%	0.1%	9.0%
Japan				
Top Managers[4]	19.6%	3.6%	3.6%	10.7%
CEOs[5]	21.2%	5.1%	3.4%	16.1%
England[6]	20.7%	5.9%	1.6%	8.8%
Latin America[7]	39.3%	1.0%	2.0%	6.0%

Note: [1]N = 37,549; [2]N = 3,798; [3]N = 1,010; [4]N = 56; [5]N = 118; [6]N = 849; [7]N = 206.

Source: [1]Osborn, Osborn, & Twillman, 1996; [2]Osborn, Osborn, & Twillman, 1996; [3]Osborn, Osborn, & Twillman, 1996; [4]Macdaid, McCaulley, & Kainz, 1986; [5]Macdaid, McCaulley, & Kainz, 1986; [6]Macdaid, McCaulley, & Kainz, 1986; [7]Macdaid, McCaulley, & Kainz, 1986.

Some cautions apply to interpretation of type tables: In all the examples in this section, the samples are presumed to be comparable but not exact; for example, even where students are at the same level of schooling, different percentages of people participate at that level in each of the countries; and the multicultural databases presented are samples of convenience. The temptation for clients is to overinterpret type distributions; thus practitioners need to emphasize the partial and tentative nature of most of the data available. Practitioners and their clients can identify patterns but need to interpret with caution.

Conclusion

This chapter has emphasized differences when the MBTI is used in multicultural settings and cautions about its use with people culturally different from those with whom it was developed. It is also important to recognize the positive experience of practitioners using the MBTI outside of the United States:

1. Both psychological type and the MBTI have been used effectively in dozens of cultures, some very different from U.S. middle-class culture.

2. Research and practitioner experience in using the MBTI multiculturally is overwhelmingly positive—clients recognize the patterns identified by psychological type, give examples of their use of preferences from their own experience, and find type's identification of normal differences very helpful in increasing their understanding of themselves and others.

3. The perspective and ethics associated with psychological type and the MBTI, summarized by Myers as "the constructive use of differences," make type and the MBTI particularly useful in cross-cultural work and in multicultural settings, where respect for human diversity is of paramount importance.

Sources and Descriptions of Samples of the 1998 Revision

Description of National Sample and National Representative Sample

National Sample

A stratified random sampling procedure was used to collect the national sample. This procedure, collected in 1996, was designed to yield a sample that would be representative of the U.S. population. However, the actual sample does not match U.S. census data. Caucasian females are overrepresented, and African American males are underrepresented, relative to the U.S. census data. Further, ethnic categories for people of American Indian, Asian/Pacific Islander, or Eskimo/Aleut descent were not available.

National Representative, or Weighted, Sample

The national representative, or weighted, sample was developed to approximate the U.S. population in terms of gender and ethnicity (African American, Caucasian, Hispanic/ Latino). Based on U.S. census data, weights for gender and ethnicity were applied to the national sample (described above) to yield the national representative, or weighted, sample.

Sample	N	Type of Sample	Age M(SD)	Gender Female	Gender Male
Test-Retest Reliability					
Consulting Psychologists Press	50	Employees	36(9)	68%	32%
Public Utilities Company	258	Employees	44(8)	50%	50%
Virginia Commonwealth University	116	College Students	25(8)	82%	18%
Validity					
The Ball Foundation	92	College Students	24(6)	55%	45%
Employee Career Enrichment Program, University of Minnesota	98	University Employees	41(9)	89%	11%
Fairview Health Services Career Resource Center	261	Health Care Employees	41	85%	14%
Iowa State University	279	College Students	21(4)	71%	29%
Middle Tennessee State University Counseling & Testing Center	198	College Freshmen	19(2)	56%	44%
Asian/Pacific American Learning Resource Center, University of Minnesota	313	College Freshmen	19	60%	40%
National Sample	3,036	Stratified Random	47(17)	54%	46%
National Representative Sample	3,009	Representative "Weighted"	46(17)	51%	49%
Trinity Lutheran Church, Minnesota	101	Community	48(18)	61%	39%
EQI Sample	139	MBA Students/Adults	34(7)	24%	72%
CRI Sample	157	Working Adults	40(11)	67%	31%

	Ethnicity Caucasian	Ethnicity African American	Ethnicity Asian American	Ethnicity Latino/Latina	Ethnicity Missing/Other	Instruments Completed
Test-Retest						MBTI Form M
Consulting Psychologists Press	na	na	na	na	na	
Public Utilities Company	156	4	2	56	40	
Virginia Commonwealth University	na	na	na	na	na	
Validity						
The Ball Foundation	63	17	1	1	10	Subscales of *Ball Aptitude Battery*
Employee Career Enrichment Program, University of Minnesota	87	2	1	1	6	*Work Environment Scale*, Ideal and Real forms
Fairview Health Services Career Resource Center	243	0	1	1	16	*Maslach Burnout Inventory, Values Scale, Salience Inventory*
Iowa State University	236	11	10	7	15	*Strong Interest Inventory, Skills Confidence Inventory, Career Factors Inventory, Adjective Check List, Positive and Negative Affectivity Scale*
Middle Tennessee State University Counseling & Testing Center	127	44	2	3	22	*Strong Interest Inventory, Career Factors Inventory, Problem Solving Inventory, Social Skills Inventory*
Asian/Pacific American Learning Resource Center, University of Minnesota	0	23	251	20	19	MBTI Form M
National Sample	2,687	139	na	106	106	FIRO-B, CPP Survey
National Representative Sample	2,203	363	na	340	103	
Trinity Lutheran Church, Minnesota	89	0	0	0	12	MBTI Forms M and G
EQI Sample	na	na	na	na	na	*Emotional Quotient Inventory*
CRI Sample	107	10	10	10	20	*Coping Resources Inventory*

Note: All sample groups completed the MBTI Form M.

Notes

Chapter 1

1. The letter "N" is used to identify Intuition because "I" is used to label Introversion. It should also be noted that Jung used the term *sensation* in his writings rather than Myers' preferred term *Sensing*.

2. A low to moderate correlation has been consistently found between the S–N and J–P dichotomies of the MBTI. Myers believed, as do many current type experts, that this relationship represents a real and natural association between the two dichotomies and is not simply attributable to measurement or sample error. Chapter 7 further explicates the rationale for this relationship.

Chapter 3

1. Myers and Briggs also use both of these terms, *attitude* and *orientation,* as equivalent when referring to Extraversion and Introversion.

2. Myers and Briggs use the term *process* interchangeably with Jung's term *function*. In his writings, Jung occasionally used the term *process* as denoting the same thing as *function*. The MBTI manual treats the two terms as equivalent but for clarity and consistency uses the term *function* in most instances.

3. This method of determining type dynamics—that is, which of the functions is dominant, auxiliary, and so on—is a distinctive feature of the MBTI. The *Jungian Type Survey* (Wheelwright, Wheelwright, & Buehler, 1964), which purports to elicit Jung's psychological types, does not include a fourth dichotomy such as J–P. Dominant versus auxiliary functions are determined by a "higher score" criterion. See Chapters 5 and 9 for a discussion of comparative clarity of preference for MBTI dominant and auxiliary functions.

4. Intellectual tradition and various research approaches have associated creativity with an Intuitive preference. When *creativity* is defined as the creation of something new that has not existed before, one can appropriately describe Sensing perception as "creative" as well. The *process* whereby Sensing develops something new may be the step-by-step, methodical, and detailed procedure characteristic of *introverted* Sensing, or the *extraverted* Sensing process of creating something new by adapting and combining whatever elements are available in the current situation. The Sensing process is in contrast to the flashes of insight that we associate with Intuition. However, the *product* created through either introverted or extraverted Sensing may be a new one that has not existed before. A likely example of introverted Sensing creativity may be Thomas Edison's inventions involving electricity, which reportedly resulted from a long series of trial-and-error efforts to find an effective conductor.

5. Measures of "shyness" are typically correlated with various measures of Introversion, including Introversion as elicited on the MBTI. This is an inevitable consequence of the overlap in content of test items used to identify Introversion and shyness. However, shyness and Introversion are not necessarily related. Some Extraverts describe themselves as socially shy, and some Introverts describe themselves as socially outgoing or gregarious. The E–I subscales of the Step II Expanded Interpretive Report (EIR) shed some light on this observation.

6. When referring to the two attitudes specified by Jung, therefore, only Extraversion and Introversion are meant. Myers and Briggs referred to their added dichotomy of Judging versus Perceiving as *attitudes* or *orientations*. The MBTI manual uses both of these terms interchangeably in referring to the Extraversion versus Introversion *attitudes* or *orientations*, and the Judging versus Perceiving *attitudes* or *orientations*.

7. This view was implied in some of Jung's writings (see previous discussion on page 28). Two other hypotheses have been advanced. One (Grant, Thompson, & Clark, 1983) sees the tertiary as taking the same attitude as the dominant function; the other (Quenk, 1993) favors the notion that the tertiary may take either attitude, depending on circumstances or individual habits. Toward the end of her life, Isabel Myers appeared to favor this latter view (Quenk, 1993; see footnote 3.8, p. 276).

8. The approach taken in the *Jungian Type Survey* (Wheelwright, Wheelwright, & Buehler, 1964) is that the orientation or attitude of both dominant and auxiliary functions is to the preferred attitude of Extraversion or Introversion. In this system, only the unconscious *inferior function* is oriented toward the less-preferred attitude.

9. An inevitable psychometric consequence of differential type development in young people, as well as incomplete development in an indeterminate percentage of adults, is that reliability estimates appear lower than would be the case if all respondents were mature and well developed in their type. See Chapter 8 for further explanation of this important aspect of type development theory.

10. Research on brain activity patterns (see Chapter 9) provides emerging empirical evidence for the innate nature of type preferences.

Chapter 4

1. These descriptions of the four temperaments were developed by L. V. Berens and appear in Berens, L. V., *Understanding Yourself and Others, An Introduction to Temperament*. Huntington Beach, CA: Telos Publications, 1998. The material was adapted with her permission.

Chapter 5

1. Word-pair items are probably a little more difficult. Presently there is no method for determining reading level of such items.

Chapter 10

1. *MBTI Applications: A Decade of Research on the Myers-Briggs Type Indicator* (Hammer, 1996b) provides a summary of the research included in the 1985 *MBTI Manual* and a detailed review of research published in the subsequent 10 years. Where available, new studies not covered in *MBTI Applications* are included in this chapter.
2. Note that more recent representative samples as discussed in Chapters 2 and 7 indicate a different proportion of Introverts in the U.S. population. Application of these newer estimates may affect this statistical result.

Chapter 14

1. The term *multicultural* in this chapter refers to using the MBTI with diverse cultural groups or with individual clients from diverse cultural backgrounds. *Cross-cultural* and *international* (the terms generally used in this chapter) refer to using the MBTI in any country or culture different from those of the group with whom the instrument was developed.

   The MBTI Form G was developed primarily with middle-class White Americans. Form M development included testing on a national representative sample in the U.S. based on census data and therefore includes a more diverse population. Form M has not yet been tested or used in cultures outside the U.S., so the data in this chapter are from use of Form G except where noted (Table 14.1).
2. Two notable exceptions are cultural anthropologists Richard Brislin and Gary Weaver, who attended, presented at, and participated in panels at "Psychological Type and Culture—East and West: A Multicultural Research Symposium," January 1993, University of Hawaii at Manoa, Honolulu, Hawaii. Their participation and comments were in the nature of "explorations," and neither indicated acceptance or evidence of psychological type's universality.

achievement measure. An assessment of competence in an area, such as the grade obtained after a course of study; a summary of the grades received in obtaining an educational degree, such as the grade point average; scores on tests that assess the degree to which a respondent has learned a particular skill or body of information.

analysis of variance (ANOVA). A statistical analysis used to determine the effects of one or more categorical independent variables on the variance of a continuous dependent variable. The analysis indicates which of the independent variables have a significant effect on the variance of the dependent variable and also identifies any statistical interactions among the independent variables that may affect the dependent variable.

ANOVA. *See* **analysis of variance.**

a posteriori. A probability that has been revised based on prior information; a probability that is conditional on a prior event or on prior knowledge.

APT. *See* **Association for Psychological Type.**

aptitude measure. A test or other device designed to assess a person's potential, either for learning in general (e.g., an intelligence test) or for learning in a specific area (e.g., a test of mechanical aptitude). Aptitude measures are in contrast to achievement measures, which assess acquired knowledge.

Association for Psychological Type (APT). A membership organization devoted to promoting the ethical use of psychological type through training workshops, international and regional conferences, and local chapters.

asymptote. A straight line approached by a given curve as one of the variables that defines the curve approaches infinity; the theoretical upper or lower limit of such a curve. A curve is asymptotic if it approaches such a limit.

attitude. Extraversion and Introversion in Jung's theory. In MBTI usage, the term *attitude* also refers to the Judging–Perceiving dichotomy. In MBTI usage, interchangeable with the term *orientation.*

auxiliary function or auxiliary process. The function or process that is second in importance and that provides balance (a) between perception and judgment and (b) between Extraversion and Introversion.

best-fit type. The type that a respondent has verified as providing the most accurate description of him- or herself, based on self-knowledge. *Contrast* **reported type** *and* **true type.**

best-fit type study. A study of a sample of 2,116 respondents to the MBTI, obtained from a variety of type workshops and in other settings over a period of several years; respondents provided assessments of their best-fit types for comparison with their reported types.

CAPT. *See* **Center for Applications of Psychological Type, Inc.**

CAPT MBTI Data Bank. A research bank of over 800,000 computer-scored MBTI answer sheets collected from 1971 to the present.

Center for Applications of Psychological Type, Inc (CAPT). A nonprofit public organization for education, research, and services relating to the MBTI, including training workshops and publications.

chi-square test. A statistical test used to determine the degree of independence or relationship between nominal and categorical variables; the test involves a comparison of the observed frequencies in each category with the expected frequencies and determines the probability that the difference between these frequencies occurred by chance.

classical test theory (CTT). A model used to construct, score, and evaluate instruments designed to measure individual differences. Classical test theory assumes that every individual has some hypothetical but unobservable *true score* on a given variable, but we estimate this true score through an *observed score* on a measuring instrument. Because the observed score is only an estimate of the hypothetical true score, CTT uses methods for determining the reliability of observed scores. CTT also includes estimates of an item's difficulty and of its discriminating ability. The forms of the MBTI that preceded Form M applied classical test theory in scale development, scoring, and evaluation of the forms.

coefficient alpha. A measure of internal consistency reliability based on the average inter-item correlation and the number of items on the scale. Also called *Cronbach's alpha.*

Comfort Scales. The seven scales of the **Type Differentiation Indicator (TDI)** that are obtained through the scoring of MBTI Form J.

Consulting Psychologists Press, Inc. (CPP). Publisher of the MBTI and related MBTI materials as well as a number of other psychological instruments.

continuous score. On forms preceding Form M, a transformation of a preference score such that the midpoint is set at 100 and the preference score for E, S, T, or J is subtracted from 100 and preference scores for I, N, F, or P are added to 100. On Form M, the continuous scores are the theta scores from the IRT scoring program. Such scores are used for research. It is not recommended that they be interpreted to respondents.

continuum. A characteristic or property that varies in size or amount, cannot be subdivided except by arbitrary division, and is measured by a series of numbers that are ordered in size from small to large or vice versa. The increments between numbers are the same size all along the continuum and represent equal amounts of the characteristics being measured. In personality measures, the categories of Likert scales are assumed to be a continuum, for example, a seven-point rating scale ranging from very dissatisfied to very satisfied.

CPP. *See* **Consulting Psychologists Press, Inc. (CPP).**

CTT. *See* **classical test theory.**

dependent variable. In a research study or statistical analysis, the dependent variable is the one that is acted upon (influenced by) other variables. Whether a given variable is considered to be independent or dependent may vary depending on the study design or the analysis being done.

Diagnostic and Statistical Manual **(DSM).** The official manual defining psychiatric and psychological diagnoses.

dichotomy. Literally, a division into two distinct parts. In type theory, the two parts are assumed to identify opposite domains of mental functioning or attitudes. Dichotomous constructs differ qualitatively as well as quantitatively from continuous variables. The four dichotomies of the MBTI are Extraversion–Introversion, Sensing–Intuition, Thinking–Feeling, and Judging–Perceiving.

DIF. *See* **differential item functioning.**

differential item functioning (DIF). An analysis based on item response theory that is designed to determine whether a test item performs similarly or differently across demographic subgroups (e.g., males versus females, or younger versus older subjects).

differentiation. The process of separation whereby distinct parts emerge from an intermingled single entity. A *differentiated type function* is one that is separate and exists by itself, so that it can operate on its own without being mixed up with or contaminated by any other function.

dominant function or **dominant process.** The function or process that is assumed to be the first developed, most conscious, and most differentiated, and which becomes the governing force dominating and unifying one's life.

DOR. *See* **dropout ratio.**

dropout ratio (DOR). A selection ratio in which the ratio compares the proportion of a type that drops out of an occupation, program, or other group being studied to the proportion in the original population.

E. *See* **Extraversion.**

EAR. *See* **Expanded Analysis Report.**

EIR. *See* **MBTI Step II Expanded Interpretive Report.**

elementary interactions. Interactions between two or more of the four type letters, *excluding* the type dynamics interactions.

elementary school. In the U.S., grades one through four; the age range of elementary school children is approximately 6 through 10.

Expanded Analysis Report (EAR). An earlier name for the **MBTI Step II Expanded Interpretive Report.**

Expanded Interpretive Report. *See* **MBTI Step II Expanded Interpretive Report.**

Extraversion (E). The attitude (orientation) that identifies the direction and flow of energy to the outer world.

Extravert, Extraverted type. An individual who has a preference for the Extraverted attitude over the Introverted attitude.

F. *See* **Feeling.**

factor analysis. A method of creating groupings of items or factors that are highly related to each other and distinct from other groups of items (factors); an underlying theme or construct unifies the items that make up a factor. A method of discovering or determining the groupings or factors inherent in a set of items or variables. A statistical technique designed to find the variables or items that are most related to one another and that are distinct from other groups. *Exploratory factor analysis* makes no assumptions about the underlying structure among the variables; *confirmatory factor analysis*, a much more rigorous procedure, tests for a specific hypothesized structure in the item set.

Feeling (F). Of the two opposite judging functions, the one by which decisions are made through ordering choices in terms of personal values.

Feeling types. People who prefer Feeling over Thinking as a way of making judgments.

forced-choice format. A style of asking questions that requires the respondent to choose one of the two options presented. It is the method used for all MBTI items.

Form AV. A discontinued self-scorable form of the MBTI that consisted of the first 50 items of Form G. The reliability of Form AV relative to Form G was unacceptable, and it has not been in use for a number of years.

Form G. This form preceded Form M as the standard form and also has a self-scorable version.

Form J. This is the current research form and takes the place of the previous Form F, which has been discontinued. Form J is used for MBTI Step III, which includes the seven Comfort Scales of the Type Differentiation Indicator (TDI)

Form K. This form contains all items needed to score for four-letter type as well as additional items needed to yield the Step II Expanded Interpretive Report.

Form M. This is the standard form of the MBTI for general use. A self-scorable version of Form M is available.

function or **process.** One of the four basic mental processes of Sensing, Intuition, Thinking, and Feeling.

function pairs. The pairs created by combining each of the two perceiving functions with each of the two judging functions. There are four function pairs—ST, SF, NF, NT.

GH procedure. A multiple comparison procedure for comparing several means post hoc in an ANOVA when the variances of the groups are unequal.

grade point average. A measure of scholastic achievement that averages a student's grades over a designated time period, such as an academic semester, total years in a degree program, and so forth.

high school. In the United States, the school that teaches students in grades 9 through 12, whose ages are approximately 14 through 18. Graduation from high school is required for admission to a college or university.

I. *See* **Introversion.**

ICC. *See* **item characteristics curve.**

independent variable. In a research study or statistical analysis, the independent variable is one whose influence on another variable is being studied. Whether a given variable is considered to be independent or dependent may vary depending on the study design or the analysis being done.

inferior function. The function opposite to the dominant function, also called the *fourth function* or *least-preferred function*. The inferior function is assumed to be the most unconscious, least experienced, and least differentiated of the functions, serving as a potential source of difficulties as well as growth.

internal consistency reliability. A measure of the reliability or consistency with which a group of respondents answer the items that make up a scale. *See also* **split-half reliability** and **coefficient alpha.**

Introversion. The attitude (orientation) that identifies the direction and flow of attention and energy to the inner world.

Introvert, Introverted type. An individual who has a preference for the Introverted attitude over the Extraverted attitude.

Intuition (N). Of the two opposite perceiving functions, the one that is concerned with meanings, relationships, patterns, and possibilities.

Intuitive type. A person who prefers Intuition over Sensing as a way of perceiving.

IRT. *See* **item response theory**.

IRT scoring. The method of scoring used with Form M of the MBTI, which involves looking at a person's response to each item on a scale and then determining the value of theta that is the most likely or probable value to have produced such a set of item responses. If the most likely theta is to the right of the midpoint, the preference is I, N, F, or P, depending on the scale. If the most likely theta is to the left of the midpoint, the preference is E, S, T, or J, depending on the scale. Theta is then converted to a preference clarity index to arrive at the numerical portion of the result.

Isabel Briggs Myers Memorial Library. A collection of over 2,700 MBTI-related books, articles, dissertations, journals, and other materials. The library is housed at the Center for Applications of Psychological Type (CAPT) in Gainesville, Florida. Library materials are available to interested persons. An updated bibliography that currently lists over 6,000 entries is also available.

item characteristic curve (ICC). In item response theory, a curve describing a test item. It shows the rate at which an item would hypothetically be endorsed by people who have varying levels of the characteristic in question. The rate of item endorsement varies from 0 to 100% and is plotted on the vertical axis of the curve. The horizontal axis shows levels of the psychological characteristic, for example, scores on a test.

item response theory (IRT). An approach to measurement that is concerned with modeling the relationship between item responses and the underlying characteristic that is assessed by the scale or test that the item is designed to measure. It can be used to select items for a test and/or to score the items. IRT is a tool of modern test theory. *Contrast* **classical test theory**.

J. *See* **Judging**.

Judging (J). The attitude (orientation) that indicates that either Thinking or Feeling is the preferred way of dealing with the outer world and is likely to appear in observable behavior.

judging functions. Thinking and Feeling.

Judging type. A person who has a judging attitude, that is, prefers to use a judging function (Thinking or Feeling) rather than a perceiving function (Sensing or Intuition) when dealing with the outer world

judgment. A term that refers to the process of making a decision or coming to a conclusion.

Likert scale. An item or question format in which a respondent is presented with a statement and is then asked to select from a number of choices that indicate his or her degree of agreement with the statement (e.g., strongly disagree to strongly agree). The number of choices can vary and the inclusion of a neutral category is optional.

LISREL. A statistical software package that is used to model and test the causal relationships among a system of variables; it allows for the simultaneous evaluation of both the measurement and the causal components in a set of variables.

logical split-half procedure. The method used to create two halves of the MBTI for use in split-half reliability studies. The MBTI items were split into halves taking all available item statistics into consideration and pairing items that most resemble each other. Logical split-halves were used for Form M as well as for forms preceding Form M.

Mantel-Haenszel statistic (M-H Δ). A statistic used to test the hypothesis that there is no differential item functioning across subgroups.

MBTI Step II Expanded Interpretive Report (EIR). A report utilizing the Step II scoring system to provide a detailed interpretation of the 20 subscales of the four dichotomies of the MBTI. MBTI Form K produces these subscales. Interpretation of this report allows exploration of individuality within type by showing a person's distinctive way of experiencing and expressing aspects of each type dichotomy.

middle school. In the United States, grades five through eight. The ages of children in middle school range from approximately 10 through 14.

midpoint. The division point on the scale for one of the four dichotomies that separates respondents into one of the two opposite categories; for example, the point that distinguishes Introverts from Extraverts or Sensing types from Intuitive types. Accurate identification of the midpoint is critical for the MBTI because the opposite categories are hypothesized to be qualitatively and not merely quantitatively different.

N. *See* **Intuition**.

national representative sample (NRS). A sample of 3,009 respondents from the national sample weighted so as to approximate the 1990 U.S. census distribution by gender and ethnic groupings.

national sample (NS). A sample of 3,009 individuals collected in 1997 by Consulting Psychologists Press, Inc., publisher of the MBTI, using a stratified random selection procedure based on random digit dialing of telephone numbers. The research form of the MBTI was given, and a number of other research questions were asked of these subjects.

NRS. *See* **national representative sample**.

NS. *See* **national sample**.

omissions. On the MBTI, questions in which neither of the two choices was selected. In research using Form M, cases are dropped if the number of omissions exceeds four on the E–I and J–P dichotomies and five on the S–N and T–F dichotomies.

orientation. Used interchangeably with the term *attitude* when referring to the MBTI dichotomies of Extraversion–Introversion and Judging–Perceiving. The E–I referent is to *orientation of energy;* the J–P referent is to *orientations to the outer world.*

orthogonal. Variables that are uncorrelated; when graphed, the variables can be visualized as forming a right angle in space.

P. *See* **Perceiving**.

pcc. *See* **preference clarity category**.

pci. *See* **preference clarity index**.

Perceiving. The attitude (orientation) that indicates that either Sensing or Intuition is the preferred way of dealing with the outer world and is likely to appear in observable behavior.

perceiving functions. Sensing and Intuition.

Perceiving type. A person who has a perceiving attitude, that is, prefers to use a perceiving function (Sensing or Intuition) when dealing with the outside world.

perception. A term that refers to the process of acquiring information.

phi coefficient. A correlation coefficient used when both variables being correlated are in the form of true dichotomies.

phrase questions. Questions in any of the forms of the MBTI that present sentences or phrases for comparison.

points. On forms of the MBTI that preceded Form M, the eight weighted sums of the values for each item on each scale, as obtained from the hand-scoring templates. For Form M, there are no points for the IRT computer-scored version. However, for the Form M self-scorable and template versions, the corresponding term is **raw points**. Neither Form G points nor Form M raw points are interpretable, being only a step in determining either the **preference score** or the **preference clarity index.**

polar opposites. Dynamic elements that are opposite to each other in both function and attitude. For example, the polar opposite of dominant extraverted Thinking is inferior introverted Feeling; the opposite of dominant introverted Sensing is inferior extraverted Intuition, and so on.

pole. Either opposite preference category of a bipolar MBTI dichotomy, such as the *Thinking pole* of the T–F dichotomy or the *Introversion pole* of the E–I dichotomy.

polychoric correlation. A correlation coefficient used when both variables being correlated represent, or have been split into, two or more categories.

prediction ratio. The formula used for item analysis of MBTI forms preceding Form M, which shows the probability that any response is given in accord with total scale score (e.g., the probability that a response designed for Extraverts is given by Extraverts and not given by Introverts). The prediction ratio is designed to indicate how well any item discriminates between choices for its scored preference.

preference. One of each pair of the four basic mental functions and attitudes that in type theory structure an individual's personality. Each type dichotomy comprises two preferences: Extraversion or Introversion, Sensing or Intuition, Thinking or Feeling, and Judging or Perceiving.

preference clarity. An estimate of the extent to which a respondent reports favoring one pole of a dichotomy over its opposite, based on responses to the MBTI. Such estimates include the *preference score* calculated on forms preceding Form M, and the *preference clarity category* and *preference clarity index* used with Form M. *See also* **preference clarity category** and **preference clarity index.**

preference clarity category (pcc). A term for a range of **preference clarity indexes** that designates the clarity of a reported preference for one or the other pole of a dichotomy. The preference clarity categories are as follows:

> *slight:*   pci = 1–5
> *moderate:* pci = 6–15
> *clear:*   pci = 16–25
> *very clear:* pci = 26–30

For template and self-scored versions of the MBTI, the pcc is obtained from the raw points associated with each preference. For the ranges used, see Table 5.4, page 112.

preference clarity index (pci). A ratio showing how consistently a person answered the questions on the scale of interest compared to the maximum possible score achievable on that scale. It is analogous to what was formerly referred to as a preference score. The pci is the basic result of scoring the MBTI. It consists of a letter to denote the direction of preference and a number to indicate the clarity or the consistency with which the person indicated that preference. The pci is derived by dividing the theta score for a person by the maximum theta possible for that preference for that scale (using the national sample as a base population), multiplying by 30, and rounding up to the nearest integer. Thus, all preference clarity indexes are standardized on a scale from 1 to 30.

preference domain. A set of characteristics that define one of the eight bipolar preferences (E, I, S, N, T, F, J, P) of the MBTI typology

preference score. On MBTI forms that preceded Form M, a number designed to show how consistently a respondent chose one pole of a dichotomy over its opposite. The corresponding term for Form M is **preference clarity index.**

PRELIS. A statistical software package used to prepare data sets for use by another statistical software package, LISREL.

process. *See* **function.**

psychological opposite. An item option that is not necessarily logically opposite to the other option, but rather is attractive to an individual who holds the preference that the option is intended to elicit. Item options serve as stimuli to evoke the desired response rather than as grammatically consistent pairings.

r. *See* **reliability coefficient.**

raw points. On the Form M self-scorable and Form M template versions of the MBTI, the sum of item responses for each preference in a dichotomy. The term *points* was also used on forms that preceded Form M. Neither the raw *points* of Form M nor the *points* of previous forms is interpretable, being only a step in determining either the **preference clarity index** or **preference score.**

reliability coefficient (r). In classical test theory (CTT), a number (a correlation coefficient or a percent agreement) indicating the consistency with which a given sample of respondents answers the test items. Reliability coefficients are calculated for consistency over time (test-retest reliability) as well as consistency among the items on a given scale (internal consistency reliability).

reported type. The four-letter type that is indicated from a person's responses to the MBTI assessment tool. Reported type is in contrast to **true type** and **best-fit**, or **verified**, **type**

rolling norms. A procedure for collecting normative data for a test or survey that involves identifying a sample from the desired population and then using contacts within that sample to lead to the next sample.

S. *See* **Sensing.**

scale. One of the four dichotomies of the MBTI, that is, the E–I scale, S–N scale, etc. Because the term *scale* tends to connote an amount of a characteristic, as is typical of trait measures, it is typically limited to discussion of the psychometric characteristics of the MBTI.

selection ratio. The ratio of the number occurring in a type or group of types compared to the number expected to occur.

selection ratio type table (SRTT). A type table on a group that has been compared to another population. The table shows the frequency, percent, selection ratio, and a probability based on a chi-square analysis for each type and type grouping.

sensation. The term used by Jung and many current Jungians that corresponds to the term **Sensing** in MBTI terminology.

Sensing. The perceiving function that is concerned with experiences available to the senses.

Sensing type. A person who prefers Sensing over Intuition as a way of perceiving.

shared facets of type. Typological characteristics that are held in common by types that share one or more preferences.

Spearman Brown formula. Formula used to estimate the reliability of a long form using the known reliabilities of a form with fewer items.

split-half reliability. A method of assessing the internal consistency of a scale based on splitting the items into two parts that are assumed to be equivalent and then correlating the scores from the two parts.

split-half scores (also called X-half and Y-half scores). Scores developed from splitting a scale into two halves; used for computing split-half reliabilities. Half of the questions are assigned to what is called the X scale and half to the Y scale.

standard error (SE). An estimate of the degree to which a score is characterized by unsystematic sources of variance. The higher the standard error, the less precise the score and the more "noise" there is in the score. Classical test theory (CTT) traditionally uses a single standard error for the entire scale; item response theory (IRT) provides a measure of standard error at each value of theta.

static level of interpretation. In contrast to the *dynamic* or *developmental* level of interpretation, a way of understanding type that is limited to definitions and characteristics of the four dichotomies considered separately, that is, with no attention to dynamic interactions among the preferences or developmental issues in the expression of type.

statistical interaction. A situation in which two or more independent (causative) variables affect a dependent variable (the one being acted upon) in ways that are different from what their separate effects on the dependent variables would be if you added them together.

Step I. A scoring system for MBTI items that yields a person's four-letter type; the letters result from the respondent's indicated preferences on each of the four MBTI dichotomies.

Step II. A scoring system for MBTI items that yields subscales that are components or facets of the underlying dichotomy of each of the four main scales. These subscales resulted from a factor analysis of a large group of MBTI items. The second-order factor analysis of the subscales yields the familiar four dichotomies of type. *See also* **MBTI Step II Expanded Interpretive Report (EIR)** and **Form K.**

Step II Expanded Interpretive Report. *See* **MBTI Step II Expanded Interpretive Report (EIR).**

Step III. *See* **Step III Type Differentiation Indicator (TDI).**

Step III Type Differentiation Indicator (TDI). A method of scoring Form J of the MBTI that yields seven additional subscales to those of Step II. These are known as *Comfort Scales.*

straws in the wind. The metaphor used by Isabel Myers to describe her approach to writing items for the MBTI. She reasoned that because people's preferences are often not consciously formulated, they probably could not report about them directly. The simple questions of the Indicator were therefore designed as observable "pointers," or "straws in the wind," that allow us to make inferences about the direction of the wind (i.e., the underlying preference) itself.

T. *See* **Thinking.**

TCC. *See* **test characteristics curve.**

TDI (Type Differentiation Indicator). *See* **Step III Type Differentiation Indicator.**

temperament. One of four categories hypothesized to be basic ways of identifying individual differences in personality. As conceptualized by modern temperament theorists, these categories are Guardian, Artisan, Idealist, and Rationalist.

tertiary function. The function opposite to the auxiliary function in the dynamics of any type. For example, if the auxiliary function is Thinking, the tertiary function is Feeling. In theory, the tertiary function is less accessible to conscious direction than the auxiliary function, but more accessible than the unconscious inferior function.

test characteristics curve. The composite of the information described by *item characteristics curves.*

test information function (TIF). In item response theory, the sum of the information found in the individual items that make up a scale, i.e., the sum of item information functions. Specifically, it is an indication of the amount of precision produced by a test at each possible value of theta (θ). The TIF is the equivalent of the reliability coefficient of classical test theory (CTT).

test standard error (TSE). The item response theory equivalent of the *standard error of measurement* in CTT (classical test theory). TSE shows the expected standard error that would be found when estimating θ scores from the observed item responses across the full range of possible θ scores.

tetrachoric correlation. A correlation coefficient used when both variables being correlated are in the form of artificial dichotomies.

theta (θ). In IRT terminology, test scores on a psychological characteristic that are roughly equivalent to the "true scores" of classical test theory. Theta scores correspond directly to MBTI continuous scores that were calculated using the prediction ratio method developed by Isabel Myers. Theta scores can be dichotomized by identifying a cut-off point or midpoint that separates individuals into two groups, associated with the poles of a dichotomy.

Thinking (T). Of the two opposite judging functions, the one by which decisions are made by ordering choices in terms of logical cause-effect and objective analysis of relevant information.

Thinking type. A person who prefers using Thinking over Feeling as a way of making judgments.

three-parameter model. In item response theory, the use of three parameters to model the relationship between item responses and the latent characteristic that the items are designed to measure. The three parameters are

a parameter: the amount of *information* available from the item; the slope of the item characteristic curve at any given value of theta; higher *a* parameters provide more information or discrimination among people with different levels of theta

b parameter: a measure of item *difficulty* based on the area on the theta scale at which a test item produces the maximum amount of information regarding the person's score on the psychological characteristic in question. Because the right end of the scale is arbitrarily defined as the keyed direction in IRT (the I, N, F, or P poles in the MBTI), items with very high *b* parameters discriminate between people with very clear preferences as compared to those with clear preferences. The most desirable MBTI items are those that provide maximum information *at the midpoint* of each dichotomy rather than at the "extremes," i.e., those that accurately identify Introverts versus Extraverts, Sensing types versus Intuitives, and so on.

c parameter: defines the baseline for item endorsement rates that would be expected from individuals who score very far to the low (left) end of the theta scale. In MBTI terms, for example, the probability that someone who is "very clear" about their preference for Extraversion would endorse the opposite, Introverted response to an EI item. In aptitude or achievement tests, this is the "guessing" parameter. In a personality instrument like the MBTI, this parameter accounts for the social desirability of the responses.

tie-breaking formula. A statistical method of labeling the type preference of respondents who obtain an equal number of points on both poles of a dichotomy. Though tied scores are rare for Form M, the tradition established for previous forms is followed when it does occur, that is, ties are broken in favor of I, N, F, or P.

trait. In the field of personality, a single personality characteristic that is present in all people in varying degrees. When personality is described in terms of traits, we assume that everyone has the same characteristics. The differences between people are due to how much they have of each of the traits that describe human personality.

trait theory. A system for explaining personality variation that postulates traits as the underlying units of descriptions. Trait theory approaches predominate among psychologists. Different trait theories vary primarily in the number and nature of the traits that are believed to be sufficient and necessary to explain human personality. In contrast to type theory and the MBTI, which rest on a specific theoretical system, most trait systems derive their sets of traits empirically and do not postulate any theoretical basis for the particular array of traits used.

transdichotomous facets of type. Typological characteristics that are "more than the sum of the parts." That is, they are not described by or included in any of the four dichotomous preferences that identify a type. These are the characteristics that make MBTI types different from trait descriptions of personality, even when the traits being described have names similar to those used with the MBTI.

true type. The personality type that is the hypothetical "true" one for the individual, in contrast to **reported type** and **best-fit, or verified, type.**

type. In the field of personality, and specifically for the MBTI, a unique combination of mental attitudes (E *or* I and J *or* P) and mental functions (S *or* N and T *or* F) that is more than the sum of its parts. Specifically, 1 of the 16 combinations of four preferences, each with specific characteristics postulated from the dynamics of the theory. *Type* is not used to denote a single preference.

type code. The four letters used to denote a type, for example, ESTJ or INFJ.

type development. In type theory, the emergence and expression of the dynamic elements that make up psychological type; the ages or developmental stages when the dominant, auxiliary, tertiary, and inferior functions may be manifested, and the roles these play in personality growth.

Type Differentiation Indicator. *See* **Step III Type Differentiation Indicator.**

type dynamics. The interaction of the dominant, auxiliary, tertiary, and inferior functions along with the attitudes of Extraversion and Introversion in which they are typically used. The dynamics of any one of the 16 types is inherent in the four-letter type code used to specify a type, such as ISTJ or ESFP.

type dynamics interactions. The theoretically predicted interactions between the E–I and J–P dichotomies that serve to identify the forms (dominant or auxiliary) and attitudes (Introverted or Extraverted) of the functions.

type table. A display of the 16 types in the format developed by Isabel Myers. The type table may have only the 16 types or may be supplemented with a column at the side showing the type groupings.

typology. A systematic way of describing types based on characteristics that are shared in various ways by the types. In the field of personality, a system of classifying personalities into qualitatively distinct groups (types) whose members share some characteristics with other groups, while at the same time possessing additional characteristics that are not shared with any other group.

unique facets of type. Typological characteristics that are "more than the sum of the parts" and are only associated with a single type. These are the typological characteristics that make each of the 16 MBTI types different from every other type.

whole type. The basic unit of type theory, being the four dynamic elements that interact uniquely to form one of the 16 types.

word-pair items. Items used in the MBTI in which two words are presented to the respondent, who must choose the word that is most appealing.

References

Adler, N. J. (1991). *International dimensions of organizational behavior.* Kent International Dimensions of Business Series. Boston: PWS-Kent.

American Psychological Association. (1990). *Guidelines for providers of psychological services to ethnic, linguistic and culturally diverse populations.* Washington, D.C.: Author, Board of Ethnic Minority Affairs, Task Force on delivery of Service to Ethnic Minority Populations.

Amis-Reichle, B. (1995). Female elementary school teachers' Myers-Briggs function preferences, child developmental belief orientations and preferences for behavior management approaches (Doctoral dissertation, University of San Francisco). *Dissertation Abstracts International, 55/08-B,* 3624.

Anchors, S., & Dana, R. (1989). Type and substance abuse in college age students. *Journal of Psychological Type, 17,* 26–30.

Anchors, S., & Hay, S. (1990). Resident assistants: Are they similar or dissimilar to students from whom they are selected? *Journal of College and University Student Housing, 20,* 2, 18–21.

Anchors, S., Robbins, M. A., & Gershman, E. S. (1989). The relationship between Jungian type and persistence to graduation among college students. *Journal of Psychological Type, 17,* 20–25.

Anchors, S., & Robinson, D. C. (1992). Psychological type and the accomplishment of student development tasks. *NASPA Journal, 29,* 2, 131–135.

Anderson, S. J. (1992). Psychological type and leadership (Doctoral dissertation, University of Calgary, Canada, 1992). *Dissertation Abstracts International, 54,* 378A.

Apostal, R., & Trontvent, R. (1989). College students' academic comfort and personality. *Journal of College Student Development, 30,* 210–212.

Arain, A. A. (1968). Relationships among counseling clients' personalities, expectations, and problems (Doctoral dissertation, Rutgers University). *Dissertation Abstracts International, 29,* 4903A-4904A. (University Microfilms No. 68-8640)

Arthur, M. B., & Rousseau, D. M. (1996). A career lexicon for the 21st century. *Academy of Management Executive, 10,* (4) 28–39.

Atman, K. S. (1993). Goal accomplishment style and psychological type: Cultural variations. *Psychological Type and Culture-East and West: A Multicultural Research Symposium,* 207–220.

Bail, F. T. (1993). An exploration of relationships among psychological type, ethnicity and computer-mediated communication. *Psychological Type and Culture-East and West: A Multicultural Research Symposium,* 221–227.

Bailey, R. S. (1991). *The Leadership Style Indicator.* Greensboro, NC: Center for Creative Leadership.

Barger, N. J., & Kirby, L. K. (1993, Fall). The interaction of cultural values and type development: INTP women across cultures. *Bulletin of Psychological Type, 16,* (4), 17–18.

Barger, N. J., & Kirby, L. K. (1995a). *The challenge of change in organizations: Helping employees thrive in the new frontier.* Palo Alto, CA: Davies-Black.

Barger, N. J., & Kirby, L. K. (1995b). INTP women across cultures. In R. Moody (Ed.), *Proceedings of psychological type and culture-east and west: A multicultural research symposium* (pp. 99–119). Gainesville, FL: Center for Applications of Psychological Type.

Barger, N. J., & Kirby, L. K. (1997a). *MBTI type and change.* Palo Alto, CA: Consulting Psychologists Press.

Barger, N. J., & Kirby, L. K. (1997b). *MBTI type and change participant's guide.* Palo Alto, CA: Consulting Psychologists Press.

Barger, N. J., & Kirby, L. K. (1997c). Enhancing leadership during organizational change. In C. Fitzgerald & L. K. Kirby (Eds.), *Developing leaders: Research and applications in psychological type and leadership development.* Palo Alto, CA: Davies-Black.

Barr, L., & Barr, N. (1994). *Leadership development: Maturity and power.* Austin, TX: Eakin Press.

Barrett, L. (1989). Impact of teacher personality on classroom environment. *Journal of Psychological Type, 18,* 50–56.

Barrineau, P. (1997). The type to drink: Undergraduate alcohol policy violators and personality type. *Journal of Psychological Type, 41,* 23–27.

Barth, R. L. (1980). *Run, school, run.* Cambridge, MA: Harvard University Press.

Bathurst, J. (1995). *Atlas of type in New Zealand.* Wellington, NZ: idic.

Battle, P. C. (1989). The effect of race and culture on Black MBTI preferences. In *Proceedings of APT VIII International Conference* (pp. 161–63). Gainesville, FL: Association for Psychological Type.

Battle, P. C. (1994). Two warring ideals in one dark body. In *Proceedings of the Third International Conference on Myers-Briggs Typology* (pp. 147–152). Montreal: International Type Users Organization.

Bayne, R. (1988). Accuracy in judging the four attitudes. *Journal of Psychological Type, 16,* 61–66.

Beck, F. S. (1973). Affective sensitivity of counselor supervisors as a dimension of growth in their trainee groups (Doctoral dissertation, University of Southern California). *Dissertation*

Abstracts International, 33, 3277A. (University Microfilms No. 73-720)

Berens, L. V. (1998). *Understanding yourself and others: An introduction to temperament.* Huntington Beach, CA: Telos Publications.

Betz, N. E., Borgen, F. H., & Harmon, L. W. (1996). *Skills Confidence Inventory.* Palo Alto, CA: Consulting Psychologists Press.

Betz, N. E., Borgen, F. H., & Harmon, L. W. (1996). *Skills Confidence Inventory Applications and Technical Guide.* Palo Alto, CA: Consulting Psychologists Press.

Beyler, J., & Schmeck, R. R. (1992). Assessment of individual differences in preferences for holistic-analytic strategies: Evaluation of some commonly available instruments. *Educational and Psychological Measurement, 52,* 3, 709–719.

Blaylock, B. K. (1983). Teamwork in a simulated production environment. *Research in Psychological Type, 6,* 58–67.

Block, J. (1978). *The Q-Sort Method.* Palo Alto, CA: Consulting Psychologists Press.

Borham, B., & Watts, J. (1994). Personality types and learning styles in undergraduate students of education and physics. In *Proceedings of the Second Biennial National Conference of the Australian Association for Psychological Type* (pp. 9–21). Melbourne: Australian Association for Psychological Type.

Bowen, J. L. (1990). The combined predictive effect of creativity level and personality type on college students' reflective judgment (Doctoral dissertation, East Texas State University). *Dissertation Abstracts International,* 51/01-A, 110.

Boyd, N. E. (1995). An examination of interpersonal relationships between student and cooperating teachers (Doctoral dissertation, University of Memphis). *Dissertation Abstracts International,* 55/10-A, 3076.

Braun, J. A. (1971). The empathic ability of psychotherapists as related to therapist perceptual flexibility and professional experience, patient insight, and therapist-patient similarity (Doctoral dissertation, Fordham University). *Dissertation Abstracts International, 32,* 2391B. (University Microfilms No. 71-26, 956)

Brehm, S., & Kassin, S. (1993). *Social psychology.* Boston, MA: Houghton Mifflin.

Bridges, W. (1980). *Transitions: Making sense of life's changes.* Reading, MA: Addison-Wesley.

Bridges, W. (1992a). *The character of organizations: Using Jungian type in organizational development.* Palo Alto, CA: Davies-Black.

Bridges, W. (1992b). *Managing transitions.* Reading, MA: Addison-Wesley.

Bridges, W. (1994). *JobShift.* Reading, MA: Addison-Wesley.

Brislin, R. (1990). *Applied cross-cultural psychology.* Newbury Park, CA: Sage.

Brislin, R. (1993). *Understanding culture's influence on behavior.* Chicago, IL: Harcourt Brace Jovanovich College & School Division.

Brislin, R., Cushner, K., Cherrie, C., & Yong, M. (1986). *Intercultural interactions: A practical guide.* Volume 9, Cross-Cultural Research and Methodology Series. Newbury Park, CA: Sage Publications.

Brocato, F. C. (1985). *Psychological type and task accomplishment in the public school management team.* Unpublished doctoral dissertation, University of Oklahoma, Norman, OK.

Brock, S. A. (1994). *Using type in selling.* Palo Alto, CA: Consulting Psychologists Press.

Brock, S. A. (1995). *Four part framework* (rev. ed.). Minneapolis, MN: Brock Associates.

Brock, S. A. (1996, Fall). A perspective on type in organizations. *Bulletin of Psychological Type, 19*(4) 5–6.

Brock, S. A., & Kummerow, J. M. (n.d.). *Valuing preferences in the workplace.* [Handout]. Gainesville, FL: Center for Applications of Psychological Type.

Brooks, F. R., & Johnson, R. W. (1979). Self-descriptive adjectives associated with a Jungian personality inventory. *Psychological Reports, 44* (3, Pt. 1), 747–750.

Brown, D. (1996). Brown's values-based, holistic model of career and life-role choices and satisfaction. In D. Brown & L. Brooks (Eds.), *Career choice and development* (3rd ed.). San Francisco, CA: Jossey-Bass.

Brown, V. L., & DeCoster, D. A. (1991). The *Myers-Briggs Type Indicator* as a developmental measure: Implications for student learners in higher education. *Journal of College Student Development, 32,* 378–379.

Brush, L. C. (1989). Training residential advisors in peer counseling: Implications of type (MBTI/PTPI). *Journal of Psychological Type, 17,* 73–78.

Burt, R. B. (1968). An exploratory study of personality manifestations in paintings (Doctoral dissertation, Duke University). *Dissertation Abstracts International, 29,* 1493B. (University Microfilms No. 68-14, 298)

Call, M. E., & Sotillo, S. (1993). Personality, culture, and field sensitivity. In R. Moody (Ed.), *Proceedings of Psychological Type and Culture—East and West: A Multicultural Research Symposium* (pp. 193-198). Gainesville, FL: Center for Applications of Psychological Type.

Campbell, D. P., & Hansen, J. C. (1981). *Manual for the SVIB-SCII Strong-Campbell Interest Inventory* (3rd ed.). Stanford, CA: Stanford University Press.

Canning, E.A.B. (1983). An analysis of cognitive style, hemispheric preference, personality type and academic achievement in a group of economically disadvantaged secondary students (Doctoral dissertation, University of Pittsburgh). *Dissertation Abstracts International,* 45/02-A, 457.

Carey, J. C., Hamilton, D. L., & Shanklin, G. (1985). Psychological type and interpersonal compatibility: Evidence for a relationship between communication style preference and relationship satisfaction in college roommates. *Journal of Psychological Type, 10,* 36–39.

Carey, J. C., Hamilton, D. L., & Shanklin, G. (1986). Does personality similarity affect male roommates' satisfaction? *Journal of College Student Personnel, 27,* 1, 65–69.

Carlson, J. (1985). Recent assessments of the *Myers-Briggs Type Indicator. Journal of Personality Assessment, 49,* 356–365.

Carlson, R. (1980). Studies of Jungian typology: II. Representations of the personal world. *Journal of Personality and Social Psychology, 38,* 801–810.

Carlson, R., & Levy, N. (1973). Studies in Jungian typology: I. Memory, social perception and social action. *Journal of Personality, 41* (4), 559–576.

Carlyn, M. (1975). *A comparison of two methods of assessing a subject's dominant process.* Paper presented at the First National Conference on the *Myers-Briggs Type Indicator,* Gainesville, FL.

Carrell, P. L., & Monroe, L. B. (1993). Learning styles and composition. *Modern Language Journal, 77,* 2, 148–162.

Carskadon, T. G. (1979). Behavioral differences between extraverts and Introverts as measured by the *Myers-Briggs Type Indicator:* An experimental demonstration. *Research in Psychological Type, 2,* 78–82.

Carskadon, T. G. (1979). Clinical and counseling aspects of the *Myers-Briggs Type Indicator:* A research review. *Research in Psychological Type, 2,* 2–31.

Carskadon, T. G. (1982). *Myers-Briggs Type Indicator* characterizations: A Jungian horoscope? *Research in Psychological Type, 8,* 87–88.

Carskadon, T. G., & Cook, D. D. (1982). Validity of MBTI type descriptions as perceived by recipients unfamiliar with type. *Research in Psychological Type, 8,* 89–94.

Carter, J. A. (1990). A comparison of personality types as determined by the *Myers-Briggs Type Indicator* with the process of separate-knowing and connected-knowing procedural processing among female undergraduate and nontraditional students (Doctoral dissertation, Michigan State University). *Dissertation Abstracts International, 51/05-A*, 1475.

Carver, C. S. (1989). How should multifaceted personality constructs be tested? Issues illustrated by self-monitoring, attributional style, and hardiness. *Journal of Personality and Social Psychology, 56*, 577–585.

Casas, E. (1990). The development of the French version of the MBTI in Canada and in France. *Journal of Psychological Type, 20*, 3–15.

Casas, E. (1995). Diversity patterns of type distributions among cultures: What do the differences mean? In R. Moody (Ed.), *Proceedings of Psychological Type and Culture-East and West: A Multicultural Research Symposium* (pp. 65–76). Gainesville, FL: Center for Applications of Psychological Type.

Casas, E., & Hamlet, J. (1984). Les types psychologiques des clients, des etudients-conseillers et des superviseurs dans un centre d'entrainement clinique: Etude sur la compatibility client-conseiller et l'apprentissage de la therapie [Psychological types of clients, student-counselors and supervisors in a clinical training center: Study of client-counselor compatibility and therapy internship]. Interim Report, CRSHC, Subvention No. 410 834 0428, University of Ottawa, Canada.

Casey, L. (1986). Personality characteristics associated with academic achievement of Hispanic high school students (Doctoral dissertation, University of California, Berkeley). *Dissertation Abstracts International, 48/05-B*, 1541.

Catoe, C. W. (1992). Developmental profiles of college students: A comparison of moral development stage and *Myers-Briggs Type Indicator* personality types (Doctoral dissertation, North Carolina State University). *Dissertation Abstracts International, 53/03-B*, 1639.

Center for Applications of Psychological Type (1995). *Profile of your MBTI results.* Gainesville, FL: Center for Applications of Psychological Type.

Chartrand, J. M. (1991). The evolution of trait-and-factor career counseling: A person x environment fit approach. *Journal of Counseling and Development, 69*, 518–524.

Chartrand, J. M., Robbins, S. B., & Morrill, W. H. (1997). *Career Factors Inventory.* Palo Alto, CA: Consulting Psychologists Press.

Chesborough, S. R. (1994). The use of the MBTI to improve opportunities for the academic success of scholarship athletes. In *Proceedings: Orchestrating Educational Change in the 90's—The Role of Psychological Type*, 119–137.

Chiang, G. C. (1991). Student ratings of teachers, teacher psychological type and teacher classroom behavior: An exploratory study in gifted education (Doctoral dissertation, Northwestern University). *Dissertation Abstracts International, 52/06-A*, 2001.

Clancy, S. G. (1997). STJs and change: Resistance, reaction, or misunderstanding? In C. Fitzgerald & L. K. Kirby (Eds.), *Developing leaders: Research and applications in psychological type and leadership development* (pp. 415–438). Palo Alto, CA: Davies-Black.

Coan, R. W. (1979). *Psychologists: Personal and theoretical pathways.* New York: Irvington.

Cohen, J. (1988). *Statistical power analysis for the behavioral sciences* (2nd ed.). Hillsdale, NJ: Erlbaum.

Comrey, A. L. (1983). An evaluation of the *Myers-Briggs Type Indicator. Academic Psychology Bulletin, 5*, 115–129.

Cooper, S. E., & Miller, J. A. (1991). MBTI learning style-teaching style discongruencies. *Educational and Psychological Measurement, 51*, 699–706.

Corlett, E. S., & Millner, N. B. (1993). *Navigating midlife: Using typology as a guide.* Palo Alto, CA: Davies-Black.

Cornett, C. E. (1983). *What you should know about teaching and learning styles.* Bloomington, IN: Phi Delta Kappa Educational Foundation.

Costa, P. Y., & McCrae, R. R. (1985). *The NEO personality inventory manual.* Odessa, FL: Psychological Assessment Resources.

Craig, D. L., Craig, C. H., & Sleight, C. C. (1988). Type preferences of decision-makers: Corporate and clinical. *Journal of Psychological Type, 16*, 33–37.

Cropley, A. J. (1965). *Originality, personality and intelligence.* Unpublished doctoral dissertation, University of Alberta, Edmonton, Alberta.

Dana, R. (1993). *Multicultural assessment perspective for professional psychology.* Boston: Allyn & Bacon.

Daugherty, P. W., Randall, K. P., & Globetti, E. (1997). Psychological types among women senior student affairs officers on college and university campuses. *Journal of Psychological Type, 41*, 28–32.

Dawis, R.V. (1996). The theory of work adjustment and person-environment-correspondence counseling. In D. Brown and L. Brooks (Eds.), *Career choice and development* (3rd ed.). San Francisco, CA: Jossey-Bass.

Dawson, B. G., & Guy, R. F. (1994). Personality type and grade performance in a TV-assisted course. *Journal of Psychological Type, 29*, 38-42.

De Beer, J. (1997). *Dealing with personal and cultural transitions.* Paper presented at APT XII, Association for Psychological Type International Conference, Boston, MA.

Delbridge-Parker, L., & Robinson, D. C. (1989). Type and academically gifted adolescents. *Journal of Psychological Type, 17*, 66–72.

Demarest, L. (1997). *Dear Deborah and John: What the gender experts can learn from type.* In Proceedings: APT XII Biennial International Conference, Boston, MA.

Denison, D. R., & Mishra, A. K. (1995). Toward a theory of organizational culture and effectiveness. *Organizational Science, 6* (2) 204–223.

DeVellis, R. F. (1991). Scale development: Theory and applications. *Applied Social Research Methods Series, 26.* Newbury Park, CA: Sage.

DiMarco, R. (1997). Using the MBTI in career pathing. In *Proceedings of APT XII*, 3–6.

DiTiberio, J. K. (1977). The strength of Sensing (Intuition preference on the *Myers-Briggs Type Indicator* as related to empathic discrimination of overt or covert feeling messages of others (Doctoral dissertation, Michigan State University). *Dissertation Abstracts International, 37*, 5599A. (University Microfilms No. 77-5789)

DiTiberio, J. K. (1996). Education, learning styles, and cognitive styles. In A. L. Hammer (Ed.), *MBTI applications: A decade of research on the Myers-Briggs Type Indicator* (pp. 123–166). Palo Alto, CA: Consulting Psychologists Press.

DiTiberio, J. K., & Hammer, A. L. (1993). *Introduction to type in college.* Palo Alto, CA: Consulting Psychologists Press.

DiTiberio, J. K., Harrison, H. A., Sim, H., & Kim, J. (1995). Culture, gender, and work role expectations as factors in type distribution. In *Proceedings of APT XI International Conference* (pp. 123–126). Kansas City, MO: Association for Psychological Type.

DiTiberio, J. K., & Jensen, G. H. (1995). *Writing and personality: Finding your voice, your style, your way.* Palo Alto, CA: Davies-Black.

Donovan, A. J. (1994). The interaction of personality traits in applied music teaching (Doctoral dissertation, University of Southern Mississippi). *Dissertation Abstracts International, 55/06-A*, 1499.

Drasgow, F. (1987). A study of measurement bias of two standardized psychological tests. *Journal of Applied Psychology, 72*, 19–29.

Drasgow, F., & Hulin, C. L. (1990). Item response theory. In M. D. Dunnette & L. M. Hough (Eds.), *Handbook of industrial and organizational psychology* (2nd ed., pp. 577–636). Palo Alto, CA: Davies-Black.

Drummond, R. J., & Stoddard, A. H. (1992). Learning style and personality type. *Perceptual and Motor Skills, 75,* 99–104.

Dunning, D. G., Lange, B. M., & Adams, A. B. (1990). Personality type and interpersonal communication behavior of senior dental students. *Journal of Psychological Type, 19,* 59–64.

Edmunds, M. (1982). Jungian personality type and imagery ability within a holistic health context (Doctoral dissertation, Pennsylvania State University). *Dissertation Abstracts International, 43* (3), 868B.

Edwards, A. L. (1954). *Manual for the EPPS.* New York: The Psychological Corporation.

Eggins, J. A. (1979). The interaction between structure in learning materials and the personality type of learners (Doctoral dissertation, Indiana University). *Dissertation Abstracts International, 40/07-A,* 3886.

Ehrman, M. (1990). Owls and doves: Cognition, personality and learning success. In J. E. Alatis (Ed.) *Linguistics, language teaching and language acquisition: The interdependence of theory, practice and research* (pp. 413–437). Washington, DC: Georgetown University Press.

Ehrman, M. (1993). Ego boundaries revisited: Toward a model of personality and learning. In J. E. Alatis (Ed.), *Strategic interaction and language acquisition: Theory, practice and research,* (pp. 331–362). Washington, DC: Georgetown University Press.

Ehrman, M. (1994a). The *Type Differentiation Indicator* and adult foreign language learning success. *Journal of Psychological Type, 30,* 10–29.

Ehrman, M. (1994b). Weakest and strongest learners in intensive language training: A study of extremes. In C. Klee (Ed.), *Faces in a crowd: Individual learners in multisection programs.* Boston: Heinle and Heinle.

Ehrman, M. (1995). *The Modern Language Aptitude Test: What does it tell us?* Unpublished manuscript.

Ehrman, M., & Oxford, R. (1989). Effects of sex differences, career choice, and psychological type on adult language learning strategies. *Modern Language Journal, 73,* 1, 1–13.

Ehrman, M., & Oxford, R. (1990). Adult language learning styles and strategies in an intensive training setting. *Modern Language Journal, 74,* 3, 311–327.

Ehrman, M. & Oxford, R. (1995). Cognition plus: Correlates of language learning success. *Modern Language Journal, 79,* 1, 67–89.

Elliott, G. R., & Sapp, G. L. (1988). The relationship between the *Myers-Briggs Type Indicator* and the *Grasha-Riechmann Student Learning Styles Questionnaire. Journal of Psychological Type, 14,* 46–50.

Elliot, G. V. (1975). A descriptive study of characteristics and personality types of counselors of runaway youth (Doctoral dissertation, University of Maryland). *Dissertation Abstracts International, 36,* 3119B-31220B. (University Microfilms No. 75-28, 741).

Embretson, S. E. (1996). The new rules of measurement. *Psychological Assessment, 8* (4), 341–349.

Erickson, C., Gantz, B. S., & Stephenson, R. W. (1970). Logical and construct validation of a short-form biographical inventory predictor of scientific creativity. In *Proceedings of the 78th Annual Convention of the American Psychological Association, 5* (1), 151–152.

Erskine, C. G., Westerman, G. H., & Grandy, T. G. (1986). Personality styles of first-year dental students. *Journal of Dental Education, 50,* 4, 221–224.

Evans, L. N. (1976). A psycho-temporal theory of personality: A study of the relationship between temporal orientation, affect, and personality type (Doctoral dissertation, United States International University). *Dissertation Abstracts International, 37,* 1875B. (University Microfilms No. 76–22, 381)

Fairhurst, A. M., & Fairhurst, L, L. (1995). *Effective teaching, effective learning: Making the personality connection in your classroom.* Palo Alto, CA: Davies-Black.

Faucett, J. M., Morgan, E. R., Poling, T. H, & Johnson, J. (1995). MBTI type and Kohlberg's postconventional stages of moral reasoning. *Journal of Psychological Type, 34,* 17–23.

Ferdman, R. L., & DiTiberio, J. K. (1996). Psychological type and the writing process of fifth graders. *Journal of Psychological Type, 38,* 24–33.

Fisher, N. M. (1994). MBTI type and writing-across-the-curriculum. *Journal of Psychological Type, 28,* 43–47.

Fitzgerald, C. (1997a). The MBTI and leadership development: Personality and leadership reconsidered in changing times. In C. Fitzgerald & L. K. Kirby (Eds.), *Developing leaders: Research and applications in psychological type and leadership development* (pp. 33–59). Palo Alto, CA: Davies-Black.

Fitzgerald, C. (1997b). Type development and leadership development: Integrating reality and vision, mind and heart. In C. Fitzgerald & L. K. Kirby (Eds.), *Developing leaders: Research and applications in psychological type and leadership development* (pp. 311–336). Palo Alto, CA: Davies-Black.

Fitzgerald, C., & Kirby, L. K. (1997a). Applying type dynamics to leadership development. In C. Fitzgerald & L. K. Kirby (Eds.), *Developing leaders: Research and applications in psychological type and leadership development* (pp. 269–310). Palo Alto, CA: Davies-Black.

Fitzgerald, C., & Kirby, L. K. (Eds.). (1997b). *Developing leaders: Research and applications in psychological type and leadership development.* Palo Alto, CA: Davies-Black.

Fleenor, J. W. (1997). The relationship between the MBTI and measures of personality and performance in management groups. In C. Fitzgerald & L. K. Kirby (Eds.), *Developing leaders: Research and applications in psychological type and leadership development* (pp. 115–138). Palo Alto, CA: Davies-Black.

Fourqurean, J., Meisgeier, C., & Swank, P. (1988). The *Murphy-Meisgeier Type Indicator for Children:* Exploring the link between psychological type preferences of children and academic achievement. *Journal of Psychological Type, 16,* 42–46.

Fourqurean, J., Meisgeier, C., & Swank, P. (1990). The link between learning style and Jungian psychological type: A finding of two bipolar preference dimensions. *Journal of Experimental Education, 58,* 3, 225–237.

Friedman, C. P., & Slatt, L. M. (1988). New results relating the *Myers-Briggs Type Indicator* and medical specialty choice. *Journal of Medical Education, 63,* 325–327.

Frederick, A. H. (1975). Self-actualization and personality type: A comparative study of doctoral majors in educational administration and the helping relations (Doctoral dissertation, University of Alabama). *Dissertation Abstracts International, 35,* 7055A-7056A. (University Microfilms No. 75-9896)

Freeman, S. C. (1994). *An investigation of psychological type and career maturity (Myers-Briggs Type Indicator).* Unpublished doctoral dissertation, University of North Carolina, Greensboro.

Fry, E. (1977). Fry's readability graph: Clarifications, validity, and extension to level 17. *Journal of Reading, 21,* 249.

Fu, J. M. (1992). The relationship between the MBTI personality types of international students and adjustment to American society (Doctoral dissertation, University of San Francisco). *Dissertation Abstracts International, 53/01-A,* 69.

Futrell, D. A. (1992). *Cognitive ability and Myers-Briggs Type Indicator preferences as predictors of group performance: An empirical study.* Unpublished doctoral dissertation, University of Tennessee.

Gallagher, S. A. (1988). An analysis of visual-spatial ability, intellectual efficiency, and learning style on mathematics achievement of gifted male and gifted female adolescents (Doctoral dissertation, University of North Carolina at Chapel Hill). *Dissertation Abstracts International, 48/07-A,* 1733.

Galvin, M. D. (1976). Facilitative conditions and psychological type in intake interviews by professionals and paraprofessionals (Doctoral dissertation, University of Florida). *Dissertation Abstracts International, 36,* 6378B. (University Microfilms No. 76-12, 078).

Garden, A. M. (1989). Organizational size as a variable in type analysis and employee turnover. *Journal of Psychological Type, 17,* 3–13.

Garden, A. M. (1997). Relationships between MBTI profiles, motivation profiles and career paths. *Journal of Psychological Type, 41,* 3–16.

Gautsch, S. M. (1993). The effects of perceptual style with mode of instruction in a hypermedia language learning environment. *Psychological Type and Culture—East and West: A Multicultural Research Symposium,* 229–240.

Gehringer, G. S. (1994). *A comparison of African American MBTI/career matches with the normative MBTI/career data in the "Atlas of Type Tables."* Unpublished doctoral dissertation, Walden University.

Gerhardt, R. (1983). Liberal religion and personality type. *Research in Psychological Type, 6,* 47–53.

Gilchrist, B. J. (1991). The *Myers-Briggs Type Indicator* as a tool for clinical legal education. *Saint Louis University Public Law Review, 10,* 601–613.

Gilligan, C. (1982). *In a different voice.* Cambridge, MA: Harvard University Press.

Ginn, C. W. (1995). *Families: Using type to enhance mutual understanding.* Gainesville, FL: Center for Applications of Psychological Type.

Golanty-Koel, R. (1978). The relationship of psychological type and mass media preferences to the values of non-academic high school students (Doctoral dissertation, University of California, Berkeley). *Dissertation Abstracts International, 38/08-A,* 4683.

Gordon, V. N., Coscarelli, W. C., & Sears, S. J. (1986). Comparative assessments of individual differences in learning and career decision making. *Journal of College Student Personnel, 27,* 3, 233–242.

Gordy, C. C., & Thorne, B. M. (1994). Proofreading ability as a function of personality type. *Journal of Psychological Type, 28,* 29–36.

Gottfredson, G. D., & Holland, J. L. (1996). *Dictionary of Holland Occupational Codes* (3rd ed.). Odessa, FL: Psychological Assessment Resources.

Gough, H. G. (1965). Conceptual analysis of psychological test scores and other diagnostic variables. *Journal of Abnormal Psychology, 70,* 294–302.

Gough, H. G. (1976). Studying creativity by means of word association tests. *Journal of Applied Psychology, 61,* 348–353.

Gough, H. G. (1981). *Studies of the Myers-Briggs Type Indicator in a personality assessment research institute.* Paper presented at the Fourth National Conference on the *Myers-Briggs Type Indicator,* Palo Alto, CA.

Gough, H. G., & Bradley, P. (1996). *CPI manual* (3rd ed.). Palo Alto, CA: Consulting Psychologists Press.

Gough, H. G., & Heilbrun, A. B., Dr. (1983). *The Adjective Check List manual.* Palo Alto, CA: Consulting Psychologists Press.

Graff, R. W., Larrimore, M., Whitehead, G. I., & Hopson, N. W. (1991). *Career counseling practices: A survey of college/university counseling centers.* Poster presented at the annual meeting of the American Psychological Association, San Francisco, CA.

Grandy, T. G., Westerman, G. H., Ocando, R. A., & Erskine, C. G. (1996). Predicting dentists' career choices using the *Myers-Briggs Type Indicator. Journal of the American Dental Association, 127,* 253–258.

Grant, W. H. (1965). *Comparability of the Gray-Wheelwright Psychological Type Questionnaire and the Myers-Briggs Type Indicator.* Auburn, AL: Research Report, Student Counseling Service, Auburn University.

Grant, W. H. (1966). *Self-description by MBTI types on the Adjective Check List.* Auburn, AL: Office of Student Development, Auburn University.

Grant, W. H., Thompson, M., & Clark, T. (1983). *From image to likeness: A Jungian path in the gospel journey.* Ramsey, NJ: Paulist Press.

Gratias, M., & Harvey, R. J. (1998, April). *Gender and ethnicity-based differential item functioning in the Myers-Briggs Type Indicator.* Paper presented at the Annual Conference of the Society for Industrial and Organizational Psychology, Dallas, TX.

Greenberg, S. E., & Harvey, R. J. (1993). *Differential item functioning on the Myers-Briggs Type Indicator.* Paper presented at the annual conference of the Society for Industrial and Organizational Psychology, San Francisco, CA.

Griffin, T. D., & Salter, D. W. (1993). Psychological type and involvement in a university residence hall judicial system. *Journal of Psychological Type, 27,* 32–38.

Grindler, M. C., & Stratton, B. D. (1990). Type Indicator and its relationship to teaching and learning styles. *Action in Teacher Education, 12,* 1, 31–34.

Grutter, J. (1990). The MBTI and Super's styles of career "maintenance." *Career Planning and Adult Development Journal, 6,* 13–17.

Grutter, J. (1993). *Counseling the less preferred MBTI functions for career transition and disengagement.* Paper presented at the Association for Psychological Type Conference, Newport Beach, CA.

Grutter, J. (1998a). *Making it in today's organizations: Career advancement using the Strong and the MBTI.* Palo Alto, CA: Consulting Psychologists Press.

Grutter, J. (1998b). *Making it in today's organizations: Career enrichment using the Strong and the MBTI.* Palo Alto, CA: Consulting Psychologists Press.

Grutter, J. (1998c). *Making it in today's organizations: Career transition using the Strong and the MBTI.* Palo Alto, CA: Consulting Psychologists Press.

Gryskiewicz, N. D., & Tullar, W. L. (1995). The relationship between personality type and creativity style among managers. *Journal of Psychological Type, 32,* 30–35.

Gryskiewicz, S. S. (1982). *Creative leadership development and the Kirton Adaption and Innovation Inventory.* Paper presented at the Occupational Psychology Conference of the British Psychological Society: "Breaking Set: New Directions in Occupational Psychology."

Guild, P. B., & Garger, S. (1985). *Marching to different drummers.* Alexandria, VA: Association for Supervision and Curriculum Development.

Hahn-Rollins, D., & Mongeon, J. E. (1988). Increasing the acceptance of the MBTI in organizations. *Journal of Psychological Type, 15,* 13–19.

Haley, U. C. V. (1997). The MBTI and decision-making styles: Identifying and managing cognitive trails in strategic decision making. In C. Fitzgerald & L. K. Kirby (Eds.), *Developing leaders: Research and applications in psychological type and leadership development* (pp. 187–223). Palo Alto, CA: Davies-Black.

Haley, U. C. V., & Pini, R. (1994). Blazing international trails in strategic decision-making research. In C. Fitzgerald (Ed.),

Proceedings of the Myers-Briggs Type Indicator and leadership: An international research conference. College Park, MD: National Leadership Institute.

Hall, W. B., & MacKinnon, D. W. (1969). Personality inventory correlates of creativity among architects. *Journal of Applied Psychology, 53* (4), 322–326.

Hambleton, R. K., Swaminathan, H., & Rogers, H. J. (1991). *Fundamentals of item response theory.* Newbury Park, CA: Sage.

Hammer, A. L. (1985). Psychological type and media preferences in an adult sample. *Journal of Psychological Type, 10,* 20–26.

Hammer, A. L. (1992). Unpublished study.

Hammer, A. L. (1993). *Introduction to type and careers.* Palo Alto, CA: Consulting Psychologists Press.

Hammer, A. L., (1996a). Career management and counseling. In A. L. Hammer (Ed.), *MBTI applications: A decade of research on the Myers-Briggs Type Indicator* (pp. 31–54). Palo Alto, CA: Consulting Psychologists Press.

Hammer, A. L. (Ed.). (1996b). *MBTI applications: A decade of research on the Myers-Briggs Type Indicator.* Palo Alto, CA: Consulting Psychologists Press.

Hammer, A. L. (1997). *Guide to the Strong and MBTI entrepreneur report.* Palo Alto, CA: Consulting Psychologists Press.

Hammer, A. L., & Huszczo, G. E. (1996). Teams. In A. L. Hammer (Ed.), *MBTI applications: A decade of research on the Myers-Briggs Type Indicator* (pp. 81–104). Palo Alto, CA: Consulting Psychologists Press.

Hammer, A. L., & Kummerow, J. M. (1992). *Strong and MBTI career development guide.* Palo Alto, CA: Consulting Psychologists Press.

Hammer, A. L., & Kummerow, J. M. (1996). *Strong and MBTI career development guide* (Rev. ed.). Palo Alto, CA: Consulting Psychologists Press.

Hammer, A. L., & Macdaid, G. P. (1992a). *Career report manual.* Palo Alto, CA: Consulting Psychologists Press.

Hammer, A. L., & Macdaid, G. P. (1992b). *MBTI Career Report: Form G.* Palo Alto, CA: Consulting Psychologists Press.

Hammer, A. L., & Marting, M. S. (1987). *Coping Resources Inventory.* Palo Alto, CA: Consulting Psychologists Press.

Hammer, A. L., & Mitchell, W. D. (1996). The distribution of MBTI types in the U.S. by gender and ethnic group. *Journal of Psychological Type, 37,* 2–15.

Hammer, A. L., Prehn, T., & Mitchell, A. (1994). [Agreement with best-fit type.] Unpublished raw data. Palo Alto, CA: Consulting Psychologists Press.

Hammer, A. L., & Yeakley, F. R. (1987). The relationship between "true type" and reported type. *Journal of Psychological Type, 13,* 52–55.

Hannah, B. (1976). *Jung: His life and work.* New York: Putnam.

Hardy-Jones, J., & Watson, M. M. (1990). Type differences over time: A ten-year study at the University of Hawaii. *Journal of Psychological Type, 19,* 27–34.

Harmon, L. W., Hansen, J. C., Borgen, F. H., & Hammer, A. L. (1994). *Strong applications and technical guide.* Palo Alto, CA: Consulting Psychologists Press.

Harris, A. H., & Carskadon, T. G. (1988). Comparative validity of the old and new scoring weights on the MBTI Thinking-Feeling scale. *Journal of Psychological Type, 15,* 54–62.

Harrison, D. F. (1984). *The temporal dimensions of Jung's psychological typology: Testing an instructional theory of future studies with middle school students.* Unpublished doctoral dissertation, University of Florida, Gainesville.

Harrison, D. F., & Lawrence, G. (1985). Psychological type and time orientation: Do middle school students differ in projecting their personal futures? *Journal of Psychological Type, 9,* 10–15.

Harrison, H. A. (1995). The relationships among Jungian psychological type preferences, problems experienced and perceived problem solving capabilities for African-Americans holding graduate degrees (Doctoral dissertation, Saint Louis University). *Dissertation Abstracts International, 55/09-A,* 2721.

Hart, H. (1991). Psychological types of students attending a high school credit remediation program for students at risk of not graduating. *Journal of Psychological Type, 22,* 48–51.

Harvey, R. J. (1996). Reliability and validity. In A. L. Hammer (Ed.), *MBTI Applications: A decade of research on the Myers-Briggs Type Indicator* (pp. 5–29). Palo Alto, CA: Consulting Psychologists Press.

Harvey, R. J. (1997, April). Computer adaptive testing, differential item functioning, faking, and the MBTI. In R. J. Harvey (Chair), *Using item response theory to address assessment challenges in I/O.* Symposium conducted at the Annual Conference of the Society for Industrial and Organizational Psychology, St. Louis, MO.

Harvey, R. J., & Murry, W. D. (1994). Scoring the *Myers-Briggs Type Indicator:* Empirical comparison of preference score versus latent-trait methods. *Journal of Personality Assessment, 62,* 116–129.

Harvey, R. J., Murry, W. D., & Markham, S. E. (1994). Evaluation of three short form versions of the *Myers-Briggs Type Indicator. Journal of Personality Assessment, 63,* 181–184.

Harvey, R. J., Murry, W. D., & Stamoulis, D. (1995). Unresolved issues in the dimensionality of the *Myers-Briggs Type Indicator. Educational and Psychological Measurement, 55,* 535–544.

Harvey, R. J., & Thomas, L. (1996). Using item response theory to score the *Myers-Briggs Type Indicator:* Rationale and research findings. *Journal of Psychological Type, 37,* 16–60.

Hawkins, C. A., Williams, M. S., & Hawkins R. C., II (1990). Psychological types of social service managers. *Journal of Psychological Type, 19,* 44-49.

Heavrin, A. R. (1998). Conscious use of the preferred mental functions in career decision making. *Journal of Psychological Type, 45,* 36–38.

Held, J. S., & Yokomoto, C. F. (1983). Technical report writing: Effects of personality differences in the laboratory. *ASEE Annual Conference Proceedings,* 197-201.

Helson, R. (1965). Childhood interest clusters related to creativity in women. *Journal of Consulting Psychology, 29* (4), 352–361.

Helson, R. (1968). Effect of sibling characteristics and parental values on creative interest and achievement. *Journal of Personality, 36* (4), 589–607.

Helson, R. (1971). Women mathematicians and the creative personality. *Journal of Consulting and Clinical Psychology, 36* (2), 210–220.

Helson, R. (1975, October). *Studying typological patterns in "real" contexts: Research styles in women mathematicians.* Paper presented at First National Conference on the Uses of the *Myers-Briggs Type Indicator,* Gainesville, FL.

Helson, R., & Crutchfield, R. S. (1970). Creative types in mathematics. *Journal of Personality, 38* (2), 177–197.

Hermon, M. V. (1993). Communication strategies of psychological types. In *Proceedings of the Association for Psychological Type 10th International Conference.* Kansas City, MO: Association for Psychological Type.

Hester, C. (1990). The differential performance of MBTI types on learning tasks. *Journal of Psychological Type, 19,* 21–26.

Hicks, L. E. (1984). Conceptual and empirical analysis of some assumptions of an explicitly typological theory. *Journal of Personality and Social Psychology, 46* (5), 1118–1131.

Hicks, L. E. (1985). Dichotomies and typologies: Summary and implications. *Journal of Psychological Type, 10,* 11–13.

Hicks, L. E. (1989). Bookishness and the null hypothesis. *Journal of Psychological Type, 17,* 14–19.

Hill, O. W., & Clark, J. L. (1993). The personality typology of Black college students: Evidence for a characteristic cognitive style? *Psychological Reports, 72,* 1091–1097.

Hinkle, K. S. (1986). An investigation of the relationships among learning style preferences, personality types, and mathematics anxiety of college students (Doctoral dissertation, University of Maryland College Park). *Dissertation Abstracts International, 47/07-A,* 2437.

Hirsh, S. K. (1990). *Using the Myers-Briggs Type Indicator in organizations.* Palo Alto, CA: Consulting Psychologists Press.

Hirsh, S. K. (1992a). *MBTI team building program.* Palo Alto, CA: Consulting Psychologists Press.

Hirsh, S. K. (1992b). *Team member's guide.* Palo Alto, CA: Consulting Psychologists Press.

Hirsh, S. K. (1995). *Exploring type with the Myers-Briggs Type Indicator* [videotape]. Palo Alto, CA: Consulting Psychologists Press.

Hirsh, S. K. (1998). *Introduction to type and teams.* Palo Alto, CA: Consulting Psychologists Press.

Hirsh, S. K., & Kise, J. A. G. (1996). *Work it out: Clues for solving people problems at work.* Palo Alto, CA: Davies-Black.

Hirsh, S. K., & Kummerow, J. M. (1989). *LIFETypes.* New York: Warner Books.

Hirsh, S. K., & Kummerow, J. M. (1998). *Introduction to type in organizations* (3rd ed.) Palo Alto, CA: Consulting Psychologists Press.

Hockersmith, P. E. (1986). A study of the relationships among personality, learning and thinking variables of student teachers at Shippensburg University (Doctoral dissertation, Temple University). *Dissertation Abstracts International, 47/08-A,* 3005.

Hoffman, J. L. (1986). Educational administrators: Psychological types. *Journal of Psychological Type, 11,* 64–67.

Hofstede, G. (1980). Culture's consequences: International differences in work-related values. Newbury Park, CA: Sage.

Hofstede, G. (1991). Cultures and organizations: Software of the mind. London: McGraw-Hill

Holland, J. L. (1994). Separate but unequal is better. In M. L. Savickas & R. W. Lent (Eds.), *Convergence in career development theories: Implications for science and practice.* Palo Alto, CA: Davies-Black.

Holsworth, T. E. (1985). Perceptual style correlates for the MBTI. *Journal of Psychological Type, 10,* 32-35.

Holtzman, F. I. (1989). An examination of the relationship between hemispheric dominance and learning styles as described by Keirseyan temperament types (Doctoral dissertation, University of Tennessee). *Dissertation Abstracts International, 50/04-A,* 853.

Hopkins, L. G. (1997). Relationships between dimensions of personality and job satisfaction. *Proceedings of APT XII,* 83–86.

Howes, R. J., & Carskadon, T. G. (1979). Test-retest reliabilities of the *Myers-Briggs Type Indicator* as a function of mood changes. *Research in Psychological Type, 2,* 67–72.

Howland, A. (1971). *Personal constructs and psychological types.* Unpublished master's thesis, University of Florida, Gainesville.

Huitt, W. G. (1989). Personality differences between Navajo and non-Indian college students: Implications for instruction. *Equity & Excellence, 24* (1), 71–74.

Huitt, W. G. (1992). Problem solving and decision making: Consideration of individual differences using the *Myers-Briggs Type Indicator. Journal of Psychological Type, 24,* 33–44.

Hulin, C., Drasgow, F., & Parsons, C. (1983). *Item response theory: Application to psychological measurement.* Homewood, IL: Dow Jones-Irwin.

Intravisit, A. (1986). *The Myers-Briggs Type Indicator: An application to the cross-cultural study of American and Thai corporate cultures.* Unpublished master's thesis, Long Island University at C. W. Post.

Ireland, M. S., & Kernan-Schloss, L. (1983). Pattern analysis of recorded daydreams, memories, and personality type. *Perceptual and Motor Skills, 56* (1), 119–125.

Isachsen, O., & Berens, L. (1991). *Working together: A personality centered approach to management* (2nd ed.). San Juan Capistrano, CA: Institute for Management Development.

Jackson, G. S. (1985). The impact of roommates on development: A causal analysis of the effects of roommate personality congruence, satisfaction and initial developmental status on end-of-quarter developmental status and grade point average (Doctoral dissertation, Auburn University). *Dissertation Abstracts International, 46/02-A,* 360.

Jacobson, C. M. (1993). Cognitive styles of creativity: Relations of scores on the *Kirton Adaption and Innovation Inventory* and the *Myers-Briggs Type Indicator* among managers in USA. *Psychological Reports, 72,* 1131–1138.

Jaffe, J. M. (1980). The relationship of Jungian psychological predispositions to the implementation of management by objectives: A sociotechnical perspective (Doctoral dissertation, University of Southern California). *Dissertation Abstracts International, 41* (11), 4833A.

James, L. R., Mulaik, S. A., & Brett, J. M. (1982). Causal analysis. Newbury Park, CA: Sage.

Jensen, G. H., & DiTiberio, J. K. (1984). Personality and individual writing processes. *College Composition and Communication, 35,* 285–300.

Jensen, G. H., & DiTiberio, J. K. (1989). *Personality and the teaching of composition.* Norwood, NJ: Ablex.

Johnson, C., Zimmerman, A., & Brooker, N. (1994). Implications and applications of type theory on a two-year technical college campus. *Proceedings: Orchestrating Educational Change in the 90's—The Role of Psychological Type,* 221–234.

Johnson, D. A. (1992). Test-retest reliabilities of the *Myers-Briggs Type Indicator* and the *Type Differentiation Indicator* over a 30-month period. *Journal of Psychological Type, 24,* 54–58.

Johnson, D. A., & Saunders, D. R. (1990). Confirmatory factor analysis of the *Myers-Briggs Type Indicator* Expanded Analysis Report. *Educational and Psychological Measurement, 50,* 561–571.

Johnson, J. A., Sample, J. A., & Jones, W. J. (1988). Self-directed learning and personality type in adult degree students. *Psychology: A Journal of Human Behavior, 25,* 1, 32–36.

Johnson, W. M. (1990). A comparative analysis of learning styles of Black and white college freshmen (Doctoral dissertation, Oklahoma State University). *Dissertation Abstracts International, 50/12-A,* 3863.

Jones, J. H., & Sherman, R. G. (1997). *Intimacy and type: A practical guide for improving relationships for couples and counselors.* Gainesville, FL: Center for Applications of Psychological Type.

Jones, J. H., Ukishima, J., Sakamoto, K., Tanouye, A., & Giron, G. (1995). Ethnicity and type of counseling center clients. In R. Moody (Ed.), *Proceedings of Psychological Type and Culture-East and West: A Multicultural Research Symposium* (pp. 77–98). Gainesville, FL: Center for Applications of Psychological Type.

Jöreskog, K. G., & Sörbom, D. (1981). *LISREL V: Analysis of linear structural relationships by maximum likelihood and least squares methods.* Chicago, IL: International Educational Services.

Jung, C. G. (1923). *Psychological types.* Princeton, NJ: Princeton University Press.

Jung, C. G. (1960). The structure and dynamics of the psyche. In *Collected Works, Vol. 8* (R. F. C. Hull, Trans.). Princeton, NJ: Princeton University Press.

Jung, C. G. (1971). Psychological types. In *Collected works: Vol. 6* (R. F. C. Hull, Trans.). Princeton, NJ: Princeton University Press. (Originally published in German as *Psychologische Typen*, Rasher Verlag, Zurich, 1921)

Jung, C. G. (1971). The structure and dynamics of the psyche. In *Collected works, Vol. 6* (R. F. C. Hull, Trans.), 23 (4), 315–331.

Kagan, J., & Snidman, N. (1991). Infant predictors of inhibited and uninhibited profiles. *Psychological Science, 2* (1), 40–43.

Kainz, R. I., & McCaulley, M. H. (1975). [Type differences in selection to medical school]. Unpublished raw data.

Kaiser, K. M. (1981). Use of the fist 50 items as a surrogate measure of the *Myers-Briggs Type Indicator* Form G. Research in *Psychological Type, 4,* 55–61.

Kalsbeek, D. (1987). Campus retention: The MBTI in institutional self-studies. In J. A. Provost & S. Anchors (Eds.), *Applications of the Myers-Briggs Type Indicator in higher education,* (pp. 31–63). Palo Alto, CA: Davies-Black.

Kalsbeek, D., Rodgers, R., Marshall, D., Denny, D., & Nicholls, G. (1982). Balancing challenge and support: A study of degrees of similarity in suitemate personality type and perceived difference in challenge and support in a residence hall environment. *Journal of College Student Personnel, 23,* 434–442.

Kandell, J. J. (1991). *The effects of group homogeneity-heterogeneity based on cognitive style on the quality of group decision making.* Unpublished doctoral dissertation, University of Maryland, College Park, MD.

Karesh, D. M., Pieper, W. A., & Holland, C. L. (1994). Comparing the MBTI, the *Jungian Type Survey,* and the *Singer-Loomis Inventory of Personality. Journal of Psychological Type, 30,* 30–38.

Katzenbach, J. R., & Smith, D. K. (1993). *The wisdom of teams.* Boston, MA: Harvard Business School Press.

Keirsey, D., & Bates, M. (1978). *Please understand me: An essay on temperament styles.* Del Mar, CA: Promethean Books.

Kelly, E. J. (1991). MBTI differences between emotionally disturbed and conduct disordered students. *Journal of Psychological Type, 21,* 23–34.

Kelly, G. A. (1955). *The psychology of personal constructs.* New York: Norton.

Kendall, B., & Carr, S. (1997). Using the MBTI with management simulations. In C. Fitzgerald, & L. K. Kirby (Eds.), *Developing leaders: Research and applications in psychological type and leadership development* (pp. 361–380). Palo Alto, CA: Davies-Black.

Kendall, B., & McHenry, R. (1998). *Technical supplement to the MBTI Manual.* Oxford, UK: Oxford Psychologists Press.

Kilburg, R. R. (Ed.). (1996). Executive coaching [Special issue]. *Consulting Psychology Journal, 48* (2).

Kilmann, R. H., & Thomas, K. W. (1975). Interpersonal conflict-handling behavior as reflections of Jungian personality dimensions. *Psychological Reports, 37,* 971–980.

Kirby, L. K. (1997). Introduction: Psychological type and the *Myers-Briggs Type Indicator.* In C. Fitzgerald & L. K. Kirby (Eds.), *Developing leaders: Research and applications in psychological type and leadership development* (pp. 3–32). Palo Alto, CA: Davies-Black.

Kirby, L. K., & Barger, N. J. (1996). Multicultural applications. In A. L. Hammer (Ed.), *MBTI applications: A decade of research on the Myers-Briggs Type Indicator* (pp. 167–196). Palo Alto, CA: Consulting Psychologists Press.

Kirton, M. J. (1987). *Kirton Adaption and Innovation Inventory (KAI) manual* (2nd ed.). Harfield, UK: Occupational Research Center.

Knapp, R. H., & Lapuc, P. S. (1965). Time imagery, introversion and fantasied preoccupations in simulated isolation. *Perceptual and Motor Skills, 20,* 327–330.

Komisin, L. K. (1992). Personality type and suicidal behaviors in college students. *Journal of Psychological Type, 24,* 24–32.

Krumboltz, J. D. (1991). *Revised Career Beliefs Inventory manual.* Palo Alto, CA: Consulting Psychologists Press.

Krumboltz, J. D. (1992). Comment: The wisdom of indecision. *Journal of Vocational Behavior, 41,* 239–244.

Krumboltz, J. D. (1996). A learning theory of career counseling. In M. L. Savickas & W. B. Walsh (Eds.), *Handbook of career counseling theory and practice.* Palo Alto, CA: Davies-Black.

Kuhn, T. S. (1970). *The structure of scientific revolutions.* Chicago: University of Chicago Press.

Kummerow, J. M. (1986). *Verifying your type preferences.* Gainesville, FL: Center for Applications of Psychological Type.

Kummerow, J. M. (1987). *Talking in type.* [Handout]. Gainesville, FL: Center for Applications of Psychological Type.

Kummerow, J. M. (1988). A methodology for verifying type: Research results. *Journal of Psychological Type, 15,* 20–25.

Kummerow, J. M., Barger, N. J., & Kirby, L. K. (1997). *WORK-Types,* New York: Warner Books.

Kummerow, J. M., & Hammer, A. L. (1995). *Strong and MBTI career development workbook.* Palo Alto, CA: Consulting Psychologists Press.

Kummerow, J. M., & Quenk, N. L. (1992). *Interpretive guide for the MBTI expanded analysis report.* Palo Alto, CA: Consulting Psychologists Press.

Kyle, J. (1985). A study of the influence of psychological type and locus of control on the academic performance of students (Doctoral dissertation, George Peabody College for Teachers of Vanderbilt University). *Dissertation Abstracts International, 46/08-A,* 2236.

Lamphere, G. I. (1985). The relationship between teacher and student personality and its effects on teacher perception of student (Doctoral dissertation, United States International University). *Dissertation Abstracts International, 46/06-A,* 1564.

Lathey, J. W. (1991). Temperament style as a predictor of academic achievement in early adolescence. *Journal of Psychological Type, 22,* 52–58.

Lawrence, G. (n.d.). *Zig-zag process for problem solving.* [Handout]. Gainesville, FL: Center for Applications of Psychological Type.

Lawrence, G. (1982). *People types and tiger stripes.* Gainesville, FL: Center for Applications of Psychological Type.

Lawrence, G. (1984). A synthesis of learning style research involving the MBTI. *Journal of Psychological Type, 8,* 2–15.

Lawrence, G., & Martin, C. R. (1996) *Profile of your MBTI results.* [Handout]. Gainesville, FL: Center for Applications of Psychological Type.

Lehto, B. A. (1990). A comparison of personalities and background of teachers using a whole language approach and a basal approach in teaching elementary reading (Doctoral dissertation, Michigan State University). *Dissertation Abstracts International, 51/03-A,* 740.

Lent, R. W., Brown, S. D., & Hackett, G. (1996). Social development from a social cognitive perspective. In D. Brown & L. Brooks (Eds.), *Career choice and development* (3rd ed.). San Francisco: Jossey-Bass.

Levell, J. P. (1965). Secondary school counselors: A study of differentiating characteristics (Doctoral dissertation, University of Oregon). *Dissertation Abstracts International, 26,* 4452. (University Microfilms No. 65-12, 227)

Levin, A. S., Krumboltz, J. D., & Krumboltz, B. L. (1995). *Exploring your career beliefs: A workbook for the Career Beliefs Inventory with techniques for integrating your Strong and MBTI results.* Palo Alto, CA: Consulting Psychologists Press.

Levin, L. S. (1978). Jungian personality variables of psychotherapists of different theoretical orientations (Doctoral dissertation, University of Oregon). *Dissertation Abstracts*

International, 39, 4042B–4043B. (University Microfilms No. 79-01, 823)

Levine, D. M. (1988). Jungian personality type and recreational reading patterns (Doctoral dissertation, University of North Carolina at Chapel Hill). *Dissertation Abstracts International, 58/12-B,* 3716.

Levy, N., Murphy, C., & Carlson, R. (1972). Personality types among Negro college students. *Educational and Psychological Measurement, 32,* 641–653.

Levy, N., & Ostrowski, B. (1983). A comparison of the Jungian personality types among Hawaiians of Japanese and Caucasian ancestry. *Research in Psychological Type, 6,* 54–57.

Lewis, R. M., Tobacyk, J. J., Dawson, L. E., Jurkus, A. F., & Means, T. L. (1996). Psychological types of male multi-line insurance agents. *Journal of Psychological Type, 39,* 37–39.

Liddell, D. L., Halpin, G., & Halpin, W. G. (1992). The measure of moral orientation: Measuring the ethics of care and justice. *Journal of College Student Development, 33,* 4, 325–330.

Lidgard, C. F., & Bates, N. W. (1988). *Do police departments in Australia, U.S.A., and the United Kingdom recruit different types of police officers?* Paper presented at the 24th International Congress of Psychology, Sydney, Australia.

Lim, T. K. (1994). Personality types among Singapore and American students. *Journal of Psychological Type, 31,* 10–15.

Loomis, M. E. (1991). *Dancing the wheel of psychological types.* Wilmette, IL: Chiron.

Lueder, D. L. (1986). The "Rising Stars" in educational administration: A corollary to psychological types and leadership styles. *Journal of Psychological Type, 12,* 13–15.

Luh, S. P. (1991). A study of learning styles, personality types and brain hemispheric preferences of teacher education majors (Doctoral dissertation, Drake University). *Dissertation Abstracts International, 51/12-A,* 4067.

Lund, S. L. (1995). Where personality meets culture: Leveraging personal and cultural diversity to improve organizational communication and teamwork. In *Proceedings of Association for Psychological Type 11th International Conference* (pp. 129–130). Kansas City, MO: Association for Psychological Type

Lynch, A. Q., & Sellers, P. A. (1996). Preferences for different educational environments and psychological type: A comparison of adult learners and traditional age college students. *Journal of Psychological Type, 39,* 18–29.

Macdaid, G. P. (1984a). Types of volunteer phone counselors in a crisis center. Unpublished paper.

Macdaid, G. P. (1984b). Recommended uses of the abbreviated version (Form AV) of the *Myers-Briggs Type Indicator* and comparisons with Form G. *Journal of Psychological Type, 7,* 49–55.

Macdaid, G. P., Kainz, R. I., & McCaulley, M. H. (1984). *The University of Florida longitudinal study: A ten-year follow-up.* Unpublished paper.

Macdaid, G. P., McCaulley, M. H., & Kainz, R. I. (1986). *Myers-Briggs Type Indicator atlas of type tables.* Gainesville, FL: Center for Applications of Psychological Type.

MacKinnon, D. W. (1960). The highly effective individual. *Teachers College Record, 61,* 367–378.

MacKinnon, D. W. (1962a). The nature and nurture of creative talent. *American Psychologist, 17,* 484–495.

MacKinnon, D. W. (1962b). The personality correlates of creativity: A study of American architects. In G. S. Nielsen (Ed.), Personality Research, *Proceedings of the XIV International Congress of Applied Psychology, 2,* 11–39.

MacKinnon, D. W. (1965). Personality and the realization of creative potential. *American Psychologist, 20,* 273–281.

MacKinnon, D. W. (1971). Creativity and the transliminal experience. *Journal of Creative Behavior, 5* (4), 227–241.

Mann, H., Siegler, M., & Osmond, H. (1968). The many worlds of time. *Journal of Analytical Psychology, 13* (1), 33–56.

Mann, H., Siegler, M., & Osmond, H. (1971). The psychotypology of time. In H. Yaker, H. Osmond, & F. Cheek (Eds.), *The future of time: Man's temporal environment* (pp. 142–178). Garden City, NY: Doubleday.

Manske, D. H. (1988). A study of the relationship of preference scores on the *Myers-Briggs Type Indicator* and the reading comprehension of adult readers (Doctoral dissertation, Memphis State University). *Dissertation Abstracts International, 49/02-A,* 227.

Marcus, S. K. (1976). Jungian typology and time orientation (Doctoral dissertation, United States International University). *Dissertation Abstracts International, 37*(03), 1409B. (University Microfilms No. 76-19-756)

Marioles, N., Strickert, D. P., Babcock, R. B., Campbell, B. R., & Cortner, R. H. (1997, July). *Type and couples: Part three.* Paper presented at the XII International Conference of the Association for Psychological Type, Boston, MA.

Marioles, N. S., Hammer, A. L., Strickert, D. P., Adams, J., Cortner, R. H., & Mareth, T. (1995). *Type and couples: Part 2.* Paper presented at the XI meeting of the Association for Psychological Type, Kansas City, MO.

Marioles, N. S., Strickert, D. P., & Hammer, A. L. (1996). Attraction, satisfaction, and psychological types of couples. *Journal of Psychological Type, 36,* 16–27.

Marrott, G. (1981), The nature of insight: A conceptual and empirical exploration of the insightful person. Unpublished doctoral dissertation, University of California.

Marshall, N. J. (1971). Orientations toward privacy: Environmental and personality components (Doctoral dissertation, University of California). *Dissertation Abstracts International, 31,* 4315B. (University Microfilms No. 71-815)

Maslach, C., Jackson, S. E., & Leiter, M. P. (1996). *Maslach Burnout Inventory Manual* (3rd ed.). Palo Alto, CA: Consulting Psychologists Press.

May, A. O. (1992). The learning styles, personality and temperament types of eighth and twelfth-grade urban African-American and white students: A comparative study (Doctoral dissertation, Seattle University). *Dissertation Abstracts International, 52/07-A,* 2472.

May, D. C. (1972). An investigation of the relationship between selected personality characteristics of eighth-grade students and their achievement in mathematics (Doctoral dissertation, University of Florida). *Dissertation Abstracts International, 33/02-A,* 555.

McCarley, N. G., & Carskadon, T. G. (1983). Test-retest reliabilities of scales and subscales of the *Myers-Briggs Type Indicator* and of criteria for clinical interpretive hypotheses involving them. *Research in Psychological Type, 6,* 24–36.

McCarley, N. G., & Carskadon, T. G. (1986). The perceived accuracy of elements of the 16 type descriptions of Myers and Keirsey among men and women: Which elements are most accurate, should the type descriptions be different for men and women, and do the type descriptions stereotype sensing types? *Journal of Psychological Type, 11,* 2–29.

McCary, P. W. (1970). The effects of small self-understanding groups on the self-concept and anxiety level when group composition has been varied (Doctoral dissertation, University of Michigan). *Dissertation Abstracts International, 31,* 2112A. (University Microfilms No. 70-20, 491)

McCaulley, M. H. (1977). *The Myers Longitudinal Medical Study* (Monograph II). Gainesville, FL: Center for Applications of Psychological Type.

McCaulley, M. H. (1978). *Application of the Myers-Briggs Type Indicator to medicine and other health professions* (Monograph I). Gainesville, FL: Center for Applications of Psychological Type.

McCaulley, M. H. (1985). The selection ratio type table: A research strategy for comparing type distributions. *Journal of Psychological Type, 10,* 46–56.

McCaulley, M. H. (1990a). The MBTI and individual pathways in engineering design. *Engineering Education, 80,* 537–542.

McCaulley, M. H. (1990b). *The Myers-Briggs Type Indicator in counseling.* Gainesville, FL: Center for Applications of Psychological Type.

McCaulley, M. H., Godleski, E. S., Yokomoto, C. F., Harrisberger, L., & Sloan, E. D. (1983). Applications of psychological type in engineering education. *Engineering Education, 73,* 5, 394–400.

McCaulley, M. H., & Kainz, R. I. (1974). *The University of Florida longitudinal study: First follow-up.* Unpublished paper.

McCaulley, M. H., & Kainz, R. I (1976). [MBTI and achievement in a Florida middle school.] Unpublished raw data.

McCaulley, M. H., Macdaid, G. P., & Granade, J. G. (1993). *Career satisfaction and type: A working paper.* Gainesville, FL: Center for Applications of Psychological Type.

McCaulley, M. H., Macdaid, G. P., & Magidson, J. (1997). *Introducing a new graphical modeling technique for profiling type tables.* Paper presented at the Association of Psychological Type XII, Boston, MA.

McCaulley, M. H., Macdaid, G. P., & Walsh, R. (1987). *Myers-Briggs Type Indicator and retention in engineering. International Journal of Applied Engineering, 3,* 2, 99–109.

McCaulley, M. H., & Natter, F. L. (1974). Psychological (Myers-Briggs) type differences in education. In F. L. Natter & S. A. Rollins (Eds.), *The governor's task force on disruptive youth: Phase II report.* Tallahassee, FL: Office of the Governor.

McCrae, R. R., & Costa, P. T., Jr. (1989). Reinterpreting the *Myers-Briggs Type Indicator* from the perspective of the five-factor model of personality. *Journal of Personality, 57* (1), 17–40.

Meisgeier, C. H., & Meisgeier, C. (1989). *A parent's guide to type.* Gainesville, FL: Center for Applications of Psychological Type.

Meisgeier, C. H., & Murphy, E. (1987). *Murphy-Meisgeier Type Indicator for Children manual.* Palo Alto, CA: Consulting Psychologists Press.

Meisgeier, C. H., Murphy, E., & Meisgeier, C. (1989). *A teacher's guide to type.* Palo Alto, CA: Consulting Psychologists Press.

Meisgeier, C. H., Poillion, M. J., & Haring, K. (1994). The relation between ADHD and Jungian psychological type: Commonality in Jungian psychological type preferences among students with Attention Deficit-Hyperactivity Disorder. *Proceedings: Orchestrating Educational Change in the 90's—The Role of Psychological Type,* 285–304.

Melear, C. T., & Richardson, S. (1994). Learning styles of African American children which correspond to the MBTI. *Proceedings: Orchestrating Educational Change in the 90'—The Role of Psychological Type,* 11–22.

Mendelsohn, G. A. (1966). Effects of client personality and client-counselor similarity on the duration of counseling: A replication and extension. *Journal of Counseling Psychology, 13* (2), 228–232.

Mendelsohn, G. A., & Geller, M. H. (1963). Effects of counselor-client similarity on the outcome of counseling. *Journal of Counseling Psychology, 10* (1), 71–77.

Mendelsohn, G. A., & Geller, M. H. (1965). Structure of client attitudes toward counseling and their relation to client-counselor similarity. *Journal of Consulting Psychology, 29* (1), 63–72.

Mendelsohn, G. A., & Geller, M. H. (1967). Similarity, missed sessions, and early termination. *Journal of Counseling Psychology, 14* (3), 210–215.

Mendelsohn, G. A., & Kirk, B. A. (1962). Personality differences between students who do and do not use a counseling facility. *Journal of Counseling Psychology, 9* (4), 341–346.

Mendelsohn, G. A., Weiss, D. S., & Feimer, N. R. (1982). Conceptual and empirical analysis of the typological implications of patterns of socialization and femininity. *Journal of Personality and Social Psychology, 42* (6), 1157–1170.

Metts, V. L. (1995). *Team type diversity and team effectiveness.* Paper presented at the 11th International Conference of the Association for Psychological Type, Kansas City, MO.

Millner, N. B. (1998). *Creative aging: Discovering the unexpected joys of later life through personality type.* Palo Alto, CA: Davies-Black.

Millon, T. (1994). *Millon Index of Personality Styles manual.* San Antonio, TX: The Psychological Corporation.

Mills, C. J., Moore, N. J., & Parker, W. D. (1996). Psychological type and cognitive style in elementary-age gifted students: Comparisons across age and gender. *Journal of Psychological Type, 38,* 13–23.

Mills, J., Robey, D., & Smith, L. (1985). Conflict-handling and personality dimensions of project-management personnel. *Psychological Reports, 57,* 1135–1143.

Miner, M. G., & Hyman, I. A. (1988). Psychological types of secondary teachers and their ratings of the seriousness of student misbehaviors. *Journal of Psychological Type, 14,* 25–31.

Minnesota Department of Economic Security. (1997). *From the DOT to O*NET: Taking occupational information into the next century.* Unpublished manuscript.

Mitchell, W. D. (in press). *MBTI Step II manual.* Palo Alto, CA: Consulting Psychologists Press.

Mitchell, W. D. (1981). *Type and social climate in a large organization.* Unpublished manuscript.

Mitchell, W. D., with Quenk, N. L., & Kummerow, J. M. (1997). *MBTI Step II: A description of the subscales.* Palo Alto, CA: Consulting Psychologists Press.

Molpus, D. (1997, December 9). *A leadership and the people issues, All Things Considered.* Upper Marlboro, MD: National Public Radio.

Montross, D. H., Leibowitz, Z. B., & Shinkman, C. J. (1995). *Real people real jobs: Reflecting your interests in the world of work.* Palo Alto, CA: Davies-Black.

Moody, R. (1988). Personality preferences and foreign language learning. *The Modern Language Journal, 72,* 4, 389–401.

Moore, D., & Bayne, R. (1997). Preference for sensing or intuition and reading for pleasure. *Journal of Psychological Type, 41,* 38–42.

Moore, L. S., Dietz, T. J., & Jenkins, D. A. (1997). Teaching about self-awareness: Using the MBTI to enhance professionalism in social work education. *Journal of Psychological Type, 43,* 5–11.

Most, R. B. (1984). [A test-retest comparison of Form AV and Form G of the *Myers-Briggs Type Indicator.*] Unpublished raw data.

Murphy, E. (1992). *The developing child: Using Jungian type to understand children.* Palo Alto, CA: Consulting Psychologists Press.

Murphy, E. (1997). Coping, adjusting, accommodating, and fostering the development of type differences in families. In *Proceedings: APT XII Biennial International Conference,* Boston, MA.

Murphy, E., & Meisgeier, C. H. (1987). *Murphy-Meisgeier Type Indicator for Children.* Palo Alto, CA: Consulting Psychologists Press.

Murry, W. D., Magidson, J., & Markham, S. E. (1997). *The MBTI cognitive functions: Using latent class and trait theory to examine the dominant and auxiliary.* Paper presented at the 12th International Conference of the Association for Psychological Type, Boston, MA.

Murry, W. D., & Markham, S. E. (1997). The MBTI and work values: The role of personality in shaping an organization's culture. In *APT XII Proceedings,* 165–170.

Myers, I. B. (1962). *Manual: The Myers-Briggs Type Indicator.* Princeton, NJ: Educational Testing Service.

Myers, I. B. (1974). *Type and teamwork.* Gainesville, FL: Center for Applications of Psychological Type.

Myers, I. B. (1977). In M. H. McCaulley, *The Myers longitudinal medical study* (Monograph II). Gainesville, FL: Center for Applications of Psychological Type.

Myers, I. B., with Kirby, L. K., & Myers, K. D. (1998). *Introduction to type* (6th ed.). Palo Alto, CA: Consulting Psychologists Press.

Myers, I. B., & McCaulley, M. H. (1985). *Manual: A guide to the development and use of the Myers-Briggs Type Indicator.* Palo Alto, CA: Consulting Psychologists Press.

Myers, I. B., with Myers, P. B. (1995). *Gifts differing: Understanding personality type.* Palo Alto, CA: Davies-Black. (original work published in 1980)

Myers, K. D. (n.d.). *Decision making and type.* [Handout]. Gainesville, FL: Center for Applications of Psychological Type.

Myers, K. D., & Kirby L. K. (1994). *Introduction to type dynamics and development: Exploring the next level of type.* Palo Alto, CA: Consulting Psychologists Press.

Nechworth, J. A., & Carskadon, T. G. (1979). Experimental validation of an assumption underlying the clinical interpretation of discrepancies between *Myers-Briggs Type Indicator* scores computed separately from word-pair and phrased question items. *Research in Psychological Type, 2,* 56–59.

Neral, S. M. (1989). Determining whether a predictive relationship exists between noncognitive characteristics and academic achievement levels of freshman medical students (Doctoral dissertation, Mississippi State University). *Dissertation Abstracts International, 50/04-A,* 906.

Newman, J. (1985). Hemisphere specialization and Jungian typology-evidence for a relationship. *Bulletin of Psychological Type, 10* (2), 13, 25–27.

Newman, L. E. (1979). Personality types of therapist and client and their use in counseling. *Research in Psychological Type, 2,* 46–55.

Nightingale, J. A. (1973). The relationship of Jungian type to death concern and time perspective (Doctoral dissertation, University of South Carolina). *Dissertation Abstracts International, 33,* 3956B. (University Microfilms No. 73-3609)

Noer, D. M. (1993). *Healing the wounds.* San Francisco: Jossey-Bass.

O'Haire, T. D., & Marcia, J. E. (1980). Some personality characteristics associated with Ananda Marga meditations: A pilot study. *Perceptual and Motor Skills, 51,* 447–452.

Ohsawa, T. (1975, October). *MBTI experiences in Japan: Career choice, selection, placement, and counseling for individual development.* Paper presented at the 1st National Conference on the *Myers-Briggs Type Indicator,* Gainesville, FL.

Ohsawa, T. (1981). *A profile of top executives of Japanese companies.* Paper presented at the 4th National Conference on the *Myers-Briggs Type Indicator,* Palo Alto, CA.

Osborn, T. N. , Osborn, D. B., & Twillman, B. (1996). MBTI, FIRO-B, and NAFTA: Psychological profiles of not-so-distant business neighbors. *Journal of Psychological Type, 36,* 3–15.

O'Shea, T., & Mamchur, C. (1989). Using a loglinear model to analyze MBTI distributions. *Journal of Psychological Type, 17,* 56–65.

Oswick, C., & Mahoney, J. P. (1993). Psychological types of first-line supervisors in the United Kingdom: A comparison of U.S. and U.K. managers. *Journal of Psychological Type, 25,* 31–38.

Oswick, C., Mahoney, J. P., & Stein, P. (1994). The fit between organizational culture and employee personality: Case evidence from three diverse organizations. In *Proceedings of the Third International Conference on Myers-Briggs Typology* (pp. 99–108). Montreal, Canada: International Type Users Organization.

Otis, G. D., & Louks, J. L. (1997). Rebelliousness and psychological distress in a sample of Introverted veterans. *Journal of Psychological Type, 40,* 20–30.

Otis, G. D., & Quenk, N. L. (1989). Care and justice considerations in "real life" moral problems. *Journal of Psychological Type, 18,* 3–10.

Owen, C. (1962). An investigation of creative potential at the junior high level. *Studies in Art Education, 3,* 16–22.

Oxford Psychologists Press (1993). *Reported to best-fit type: Changes during the Oxford Psychologists Press qualifying workshops, February 1991–April 1993.* Unpublished report.

Oxford, R., & Ehrman, M. (1988). Psychological type and adult language learning strategies: A pilot study. *Journal of Psychological Type, 16,* 22–32.

Oxford, R., Nyikos, M., & Ehrman, M. (1988). Vive la difference? Reflections on sex differences in use of language learning strategies. *Foreign Language Annals, 21,* 4, 321–329.

Palmiere, L. (1972). Intro-Extra-version as an organizing principle in fantasy production. *Journal of Analytical Psychology, 17* (2), 116–131.

Park, J. S. (1996). Paper presented at *Psychological Type and Culture-East and West: A Multicultural Research Symposium.* University of Hawaii at Manoa, Honolulu.

Pearman, R. R. (1993). *Diversity denied: Type bias in manager selection.* Paper presented at the 11th international conference of the Association for Psychological Type, Kansas City, MO.

Pearman, R. R., & Albritton, S. C. (1997). *I'm not crazy, I'm just not you: The real meaning of the sixteen personality types.* Palo Alto, CA: Davies-Black.

Pearman, R. R., & Fleenor, J. (1996). Differences in observed and self-reported qualities of psychological types. *Journal of Psychological Type, 39,* 3–17.

Penley, J. P., & Stephens, D. W. (1994). *The M.O.M.S.^SM Handbook: Understanding your personality type in mothering.* Gainesville, FL: Center for Applications of Psychological Type.

Penn, B. K. (1992). Correlations among learning styles, clinical specialities, and personality types of U.S. Army nurses (Doctoral dissertation, University of Texas at Austin). *Dissertation Abstracts International, 53/02-A,* 393.

Percival, T. Q., Smitheram, V., & Kelly, M. (1992). *Myers-Briggs Type Indicator* and conflict-handling intention: An interactive approach. *Journal of Psychological Type, 23,* 10–16.

Perelman, S. G. (1978). A phenomenological investigation of the counselor's personal experience of his counseling practice and its relationship to specific constructs in Jungian analytical psychology (Doctoral dissertation, University of Pittsburg). *Dissertation Abstracts International, 38,* 5258A. (University Microfilms No. 7801874)

Perry, H. W. (1975). Interrelationships among selected personality variables of psychologists and their professional orientation (Doctoral dissertation, Notre Dame University). *Dissertation Abstracts International, 35,* 6080B. (University Microfilms No. 75-13,100)

Peterson, L. (1995). *Starting out, starting over: Finding the work that's waiting for you.* Palo Alto, CA: Davies-Black.

Petty, M. L. (1985). A profile of college student leaders relating personality types, learning styles, and leadership approaches (Doctoral dissertation, Florida State University). *Dissertation Abstracts International, 46/12-A,* 3621.

Pollard, C. K. (1989). The relationship of GPA to personality factors of students as measured by the MBTI and the 16PF (Doctoral dissertation, Baylor University). *Dissertation Abstracts International, 49/10-A,* 3006.

Power, S. J., & Lundsten, L. L. (1997). Studies that compare type theory and left-brain/right brain theory. *Journal of Psychological Type, 43,* 22–28.

Price, P. M. (1993). An examination of response to literature and Myers-Briggs personality preferences in high-ability secondary school students (Doctoral dissertation, University of Virginia). *Dissertation Abstracts International, 54/05-A,* 1660.

Pritchett, P. (n.d.). *The employee handbook of new work habits for a radically changing world: 13 ground rules for job success in the information age.* Dallas, TX: Pritchett & Associates, Inc.

Provost, J. A. (1985). Type watching and college attrition. *Journal of Psychological Type, 9,* 16–23.

Provost, J. A. (1990). *Work, play, and type: Achieving balance in your life.* Palo Alto, CA: Consulting Psychologists Press.

Provost, J. A. (1991). Tracking freshman difficulties in the class of 1993. *Journal of Psychological Type, 21,* 35–39.

Provost, J. A. (1992). *Strategies for success: Using type to do better in high school and college.* Gainesville, FL: Center for the Applications of Psychological Type.

Provost, J. A. (1993). *Applications of the Myers-Briggs Type Indicator in counseling: A casebook.* Gainesville, FL: Center for Applications of Psychological Type.

Provost, J.A. & Anchors, S. (1987). Student involvement and activities. In J. A. Provost & S. Anchors (Eds.), *Applications of the Myers-Briggs Type Indicator in higher education* (pp. 91–106). Palo Alto, CA: Davies-Black.

Provost, J. A., Carson, B. H., & Beidler, P. G. (1987b). Teaching excellence and type. *Journal of Psychological Type, 13,* 23–33.

Quenk, A. T. (1985a). *Psychological types and psychotherapy.* Gainesville, FL: Center for Applications of Psychological Type.

Quenk, A. T., and Quenk, N. L. (1982). The use of psychological typology in analysis. In M. Stein (Ed.), *Jungian analysis.* La Salle, IL: Open Court Press.

Quenk, N. L. (1966). Fantasy and personal outlook: A study of daydreaming as a function of optimism, pessimism, realism and anxiety (Doctoral dissertation, University of California, Berkeley). *Dissertation Abstracts International, 27,* 970B. (University Microfilms No. 66-8364)

Quenk, N. L. (1985b). Directionality of the auxiliary function. *Bulletin of Psychological Type, 8,* (1).

Quenk, N. L. (1989). Jung's theory of psychological types and the self-contained patient. In E. M. Stern (Ed.), *Psychotherapy and the self-contained patient.* New York: Haworth Press.

Quenk, N. L. (1993). *Beside ourselves: Our hidden personality in everyday life.* Palo Alto, CA: Davies-Black.

Quenk, N. L. (1996). *In the grip: Our hidden personality.* Palo Alto, CA: Consulting Psychologists Press.

Quenk, N. L., & Albert, M. (1975). *A taxonomy of physician work settings* (Study Report #2 to Bureau of Health Resources Development, Health Resource Administration, Contract No. 1-MI-24197). Albuquerque, NM: University of New Mexico.

Quenk, N. L., & Kummerow, J. M. (1996). *MBTI Step II expanded interpretive report: Form K.* Palo Alto, CA: Consulting Psychologists Press.

Quenk, N. L., & Quenk, A. T. (1996). Counseling and psychotherapy. In A. L. Hammer (Ed.), *MBTI applications: A decade of research on the Myers-Briggs Type Indicator* (pp. 105–122). Palo Alto, CA: Consulting Psychologists Press.

Random House dictionary of the English language (2nd ed., unabridged). (1987). New York: Random House.

Reynierse, J. H. (1993). The distribution and flow of managerial types through organizational levels in business and industry. *Journal of Psychological Type, 25,* 11–23.

Reynierse, J. H. (1997). An MBTI model of entrepreneurism and bureaucracy: The psychological types of business entrepreneurs compared to business managers and executives. *Journal of Psychological Type, 40,* 3–19.

Reynierse, J. H., & Harker, J. B. (1995). The psychological types of line and staff management: Implications for the J–P preference. *Journal of Psychological Type, 34,* 8–16.

Rich, B. (1972). *A correlational study of the Myers-Briggs Type Indicator and the Jungian Type Survey.* Unpublished paper.

Rigley, D. A. (1993). The relationship between personality type, academic major selection and persistence (Doctoral dissertation, Illinois State University). *Dissertation Abstracts International, 54/04-A,* 1333.

Roberds-Baxter, S. L., & Baxter, W. D. (1994). Student MBTI type-characteristic behavior: Correlations with the *Adjective Check List* and teacher and school psychologist judgment of social acceptance and emotional health. In *Proceedings: Orchestrating Educational Change in the 90's—The Role of Psychological Type,* 305–319.

Robinson, D. C. (1994). Uses of type with the 1990 United States Academic Decathlon program. In *Proceedings: Orchestrating Educational Change in the 90's—The Role of Psychological Type,* 35–41.

Rollock, D., & Terrel, M. D. (1996). Multicultural issues in assessment: Toward an inclusive model. In J. L. Delucia-Waack (Ed.), *Multicultural counseling competencies: Implications for training and practice* (pp. 113–153). Alexandria, VA: Association for Counselor Education and Supervision.

Rosati, P. (1997). Psychological types of Canadian engineering students. *Journal of Psychological Type, 41,* 33–37.

Rosin, P. L. (1995). A psychological type comparison of Cree and non-native junior high students: Implications for education (Master's thesis, University of Alberta). *Master's Abstracts International, 33/01,* 37.

Ross, J. (1961). *Progress report on the College Student Characteristics Study: June 1961* (Research Memorandum 61-11). Princeton, NJ: Educational Testing Service.

Ross, S. I. (1994). The relationship between cognitive style and academic achievement in African-American high school students (Doctoral dissertation, Fordham University). *Dissertation Abstracts International, 55/04-A,* 914.

Roush, P. L. E. (1989). MBTI type and voluntary attrition at the United States Naval Academy. *Journal of Psychological Type, 18,* 72–79.

Ruane, F. V. (1973). An investigation of the relationship of response modes in the perception of paintings to selected variables (Doctoral dissertation, Pennsylvania State University). *Dissertation Abstracts International, 34,* 5031A. (University Microfilms No. 74-4285)

Ruble, V. E., Mahan, M. P., & Schurr, K. T. (1987). *Multiple uses of the MBTI within an athletic program.* Paper presented at the 4th Annual Conference on Counseling Athletes, Springfield, MA.

Ruhl, D. L., & Rodgers, R. F. (1992). The perceived accuracy of the 16 type descriptions of Myers and Keirsey: A replication of McCarley and Carskadon. *Journal of Psychological Type, 23,* 22–26.

Ruppart, R. (1985). *Psychological types and occupational choices among religious professionals: A psychosocial, historical perspective.* Unpublished doctoral dissertation, New York University.

Russel, M. T., & Karol, D. L. (1994). *16PF fifth edition administrator's manual.* Champaign, IL: Institute for Ability and Personality Testing.

Rytting, M., Ware, R., & Prince, R. A. (1994). The impact of family ownership and CEO type on the character of companies. *Journal of Psychological Type, 31,* 32–40.

Samovar, L. A., & Porter, R. E. (Eds.). (1991). *Intercultural communication: A reader* (6th ed.). Belmont, CA: Wadsworth.

Sample, J. A., & Hoffman, J. L. (1986). The MBTI as a management and organizational development tool. *Journal of Psychological Type, 11,* 47–50.

Satava, D. (1996). Personality types of CPAs: National vs. local firms. *Journal of Psychological Type, 36,* 36–41.

Satava, D. (1997). Extraverts or Introverts: Who supervises the most CPA staff members? *Journal of Psychological Type, 43,* 40–43.

Saunders, D. R. (1987). *Type differentiation indicator manual*. Palo Alto, CA: Consulting Psychologists Press.

Saunders, D. R. (1989). *MBTI Expanded Analysis Report manual*. Palo Alto, CA: Consulting Psychologists Press.

Saunders, F. W. (1991). *Katharine and Isabel: Mother's light, daughter's journey*. Palo Alto, CA: Davies-Black.

Schacht, A. J., Howe, H. E., & Berman, J. J. (1989). Supervisor facilitative conditions and effectiveness as perceived by Thinking- and Feeling-type supervisees. *Psychotherapy, 26*, 475–483.

Schadt, D. O. (1997). The relationship of type to developmental issues of midlife women: Implications for counseling. *Journal of Psychological Type, 43*, 12–21.

Schaefer, G. L. (1994). Relationship of *Myers-Briggs Type Indicator* personality profiles to academic self-esteem (Doctoral dissertation, University of the Pacific). *Dissertation Abstracts International, 55/05-A*, 1228.

Scherdin, M. J. (1994). Vive la difference: Exploring librarian personality types using the MBTI. In M. J. Scherdin (Ed.), *Discovering librarians: Profiles of a profession*. Chicago: Association of College and Research Libraries, American Library Association.

Schilling, K. L. (1972). *Myers-Briggs Type Indicator and the helping person*. Unpublished master's thesis, University of Florida, Gainesville.

Schnell, E. R., & Hammer, A. L. (1997). Integrating the FIRO-B with the MBTI: Relationships, case examples, and interpretation strategies. In C. Fitzgerald & L. K. Kirby (Eds.), *Developing leaders: Research and applications in psychological type and leadership development* (pp. 439–464). Palo Alto, CA: Davies-Black.

Scholl, J. S. (1975). *Task performance of small groups composed on the basis of Jung's psychological types* (Doctoral dissertation, Temple University). *Dissertation Abstracts International, 75* (28), 141A.

Schroeder, C. C., & Jackson, S. (1987). Designing residential environments. In J. A. Provost & S. Anchors (Eds.), *Applications of the Myers-Briggs Type Indicator in higher education*, (pp. 65–88). Palo Alto, CA: Davies-Black.

Schurr, K. T., Henriksen, L. W., Alcorn, B. K., & Dillard, N. (1992). Tests and psychological types for nurses and teachers: Classroom achievement and standardized test scores measuring specific training objectives and general ability. *Journal of Psychological Type, 23*, 38–44.

Schurr, K. T., Houlette, F., & Ellen, A. (1986). The effects of instructors and student *Myers-Briggs Type Indicator* characteristics on the accuracy of grades predicted for an introductory English composition course. *Educational and Psychological Measurement, 46*, 4, 989–1000.

Schurr, K. T., & Ruble, V. E. (1986). The *Myers-Briggs Type Indicator* and first-year college achievement: A look beyond aptitude test results. *Journal of Psychological Type, 12*, 25–37.

Schurr, K. T., & Ruble, V. E. (1988). Psychological type and the second year of college achievement: Survival and the gravitation toward appropriate and manageable major fields. *Journal of Psychological Type, 14*, 57–59.

Schurr, K. T., Ruble, V. E., & Ellen, A. S. (1985). Myers-Briggs Type Inventory and demographic characteristics of students attending and not attending a college basketball game. *Journal of Sport Behavior, 8*, 4, 181–194.

Schurr, K. T., Ruble, V. E., & Henriksen, L. W. (1988). Relationships of *Myers-Briggs Type Indicator* personality characteristics and self-reported academic problems and skill ratings with scholastic aptitude test scores. *Educational and Psychological Measurement, 48*, 187–196.

Schurr, K. T., Ruble, V. E., & Henriksen, L. W. (1989). Effects of different university admission practices on the MBTI and gender composition of a student body, graduation rate, and enrollment in different departments. *Journal of Psychological Type, 18*, 24–32.

Schurr, K. T., Ruble, V. E., Palomba, C., Pickerill, B., & Moore, D. (1997). Relationships between the MBTI and selected aspects of Tinto's model for college attrition. *Journal of Psychological Type, 40*, 31–42.

Schurr, K. T., Wittig, A. F., Ruble, V. E., & Ellen, A. S. (1988). Demographic and personality characteristics associated with persistent, occasional, and non-attendance of university male basketball games by college students. *Journal of Sport Behavior, 11*, 1, 3–17.

Schutz, W. (1978). *FIRO Awareness Scales manual*. Palo Alto, CA: Consulting Psychologists Press.

Scott, T. H., & Scott, J. C. (1996). Psychological types of outstanding high school basketball officials. *Journal of Psychological Type, 39*, 40–42.

Seiden, H. M. (1970). Time perspective and styles of consciousness (Doctoral dissertation, New School for Social Research). *Dissertation Abstracts International, 31*, 386B (University Microfilms No. 70-11, 275)

Severino, C. J. (1989). Helping nontraditional students achieve college literacy: A context-based study of the uses of text and teacher-student interaction (Doctoral dissertation, University of Illinois at Chicago). *Dissertation Abstracts International, 50/06-A*, 1585.

Shelton, J. (1996). Health, stress, and coping. In A. L. Hammer (Ed.), *MBTI applications: A decade of research on the Myers-Briggs Type Indicator* (pp. 197–215). Palo Alto, CA: Consulting Psychologists Press.

Sherman, R. G. (1981). Typology and problems in intimate relationships. *Research in Psychological Type, 4*, 4–23.

Shiflett, S. C. (1989). Validity evidence for the *Myers-Briggs Type Indicator* as a measure of hemispheric dominance. *Educational and Psychological Measurement, 49*, 3, 741–745.

Short, G. J., & Grasha, A. F. (1995). The relationship of MBTI dimensions to perceptions of stress and coping strategies in mangers. *Journal of Psychological Type, 32*, 13–22.

Shuck, J., & Manfrin, C. (1997). Client verification of reported type at onset and after six months of continuous treatment in an abstinence-based chemical dependency treatment program. Unpublished research.

Sim, H.-S., & Kim, J.-T. (1993). The development and validation of the Korean version of the MBTI. *Journal of Psychological Type, 26*, 18–27.

Simmons, G., & Barrineau, P. (1994). Learning style and the Native American. *Journal of Psychological Type, 28*, 3–10.

Singer, M. (1989). Cognitive style and reading comprehension. *Journal of Psychological Type, 17*, 31–35.

Sipps, G. J., Alexander, R. A., & Friedt, L. (1985). Item analysis of the *Myers-Briggs Type Indicator*. *Educational and Psychological Measurement, 45*, 789–796.

Smith, A., Irey, R., & McCaulley, M. H. (1973). Self-paced instruction and college student's personality. *Engineering Education, 63* (6), 435–440.

Smith, N. P. (1976). The influence of structural information characteristics of Jungian personality type on time horizons in decision-making (Doctoral dissertation, University of California). *Dissertation Abstracts International, 37*, 2297A–2298A. (University Microfilms No. 76-22, 715)

Spielberger, C. D. (1983). *Manual for the State-Trait Anxiety Inventory (Form Y)*. Redwood City, CA: Mind Garden.

Spokane, A. R. (1996). Holland's theory. In D. Brown & L. Brooks (Eds.), *Career choice and development* (3rd ed.). San Francisco: Jossey-Bass.

Squyres, E. M. (1980). *Time orientation and Jung's concept of psychological wholeness*. Unpublished master's thesis, Georgia State University.

Steele, G. E. (1986). An investigation of the relationship between students' interests and the curricular practices of an alternative high school, through the perspective of Jung's theory of psychological types (Doctoral dissertation, Ohio State University). *Dissertation Abstracts International, 47/10-A,* 3616.

St. Germain, C. J. (1988). A comparative analysis of Jungian psychological type using measures of academic achievement, ability, grades and perceptions of classroom practice tasks of middle school students (Doctoral dissertation, University of Texas at Austin). *Dissertation Abstracts International, 48/10-A,* 2531.

Stenberg, G. (1990). *Brain and personality: Extraversion/Introversion in relation to EEG, evoked potentials and cerebral blood flow.* Unpublished doctoral dissertation, University of Lund, Sweden.

Stephens, W. B. (1975, April). *University art department and academies of art: The relation of artists' psychological types to their specialties and interests.* Paper presented at the National Art Education Association Conference, Miami, FL.

Sue, D. W. (Ed.). (1998). *Multicultural counseling competencies: Individual and organizational development.* Newbury Park, CA: Sage.

Sundstrom, E., & Busby, P. L. (1997). Co-workers' perceptions of eight MBTI leader types: Comparative analysis of managers' SYMLOG profiles. In C. Fitzgerald & L. K. Kirby (Eds.), *Developing leaders: Research and applications in psychological type and leadership development* (pp. 225–265). Palo Alto, CA: Davies-Black.

Super, D. E. (1970). *The Work Values Inventory.* Boston, MA: Houghton Mifflin.

Super, D. E., Savickas, M. L., & Super, C. M. (1996). The life-span, life-space approach to careers. In D. Brown & L. Brooks (Eds.), *Career choice and development* (3rd ed.). San Francisco: Jossey-Bass.

Swanson, J. L., & O'Saben, C. L. (1993). Differences in supervisory needs and expectations by trainee experience, cognitive style, and program membership. *Journal of Counseling & Development, 71,* 457–464.

Taggart, W. M., Kroeck, K. G., & Escoffier, M. R. (1991). Validity evidence for the *Myers-Briggs Type Indicator* as a measure of hemisphere dominance: Another view. *Educational and Psychological Measurement, 51,* 775–783.

Taylor, F. L. (1990). The influence of an outdoor adventure recreation class on personality type, locus-of-control, self-esteem, and selected issues of identity development of college students (Doctoral dissertation, University of San Francisco). *Dissertation Abstracts International, 51/04-A,* 1122.

Terrill, J. L. (1970). Correlates of counselor role perception (Doctoral dissertation, University of Colorado). *Dissertation Abstracts International, 31,* 166A. (University Microfilms No. 70-5898)

Tharp, G. D. (1992). Relationship between personality type and achievement in an undergraduate physiology course. *American Journal of Physiology, 262,* 6, 1–3.

Thomas, L. (1996a). *The work style inventory* (unpublished items). Palo Alto, CA: Consulting Psychologists Press.

Thomas, L. (1996b). *The work style inventory.* Unpublished master's thesis, Virginia Polytechnic and State University.

Thomas, L., & Harvey, R. J. (1995, May). *Improving the measurement precision of the Myers-Briggs Type Indicator.* Paper presented at the annual conference of the Society for Industrial Organizational Psychology, Orlando, FL.

Thomason, R. S. (1983). Relationships of chronological age, psychological type, and reading comprehension of college students (Doctoral dissertation, University of Florida). *Dissertation Abstracts International, 45/04-A,* 1086.

Thompson, B., & Borrello, G. M. (1986). Construct validity of the *Myers-Briggs Type Indicator. Educational and Psychological Measurement, 46,* 745–752.

Thompson, B., & Borrello, G. M. (1989, January). *A confirmatory factor analysis of data from the Myers-Briggs Type Indicator.* Paper presented at the annual meeting of the Southwest Educational Research Association, Houston, TX.

Thorne, A. (1987). The press of personality: A study of conversations between Introverts and Extraverts. *Journal of Personality and Social Psychology, 53* (4), 718–726.

Thorne, A., & Gough, H. (1991). *Portraits of type: An MBTI research compendium.* Palo Alto, CA: Consulting Psychologists Press.

Tieger, P. D., & Barron-Tieger, B. (1992). *Do what you are.* Boston: Little, Brown

Tischler, L. (1994). The MBTI factor structure. *Journal of Psychological Type, 31,* 24–31.

Tischler, L. (1996). Comparing person-organization personality fit to work success. *Journal of Psychological Type, 38,* 34–43.

Tobacyk, J. J., Hearn, R. E., & Wells, D. H. (1990). Jungian type and California Achievement Test performance in junior high school students at high risk for dropout. *Journal of Psychological Type, 19,* 13–20.

Tobacyk, J. J., Wells, D. H., & Springer, T. P. (1988). Jungian type and self-concept in junior high school students at high risk for dropout. *Journal of Psychological Type, 16,* 47–53.

Tzeng, O. C. S., Outcalt, D., Boyer, S. L., Ware, R., & Landis, D. (1984). Item validity of the *Myers-Briggs Type Indicator. Journal of Personality Assessment, 48,* 255–256.

Toothaker, L. E. (1991). *Multiple comparisons for researchers.* Newbury Park, CA: Sage.

Vaccaro, A. J. (1988). Personality clash. *Personnel Administrator,* 88–92.

Van Ham, L. B. J. (1994). *Psychological variables related to the management progress of women employed as registered nurses in a hospital setting: Implications for career counseling and consulting.* Unpublished doctoral dissertation, University of Nebraska, Lincoln.

Van Rooyen, J. (1994). Creativity: An important managerial requirement, a South African perspective. In C. Fitzgerald (Ed.), *Proceedings of the Myers-Briggs Type Indicator and Leadership: An International Research Conference* (pp. 49–60). College Park, MD: National Leadership Institute.

Van Sant, S., & Payne, D. (1995). *Psychological type in schools: Applications for educators.* Gainesville, FL: Center for the Applications of Psychological Type.

Van Velsor, E., & Fleenor, J. W. (1997). The MBTI and leadership skills: Relationships between the MBTI and four 360-degree management feedback instruments. In C. Fitzgerald & L. K. Kirby (Eds.), *Developing leaders: Research and applications in psychological type and leadership development* (pp. 139–162). Palo Alto, CA: Davies-Black.

Vaughan, J. A., & Knapp, R. H. (1963). A study in pessimism. *Journal of Social Psychology, 59,* 77–92.

Veach, T. L., & Touhey, J. C. (1971). Personality correlates of accurate time perception. *Perceptual and Motor Skills, 33* (3), 765–766.

Vollbrecht, F. E. (1991). A study of selected personality characteristics of vocational trade and industrial education teachers (Doctoral dissertation, Texas A&M University). *Dissertation Abstracts International, 52/06-A,* 1990.

Vondran, K. A. (1989). A study of the relationship between personality type and the expressive, explanatory, and persuasive writing of seventh and eighth-grade students (Doctoral dissertation, Temple University). *Dissertation Abstracts International, 49/10-A,* 2920.

von Franz, M. L. (1971). The inferior function. In M. L. von Franz & J. Hillman (Eds.), *Lectures on Jung's Typology* (5th corrected printing) (pp. 1–72). Dallas, TX: Spring Publications.

Walck, C. L. (1992a). Psychological type and management research: A review. *Journal of Psychological Type, 24,* 13–23.

Walck, C. L. (1992b). The relationship between Indicator type and "true type": Slight preferences and the verification process. *Journal of Psychological Type, 23,* 17–21.

Walck, C. L. (1996). Management and leadership. In A. L. Hammer (Ed.), *MBTI applications: A decade of research on the Myers-Briggs Type Indicator* (pp. 55–80). Palo Alto, CA: Consulting Psychologists Press.

Walck, C. L. (1997). Using the MBTI in management and leadership: A review of the literature. In C. Fitzgerald & L. K. Kirby (Eds.), *Developing leaders: Research and applications in psychological type and leadership development* (pp. 63–114). Palo Alto, CA: Davies-Black.

Waller, N. G., & Reise, S. P. (1989). Computerized adaptive personality assessment: An illustration with the Absorption Scale. *Journal of Personality and Social Psychology, 57* (6), 1051–1058.

Walter, K. M. (1984). Writing in three disciplines correlated with Jungian cognition styles (Doctoral dissertation, University of Texas at Austin). *Dissertation Abstracts International, 46/02-A,* 414.

Walters, N. J., Wilmoth, J. N., & Pitts, C. A. (1988) Personality traits of high school HOSA officers. *Journal of Health Occupations Education, 3,* 2, 80–105.

Waltz, E. E., & Gough, H. G. (1984). External evaluation of efficacy by means of an *Adjective Check List* scale for observers. *Journal of Personality and Social Psychology, 46,* 607–704.

Ware, R., & Yokomoto, C. (1985). Perceived accuracy of *Myers-Briggs Type Indicator* descriptions using Keirsey profiles. *Journal of Psychological Type, 10,* 27–31.

Watson, D., Clark, L., & Tellegen, A. (1988). Development and validation of brief measures of positive and negative affect: The PANAS scales. *Journal of Personality and Social Psychology, 54,* 1063–1070.

Waymire, C. H. (1995). An analysis of first year dropouts from two church-related universities as profiled according to the *Myers-Briggs Type Indicator* (Doctoral dissertation, University of Mississippi). *Dissertation Abstracts International, 55/11-A,* 3430.

Webster, K., & Howard, P. J. (1989). MBTI-type heterogeneity and business game results. In N. L. Quenk (Ed.), *Eighth Biennial International Conference of the Association for Psychological Type* (pp. 149–152). University of Colorado: Association for Psychological Type.

Wederspahn, A., & Barger, N. J. (1988, Winter). Implications for using the MBTI with non-native English speakers. *Bulletin of Psychological Type, 11,* 12, 21.

Weir, D. M. (1976). The relationship of four Jungian personality types to stated preference for high unconditional positive regard as a counseling approach (Doctoral dissertation, Southern Illinois University). *Dissertation Abstracts International, 36,* 7881A. (University Microfilms No. 76-13, 298)

Weisbord, M. (1992). *Discovering common ground.* San Francisco, CA: Berret-Koehler.

Wellins, R. S., Byham, W. C., & Wilson, J. M. (1991). *Empowered teams.* San Francisco, CA: Jossey-Bass.

Wheelwright, J. B., Wheelwright, J. H., & Buehler, H. A. (1964). *Jungian type survey: The Gray-Wheelwright test* (16th ed.). San Francisco, CA: Society of Jungian Analysts of Northern California.

Whittemore, R. G., & Heimann, R. A. (1965). Originality responses in academically talented male university freshmen. *Psychological Reports, 16,* 439–442.

Williams, B. T. & Carskadon, T. G. (1983). Validity of three MBTI clinical interpretive hypotheses in normal and psychosomatically stressed adults. *Research in Psychological Type, 6,* 81–86.

Williams, R. (1992). Personality characteristics of gifted and talented students as measured by the *Myers-Briggs Type Indicator* and the *Murphy-Meisgeier Type Indicator for Children* (Doctoral dissertation, East Texas State University). *Dissertation Abstracts International, 53/03-A,* 762.

Williams, R. L., Verble, J. S., Price, D. E., & Layne, B. H. (1995). Relationship between time-management practices and personality indices and types. *Journal of Psychological Type, 34,* 36–42.

Wilson, M. A., & Languis, M. L. (1989). Differences in brain electrical activity patterns between introverted and extraverted adults. *Journal of Psychological Type, 18,* 14–23.

Wilson, M. A., & Languis, M. L. (1990). A topographic study of differences in the P300 between introverts and extraverts. *Brain Topography, 2,* 4, 269–274.

Wilson, M., Laposky, A. D., & Languis, M. L. L. (1991, July). *A topographic study of electrophysiological differences between Sensing and Intuitive types.* Paper presented at 10th meeting of the Association for Psychological Type, Richmond, VA.

Wittig, A. F., Schurr, K. T., & Ruble, V. E. (1986). Gender, personality characteristics and academic preparation as factors accounting for achievement and attrition of honors students. *Forum for Honors, 17,* 1, 26–35.

Wittig, A. F., Schurr, K. T., Ruble, V. E., & Ellen, A. (1994). Relationship of *Myers-Briggs Type Indicator* Thinking-Feeling preferences with physical activity choices. *Journal of Psychological Type, 28,* 21-28.

Witzig, J. S. (1978). Jung's typology and classification of psychotherapies. *Journal of Analytical Psychology,* II Biennial International Conference, Boston, MA.

Woodruff, R. G. V., & Clarke, F. M. (1993). Understanding the academic needs of minority students at the University of Hawaii, Manoa. *Psychological Type and Culture—East and West: A Multicultural Symposium,* 199–205.

Yang, A. I. (1981). Psychological temporality: A study of temporal orientation, attitude, mood states, and personality type (Doctoral dissertation, University of Hawaii). *Dissertation Abstracts International, 42* (4), 1677B.

Yao, Y. (1993). Analyses of the MBTI personality types of Chinese female school administrators in Liaoning province, the People's Republic of China (Doctoral dissertation, Mississippi State University). *Dissertation Abstracts International, 55,* 32.

Yeakley, F. R. (1982). Communication style preferences and adjustments as an approach to studying effects of similarity in psychological type. *Research in Psychological Type, 5,* 30–48.

Yeakley, F. R. (1983). Implications of communication style research for psychological type theory. *Research in Psychological Type, 6,* 2–13.

Zietsmann, G. (1996). *The validation of the MBTI on a South African sample: A summary of the results.* Paper presented at International Type Users Conference, South Africa.

Contributors

Nancy J. Barger, M.A., works as an independent consultant in Littleton, Colorado, focusing on organizational transition, leadership and management development, and team building. She has led training programs and consulted with organizations in the United States, Canada, the United Kingdom, Finland, Singapore, New Zealand, and Australia. Her publications include *MBTI Type and Change: Leader's Resource Guide* and *Participant's Guide* (1997), "Multicultural Applications" in *MBTI Applications: A Decade of Research on the Myers-Briggs Type Indicator* (1996), *The Challenge of Change in Organizations: Helping Employees Thrive in the New Frontier* (1995), and *The Interaction of Culture and Type: INTP and ESFJ Women, INFP and ESTJ Men Across Cultures* (1996), all coauthored with Linda K. Kirby, and *WORKTypes* (with J. Kummerow and L. K. Kirby, 1997).

John K. DiTiberio, Ph.D., is associate professor and chair in the Department of Counseling and Family Therapy at St. Louis University. He has taught high school history and courses for undergraduates in education, and he currently teaches courses for master's and doctoral students in counseling and family therapy. DiTiberio serves on the faculty of the Association for Psychological Type's MBTI qualifying program and on the MBTI Research Advisory Board for Consulting Psychologists Press. He is author of "Education, Learning Styles, and Cognitive Styles" in *MBTI Applications: A Decade of Research on the Myers-Briggs Type Indicator* (1996) and coauthor of *Writing and Personality* (1995), *Introduction to Type in College* (1993), and *Personality and the Teaching of Composition* (1989).

Allen L. Hammer, Ph.D., is senior scientist at Consulting Psychologists Press. His own research on the MBTI focuses on careers, couples, stress and coping, and media preferences. He is author of *Introduction to Type and Careers* (1993), the *MBTI Team Report* (1994), the *MBTI Relationship Report* (1987), and the *Strong Professional Report* (1994), and coauthor of the *MBTI Career Report* (1992), *Introduction to Type in College* (1993), the *Strong and MBTI Career Development Guide* (1996), the *Strong Interpretive Report* (1994), and *Introduction to the FIRO-B in Organizations* (1993). He is editor of *MBTI Applications: A Decade of Research on the Myers-Briggs Type Indicator* (1996). He also serves on the editorial board of the *Journal of Psychological Type.*

Linda K. Kirby, Ph.D., is director of the Association for Psychological Type's MBTI qualifying program. She works as a writer, editor, researcher, and trainer in Littleton, Colorado. With Katharine D. Myers, she edited *Introduction to Type* (6th ed., 1998) and authored *Introduction to Type Dynamics and Development* (1994). With Nancy J. Barger, she wrote *MBTI Type and Change: Leader's Resource Guide* and *Participant's Guide* (1997), "Multicultural Applications" in *MBTI Applications: A Decade of Research on the Myers-Briggs Type Indicator* (1996), *The Challenge of Change in Organizations: Helping Employees Thrive in the New Frontier* (1995), and *The Interaction of Culture and Type: INTP and ESFJ Women, INFP and ESTJ Men Across Cultures* (1996). She is also coauthor of *WORKTypes* (with J. Kummerow and N. J. Barger, 1997).

Jean M. Kummerow, Ph.D., is a psychologist, consultant, and author in St. Paul, Minnesota. She applies type in career counseling, leadership and management development, and team building. Kummerow trains professionals internationally in the use of several psychological instruments including the MBTI, the MBTI Step II, and the *Strong Interest Inventory.* She is coauthor of *Introduction to Type in Organizations* (3rd ed, 1998), the MBTI Step II Expanded Interpretive Report (1996), the *Strong and MBTI Career Development Guide* and *Workbook* (1996), "Using the MBTI Step II with Leaders and Managers" in *Developing Leaders: Research and Applications in Psychological Type and Leadership Development* (1997), *LIFE-Types* (with S. K. Hirsh, 1989), and *WORKTypes* (with N. J. Barger and L. K. Kirby, 1997), and editor of *New Directions in Career Planning and the Workplace* (1991). She also serves on the editorial board of the *Journal of Psychological Type.*

Roger R. Pearman, Ed.D., is president of Leadership Performance Systems, Inc., a training and consulting firm providing management and business development services in Pfafftown, North Carolina. Through this company, he works with organizations in the United States, Canada, and Europe. Winner of the 1995 Isabel Briggs Myers Research Award, he is a member of the MBTI Research Advisory Board and a past president of the Association for Psychological Type. Pearman is coauthor of *I'm Not Crazy, I'm Just Not You: The Real Meaning of the Sixteen Personality Types* (with Sarah Albritton, 1997); author of *Hardwired Leadership* (1998), and *Enhancing Leadership Development Through Psychological Type* (1998); and editor of *The Best of the Bulletin: Nineteen Years of Psychological Type* (1998).

Naomi L. Quenk, Ph.D., is a licensed clinical psychologist in independent practice in Albuquerque, New Mexico. She is past president of the Association for Psychological Type and former Director of Training for the MBTI qualifying program. She has written numerous articles on psychological type and is author of *Beside Ourselves: Our Hidden Personality in Everyday Life* (1993) and *In The Grip: Our Hidden Personality* (1996). Quenk is coauthor of the *MBTI Step II Expanded Interpretive Report* (1996), *Dream Thinking: The Logic, Magic, and Meaning of Your Dreams* (1995) and *True Loves: Finding the Soul in Love Relationships* (1997).

Index